We the People

A Brief American History
Volume 1   To 1877

Paul Revere's Ride
on the Night
of April 18, 1775.

We the People

A Brief American History
Volume 1   To 1877

Peter N. Carroll
Stanford University

Australia • Canada • Mexico • Singapore • Spain • United Kingdom • United States

WADSWORTH

THOMSON LEARNING

WADSWORTH
★
™
THOMSON LEARNING

History Publisher: Clark Baxter
Senior Development Editor: Sue Gleason
Assistant Editor: Kasia Zagorski
Editorial Assistant: Jonathan Katz
Executive Marketing Manager: Caroline Croley
Print/Media Buyer: Karen Hunt
Permissions Editor: Stephanie Keough-Hedges
Production Service: Johnstone Associates
Text and Cover Designer: Lisa Devenish
Photo Researcher: Susie Friedman
Maps: Thompson Type

Map, p. 138: Pat Rogondino
Cover Image: Miners in the Sierras, 1951–52. Charles Christian Nahl and Frederick August Wenderoth. Smithsonian American Art Museum. Washington, DC/Art Resource, New York.
Cover Printer: Phoenix Color Corporation
Compositor: Thompson Type
Printer: QuebecorWorld, Taunton
For photo credits and further information on chapter-opening photos, see the Photo Credits on page 380.

Wadsworth/Thomson Learning
10 Davis Drive
Belmont, CA 94002-3098
USA

For more information about our products, contact us:
Thomson Learning Academic Resource Center
1-800-423-0563
http://www.wadsworth.com

International Headquarters
Thomson Learning
International Division
290 Harbor Drive, 2nd Floor
Stamford, CT 06902-7477
USA

UK/Europe/Middle East/South Africa
Thomson Learning
Berkshire House
168-173 High Holborn
London WC1V 7AA
United Kingdom

Asia
Thomson Learning
60 Albert Street, #15-01
Albert Complex
Singapore 189969

Canada
Nelson Thomson Learning
1120 Birchmount Road
Toronto, Ontario M1K 5G4
Canada

*This book is dedicated to my coworkers
at the Abraham Lincoln Brigade Archives,
a nonprofit educational organization.*

Contents

CHAPTER 12

Manifest Destiny and the National Identity, 1844–1850 • 247

CHAPTER 13

The Collapse of the Union, 1850–1861 • 269

Maps

Peter N. Carroll was born in The Bronx, New York, and received his A.B. from Queens College and his history Ph.D. from Northwestern University. He has taught the U.S. history survey course at the University of Illinois, the University of Minnesota, and San Francisco State University; consulted on dozens of textbooks; and worked with survey course teachers for the National Faculty in the 1990s. He has also taught U.S. cultural history, American studies, and creative writing at the University of Minnesota, Stanford University, the University of San Francisco, and the University of California at Berkeley. Carroll's publications include *It Seemed Like Nothing Happened: America in the 1970s,* rev. ed. (Rutgers University, 2000); *Keeping Time: Memory, Nostalgia, and the Art of History* (University of Georgia Press, 1990); *The Odyssey of the Abraham Lincoln Brigade: Americans in the Spanish Civil War* (Stanford University Press, 1994). In addition, he co-authored *They Still Draw Pictures: Children's Art in Wartime* (University of Illinois Press, 2002). Carroll and his partner, author Jeannette Ferrary, live in Belmont, California.

We the People is written for contemporary college students who are inhabiting a world of unprecedented cultural complexity. They have grown up in a society of racial and ethnic diversity, are participating in a technological revolution based on electronic globalization, and look somewhat askance at the promises and bromides of their leaders. Many instructors lament the "aliteracy" of this generation, but this book presents the nation's history from a fresh perspective that will resonate with current undergraduate interests.

What are this book's priorities?

- Good, clear writing
- Brevity and succinctness (leaving abundant reading time for outside assignments)
- The integration of political, social, and cultural history, with a clear political chronology framing the major economic, social, and cultural topics
- The human dimension: a multicultural perspective that reflects the demographics of today's student experience
- Brief quotations that illuminate the concerns of both political leaders and plain folk

At the dawn of the twenty-first century we no longer need to justify a multicultural approach to U.S. history. Today's students expect no less. Besides, historians know that America has always been a pluralistic land. Even before Columbus's ships touched these shores, Native Americans spoke about 2,000 languages, some as different from each other as English is from Chinese. Yet, despite vast linguistic diversity, the word that each of them used to describe its own group, society, or nation was equivalent to the English words "the people."

We the People, as the title suggests, presents the history of diverse cultural groups as a basic ingredient of the national narrative. In this book, women, minorities, and ordinary people find their distinctive voices, often in vivid, pithy language, along with the more familiar words and ideas expressed by politicians, business leaders, and other prominent citizens. Rather than isolating different groups, this book invites comparisons among them by describing issues and themes that affected them all.

For reasons of clarity and simplicity, *We the People* follows a political chronology, assuming the structure of most U.S. history survey courses. Students will follow a familiar sequence of events from the pre-Columbian societies of North America through the founding of the United States and its social, economic, and political development in the nineteenth and twentieth centuries. Yet the book's multicultural perspective also encourages an intertwining of what historians call "social history" within that political framework. Rather than placing social, economic, and cultural topics in separate chapters, *We the People* carefully blends those subjects into the nation's political history. In every chapter, politics, society, economics, and culture form the threads of a single tapestry— a coat of many colors—that tells the story of this country's diverse inhabitants.

Within this broad structure, *We the People* addresses several specific themes that are woven through this nation's history. First, the history of the United States has always been a pluralistic experience, a complicated interaction of women and men from diverse ethnic and cultural groups, involving many races, religions, and national origins. The relationships among these groups have changed dramatically during five centuries of history. The sheer diversity of the population has obliged all cultural groups to accommodate one another and thereby redefine their own identities. Second, because the history of this people involves members of diverse economic and social groups, this book endeavors to describe connections between society and politics, between ordinary people and their leaders. It explores how the country's political system has reflected and represented larger social and economic trends. Third, this book asks the reader to consider how interactions among groups have produced changes in the larger common culture. Taken together, these themes describe the evolution of a distinct national identity and enable us to discuss what it is to be a nation, to have a history, and to live in a specific time and place. From this common past, we can begin to answer the question, asked from the very beginnings of our country's history: What is an American? Going further: Who are we? What do we stand for? What is the meaning of our society, of our culture, and of our individual lives?

For the Instructor

Instructor's Manual and Test Bank

Prepared by Laura Matysek Wood, Tarrant County College, this manual features chapter outlines, lecture/discussion topics, student projects, multiple-choice and essay questions, Web addresses that link you to additional resources, and a *Resource Integration Guide* that features chapter-by-chapter ideas for instruction, as well as suggestions for incorporating CD-ROMs, print resources, and Internet and video resources into

your course. With this easy-to-use tool, you can quickly compile a teaching and learning program that complements both the text's coverage and your own personal instructional style.

ExamView®

Cross-platform computerized testing. Create, deliver, and customize tests and study guides (both print and online) in minutes with this easy-to-use assessment and tutorial system. ExamView offers both a Quick Test Wizard and an Online Test Wizard that guide you step by step through the process of creating tests, while its "what you see is what you get" capability allows you to see the test you are creating on the screen exactly as it will print or display online. You can build tests of up to 250 questions using up to twelve question types. Using ExamView's complete word processing capabilities, you can enter an unlimited number of new questions or edit existing questions.

U.S. History Transparency Package

This package contains nearly 200 color transparencies that include maps, charts, graphs, and cartoons from the text and other sources. The transparencies are keyed to chapters of the text for ease in lecture planning.

Historic Times: The Wadsworth History Resource Center (http://history.wadsworth.com)

Both instructors and students will enjoy this Web-based resource center. From this full-service site, instructors and students can access such selections as a career center, lessons on surfing the Web, and links to great history-related Web sites. Students can also take advantage of the online Student

Guide to InfoTrac® College Edition, featuring lists of article titles with discussion and critical-thinking questions linked to the articles to invite deeper examination of the material. Students can access chapter-by-chapter resources for this book (including interactive quizzes), and professors can browse Historic Times to learn more about our other history texts and supplements.

We the People Web Site

Provocative, exciting, and interactive, this site has something for everyone: instructors, students, and U.S. history buffs. Includes a wealth of documents and visuals with related activities, tutorial quiz questions, hyperlinks, and Internet and InfoTrac College Edition exercises for each chapter. Also features link searches for American Journey Online (see below) for each chapter of the text, as well as extended descriptions of the text's chapter-opening photographs. Each chapter opener in the text carries the Wadsworth History Resource Center address to remind readers of the availability of these American Journey searches. http://history.wadsworth.com.

WebTutor™ on WebCT and Blackboard

A great study tool, a great course management tool, a great communication tool! For students, Web-Tutor offers real-time access to a full array of study tools, including flashcards (with audio), practice quizzes, online tutorials, and Web links. Use Web-Tutor to provide virtual office hours, post your syllabi, set up threaded discussions, track student progress with the quizzing material, and more. WebTutor provides rich communication tools, including a course calendar, asynchronous discussion, "real-time" chat, whiteboard, and integrated email system. Professors who have tried WebTutor love the way it allows students—even those in very large classes—to participate actively in class discussions online. This student-to-student interaction has enormous potential to enhance each student's experience with the course content.

WebTutor is filled with preloaded, text-specific content (including interactive simulations, Power-Point files, and much more) and is ready to use as soon as you and your students log on. At the same time, you can customize the content in any way you choose, from uploading images and other resources, to adding Web links, to creating your own practice materials. Contact your Wadsworth/ Thomson Learning representative for information on bundling options.

Multimedia Manager for U.S. History: A Microsoft® PowerPoint® Link Tool

This cross-platform digital library and presentation tool is available on one convenient multi-platform CD-ROM. With its easy-to-use interface, you can take advantage of Wadsworth's already-created text-specific presentations, which consist of map images, slides of art and architecture photos, interactive map and timeline images, and much more. You can even customize your own presentation by importing your personal lecture slides or other material you choose. The result is an interactive and fluid lecture that truly engages your students.

The Wadsworth U.S. History Video Library

This completely new selection of videos, from Films for the Humanities and Sciences and other sources, includes a variety of titles, including *Colonialism, Nationalism, and Migration; From Workshops to Factory; Revolution, Progress: Politics, Technology, and Science;* and many more. Contact your Wadsworth/Thomson Learning representative for additional information on requesting videos. Available to qualified adopters.

American Heritage Reader

In partnership with *American Heritage,* the pre-eminent magazine of the American experience, Thomson Custom Publishing is offering instructors the opportunity to build their own Custom *American Heritage* reader. The process is simple: contact our Custom group at 1-800-335-9983 or ask your Thomson Sales Representative for details. From there we can share a list of articles available for the reader. For nearly half a century, *American Heritage* has been the nation's memory, telling our shared story with verve, humor, passion and, above all, authority. Our wars and our songs, our heroes and our villains, our art and our technology—all are brought to vivid and immediate life through incisive prose and a wealth of original images.

For the Student

Study Guide

Prepared by Mary Ann Heiss, Kent State University, this valuable resource for students includes chapter summaries, chapter outlines, chronologies, identifications, matching, multiple-choice, fill-in-the-blank, questions for critical thought, and map exercises. Available in two volumes.

American Journey Online (http://www.americanjourney.psmedia.com)

The landmark events of American history recorded by eyewitnesses, the great themes of the American experience according to those who lived it—these are captured in the fifteen primary source collections that make up American Journey Online. Each key topic in American history and culture addressed by the series encompasses hundreds of carefully selected, rare documents, pictures, and archival audio and video, while essays, headnotes, and captions by

scholars set the sources in context. Full text searchability and extensive hyperlinking provide fast and easy access and cross-referencing. The scope of the collections and the power of online delivery make American Journey Online a unique and unprecedented tool for historical inquiry for today's researchers. For more information and sample searches, see the inside back cover of this volume.

InfoTrac® College Edition

Ignite discussions or augment your lectures with the latest developments in history. InfoTrac College Edition provides free online access to hundreds of journals and periodicals. A free four-month subscription to this extensive online library is enclosed with every new copy of the book, giving you and your students access to the latest news and research articles online—updated annually and spanning four years! This easy-to-use database of reliable, full-length articles (not abstracts) from hundreds of top academic journals and popular sources is available twenty-four hours a day, seven days a week, and includes such journals as

- *American History*
- *Antiquity*
- *Biography*
- *History Today*
- *Past & Present*
- *Smithsonian*
- and many more!

(Available only to college and university students.)

American History Atlas

An invaluable collection of more than fifty clear and colorful historical maps covering all major periods in American history. Please contact your local sales representative for information.

History: Hits on the Web

Recently revised for 2002, Hits on the Web (HOW) is an exciting, class-tested product specially designed to help history students utilize the Internet for studying, conducting research, and completing assignments. HOW is approximately eighty pages of valuable teaching tools that can be bundled with any Wadsworth textbook at an affordable price. Available through Thomson Custom Publishing.

Acknowledgments

I have benefited immensely from the advice and suggestions of many active teachers, including: Terry L. Alford, Northern Virginia Community College; Stephen Armes, Fresno City College; Thomas E. Blantz, University of Notre Dame; John D. Buenker, University of Wisconsin—Parkside; Tony Edmonds, Ball State University; Carolyn Eisenberg, Hofstra University; Shirley M. Eoff, Angelo State University; Emmett M. Essin, East Tennessee State University; Melanie Gustafson, University of Vermont; Mary Ann Heiss, Kent State University; Chuck Hope, Tarrant County College, Southeast; Lisa M. Lane, Miracosta College; Gaylen Lewis, Bakersfield College; Barbara Melosh, George Mason University; Carl H. Moneyhon, University of Arkansas at Little Rock; James O'Donnell, Marietta College; J'Nell L. Pate, Tarrant County College, Northeast; Daniel Pope, University of Oregon; R. B. Rosenburg, University of North Alabama; David Sloan, University of Arkansas at Fayetteville; Ron Stocker, Tarrant County College, South; Richard M. Ugland, Ohio State University; Ken Weatherbie, Del Mar College; Lynn Weiner, Roosevelt University; Daniel Wilson, Muhlenberg College; David Wilson, Southern Illinois University; Laura Matysek Wood, Tarrant County College, Northwest.

I thank David A. Horowitz of Portland State University, who read an early draft and gave valuable advice, and especially acknowledge the help of Michael Batinski of Southern Illinois University, whose support made this entire project possible. My editor, Sue Gleason, earns special thanks for her astute criticism of the manuscript and imaginative suggestions for its improvement. Judith Johnstone provided excellent copyediting and overall production management. Hal Humphrey at Wadsworth extended many courtesies. Clark Baxter, former student and now editor, merits a medal for loyalty. My daughter, Natasha Carroll-Ferrary, who passed AP U.S. history while this work was in progress, cleansed the book of literary clichés, such as "tip of the icebeg" and "scratching the surface." Jeannette Ferrary, as ever, was a stalwart friend, a wise critic, and (come to think of it) everything else that matters.

Peter N. Carroll
Belmont, California

When a book advertises itself as a history of the American people, readers are entitled to ask, "Which people?"

"We the people," I answer. "All of us."

"We the people," the first words of the U.S. Constitution, tell much about the nation's values, expectations, and history. The phrase is inclusive, rather than exclusive. It suggests that all citizens have a voice and should be heard. We know, to be honest, that the signers of the Constitution did not listen to the voices of all Americans, but later amendments to the document broadened its meanings to bring more people into its framework.

This history seeks the same inclusiveness. To speak about "the American people," *We the People* uses a multicultural approach that embraces all people—rich and poor, men and women, and the rainbow of ethnic groups. From its historical beginnings, long before Columbus sailed in 1492, the land that became the United States supported many different cultures. Migrations from Europe, Africa, and Asia added to that multiplicity. Because of this historical diversity, Americans have struggled with questions of self-definition. In other parts of the world, most people do not question which nation or culture they belong to: "French," "Korean," or "Egyptian" suffices as a self-descriptive term. For those who inhabit the United States, however, self-definitions have been more complex. Part of the story that follows examines changing self-definitions.

It is important to remember that every history has three elements. First, there are the *people,* those who inhabit the realm of history. Second, history is about *place,* where events happen, how one place relates to another, how places change over time as people pass over them. Third, history is about *time,* chronology, sequence, putting first things first and

second things second. Dates make this mental operation easier, especially because some events occur simultaneously, and others may cause additional events to follow. This book presents these three elements as a constantly changing interaction, a juggling act, as people experience time and place during five centuries and more.

Because of the great diversity of their origins and their willingness to intermix, the *people* who call themselves "Americans," "North Americans," or "U.S. citizens" have been uncertain about how to define their national identity. In fact, to speak about Americans requires thinking in plural terms which include Native Americans, African Americans, European Americans, Asian Americans, Latin Americans, male Americans, female Americans, and so on. Even more important, we need to remember that being American is not an absolute, unchanging category, but an evolving, often-ambiguous concept that enables us to define ourselves as part of a larger national group and as part of the human species.

The *place* of this book is the portion of North America that today is called "The United States of America." Yet the borders of that place have changed over the centuries as various peoples have come to consider America their home. Part of the story that follows involves the changing meaning of America as a place. To some extent, these changes involve redrawing the lines on a map, establishing boundaries with other nations, creating internal borders (colonies, states, territories), and transforming the land for different economic and social purposes (reservations, cities, suburbs). A major theme of this book examines how places have changed as populations have migrated from sea to shining sea. Such migrations also involve different types of transportation (from prehistoric canoes to railroads and automobiles),communications (oral messages, telegraph, mass media), and ideas or values (the things people say or believe). Underscoring this theme of place over the passage of time, we have inserted in the front of the Comprehensive Volume and Volume 1 of this textbook two acetate overlays of the 48 contiguous states. These volumes cover the period before which most present-day state boundaries had taken shape. You may place these acetates over specially labeled maps in the textbook to help you determine, for example, which current states arose out of the Louisiana Purchase.

As for the discussion of *time,* this book follows a familiar chronology—the dates that give history a logic and a sequence, though *not* a sense of inevitability. Life does not change abruptly every December 31 or at the end of each decade and century. *People,* not dates, make history. Indeed, human beings generally stress the continuity of their lives—their connections to ancestors and descendants, their heritage and their expectations for the future.

History, however, also involves those occasions when abrupt events disturb the ordinary flow of time. For Americans, the date 1492 immediately implies the idea of a "before" and an "after." So does December 7, 1941, the "day of infamy" that brought the United States into World War II. Other dramatic events—George Whitefield's preaching that sparked the Great Awakening in the 1740s or Henry Ford's development of mass production during the first decades of the twentieth century—may not be pinpointed so precisely, but they highlight the discontinuities of time, the sense of before and after, that illuminate historical change.

At the same "time," events occur at different places that may or may not be related to each other. Who creates those events or witnesses them often determines whether they are considered historically important. On the day Neil Armstrong became the first human being to touch the surface of the moon, his country was fighting a war in Vietnam. Two human events have never occurred so far away from each other—yet one date, July 20, 1969, binds them inextricably together. And both events, seemingly so far apart, reflect the same industrial-technological culture of the 1960s.

This book also deals with the changing meaning of time itself. From the cultures of Native Americans, who measured time by observing the changing natural cycles and seasons, to our world of digital watches and clocks, which divide time into linear microseconds, Americans have increasingly rationalized the use of time. This growing consciousness of time has helped Americans define themselves. Captain John Smith had to institute martial law to make the first Virginia colonists work six hours a day; a century-and-a-half later, Benjamin Franklin extolled the efficiency of an eight-hour work day. In the nineteenth century, factory owners imposed a twelve-hour day on their workers. By the twentieth century, labor unions forced a reduction of the work day so that workers would have more leisure. Yet, in today's society, people are busier (that is, are *choosing* to have less "free" time) than ever before. One must ask: How does the use of time reflect other cultural and historical values?

Issues of time and place help to define a people's common identity, the sense of living as part of a community. Although each person is as different as his or her fingerprints and DNA, we all coexist and share our individuality with social and cultural groups. In the times and places described in the pages that follow, Americans defined themselves by who they were and who they were not. To be an "American" meant different things, depending on a person's race, gender, class, or values, and these meanings changed greatly over time and in different places. This history, then, is about us, all of us: where we have come from, where we are heading.

Such ideas help us to understand not only the people of the past but also "We the people" today. Our own identities—as students and teachers, historians all—reflect our own sense of time and place: where we live, where we came from, who we are.

We the People

A Brief American History
Volume 1   To 1877

In the Beginning: The World of Native Americans

In the beginning, there were only Earthmaker and his creations. Standing on a plain in the midst of the void, facing his maker, Coyote howled aloud on behalf of his fellow beings:

> "How, I wonder—how, I wonder—
> in what place, I wonder—
> where, I wonder—
> in what sort of place might we two see a bit of land?"

"Each of you will have a place to be," replied Earthmaker to his children. "Each and every one . . . will have a name." He went on:

> "You are creatures who speak differently—
> creatures who look different.
> You also will have a place of your own. . . ."

Then he divided out the lands among them.

> "You take the land over *that* way,
> And you others, go to *that* country.
> All of you various creatures will be called different things."

So it was sung, as part of a creation myth of the Maidu people, who inhabited the northern ridge of the Sierra Nevada, in what is now California.

http://history.wadsworth.com

The Maidu creation story emphasizes how diverse was human life in the Western Hemisphere long before Europeans, Africans, and Asians reached what became known as America. By 1492, when Europeans first landed on American shores, the population of the Western Hemisphere was considerable. Statistical estimates, based on archeological evidence, European observations, and belated oral testimony, remain inexact. Yet the total population of the American continents in 1492 probably approached 50 million people (the combined present-day populations of California and New York State), about one-half of whom inhabited Central America. Residents of North America reached 5 to 10 million. The Algonquian-speaking nations of New England numbered well over 100,000 before the arrival of French and English explorers. Around Chesapeake Bay, the groups led by Powhatan totaled at least 20,000. The Cherokees of the Southeast comprised some 30,000 people; Florida's rival nations, the Timucuas and Apalachees, together reached 75,000. Farther inland, Huron and Iroquois villages contained 1,500 to 2,000 residents at a time when most European villages held about 500 persons.

The American continent, in other words, was hardly a vacant territory waiting to be discovered, but was the home of many diverse organized societies. This dense population included thousands of different cultures and subcultures, each pursuing distinctive activities and values. Terms like *Native American* and *American Indian* tend to obscure such differences, just as the word *European* refers to a diversity of Catholics and Protestants, rich and poor, Spanish, French, Italian, English, and Dutch.

As the Maidu creation story indicates, Native American peoples had a strong sense of place; they knew where they belonged. This knowledge of place enabled them to interact well with their natural en-

The American continent was hardly a vacant territory waiting to be discovered.

vironments—exploiting local resources, integrating human culture into natural cycles, changing the land as it changed them. The harmony between nature and the native cultures may seem idealized, but relations among geography, climate, and society were not static. Droughts, poor harvests, disease, and warfare could quickly destroy any sense of security; all too frequently, natural disasters provoked the fear—and sometimes the reality—of extinction.

The diversity of Native American life invites comparison and contrast among the multitude of tribes and nations that inhabited the Western Hemisphere. Indeed, to acknowledge that the Native American population in 1500 comprised so many people, speaking at least 2,000 languages, some as different from one another as English is from Chinese, suggests the magnitude of the subject. Among Native American groups, differences of size were most obvious. Some bands, such as the Ute-speakers of the desert plains, numbered only in the dozens as recently as the 19th century, reflecting the difficulty of sustaining large populations in arid territory. Other Native American communities, such as the Mississippian mound-building people at Cahokia, just east of modern St. Louis, enjoyed a beneficent environment that supported a community of 20,000 around A.D. 1000. Such numbers imply diversity, not a hierarchy of superior and inferior groups. Many small groups, such as the Utes, were still flourishing when the Europeans arrived; some large ones, like the Mississippian moundbuilders, had disappeared.

After contact between Europeans and Native Americans, startled observers on both sides were preoccupied by their similarities and differences—by the very existence of strange beings from distant worlds. And such primary contacts recurred constantly as men and women, exhibiting biological and cultural differences, met again and again over a vast landscape of time and place. The shock was always mutual, and focused on unexpected physical appearances, social customs, and inferred attitudes. Yet both sides attempted to locate common human qualities. Indeed, the desire to *understand* the other—however futile or dangerous—emerges as a major theme of cross-cultural contact.

The First Migration

Ironically, Europeans and Native Americans shared the experience of long journeys. Although Native peoples stressed their deep attachments to particular places, their creation myths and traditional storytellers often depicted their origins with legends of distant migrations, guided by spiritual visions, that led their ancestors to their "natural" homes. Such tales reinforce the most recent archeological and anthropological evidence about the origins of the first Americans. For Native Americans were not truly "native" to America; at least no fossil evidence has been found to indicate the presence of ancient types of human beings in the Western Hemisphere. Rather, the first Americans appear to have been modern *Homo sapiens,* who migrated to a "new" world during the later stages of the last Ice Age, beginning about 15,000 years ago, but possibly even 10,000 years before that.

Geological evidence supports the theory that the first Americans came from Asia. During the last Ice Age, when huge glaciers absorbed oceanic waters, the levels of the seas fell, creating a 750-mile-wide subcontinent, known today as Beringia, where the Bering strait now separates Siberia from Alaska. This grassy, shrubbed land bridge between Asia and North America attracted large mammals such as mammoths, mastodons, and bison, as well as smaller animals, including seals and birds. Asian hunters apparently pursued these animals across this temperate territory, eventually entering the American continent as the largest glaciers melted and created overland routes toward the east. Such migrations occurred in waves, interrupted by climate changes and the wanderings of the mammals. Indigenous peoples such as Eskimos and Aleuts, who currently inhabit the most northern regions, probably arrived during the last waves of migration. When the glaciers finally melted 10,000 to 15,000 years ago, the land route from Asia was submerged, as it remains today.

Archeological evidence also reinforces the theory of Asian origins. Until recently, the oldest evidence of a human presence in America was a distinctively shaped type of stone spear point that was first excavated at Clovis, New Mexico.

These so-called Clovis points were found embedded in the bones of a mammoth killed by prehistoric hunters. Measuring the rate of radioactive carbon disintegration of the mammoth bones dated the Clovis site as 11,200 years old. The discovery of similar Clovis points throughout North and Central America reinforced the theory that the first hunters spread through the hemisphere in search of mammals. Not until 1996 did archeologists working in Siberia discover similar Clovis points, which were dated 8,300 years old. Since by then Beringia was under water, this discovery suggests that Asia was indeed the source of Clovis points and of the people who used them. Other biological data—common shovel-shaped incisor teeth, a few rare blood enzymes, and some typical body characteristics such as sparseness of facial hair—support the view that the first Americans originated in Asia.

Because glacial conditions prevented direct overland migration south from Alaska, archeologists

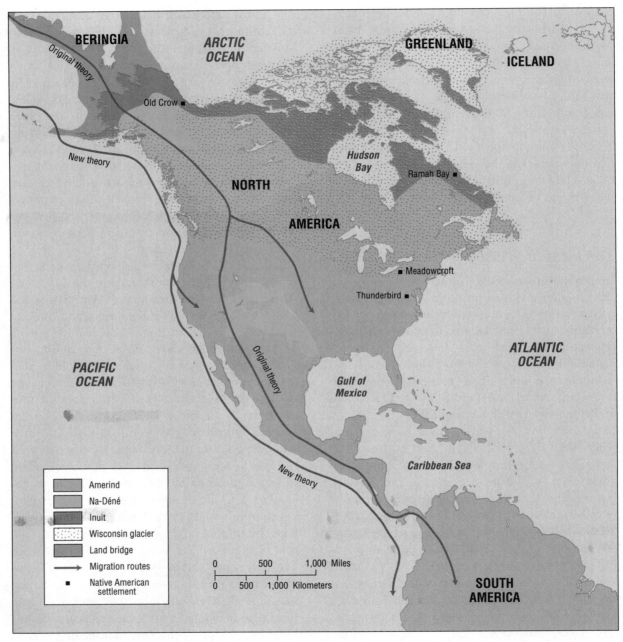

Early North American Migrations and Settlement. There have been two prevailing theories of the settlement of North America. According to the old theory, the original Americans traveled across the Bering Strait from Mongolia. However, the new theory holds, based on new archaeological finds, that migration moved by both land and sea from Asia.

These distinctively shaped stone tips, known today as Clovis points because they were found at Clovis, New Mexico, were attached to wooden shafts and used to hunt animals.

have long believed that the first American hunters migrated east across Beringia, then south and east of the Rocky mountains to places as diverse as Clovis, New Mexico, the Atlantic seaboard, and the southern reaches of South America. Over the years, tantalizing evidence of earlier human occupation has called into question the theory of overland migration but never with convincing proof. But in 1997, archeologists confirmed the dating of a site called Monte Verde in southern Chile to be 12,500 years old, more than 1,000 years older than Clovis. Evidence at this site included DNA specimens from a mastodon, seeds and nuts, and the single footprint of a human child. Since geologists believe that northern glaciers prevented an overland migration at that time, the hunters or their ancestors who arrived in Chile probably followed a coastal route that took them by sea from Beringia to South America. In 1998, archeologists discovered two sites in coastal Peru, both 12,000 years old, that provided evidence that humans lived on seabirds and small fish. Another recent discovery of 9,700-year-old human bones in an Alaskan coastal cave, together with seal bones dated 17,565 years old, suggests the possibility that mammals could have survived and traveled by a water route. Perhaps, then, other claims that humans occupied America 25,000 to 30,000 years ago may not be wrong.

More recently, archeologists have found other pre-Clovis sites in Pennsylvania, Virginia, and South Carolina. These discoveries are forcing a reevaluation of migration theories. The sites, which have been dated up to 17,000 years old, contain the oldest stone tools found in America. Their existence, dating to a time when glaciers would have prevented overland migrations, raises questions about the origins of the first humans in America. Rather than accepting the theory that all prehistoric Americans originated in Asia, some archeologists speculate that some migratory people began their journeys in Europe and traveled in boats near the icy shorelines westward across the North Atlantic to the east coast of America. Low sea levels would have minimized long voyages on the open seas. Whether such people survived, became extinct, or mixed with other humans from Asia is unknown. Archeologists now believe that multiple migrations probably occurred, some from Asia or Polynesia and others, perhaps, from Europe.

Establishing Local Cultures

Long-distance migrations over many centuries brought the first Americans into diverse environments, which in turn stimulated the development of multiple local cultures. Archeological evidence has suggested human occupation in the Ohio River valley near Pittsburgh at least 12,000 years ago; excavation of a man's gravesite near Sarasota, Florida, demonstrates human habitation there 10,000 years ago. Such wide and rapid geographical dispersal suggests that these early American residents were opportunistic migrants, seeking animals to hunt, fish to snare, or wild plants to gather. Around 11,000 years ago, moreover, climatic warming and human hunters hastened the extinction of the largest mammals, such as mammoths and mastodons. To survive, humans had to adapt to smaller sources of food. Instead of searching widely for big game, they learned to exploit the varieties of local regions. As hunters and gatherers of edible vegetation, Native Americans became a settled people.

Diverse California Communities

The diversity of local habitats can be seen even in a single area, such as modern-day California. "You will live here," Earthmaker told the Maidu to explain their settlement in a land of abundance. "Living in a country that is little, not big, you will

be content." And when he created more people, Earthmaker promised them "a small country [called] by different names." California, apparently known even in prehistoric times for its good climate and ample food, attracted diverse groups. The region's languages reflected their separate origins. At the time Europeans first met Native Californians, the population spoke over 100 languages. Some of these languages were related to those spoken in Canada; some came from the southwestern regions of what is now the United States; other dialects were similar to the Algonquian spoken on the east coast. Whatever the geographic origins or linguistic roots, each Native American group simply called itself "the people."

The first settlers of North America's Pacific coastal regions made their lives in a land of plenty. In the high country of the Maidu, thick forests sheltered abundant populations of deer, elk, rabbits, and mountain lions, and produced crops of protein-rich acorns that provided the dietary staple. Armed with chiseled stone arrows, spears, and woven snares, Maidu men pursued their primary occupation of hunting. They prepared for the hunt with ritualistic smokehouse ceremonies—fasting, purifying themselves, appealing to the spirits of the animals to ensure the success of their task. Then, wearing animal heads and skins as camouflage, the hunters approached the game for the kill. The slain animals became communal property to be shared by all, and the carcasses were treated with utmost respect—the hunters never chewed the bones or carelessly discarded remnants—lest the animal spirits become offended and withdraw from the forests.

California Native American Languages

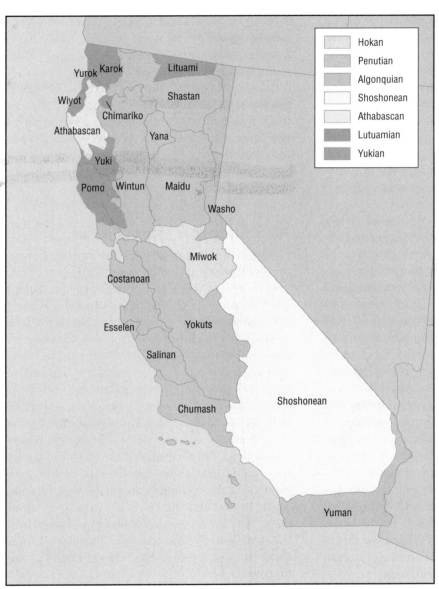

Most women of the Pacific region assumed responsibility for the vegetable harvest. Their task began in the spring with the gathering of willow shoots and stringy roots. After participating in religious ceremonies that gave them spiritual vi-

sions, the women wove the plant fibers into beautiful baskets, some patterned after the skins of snakes, lizards, or deer. Woven so tightly that water did not leak out, the baskets served as utensils for cooking and carrying. To heat water in this nonmetallic society, the women made fires, heated stones, and dropped them into the water baskets. Women also gathered the acorn harvest, placed the dried seeds in baskets lined with herbs to repel insects and mold, and stored them underground or in granaries built on stilts. For food, women pounded acorns with stone pestles into fine powdery flour, leached out the bitter tannins with hot water, and cooked the grain into a watery mush or made acorn bread. In the fall, harvests of wild seeds such as fennel made pungent and easily preserved seed cakes.

Native California architecture revealed diverse interrelations between the natural environment and the customs of the inhabitants. In the redwood and pine forests near the Northwest coast, for example, the Karuk people constructed plank houses by splitting logs with stone wedges to form flat boards; lacking metal nails, they used knotted wild grapevine roots and gravity to hold the structures together. Here families gathered for meals and communal activities, although men slept apart from women in their sweathouses. The Miwok people of California's central valley dug circular houses into the earth, joined wood poles at the top to form a steeple, and covered the surface with soil to keep out water. On the central coast marshlands, the Ohlones built small circular houses from the native tule grass, while the Chumash of Santa Barbara used willow poles for houses that accommodated as many as fifty occupants. Some groups erected other special structures, such as huts in which menstruating women were segregated from contact with men.

The architecture of transportation was equally varied. At the mouth of the Klamath River, the Yuroks cut tough dugout canoes from redwood logs, sturdy enough to withstand the pummeling of coastal rocks and gravel river bottoms, yet, according to one observer, "smooth as if they had been sandpapered." The Modocs, by contrast, built light, thin-shelled dugouts to sail on the calmer waters of the interior lakes. Around San Francisco Bay, the Ohlones went fishing in canoes made from woven tule grass, the same fibers used for their houses and skirts. California's premier mariners were the Chumash, who built 30-foot long oceangoing boats of plank, sewn together with deer sinew and caulked with natural asphalt found on the beaches. In such vessels, Chumash sailors embarked on voyages as far as sixty-five miles from shore.

The Spirit World of Native California

Native Californians were astute students of the cycles of nature and understood the habits of natural creatures. Those who lived near the Pacific coast learned to exploit the abundance of fish, shellfish, waterfowl, and the occasional beached whale, thus assuring a generous food supply that encouraged population growth. Native peoples even measured the calendar by seasonal phenomena, such as the running of the salmon upriver to spawn (an excellent time to trap the abundant fish) or the annual autumn migration of geese (best lured by decoys and caught in nets woven of tule grass). In the Native American world, such food-gathering activities demanded spiritual awareness: the communication between the spirit of the hunter and the spirit of the prey, in which there was agreement that one should kill, the other be killed. That was why hunters adopted strict rules prohibiting the indiscriminate killing of game.

Underlying this sensitivity to natural cycles was the belief held by most Native American peoples that all the world was alive. "These mountains, these rivers hear what you say," a Modoc woman learned from her parents, "and if you are mean they will punish you." Native Californians treated not only animals but also plants and inanimate objects as living entities. "This rock did not come here by itself," declared a Yuki holy man. "This tree does not stand here of itself." Rather, human beings were surrounded by aspects of the natural creation. And if everything was alive, created by an Earthmaker, then animals were related to humans as kin.

In contrast to Europe's Judeo-Christian traditions and the Bible's Book of Genesis, which said that humans "have dominion . . . over every living thing," Native Americans saw themselves as members of animal clans. They identified, for example, with the families of Bears or Hummingbirds or Turtles, each of which had their own special qualities. Animal clans helped define who were a person's relatives and whom one could marry. Believing in spiritual communication with other species, humans might sing to animals or plants. Indeed, many songs had no words, but their melodies were sung or played on bone whistles or flutes to be understood by different animals. Many tunes have vanished and only the lyrics remain: "I dream of you," sang the Ohlones.

I dream of you jumping.
Rabbit. Jackrabbit. Quail.

The Rise of Agriculture

In areas of natural abundance, such as California, hunter-gatherer societies had sufficient food to survive without drastically altering the environment around them. Observation of natural phenomena enabled some men and women who were considered healers to use the medicinal properties of native vegetation to treat illness and injury. Indeed, Native American medicine men and women identified over 170 pharmaceutical ingredients that are still used today. Such botanical wisdom eventually led to a major transformation

of some societies. Experimenting with wild seeds, prehistoric Americans learned the ways of agriculture—planting, weeding, and irrigating to produce larger crops. Domestic agriculture offered a stable food supply, stimulated population growth, and encouraged more settled habits, at least during the planting and harvest seasons. Yet few societies relied exclusively on agriculture. Most continued to gather wild foods and to hunt. Having different sources of food protected human groups from natural calamities such as drought or the disappearance of game. And, within most societies, certain groups became more expert in exploiting specific resources. Typically, women worked at agriculture while men specialized in hunting.

Early Agricultural Societies

The cultivation of maize, or yellow corn, probably began in central Mexico about 4,500 years ago. Domesticated lima beans appeared in Peru 3,500 years ago, and green beans emerged in the Andes 1,000 years later. As native farmers developed improved varieties of these crops, food supplies increased dramatically. The absence of written records has left huge gaps in the historical chronology, but archeological remains show that by about 2,000 years ago agriculture was supporting a flourishing Maya civilization in southern Mexico and Guatemala. With sufficient resources for a dense population, the Mayans built temples and cities, established wide trade networks, encouraged skilled artisans to produce silver and gold jewelry, and included intellectuals who invented a written hieroglyphic language and sophisticated astronomical calendars that could predict eclipses for centuries.

Supported by its extensive agricultural base, Mayan wealth attracted other groups. Among these newcomers were a migratory people called the Toltecs, who invaded from the north about 1,000 years ago and reigned in the region for about 200 years. Another migratory people, the Incas, entered the Andes region about 900 years ago, established extensive trade routes, built lavish cities, and flourished for 400 years.

Other invaders penetrated Central America, including the long-migrating Aztecs, who followed the spiritual guidance of the Hummingbird god into Toltec territory in Mexico. After acting as mercenary warriors for the Toltecs, the Aztecs intermarried with a royal family. But when they executed a Toltec princess in the expectation that she would become a goddess, the Toltecs expelled them. The Aztecs then moved to the shores of a swampy lake and proceeded to build a magnificent city called Tenochtitlan on the site of today's Mexico City. By the 15th century, the Aztecs were rulers of the region, dominating the core city with a population of a quarter of a million and demanding tribute from subordinate peoples of Central America. Elaborate irrigation systems made possible seven crops each year, and engineering feats included aqueducts, roadways, masonry buildings, and the fabulous Great Temple where human sacrifices took place. Aztec leaders enjoyed great wealth, exotic foods, and fine crafts and literature. Subject peoples faced mass religious sacrifices to satisfy Aztec gods; over 20,000 were killed in one celebration. Such subordinates were all too willing to betray their Aztec masters when later invaders arrived.

North American Agriculture

Agricultural knowledge probably moved from Central America in a northeasterly direction. Maize cultivation appeared in the southwestern areas of what are now Arizona and New Mexico about 3,000 years ago, followed soon after by squash and beans. About 1,500 years ago, the Hohokam people introduced irrigation to the desert lands to harvest crops twice annually. Five hundred years later, the Anasazi people ("old ones" in Navajo) adopted irrigated agriculture, developed an elaborate road system, and dominated southwestern culture. Anasazi architecture included *kivas,* underground circular chambers in which men held religious ceremonies, and rectangular apartment-style dwellings still imitated by their Pueblo descendants. Archeologists believe that soil erosion and droughts forced the Anasazi to abandon their pueblos and migrate to other parts of the Southwest.

Agriculture also supported thriving societies in the Ohio and Mississippi river valleys. Beginning about 2,500 years ago, groups known to anthropologists as the Adena and Hopewell peoples established extensive community networks. Mixing hunting, gathering, and farming, these societies built large earthen mounds, apparently as religious sites and fortifications. By about 1,000 years ago, this so-called Mississippian culture dominated what is now the southeastern United States. Most of these settlements remained small villages, but at least one site at Cahokia in western Illinois contained an extensive metropolitan culture with a population density of 4,000 people per square mile.

At Cahokia, hundreds of acres of crops (maize, beans, squash) provided food for residents of the urban center, who also domesticated turkeys and tended herds of deer. Living in square wooden and mud houses, these Mississippians constructed enormous earthen pyramids, some 100 feet high, on which the chiefs and religious leaders lived. A continental trade network linked Cahokia to copper from Lake Superior and conch shells from the Atlantic seaboard. But wood supplies ran short, and the population began to decline 700 years ago. Drought, food shortages, and conflicts with neighboring groups led the Mississipians to migrate to the Southeast about 500 years ago. Their descendants continued as the Natchez, Choctaw, Chickasaw, Creek, and Cherokee peoples. Evolving as separate cultures, these southeastern groups developed societies based on agriculture and hunting, with a division of labor based on gender.

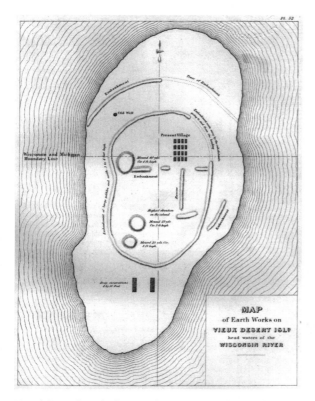

Pl. 52

MAP
of Earth Works on
VIEUX DESERT ISLᵀ
head waters of the
WISCONSIN RIVER

Map of the earth works discovered on Vieux Desert Isle, at the headwaters of the Wisconsin River, at the boundary of Wisconsin and Michigan. This encampment appears to have been designed as a retreat and a stronghold. No enemy could approach it except by water, and an elliptical embankment at its center seems to have served as the foundation for pickets. There were small mounds or barrows within the enclosure.

Among the Cherokees, for example, agriculture was a female task and hunting was male. Consequently, Cherokee men and women had equal economic and spiritual importance.

The Settled Cultures of the Northeast

Native societies in the Northeast also mixed agriculture and hunting. According to the Algonquian-speaking people who lived east of the Appalachian mountains, a sacred crow brought them the first kernels of corn and beans. Northeastern men still pursued animals to hunt, but women coordinated the tasks of planting, watering, and weeding with the responsibilities of childcare. Reliance on agriculture and gathering meant that women often contributed more to the household's diet than did men. Among these Algonquians, agriculture affected both social relations and their broader cultural outlook. Thus, while hunting tribes such as the Micmac regulated their social activity by the annual changes among animal populations (naming lunar months with reference to salmon runs, the migration of birds, or the hibernation of bears), New England agricultural people adopted a calendar describing activities involved in growing crops.

Agricultural communities in this region remained mobile, however, not only to accommodate the men's hunting and fishing seasons but also because it was easier to abandon old fields than to fertilize the soil. (The practice of using fish heads as fertilizer, a technique taught to the Pilgrim settlers in the 1620s, appears to have been unusual, partly because of the difficulty of transporting fish to fields.) In winter, entire communities moved from the planted areas into wooded valleys, where fuel was more convenient. The frequency of moves from field to forest encouraged the development of simple wigwam structures, which could easily be dismantled, moved, and reassembled.

Although the Algonquians' spiritual outlook encouraged the protection of natural resources, hunters and farmers left their mark on the land. To clear fields for agriculture, the men burned the woods twice annually to remove underbrush and dead wood. Such practices made it easier to track game and encouraged the growth of pine trees, which survived the fires to become the tallest trees in New England, some as high as 250 feet. Burning had the ecological advantage, probably unknown to the hunters, of accelerating the recycling of nutrients into the forest floor, opening areas to sunlight, killing plant diseases, and eliminating such omnipresent pests as fleas.

As in California, the hunters of the eastern woodlands understood the migratory habits of fish,

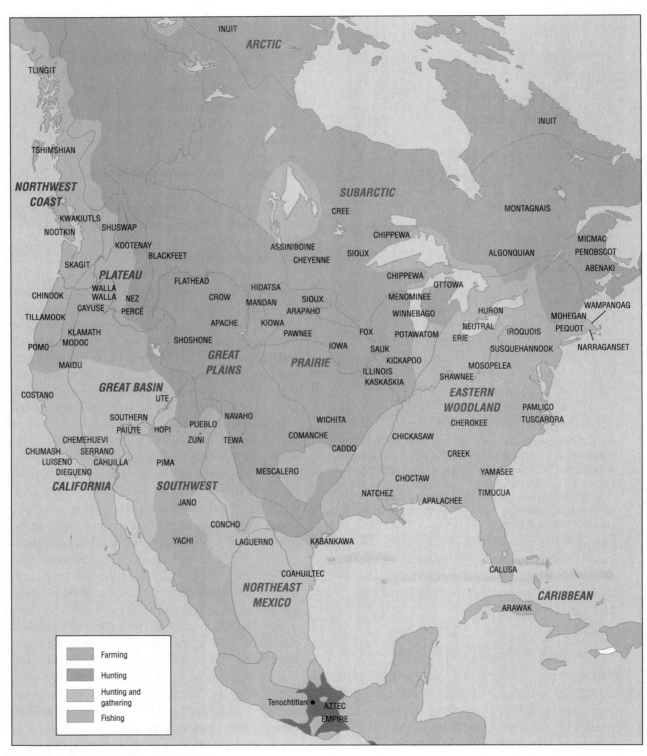

INUIT

ARCTIC

TLINGIT

INUIT

TSHIMSHIAN

SUBARCTIC

NORTHWEST COAST

CREE

MONTAGNAIS

KWAKIUTLS

SHUSWAP

CHIPPEWA

NOOTKIN

KOOTENAY

ASSINIBOINE

SIOUX

ALGONQUIAN

MICMAC

PENOBSCOT

BLACKFEET

CHEYENNE

ABENAKI

SKAGIT

PLATEAU

FLATHEAD

CHIPPEWA

CHINOOK

WALLA WALLA

NEZ

CROW

HIDATSA

OTTOWA

MENOMINEE

HURON

WAMPANOAG

CAYUSE

PERCÉ

MANDAN

SIOUX

ARAPAHO

WINNEBAGO

NEUTRAL

MOHEGAN

PEQUOT

TILLAMOOK

APACHE

KIOWA

FOX

POTAWATOM

ERIE

IROQUOIS

KLAMATH

PAWNEE

SAUK

SUSQUEHANNOOK

NARRAGANSET

POMO

MODOC

SHOSHONE

IOWA

KICKAPOO

MOSOPELEA

MAIDU

GREAT PLAINS

PRAIRIE

ILLINOIS

KASKASKIA

SHAWNEE

COSTANO

GREAT BASIN

UTE

EASTERN WOODLAND

PAMLICO

SOUTHERN PAIUTE

NAVAHO

WICHITA

CHEROKEE

TUSCARORA

CHEMEHUEVI

HOPI

PUEBLO

ZUÑI

TEWA

COMANCHE

CHICKASAW

CHUMASH

SERRANO

CADDO

CREEK

LUISENO

CAHUILLA

PIMA

YAMASEE

DIEGUENO

CALIFORNIA

SOUTHWEST

MESCALERO

CHOCTAW

TIMUCUA

JANO

NATCHEZ

APALACHEE

CONCHO

YACHI

LAGUERNO

KABANKAWA

CALUSA

NORTHEAST MEXICO

COAHUILTEC

CARIBBEAN

ARAWAK

Tenochtitlan ● AZTEC EMPIRE

	Farming
	Hunting
	Hunting and gathering
	Fishing

Native American Regions, 1492 OVERLAY 2

fowl, and other animals. At one remarkable site in Boston, dating from about 2,500 B.C., the inhabitants built a fish trap made of 65,000 stakes and intertwined brush that covered two acres. Fishermen of the Southeast developed poisons made from buckeyes or walnut bark that, when dumped in small lakes, temporarily paralyzed the fish. Native hunters simply scooped the floating fish into their nets. The pursuit of larger game, deer or bear, required equally subtle strategies—stalking, trapping, working as teams to drive the prey toward ambushes of tribesmen. The catch provided large quantities of meat that, when smoked or dried, could feed the people all winter. Women fashioned animal skins into clothing and moccasins.

The mixed economies of hunting, gathering, and agriculture reinforced a sense of territoriality. Although Native Americans considered the personal ownership of land as absurd (how could anyone own the natural creation?) they believed that organized groups possessed the right to use the resources of a specific geographic area. Custom dictated tribal boundaries. Claims to the land gave a people rights to hunt, fish, farm, and gather natural resources. Outsiders did not enjoy such privileges. A hungry stranger might be permitted to kill animals for food, but not for the skins. Usually, natural geography—a river, mountain, or valley—defined borders, and the perennial harvesting of resources justified the continued presence of a people. Native American maps, later copied by Europeans, reveal considerable knowledge of distant places, far beyond the range of an individual's personal travel.

Leadership and Warfare: Political Organization in Native Groups

Within their territorial communities, Native peoples accepted the leadership of a select few, but even hereditary leaders ruled by earning the respect and consent of their people; they could not coerce people to obey, relying instead on the power

Inhabitants built a fish trap made of 65,000 stakes and intertwined brush that covered two acres.

of persuasion. "Neither anger nor fury shall find lodgement in their minds," a European described the Iroquois chiefs, "and all their actions shall be marked by calm deliberation." Many societies deferred to their older men and women, acknowledging the wisdom of age.

This idea of a community consensus did not extend to outsiders who threatened precious natural resources. Among the eastern groups, warfare was violent, cruel, and seemingly perpetual, largely because conflict had both spiritual and political meaning. "They firmly believe," a European said of the Catawba, fierce fighters of the Carolina hill country, "that the spirits of those who are killed by the enemy, without equal revenge of blood, find no rest, and at night haunt the houses of the tribe to which they belonged." Among the Iroquois, another people feared as warriors, warfare served literally to revitalize the community by replacing the dead with captives, who might be either adopted into an Iroquois family to replace a recently deceased member or ritually tortured to ease the grief of a dead person's family. Native American warfare preceded the arrival of Europeans; palisaded villages and circular fortifications were part of the landscape throughout the eastern woodlands. But, while warfare was brutal, it did not involve extermination or genocide. Women, children, and the elderly were usually spared from death, and even enemy warriors were preferred as captives.

Among the most complex political arrangements in North America was the Iroquois Confederation, whose territorial influence ranged from the Adirondack Mountains to the Great Lakes. Consisting of five major societies or nations—Mohawk, Onondaga, Oneida, Cayuga, and Seneca (and later a sixth nation, the Tuscarora)—the Iroquois League emerged in the 1400s as an alternative to intertribal warfare and persistent blood feuds.

According to Iroquois tradition, a supernatural creature named Dekanawidah appeared before the Mohawk chief Hiawatha and proposed a union of the tribes that forbade blood revenge. Persuading other chiefs of his vision, Hiawatha developed a plan of confederation for the separate villages. A council of forty-nine elders assumed responsibility for diplomatic affairs, although it could not interfere with the internal problems of the separate groups. In this way, the Iroquois achieved a powerful unity to challenge the neighboring Hurons and Algonquians, with whom they were chronically at war. Later, when Europeans entered their territories, the Iroquois could offer a united front against the newcomers.

Central to Iroquois society was a matrilineal family system, or "fireside," in which social relations followed the female line. Married men entered the households of their wives, and women alone could initiate divorce. Networks of related women formed the clans. Women also participated in political decisions. The female elders named the 49 male representatives on the Iroquois council. Men dominated political speeches, but the matriarchs advised and consented about political matters. Women could also initiate wars by sending male war parties to capture an enemy to replace a dead member of the extended family, and women could determine the fate of the captive, either death or adoption. Women could also replace the male counselors or veto military attacks. Shared power between men and women underscored the values of consensual government.

The World View of Native Americans

Political consensus strengthened group identity. Since the Americas were so large and the local en-

vironments so diverse, each location encouraged a unique sense of place and reinforced the distinct development of each group. Yet, despite great variations of language, customs, and spiritual ideas, most Native Americans shared similar beliefs that framed their cultural views. Living close to the natural world, Native Americans held a holistic image of life, believing that all aspects of the universe were interconnected like the threads of a web. Time could be measured by moons and seasons; societies could be divided into clans that shared an identity with animals; individual development followed the biological life cycle of birth, growth, decay, and death. Such a perspective deemphasized individuality, but valued communal obligations. Native Americans saw the world as cyclical, moving from season to season and birth to birth, because, as one Native American prophet put it, "everything is round." Yet because their world appeared complete, Native Americans were unprepared for their encounters with utterly different peoples and failed to appreciate the threat that Europeans posed to their way of life.

Respect for Place

Among Native peoples, group identity was closely linked to where they lived. When they thought of history, they emphasized place rather than time. *Where* things happened appeared more important than *when*. "Instead of records and chronicles," explained one observer of the New England inhabitants, they used the physical environment to stimulate oral traditions. "Where any remarkable act is done, in memory of it, either in the place or [nearby], they make a round hole in the ground." When others passed the hole, "they inquire the cause and occasion of the [hole], which being once known, they are careful to acquaint all men. . . ; and lest such holes should be filled or [overgrown] by accident, as men pass by, they will often renew the same; by which means many things of great antiquity are fresh in memory." Residents of the Appalachian region made small piles of stones to commemorate historical events. Thus history was not about chronological time—a date or year—but a recognition of an important place.

Native Americans also embraced the past by respecting traditions. They were conservative people, dedicated to preserving the "truths" of their elders, because local custom reflected accumulated wisdom and contributed to their survival. Abundant food in most of North America assured adequate subsistence. In New England, adults consumed about 2,500 calories daily, comparable to the modern U.S. diet. But seasonal shortages and crop failures reinforced the values of mutual support for survival. And so proven traditions—customs, habits, "the old ways"—assumed paramount importance for preserving a society. Men hunted the same way their great-grandfathers hunted, and caught the descendants of the animals their great-grandfathers had killed. Innovation and independence were less valued than perfecting the known arts and crafts, observing community restrictions, and accepting one's place in the cosmic order.

Family Relations

Marriage also forged connections to the past, serving to bind together not only two individuals but also their families. Native couples sang love songs and experienced the pangs of passion. "I am a fine-looking woman; still, I am running with my tears" were the words of a traditional Maidu song. Successful marriage required the approval of both families and was sealed by the exchange of gifts, which symbolized the mutual obligations of the two clans. Because marriage was a shared commitment, either spouse could usually initiate a divorce. And, rather than establishing independent households, newly married

Native couples sang love songs and experienced the pangs of passion.

couples took up residence in one of their parents' homes, depending on whether that community emphasized fathers' or mothers' lines of descent. These extended families reinforced community loyalties for mutual assistance.

"Single fornication they count no sin," observed one European of the Rhode Island Narragansetts, "but after marriage . . . then they count it heinous for either of them to be false." Sexual relations were usually controlled by strict rules. Understanding that unrestrained sexuality could be disruptive, societies imposed restraints, or taboos, that obliged people who were preparing to hunt or participate in religious ceremonies or collect medicinal herbs to avoid sexual contacts. Nursing mothers, concerned about producing sufficient milk, abstained from sexual relations, sometimes for years. Native women also used herbs and medicines to avoid pregnancy or induce miscarriages and, in times of war or famine, might practice infanticide.

Warnings about reckless sexuality appeared frequently in tribal folklore, such as the Maidu story of the young mother who left her child to pursue a beautiful butterfly, only to have the insect turn into a man, who led her into strange valleys where she was lost. "When people speak of the olden times," was the moral of the story, "people will say that this woman lost her lover, and tried to get others but lost them, and went crazy and died." Even with these strict heterosexual codes, many tribes permitted certain men (rarely women) to dress and live as members of the opposite sex. According to French observers, such people might be "as much esteemed as the bravest . . . men in the country."

Among the Cherokees, men who crossed customary gender boundaries became the objects of jokes—a way of reaffirming traditional roles. But Cherokee women who took male roles (as warriors, for example) might be honored.

Most Native mothers clung closely to their children. Soon after birth, infants were swaddled tightly in soft skins and attached to a cradleboard, which could be carried on the mother's back. Women used the fluff of cattails or the powdery core of rotten wood to keep the babies dry and clean. Some cultures saw beauty in the flat shape of the face and literally molded the skulls of their offspring to create the desired appearance. Children were breast-fed for years and weaned on a porridge of boiled corn. In the absence of domestic cows and goats, Native people lacked a milk substitute and it was unusual to use wet nurses. Even today, people of Native American descent are more likely than the descendants of Europeans to develop allergies to dairy products.

Contrasts of Childhood. In most Native American cultures, the end of childhood came with a naming ceremony. "They never invent new names," observed a French traveler, explaining that each clan used certain names to reinforce kinship ties. Yet a person's name did not necessarily remain the same through an entire lifetime. Instead, names indicated not only one's individual identity but also a social role or status as a member of the community.

Native American naming practices contrasted with European customs. In medieval Catholic countries, at a time when Paris and London were no larger than Cahokia, families usually named their offspring after saints or holy figures, and children celebrated their birthdays on the nameday of their saint. By the 1500s, however, parents in some parts of Protestant Europe, such as England, began more frequently to name their children after themselves or some favored secular person. To assure the perpetuation of a particular

name at a time of high infant mortality, some English families even gave two children the same name. At about the same time, England instituted formal birth registration. With secular names and legal records, birthdays became personal events rather than occasions to celebrate the sacred calendar of the saints. Unlike Native American practices, which linked names to communities, Europeans increasingly stressed individuality.

Native Americans also differed from Europeans in rejecting corporal punishment of the young. At a time when European parents believed that to spare the rod spoiled the child and used beating to discipline the youngest children, Native American parents relied on more gentle practices to instill respect. Splashing water on a child's face was considered an ultimate penalty, which gave great shame to the young. Typically, elders held up positive role models for children to imitate and gave greater latitude in personal behavior.

Contrasting Rites of Passage. Elders also supported their children through personal rites of passage. "You are a girl no more," sang the Wintu of northern California as part of a menstrual ritual. "The chief, the chief, honors thee." Throughout Native America, elaborate ceremonies brought young women through puberty into adult status. Believing that menstruation gave women extraordinary powers—not just the capability of procreation, but also magical energy that could inflict harm or illness—many societies required a woman to live apart during her period, to abstain from certain foods and sexual relations, and to avoid eye contact with everyone. The husband of a menstruating woman might be prohibited from hunting because her condition could weaken his prowess or turn his luck.

Such magical beliefs about menstruation had analogies in European customs. Traditional Jews required women to undergo a ritual bath after menstruating and before resuming sexual relations with their husbands. In medieval Christianity, a menstruating woman was considered spiritually unclean and could be refused religious communion. After childbirth, women were required to undergo "churching," or purification, before returning to normal life. Only with the rise of Protestantism in the 16th century did reformers begin to challenge rituals that implied that sexually active women were unclean. Criticizing Catholic traditions, one Protestant asked indignantly, "Why do they separate her? Why do they cleanse her? Why may she not return to Church . . . before her month be expired?" These protests show that magical beliefs, not very different from those of Native Americans, persisted in Europe.

Other contrasts could be seen in male rites of passage. Except for the sons of aristocrats, European boys engaged in manual work as soon as they were able. Poorer families usually gave their children as apprentices or servants to other families. For boys in England, apprenticeship began at about age 7, and youngsters were expected to serve a master until reaching adulthood. Yet, because of limited economic resources in Europe, boys were not considered men until they could support an independent household. Although statistics are imprecise, the average age of marriage for men in England was in the late twenties, around age 28. For women, it was slightly younger, about 26. English children thus endured a long period of dependence before they could claim to be full-fledged adults.

Among Native Americans, boys also began preparation for adulthood at a young age, learning hunting skills with small bows and arrows and forming a friendship with a male comrade who would become a constant companion. The onset of puberty brought more elaborate rituals, some requiring extraordinary ordeals by which a boy proved his manhood. Taken blindfolded into the forest at night by an older male relative, a New England boy would be left alone to survive by his own ingenuity for an entire winter. Then he would undergo a ritual purging by drinking a brew made from poisonous herbs. "If he is able to stand it all well, and if he is fat and sleek, a wife is given to him." The first successful hunt was another important male rite of passage.

Hallucinogenic drugs also initiated young men into tribal mysteries. Among southern California peoples, such as the Luiseno and Chumash, boys were taken at night to consume *toloache,* a beverage made from Jimson weed, and then they danced until they lost consciousness. This state might last for days, during which the initiate experienced visions. As the heightened sensitivity was prolonged by weeks of fasting, the elders taught young people sacred songs, dances, and wisdom. As a final rite, the men produced sand paintings on the ground to depict the universe and lectured about the meaning of astronomical and natural phenomena. The influence of *toloache* can still be seen in the colorful Chumash rock paintings, found in caves and outcroppings throughout southern California.

On the opposite side of the continent, the Powhatans of Virginia and the Carolinas selected their religious and political leaders by putting boys through rigorous tests called *huskanaws,* which included the use of intoxicating drugs that caused amnesia. "This violent method of taking away the memory," a visitor was told, "is to release the youth from all their childish impressions. . . and unreasonable prejudices which are fixed in the minds of children." Purged of personal bias, a man could then qualify as a political leader. Such impartial men assumed responsibility for dividing food, settling disputes, and initiating diplomacy and war.

The World of Spirits

Besides respecting their political leaders, Native Americans recognized the power of spiritual guides, or shamans. These religious leaders served as intermediaries between humans and the world of spirits. Their skills could be used for good or ill—they could cure or curse—and were seen as extremely dangerous and potent. Bear shamans might not only prophesy a successful hunt but also participate by luring the animals out of their retreats. In regions of drought, the weather shaman would conduct rituals to hasten the arrival of rain. Shamans also conducted religious ceremonies (such as annual mourning rites), treated those afflicted by ghosts, and preserved traditional spiritual practices.

Shamans were valued, above all, for their power to cure. Among Native Americans, illness was seen as a physical entity ("pain," "poison") deposited in the body by an enemy or evil spirit or because the sick person had violated a rule. To remove such ills, the shaman used herbs or animal parts, or manipulated sacred objects such as a secret amulet. Cuts might be made between the eyes to heal headache or other pains. Blowing tobacco smoke into an ill person's face might cure a fever. Among the Yurok and northwestern California people, most shamans were women who underwent rigorous trials, fasting and dancing for ten days until unconscious, before they claimed control of the sacred powers. These practices mirrored unorthodox religious behavior throughout medieval Europe, where "wise men" and "wise women" employed astrology, made amulets, and dispensed herbs to cure disease, change the weather, or predict the future.

The Meeting of Unexpected Peoples

Religion, spiritual prophecy, and a sense of cosmic unity enabled people of all cultures to explain the world according to their beliefs. When the Italian navigator Christopher Columbus saw the naked Taino people in the Caribbean in 1492, he concluded that he had met exactly what he had been looking for: "Indians" from East Asia. Meanwhile, the Taino, Columbus reported, "believe very firmly that I, with these ships and people, came from the sky." Similarly, when Spanish explorers encountered Zuni elders in the southwestern desert in 1540, they reported that "it was foretold . . . more than fifty years ago that a people such as we are would come, and from the direction we have come, and that the whole country would be conquered." Native prophets on the Mississippi River and the Atlantic coast recalled similar predictions of the coming of "a white race."

Such impressions reflected the difficulty of explaining the existence of mutually unknown beings. Prior to direct contact, both Europeans and Americans considered their worlds complete and finished. Just as Christianity assumed that God had created the world in six days, so the Maidu believed that the Earthmaker had shaped the primordial waters into familiar patterns of life. Or, to use another example, the Iroquois of northeastern America thought the Great Spirit ordered the Great Turtle "to get from the bottom of the waters some slime on its back" to form an earthly foundation. Even today, many "Indians" call America "Turtle Island."

The European "discovery" of new humans raised basic questions about the Garden of Eden and the descendants of Adam and Eve. One Spanish writer even proposed the theory of an ancient land bridge connecting the "old world" and the new as a way of preserving his faith in the known universe. Some writers suggested that the natives were one of the "lost" tribes of Israel. Like the Europeans, Native Americans incorporated new beings into their world view by perceiving the strangers as heavenly spirits (*manitous,* in the Algonquian vocabulary) who could communicate with humans.

A Clash of World Views

One day in 1609, the Delawares and Mohicans who inhabited the area of what is now New York and

New Jersey observed something immense floating in the water and debated whether it was an animal or a house. They concluded that "the great Mannitto [the great or Supreme Being]. . . probably was coming to visit them." While the spiritual conjurors wavered "between hope and fear," the women prepared a welcoming feast. Soon the crew of Henry Hudson's *Half Moon* was among them. The sight of the first Dutch visitors provoked wonder at the whiteness of their skin. But the chiefs hesitated to drink the strangers' mysterious brew—believing it to be blood or poison—until one man, fearing that such a rejection would infuriate the Great Spirit, drank the offered cup of wine.

The resulting intoxication proved amazing. For people already fascinated by dream-visions and spiritual quests, alcohol opened a realm of mind-altering substances. Later, alcohol abuse would contribute to the loss of cultural integrity, but initially Native Americans believed that the European traders were gods. A subsequent exchange of gifts, iron axes and stockings from the Europeans, established friendly relations. Yet while the Americans admired European goods, they adapted them to their needs, wearing the axe heads as ornaments around their necks and using the stockings as tobacco pouches. Significantly, the Iroquois word for *European* translated as "ax-maker."

Even a century later, encounters between Native Americans and Europeans continued to be characterized by fear and bewilderment. "We came upon a poor Indian who was coming very carelessly along, carrying a bunch of grass such as they eat," reported a Spanish priest who accompanied an exploratory expedition south of San Francisco Bay in 1776. "But as soon as he saw us he manifested the greatest fright that it is possible to describe. He could do nothing but throw himself at full length on the ground, hiding himself in the grass in order that we might not see him, raising his head only enough to peep at us with one eye." When a Spaniard approached with

glass beads, the Ohlone "was so stupefied that he was unable to take the gift. . . . Completely terrified, and almost without speaking," the man offered his bundle of grass to the strange creatures on horseback, "as if with the present he hoped to save his life, which he feared was lost. He must never have seen Spaniards before," concluded the priest, "and that is why we caused him such surprise and fear." Indeed, the Ohlone had never seen a horse either, and probably believed that the man on horseback was not even human.

Early commercial relations between Native Americans and Europeans underscored profound differences of cultural perspective. Even simple transactions, such as trade and barter, revealed complex distinctions. Just as Europeans saw Americans as a source of natural resources (animal skins, access to gold mines, valuable plants such as sassafras), Native traders saw Europeans as a source of kettles, guns, and fishhooks. But for Native Americans trade was not merely an economic transaction; it was also a form of gift giving, representing friendship and alliance, mutual obligations, and trust. To engage in commercial relations, therefore, Europeans had to give gifts, ranging from beads and "trifles" to manufactured goods, to tribal leaders. The chiefs then dispensed these goods to others in their communities to strengthen their own social relationships. Europeans also had to learn how to measure goods by American standards—an arm's length of beads, for example, or a mouthful of rum. Reciprocal gifts sometimes gave European men access to women as wives or temporary partners. Although these personal arrangements resulted in economic advantages, Native Americans complained frequently that Europeans considered only profits, not communal responsibility, in business relations.

Measuring Place and Time

Cultural differences shaped the way people literally looked at their worlds. European explorers well understood the importance of reliable compasses in navigating the oceans and trekking through unknown country. Indeed, the invention in the 15th century of the astrolabe, a device that measured longitude by the stars, greatly facilitated ocean voyages. Europeans also relied on their own bodies to express direction. "From the summit of this range we saw the magnificent estuary, which stretched toward the southeast," wrote the first Spaniard to see San Francisco Bay. "We left it on our *left* hand, and, turning our *backs* on the bay, advanced to the south-southeast." By contrast, Native Americans never used the egocentric "left-hand, righthand" to give directions. A person walking north might say a mosquito had bitten her "east hand"; later, walking south, she would scratch her "west hand." Native American maps did not locate north at the top, but used the course of the sun from east to west to depict both direction and distance. Equally common was the use of geographical landmarks to describe directions: upriver/downriver might mean north/south; or specific places would be used instead of universal compass points.

The sense of living close to the natural world also influenced the Native Americans' measurement of time. While European traditions emphasized the linearity of time—the chronological calendar moving forward day-by-day, year-by-year—Native Americans generally perceived a cyclical pattern in which time moved with the changing seasons. Each year began in the spring. In fact, Europeans in the age of Columbus shared that perspective. Not until 1582 did Pope Gregory introduce a new calendar that began the new year on January 1 rather than at the spring equinox in March. Protestant countries did not accept the changes until the 18th century. During most of the English colonial period, Anglo Americans used a double-year system; for example, 1630/31 would be used in 1631 between January 1 and the

spring equinox. Native Americans, moreover, marked time by seasonal events; among southeastern people, the herring month was equivalent to March, the strawberry month was June.

Native Americans and Europeans also expressed different views about the spirituality of the land. Although some Native rituals occurred inside specific structures—underground kivas and sweathouses, for example—these edifices were located on geographical places that were endowed with spiritual meaning. But many ceremonies took place outside human architecture. Europeans no longer worshipped outdoors. Instead, they marked religious places with consecrated buildings (churches, chapels, shrines), many of them built on sites considered sacred since pre-Christian times. By 1600, the European countryside had sprouted some 500,000 Christian structures. The first European explorers saw no comparable architecture in America and, without evidence of Christian churches, concluded that Native Americans lacked any religion. "I believe that they would easily be made Christians," wrote Columbus of the first Americans he encountered, "for it appeared to me that they had no creed." The Italian navigator Amerigo Vespucci, for whom the continent was eventually named, agreed that "they are worse than heathen; because we did not see that they offered any sacrifice, nor yet did they have [any] house of prayer." Later, when Europeans did learn of Native American religious practices, they concluded that these heathen worshiped the devil and vowed to convert them to the "true" faith.

Encountering Strange Diseases

Differences of culture and perspective led to multiple misunderstandings, confusion, and disappointment, but nothing after 1492 more powerfully dramatized the collision of worlds than the arrival

An epidemic in 1616–1618 killed 90 percent of the population, effectively exterminating the Massachusetts people.

of deadly diseases for which neither Native American shamans nor European "doctors" could offer a cure. "A few days after our departure," wrote one 16th-century English explorer, "people began to die very fast. . . . The disease . . . was so strange that they neither knew what it was, nor how to cure it." From the first major epidemic that swept through the Caribbean islands and Mexico in 1519, Native Americans succumbed in huge numbers to respiratory infections, typhus, diphtheria, smallpox, measles, mumps, and other illnesses against which their immune systems had no antibodies.

Mortality figures are at best rough estimates, but the population of Aztec Mexico probably dropped from 25 million to 16 million in a single decade. Inhabitants of many Caribbean islands became extinct. In New England, an unspecified epidemic in 1616–1618 killed 90 percent of the population, effectively exterminating the Massachusetts people and removing most of the Native claimants to the land. People "died on heaps, as they lay in their houses," reported one European colonist, who saw human "carcasses lie above the ground without burial."

Native medicine compounded the problem. The custom of crowding around a patient, blowing smoke, and sharing a sweathouse merely exposed more people to infection. Moreover, because the shamans dutifully responded to the needs of the sick, they too became victims, dying suddenly and disrupting the expected treatment of illness. When they saw that Europeans showed no signs of disease, Native Americans concluded that these god-like creatures indeed held powerful weapons that could destroy them at a distance. Ironically, Europeans accepted that interpretation of divine intervention, claiming that the epidemics proved God had cleared away the Native rivals for their settlements.

A Shattered World Survives

Raging epidemics destroyed the very structure of Native societies, killing leaders and followers, shamans and chiefs, adults and children. In addition to foreshadowing the arrival of more strangers who held powerful technological inventions (firearms, fishhooks, knives, cloth, beads, and alcohol), the appearance of diseases without cure created profound demoralization. A world that had seemed orderly and spiritual quickly became fragmented and chaotic.

"There was then no sickness," remembered the Aztec survivors of a lost age. "They had no aching bones; they had then no high fever; they had then no burning chest; they had then no abdominal pain; they had then no consumption; they had then no headache." Instead, sang the Aztecs, "the course of humanity was orderly. The foreigners made it otherwise when they arrived here." A century later, in the 1640s, a New England Narragansett repeated the lamentation: "Our fathers had plenty of deer and skins, our plains were full of deer, as also our woods, and of turkeys, and our coves full of fish and fowl. But," he exclaimed, "these English having gotten our land, they with scythes cut down the grass, and their hogs spoil our clam banks, and we shall all be starved." Ninety years after that, the Natchez leader Tattooed Serpent complained that before the French came "we lived like men who are satisfied with what they have; whereas at this day we are like slaves."

The competition between Native Americans and Europeans for the land and resources of North America would last for centuries. In the beginning, the outcome was not so clear, for the indigenous peoples had developed flourishing societies and lived in harmony with the environment. The early European arrivals, uprooted from their homes and familiar places, depended heavily on the Native Americans' generosity, knowledge of the country, and eagerness to exchange gifts and produce. Neither people expected to abandon their beliefs, but neither could avoid the presence of the other. Steadily, however, European diseases, technologies, and an expansionist ideology shifted the balance of power from Native Americans to invading colonizers. In the end, Europeans and their descendants prevailed, though not completely, and the histories of the rival cultures remained forever intertwined.

INFOTRAC® COLLEGE EDITION EXERCISES

● For additional reading go to InfoTrac College Edition, your online research library, at *http://web1.infotrac-college.com.*

Subject search: early Native Americans

Keyword search: maize

Keyword search: Anasazi

Keyword search: Stone Age America

Keyword search: Amerindian

Keyword search: Indian converts

Keyword search: Aztec

Keyword search: Maya

Keyword search: Iroquois

ADDITIONAL READING

The First Migration

Brian M. Fagan, *The Great Journey: The Peopling of Ancient America* (1987). An archeological analysis of the first Americans, though the most recent discoveries have modified the author's chronology.

Establishing Local Cultures

Alice B. Kehoe, *North American Indians: A Comprehensive Account* (1992). A thorough anthropological survey of the history and culture of diverse societies and peoples; a basic resource for the field.

Diverse California Communities

Malcolm Margolin, *The Ohlone Way* (1978). Written for the lay reader, this work examines Native Americans who inhabited the region around San Francisco Bay.

The World View of Native Americans

Colin G. Calloway, *New Worlds for All: Indians, Europeans, and the Remaking of Early America* (1997). The author explores the interaction of environment, biology, and culture.

Theda Perdue, *Cherokee Women: Gender and Culture Change, 1700–1835* (1998). The first chapters describe the world view of one southeastern nation.

Marion Schwartz, *A History of Dogs in the Early Americas* (1997). A survey of Native Americans' views and uses of the only domesticated animal in America before 1492.

The Meeting of Unexpected Peoples

William Cronon, *Changes in the Land: Indians, Colonists, and the Ecology of New England* (1983). Contrasts Native American and European views of the natural environment.

Alfred W. Crosby, Jr., *The Columbian Exchange: Biological and Cultural Consequences of 1492* (1972). This pioneering work describes the impact of European diseases on Americans and the diffusion of plants and animals between Old World and New.

Karen Ordahl Kupperman, *Indians and English: Facing Off in Early America* (2000). Depicts the earliest cross-cultural encounters between Native peoples and English and how they viewed each other.

Daniel K. Richter, *The Ordeal of the Longhouse: The Peoples of the Iroquois League in the Era of Colonization* (1992). This study of Iroquois culture and diplomacy explains underlying values and changes induced by Europeans.

Anthologies of Primary Sources

James Axtell, ed., *The Indian Peoples of Eastern America: A Documentary History of the Sexes* (1981).

Malcolm Margolin, ed., *The Way We Lived: California Indian Reminiscences, Stories, and Songs* (1994).

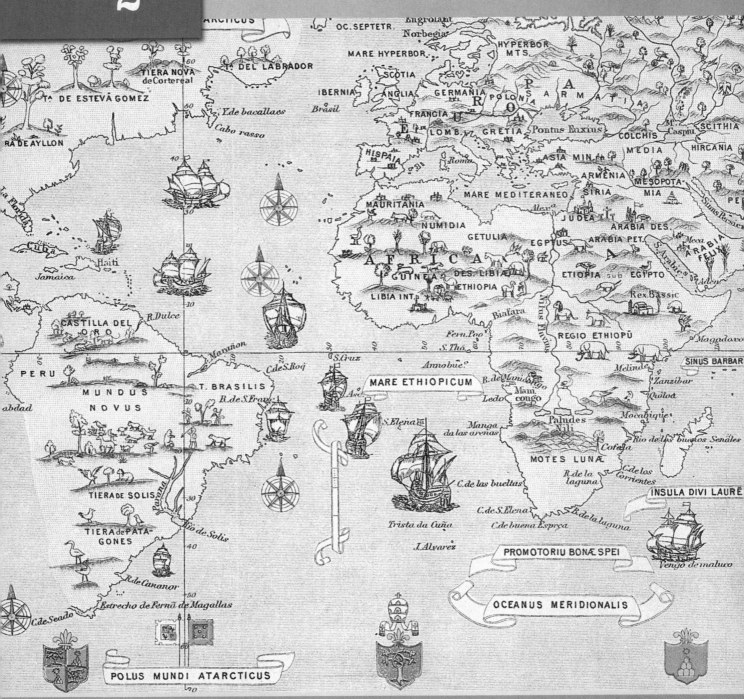

Europe's Quest for Empire in America

CHRONOLOGY

1444	Portuguese sailors reach the Senegal River in West Africa
1450s–1480s	Portugal and Spain seize Atlantic islands
1492	Columbus touches land in the Caribbean
1494	Treaty of Tordesillas divides the Western Hemisphere between Portugal and Spain
1497	John Cabot establishes English claim in North America
1498	Portuguese sail around tip of southern Africa
1500	Portuguese accidentally reach Brazil
1513	Ponce de Leon lands in Florida
1519–1521	Hernan Cortes conquers Aztec empire in Mexico
1539–1543	Hernando de Soto and Francisco Coronado explore North America for Spain
1558	Elizabeth I becomes Queen of England
1565	Spain establishes St. Augustine in Florida
1585	Walter Raleigh plants first English colony at Roanoke
1588	England defeats Spanish Armada
1598	Juan de Onate claims New Mexico for Spain
1608	Samuel de Champlain founds French settlement at Quebec
1624	Dutch plant colony at Manhattan Island

"What is it for?" inquired Queen Isabella peevishly in 1492.

A member of the royal court, who had just presented her with the first printed grammar of the Spanish language, was taken aback for a moment.

"Your majesty," responded the donor, with all the presence a courtier could muster, "language is the perfect instrument of empire."

Although the young queen could not have known it in 1492—the year Spain's monarchs sponsored Christopher Columbus's historic quest for a water route to the "Indies"—Spanish names were destined to appear in all corners of the globe. Soon the words of the Spanish empire would be stamped on places called "San Salvador" in the Caribbean, "La Florida" in southeast North America, and "California" on its western coast.

This quest for empire, dramatized by the startling "discovery" of America in 1492, reflected a longer process of European expansionism. Unlike most Native American peoples who exploited local natural resources, Europeans had probed beyond their own continent for centuries, seeking commerce, commodities, and technology from distant lands. This interest in expansion stemmed in part from the lack of a self-sufficient economy in Europe, and from the desire to obtain valuable products from Asia and Africa, such as spices to preserve food.

Geographic expansion also expressed a competitive impulse as Europe's Christian monarchs undertook military and religious crusades to end Muslim domination of the Mediterranean world. Indeed, European Christians assumed that God approved their worldly conquests and they needed no further justification for waging wars against the "infidels." Expansionism also reflected persistent rivalries within Europe, particularly conflicts among the monarchs about national wealth, political prestige, and religious truth. After the Protestant Reformation shattered the religious uniformity of Europe in the early 1500s, Catholics and Protestants competed aggressively to expand the "true" religion around the world.

Expansionism inevitably involved cultural confrontation. Just as the Europeans who first penetrated the Western Hemisphere carried cultural and biological baggage (metal swords, infectious diseases) that transformed Native American life, so the natural resources of the Western Hemisphere (gold, silver, tobacco, maize, animal skins, human labor, and the often-fatal syphilis bacterium) changed European society. The importation of gold and silver from America to Spain, for example, produced an inflation of prices in western Europe, which encouraged landlords to raise rents. Many poor agricultural workers lost their homes and wandered the countryside in search of work. Believing that Europe had a surplus population, some writers advocated colonization to ease the misery of the poor. Yet, ironically, the first cargo of workers to cross the Atlantic in 1495 sailed from west to east. These were the enslaved Caribbeans who were shipped to Spain.

European contacts with the peoples of Africa stimulated similar exchanges of commerce and culture and produced similar problems. Trade for west African peppers, gold, and slaves enriched both European and African rulers and the merchants who transacted overseas business. But the result was the enslavement of vast numbers of Africans, of whom more than 10 million were shipped across the Atlantic to populate America and exploit its resources. The overwhelming majority went to South America and the Caribbean; about half a million—5 percent of the total—landed in North America.

Native Americans, Europeans, and Africans thus shared an intricate relationship in America's development. Biological differences among them included skin color, facial characteristics, blood enzymes, and antibodies against various diseases. But intermarriage and sexual relations, voluntary or forced, soon diluted the genetic purity of all races. Among this multitude of groups, moreover, differences in social structure, culture, and political organization could be matched by innumerable similarities. Hereditary monarchies, for example, existed in England, Mexico, and the Kongo; meanwhile, trading empires flourished among the Dutch of northern Europe, the matriarchal Iroquois who inhabited the northern Adirondack regions in North America, and the Ibibio-speaking Efiks of Biafra in western Africa. Yet, in America after 1492, the steady expansion of European political power over Native Americans and Africans created unequal relationships. Political institutions that were imposed by European kings, bishops, and merchants limited the cultural independence of other peoples, as well as of European men and women who lacked a political voice.

The Cultures of West Africa

Africans shared with Europeans and Native Americans an enthusiasm for commerce. The diversity of African societies had encouraged trade for centuries. In the region between the Senegal and Gambia rivers, for example, one of the first areas reached by the Portuguese during the 15th century, inhabitants of Mali had long exchanged "clothes of fine cotton" for salt brought by coastal traders. Although Africans spoke some 800 distinct languages, many had related grammars and vocabulary that were mutually intelligible, and politically separate groups often participated in trade networks along the rivers. Even when groups were linguistically diverse, such as the people of Upper Guinea, their shared Islamic influences and geographical proximity facilitated trade. In Lower Guinea, the Yoruba language and traditions prevailed on the coast, while those of Benin dominated the interior, in each case establishing a common culture for trade. On the Angola coast, by contrast, similar Bantu languages encouraged cultural homogeneity, but strong political rivalries produced continuing conflict and warfare.

A World of Spirits

Christian and Muslim traders often sought to gain the religious conversion of African "heathens" to facilitate commercial transactions, and some African leaders, such as the king of the Fetu, became Christians to gain access to western goods. But most west Africans resisted such efforts, because they already held religious views that acknowledged a supreme being, or creator, and a world of spirits that included the living and the dead, plants and animals, and even inanimate objects. Although some groups, like the Ashanti, built shrines to the high god, Africans generally revered the lesser spirits, particularly those of ancestors and elders. Central to the African world view was respect for the past and for the founders of the lineage clans with which each individual identified. Like Europeans, Africans named their children after grandparents and other elders who defined their place in the clan.

West African religions linked individuals with ancient ancestors as well as recently deceased relatives. According to African beliefs, such predecessors remained intimately involved in the affairs of this world, for good or evil. Communication with the spirits of the dead required knowledgeable priests, skilled in magic and medicine, who made offerings to these ancestors. Like Native American shamans, these spiritual guides used amulets, charms, and herbs to negotiate with the spirit world, to counter witchcraft, and to treat those afflicted by evil ghosts. Centuries later, some Africans in America placed glass bottles in trees to ward off bad spirits.

West African religious ceremonies involved intense musical expression, including dancing, clapping, drumming, and singing. Africans believed that each spirit responded to personal melodies or rhythms. Among the common elements of west African cultures was the circular counterclockwise dance (following the direction of the sun in the Southern Hemisphere), which appeared in the rituals of the life cycle associated with birth, coming of age, and death. Such beliefs, shared by many different cultures, would endure in America and

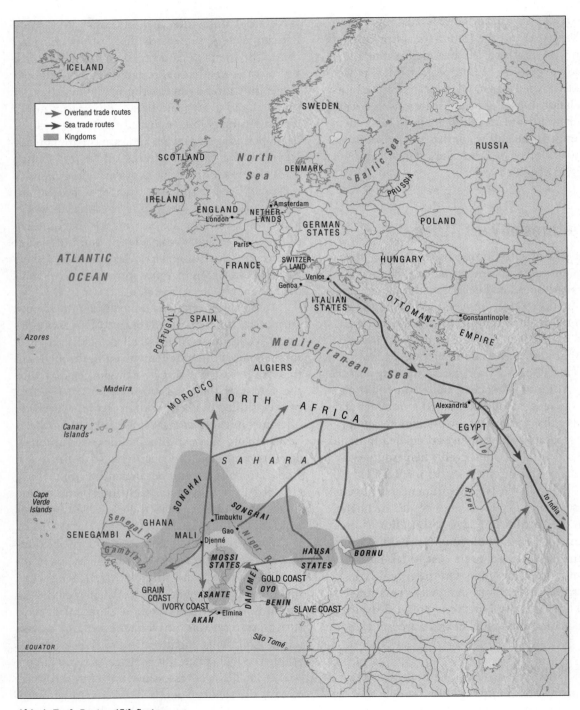

Africa's Trade Routes, 15th Century

establish common grounds for diverse Africans to form an African American identity.

Political Diversity and Commercial Rivalry

Despite their shared spiritual universe, west African societies remained politically fragmented. Some were little more than a cluster of villages claiming a common ancestry and a central place where elders met to settle disputes. Others developed broader geographical ties and emerged as kingdoms and empires. Most Africans lived in decentralized political units with a population ranging from 3,000 to 30,000. This small scale underscored the importance of belonging to a particular place—having a sense of home ground—where, upon death, a person's spirit was believed to return. Most west African societies were hierarchical, controlled by a single ruler or ruling family with extensive power. Yet political diversity encouraged competition between villages and regional groups for trade. Commercial rivalry, in turn, provoked persistent warfare, even before the arrival of European merchants whose desire for African commodities, including slaves, intensified competition.

Slavery and Africa

Long before they had contact with Europeans, many African states accepted slavery as a social institution. The Ashanti, for example, used five different words to describe degrees of servitude. A criminal might be sentenced to slavery or a debtor might settle a payment through voluntary enslavement; more frequently, prisoners of war became slaves of their captors. Usually slavery implied some type of kinship between owner and captive, a relationship involving mutual responsibilities that did not necessarily pass on to the children of slaves. As in many Native American societies, a prisoner might be adopted by the captor and permitted to intermarry and raise children who participated in community life. Yet such a person would remain subordinate within the captor's family. African slaves also retained basic rights to earn wealth and own property, even to inherit their owner's assets.

Slavery and long-term servitude flourished in African societies because cultural values permitted limited opportunities for individuals to acquire wealth. As in Native American cultures, African law generally rejected private ownership of land. Rather, land belonged to the state or community and was appropriated according to its use by particular households. But a family could increase its economic productivity, and thus improve its wealth, status, and power, by using slaves to tend larger fields or weave more cloth. Often slaves captured in war might be conscripted into the armies of their conquerors, and some were employed as public officials. Rather than joining a family or clan, public servants became slaves of the ruling household.

Because slaves might easily escape to their home countries, African leaders often took the precaution of trading their captives to more distant places. Before Europeans arrived in west Africa, a substantial overland trade in gold and slaves linked that region with the Muslim states of northern Africa. In fact, the very expansion of trade created a demand for labor to produce commodities and transport them to market, a demand that stimulated the sale and purchase of human beings.

European Involvement in the Slave Trade

European involvement in the Atlantic slave trade built upon African precedents and required the cooperation of African merchants. Although early European slave traders simply kidnapped Africans from coastal areas, by 1450 Europeans generally purchased African slaves from previous African

TABLE 2.1	
Portuguese Slave Imports, 1450–1870	
1450–1500	33,500
1500–1600	241,400
1600–1700	560,000
1700–1810	1,909,700
1810–1870	1,445,400
	4,190,000

Source: James A. Rawley, *The Transatlantic Slave Trade*, New York, 1981.

owners, who acquired slaves specifically for the purpose of resale.

The Portuguese first acquired African slaves by purchase from caravans heading north, effectively diverting the human traffic from the Sahara to the Atlantic coast. Even though the European market for slaves remained limited, the Portuguese traded about 2,500 per year during the 15th century; by 1500, Portuguese exports totaled 33,500 slaves. During the next century, the Portuguese traded 240,000 slaves. And, despite increasing competition from other European nations, Portuguese purchases exceeded half a million slaves during the 17th century and doubled again in the next hundred years (Table 2.1).

The most obvious change wrought by Europe's entry into the slave trade lay in the racial and religious differences between white Christian owners and black non-Christian slaves. The growing market for slaves also intensified competition among African slave catchers. "Every day people are kidnapped and enslaved," complained the Kongo's King Afonso in 1525, "even members of the king's family." Like earlier Muslim slave traders, the Catholic church accepted slavery as a fair punishment for prisoners taken in a "just" war. Now African leaders fought wars simply to acquire slaves for Europeans.

By treating African slaves as economic commodities, rather than as family members, European traders could disregard traditional cultural restraints on the treatment and status of slaves. Of course, it was in the economic interests of merchants to protect their investments. But a growing demand for slave labor greatly increased the profitability of the slave trade, so that Atlantic merchants could focus on gross benefits rather than the condition of individuals. In any event, the journey of slaves from Africa to Europe, to the Atlantic islands, and eventually, for most slaves, to the lands of the Western Hemisphere—the so-called Middle Passage—proved extremely brutal.

The Ordeal of Enslavement

During the four centuries in which the Atlantic slave trade flourished, 10 to 12 million Africans were forcibly uprooted from their homes and shipped to America. Mortality rates, which varied according to the length of voyage (typically from one month to six weeks, or more), ranged from 5 to 20 percent. So appalling were conditions aboard slave ships that even European crews died at high rates. Tightly packed in suffocating quarters below decks, shackled slaves lacked fresh air and sufficient space to lie on their backs. Slave women, fewer in number, were sometimes permitted to remain on the decks, but fell prey to sexual assault by European sailors. Faced with dehydration, malnutrition, and such diseases as smallpox, dysentery, measles, scurvy, yaws, and worms, even the strongest slaves experienced profound suffering during the passage to America.

"What heart could be so hard," wrote Gomes Eannes de Zurara, a courtier who witnessed the arrival of the first African slaves in Portugal in 1444, "as not to be pierced with piteous feelings to see that company? For some kept their heads low, and their faces bathed in tears, looking one upon another. Others stood groaning very dolorously, looking up to the height of heaven, fixing their eyes upon it, crying out loudly, as if asking help from the Father of nature; others struck their faces with the palms of their hands, throwing themselves at full length upon the ground; while others made lamentations in the manner of a dirge, after the custom of their country."

Three hundred years later, an Ibo man named Olaudah Equiano described the same sense of fear and despair, believing that he "had gotten into a world of bad spirits, and that they were going to kill me." Observing a large copper pot boiling with water "and a multitude of black people of every description chained together, every one of their countenances expressing dejection," he was convinced that he would be eaten by the crew. Some slaves were stunned into melancholy by the ordeal and refused to eat; others jumped overboard to die and thus facilitate the return of their spirits to Africa before they lost their way. Still others attacked their captors, which led ship captains to keep the men (seldom the women) in chains through the entire passage. Once landed, the weakened slaves endured additional indignities, such as branding, whipping, and separation from family and friends.

Sugar and Slaves

Despite the high death toll of the Atlantic slave trade, profits in America promised to more than offset any economic losses. Within only two decades of Columbus's first voyage to America, Spain's colonial settlements in the Caribbean were returning great wealth by satisfying Europe's sweet tooth, the craving for sugar. Portugal and Spain first developed profitable sugar manufac-

An Ibo man named Olaudah Equiano was convinced that he would be eaten by the crew.

turing on the Atlantic islands. The formation of colonies in America merely increased the economic opportunities. Indeed, Spain's Caribbean colonies of Santo Domingo, Jamaica, and Puerto Rico and Portugal's Brazil offered unprecedented profits for European sugar investors, but only if the American plantations could find an adequate supply of labor.

Having already developed the slave trade in west Africa, Portugal and Spain looked there for a labor force to work the sugar plantations in America. Although Spain's Catholic monarchs promulgated many laws against Native American slavery, few Spaniards objected to the enslavement of Africans. Since the Middle Ages, Spanish law had permitted the enslavement of Muslims and other "heathen," and Muslims in turn had seized Europeans to become slaves. Beginning in the 15th century, both Portugal and Spain had used African slaves to manufacture sugar for decades. Ironically, the Africans' immunity to yellow fever and malaria, due to a genetic factor known as sickle-cell hemoglobin, made them hardier tropical workers than either Native Americans or Europeans. By the early 1500s, the Caribbean islands had become a profitable market for African slaves; by the end of that century, the demand for sugar workers had spread from Spain's island plantations to Portugal's Brazil.

The economics of sugar production intensified the misery of African workers. In 1530, in a typical mix of cultures, 3,000 African slaves worked on sugar plantations in Puerto Rico, but only 327 Europeans inhabited the island. The vastly outnumbered Europeans had little personal interest in their laborers. The slave population was overwhelmingly male and not expected to live long. But rather than seeking a sexual balance to encourage natural reproduction, sugar planters found it much cheaper to import new slaves to replace those who died. Nor did the planters wish to waste profitable sugar acreage by growing food, preferring to import dried fish and other commodities, even though the resulting poor diet increased mortality rates. High sugar profits easily offset the labor costs. For the next three centuries, sugar and slaves were inextricably connected, enriching European investors while consuming African workers.

The Origins of European Expansionism

European expansion of the slave trade was inseparable from Europe's political expansion into the Western Hemisphere. During the 15th and 16th centuries, several factors stimulated exploration, trade, and colonization beyond Europe's borders. This expansion first emerged among the centralized monarchies, which were capable of expending large national resources to finance overseas endeavors. That was one reason why Portugal and Spain initiated colonial development, why England and the Netherlands, delayed by domestic upheavals, came later, and why other countries, such as Italy and Germany, barely participated in the great adventure. Colonies, in other words, were an extension of national power.

Successful expansion also depended on new commercial practices, which could produce the capital and credit to support such expensive and risky undertakings. Overseas investments initially promised to add to private and national wealth. In addition, the search for new trade and new

lands expressed an intellectual curiosity associated with a cultural movement known as the Renaissance, a rebirth of learning during the 15th and 16th centuries. The desire for more knowledge about the world, for technological innovations, and for new experiences created the mental impulse that made European expansion possible. Trade and colonies rewarded those who made daring choices.

Finally, these expansionist values presumed the absolute superiority of western European culture. "Colonies degenerate," advised an English promoter of overseas settlement, "when the colonists imitate and embrace the habits, customs, and practices of the natives." Europe remained the standard by which explorers and colonizers measured the peoples of the world. European modes of thought—European ideas about food, clothing, and shelter; European notions of time, place, and justice—defined their relationships with the inhabitants of other parts of the world.

Western Europe Takes the First Steps

Geographical location prompted Portugal and Spain to embark on the road to empire in the 15th century. Both nations had competed for centuries with Islamic peoples on the Iberian peninsula and in North Africa for political dominance and control of Mediterranean trade. Religious differences between Catholic and Islamic rivals added intellectual and emotional intensity to European expansionism. Both Spain and Portugal had participated in religious crusades to free Jerusalem from its Islamic occupants. These endeavors had introduced Europeans to valuable commodities from Asia: silk, spices, gold, sugar, and precious stones. But commerce to Asia was dominated by merchants in the Italian city-states, such as Venice, who operated between western Europe and the Middle East and made immense profits as middlemen. Because of the Italian control of this trade, Asian products remained scarce and expensive in western Europe.

To break the Italian trade monopoly, the monarchs of Portugal and Spain sought an alternative route to the riches of Asia. Portugal's Prince Henry the Navigator, a visionary empire builder, also wanted to bypass the Muslim merchants of Morocco, who controlled trade with sub-Saharan west Africa, particularly to gain access to the celebrated gold fields and the "grains of paradise" (peppers) that grew on the Atlantic coast. During the early 1400s, Portugal and Spain began to explore and settle the Atlantic islands—the Canaries, Madeiras, and Azores. In the mid-1400s, Portugal occupied the uninhabited Madeiras and Azores, and Spain seized the Canary Islands, enslaving the native population. Taking advantage of the fertile lands, both countries established sugar plantations and wine production and imported African slaves as a labor force. Meanwhile, Portuguese sailors advanced along the west coast of Africa, reaching the Senegal River ("river of gold") and Cape Verde in 1444. By the end of the century, Portuguese navigators had rounded the Cape of Good Hope at the southern tip of Africa and found a direct water route to the Indian Ocean.

The Portuguese on the African Coast

This gradual expansion along the African coast introduced Europeans to vast commercial opportunity. Portuguese maps described the shoreline by its commodities: the Grain Coast, the Ivory Coast, the Gold Coast, the Slave Coast. Portugal's success came from superior navigational technology, including new ocean-going vessels, such as the speedy caravel, which sailed efficiently into the head winds; an improved box compass, borrowed from Arab sailors; the astrolabe to measure latitude; and sophisticated charts of ocean currents and maps of the Atlantic coast.

Such technological advantages allowed the Portuguese to attack west African shores and raid coastal communities for gold, pepper, and slaves. But although European ships could dominate the high seas, Africans successfully defended coastal waters from the invaders. The tropical disease environment caused high mortality among Europeans, further discouraging military raids. Unlike the Atlantic islands, west Africa could not be conquered and settled by Europeans. (Thanks to a lucky accident, however, Portugal's expansion toward Africa did lead to a single colony in America. Blown off course in a storm in 1500, a Portuguese crew landed in South America, establishing claims to what later became Brazil.)

Unable to conquer Africa, Portugal's empire consisted of a network of trading posts. Africans participated equally in this coastal trade, collecting tribute and customs duties for local transactions. African preferences for European textiles, metal products (iron knives, copper bowls), shells, and beads—items which were already available in Africa—underscore the voluntary nature of this trade. To conduct business, European visitors had to follow African protocol, bring gifts to rulers, obtain permission, and pay taxes.

While African rulers negotiated commercial arrangements with Portuguese officials, they also conducted business unofficially with private traders, known by the Portuguese word *lancados*, who settled in small numbers along the coast. Intermarrying with African women, these Afro-Portuguese traders and their mulatto descendants served as intermediaries in coastal commerce and came to dominate the local markets. They established trade networks along the African river systems that led into the interior of the continent. By exchanging European goods for commodities that previously had gone overland by caravan to Morocco, the Portuguese accomplished their plan to break Muslim control of the African trade. By the

16th century, Portugal had extended its commercial transactions into east Africa on the Indian Ocean and to the islands still further east in Asia.

Spain Challenges the Portuguese Empire

Portugal's burgeoning empire—the sugar plantations on the Atlantic islands, the spice trade near Senegal, and a thriving slave trading center on the island of Sao Tome—brought immense profits and excited Europe's interest in exotic commodities. Among the most ambitious dreamers of expanding global trade was a Genoese mariner, Christopher Columbus, who had sailed three times under the Portuguese flag to the Guinea coast. Like all educated sailors of his time, Columbus knew the world was round and speculated that he could find a water route to the Asian markets by sailing west across the Atlantic. But unlike most geographers, he drastically underestimated the circumference of the globe. The Portuguese court, content with its commercial success, promptly rejected Columbus's plans. He took them to Spain, where he obtained royal approval from Queen Isabella and King Ferdinand to launch three ships in search of Asian markets.

Columbus was unaware that other European sailors had preceded his western voyage. According to archeological evidence and oral tradition, Norse explorers led by Leif Erickson had landed in "Vinland" (today's Newfoundland, Canada) in the 11th century, but made no effort to build a settlement. Four hundred years later, Basque sailors had probably discovered the rich cod fisheries off the Newfoundland coast and may have built smokehouses and traded with local inhabitants. Such contact remained haphazard because Europeans lacked an incentive to develop trade or settlement on such isolated terrain. Columbus's promise of access to Asian commodities, by contrast, appealed to an existing demand. Indeed, in the decade prior to Columbus's voyage, merchants in Bristol, England, had sent exploratory vessels westward across the Atlantic toward a place they called "Brasil," though the voyages proved futile.

The Search for Wealth

Columbus's four voyages to America followed the pattern of Portuguese exploration and commerce. Like his first employers, Columbus's Spanish sponsors were interested less in establishing colonies than in opening trade. Soon after landing in what he thought were the "Indies" (really the island of San Salvador in the Bahamas), Columbus began to search for valuable commodities, especially gold, and for places to build fortified trading posts like those he had visited in west Africa.

As for the native inhabitants he encountered, Columbus quickly tested the market advantages. On the very first day of contact, he recorded giving the Taino natives red caps and glass beads "in which they took so much pleasure." Later, the Taino reciprocated with parrots, cotton threads, and spears, for which the Europeans exchanged small glass beads and bells. Columbus was obviously disappointed by their limited resources, describing them as "people very poor in everything." They had no iron and knew nothing of arms; when the Spanish showed them swords the Taino grasped the blades with their hands and cut themselves. Yet even in these deficiencies, Columbus perceived commercial opportunities. "They ought to be good servants," he wrote in his journal. "Our Lord pleasing, I will carry off six of them at my departure. . . in order that they may learn to speak." When Columbus departed for Spain, he carried thirty Taino aboard ship; only seven survived the voyage.

Having discovered no obvious wealth, Columbus was already envisioning another type of com-

> **"They ought to be good servants. Our Lord pleasing, I will carry off six of them at my departure . . . in order that they may learn to speak."**

mercial enterprise, similar to the Portuguese and Spanish settlements of the Atlantic islands. The natives "are fit to be ordered about and made to work, plant, and do everything else that may be needed," he assured the Spanish monarchs, "and build towns and be taught our customs, and go about clothed." After receiving a royal reception in Spain, Columbus began to prepare for a second voyage. Instead of viewing America as a unique place with a distinctive environment, the Spanish planned to remake the Western Hemisphere in the image of Europe. Among the cargo on the second voyage would be horses, cows, goats, sheep, and pigs; seeds for vegetables and fruit trees; and wheat to serve as a food staple. New Spain would become an extension of the Old World.

News of Columbus's voyage aroused Portuguese protests against intrusion into its empire. But in 1493 the two Catholic monarchies accepted mediation from the Pope, who drew a demarcation line dividing the heathen world between the two kingdoms. In 1494, the Treaty of Tordesillas gave control of the African and Asian trade to Portugal and confirmed Spain's claims to most of the Western Hemisphere. The boundary line left a large portion of South America to Portugal, the area later claimed because of the accidental landfall in 1500. Other European nations, not parties to the treaty, simply ignored it.

Spain's Early Colonization

On his second voyage to the Caribbean in 1493, Columbus brought 1,500 Spanish settlers to His-

paniola in the Caribbean and planned to establish regular trade with Spain, including the sale of Native American slaves, whom he described as cannibals. Resistance from the native Caribs resulted in the first struggle between Americans and Europeans, which the Spanish won. Columbus subsequently gave one captured woman to his friend Cuneo, who recorded the ensuing rape with clinical amusement. By 1515, the Spanish had planted settlements on the islands of Puerto Rico, Jamaica, and Cuba.

To encourage development of these settlements, the Spanish crown established a system of forced labor, known as *encomienda,* and gave private citizens rights to use both the land and the labor of the inhabitants. As an *encomienda,* an entire native village might be assigned to work for a single landowner. Intended to Christianize and civilize the native peoples, the system instead brought calamity, forcing the Native Americans to perform hard labor in agriculture, mining, road building, and public works. As a result of overwork and vulnerability to European diseases, the Native American labor force began to decline. Of a Caribbean population that numbered about 1 million in 1492, fewer than 50,000 survived 30 years later.

Some Catholic missionaries, most famously the friar Bartholome de Las Casas, protested the mistreatment of native peoples. The Spanish monarchy shared those concerns and rejected the enslavement of Native Americans, viewing them instead as subjects to be converted to the Catholic faith. But the royal authority could not prevent abuses in distant America. In 1530, two Spanish judges reported that Native Americans "treat slaves as relations, while the Christians treat them as dogs."

Spaniards continued to seek easy wealth. Still believing that the newfound lands were a part of Asia, explorers embarked on numerous voyages to find a water route to the Indies. In 1513, Vasco de Balboa crossed the Isthmus of Panama and became

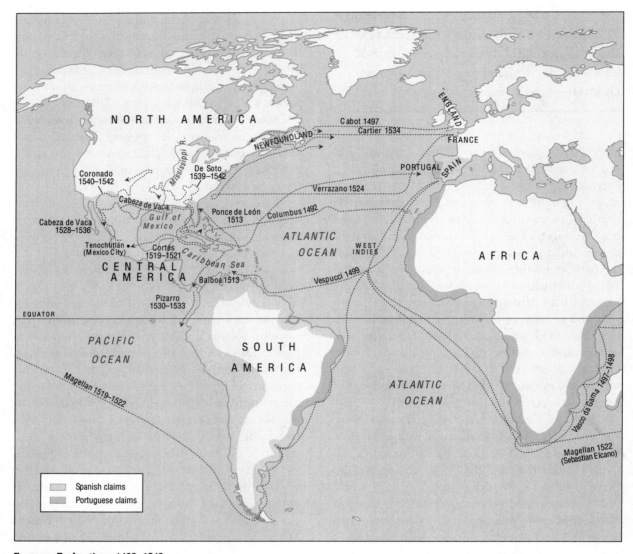

European Explorations, 1492–1542

the first European to glimpse the Pacific Ocean. But the first explorer to suggest the existence of a separate continent was Amerigo Vespucci, a Florentine navigator who sailed under Spanish flags; by the second decade of the century, he had placed his name on maps of the New World. Yet only after

Ferdinand Magellan sailed through the straits of South America into the Pacific and proceeded to circumnavigate the globe between 1519 and 1522 did Europeans generally understand that America was a separate continent with potential riches far more valuable than the spice trade with Asia.

Other Spanish adventurers, members of the lower aristocracy who became known as *conquistadores* (conquerors) came to America to find wealth by plundering the more affluent Native American societies. In 1519, a Spanish official, Hernan Cortes, led an expedition to the coast of Mexico, where the native peoples told of the vast wealth of their Aztec rulers. Forming alliances with these dissatisfied subjects and benefiting by the Aztecs' belief that the Spaniards were mythical white gods, Cortes overpowered the Aztec capital at Tenochtitlan. The Spanish conquest succeeded because of some technological advantages, particularly European guns and soldiers who rode on horses, animals previously unknown in America. But the decisive factor was the presence of a microscopic virus, smallpox, which devastated Mexico's population. "The streets, squares, houses, and courts were filled with bodies," said one observer. "Even Cortes was sick from the stench in his nostrils."

The splendor of the Aztec metropolis, with its elaborate aqueducts, silver and gold statuary, and masonry buildings, astonished the invaders. "Some of our soldiers even asked whether the things that we saw were not a dream," declared one of the victors. Cortes proceeded to confiscate the precious metals and jewels, destroy the temples where the Atzecs had conducted human sacrifices, and enslave the survivors. By 1521, the Aztec emperor Moctezuma was dead. Out of the ashes of the capital, Spain's Mexico City would rise. And the quest for gold continued. In 1531, Francisco Pizarro led an expedition against the Incas of Peru, accomplishing the conquest of this rich empire with the aid of European diseases.

Competition for North America

As Spain extracted great wealth from Central and South America and founded a sugar empire in the Caribbean, the hope of finding precious minerals lured explorers into the unknown territories of what is now the United States. Spain's interest in North America also emboldened other Europeans—French, Dutch, and English—to seek similar acquisitions. Like the Spanish and Portuguese, these interlopers searched primarily for trade advantages, particularly a sea route to Asia, and only belatedly recognized the economic and political benefits of colonization. Viewing America as a map rather than a landscape, they drew artificial boundaries, made extravagant territorial claims, and disregarded the prior rights of the Native peoples.

Spain Explores North America

Despite fabulous tales told by Native Americans to Spanish explorers, none of the *conquistadores* found the mythical cities of gold in North America. Their efforts did inspire great sagas of adventure. Ponce de Leon, for example, landed on the Florida coast in 1513, seeking gold and the "fountain of youth," but met resistance from the native Calusas and withdrew without finding any treasure. When he returned eight years later, the Calusas again repelled the invasion. Later Spanish *conquistadores* raided the South Carolina coast for Native American slaves, and Spaniards built houses and a church among the Guales in Georgia in 1526, but soon abandoned the colony. Exploratory voyages by Juan Cabrillo along the Pacific coast during the 1540s extended Spain's claim to the western shores of North America.

By the mid-16th century, Spanish explorers were penetrating the interior of the northern continent. "They wore coats of iron, and war bonnets of metal, and carried for weapons short canes that spit fire and made thunder," remembered the Zuni people who lived in what is now New Mexico. In 1540, the arrival of a Spanish expedition on horseback, led by Francisco Vasquez de Coronado, prompted a Zuni attack with bows and arrows. The invaders retaliated with gunpowder, enabling Coronado to occupy the Native village he called "Cibola," which consisted of adobe apartment-like structures. The party proceeded to explore surrounding regions, including the Grand Canyon, but found no gold and abandoned the search in 1541. Meanwhile, an expedition under Hernando De Soto marched from Florida to the Mississippi River, plundering Native villages, raping, maiming, and murdering with impunity. Seeking gold, these campaigns acquired little systematic information about North American geography, except that the interior of the continent was vast and diverse.

Rival Claims to North America

"Without settlement," warned a 16th-century Spanish official, "there is no good conquest." Focusing on the plunder of Native American societies, fabled water routes to the Indies, and the mythical cities of gold, Spain claimed rights to all of North America, but failed to establish colonial settlements to protect its authority. Soon other countries arrived to challenge Spanish claims. Like Spain, these European rivals sought wealth through theft or trade with Native Americans rather than the creation of permanent settlements. During the 16th century, most European activity in North America involved temporary territorial encroachment and military raids. Looking at America as a map, European soldier-explorers enabled their countries to claim ownership of areas that were already inhabited by other people, mostly Native Americans. Possession of those lands was another matter.

Since Spanish treasure ships sailing from Mexico passed close to Florida's shores, French pirates used the peninsula as a base of attack. But the first efforts at French settlement appeared on the coast of what is today South Carolina in 1562. As French Protestants, known as *Huguenots,* sought refuge from religious persecution at home, an expedition of 150 men built a fort at "one of the greatest and fairest havens in the world." Two years later, another group of French Huguenots landed at Fort Caroline on the St. John's River in Florida.

Responding to these territorial threats, Spain sent Pedro Menendez to start a settlement at what is now St. Augustine, Florida, in 1565. Believing that Huguenots and Native Americans "held similar beliefs, probably Satanic in origin," Menendez decided to become "free from this wicked sect." Two weeks after landing, he attacked the French, killing even those who surrendered. The next year, Spain eliminated the French settlement in South Carolina. While continuing to search for precious metals, Menendez planted small garrisons around Florida, most of which failed to survive. By the end of the century, St. Augustine stood as a lonely outpost of the Spanish empire.

While Spain and France engaged in petty warfare on the Atlantic coast, 2,000 miles to the west in the desert country near what is now Albuquerque, a Spanish official named Juan de Onate stood among the native Pueblo peoples in 1598 and invited them to become subjects of Spain in the new province of New Mexico. The Spanish hoped that the settlement would lead to the discovery of silver mines and provide access to the Pacific Ocean, an expectation that soon clashed with the geographical reality. Spanish oppression of the Pueblos also provoked retaliatory attacks, which brought even harsher retribution. But limited natural resources and the difficulty of survival in the dry environment discouraged further settlement. Onate was recalled to Mexico in disgrace, partly for abusing the Pueblos, and the outpost was left to Franciscan missionaries to Christianize the natives. Spain's North American colonies would grow slowly during the next two centuries.

The French Seek Permanent Settlement

While Spain concentrated on the southern areas of North America, close to the colonies of Central America, France tried to build permanent colonies in the Northeast. French exploration began with the 1524 voyage of Giovanni da Verazzano, who sailed along the Atlantic coast seeking the "Northwest Passage," a direct water route to Asia. Ten years later, Jacques Cartier sailed around Newfoundland, then entered the St. Lawrence River, believing he had found the elusive waterway. In 1541, the French erected a fortified settlement in Canada, but conflicts with the local peoples and outbreaks of disease ended the experiment. Yet, by 1600, French fishermen were exploiting the cod waters off Newfoundland, while fur traders tapped the market for beaver skins along the St. Lawrence.

Seeking an extensive trade network with the Native Americans for fish and furs, Samuel de Champlain founded the first permanent French settlement at Quebec in 1608. From this base, French explorers, traders, and religious missionaries followed the river routes inland to acquire the precious beaver furs and to redeem the souls of the local Hurons. Later in the century, French explorers traced the Mississippi River to its mouth in the Gulf of Mexico and built trade networks that extended through the Great Lakes and the Mississippi valley. Forming commercial alliances with native inhabitants and accepting intermarriage between Europeans and Native Americans, the French established their dominance of eastern Canada and the hinterland even though their numbers remained fairly small. As in west Africa, where the *lancado* offspring of interracial marriage conducted the slave trade between Europeans and African rulers, in French America, a class of half-French, half-Native Americans, called *metis,* served as intermediaries of French-Native culture and trade.

The Dutch in America

Competition for empire also attracted the Low Countries of northern Europe. Superiority in shipbuilding, navigation, banking, and military aggression enabled the small Dutch nation to emerge as a powerful commercial rival. Having rebelled from the Spanish empire in 1580, the Dutch created the East India Company, which successfully challenged Portuguese business in Asia, while the Dutch West India Company broke the Portuguese slave trade monopoly in Africa. Lacking sufficient population to colonize extensively, the Dutch built trading communities on the African Gold Coast, on islands in the Indian Ocean, in Brazil, in Barbados in the Caribbean, and along the Hudson river (named for Henry Hudson, who explored the region in search of the Northwest Passage in 1609).

Planting a town named New Amsterdam at the foot of Manhattan Island in 1624, and a trading post at Fort Nassau (now Albany) in the Hudson valley, the Dutch West India Company competed with the French for control of the northern fur trade. Limited by a small population, the company tried to attract settlers by offering large land grants (called "patroonships") to investors who, in turn, promised to transport tenant farmers to the colony. But few colonists wanted to be tenants when free land abounded. Yet, because the Dutch trading empire reached across Europe, Africa, Asia, and the Caribbean, the New Netherlands colony attracted a multiethnic population, including Jews, Catholics, Africans (free and slave), and other European nationalities. Yet the establishment of a Swedish trading settlement at the mouth of the Delaware River alarmed the Dutch leaders, who sent a war party to annex the region to New Netherlands. During the 1640s and 1650s, persistent wars with Native Americans accentuated the colony's vulnerability. Despite economic success, the Dutch could not prevent the settlement of Long Island by English colonists nor defend themselves against the English navy.

England Reaches for America

England was late in entering the race for empire in America. Although King Henry VII sponsored a voyage of exploration to North America by John Cabot in 1497, just five years after Columbus's first voyage, dynastic problems during the 16th century distracted England from pursuing colonization. When Henry VIII broke with the Roman Catholic church in 1534 in order to divorce his wife, Catherine of Aragon, he placed England on the side of Protestants who denied the spiritual leadership of the Catholic pope and refused to accept Spain's claims to America.

The English monarchy also encouraged foreign trade. By the mid-16th century, English merchants were forming privately owned "joint-stock companies," the predecessor of the modern corporation, to pool their investments and share the risks and profits of overseas enterprise. By 1600, English trade with Spain and the West Indies brought great profits to adventurous merchants. Although foreign trade encouraged English landowners to shift to wool production, thereby displacing many agricultural workers, merchants claimed that commercial profits would benefit the entire nation. Influential writers such as Richard Hakluyt, who wrote a *Discourse Concerning Western Planting* in 1584, supported colonization as a way of increasing foreign trade while relieving England of its landless population.

Interest in overseas colonies aggravated the rivalry between England and Spain. The conflict

The Roanoke colonists wasted their energy searching for gold instead of planting fields.

flared during the reign of Elizabeth I (1558–1603), who supported attacks on Spanish shipping in the Atlantic. During the 1560s, the buccaneer John Hawkins violated Portugal's trade monopoly in west Africa to acquire slaves and then ignored Spain's commercial prohibitions to sell his cargo in the Caribbean. Hawkins's cousin, Francis Drake, also raided Spanish treasure ships during the 1570s, in one voyage burning Florida's St. Augustine, in another capturing Spanish gold ships in the Pacific, refitting on the California coast near San Francisco, and proceeding to circumnavigate the world (1577–1580).

In defying Spain, Elizabeth also supported colonization in North America during the 1580s under the auspices of Humphrey Gilbert and his half-brother Walter Raleigh. With a royal charter from the queen, Raleigh planted the first English colony on Roanoke Island off the coast of North Carolina in 1585. The artist John White, who accompanied the settlers, produced drawings to document Native American life, while the naturalist Thomas Hariot wrote detailed descriptions of the vegetation and animals. But the Roanoke colonists wasted their energy searching for gold instead of planting fields. When Francis Drake visited the colony the next year, the settlers abandoned the effort and returned to England. Raleigh sent a second expedition to Roanoke in 1587, though once again the colonists quarreled with the local tribes and imperiled their food supply.

While the Roanoke colonists clung precariously to their island outpost, England lost contact with the settlement. In 1588, Spain responded to English

The English artist John White visited Roanoke Island in 1585 and drew careful illustrations of the Native people. The circular palisaded village provided protection from enemies and suggested a preference for circles rather than squares.

attacks in America by sending its fleet, known as the *Armada,* to war against England. But in a remarkable victory, the English navy defeated the Armada, opening the way for colonial development in North America. But, because of warfare with Spain, no ships sailed from England to Roanoke until 1590. When English ships reached the colony, they found no settlers, only the word CROATOAN, the name of a nearby island, scratched on the bark of a tree. Whether the English had been killed, died of natural causes, or joined a Native community remains unknown. But the failure of the "lost colony" demonstrated the importance of maintaining contact between colonial outposts and the home country and providing adequate resources in planting overseas settlements.

The Ideology of Empire

"Religion stands on tip toe in this land," wrote the English poet George Herbert, "ready to pass to the American strand." In speaking about the colonization of America, promoters in every country emphasized trade, commodities, economic profit, and the resulting expansion of national power. Equally prominent in every country's justification of overseas settlement was the language of religion. Whether Catholic or Protestant, Europeans viewed the world through a religious lens. Just as Native Americans and Africans saw connections between the visible world on earth and an invisible world of spirits, so Europeans believed that God ordered the universe, scrutinized human behavior, and judged individuals worthy of everlasting immortality or damnation. Of course, not everyone had the same religious beliefs: Catholics and Protestants, though Christians, hated each other. But it was precisely because Europeans took religion so seriously that they were prepared to wage bloody wars against those who worshiped in a different faith or, like Native Americans and Africans, who seemed to Europeans to have no faith at all.

Naming the Land

This sense of a God-given superiority allowed Europeans to dismiss the competing claims of other peoples. Wherever European adventurers discovered unfamiliar geography—rivers, lakes, islands, or mountains—they instantly affixed their own names to the lands and waters, even to the people, they encountered. Thus the Caribbean Taino became the first Americans to be labeled "Indians" and their home was called "San Salvador" in the vocabulary of Spanish Christianity. Three decades later, Verrazzano summarily dealt European names to the islands of the north Atlantic coast: "Arcadia" and "Le Figli di Navarra" (daughters of Navarre). When the English settled the same portions of North America, they paid homage to their own royalty, naming Virginia for Elizabeth I, the virgin queen, and other coastal areas—Maryland, New York, and Carolina—for other aristocrats.

This naming suggested important power relationships. Spain's elimination of French settlers in Florida in 1566 transformed "Fort Caroline" into "San Mateo." After the English defeated the Pequots in New England, they promptly renamed Pequot village "New London" and called the nearby river the "Thames." When the Spanish explorer Juan Bautista De Anza punished a runaway servant with a severe whipping near the Gila River in Arizona, his soldiers named the place El Azotado for "the one who got the beating." As the names of European places and princes dotted the maps of North America—New Amsterdam, Boston, New Orleans, Albuquerque—Europeans not only established continuity of their culture and values but also strengthened their claims to the land.

Maps and National Power

Given the Europeans' ignorance of American geography (to his dying day, for example, Columbus never accepted the fact that he had failed to reach the Indies), naming the land became a means to control the unknown, the so-called terra incognita. Detailed maps established claims of ownership and political rights. During the 15th century, maps assumed new importance as European nations competed for knowledge of uncharted seas and places. Portugal's Henry the Navigator treated his maps as state secrets, threatening the death penalty for any mariner who divulged cartograph-

> To his dying day, Columbus never accepted the fact that he had failed to reach the Indies.

ical information to a foreigner. Although Native American guides drew sketches and maps for European visitors, explorers like Captain John Smith not only ignored Native place names but also drew maps that left vast areas blank. Thus, the continent appeared largely uninhabited. And empty lands validated European claims. "In a vacant soyle," wrote an English preacher, "he that taketh possession of it . . . his Right it is."

After the invention of the printing press by Johann Gutenberg in the 15th century, European travel accounts spread rapidly in intellectual circles. These writings often blurred reality with fantasy, but a major topic in this literary genre was the description of exotic commodities—plants, such as sassafras and tobacco; an abundance of birds, fish, and fur-bearing animals; and the fertility of the land, which also became a commodity. Maps, such as the 16th-century Mercator Projection, not only reduced the unknown world to manageable proportions but also provided Europeans with valuable information about distant places. Thus maps, ocean charts of winds and currents, and travel literature became crucial ingredients in the continuing pursuit of overseas trade and national power.

A Passion for Colonization

To Europeans, the ideology of empire expressed the sense of cultural superiority. Such beliefs did not inspire toleration of others. Rather, Europeans continued to believe in a singular world view, which could embrace all knowledge, all truth, all

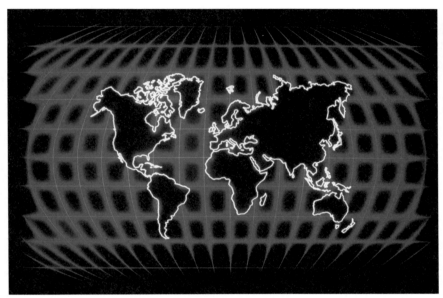

The 16th-century Flemish mapmaker, Gerardus Mercator, created a linear format for picturing the globe, but his pattern exaggerated the size of the Northern Hemisphere.

beings. When they discovered aspects of the world that did not fit their beliefs, they did not change their minds, but instead sought to change the world. This arrogance enabled European adventurers to endure incredible hardships to fulfill deeply held beliefs. To be sure, exploration, trade, and colonization required careful calculation, economic wisdom, and distinct material objectives. But it also demanded passionate commitment from those who risked not only material possessions but also life and limb—and, in their eyes, immortal souls as well.

The first European explorers, traders, and colonizers to reach America had no idea of the vastness of the continent or the difficulty of fulfilling the goals of conquest and settlement. Indeed, most individuals had smaller objectives, such as profit from trade in furs, sugar, spices, and slaves, though some, no doubt, sought the promised immortality of success. Like Columbus, they expected approval by European standards—a title, a coat of arms, hard cash, and a great reputation.

But most Europeans failed to find what they sought; most did not even survive to return home. Although European expansion brought gold and glory to a lucky few, exploration and colonization also created misery and suffering for millions of Native Americans and Africans as well as for those anonymous sailors, traders, and colonists who disappeared from history in faraway places. Yet Europeans continued to sail to unknown lands in increasing numbers, built beachhead communities on the Atlantic shores of the western world, and eventually, by the 17th century, even began to call America their home.

INFOTRAC® COLLEGE EDITION EXERCISES

 For additional reading go to InfoTrac College Edition, your online research library at http://web1.infotrac-college.com.

Keyword search: Portugal history

Subject search: slave trade

Subject search: Spanish colonies
Subject search: British colonial
Keyword search: colonial France
Subject search: Vikings in America
Subject search: triangular trade
Keyword search: Jamestown
Keyword search: Coronado
Keyword search: Spanish Armada
Subject search: East India Company
Keyword search: Walter Raleigh

ADDITIONAL READING

European Involvement in the Slave Trade

John Thornton, *Africa and Africans in the Making of the Atlantic World, 1400–1680* (1992). The author analyzes the role of Africa in the formation of European empires, examining the slave trade and its consequences.

James A. Rawley, *The Transatlantic Slave Trade: A History* (1981). A detailed analysis of slavery in the commercial activities of the major slave-trading nations.

Hugh Thomas, *The Slave Trade: The Story of the Atlantic Slave Trade: 1440–1870* (1997). An overview of slave trading that emphasizes the industry's economic complexity and discusses the struggle for its abolition.

The Origins of European Expansionism

J. H. Parry, *The Age of Reconnaissance* (1963). An overview of European expansionism, linking ideology, exploration, trade, and empire.

David B. Quinn, *North America from Earliest Discovery to First Settlements: The Norse Voyages to 1612* (1977). A comprehensive account of exploration and colonization, including a thorough bibliography.

Spain Challenges the Portuguese Empire

William D. Phillips, Jr. and Carla Rahn Phillips, *The Worlds of Christopher Columbus* (1992). With a critical eye, this study places Columbus's career in the context of his times.

Spain Explores North America

David J. Weber, *The Spanish Frontier in North America* (1992). A thorough description of Spain's colonial activities north of Mexico.

England Reaches for America

Harry Kelsey, *Sir Francis Drake: The Queen's Pirate* (1998). A lively account of the voyages of England's premier sailor.

David Harris Sacks, *The Widening Gate: Bristol and the Atlantic Economy, 1450–1700* (1991). A detailed study of one of England's major port cities, examining the expansion of trade and its impact on one community.

Maps and National Power

Emerson W. Baker, et al., eds., *American Beginnings: Exploration, Culture, and Cartography in the Land of Norumbaga* (1994). This collection of essays examines Europe's image of the Atlantic coast and the development of northern New England and Canada.

3

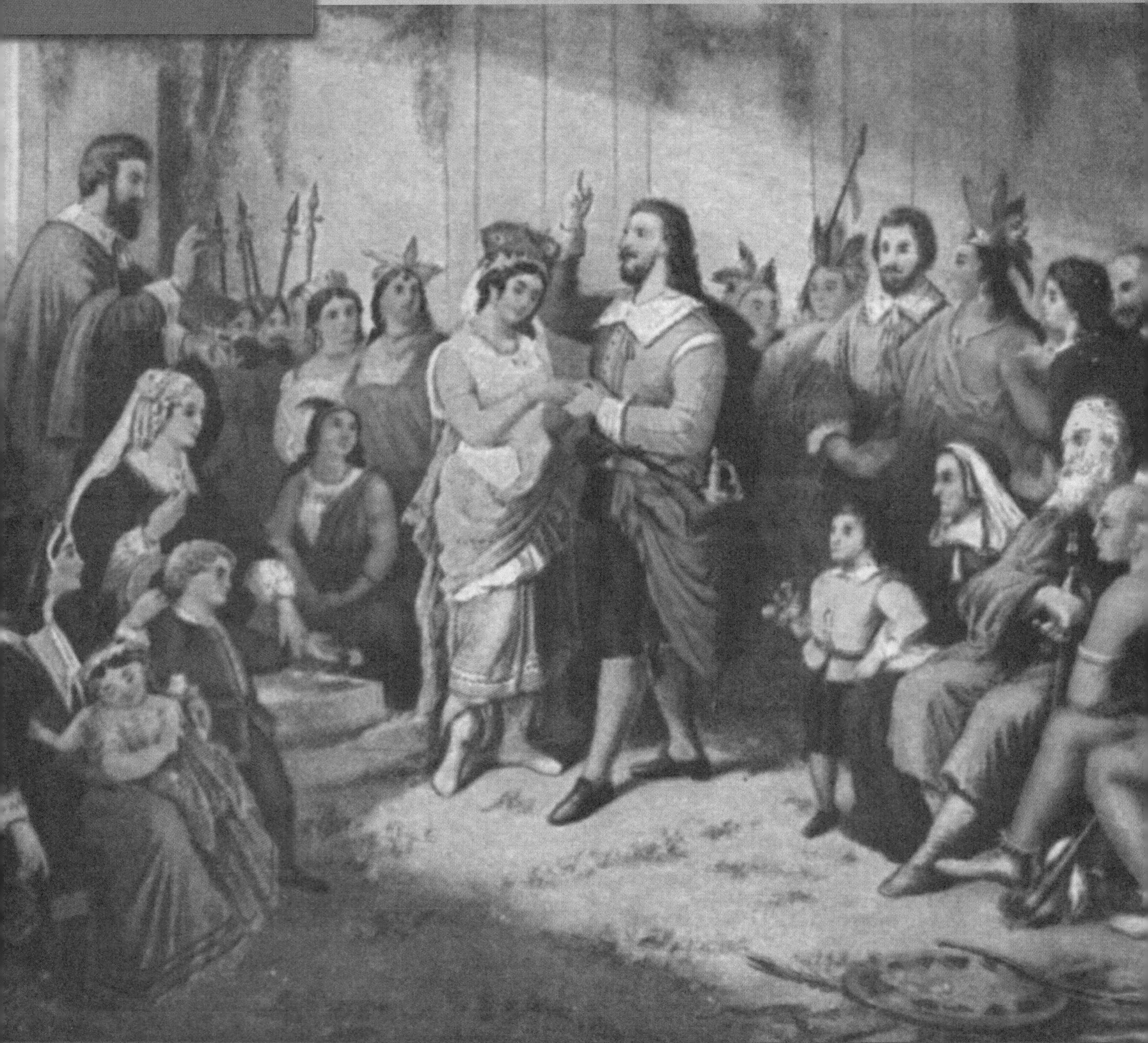

Colonial Competition and Cultural Struggle, 1598–1700

CHRONOLOGY

1598	Spanish establish settlement in New Mexico
1607	Virginia Company founds colony at Jamestown
1619	First Africans brought to Virginia
1620	The *Mayflower* lands at Plymouth, Massachusetts
1622	Powhatans attack Virginia settlements
1630	Puritans begin colony at Massaschusetts Bay
1634	English colonists arrive at Maryland
1635	Roger Williams establishes settlement at Rhode Island
1640–1660	English civil war between king and parliament
1651	Parliament enacts first navigation law
1660	Charles II restored to monarchy
1663	Charles II grants proprietorship in South Carolina
1664	English conquer Dutch New Netherlands
1675–1676	King Philip's war devastates New England
1680	Pueblos rebel against Spanish in New Mexico
1681	William Penn launches Quaker colony in Pennsylvania

Long at sea and weary of seeing little but waves and sky, two English sea captains, Philip Amadas and Arthur Barlow, at last approached the coast of North Carolina as part of the doomed expedition to Roanoke in 1584. The lush green coastline beckoned with its low, sandy beach.

They later recalled, "We smelt so sweet, and so strong a smell, as if we had been in the midst of some delicate garden abounding with all kind of odoriferous flowers. . . . [We landed on a beach,] very sandy and low towards the water's side, but so full of grapes, as the very beating and surge of the sea overflowed them."

It seemed they had found paradise itself. Soon welcomed by the native people, "We were entertained with all love and kindness, and with as much bounty (after their manner) as they could possibly devise. We found the people most gentle, loving, and faithful, void of all guile and treason, and such as live after the manner of the golden age."

Such explorers' reports sent from America to Europe during the 1500s may be seen as an early form of mass advertising. Although published descriptions of the "new world" often depicted the absence of "civilized" institutions—no churches, farms, or settled towns—most commentators praised the natural bounty of uninhabited lands waiting to be developed. An abundance of gold and silver awaited visitors. Claimed Sir Walter Raleigh of Guiana, "The graves have not been opened for gold, the mines not broken with sledges, nor their images pulled down out of their temples." Such chronicles usually downplayed the presence of native inhabitants and whetted the European appetite for colonies in North America. Colonists from western Europe seized the bait. By the end of the 17th century, Spain had settlements in Florida and New Mexico; English men and women lived along the Atlantic coast; French colonists inhabited eastern Canada and the Mississippi River valley; and the Dutch held outposts in what are now New York and New Jersey.

The hopes that prompted colonization often collided with American realities. For the first colonists, survival in a strange land remained problematic, with success or failure often depending on their relationships with Native peoples. As in England's "lost" colony at Roanoke, antagonism between settlers and the indigenous people could spell disaster. Relations with Native American groups also reflected the policies of the home countries that sent colonists overseas. Indeed, each European nation had a distinctive approach toward the native inhabitants. Thus, Spaniards in New Mexico characterized the Pueblo people under their control as "stupid" and "of poor intelligence." Accordingly, the conquistadors expected them to adopt European dress, religion, and customs. By contrast, the French colonists in Canada, fewer in number and lacking the power to impose their will on the native villages, treated their Huron and Algonquian neighbors as allies and trading partners and emphasized their voluntary cooperation. Meanwhile, English and Dutch encroachment on Native American lands frequently provoked quarrels, violence, and warfare. By the end of the 17th century, however, the balance of power between Europeans and the coastal tribes had shifted forever, and the colonial outposts worried less about survival than about competition from neighboring colonies.

As Europeans gained control of the Atlantic territories, the colonists increasingly exerted their cultural domination. The introduction of European manufactured goods such as guns, iron kettles, and woven shirts demonstrated technological advantages that encouraged Native peoples to participate in vigorous trade relations. Such products altered traditional tribal practices; for example, to satisfy the European demand for beaver pelts, Native hunters no longer limited their kill to those animals that could be eaten, but began to overkill the animals for their furs. The European demand for leather and venison drastically reduced the number of white-tailed deer in the Chesapeake area; as early as 1699, the southern English colonies enacted laws banning the hunting of white-tails during certain seasons. Such conservation laws appeared infrequently during the colonial era, but indicated how quickly the pressure of European trade threatened the environmental balance. And, wherever Europeans went, the accompanying diseases devastated the human population.

The technological dominance of Europeans also revealed fundamental differences in cultural perspectives among the colonists, Native Americans, and Africans. One of the mechanical wonders brought to New France during the 17th century was a clock that chimed the hours. According to a French priest, when as a joke one of the Frenchmen "calls out at the last stroke of the

As Thomas Harriot put it, "Manie other thinges that we had, were so strange unto them, and so farre exceeded their capacities to comprehend . . . that they thought they were rather the works of gods than of men."

hammer, 'That's enough,' and then it immediately becomes silent," the amazed Native observer believed that the clock could hear. Similarly, the Virginia slave Olaudah Equiano found himself in his master's bedroom with orders to fan the sleeping man. "The first object that engaged my attention was a watch which hung on the chimney," he recalled. "I was quite surprised at the noise it made, and was afraid it would tell the gentleman anything I might do amiss." Meanwhile, in Spanish New Mexico, Franciscan missionaries sounded bells to summon Native Americans to religious worship. To Native Americans and Africans, accustomed to living by the natural time of sunrise and sunset, who ate when hungry and slept when tired, European timekeeping seemed inherently authoritarian. Indeed, the Algonquians in French Canada called the chiming clock "the Captain of the day" because the timepiece dictated when social activities, such as prayers and meals, would

occur. Yet, by the 17th century, Europeans considered clock time natural and used the measurement of hours to discipline their own lives as well as those of the Africans and Native Americans under their control. Timekeeping, in other words, became a form of cultural domination.

The Europeans' authority and power—their control of time or seizure of the land—created severe tensions with other peoples. While both Native American and African traditions denied that individuals should own the land, European nations claimed land titles from "sea to sea," drew straight boundary lines on their maps, and occupied Native American territory. And, since land in America usually had no value to Europeans unless it was "improved" to produce crops, the effort to reap agricultural profits justified the enslavement of Africans and Native Americans as a labor force. By the end of the 17th century, moreover, land itself had become a commodity.

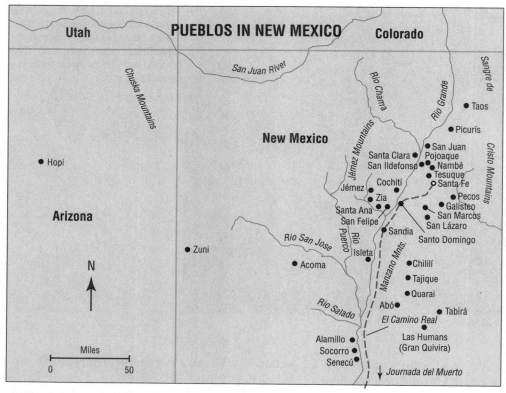

PUEBLOS IN NEW MEXICO

Utah

Colorado

San Juan River

Chuska Mountains

Sangre de Cristo Mountains

Rio Chama

Rio Grande

New Mexico

• Taos

• Picurís

• Hopi

Jémez Mountains

Santa Clara • San Juan
Pojoaque •
San Ildefonso • • Nambé
• Tesuque
Cochití • ○ Santa Fe

• Jémez
• Zia
Santa Ana •
San Felipe •

• Pecos
• Galisteo
• San Marcos
• San Lázaro

• Sandia

Santo Domingo

Arizona

Rio San Jose

Rio Puerco

Manzano Mnts.

• Zuni

N

• Acoma

• Isleta

• Chililí

• Tajique

• Quarai

Abó • • Tabirá

Rio Salado

El Camino Real

Alamillo •
Socorro •
Senecú •

Las Humans
(Gran Quivira)

↓ Journada del Muerto

Miles

0   50

Missions in New Mexico, 1650–1675

Unlike Native Americans, who saw the land as a home, or Africans, who regarded their homelands as sacred places to which their souls would return, European colonists saw the land as real estate—property to be bought, used, and sold. Since Europeans shared this cultural perspective, rivalries among nations (English, French, Dutch, and Spanish) produced constant competition and conflict. Government policies made in Europe, such as royal land grants to colonial investors or treaties that artificially divided natural geography, determined which country's settlers could claim American land and how they would exploit its value. This persistent discord about the land and its resources meant, finally, that some European nations

would lose their colonies in America and others would determine the future of the continent.

Spain's Empire of Souls

After the first conquistadors failed to find gold on the dry lands of New Mexico, the sparsely settled area offered few attractions for Spanish settlement. In 1573, the Spanish monarchy disavowed military conquest of Native peoples and demanded that further discovery "be carried out peacefully and charitably." The Pueblos thus emerged as ideal targets for Spain's religious missionaries, the Franciscan monks who resolved to convert the "heathen" on

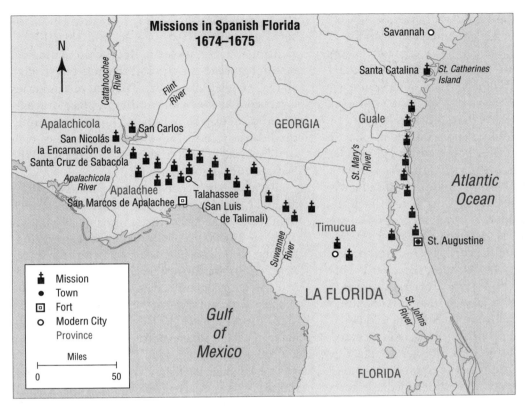

Missions in Spanish Florida 1674–1675

Savannah ○

Santa Catalina ✚ *St. Catherines Island*

Cattahoochee River

Flint River

Apalachicola

San Carlos

San Nicolás
la Encarnación de la
Santa Cruz de Sabacola

Apalachicola River

Apalachee

San Marcos de Apalachee

Talahassee
(San Luis
de Talimali)

GEORGIA

Guale

St. Mary's River

Atlantic Ocean

Timucua

Suwannee River

LA FLORIDA

Gulf
of
Mexico

St. Augustine

St. Johns River

FLORIDA

Legend:
- ✚ Mission
- ● Town
- ▣ Fort
- ○ Modern City
- Province

Miles
0   50

N

Missions in Florida, 1650–1675

the northern fringes of the Spanish empire. Establishing the first mission in New Mexico in 1598, the Franciscans built some fifty churches and baptized 85,000 individuals during the next thirty years. Meanwhile, on the eastern side of the continent, the Franciscans established missions in northern Florida and along the Atlantic coast of Georgia and South Carolina. Such religious expansion bolstered Spain's North American claims; missionaries rather than soldiers protected the northern frontiers.

Imposing Spanish Culture

Spain's missionary goals made few allowances for the traditions of indigenous peoples. Instead, the Franciscans forced the Pueblos to construct the mission churches: men under Spanish supervision performed the carpentry; women made the adobe walls. Even church design reflected a conflict of cultures. Where the Pueblos traditionally worshipped in circular underground chambers called *kivas*, Catholic architecture—indeed, the very adobe bricks used to build the structures—was uniformly rectangular in shape. The churches also brought sacred ceremonial space indoors and sheltered religious ritual from the natural environment. Thus, while Pueblo religions observed the cycles of seasons and the movement of celestial bodies, Spanish church bells summoned converts indoors at fixed hours and marked sacred time by calendars and holidays ("holy days"). Of course, the Pueblos never completely abandoned their own spiritual beliefs, but accepted a fusion of ceremonies. Thus Franciscan Christmas rituals became mixed with Pueblo ceremonies honoring the winter solstice.

The mission schools taught the elements of Christianity to both adults and children but focused on converting the young. Besides teaching Catholic catechism, prayers, and hymns, the missionaries demanded that the Pueblos "live in a civilized manner," which meant that they wear European clothing and shoes, cultivate European crops such as wheat and fruit trees, and raise domesticated animals imported from Europe, including horses, cattle, sheep, and pigs. Although Spaniards emphasized that conversion to Christianity was a voluntary act, they used elaborate gifts to entice converts and undermine the authority of traditional spiritual leaders. Moreover, once a person accepted Christian baptism, the convert became subject to Catholic discipline. Converts who violated religious rules, neglected the mass, or participated in Native ceremonies were severely punished.

Oppression and Resistance

Emphasis on religious conversion severely disrupted Pueblo society, dividing communities between converts and traditionalists. Worse, the missionaries inadvertently brought diseases that killed in epidemic numbers. By 1680, the Pueblos had been reduced by half; the Florida Apalachees had dropped 60 percent. High mortality compounded the difficulties of mission life. As subjects of the Spanish crown, the Pueblos were required to pay tribute in the form of goods and labor to the landowners. Public works projects, such as the building of roads, forts, and the town of Santa Fe, obliged the Pueblos to perform extraordinary labor. In addition, Spanish settlers vio-

lated royal orders by occupying Native lands, enslaving non-Christian people, and sexually assaulting Pueblo women. Recent archeological research among the skeletal remains of Florida's Native peoples shows that Spanish missionaries imposed a new cornbread diet in place of traditional protein-rich fish-based foods, weakening the health of local inhabitants. The use of well water instead of natural streams also increased the Natives' illness and mortality.

Resisting such changes, Native groups in Florida and New Mexico organized rebellions. In 1680, the Pueblos staged a surprise uprising, coordinating some 17,000 people from numerous communities and culture groups. Led by the spiritual leader Popé, whom the Spanish had previously punished in a witch hunt, the Pueblos killed a quarter of the Spanish settlers and drove the survivors out of New Mexico. The uprising particularly targeted Christianity. Pueblo converts destroyed Spanish churches and religious objects and plunged into rivers to wash away their baptism. During the same period, Florida's Native peoples, goaded by nearby English traders, rebelled against the Spanish missions, killing Christianized Natives as well as Spanish settlers. Among the rebels were some who rejected their baptism, slapping their foreheads and shouting "I am no Christian!"

The Spaniards fought their way back into New Mexico in 1693, using military force to overcome Pueblo resistance. In Florida, Franciscans and soldiers clung to isolated bases at St. Augustine and Pensacola. Thus the Spanish empire in North America remained fragmentary, dispersed, and sparsely populated by Europeans through the next century. These military outposts, which by the 1770s extended into Texas, Arizona, and northern California, served primarily as territorial claims against Spain's European rivals. But the poverty of the Spanish settlements offered little competition to English and French traders, and the mission system proved immeasurably oppressive to Native peoples. Visitors compared the regimen of mission life to the slave plantations of the West Indies; others noted that the Natives wore their hair singed short—a sign of mourning. "I have never seen one laugh," wrote a French observer. "They look as though they were interested in nothing."

English Colonies on the Chesapeake

The sparseness of New Spain's settlements in North America would eventually contrast with the growth of England's colonies, but from the beginning both nations faced similar problems of attracting residents. Although England had failed to establish a permanent colony at Roanoke during the 1580s, English commercial investors continued to view Virginia as a site for colonial development. Such a colony would assert Protestant England's challenge to Catholic Spain, while offering the prospect of trade in the region's natural resources, which included lumber, sassafras (believed to be a cure for syphilis), and gold. Interest in colonization also expressed long-term economic developments that were changing England from a rural society into an expanding capitalist nation. As English merchants increasingly traded manufactured goods overseas for spices, sugar, and other commodities, landowners shifted from growing crops to raising sheep for wool to be made into cloth. Consequently, many farm workers lost their lands and migrated to English cities; London tripled in size between 1560 and 1625. Widespread poverty made colonization attractive to people without prospects of betterment at home.

The Background of English Colonization

The political situation in England also encouraged colonization. After Henry VIII separated from the Roman Catholic Church in 1534, the monarchy wavered between accepting Protestantism or returning to the Catholic faith. Queen Elizabeth (1558–1603) adopted a middle course, strengthening the national Church of England while rejecting extreme Protestants who wished to eliminate certain prayers and church offices that remained from Catholic days. Those who wished to purify the Church of England by removing all traces of its Catholic heritage were called *Puritans*. Significantly, puritanism had a strong appeal among those English people who experienced social uprooting. By emphasizing godliness over materialism, spiritual purity over worldly corruption, puritanism offered unfortunate people religious security in the next world, if not on earth. Such self-assurance would inspire many English Puritans to pursue their beliefs in America.

Despite widespread social upheaval, most people in Elizabethan England idealized the harmony and orderliness of society. As William Shakespeare wrote, all the elements of the world "observe degree, priority, and place." Elizabethans assumed that certain people were naturally better than most and expected these superiors to rule their inferiors. Status distinctions divided English society into a hierarchy. At the top stood the ruling monarchy and aristocracy; then came the well-to-do gentry—gentlemen and gentlewomen—who did not have to work with their hands; below them were the yeomen, who owned land but had to work on it; and finally the landless poor, the overwhelming majority of whom could not vote and barely earned enough to survive. These status distinctions remained patriarchal at all levels. Men were considered heads of their households; women assumed the status of their fathers or husbands.

Although the privileged aristocracy and gentry amounted to only 5 to 7 percent of the population, Elizabethans claimed that the interests of

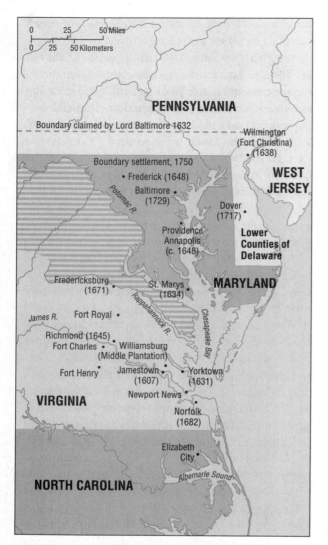

English Colonies in Maryland and Virginia, early 1600s

ciety and politics would be transferred to England's colonies during the 17th century.

Founding Virginia

In 1607, a 60-year old Algonquian leader named Powhatan claimed authority over 14,000 people who lived in small groups around Chesapeake Bay. That year, the Virginia Company, a London-based joint-stock investment corporation sent three ships with settlers and supplies to plant a colony north of Spain's Atlantic settlements. Their objectives were to establish English claims in the area, find precious metals, seek the fabled Northwest Passage to the Pacific, and convert the Algonquians from the worship of devils to Protestant Christianity. Selecting a site on the newly named James River, the English constructed a base at Jamestown and laid claim to Powhatan's territory. The leader, fearful of the armed intruders, maintained friendly but cautious relations, exchanging goods and information to avoid open conflict.

When Powhatan's generosity wavered, however, Virginia leaders such as Captain John Smith used military force to take the food they wanted. Jamestown's settlers also copied Algonquian architecture, using bark and grass mats to insulate their drafty dwellings. But when Smith returned to England in 1609, the colonists' discipline collapsed. As the ill-prepared, mostly male colonists paid less attention to planting fields and more to raiding Native-grown crops, Powhatan withdrew his support. The "starving time" commenced during the winter of 1609–1610, when, without Native assistance, the English died of famine and disease, and some resorted to cannibalism. Of 900 English settlers, scarcely 60 survived until the arrival of reinforcements in the spring. According to the relief group, the survivors "looked like anatomies, crying out, we are starved, we are starved."

all groups could be protected by these wealthy few, who were responsible for preserving fair prices for food and fuel. Only male property holders with a stake in society were allowed to vote, and they elected their betters to represent them in the national Parliament. These ideas about so-

The Virginia Company continued to send fresh colonists and instituted martial law to force them to work. Even then Captain Smith required only six hours of daily labor, leaving the rest of the day for "pastime and merrie exercises." But as Powhatan's people continued to withhold supplies, the English used military force to seize lands along the James River. In 1614, Powhatan accepted a truce and permitted his daughter Pocahontas to marry John Rolfe, symbolizing the uneasy alliance between the two peoples. Her death of disease while visiting England indicated the fragility of such relationships. Saddened by her loss, the elderly Powhatan transferred his authority to his brother Opechancanough.

By 1613, Powhatan's English son-in-law, John Rolfe, had laid the basis for the colony's survival. Experimenting with a locally grown plant, he introduced Virginia's first profitable commodity: tobacco. As the demand for tobacco increased in England, Rolfe's hybrid variety brought revenue to the Virginia Company's investors. But to maximize tobacco production, the company needed additional laborers and began to offer fifty acres of land to anyone who paid the passage of a worker—an arrangement known as a "headright." The policy enabled wealthy merchants and ship captains to acquire large land holdings by transporting servants to Virginia. Between 1619 and 1622, 3,000 new settlers arrived in the colony. By 1622, however, the total number of surviving colonists was only 1,200.

The high colonial death rate encouraged Virginia leaders to seek an alternative labor supply. By 1619, people of African descent were working in the colony. That year John Rolfe reported that a Dutch ship had deposited a cargo of "twenty Negars." Whether these Africans were slaves or free, or what became of them in Virginia, remains unknown. Through the first four decades of Virginia's settlement, the legal status of Africans remained extremely fluid, varying greatly in individual cases. Certainly, given England's tradition of social hierarchy and a belief that black Africans were inferior to white Europeans, those first black Virginians entered a society that treated all workers as commodities to be bought, traded, and sold.

Although tobacco provided some financial security for landowners, the plant rapidly depleted the soil, usually within three years. Virginians found it cheaper to acquire new lands than to fertilize old soil, and the colony began to expand along the rivers, maintaining proximity to ocean-going vessels. To consolidate the colony, the Virginia Company ordered the summoning of the first legislative assembly, the House of Burgesses, in 1619. Composed of two delegates from each geographic district, this legislature participated in company decisions, an early example of representative government.

As tobacco planters continued to encroach on Algonquian territory, the Native people recognized the threat to their way of life. In 1622, the Powhatans attacked the settlements, killing over 300 colonists, including the leading missionary, and forced the survivors to retreat to fortified sites. The colonists soon retaliated, slaughtering people, destroying crops, and smashing villages. Now Virginians could claim Algonquian lands by "right of conquest." Yet one casualty of war was the Virginia Company itself. Although more than 8,500 colonists had sailed to Virginia by 1624, the surviving population numbered only 1,300. Frustrated by the colony's failure to prosper, the king revoked the Company's charter in 1624, making Virginia a royal colony. Hereafter, a governor appointed by the crown would govern the colony, assisted by an appointed council and the elected House of Burgesses.

After a decade of warfare, Opechancanough agreed to peace and withdrew beyond the edges of colonial settlement. During the 1630s, the English population began to grow, devouring fertile acreage along the rivers for tobacco. By 1640, Virginians numbered 10,000, about the same as the declining Powhatans. In 1644, Opechancanough launched another attack, killing nearly 500 colonists. But Virginians under Governor William Berkeley suppressed the uprising, executed the Native leader, and imposed a punitive peace that forced the Powhatans to migrate to the western part of the colony. By 1675, when Virginia's colonial population exceeded 40,000, the remaining Powhatans totaled 2,000. Fifty years later, they would number in the hundreds.

Maryland, a Proprietary Colony

While Virginians struggled to build a tobacco economy, King Charles I granted the northern portions of Chesapeake Bay, later named Maryland, to George Calvert, Lord Baltimore, in 1632. Unlike Virginia, which was first controlled by an investment company and then by the king, Maryland was the private property of the proprietor. Calvert owned all the land, controlled trade, and held extensive political power. First settled at St. Mary's in 1634, the colony produced good harvests of corn and wheat but, as in Virginia, tobacco emerged as the main crop. By 1640, Calvert introduced headrights to encourage the transportation of workers. Although the Catholic proprietor intended the colony as a haven for his co-religionists, most settlers were Protestants. Forced by the colonists to establish a local legislature, Calvert attempted to protect the Catholic minority with the Toleration Act of 1649, a landmark law that established religious liberty for all Christians.

The tobacco economy defined not only the nature of work in the Chesapeake region but also the geography of settlement. Since overland transportation was difficult, the local river systems provided convenient lines of communication.

Nearly all colonists lived within a half mile of a river, and most were even closer. In laying out property sites, surveyors used the riverfronts as one boundary line and drew rectangular straight lines for the other three sides. Each 1,000 acre holding entitled a landowner to a mile and a half of riverfront. This type of settlement encouraged population dispersal. Most households had few close neighbors or common buildings, such as churches. Unlike village society of England or crowded London, Chesapeake settlers were more isolated and had fewer obligations to society.

Chesapeake Society

Settled along rivers and based on commercial agriculture, Maryland and Virginia produced similar economic and social patterns. As in the mother country, 17th-century English settlers believed that society was naturally hierarchical, though conditions in the Chesapeake encouraged greater social mobility. In England, a titled aristocracy governed the country, held most economic wealth, and enjoyed the privileges of high social status, but few aristocrats migrated to the colonies, and most of those who did died soon. Indeed, the extraordinarily high mortality rates, due to unfamiliar diseases and malnutrition, left few propertied colonists to prosper during the early decades of colonization.

Most 17th-century immigrants to the Chesapeake were propertyless young adults whose primary asset was the ability to work. Most journeyed to America by becoming indentured servants, meeting the cost of their transportation by contracting to work for a master for a period of time (usually around five years) after which they would receive their freedom and a small payment. About 40 percent of those indentured did not live long enough to collect. Colonists who had the money to pay the passage of other settlers not only acquired the services of indentured workers but also accumulated substantial acreage through headrights. Such landowning investors, who controlled agricultural supplies and food, also controlled the lives of their workers and could sell their labor contracts to others.

Most indentured servants were males in their late teens or early twenties, and they faced backbreaking labor six days a week. At the end of their contracts, servants achieved freedom to work for themselves, but few had accumulated sufficient wealth to purchase their own lands. However, since tobacco prices remained high until about 1660, a free worker might save enough during a year's labor to afford modest acreage. In this way, a poor English immigrant might become a person of property—a goal that was much harder to achieve in England. Despite opportunities for social mobility, most former servants improved their position only slightly, if at all, in one generation. Chesapeake society remained only slightly less stratified or hierarchical than England's and became even less fluid during the 17th century as new leaders consolidated their wealth.

One important difference between England and the Chesapeake was the sexual composition of society. In England, where sex ratios were approximately equal, economic limits forced young people to delay marriage until they could afford independent households, usually in their mid- to late twenties. With limited years of marital fertility, English families had from five to seven live births, of whom perhaps half lived to adulthood. By contrast, most Chesapeake colonists were unmarried young adults, with at least three times as many men emigrating as women. In early Maryland, 70 percent of males died before age 50; for women, who were particularly vulnerable to malaria while pregnant, life expectancy was even shorter. Few marriages lasted ten years before one spouse died. Since women who came to the colony

as servants had to delay marriage until they finished their indentures—penalties for pregnancy included additional years of servitude and sometimes the seizure of their babies—they enjoyed fewer years of marital fertility than English women and had fewer children. Yet the scarcity of females encouraged widows to remarry, sometimes more than once. A woman might thereby inherit considerable property. Indeed, a good marriage was one way a former indentured servant of either sex might ascend the social ladder. The precariousness of life thus produced a volatile social order that would explode before the end of the century.

French North America

Unlike the Spanish and English colonies in North America, French settlements in Canada remained lightly populated by Europeans, largely because their home population felt little pressure to leave Europe. But French Protestants, known as *Huguenots,* did face religious persecution, both in France and in French colonies, and they frequently sought refuge in the colonies of other countries, such as New Netherlands. Because the French lacked the numerical strength to dominate Native American people as the Spanish or English did, their colonies emphasized economic and cultural reciprocity, particularly with the Algonquians and Hurons of the Northeast and the Choctaws of the lower Mississippi valley. Although the French sent Jesuit missionaries to convert the American "heathen" to the Catholic faith, they also permitted French fur traders and trappers, known as *coureurs de bois* ("travelers of the woods"), to form partnerships with Native American traders and to marry Native American women.

After Samuel de Champlain established Quebec in 1608 (see Chapter 2), French traders supported the local Huron nation against the Mohawk

Iroquois to gain access to the interior beaver trade. During the 17th century, French fur traders extended their influence around the Great Lakes and the Ohio River valley. By 1672, the Jesuit Jacques Marquette and the trader Louis Joliet explored 1,200 miles of the Mississippi River; a decade later, the explorer Sieur de La Salle reached the Gulf of Mexico and claimed the Mississippi valley for France, naming the territory *Louisiana* after King Louis XIV. By the end of the century, the French were planting small outposts near the mouth of the Mississippi, close to the present site of New Orleans.

These extensive commercial networks discouraged concentrated settlements in Canada. Royal plans to establish agricultural estates in the St. Lawrence valley failed to develop because of a chronic shortage of labor, and efforts to stimulate the immigration of indentured servants to work the land could not compete with the attraction of fur trading. French fur traders, who spent long seasons among the Native Americans of the interior, remained loosely attached to the colonial government in Quebec.

Based on alliances with Algonquians and Hurons, the French fur traders remained vulnerable to attacks from the aggressive Iroquois. Decimated by European diseases, the Iroquois nations embarked on war against the Hurons in order to repopulate their clans with captives. Such violence threatened Canadian trade and led the French to give military aid to their Huron allies. The Mohawk Iroquois responded by attacking New France. By 1650, the Mohawks had crushed the Hurons, opening the way for peace negotiations with the French. But frequent violations of the truce led the French government to dispatch a military expedition that destroyed several Iroquois villages. Further weakened by epidemic diseases, the Iroquois accepted peace, enabling the French fur trade to prosper. But the Iroquois remained implacable foes of French expansion and

allied themselves with other Europeans to limit French influence.

Puritanism Comes to New England

Unlike the Spanish missionaries, who focused on converting the native peoples, or the dispersed tobacco growers of the Chesapeake, or the scattered fur traders of French Canada—all of whom were overwhelmingly male—the founders of New England migrated to America to build stable communities. Governor John Winthrop called New England "a city upon a hill" to demonstrate to the world (especially a decadent England) the values of a godly Puritan society. Thus, the Puritans transplanted strong social institutions, including families, churches, and town government to assure common standards of behavior. But not all New England colonists were Puritans, and many quarreled with the leadership. Some Puritans also challenged specific religious doctrines and departed to establish colonies in Connecticut and Rhode Island.

The Origins of Puritanism

Puritanism arose within the Church of England during the late 1500s as a protest against the continued use of Catholic prayers and officers such as bishops. Influenced by the Protestant theologian John Calvin of Geneva, reform-minded ministers in England sought to simplify religious services and establish the independence of each congregation. They insisted that a person's salvation depended not on church rituals but on the quality of an individual's faith in God. Their opponents called them *Puritans* as a term of scorn.

Besides its religious argument, puritanism expressed strong emotional elements. Making a distinction between those people whose souls were saved for all eternity and those who were destined for eternal damnation, Puritans insisted that the

Their opponents called them *Puritans* as a term of scorn.

issue remained entirely in God's hands. This idea of *predestination*—the belief that a person's fate was determined before birth—could cause great anxiety. But from that inner stress most Puritans discovered in a moment of religious conversion that they were among the Elect, those chosen by God for salvation. And while Puritans believed that their fate rested entirely with God, they taught that individuals should strive to "prepare" themselves to receive God's grace. It was the conversion experience, the realization of one's total dependence on God and the sense of a spiritual rebirth, that ever after separated the "saved" from the damned. Those who were saved formed Puritan congregations in England and denied that the bishops should oversee their affairs. While demanding reforms of the Church of England, most Puritans did not believe that the national church was beyond redemption; those extremists who did were called *Separatists*.

Although puritanism began as part of a theological dispute, the movement spread rapidly during the reign of Elizabeth I. Puritanism appealed especially to people whose lives had been affected by the dislocations of English society. Although Puritans admitted that no one could ever know God's will, most were confident about their own salvation. Thus puritanism created a feeling of community. This enthusiasm, the feeling of divine inspiration, gave Puritans courage to criticize England's religious practices and to found godly communities in America.

The Pilgrim Colony

To Puritan eyes, God's grace could be seen in the effects of an epidemic that killed "great multi-

tudes of natives" in New England in order to "make room for us." So reported a leader of the group that sailed aboard the *Mayflower* and landed at Plymouth on the Massachusetts coast in 1620. The group's leaders were Separatists, or *Pilgrims,* representing a form of puritanism that rejected the Church of England as totally corrupt. These religious dissenters had lived in the Netherlands since 1607 before deciding to establish an independent community in America. They had obtained a grant of land from the Virginia Company, and their financial support came from a joint-stock company, a mix of London investors and actual settlers who traded their labor for a share of stock. Only one-third of the *Mayflower*'s passengers were Separatists (the others were called "strangers") but the colony leaders persuaded all to sign the "Mayflower Compact," by which they agreed to abide by laws of their own making. The agreement enabled the Pilgrim minority to exercise some control over the outsiders.

Touching Plymouth Rock just as winter descended, the Pilgrims were scarcely prepared for the hardships of settlement. Only the timely assistance of Massasoit, a local Native leader, and his translator Squanto, who had learned English after being kidnapped by earlier explorers, saved the Pilgrim community from starvation. Some Pilgrim merchants tried to develop trade in furs, fish, and lumber; most settlers turned to small-scale farming. Few outsiders were attracted to the colony, and the population grew slowly. Eventually, the Pilgrim colony merged with a larger settlement at Massachusetts Bay.

The Great Puritan Migration

As Separatists from the Church of England, the Pilgrims left Europe to escape from religious corruption, but the ascension of King Charles I in 1625 aroused concern among even the non-Separatist Puritans, who still hoped to purify the Church of

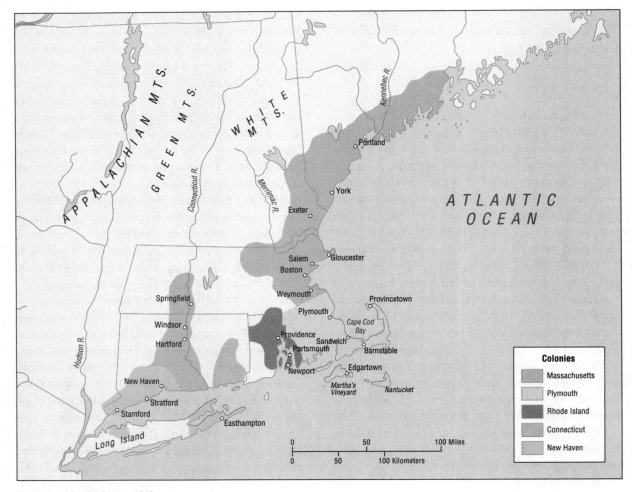

The New England Colonies, 1640

England. As the king silenced Puritan ministers and ignored protests in Parliament, Puritan leaders made plans to migrate to America to preserve their religious principles, perhaps as a model for England to imitate. In 1630, the Puritans began the "great migration" to New England when 1,000 settlers landed near Boston under the leadership of John Winthrop. Within a decade, 20,000 English had flocked to Massachusetts Bay and extended settlements into Rhode Island, Connecticut, and the towns of western Massachusetts. This remarkable growth reflected not only the power of Puritan idealism—the desire to create a "wilderness zion," a spiritual community in America—but also the related decision to migrate as families, rather than as individuals.

Unlike the Chesapeake colonies, which were settled by young, unattached people, the Puritans carried strong community values. Seeking to live in geographic clusters, they granted land not to individuals but to townships consisting of families and a minister, who then subdivided the land among the settlers. As in the southern colonies, New Englanders expected their "betters" to own more land than the common sort, but local leaders remained closely connected to the towns in which they dwelled. By law no one could live more than a mile from a church or "meeting house."

The government of Massachusetts originated in the joint-stock Massachusetts Bay Company. Corporate rules permitted only stockholders, known as *freemen,* to vote. But Puritan leaders preferred a consensual type of government that would bind people to community decisions. In 1631, the definition of freemen was altered to mean "citizen," which expanded the base of political participation. Yet Puritans allowed only church members to become freemen with full rights of citizenship such as voting and holding office. And, although religion and government remained legally separate, Puritans controlled who could become full church members. After 1634, men had to testify publicly to having had a conversion experience before they could join a church; women could describe such personal experiences privately. As in England and other English colonies, women, whether or not they were church members, could not vote. On the town level, where open meetings supervised local government, all property-holding men could vote or hold office, and in 1634 the colony legislature ordered the towns to elect delegates to a representative assembly.

Puritan Families

The social basis of Puritan government began in the family. Puritans saw their households as a microcosm of society and required all unmarried people to live in "well-governed families." They assumed that parents were superior to children, husbands to wives, and masters to servants. Puritan leaders believed that such a hierarchy assured a balance of obligations and responsibilities. "The husband should love, provide for, and be tenderhearted to the wife," a Puritan minister explained. "The wife should reverence the husband, obey him, and endeavor to be an help[mate] for him."

As in England and the Chesapeake, the legal status of married women was subsumed by their husbands. Married women could not own property independently; married women therefore were not responsible for their debts, even when contracted prior to marriage. Ironically, when a wife was fined for sexual misbehavior with another man, her husband was required to pay her fine. In protecting these patriarchal households, Puritans treated the rape of a married woman more seriously than other sexual offenses, even the rape of a child, because such crimes threatened their basic social unit. In contrast to the Chesapeake colonies, where the family structure was constantly shifting because of high mortality and frequent remarriages, the Puritan governments considered household life subject to public scrutiny. Thus Puritans viewed sexual misbehavior by either gender as both sinful and criminal.

The healthy environment in New England—a sharp contrast with the Chesapeake colonies—encouraged population growth, and the abundance of land encouraged people to marry younger, averaging in their early twenties. With a longer time of marital fertility, the birthrate in 17th-century New England increased, averaging from six to eight children per family. Believing that even babies were naturally evil because of Adam and Eve's Original Sin, Puritans emphasized discipline of young children.

From early childhood, youngsters learned moral lessons along with the alphabet from the

In *Adam's* Fall We Sinned all.

Thy Life to Mend This *Book* Attend.

The *Cat* doth play And after flay.

A *Dog* will bite A *Thief* at night.

An *Eagles* flight Is out of sight.

The Idle *Fool* Is whipt at School.

A page from the *New England Primer,* first published in 1690.

New England Primer: "In Adam's fall / We sinned all" and "The idle fool / Is whipt at school." Puritan attitudes toward sexuality were not necessarily "puritanical." Evidence from Puritan diaries shows that marital sexuality was welcome, and even premarital sexuality between engaged couples was often considered acceptable.

Expanding into Connecticut

New England's growing population created pressure for geographical expansion. Although epidemic diseases had eliminated the coastal tribes, numerous interior peoples occupied the fertile acreage coveted by Puritan farmers. Among these groups were the

Puritan attitudes toward sexuality were not necessarily "puritanical."

Pequots of Connecticut, who had developed extensive trade with the nearby Dutch settlements. Using the murder of an English trader as an excuse, the Puritans sent a military expedition against the uncooperative Pequots and proceeded to burn their village, killing inhabitants as they tried to escape. Pequot men who survived the ensuing battle were executed; captured Pequot women and children were enslaved and sold in the West Indies. There they were traded for the first African slaves to arrive in New England, in 1638. But small farms and cohesive family life limited the economic viability of slavery in the northern colonies. A few Pequots who survived the massacre lived on as stragglers, too few in number to resist the migration of Puritans from Massachusetts, who founded separate colonies at Connecticut and New Haven.

Puritan aggression against the Pequots reflected a wider European intolerance of cultural differences. Believing that Native Americans worshipped false gods, if not the devil, Puritans, like other European colonials, professed a desire to convert them to Christianity. Yet, unlike the Franciscans of New Spain and the Jesuits in French Canada, only a few Puritan missionaries attempted to preach to Native groups. Apostles like Massachusetts' John Eliot baptized some converts, and Eliot even translated the Bible into Algonquian in 1661. But Protestants no less than Catholics expected the converts to abandon their own culture, move into "praying villages," and accept European values.

Expressing Religious Dissent

Although the Puritans sailed to New England to protect their religious beliefs, they opposed extending similar liberties to other dissenters. When the pastor at Salem, Roger Williams, demanded a complete separation of church and state (because, he argued, politics would inevitably corrupt religion), Governor Winthrop arranged for his expulsion. In 1635, Williams fled to Rhode Island, where he took refuge among the Narragansetts and later purchased land to establish an independent colony dedicated to religious toleration. His book *A Key into the Language of America* (1643) remains a valuable source for Native American historians and anthropologists. Rhode Island became a haven for other Puritan nonconformists.

Another challenge to Puritan orthodoxy emerged in 1636 when a parishioner of the Boston church, Anne Hutchinson, began to hold private religious meetings in her home and included women in the discussions. Hutchinson even dared to question the ministers' emphasis on "moral" behavior, such as attending sermons, as a condition for salvation. Her position was a logical extension of puritanism, for it assumed that God's grace, not a person's actions, determined who would be saved. But in two ways Hutchinson challenged Puritan authority. First, she stated that God had spoken to her directly (a heresy known as *antinomianism*) and so diminished the importance of the ministers. Second, she defied the traditional subordination of women to the male clergy. "The woman is more subject to error than a man," announced her pastor, John Cotton. "You have stepped out of your place," said another minister. "You have rather been a husband than a wife, and a preacher rather than a hearer, and a magistrate rather than a subject." For defying the social order, Anne Hutchinson was banished from Massachusetts in 1638. She fled to Rhode Island, where she gave birth to a deformed fetus, which the Puritans considered proof of her diabolical purposes. Massachusetts also expelled a group of Quakers and executed a few, who, like Williams and Hutchinson, expressed heretical religious views.

Although the Puritans placed great emphasis on instilling their religious values in the young and founded Harvard College in 1636 to provide educated ministers, they discovered that the proportion of young people who qualified for church membership by undergoing a conversion experience was steadily declining. Perhaps the social conditions that inspired puritanism, religious anxiety, and conversion experiences had vanished in America. By mid-century, Puritan ministers were bemoaning the decline of religion and the rise of material values. Meanwhile, the outbreak of civil war in England during the 1640s reduced interest in colonial affairs and slowed immigration, precipitating an economic depression in New England and a feeling of spiritual loss among Puritans. While old England struggled with internal problems, New England remained a distant outpost, no longer the beacon on the hill.

The Restoration Touches America

In the Old World, the English civil war pitted Charles I against a pro-Puritan Parliament, which demanded the right to control taxation and criticized the king's religious views. The execution of the king in 1649 opened a brief era of parliamentary rule under the Puritan Oliver Cromwell. But in 1660, Parliament agreed to restore the monarchy in the person of the dead king's son, Charles II, whose subsequent reign was called the *Restoration*. Having defeated his opponents, the restored king proceeded to tighten royal control over England's growing empire in America. At the king's bequest, wealthy aristocrats received title to vast tracts of land on the Atlantic seaboard to establish colonies, including the Carolinas, New York, and Pennsylvania. The crown also gave more attention to regulating trade between the colonies and the mother country.

Settling the Carolinas

Charles II repaid his political supporters by giving them large "proprietary" grants in America. The first of these gifts, given to a group of eight lords in 1663, comprised the region known as Carolina. Expecting to produce expensive exports, such as silk and wine, the proprietors envisioned a country of large estates. Their secretary, the philosopher John Locke, proceeded in 1669 to draft a blueprint, known as the Fundamental Constitutions, proposing a hereditary nobility based on large landholdings and slave labor. This scheme was never implemented because few colonists wanted to live as peasants rather than on their own lands. Already the northern part of Carolina around Albemarle Sound had attracted small farmers from Virginia who rejected proprietary rule. This area later formed the independent colony of North Carolina in 1712.

The Carolina proprietors did attract another class of settlers who already had wealth in America, particularly sugar planters from Barbados, who migrated with their slaves to the area around Charles Town (later Charleston) in 1670. Some began raising cattle, using Africans who had acquired herding skills in their homelands of west Africa. More profitable was the trade for deerskins with the populous Southeast nations—Creeks, Chickasaws, Chocktaws. By 1700, Carolina's commerce extended to the Mississippi River, where the English competed with Spanish and French fur traders.

Carolina merchants found even greater profits in the slave trade among Native Americans. Encouraging rival tribes to war among themselves, white Carolinians offered firearms and other manufactured goods in exchange for Native American captives. Beginning in the 1670s, Carolina's Yamasee and Creek allies conducted slave raids against the Spanish missions in Florida. But because Native American captives often fled into the woods, Carolinians preferred to ship these slaves to other colonies. By 1710, Charleston had exported 12,000 Native American slaves to Virginia, New England, and the West Indies. Warfare and European diseases took an additional toll on the Native inhabitants. Between 1685 and 1700, the Native population dropped 25 percent, to about 15,000. Thirty years later, with continuing slave raids and wars, only 4,000 survived. Thus passed such thriving groups as the Westos, Savannahs, Tuscaroras (who found refuge among the Iroquois of New York), and Yamasees. Meanwhile, Carolina merchants built fortunes to invest in rice plantations in the next century.

Seizing the Dutch Colonies

Consolidating English possession of the mid-Atlantic seaboard, Charles II sent a military expedition in 1664 to seize the single outpost of Dutch competition in North America, the small colony of New Netherlands. Linked in a fur trading alliance with the Iroquois confederacy, the Dutch were competing effectively against French traders in Canada, who aligned with Algonquians. But the colony was sparsely populated and unable to defend itself. Already New Englanders had taken Dutch territory in Connecticut. The English fleet proceeded to conquer the Dutch colony without firing a shot, and Charles II granted proprietary rights to the area to his brother, the Duke of York. The Duke then granted the southern portions of his domain (now New Jersey) to two other proprietors. In 1670, the Dutch would recapture New York, but they later returned it as part of a peace settlement with England.

English rule brought little change to the settlements on the Hudson. With a heterogeneous population and a shared commitment to commerce, Dutch and English coexisted peacefully throughout the colonial period. However, the replacement of Dutch legal traditions with English customs altered the status of married women. Under Dutch law, married women could own property independently of their husbands, and wives maintained rights to half their family's estates. The conquest of 1664 did not immediately change Dutch practices, but as Dutch families adopted English customs, the English limits on married women's rights prevailed.

New York and New Jersey continued to attract land-hungry settlers from New England as well as English Quakers seeking religious freedom. By the end of the 17th century, over 10,000 settlers inhabited the two colonies. New York's primary economic activity was trade, first in beaver furs brought by Iroquois allies and later in the export of wheat and corn. By 1700, New York City was already a thriving metropolis.

Founding Pennsylvania

To settle another political debt, Charles II granted a proprietary colony to William Penn, a wealthy English Quaker, in 1681. The Society of Friends, or Quakers, had emerged in England as a radical offshoot of the Puritan movement; but, instead of emphasizing Original Sin and the limits of human achievement, the Quakers stressed the "inner light" of divinity within each person and the importance of achieving a spiritual community on earth. Believing that all humans were spiritual equals, the Quakers rejected worldly authority, refusing to tip their hats to their betters or to engage in warfare. Quakers also acknowledged the spiritual equality of women, who spoke freely at the Friends' religious "meetings." Such beliefs had led to their persecution both in England and New England. Now, in Pennsylvania, William Penn hoped to create a godly society and a sanctuary for his co-religionists.

To administer the colony, Penn granted a charter called the First Frame of Government in 1682, which established the principles of religious freedom and representative government. Penn also took pains to purchase the lands given to him by the king from the Delaware people who inhabited the area. Such fair dealing earned Penn the appreciation of the Native groups and facilitated subsequent trade for furs.

Penn's religious toleration, together with liberal opportunities for land purchase, attracted colonists throughout Europe. By 1700, German and Scottish settlers contributed to Pennsylvania's heterogeneous population. Since most immigrants arrived as families, the colony boasted a high birthrate comparable to New England's. By 1700, the population numbered 12,000. Penn planned the colony's chief city, Philadelphia, as a grid with right-angle intersections and park areas, typical of his desire for orderly development. With choice agricultural land to grow wheat, corn, and rye, and the port at Philadelphia to ship exports abroad, Pennsylvania emerged as America's breadbasket during the 18th century.

Mercantilism and English Commercial Policy

Although private proprietors controlled the Restoration colonies, the English government recognized the great economic value of colonial development. During the civil war, English merchants had worried about the loss of commerce in America to Dutch traders who bought West Indian sugar, Virginia tobacco, and North American furs and sold European commodities and African slaves. Such interloping by foreign traders violated the economic principles of *mercantilism,* which held that a nation's wealth depended on the amount of gold and silver it possessed. Mercantilists believed that countries could become richer at the expense of other countries by engaging in trade that produced more exports than imports. Accordingly, colonies could serve as sources of raw materials and as markets for products of the mother country. Such trade promised prosperity to both trade parties, and any apparent conflicts of interest between specific groups would be compensated by the economic benefit to the nation as a whole. Parliament therefore responded to Dutch competition by passing the first Navigation Act in 1651. The law required that all goods shipped to and from the colonies be carried by English or English colonial ships; furthermore, all non-English products, including colonial exports such as tobacco, had to be brought directly to England from the point of origin. By including English colonists as bona fide shippers, the measure supported colonial merchants and shipbuilders.

After the restoration of the monarchy in 1660, Parliament passed a second Navigation Act in 1660, eliminating some loopholes in the original law. English vessels now had to be manned by crews of which three-quarters were English or English colonials. The law also "enumerated" certain colonial products (tobacco, sugar, cotton, indigo) that could only be exported to England. Later navigation acts added to the enumerated list to include rice, furs, iron, lumber, and naval stores. But, because colonial producers could sometimes sell these items illegally to other countries at greater profit, many shippers ignored the law, much to the frustration of English officials. To prevent such violations, Parliament passed additional laws of enforcement. These included provisions that required all European trade headed for the colonies first to pass through English ports before being trans-shipped (1663); required merchants to post bonds assuring that goods would not be shipped to illegal destinations (1673); and created naval courts (which omitted juries) to punish smugglers (1696). These various navigation acts, though frequently ignored by colonists and royal officials alike, represented a conscious effort by English administrators to coordinate colonial policy.

The mercantile system thus forced the colonists to trade with the mother country, but such trade probably would have occurred anyway. In an age when most commercial activity required familiarity with trusted agents overseas, English-speaking merchants would most likely have created arrangements with people of similar backgrounds. Moreover, England's manufactured products were of superior quality, were much preferred over other European goods by both colonists and Native American traders, and were much cheaper. The enumeration of goods also gave England's colonists a monopoly of the English market for such products as tobacco, naval stores, and indigo. Although some of these products might have been sold at higher prices in other countries, the total cost was not excessive. Yet economic analysis shows that England's navigation system had its greatest impact on the colonies at the end of the 17th century, when law enforcement was strict and the young economies were most susceptible to extra costs.

English intervention in the colonies during the late 17th century also brought new political problems, especially in Puritan New England. After the Restoration, a royal commission, sent to investigate New England's trade policies, found widespread violations of the navigation acts. To exercise greater control, the crown revoked Massachusetts' charter in 1684, removing the legal basis of self-government. When the Duke of York ascended the throne as King James II, he incorporated the New England colonies and New York in a larger administrative unit known as the Dominion of New England. This political system lacked a representative government. English officials also threatened New England's independence by questioning the legality of old land grants, enforcing the navigation acts more strictly, levying new taxes, and allowing the Church of England to hold services in Puritan Boston.

By 1689, therefore, New Englanders welcomed the news from England that Parliament had overthrown the king in a so-called Glorious Revolution. New Englanders spontaneously supported

Parliament by revolting against the Dominion of New England and seeking a new royal charter from the new monarchs, William and Mary. Residents of New York, equally hostile to the Dominion, joined the rebellion. In America, the Glorious Revolution stood as a benchmark in political liberty, long a reminder that royal power had to respect colonial rights.

The Clash of Cultures

By 1689, the growth of colonial society was impressive. At the beginning of the century, Powhatan had reminded John Smith that "we can plant anywhere. . . and we know that you cannot live if you want [i.e., lack] our harvest, and that relief we bring you." Two generations later, an English negotiator could reverse the claim, telling an Iroquois leader "You know that we can live without you, but you cannot live without us." By then, Iroquois hunters had come to depend on European goods, such as guns to hunt animals and defend themselves from equally supplied enemies. Yet despite their dependence on European weapons, the Native American nations remained a potent factor in the development of the colonial economies.

Nothing showed the power of Native Americans more clearly than the continuing competition for the fur trade. Although the French in Canada had developed ties with the Hurons and Algonquian groups to dominate the Great Lakes beaver supply, by the mid-17th century the rival Iroquois, armed by Dutch and English colonies, threatened this valuable commerce. Moreover, after the Iroquois defeated the Hurons in 1650, scattering their tribal remnants into the Ohio valley, French traders had difficulty maintaining the lucrative commerce. Under Iroquois control, beaver furs moved in greater quantity toward the Dutch and English traders of Albany, New York, rather than to New

> **"You know that we can live without you, but you cannot live without us."**

France. Hostility between Iroquois and Algonquians thus paralleled the rivalry between England and France, laying the basis for intercolonial warfare that would last for another century.

King Philip's War

The strategic position of the Iroquois played an important role in the defeat of a major Algonquian uprising against the Puritan colonies. Since the Pequot war of 1637, New England colonists had avoided warfare with the local peoples, though war scares occurred frequently. Territorial disputes between New England and the Narragansetts finally erupted in open warfare in 1675, when the colonists responded to the murder of an English settler by invading Native lands, burning villages, and destroying the growing crops. When the local tribes fought back, organizing coordinated attacks against English towns, New Englanders realized they were fighting for the right to live in western New England.

Under the leadership of Metacomet, known to the English as King Philip, the Wampanoags were joined by many other Algonquian groups to attack colonial settlements, killing and kidnapping inhabitants, and burning English homes and fields. Exposed to surprise attack, the colonists abandoned twenty-five towns, more than half of all their communities, and feared for the survival of the English colonies. Although the colonial militia organized counterattacks, Metacomet avoided entrapment for more than a year. But his hope of creating a Native American alliance against the English failed to gain support from the rival Iroquois, who wanted to preserve their fur trade with the colonists. Instead of supporting the uprising, Iroquois warriors helped the Puritans pursue Metacomet, killing him in battle in 1676. Then the Iroquois joined the English in forcing the Algonquians to accept a harsh treaty that took away their lands. Despite the Puritan victory, New England suffered 2,000 casualties and severe economic losses that retarded colonial development for decades.

The Iroquois Covenant Chain

In 1677, Iroquois and English negotiators agreed to a formal alliance known as the "Covenant Chain," which protected peace between these trading empires for nearly a century. Meanwhile, the French restored commercial relations with scattered Algonquian groups, who had resettled west of the Iroquois in the Ohio valley. In this competition for the fur trade with Europeans, the Native chiefs demonstrated considerable diplomatic skill, forcing both the French and English to make concessions. Successful colonial traders recognized the importance of ritualistic language and gift giving in forging alliances with their trading partners. All parties understood that allies were independent and could be swayed by competitors to become deadly enemies. When, for example, the Iroquois learned that the French were building a fort at Detroit, they expected the English to challenge their common enemy. Indeed, the English failure to act persuaded the Iroquois to sign a peace treaty with New France in 1701.

An Emerging North American Society

The clash of cultures in 17th-century North America thus involved high political stakes for the competing European empires as well as for the Native American nations that struggled to benefit from this international conflict. But as the complicated

diplomatic drama unfolded, most colonials were more concerned with their mundane activities—farming, raising children, and building communities. Although most colonists who landed on the Atlantic coast expected simply to transplant familiar social customs and economic practices, their great distance from Europe forced the settlers to create societies different from the ones they had left behind. The cultural diversity that appeared in many colonies—the presence of people from different areas of the home country as well as strangers from other parts of Europe and Africa—required adjustments of traditional views. Moreover, the lack of established traditions (the absence of churches in 17th-century Virginia, for example, or titled aristocrats in New England) encouraged the colonists to improvise as they organized new societies. Such changes created a distinct provincial environment and the sense of being only a small part, a province, of a larger empire.

INFOTRAC® COLLEGE EDITION EXERCISES

 For additional reading go to InfoTrac College Edition, your online research library, at http://web1.infotrac-college.com.

Keyword search: Spanish colonization
Subject search: Champlain
Keyword search: colonial Spain
Keyword search: Puritans
Subject search: Pilgrims
Subject search: Anne Hutchinson
Keyword search: Oliver Cromwell
Keyword search: mercantilism

ADDITIONAL READING

Spain's Empire of Souls

Ramon A. Gutierrez, *When Jesus Came, the Corn Mothers Went Away: Marriage, Sexuality and Power in New*

Mexico, 1500–1846 (1991). An excellent analysis of cultures in conflict, depicting Spain's impact on the Pueblo peoples.

David J. Weber, *The Spanish Frontier in North America* (1992). Describes Spanish colonization from Florida to New Mexico and California.

The Background of English Colonization

David Hackett Fischer, *Albion's Seed: Four British Folkways in America* (1989). Focusing on four regions in Britain, this book examines the social origins of English colonial customs.

Founding Virginia

Kathleen M. Brown, *Good Wives, Nasty Wenches, and Anxious Patriarchs: Gender, Race, and Power in Colonial Virginia* (1996). Tracing the transfer of English values to Virginia, this book describes the emergence of white male leaders at the expense of women, Africans, and Native Americans.

Edmund S. Morgan, *American Slavery, American Freedom: The Ordeal of Colonial Virginia* (1975). Examining the labor system of early Virginia, this volume reveals the rigors of early settlement that paved the way for slavery.

Chesapeake Society

Gloria L. Main, *Tobacco Colony: Life in Early Maryland, 1650–1720* (1982). Based on probate records and demographic statistics, this work provides a lively analysis of social life on the Chesapeake.

Timothy Silver, *A New Face on the Countryside: Indians, Colonists, and Slaves in South Atlantic Forests, 1500–1800* (1990). Studies the human impact on southern natural resources during the first two centuries of European settlement.

French North America

James Axtell, *The Invasion Within: The Contest of Cultures in Colonial North America* (1985). A lively analysis of English and French competition among Native Americans.

Puritanism Comes to New England

Edmund S. Morgan, *Puritan Dilemma: The Story of John Winthrop* (1958). This classic biography of the Massachusetts governor offers a lucid explanation of Puritan objectives in New England.

Puritan Families

Mary Beth Norton, *Founding Mothers and Fathers: Gendered Power and the Forming of American Society* (1996). A study of gender values in English America, exploring the legal and political implications of 17th-century attitudes.

The Clash of Cultures

Jose Antonio Brandao, *Your Fyre Shall Burn No More: Iroquois Policy toward New France and Its Native Allies to 1701* (1997). A study of Iroquois warfare, emphasizing the cultural context of Native American diplomacy.

Francis Jennings, *The Ambiguous Iroquois Empire: The Covenant Chain Confederation of Indian Tribes with English Colonies from its beginnings to the Lancaster Treaty of 1744* (1984). An exhaustive study of diplomacy that stresses the ability of the Iroquois to negotiate with Europeans.

Francis Jennings, *The Invasion of America* (1975). A detailed analysis of Puritan relations with native tribes, stressing the role of European aggression and greed.

Jill Lepore, *The Name of War: King Philip's War and the Origins of American Identity* (1998). Analyzes the cultural context of the deadly New England war.

James H. Merrell, *The Indians' New World: Catawbas and Their Neighbors from European Contact through the Era of Removal* (1989). Discusses the interaction of the southern tribes and English settlers in the Carolinas.

Neal Salisbury, *Manitou and Providence: Indians, Europeans, and the Making of New England, 1500–1643* (1982). A careful study of competition for land and resources during the formative period of colonization.

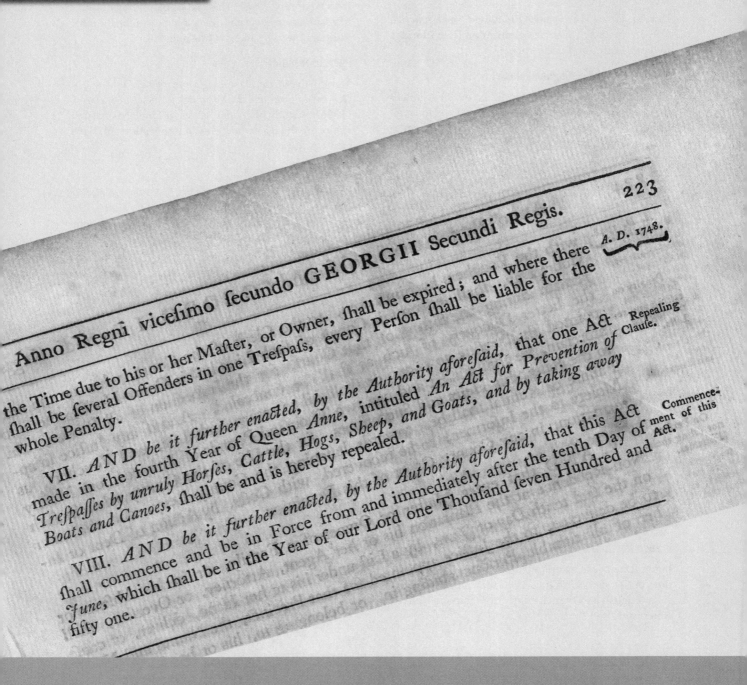

4

Anno Regni vicesimo secundo GEORGII Secundi Regis.   223

A. D. 1748.

the Time due to his or her Master, or Owner, shall be expired; and where there shall be several Offenders in one Trespass, every Person shall be liable for the whole Penalty.

VII. AND be it further enacted, by the Authority aforesaid, that one Act made in the fourth Year of Queen Anne, intituled *An Act for Prevention of Trespasses by unruly Horses, Cattle, Hogs, Sheep, and Goats, and by taking away Boats and Canoes*, shall be and is hereby repealed.

Repealing Clause.

VIII. AND be it further enacted, by the Authority aforesaid, that this Act shall commence and be in Force from and immediately after the tenth Day of *June*, which shall be in the Year of our Lord one Thousand seven Hundred and fifty one.

Commencement of this Act.

The Emergence of Colonial Cultures, 1675–1765

CHRONOLOGY

1675–1676	Nathaniel Bacon leads a rebellion in Virginia
1692	Salem witchcraft trials begin
1699	France establishes settlements in Louisiana
1705	Virginia enacts comprehensive slave code
1723	Virginia prohibits free blacks from voting
1732	Colony of Georgia founded
1739	Slave rebellion erupts in Stono, South Carolina
1739–1742	George Whitefield sparks Great Awakening
1743	Benjamin Franklin founds American Philosophical Society
1750s	South Carolina settlers impinge on Catawba lands

Looking out upon his flock from the heights of a rough-hewn pine pulpit, Connecticut pastor Samuel Wakeman turned his eyes heavenward. Where was the humility that faith demanded of his people?

He could see the more richly clad of the colony's leaders seated comfortably, footwarmers at their toes, in the front pews. Toward the rear, in the chillier reaches of the church, sat the humbler ones with aspirations to the front. More and more, these folk, he thought, felt that "every nobody would be a somebody, and that persons of a commoner rank look. . . too earnestly towards the upper end of the world: men know not their places. . . . Men's conditions sit uneasy, and their callings suit them not." He felt, in short, that people had forgotten their proper places in society, in God's eyes.

Although the first colonists had struggled to transplant their familiar society in America, they could never reproduce what they had left behind in Europe. Population dispersal, the mixture of cultural groups, and shortage of labor—all brought changes to the social order. The absence of a hereditary aristocracy, for example, allowed men of lesser status to assume leadership, causing resentment among those who were expected to defer to their "betters." At the opposite end of the hierarchy, the introduction of slavery created a new caste that divided workers along racial lines. How colonials adjusted to these social changes usually depended on the benefits and losses they experienced.

During the first century of settlement, the North American colonies developed a new social order. New leaders emerged and consolidated their wealth and power. By 1750, they formed an established colonial elite that claimed the respect and allegiance of people of lesser status, at least among whites. "A man who has money here," remarked a Rhode Island colonist, "no matter how he came by it, he is everything." Although the distance between the richest and the poorest was not as wide as in Europe, property holding remained the prime standard of citizenship, a category that excluded women, slaves, and other economic dependents who could not legally own property. Yet even small property holders could aspire for success as merchants, politicians, or "gentlemen."

Colonial society also differed from Europe's in the diversity of its population. In 1700, 250,000 non-native people inhabited British North America; three-quarters of a century later, the population had multiplied tenfold to 2.5 million. Only one-quarter of this growth resulted from immigration; the remainder reflected natural increase, which created denser communities and encouraged internal migration to unsettled areas.

This population explosion involved complicated changes in social composition. As the number of Africans increased tenfold, whites in all colonies met west Africans of diverse backgrounds who spoke dozens of dialects and possessed distinct cultural experiences. European immigrants included ever larger numbers from Scotland, Ireland, Wales, and the West Indies, who mingled with settlers who spoke German or Dutch or French. Native communities, especially those near the fringes of European settlement, often consisted of remnants and survivors of decimated groups, linked together by distant ties of kinship or political dependence. Yet the leadership in British North America remained overwhelmingly English, eager to imitate the values of the mother country.

Transforming Chesapeake Society

The transformation from a European social order could be seen clearly in colonial Virginia during the last quarter of the 17th century. In 1675, the colony's royal governor, Sir William Berkeley, stood at the apex of society. As the highest government official, Berkeley and his appointed advisers in the colony's council dominated the tobacco economy. They controlled all grants of land, collected export revenues, and levied taxes. This powerful group consisted of those who had survived the ravages of colonization: economic uncertainty, conflict with the Powhattan natives, and high mortality. By vigorously exploiting the labor of white indentured servants and black slaves and by using their connections with royal power they had amassed large landholdings, taken control of the fur trade with the Susquehanna hunters, and exported much of the colony's annual 15 million pound tobacco crop to England. Despite their great wealth and power, however, Virginia's leaders were "new men," products of rapid social mobility rather than the inherited status that prevailed in England.

Bacon's Rebellion

Challenges to the leadership group began in the 1660s. The end of the English civil war had encouraged immigration to the Chesapeake at the same time that many indentured servants were completing their terms of labor. The result was an overproduction of tobacco, which brought a drop in prices. Yet new planters and former servants continued to seek land to become tobacco farmers. They soon confronted two obstacles: first, Governor Berkeley and his entrenched advisers opposed the ambitions of potential rivals; second, the Susquehannas and their allies, who traded animal skins with the English, resisted a further loss of their land. When Virginia settlers encroached on Native territory in 1675, minor disputes flared into violence. Angry Chesapeake colonials, under the leadership of a recent well-born immigrant named Nathaniel Bacon, marched against the Susquehannas, seeking an opportunity to seize their lands.

Governor Berkeley refused to provide military assistance to Bacon and his allies, opposing their desires to obtain western lands. Bacon then led his armed followers to Jamestown, where he defied the governor's authority and forced the House of Burgesses to enact laws providing for tax reforms and authorizing an attack on the Susquehannas. Backed by indentured servants who coveted western lands and African slaves who fought for their freedom, Bacon's insurrection threatened both the legal government and the social order that had evolved during the first generation. But Bacon's sudden death from illness and the arrival of British military forces ended the up-

> ## "Like one of the patriarchs, I have my flocks and my herds, my bond-men and bond-women."

rising. Berkeley proceeded to crush the remaining rebels, executing twenty-three for treason, reenslaving Africans and bond servants, and confiscating the rebels' property.

Although Bacon's rebellion indicated widespread dissatisfaction with the colonial leadership, the old order triumphed and persisted. After 1676, the House of Burgesses would share authority with the governor and council in making grants of land. But the Burgesses also reversed recent laws that permitted all free white men to vote and limited suffrage to "freeholders," that is, to property owning free men. Maintaining control over land and trade with Native peoples, affluent planters continued to dominate political power, and in time their leadership came to appear stable and respectable. With wealth and power, leading families intermarried and formed the "first families" of the colony. This elite self-consciously imitated the English gentry, building elegant capitals at Annapolis, Maryland, and Williamsburg, Virginia, founding the College of William and Mary in 1693, and adopting English fashions and architectural models. By 1726, one Virginia planter could boast: "Like one of the patriarchs, I have my flocks and my herds, my bond-men and bond-women, and every sort of trade among my servants, so that I live in a kind of independence of every one, but Providence."

The drive of the Chesapeake leadership to consolidate wealth, power, and status was made easier by other changes in society. If Bacon's rebellion expressed the frustrations of landless workers and slaves, the decline of tobacco prices during the late 17th century further diminished Virginia as a land of opportunity. With new colonies opening in the Carolinas and Pennsylvania, fewer white laborers migrated to the Chesapeake region. To the established leadership, reduced migration meant less competition, but it also aggravated the colony's labor shortage. The result was a major transformation of tobacco society and culture.

Defining Slavery in the Colonies

Virginia's labor problems prompted a reconsideration of the colony's African residents. The status of the first Africans in Virginia and Maryland remains uncertain, though like all servants, whether slave or free, most were males, and their conditions were undoubtedly poor. Probably most Africans entered the colony as slaves; but within a few years some had obtained both freedom and property, perhaps because they were treated as indentured servants. Whatever their exact status, surviving court records suggest that the legal system treated blacks differently than whites and occasionally punished black offenders with lifetime servitude. Africans, unlike European settlers, were generally listed only by their first names in the local census. Such practices reflected English ideas about the inferiority of nonwhite peoples—the belief that Africans lacked both Christianity and civilization, that their skin color indicated both sin and savagery. When, for example, a New Englander criticized another white woman for "the black side of her actions," she meant that the behavior was evil. When Africans came to be treated as slaves, their social debasement perpetuated these cultural prejudices.

During the mid-1600s, Chesapeake law steadily undermined Africans' civil rights. In 1643, Virginia imposed a tax on landowners who employed African women, thus placing black women (but not white women) in the same category as male

workers both black and white. At around the same time, Maryland prohibited Africans from bearing arms. Both colonies banned interracial sexual relations, with a Maryland law of 1664 stating that all "English women [who are] forgetful of their free condition and to the disgrace of our nation do intermarry with Negro Slaves . . . shall serve the master of such slaves during the life of her husband." The children of such women also became slaves. In 1669, Virginia legislated that a master who killed a slave while administering punishment would not be charged with murder.

The political consequences of a permanent slave population emerged during Bacon's rebellion. The interracial insurrection, allying white indentured servants and black slaves, was especially dangerous to political leaders, not only because of the number of organized rebels but also because by then African Americans had the least to lose by rebelling. Indeed, of the last 100 rebels who confronted Governor Berkeley, 80 were black.

As more English immigrants settled in other colonies, where opportunities for owning land were better, the decline of indentured servitude encouraged a rise in the number of black slaves. In 1660, Africans in Virginia numbered 1,700; twenty years later, they comprised 4,600; in another twenty years, their number had grown to nearly 13,000; and by 1710, the figure touched 30,000. To put it another way, in 1680 Africans represented 7 percent of the total Chesapeake population; by 1720, they comprised 25 percent.

During this period of increasing slave importation, the Chesapeake colonies adopted additional measures to restrict slave activity. Serious slave offenses were tried by separate tribunals. Slaves convicted of capital crimes, such as violence against whites, were often hanged or burned alive, their bodies dismembered and displayed publicly as a warning to others. Chesapeake laws declared that conversion to Christianity did not liberate a slave;

nor could free Africans, mulattos, or Natives own another person, except of their own "complexions." In 1699, Virginia ordered all free Africans to leave the colony, though the measure was seldom enforced. In 1705, these various statutes were reenacted as a comprehensive slave code.

The effect of Virginia's slave laws was not just to keep Africans in a subordinate position. More subtly, laws that restricted blacks reminded free whites of who they were *not*. Although poor whites had aligned with black slaves during Bacon's rebellion, by 1700 even the most oppressed white could claim a superior position to virtually any black person. During the 1680s, moreover, interracial sexual relations became illegal, and white women were prosecuted for having intercourse with black men (but the rape of black women by white men was not treated as a crime). In 1723, even free Africans were denied the right to vote. By the middle of the century, only 4 percent of Virginia's population consisted of free Africans, most of whom lived in female-headed households because slave-owners emancipated more women than men.

Slave Trading. Although the first slaves imported into the Chesapeake originated in the West Indies, tobacco planters disliked these "refuse" or "rogue" slaves, who had apparently been rejected by sugar planters for reasons of poor health, old age, or bad behavior. After 1680, as British merchants dominated the Atlantic slave trade, North Americans imported most slaves directly from Africa. Some colonies, such as New York and South Carolina, taxed slave imports from Africa at a lower rate than those from the West Indies. Yet until 1697, the Royal African Company, chartered by the English crown, held a monopoly of England's slave trade and limited sales in North America to keep prices high. Once English and colonial merchants broke that monopoly, slave prices fell and imports rose.

In purchasing slaves from Africa, colonial slave-owners expressed distinct ethnic preferences, favoring Africans from the Gold Coast and Windward Coast to those from other areas. Slaves who were Calabar or Ibo were less attractive because colonials believed they were more likely to commit suicide or try to escape. Southern planters preferred strong young men capable of hard field work, while whites in urban areas looked for younger boys and girls who could be trained as domestics or artisans.

In the Carolinas, African slaves had a great influence on the colony's economic development. Carolina's first planters came from the Caribbean, bringing slaves who had learned about herding and stock raising in Guinea along the Gambia River. Their skills, including seasonal burning of forests to stimulate the growth of grasses, enabled the planters to prosper. Later, as Carolina planters searched for a staple crop suitable for the colony's semi-tropical lowlands, west Africans contributed their experience with rice cultivation. The Africans' resistance to malaria and yellow fever also enabled them to survive in the swampy rice fields. Using African types of hoes and dikes, Carolina's slaves made rice the major cash crop after 1700. Exports jumped from 1.5 million pounds in 1710 to 20 million in 1730. Carolinians also used slaves to cultivate indigo dyes, based on the experiments of a white woman named Eliza Lucas, but that crop depended on continued economic subsidies from England. Reliance on African labor turned South Carolina into a black majority (about 60 percent), while Charleston became a slave trading center. Nevertheless, a high percentage of small farmers, especially in the western regions of the Carolinas, owned no slaves.

Unlike Carolina, the colony of Georgia, founded in 1732 by James Oglethorpe as a philanthropic experiment, explicitly prohibited slavery. But slow economic growth led the colonists to protest the ban. Arguing that it was "simply impossible to manufacture the rice by white men," and that blacks were "as essentially necessary to the cultivation of Georgia, as axes, hoes, or any other utensil of agriculture," the colonists won the right to own slaves in 1750. Carolina rice planters, eager to expand their holdings, promptly moved south with their slaves. By 1773, Georgia's African population numbered about 15,000—about the same as the white population.

Slavery in the North. Northern slaveowners experimented with Native American slaves imported from South Carolina, but found these servants "malicious, surly, and revengeful" and banned this trade in 1715. Africans comprised only 3 percent of New England's population: 10–15 percent in the middle colonies, but nearly 20 percent in the cities (Newport, Rhode Island; New York). On family farms, blacks worked closely with whites and shared their meals and housing, and so had fewer opportunities for privacy and anonymity than slaves on larger southern farms. Most northern Africans were male; most surviving Native Americans in the northern colonies, free or slave, were female. Intermarriage resolved those demographic imbalances, though not without arousing strong objections from white political leaders.

In northern cities, African occupations included skilled trades, such as sail making, brewing, and carpentry, as well as hard dockside labor and domestic servitude. Because of the relatively small African population, the northern colonies permitted more mobility to slaves. But certain crimes—sexual relations with whites, for example—were punished severely, and a Massachusetts law banished convicted Africans to the West Indies. Northern slaveowners showed their disdain for Africans by giving them, as one writer reported, "such-like names they give their dogs and horses." In the cities, where there were small populations of free blacks, African behavior was limited by curfews and prohibitions of alcohol. During economic slow-

Cotton Mather, who said of early smallpox inoculations "ye Method of Inoculation, I had from a Servant of my own, an Account of its being practiced in Africa. Enquiring of my Negro-Man Onesimus, who is a pretty Intelligent Fellow, Whether he ever had ye Small-Pox, he answered Yes and No; and then told me that he had undergone an Operation, which had given him something of ye Small-Pox, and would forever preserve him from it."

downs, competition between white workers and black slaves sometimes produced violent conflict. Yet cultural exchange occurred frequently. Indeed, it was an African slave who taught Boston's minister, Cotton Mather, the secrets of smallpox inoculation that, when introduced in Boston during an epidemic in the 1720s, limited the mortality rate.

Creating an African American Culture

Africans in America found themselves among people who spoke different languages and dialects. Those from neighboring African homelands tended

"If my slaves go to heaven, must I see them there?"

to group together, speaking "creole" languages that blended English and African tongues. But conditions of slavery determined which African traditions survived. In the scattered rural areas of the north, Africans remained isolated, meeting others only occasionally. Yet, even with few blacks around, Puritan churches maintained racial segregation during religious services and in churchyard burials. Southern Christians also established racial segregation in their churches, leading one troubled parishioner to ask "If my slaves go to heaven, must I see them there?" But in the southern colonies, where large numbers of Africans lived close together, racial segregation encouraged the preservation of African cultures and traditions. Within the separate slave quarters, Africans from diverse backgrounds were obliged to construct new lives. Exposure to different African languages, marriage into new kin networks, the sharing of work and leisure—all had a homogenizing effect, laying the basis for a common African American culture.

African American Kinship

In the decades before 1720, slave importations created a lopsided male population in North America. With few African women to marry and with prohibitions on interracial sex, most slaves lacked the opportunity to form families, and the African birthrate remained low. Yet Africans took pains to travel between plantations, sometimes walking as many as thirty or forty miles, to gather in the evenings, on Sundays and holidays or, as one planter complained, "beating their Negro drums by which they call considerable numbers of Negroes together in some certain places." Since enslavement drastically disrupted networks of family, kin, and clan, Africans developed extended relationships with neighbors and friends, who offered emotional support, assistance, and cultural continuity. "Uncles" or "Aunties" who were not blood relatives served as surrogates and role models for children in the event of the death or sale of a parent.

Around 1720, as declining tobacco prices reduced slave imports, the gender balance among Africans improved, and the African birthrate began to rise. In 1700, the African population of British North America totaled 28,000; by 1776, it exceeded half a million. That growth, far higher than increases in other parts of the slave world, reflected a healthier environment, better nutrition, and a sex ratio that stimulated natural increase. Because of work obligations, male slaves often resided apart from their wives and children, leaving childrearing to the women. Despite laws prohibiting interracial sex, slave women were vulnerable to sexual exploitation by their masters. Mulattos, children born to slave women by white men, followed their mothers' status into slavery. Meanwhile, slaveholders denied the legality of slave marriages, and allowed mothers with infants to be sold "together or apart." Yet Africans respected their family ties, choosing names for their children that established parental lineage. Advertisements for runaway slaves in Virginia before 1775 reveal that one-third had departed in search of their relatives.

African American Religion

"Talk to a planter about the soul of a Negro," wrote a traveler in 1705, and he will respond that although the body is worth twenty pounds, "the souls of a hundred will not yield him one farthing [penny]." Slaveholders feared that conversion to Christianity might stimulate interest in freedom. Consequently, most Africans had little exposure to organized Christianity, and most preserved the spiritual beliefs of their own cultures.

The racial segregation of burial grounds, seen at George Washington's Mount Vernon plantation, enabled African Americans to preserve their traditional burial customs. The monument's inscription reads "In memory of the Afro-Americans who served as slaves at Mount Vernon this monument marking their burial ground dedicated September 21, 1983, Mount Vernon Ladies' Association."

The survival of African religious beliefs took many forms. Believing that spirits abounded in the natural world and could intervene in human activities for good or evil, Africans resorted to conjurors (people skilled in magical powers) to calm antagonistic spirits with charms, amulets, or herbal potions. (Similar magical beliefs existed among some European colonists, particularly those who did not belong to traditional churches; cross-cultural beliefs regarding witches would later form common ground for accusations of witchcraft in New England.) Because of the importance of ancestor worship, Africans took pains to uphold their traditional funeral rites and burial services. Long funeral processions, alive with song and dance, escorted the dead to their graves. This practice was outlawed in Boston because it was considered both unseemly and un-Christian. Recent excavations of an 18th-century African cemetery in New York City revealed that the dead were buried with care—shrouded, placed in wooden coffins, and aligned as in Africa with their heads toward the west.

Despite claims that slavery would Christianize the "heathen," English churches made few converts among transplanted Africans. In New England, requirements for baptism demanded both theological knowledge and Christian deportment, a formality that did not exist in African traditions and discouraged membership in Puritan churches. In the southern colonies, interest in converting Africans conflicted with the fear that Christianized slaves would claim spiritual equality and demand their freedom. Moreover, since slaves lived in large groups segregated from whites, they had more freedom to define their religious life. Missionaries who did preach among slaves usually emphasized the importance of Christian obedience and humility. To be baptized in South Carolina, a slave had to swear to remain obedient.

Evangelical preachers, who tapped African traditions of spiritual rebirth and whose sermon styles evoked African call-and-response rhythms, won many Christian converts in the mid-18th century. During a larger religious revival known as the "Great Awakening," Africans responded to a familiar feeling of spirit possession marked by dancing, clapping, shouting, and singing, and came forward in large numbers to be baptized. "They feel themselves uneasy in their present condition," remarked Samuel Davies, a white revivalist preacher, "and therefore desire a change."

Interpreting Christianity selectively, Africans drew parallels between going to heaven and returning to the spirits of their ancestors. In the emerging Baptist churches, moreover, whites and blacks, free and slave, created mixed congregations that permitted equal participation in church affairs. By the end of the colonial era, some of these churches, together with the Quakers, were calling for an end to slavery. Yet the overall proportion of slaves who became Christians remained very small.

Resisting Slavery

Christian sermons typically advised slaves to submit to their owners, but Africans demonstrated considerable skill, both personal and collective, at thwarting the demands of their masters. By controlling the pace of their labor, slaves could define their daily lives. Black slave drivers, respected leaders within African communities, emerged as intermediaries between workers and white overseers, ensuring the reasonableness of the work. On rice plantations, a task labor system focused on the completion of specific tasks, leaving slaves free time to tend their own gardens. Such produce would be used for personal consumption or traded in markets. Masters who ignored customary holidays (Sundays, summer nights, harvest feasts, Christmas) faced retaliation such as arson that imperiled an entire season's work.

Efforts to escape from slavery were omnipresent. Newly arrived Africans tended to flee in groups, while slaves who were familiar with the English language usually ran off alone. African-born slaves were more likely to become fugitives; American-born slaves were less likely to be caught. Newspaper advertisements for runaway slaves often mentioned their ethnic origins, reinforcing white opinions that certain African areas, such as Angola, produced less compliant slaves. Angolans, with some knowledge of Portuguese, often fled from the Carolinas to Spanish Florida, gaining sanctuary with Native Americans in mixed ethnic communities. Members of the Catawba nation that lived on the western fringes of the Carolinas sometimes acted as slave catchers, protecting their relations with white settlers by returning fugitives. Punishment for running away might include bodily mutilation, which served as a warning to others.

The dispersal of Africans inhibited slave rebellions in North America, but wherever slaves lived in dense communities, owners faced (and feared) the possibility of insurrection. A group of twenty slaves in New York City, including women and Native Americans, fomented an uprising in 1712, burning buildings and killing whites, before being crushed by military forces. The ensuing penalties—torture, execution, or deportation to the West Indies—and passage of a new slave code that curtailed blacks' activities pacified the city. But in 1740, rumors of another slave plot to destroy the city set off investigations, backed by torture, that produced confessions from accused Africans. Although dozens were executed and punished, evidence of conspiracy remained sketchy.

Some uprisings were less ambiguous. In 1739, slaves near the Stono River in South Carolina organized a mass rebellion, seized weapons and ammunition, and attracted dozens of recruits by beating drums. The rebels headed south toward

Florida, but a white militia intercepted them and defeated the fugitives in battle. It took months before all the rebels were caught and killed. After the Stono rebellion, rumors and fear of slave uprisings circulated in all the colonies.

Economic Expansion and Social Conflict

The widespread use of slavery in North America underscored the commercial basis of colonial society. With the exception of a small minority of household servants, who comprised only 5 percent of all bound workers, most slaves worked to produce goods that were sold in an expanding Atlantic marketplace. Such commercial activity obviously preoccupied their employers. Even small farmers, who prided themselves on being "self-sufficient," were dependent on neighbors and crossroads markets for certain products and trade. During the 18th century, colonial enterprise developed an international network that linked North American markets to England, continental Europe, the West Indies, and West Africa. And, although English navigation acts endeavored to regulate and restrict this trade (see Chapter 3), colonial merchants showed remarkable initiative in exporting American goods such as lumber, grain, fish, and rum around the world, while importing finished products from England, sugar from the West Indies, and slaves from west Africa.

Economic activity permeated colonial society. Slaveowners harnessed workers to produce tobacco, rice, and indigo, and small farmers labored to maximize agricultural production. Farm households in all regions typically had women working with men in barns and fields, at least during harvest time, in addition to performing domestic chores. During the 18th century, farm women specialized in dairy and poultry products (butter, cheese, eggs, feathers for bedding) for sale in the marketplace. In this way, small-scale agriculture was tied to market activity.

The search for economic success won reinforcement in the popular writings of Philadelphia's premier self-made man, Benjamin Franklin. His widely read *Poor Richard's Almanack,* first published in 1732, and his pamphlet *The Way to Wealth,* offered practical advice for business success. His famous aphorisms, such as "A penny saved is a penny earned," emphasized values of individual initiative and personal advancement. Franklin also advocated the strict measurement of daily time to ensure the improvement of one's life.

Franklin's advice appealed to an ambitious society because he insisted that America, in contrast to England, was a land of opportunity. "The only principle of life propagated among the young people," agreed one of Franklin's New York friends, "is to get money, and men are only esteemed according to what they are worth—that is the money they are possessed of." Most leading families had achieved their status during the early years of colonization, a time of social fluidity, and later generations consolidated their positions. To be sure, rapid social mobility remained possible. Franklin had begun his career as an apprentice printer and rose to become a leading tradesman, politician, and intellectual. Virginia's George Washington had obtained a fortune through land speculation and marriage to a wealthy widow. But most colonials could only hope for modest advancement.

The relative ease of achieving land ownership in America encouraged the appearance of small independent farmers. In the cities, artisans and shopkeepers formed a thriving middle class, though urban dwellers comprised only 5 percent of the total population. Beneath middle-class property owners on the social scale were propertyless farm workers (including, in descending order of wealth, tenants, free workers, and indentured servants)

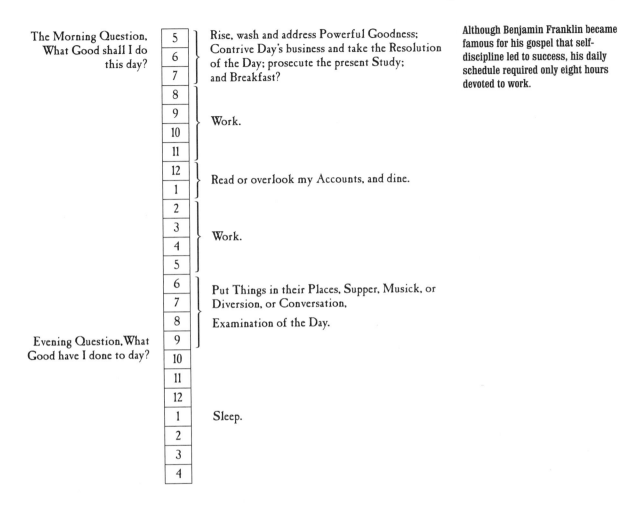

The Morning Question, What Good shall I do this day?	5 6 7	Rise, wash and address Powerful Goodness; Contrive Day's business and take the Resolution of the Day; prosecute the present Study; and Breakfast?
	8 9 10 11	Work.
	12 1	Read or overlook my Accounts, and dine.
	2 3 4 5	Work.
	6 7	Put Things in their Places, Supper, Musick, or Diversion, or Conversation,
	8	Examination of the Day.
Evening Question, What Good have I done to day?	9 10 11 12	
	1 2 3 4	Sleep.

Although Benjamin Franklin became famous for his gospel that self-discipline led to success, his daily schedule required only eight hours devoted to work.

and, in urban areas, day workers and apprentices. Lowest in the social order were racial minorities, free as well as slave. Although women worked on family farms and city shops, they assumed the social status of their fathers and husbands. Widows, particularly those with young children, were usually the poorest individuals, though some successfully continued their husbands' businesses.

Colonials well understood and respected these degrees of status and rank. In New England, for example, seating in the meeting house reflected a per-

son's social position; so, too, did the annual ranking of students at Harvard and Yale. In the southern colonies, middle-class farmers, even nonslaveowners, recognized a leadership of wealth and assumed their own superiority to Africans and Native peoples. These assumptions enabled the wealthy minority to claim the privileges of a "natural" aristocracy. Yet, precisely because the colonial leadership was based on wealth and not inherited aristocracy, contention sometimes exploded into social conflict. Such outbursts were rare and short-lived, indicative of frustration but seldom a real threat to colonial authorities.

Social Stress in New England

Concern about changing social values appeared dramatically in New England at the end of the 17th century. Unable to develop a staple cash crop, early New Englanders had gone to sea, exporting huge quantities of Newfoundland cod to feed slaves on the sugar plantations of the West Indies, and shipping lumber from local forests to build barrels for tobacco, rum, rice, and other goods. This commerce stimulated a shipbuilding industry as well as bringing profits to shippers. Successful Boston merchants emerged as a wealthy elite who owned choice urban real estate and houses, mahogany furniture, imported linens, and fine clocks that chimed quarter hours. Meanwhile, as a high birthrate created population pressure on old lands and encouraged younger generations to migrate to new towns, land prices rose and speculators reaped profits. By the 1690s, the top tenth of New England society controlled 40 percent of local wealth.

Although Puritan ministers continued to uphold communal values, the pursuit of profits and the disparities of wealth disturbed the traditional social order, resulting in local conflicts about taxes, political representation, and the sites of new churches. Such contention occasionally led to accusations of witchcraft. Belief in witchcraft permeated the folk culture of all colonies, and witchcraft cases had appeared sporadically. But the patterns of the accusations indicated unspoken conflicts involving gender relations, especially in Puritan New England. In 1692, such tensions exploded in Salem, Massachusetts, when over 200 people were accused of witchcraft—and twenty were sent to their deaths.

Although men were occasionally accused of sinful contact with the devil, the overwhelming majority of accused witches were women. One of them, Katherine Harrison of Connecticut, defended herself by saying she was "a female, a weaker vessel, subject to passion." As her words reveal, women were believed more likely to succumb to the devil and, like the original Eve, seduce others into sin. Such assumptions reinforced women's subordination within the churches and the larger society. Indeed, while most of the *accusers* were young women, most of the *accused* were middle-aged women who were considered misfits by their neighbors. The accusers were poorer, often widowed, and known for abrasive conduct; some of the so-called witches had publicly criticized their neighbors' uncharitable behavior.

The Salem trials also illuminated new economic conflicts within colonial society. Some historians have seen the Salem case as an example of conflict between two types of communities—backward agricultural Salem Village, where most of the accusers lived, and prosperous commercial Salem Town, where most of the accused resided. These scholars speculate that social resentment may have provoked rural villagers to criticize the more worldly townspeople. Other historians have emphasized the decline of economic opportunity as population growth caused greater competition for available land. Many accused witches had been involved in legal disputes with family members and neighbors about inherited property. Their economic independence, or the possibility of their achieving such independence, threatened the interests of competing families and challenged the prevailing belief that women should remain subordinate to men. Thus the witch trials could be seen as efforts of male authority figures to keep women in their place.

What distinguished the Salem outbreak were not the accusations, but the number of people implicated, including members of wealthy families. The case thus aroused the interest of the colony's leaders, an elite composed of wealthy merchants,

> **The witch trials could be seen as efforts of male authority figures to keep women in their place.**

who intervened to halt the trials. Thereafter, charges of witchcraft abruptly ceased. Old Puritans might dislike the materialism of New England society, but they no longer looked to the devil to find an explanation for their problems.

Conflicts in Boston appeared less subtle. During the 17th century, New England towns had regulated the price of food and fuel to protect the poor. But when a leading Boston merchant ignored this tradition in 1710, acquired a monopoly of grain, and caused bread prices to soar, a mob attacked his warehouses and took the stored grain. Although a conservative townsman claimed that the rioters were "not God's people, but the Devil's people," the poor had effectively challenged the new law of supply and demand. None were prosecuted for the violence. Commercial values continued to triumph, however, and Boston society became increasingly polarized between rich and poor. The old "publick spirit," one clergyman subsequently complained, had been replaced by a "greedy desire of gain." New England preserved its hierarchical character to the end of the colonial era.

Pluralism and Conflict in the Middle Colonies

Society in the middle colonies appeared more heterogenous than New England's, but also experienced growing stratification. William Penn's liberal offers of land and religious toleration attracted considerable non-English immigration, particularly among German religious groups such as the Moravians and Amish, who fled persecution and European wars. In addition, Scots-Irish Presbyterians from northern Ireland also migrated to Pennsylvania, New York, and New Jersey in search of economic opportunity. Coming initially as indentured servants, many Germans and Scots-Irish provided manual labor in Philadelphia; New York City, by contrast, relied more on African slaves. Immigrant farmers obtained cheap land and produced corn, wheat, beef, and pork for export. As eastern areas became crowded, later settlers moved west toward the Appalachians and then south into the Carolinas and Georgia. Their desire for land often led to conflicts with Native Americans such as the Catawbas, who traded deerskins with colonial merchants.

Other non-English Europeans included French Huguenots and Mediterranean Jews, who settled as merchants in the port cities. Along with Quaker and English merchants, they participated in the Atlantic trade, exporting food to the West Indies and Europe, selling beaver fur to England, and importing slaves to the colonies. Such merchants also traded with England's French and Spanish colonial rivals, even in times of war. By the mid-18th century, immigration and natural increase saw Philadelphia and New York emerge as major cities, bringing prosperity to shopkeepers and skilled artisans like Benjamin Franklin. Yet city workers faced seasonal unemployment and price inflation and found small opportunity for social mobility. During the colonial era, these cities experienced greater social stratification as wealth became concentrated in fewer hands and the poor became more dependent on public assistance.

Mixed populations contributed to social conflict. Pennsylvania's German immigrants tended to cluster in cohesive communities, avoiding the English language, the English legal system, and English-speaking churches. Their economic success troubled Anglophiles like Franklin, who feared that the colony would become Germanized. Other ethnic and economic rivalries created political crises. In 1763, the Scots-Irish who lived in western Pennsylvania demanded military assistance from the pacifist Quaker legislature to wage war against the Delaware people. When Quakers hesitated to support these frontier farmers, Scots-Irish rebels, known as the Paxton Boys, massacred a village of peaceful Conestogas, then marched to Philadelphia to protest their lack of representation in the legislature. Only Franklin's negotiations thwarted an insurrection against the government. Meanwhile, in New York's Hudson valley, where wealthy Dutch landlords rented property to English tenant farmers, eviction orders provoked an armed rebellion in the 1760s, which was finally crushed by the British military.

Anxieties in Southern Society

Society in the southern colonies appeared more stable as commercial agriculture dominated social relations. Tobacco planters with access to the rivers served as merchants for their neighbors—exporting crops and importing finished goods, and thus made urban centers unnecessary. Overproduction continued to lower tobacco prices, and planters responded by intensifying cultivation, only lowering prices more. Although large landowners with more than five slaves comprised less than 5 percent of the population, they owned nearly 50 percent of the total wealth. This elite built spacious brick houses, employed slaves as domestic servants, and purchased luxury items (furniture, libraries, silver dinnerware) to show their high status. Their assets set the tone of Chesapeake society, and smaller farmers deferred politically to these leaders. "Before a boy knows his right hand from his left," remarked one visitor about the children of the rich, "he is a Gentleman."

By the mid-18th century, however, Chesapeake planters lived amidst ever growing debt to English and Scottish merchants who sold them imported goods. Whipped by fluctuating tobacco prices, some frustrated planters, such as George Washington, finally abandoned the crop to plant more wheat and corn, but most grew tobacco out of habit and its implied prestige. Virginia planters also engaged in land speculation, using political connections to profit from westward expansion. But despite their best efforts, falling tobacco prices and rising consumption of English goods created a crisis of indebtedness, which was aggravated after 1760 when British creditors began to demand payment.

Planters in South Carolina and Georgia enjoyed more stable prosperity, exporting rice, indigo, deerskins, and naval stores. To avoid the malarial lowlands, wealthy landowners resided in Charleston and Savannah, employing overseers to manage their holdings. Supported by commercial agriculture and surrounded by a black majority of slaves (in some areas more than twice the white population), this elite of planters, merchants, and lawyers pursued an aristocratic lifestyle and supported diverse cultural activities. But the western regions of those colonies were settled by small farmers who objected to the eastern elite's indifference to their problems. Angered by dishonest tax collectors and a poor judicial system, western farmers in North Carolina formed a "Regulator" movement in the 1760s and challenged government authority. The Carolina leadership used the militia to crush the rebellion, but the protests, together with constant fear of slave revolts, created a mood of intense insecurity among southern leaders.

Social tension thus percolated through the English colonies, occasionally erupting in urban riots to protest bread prices or election frauds, and sometimes prompting western farmers to disobey laws against selling alcohol to Native people. Such outbursts were exceptional, symptoms of stress rather than rebellious intentions. Most inhabitants of British origin accepted the hierarchical social order and allowed their "betters" to rule. Yet by English standards, the self-made leadership groups in America appeared as pseudo-aristocrats, big fish in a small pond, rather than members of a hereditary elite. Ironically, many American leaders shared that feeling of inferiority. By the mid-18th century, the sense of being provincial—cultural outsiders compared to the English aristocracy—defined the identity of the colonial leadership.

The Paradoxes of Colonial Culture

The sense of provincialism was accentuated by the flourishing commerce between American wharves and the mother country, which involved not only economic goods but also ideas and values. Imitating English leaders, the colonial elite read English books, magazines, and newspapers, copied English fashions and architecture, and reproduced English curricula in American schools and colleges. American scientists, such as the Quaker John Bartram and Benjamin Franklin, who together founded the American Philosophical Society in Philadelphia in 1743, still communicated their research to the Royal Society of London. Provincialism—the sense of England's cultural superiority—thus served as an intellectual common denominator, whether a colonial lived in a Boston townhouse or presided over a Virginia plantation.

Although the colonial elite took pride in its cultural sophistication, few Americans were really qualified to discuss the contemporary Enlightenment. Basing their ideas on the scientific theories of Sir Isaac Newton, Enlightenment thinkers viewed the universe as a clock, which God had wound up at the Creation and which ran eternally according to the natural laws of physics. Accordingly, they believed that God no longer had to intervene in human affairs. But while a small intellectual elite pondered these ideas, most colonials simply accepted the Protestant faiths. By the mid-18th century, the spirit of religion had flattened; proportionately fewer people attended worship services. Criticism of religious indifference permeated the

land, but most inhabitants ignored the preaching, allowing their spiritual feelings to subside.

These subdued passions suddenly erupted into a major religious revival when an English evangelist named George Whitefield arrived in America in 1739, urging sinners to "fly to Christ." Earlier revivals in the middle colonies and in Jonathan Edwards' church at Northampton, Massachusetts had touched local congregations. But Whitefield's public oratory (Franklin estimated in one open-air meeting in Philadelphia that his voice could reach 25,000 people) sparked what was known as the "Great Awakening." Whitefield's message stressed the futility of achieving worldly success without obtaining spiritual redemption. Instead, Whitefield and his "New Light" disciples summoned individuals to experience a religious rebirth and create a Christian community on earth.

Such preaching, filled with hellfire and brimstone, aroused many colonials from spiritual sleep. Facing eternal damnation, frightened souls shouted out "Oh, I am going to hell! What shall I do to be saved?" And they experienced a spiritual "rebirth" from sinner to saint, joining the churches in great numbers. Although the revivalists were effective in all regions and among all classes, they proved most successful in areas undergoing rapid change, such as newly settled parts of Connecticut, or among groups facing particular problems, such as epidemics or the prospect of war. Since women outnumbered men in church membership (a shift from the early days of colonization), new converts were disproportionately male, young adults in their late twenties. Perhaps the problems of finding one's place in a new society (what today might be called an identity crisis) explains why young men responded to the evangelical call. The Awakening also attracted young women, often during pregnancy when the fear of death was close. "I was . . . brought to the very brink of eternity," said one woman of her conversion, "and then I received comfort." In churches that embraced the revival, women sometimes assumed greater responsibility in church affairs. The revival also attracted Africans, who discovered a parallel between the Christian rebirth and African beliefs of continuing spiritual revelation.

The Awakening's promise of spiritual equality challenged the religious status quo. "It is impossible to relate the convulsions into which the whole country is thrown," complained one clergyman, "for men, women, children, servants, and Negroes are now become (as they phrase it) exhorters." Revivalists boldly rejected traditional styles of worship, even holding services outdoors. As Christians debated the revival, the Presbyterian and Congregational churches split into bitter factions—anti-revivalist "Old Side" Presbyterians and "Old Light" Congregationalists versus evangelical "New Sides" and "New Lights"—resulting in a proliferation of denominations and sects. Methodists and Baptists, who embraced the revival, increased substantially, particularly in areas that previously lacked churches. The willingness of Baptists to accept African American converts as spiritual equals also defied religious justifications for enslaving "heathen" peoples.

Denominational competition inspired the founding of new colleges: the College of New Jersey (now Princeton) by evangelical Presbyterians; King's College (Columbia) by Anglicans; Brown by Baptists; and Queen's College (Rutgers) by Dutch Reformed. Such competition indicates that colonial Americans took religion seriously, even passionately. But when, eventually, these denominational rivals realized that no one group could achieve religious supremacy, they grudgingly accepted the reality of religious pluralism, at least for Protestants. (Only Rhode Island and Pennsylvania accepted religious freedom in principle.) Thus religious toleration—not equality—gradually emerged in American society. Although privileged churches continued to receive tax support, dissenters began to demand separation of church and state.

Preserving a Native American Identity

Colonial Protestants and white ethnic minorities learned to coexist, but toleration did not often cross boundaries of race. Colonial law and social custom kept Africans in subordinate positions, while Native peoples, when they were not enslaved, remained either dependents or cultural outsiders. By 1700, the coastal groups had virtually disappeared, decimated by disease and war or driven by colonial expansion to seek homes beyond the fringe of white settlement. Other Native nations continued as partners in the fur and skin trade with English, French, and Spanish merchants, contributing to the flow of goods overseas. They also served as military allies of the warring European colonies, balancing their own interests in a struggle to maintain their cultural independence.

Dependent Peoples

The coastal peoples, or what was left of them, faced grave problems of maintaining a group identity. Defeated in warfare during the 17th century and plagued by disease and social upheaval, groups like Massachusetts' Nantuckets or Carolina's Catawbas reluctantly sought refuge near colonial settlements, accepting subordination as the price of survival. Known as "settlement Indians" in the southern colonies and "praying Indians" in New England, they exchanged their autonomy for protection from their enemies and accepted marginal employment as hunters, traders, tanners, transporters, and slave catchers. Many lived in mixed groups, composed of members of different nations, a situation that complicated their cultural identity.

Targeted by Christian missionaries, these Natives absorbed European beliefs and habits, but usually within a Native context. In New France, for example, Catholic priests instituted masses, prayers, and confession, but Iroquois converts continued to use shamans, charms, animal sacrifices, ecstatic dances, and festivals to express spiritual concerns. Such mixing of customs reflected not only pragmatic accommodation but also a permanent loss of cultural continuity. "They have forgot most of their traditions," explained one Carolina settler of the southern nations in 1710. "They keep their festivals and can tell but little of the reasons: their Old Men are dead."

Surviving members of the disrupted groups became targets for exploitation by unscrupulous traders, who used alcohol, sexual violence, and dishonest dealing to reduce Native peoples into indebtedness, claimed their labor, and stole their land. With irregular boundary lines separating Native and colonial settlements, common crimes such as trespassing, poaching, and squatting exaggerated tensions. Native disrespect of private property—the killing of livestock, burning of fences, and petty theft—caused conflicts with farmers, while colonials encroached on Native territory to cut wood or feed their livestock.

Inhabiting the Borderlands

While some Native groups surrendered their autonomy, others migrated into the interior to form new communities, hoping to preserve their economic independence and identity. By the 1720s, Shawnees, Delawares, Senecas, and other multiethnic tribes had found refuge in the Ohio valley, an area rich with game and fertile acreage, seemingly remote from European intruders. These tribal clusters established self-sustaining kinship-based societies. Women engaged in agriculture and men pursued hunting. During the next three decades, male leaders continued to trade with colonial merchants, exchanging furs for manufactured goods. And, although colonial traders used rum and extended credit to make the Ohio Natives dependent on their goods, the resettled tribes formed stable communities and profited from this commerce.

These inland settlements did not long preserve their independence. As early as 1699, the French had begun to settle the Louisiana territory at the mouth of the Mississippi River. The small colony, based on African slave labor and trade as far east as Carolina and west to Texas and Nebraska, anchored France's southern claims to North America. To the north, French settlements on the St. Lawrence formed an elaborate trade network with the Native peoples around the Great Lakes and in Illinois. Together, France's colonies created an arc of settlement that effectively contested English expansion west of the Appalachians. Thus when English traders from Virginia, Pennsylvania, and New York entered the Ohio valley to deal with the resettled nations, they knowingly threatened France's territorial claims. By the 1740s, the French government began to send military expeditions to block English colonial interlopers. The Ohio nations now found themselves caught in the middle of an explosive imperial rivalry. Soon war would come to the Ohio valley, forcing them to choose sides.

Competing for the Continent

In contrast to the sparsely populated French settlements, some of which were little more than trading posts, the English colonies had achieved considerable economic and cultural strength during the 18th century. Yet the land still appeared overwhelmingly undeveloped. In Virginia, for instance, the dense woods between tobacco plantations served as an alternative territory for African slaves, a sheltered place to hold religious ceremonies and feasts or simply a refuge to hide from their owners. Even around the tamest communities of New York and New England, Native peoples remained a presence, if not a threat to peace.

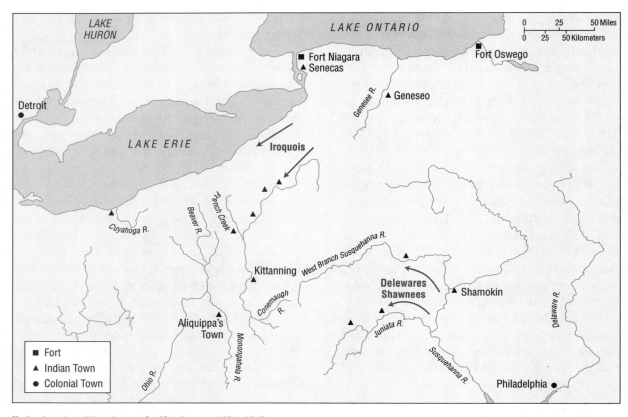

Native American Migrations to the Ohio Country, 1724–1745

Thus as English provincials emphasized their advanced social development, they perched precariously on the edges of the continent, looking more to Europe for trade, values, and purpose than to the western interior. Facing the Atlantic, they referred to the West as the "back country." With their eyes on England, moreover, colonial leaders remained acutely dependent on merchants and politicians in the mother country who could threaten their political and economic interests. Yet by the mid-18th century, western lands were increasingly summoning colonial surveyors and speculators, traders and settlers, to seek opportunity. As England and France simultaneously looked to the future in the Ohio val-

ley, colonists and native inhabitants understood the stakes of this competition. The winner would control the continent.

INFOTRAC® COLLEGE EDITION EXERCISES

 For additional reading go to InfoTrac College Edition, your online research library at *http://web1.infotrac-college.com*.

Subject search: William Berkeley

Keyword search: Bacon's Rebellion

Subject search: slavery

Subject search: slavery, religious aspects

Keyword search: slave culture
Subject search: colonial America
Subject search: Great Awakening, related subjects
Keyword search: American philosophy
Keyword search: wars of religion

ADDITIONAL READING

Jon Butler, *Becoming America: The Revolution before 1776* (2000). A convenient summary of colonial social history.

Bacon's Rebellion

Stephen Saunders Webb, *1676: The End of American Independence* (1984). An analysis of Bacon's rebellion, placing colonial conflicts within the context of British and Native American affairs. See also Edmund Morgan's *American Slavery, American Freedom,* listed in Chapter 3.

Defining Slavery in the Colonies

Ira Berlin, *Many Thousands Gone: The First Two Centuries of Slavery in North America* (1998). A comprehensive study of the development of slavery in the Atlantic colonies and Louisiana. See also Philip D. Morgan, *Slave Counterpoint: Black Culture in the Eighteenth-Century Chesapeake and Low Country* (1998).

Michael A. Gomez, *Exchanging Our Country Marks: The Transformation of African Identities in the Colonial and Antebellum South* (1998). Analyzes ethnic diversity in Africa and its continuities among American slaves.

Winthrop Jordan, *White over Black: American Attitudes toward the Negro, 1550–1812* (1968). A classic study of the origins and forms of race prejudice and slavery in North America, whose focus is on white thinking about blacks.

Economic Expansion and Social Conflict

Richard L. Bushman, *From Puritan to Yankee: Character and the Social Order in Connecticut, 1690–1765* (1967). Describes social changes in rural Connecticut and their effect on religion and politics.

Jack P. Greene, *Pursuits of Happiness: The Social Development of Early Modern British Colonies and the Formation of American Culture* (1988). A comparative analysis of colonial history, linking economic changes to social structure.

Rhys Isaac, The *Transformation of Virginia, 1740–1790* (1982). The author explores the interaction of social relations, religious controversy, and political values.

Gary B. Nash, *The Urban Crucible: Social Change, Political Consciousness, and the Origins of the American Revolution* (1979). Focusing on Boston, New York, and Philadelphia, Nash explains the relationship of economic and social issues to the emergence of political conflict.

Laurel Thatcher Ulrich, *Good Wives: Images and Reality in the Lives of Women in Northern New England, 1650–1750* (1982). This book, studded with details about everyday life, describes the life cycle of ordinary colonial women.

Social Stress in New England

Carol F. Karlsen, *The Devil in the Shape of a Woman: Witchcraft in Colonial New England* (1987). This analysis of New England witchcraft emphasizes underlying gender issues.

Preserving a Native American Identity

John Demos, *The Unredeemed Captive: A Family Story from Early America* (1994). Focusing on a Puritan girl who was captured by Iroquois warriors, the book examines the ensuing cultural interactions.

Daniel R. Mandell, *Behind the Frontier: Indians in Eighteenth-Century Eastern Massachusetts* (1996). Examining the period after King Philip's War, this book describes the cultural pressures faced by Native survivors.

Michael N. McConnell, *A Country Between: The Upper Ohio Valley and Its Peoples, 1724–1774* (1992). Describes the complicated Native cultures west of the Appalachians.

Richard White, *The Middle Ground: Indians, Empire, and Republics in the Great Lakes Region, 1650–1815* (1991). A thorough study of Native American society, politics, and diplomacy, emphasizing cross-cultural relationships.

5

Patriarchal Politics and the Colonial Crisis, 1689–1776

CHRONOLOGY

1689–1697	King William's War fought against New France
1701–1713	Queen Anne's War waged against French Canada and Spanish Florida
1744–1748	King George's War embroils England against France
1754–1763	Seven Years' War results in expulsion of France from North America
1754	Benjamin Franklin proposes plan of union at Albany congress
1761	James Otis argues against writs of assistance
1763	Proclamation Line limits western expansion
1763–1764	Pontiac leads uprising against Anglo American posts
1764	Parliament passes Sugar and Currency acts
1765	Stamp Act provokes colonial protests
1766	Declaratory Act affirms Parliament's right to legislate
1767	Townshend acts seek alternative source of revenue; John Dickinson publishes protest
1770	Conflict with British troops sparks Boston Massacre
1773	Parliament passes Tea Act; Boston stages "tea party"
1774	Passage of Coercive acts prompts first Continental Congress
1775	Minutemen battle redcoats at Lexington and Concord; Second Continental Congress convenes
1776	Congress approves Declaration of Independence

On a sunny Thursday morning in 1765, thirty-nine of Virginia's most powerful leaders sat transfixed in the chamber of the House of Burgesses, the colony legislature. The 29-year-old delegate from Hanover, Patrick Henry, stood before them, his voice ringing through the hall, his words stirring their hearts.

In vivid patriotic language, like none ever before uttered in the legislature, Henry eloquently defended his countrymen's exclusive right to tax themselves rather than accept the latest proposals of the English Parliament. He urged his colleagues to remember that history's tyrants, including the kings of England, had always faced strong opposition. Now, in a new moment of peril, he hoped simply that "some good American would stand up in favor of his country."

But, just as Henry paused to take a breath, another more-cautious representative startled the delegates: "Treason! Treason!" he shouted.

That verbal duel underscored the immense changes in colonial politics since the founding of England's colonies in the previous century. The 3,000 miles that separated Americans from Europe had encouraged the birth, and growth, of a distinct political perspective. As the mother country pursued a policy of "salutary neglect," the colonists developed considerable self-government—in practice, if not in principle. Most colonies had established a political order based on England's system of government. They celebrated a heritage that preserved individual legal rights, such as trial by jury, and constitutional protections, which limited the power of the monarchy with an elected representative legislature. But, ironically, these much-honored "rights of Englishmen" would eventually lead colonials to defend their *own* rights when challenged by the mother country. From being loyal Englishmen, colonials like Virginia's Patrick Henry and Thomas Jefferson, Massachusetts's Sam Adams and John Adams, Maryland's Daniel Dulany, and Pennsylvania's Benjamin Franklin, would slowly but surely become loyal *Americans*.

This evolving political identity mirrored the colonists' social views. The key to understanding colonial politics could be found in the belief that the family was a miniature of society. "Families are the nurseries for church and commonwealth," said one New England minister. "Ruin families, and ruin all. Order them well and the public state will fare better." To people living in colonial America, both family and government existed as patriarchal institutions dominated by powerful father figures. Fathers were expected to rule their households, just as political leaders governed society and the state. The Fifth Commandment—"Thou shalt honor thy father and thy mother"—established the moral underpinnings of both private and public life. Yet, to colonials, a patriarchal society was

Only as a last resort did Americans attack King George directly.

not oppressive—indeed, just the opposite. Fathers, whether biological or political, were expected to protect the entire family.

Although political leaders assumed that families, societies, and governments should be hierarchical (that is, that some should be higher than others) they believed that no segment of society could flourish unless the entire society did. Such views justified, in their eyes, colonial dependence on the patriarchal king and the mother country. Even when the English Parliament passed laws that were unpopular in America, colonial leaders usually expressed affection for the king and appealed to him to correct injustices. Only as a last resort did Americans attack King George directly. And then, in 1776, leading colonists announced to the world that the Anglo American political family no longer satisfied the needs of all its members. The result was political divorce and American independence.

Patriarchy and Political Power

Patriarchal politics had its roots in local governments—the towns in New England and counties elsewhere—that were most closely tied to family life. Local officials, including sheriffs, justices of the peace, and coroners, provided all the government services that most people needed. Their duties included the probate of wills, assessment of taxes, dispensing of charity, and supervision of elections to the colonial legislatures. According to English custom and provincial laws, political leaders were chosen from the local elite; they were men of property who acted as "fathers" of their communities. Because land ownership was widespread among free white men, English colonials formed a larger electorate than in other countries. Yet voters accepted a patriarchal view of government and chose their "betters" to exercise power.

Gender and Politics

"Parents should be very careful to uphold a prudent government of their children," remarked a New Englander in 1737. "A steady, mild, yet close and taut government is the best." Believing that infants were born corrupted by original sin, many colonial parents began to discipline their children at a very young age. Children of both sexes were dressed in gowns or petticoats, which covered their feet and so restricted their mobility. At the age of about six, boys began to wear the breeches or pants of adult male garb. The change was significant, for while boys achieved greater liberty of movement, girls' skirts hobbled their ability to run and ride. Boys obtained more education; male literacy remained substantially higher than female during the colonial period: 85 percent of males to 50 percent of females in New England; 60 percent to 25 percent in the other colonies.

The division of male and female roles reflected popular assumptions about gender differences. According to conventional wisdom, men possessed "wisdom, strength and courage, fit to protect and defend," whereas women appeared "weaker . . . more fearful, and more affectionate [i.e., more emotional]." The consequences of such beliefs were substantial. Men were seen as active, women as passive; men were expected to be leaders, women their followers. In advising his son to prepare for public

Colonial portraits pictured children as miniature adults. Such images reinforced the idea that even youngsters were burdened by the "original sin" of Adam and Eve and were not born innocent.

life, Maryland's Charles Carroll urged the young man to find a wife who was "virtuous, sensible, good natured, complaisant, complying, and of a cheerful disposition."

Colonial laws, based on English precedents, reinforced this emphasis on female passivity by restricting women's legal identity. Upon marriage, a woman's property legally passed to her husband, her income belonged to him, and anything she inherited became his. Fathers controlled the custody of their children, which was in significant contrast with Native practices (and sometimes an impediment to legal marriages between Native women and English men). Colonial inheritance laws gave widows the use of one-third of their husbands' property, but seldom the independent ownership of that property; children received the remainder. Sons received larger amounts than daughters, whose inheritances passed to their own husbands. Since divorces and legal separations were extremely difficult to obtain, colonial women understandably worried about their marital choices. "If we happen to judge wrong," complained the widowed South Carolina indigo planter Eliza Lucas Pinckney, "there is an end of all human felicity." Yet the independent, educated, and spirited Mrs. Pinckney would, on her own, successfully manage her extensive plantations and raise two sons, Charles and Thomas, to become political leaders and statesmen.

Local Politics and Political Participation

Patriarchal politics began on the local level of government, where property qualifications restricted the right to vote. The ease of land ownership in America (only New York, New Jersey, and Maryland had large numbers of tenant farmers) enabled most adult white men to meet the voting requirements (75 percent in the northern colonies, 50 percent in the southern colonies). By comparison with other countries, including England, Americans enjoyed wide suffrage. But nearly all women, servants, tenants, day laborers, slaves, and children—individuals who were dependents on a male head of household—could not vote because they owned no property and therefore did not have sufficient "stake" in society. For reasons of religious bigotry, most colonies denied the vote to Jews, Catholics, and other non-Protestants.

Since local officials oversaw the voting process, patriarchal assumptions diminished the importance of the right to vote. Most political candidates came from the local elites, either because of higher property qualifications for holding public

office or because their neighbors already recognized the nominees as leaders. Lacking significant political choices, many eligible voters simply did not vote. Those who did found their options limited. During the 18th century, most legal affairs, even the filing of court documents, were conducted orally. So, too, was voting. A voter approached the polling place and was greeted by the rival candidates, asked to express his choice aloud, and then treated to a glass of rum by his preferred candidate. Such open balloting hardly encouraged defiance of local leaders. Yet except at times of crisis, voters seldom protested this system of elite rule. Slaveowning rice planters in the Carolinas, tobacco aristocrats on the Chesapeake, wealthy landlords in the middle colonies, Atlantic merchants in Philadelphia, New York, and Boston—in all colonies, a respectable leadership emerged to dominate local governments.

The power of patriarchy in the English colonies contrasted with a more balanced gender system in many Native American communities. The Cherokees who lived on the borders of Georgia and the Carolinas, for instance, had a matriarchal clan system in which women played a major role in community decisions. Since control of property and crops followed the mother's lineage, women had considerable voice in determining how resources would be distributed. Cherokee men, who traditionally controlled trade in deerskins and diplomacy, had more contact with colonial leaders. When a Cherokee head man met with the South Carolina government in 1757, he was surprised at the absence of women in the council meeting, remarking in confusion to the governor that "White men as well as Red were born of women." Colonial leaders preferred to negotiate with male warriors and traders, and their views eventually altered Cherokee customs. As Cherokee men became more economically important in tribal life, women's status declined. Thus for Cherokees, as for Anglo Americans, control of property was linked to political power. Lacking the Cherokee women's access to land ownership, colonial women had no public voice.

The Structure of Provincial Power

The political system in America deliberately paralleled the structure of power in the mother country. Most colonies operated with a three-part government, consisting of a governor, council, and assembly, echoing the English system of king, House of Lords, and House of Commons. The governor (usually appointed by the crown or, as in Pennsylvania, by the proprietor) acted as the executive branch. Governors were responsible for approving legislation, enforcing the navigation acts, and serving as commanders-in-chief of the militia. Governors selected members of the council, who acted as the upper house of the legislature. The Council served with the governor as the highest court of appeal, authorized land grants, and confirmed judicial appointments. Yet, the councilors' dependence on the governor's favor limited their legislative independence. Political leaders who did not curry favor or enjoy the governors' friendship often sought political power in the elected assembly (lower house of the legislature).

While the governors defended the king's power, the lower house strove to protect colonial rights. (It was, for example, no surprise that Patrick Henry challenged the rights of Parliament in Virginia's assembly, the House of Burgesses.) These legislative bodies consisted of elected representatives, chosen by the adult white men in the towns and counties. During the colonial period, the assemblies had consciously imitated Parliament and won the right to enact taxes to finance government activities. With that right, the legislatures could challenge the governors' efforts to impose royal policies. By controlling taxes, for example, the assemblies could withhold approval of specific expenditures—even the governor's own salary—until he agreed to their terms.

In nearly every colony, the assemblies fought with the governors at one time or another about taxes, the payment of salaries, land grants, the appointment of government officers, issuance of paper money, access to trade with Native peoples, and military defense. These issues were closely related to economic success, since passage of a law could make the difference between a family's prosperity or failure. Land grants, for example, promised great profits as population increased and residents sought land for their children to inherit. Issuance of paper money, which usually was worth less than its face value, could become a bonus for those who had to repay debts. The appointment of friendly tobacco inspectors might benefit particular planters, and a wartime contract for warm blankets might reward cloth merchants.

More important than the advantages of specific laws, however, was the way colonial politicians viewed these political struggles. Among the most popular reading in the British colonies were the essays titled *Cato's Letters,* by John Trenchard and Thomas Gordon, first published in 1733 and frequently reprinted in colonial newspapers. The two writers had not benefited by the patronage system in the mother country and warned Englishmen on both sides of the Atlantic that conspiratorial politicians were attempting to undermine the English constitution. Suggesting that the king's advisors were using patronage to influence the other branches of government, they reminded readers that legislators had to remain independent of executive pressure to preserve the constitutional balance. The title of one of Cato's letters expressed their extreme suspicion of the political system:

"What Measures Are Actually Taken by Wicked and Desperate Ministers to Ruin and Enslave Their Country." To preserve the beloved English "liberty," they urged citizens to exercise utmost vigilance against the expansion of royal power.

English Interference in Colonial Affairs

Such advice made sense to colonial politicians, who lived 3,000 miles from the centers of power in England. Despite the efforts of provincial assemblies to assume the same rights that the British parliament enjoyed, colonial politics remained subordinate to England's interests. Patronage issues in the mother country often caused the recall of the royal governor and the appointment of his replacement. Many colonial assemblies hired agents to look out for their affairs in London. Even so, new royal governors arrived in America with fresh instructions to levy taxes, enforce trade laws, or raise an army without considering colonial concerns. Such arrivals and departures disrupted the political process, as colonial politicians formed coalitions to work with or against the governors. In addition, British regulations required that all legislative acts be approved in England before they could become law. Although the king's Privy Council seldom vetoed these laws, delays and uncertainty stirred colonial fears of the abuse of power.

English supervision of colonial politics also had economic consequences. The theory of mercantilism assumed that the advantages of empire would be reciprocal: both the colonies and the mother country would benefit from the regulation of trade. Thus the navigation acts had stimulated shipbuilding in New England and supported South Carolina's indigo industry with English bounties. But sometimes English policy threatened colonial prosperity. When falling tobacco prices prompted Virginia legislators to limit production by stopping the slave trade in the 1730s, the English Privy Council vetoed the measure, explaining that only Parliament could enact laws of trade. To protect English merchants from having to accept depreciated paper money as payment for imported goods, Parliament restricted the use of paper money, first in New England in 1750 and later in all colonies. The Hat Act (1732) favored England's hatmakers by halting colonial manufacture of finished hats, while the Iron Act (1750) limited colonial production to merely bar and pig iron. Such measures underscored the subordinate economic role of England's colonies.

Although many colonists disliked English interference and secretly defied some restrictions by smuggling and by bribing officials to close their eyes to violations (such as trade with French colonies), colonial protest usually remained only rhetorical and theoretical. In fact, colonial leaders typically asserted their allegiance to England's monarchy, reiterating their "obligations to duty, loyalty, and affection" in exchange for the king's "paternal care." Nonetheless, by the mid-18th century, colonial leaders well understood their subordinate position in the British empire.

Other colonials, less well placed than the political elite, could not always afford to accept England's authority. Although most 18th-century Americans accepted elite rule, economic or political grievances sometimes spurred political action outside the legal system. During the 1740s, for example, the royal navy provoked popular opposition in Boston by forcing colonial sailors to serve on British warships. On several occasions, spontaneous but purposeful crowds used violence to interfere with this British policy. Similarly, disputes about paper money in Boston created so much hostility among workers that when the house of a leading politician, Thomas Hutchinson, mysteriously caught fire, a crowd surrounded the blaze, cursed the unpopular leader, and roared "Let it burn! Let it burn!"

Such cases of organized violence were exceptions to the rule of voluntary obedience. Africans in the north also created an unofficial political system to settle disputes. On colony election days, Africans voted for their own "governors" and "kings," respected leaders who would provide guidance for their community. Only partly a satire of colonial rituals, these elections allowed Africans to choose leaders to resolve internal problems.

Imperial Wars Disrupt the Public Order

The general acceptance of the English colonial system could be seen in the colonists' sacrifices during time of war. As loyal subjects, Americans accepted the crown's control of foreign diplomacy and rallied to the king's defense. Four times between 1689 and 1763, the mother country engaged in war with European rivals, especially France; four times Americans shared the burdens of these wars. Because the European powers drew Native allies into these struggles, the wars also affected Native societies, disrupting trade, threatening territorial boundaries, and causing countless deaths. Among colonials, the wars had a strong economic impact, fostering brief booms and inflations that were followed by layoffs and depressions. Most important, these imperial conflicts underscored the colonies' dependence on English policies; decisions about war and peace were made in Europe, never in America. The colonials might well share English victories, but just as surely would they fear and suffer from military upheaval.

Europe's American Wars

The first colonial war, King William's War (1689–1697) pitted England against France on the northern borders of New England and New York. When English plans to invade French Canada failed in 1689, the conflict turned into a series of border raids. English, French, and Dutch settlers suffered grievous losses when Native warriors burned towns or kidnapped civilians to replace their own dead. Although some European captives managed to escape, becoming famous for preserving their faith amid "savage" conditions, many spent the remainder of their lives among their captors, assimilating into Native communities.

King William's War also brought heavy losses to the Iroquois, whose Algonquian and Abenaki enemies continued to fight even after the European treaty formally ended the war in 1697. By 1701, the weakened Iroquois negotiated with the French and their Native allies to preserve access to the western fur trade in exchange for limiting their military alliance with England. Despite losing 20 percent of their population, the Iroquois would remain an important military presence on the borders between New France and New England.

The second colonial war, Queen Anne's War (1701–1713), revived English-French hostility in the northern colonies and English-Spanish conflict between Florida and South Carolina. Once again, civilians on the outskirts of settlements suffered attacks, murders, and kidnappings. In colonial cities, war profiteering by wealthy merchants caused an inflation of prices and shortages of food. But the peace treaty gave England control of Hudson's Bay, Newfoundland, and Acadia (Nova Scotia), which had the effect of protecting New England's lucrative fishing industry.

In 1739, a dispute over trading rights in the West Indies (which became known as the War of Jenkins' Ear because a Spanish officer allegedly mutilated the English Captain Jenkins) erupted into a third conflict between England and its enemies, France and Spain, known as King George's War (1744–1748). As England organized military campaigns against Spanish shipping and Canadian towns, the colonial economy benefitted by shipbuilding, privateering, and war contracts. Three thousand Massachusetts men, a rough band drawn heavily from among Boston's poor, enlisted in an expedition against the French fortress at Louisbourg. All colonials celebrated their victory in 1745.

From England's point of view, however, glory in America was worth less than achieving dominance in Europe. To the dismay of colonials, the peace treaty of 1748 returned all conquered territories to their previous claimants. The social costs were less easily remedied. Recent estimates suggest that Massachusetts lost 2 percent of its population, 8 percent of its men over the age of 16. Such heavy casualties, the result of disease and malnutrition more than enemy bullets, left large numbers of widows, many with children, who became destitute. Such problems encouraged public efforts to help the poor. But when Boston caretakers introduced a textile workhouse for poor women, the beneficiaries rebuffed the scheme, preferring to spin wool at home, where they could labor in a familiar environment, supervise their children, and earn a meager living by taking in laundry and boarders. Although prosperity returned to the colonies in the 1750s, unemployment remained high in Boston.

The War for Empire

The peace was short lived. The outbreak of the Seven Years War (1754–1763) reminded colonials that the cherished rights of Englishmen demanded sacrifice. As France moved to protect its access to the rich fur trade of the Ohio valley and English colonials penetrated the same region for settlement and trade with the Ohio nations, both European powers understood that the contest involved nothing less than control of the continent. At the remote borderlands of the Ohio river valley, on territory occupied by various refugee peo-

Here was the threshold to all the natural riches of America.

ple including Delawares, Shawnees, and Mingos, but claimed by Iroquois, French, Virginians, and Pennsylvanians, the two European rivals drew lines on a map and fought to protect their claims. Here, after all, was the threshhold to all the natural riches of America.

In 1749, King George II had granted unknown acreage to the Ohio Company of Virginia, a private investment company, which employed a young land speculator named George Washington to survey the area. Pennsylvania's land speculators soon moved to secure their own claims to the region. Both colonial groups had dealt directly with the small Ohio nations, ignoring the Iroquois, who claimed to speak for their Ohio "cousins" and who also wanted a share of the interior trade. English activity in the region prompted the French to send an army to begin building a chain of forts in 1753 to keep English colonials east of the Appalachian mountains. Amid these competing interests, one view emerged clearly: the local Ohio nations wanted to remove all invading groups—English, French, or Iroquois—and tried to juggle their neutrality for their own benefit. Washington's appointment as a Virginia militia officer merely antagonized the Ohio people because of his tendency "to Command the Indians as his slaves."

Negotiations to form an alliance with the Native groups climaxed when seven English colonies sent delegates to Albany, New York, in 1754 to meet with the Iroquois and plan for mutual defense. Frustrated by intercolonial rivalry and broken promises, the Iroquois refused to join an alliance. Benjamin Franklin took the opportunity to introduce a "Plan of Union," proposing the cre-

The mortally wounded Major General Edward Braddock retreating with his army after being attacked by French and Indian forces near Fort Duquesne on July 9, 1755.

ation of a Grand Council that would represent all colonies to administer military defense, coordinate land and trade relations with Native nations, and levy taxes. Although approved by the Albany congress, the plan challenged the existing political leadership and was rejected by the colonial assemblies. In any event, royal officials in England had no intention of turning over such profitable business to colonial politicians.

In 1754, skirmishes between English and French troops signaled the outbreak of open warfare. Both European nations promptly transported their armies to America. But when the English General Edward Braddock notified the Ohio nations that "no Savage should inherit the land," Native leaders decided that English expansion represented more of a threat than French forts and trading posts. The result was a British military disaster. As Braddock marched his troops toward the French forts in western Pennsylvania in 1755, French and

"Our exalted ideas of the prowess of British regulars had not been well founded."

Native warriors sprang from an ambush and forced the redcoats to retreat. "This whole transaction," Franklin later wrote, "gave us Americans the first suspicion that our exalted ideas of the prowess of British regulars had not been well founded."

In addition to humiliating Braddock and the English, the flight of English forces from the Ohio region gave the French great power over the Native nations. Threatening to destroy their villages, the French coerced the Natives to join them in attacking English settlements in Pennsylvania, Virginia, and the Carolinas. This alliance gave the conflicts its popular name: French and Indian War.

Pennsylvania Quakers, famous for their pacifism, faced pressure from their Scots-Irish and German neighbors to vote for taxes to finance retaliatory attacks. Although Quaker leaders quickly approved funds "for the king's purposes," a few Quakers resigned from the assembly to preserve their pacifist consciences. The Quakers also insisted on peaceful negotiations to end the brutal warfare. Indeed, Quaker criticism of previous unfair dealing with the Delawares and generous gifts to Native leaders eased tensions on the colony's western borders. "In all the desolation on our frontiers," remarked one pacifist politician in 1758, "not one Friend we have heard of has been slain nor carried captive."

The early failure of English military forces enabled the French to gain control of the borders of New York and Canada. But French success alarmed the Iroquois and Ohio nations. A complete victory by one European power would mean that the Native nations would fall subordinate to the victor and lose their independence. By 1758, Native leaders were eager to negotiate a neutral position with the English. Their withdrawal from the war coincided with the rise of a new English leader, William Pitt, who reinvigorated British military activity. Instead of sending fresh troops to America, Pitt agreed to finance the cost of the war if the colonies provided the manpower. Under the leadership of British officers, colonial militiamen recaptured the French forts in western Pennsylvania, New York, and Canada. The hostilities climaxed in the battle of Quebec, where General James Wolfe defeated the French General Montcalm in 1759. Four years later, the Treaty of Paris ended the war; France surrendered all its American possessions except for two sugar islands in the West Indies.

Benjamin Franklin delighted in the colonial contribution to England's victory. "The growth of the children," he gloated, expressing pride in America's sacrifices, "tends to increase the growth of the mother." The colonists had also gained considerable benefits. War contracts had brought prosperity to colonial cities; farmers found markets for their produce. And, once colonial privateers had swept the French navy from the seas, merchants resumed the profitable illegal trade with the French and Spanish sugar islands. But when Parliament attempted to stop such smuggling by permitting the issuance of general search warrants, called "writs of assistance," colonial merchants rose in protest. Attacking the use of such writs in 1761, Massachusetts lawyer James Otis suggested that Parliament lacked the *right* to legislate for the colonies. Although the Massachusetts courts ruled against him, Otis's argument foreshadowed new challenges to Parliament's power.

Not everyone in the colonies had profited from the war. In Maryland, Catholics (presumed allies of the French Catholics) were shouldered with double property taxes to finance the war. Boston soldiers again suffered heavy casualties, leaving large numbers of widows and orphans. From South Carolina, the Catawbas had sent warriors to battle with the English, only to have them return infected with smallpox that devastated the population. Drastically reduced in numbers and dependent on colonial trade, the survivors accepted reservation lands in the western parts of the colony as a way of preventing complete encroachment by colonial settlers.

Colonial Expansion Provokes Resistance

Other Native groups also faced an uncertain future. Although the removal of France from North America promised to end border warfare in the Ohio valley, the diverse Native nations now had to confront uncontested English power. To the dismay of Delawares, Shawnees, Ottawas, Miamis, Chippewas, and Iroquois, British General Jeffrey Amherst did not follow the defeated French in retreat from

British soldiers presented the Delawares gifts of blankets and handkerchiefs that had deliberately been contaminated with smallpox.

Fort Duquesne; instead, he built an English fort on the ruins at Pittsburgh. The British even violated the custom of diplomatic reciprocity, such as gift giving. During negotiations with Delaware diplomats, British soldiers presented gifts of blankets and handkerchiefs that had deliberately been contaminated with smallpox. "I hope it will have the desired effect," reflected a British soldier coldly.

Nor could British officials curb the appetite of colonial land grabbers. As colonials illegally occupied Native territory, one Delaware warrior complained that "the white people covets the land and eats them out by inches . . . which [is] against the will of God." Property disputes between colonial settlers and Native peoples provoked violence and intensified racial hatred. Meanwhile, the royal government in England also coveted Native lands and tried to restrict colonial land speculation and trade with Native groups. The royal government now issued the Proclamation of 1763, which prohibited colonial settlement west of the Appalachian mountains. The policy ignored both Native and colonial claims in the region.

"If you suffer the English among you, you are dead men," warned the frustrated Delaware prophet Neolin. "Sickness, smallpox, and their poison will destroy you entirely." Pointing to the disappearance of deer herds, the seizure of tribal lands, and the English refusal to trade gunpowder, Neolin called for a revitalization of traditional values, the rejection of "white people's ways and nature," including rum, and the display of friendship by shaking hands with the left hand, not the European's customary right hand. "Drive them away," Neolin urged. "Wage war against them."

During the spring of 1763, Native hostility spread through the Ohio valley, igniting another war. Under the leadership of the Ottawa chief Pontiac, Native groups in the Ohio valley attacked British forts and trading posts as well as frontier settlements in Pennsylvania and Virginia. But without French assistance, Pontiac's rebellion collapsed once British troops arrived. Although the royal government still hoped to control the western lands, colonial speculators won some revisions of the Proclamation Line. Colonials continued to stake claims in Kentucky and Tennessee, but legal title to these lands remained uncertain, contributing to dissatisfaction with England's policies.

England's Imperial Crisis

England's victory over France, instead of bringing peace and security to America, actually inspired new grievances that set the colonies on the road to independence. Of course, no one in 1763 actually spoke about the separation of the colonies from the mother country, nor did anyone envision the long and tricky route that led to the Declaration of Independence thirteen years later. Indeed, it would be a mistake to assume that the creation of an American nation was inevitable. And yet the French and Indian War had revealed serious problems within the British Empire. Despite the military emergency, the colonies had been slow to support England's efforts. Yet the war had increased England's indebtedness, and royal officials resolved to tax the colonies to pay for future military defense and administrative costs. England also had decided, even before Pontiac's rebellion, to station 10,000 regular troops (redcoats) in America, at the colonies' expense.

England's plans came at an inopportune time. The war's end had brought with it an economic depression that slowed business, lowered wages, and eliminated jobs. As credit contracted, English merchants demanded that colonists pay their outstanding debts; one result was a financial crisis in Virginia, where heavily indebted tobacco planters scrambled to avoid bankruptcy. Concern about British interference in colonial affairs surfaced when the king's Privy Council vetoed a Virginia law that would have lowered the salaries of clergymen. Defending the bill in 1763, an impassioned Patrick Henry denied the king's right to veto colonial laws, calling him a tyrant. Moved by the speech, a jury awarded the clergymen a single penny in damages; Henry soon won election to the Virginia House of Burgesses.

England Seeks Revenue, Colonists Dissent

Objections to Parliament's control of the colonies became precedents for further protests when England resolved to introduce new taxes to pay for colonial defense. Reasoning that the colonists who had benefited from the war with France should share the costs of empire, Parliament passed the Sugar Act in 1764—for the first time using a navigation law *not* to regulate trade but to raise revenue. Although the measure lowered customs duties on imported molasses, it also attempted to increase revenue collections with better enforcement provisions to end colonial smuggling. Yet the law deprived shippers of the traditional legal protections, such as trial by a local jury and presumption of innocence rather than guilt. Despite protests from colonial merchants, an indifferent Parliament also passed the Currency Act of 1764, which prohibited the use of paper money and thus reduced the supply of currency just as English creditors were recalling debts and tax collectors were seeking more revenue.

Parliament then passed a broader tax law, the Stamp Act, in 1765. Requiring revenue stamps to be attached to legal documents, such as wills and deeds, newspapers, and printed matter, the law

proposed to tax colonials without relying on the colony legislatures, which customarily had approved all revenue bills. Parliament also passed the Quartering Act of 1765, requiring colonials to provide food and housing for British troops in America. Since the redcoats were notoriously abusive to civilians, the law seemed doubly obnoxious: colonials would have to pay for protection they did not want or need. In fact, only New York faced a significant tax burden and finally simply refused to comply with the law.

The new taxes aroused storms of protest, particularly from the lawyers, merchants, and printers who would have to use the new revenue stamps. The Maryland lawyer Daniel Dulany led the attack. In a widely read pamphlet, *Considerations on the Propriety of Imposing Taxes in the British Colonies* (1765), he argued that by passing new taxes Parliament threatened a basic right of Englishmen. Although Parliament claimed that it "virtually" represented the entire empire, Dulany insisted that only "actual" representation by specific delegates was legal (though no one really wished to send delegates to England), and he declared that Parliament's interests no longer coincided with colonial rights.

In Virginia, Dulany's constitutional arguments translated on the popular level into a fear that English politicians intended to destroy colonial self-government. The Stamp Act prompted young Patrick Henry to advocate resolutions that denounced Parliament's supremacy. His fiery condemnation of the king made him instantly famous in all the colonies. Other protesters did not stop with words. Aware of the economic impact of the new taxes, merchants, artisans, and workers in the port cities formed secret groups called "Sons of Liberty" to prevent the use of the government stamps. In Boston, New York, Newport, and Philadelphia, angry crowds visited the appointed stamp officials and demanded their resignations. When the government officials refused, the mobs attacked their property and threatened their lives. Once again, the unfortunate Thomas Hutchinson lost his Massachusetts house to mob violence. In New York, another mob tore apart a theatrical playhouse frequented by the wealthy. Backed by such popular sentiment, nine colonial assemblies sent delegates to a Stamp Act Congress in New York in 1765, which drafted a Declaration of Rights and Grievances, denying Parliament's right to tax the colonies.

Adding muscle to these protests, colonial merchants agreed to boycott English goods until the Stamp Act was repealed. Believing that luxury imports contributed to a loss of morality, supporters of the boycott promised not only to persuade Parliament to repeal the law but also to restore the public virtue. More practically, the nonimportation and nonconsumption agreements threatened English commercial interests that had considerable influence in Parliament. To reinforce such pressure, the assemblies also appointed colonial agents to lobby Parliament to rescind the unpopular taxes.

Parliament Defends Its Sovereignty

By 1766, this combination of economic pressure, political lobbying, and constitutional argument convinced Parliament to repeal the Stamp Act. Americans rejoiced at the news. But England's reversal also fueled colonial suspicions of the mother country. Reasoning that Parliament would not have repealed a good law, colonials concluded that their fear of an evil conspiracy among English politicians had been correct. "We always have had enemies," declared a wary preacher. "We may depend upon it that they will lay new schemes." Such skepticism seemed confirmed when Parliament passed the Declaratory Act in 1766, affirming its right to legislate for the colonies. Although Parliament conceded the failure of the Stamp Act, the principle of legislative sovereignty remained in place.

The argument started again in 1767, when Parliament, still seeking revenue from the colonies, adopted a series of laws known as the Townshend

Burning the Stamps.

American colonists protesting the Stamp Act by burning the British tax stamps in a bonfire in 1765.

acts. Making a distinction from the Stamp Act, which levied *internal* taxes, the new laws claimed merely to enact *external* taxes, that is, taxes on trade and commerce, which Parliament had always controlled. The first new law introduced customs duties on such products as glass, paper, and tea; the second tightened enforcement of the navigation system by permitting trials without jury of suspected smugglers; the third permitted the use of customs taxes to pay government salaries, thus bypassing the colonial assemblies that had traditionally voted for such funds; the fourth, which was not related to taxes, suspended the New York Assembly for its earlier rejection of the Quartering Act. By the time news of the laws reached the colonies, New York had already complied with the Quartering Act, but Parliament's attack on a colonial government seemed menacing to all colonies.

Rejecting Parliament's Rights

Colonial leaders quickly challenged the new laws. In 1767, a Philadelphia lawyer named John Dickinson published twelve essays, entitled *Letters from a Farmer in Pennsylvania,* which provided a legal argument against the Townshend acts. Dismissing any difference between an "internal" tax, such as revenue stamps, and an "external" tax, such as a trade law, Dickinson denied that Parliament had the right to legislate for the colonies or to raise money without the consent of the taxpayers. Political leaders in Massachusetts authorized two Sons of Liberty, Samuel Adams and James Otis, to write a "Circular Letter" in 1768 to the other colonies, denouncing Parliament's threat to self-government while "expressing their firm confidence in the king our common head and father." Meanwhile, to pressure English merchants, colonial businesses renewed the nonimportation agreements, appealing to popular dislike of luxury goods and their implied immorality.

Such peaceful boycotts drew women into the political crusade. "The great difficulty of all," remarked South Carolina's Christopher Gadsden, "is to persuade our wives to give us their assistance, without which it is impossible to succeed." While refraining from purchasing such products as tea, women also organized spinning bees to increase domestic production of cloth and so reduce dependence on English trade. The entire graduating class of Yale College came to the 1769 commencement "wholly dressed in the manufactures of our own country." But ironically, in light of women's central importance to the effort, political leaders like Mass-

achusetts's John Adams defined the boycott as an assertion of "manly and warlike virtues" against the English "elegance, luxury and effeminacy" that threatened American virtue. Meanwhile, in Boston and New York, street mobs coerced reluctant importers to respect the boycott.

As colonial leaders waged moral warfare against Parliament, city merchants continued to smuggle goods into the ports, although they encountered greater obstacles from England's newly appointed customs collectors. Street crowds occasionally recaptured confiscated goods. One night in 1768, a mob attacked the customs officers who had seized Boston merchant John Hancock's vessel *Liberty* for failing to pay a duty on wine. Such violence moved the English government to send four regiments of redcoats to Boston. These troops further antagonized the city's workers by taking odd jobs during their free time. Street brawls between soldiers and civilians erupted sporadically, climaxing on March 5, 1770, when the redcoats fired into a crowd, killing five people, including the mulatto sailor Crispus Attucks. To colonists, this Boston "massacre" epitomized the tyranny of English authority.

While Boston mourned its dead, news arrived in America in 1770 that Parliament had repealed the Townshend duties, retaining only the tax on tea as a sign of legislative supremacy. Jubilant colonials, vindicated in their defiance of English policy, resumed business as usual—except for the boycott of English tea. As one anonymous woman wrote,

Let the Daughters of Liberty, nobly arise,
And tho' we've no Voice, but a negative here,
The use of the Taxables, let us forbear.

"Thus acting," she added with a pun, "we point out their Duty to men."

With provincial trade expanding, however, tranquility returned to American politics. But the peace was fragile, easily disrupted by mutual suspicion. When the British patrol ship *Gaspée* ran aground while chasing smugglers in Rhode Island in 1772, a mob ignored the sacred English rights of property and set the vessel afire. To reassert royal authority, the governor of Massachusetts announced that the salaries of certain judges would hereafter be paid by the treasury rather than by the colony's legislature. The decision offended the colonial sense of justice. "An independent ruler," responded the indignant lawyer John Adams, was "a monster in a free state." Sensing an attack on colonial rights, Boston's Samuel Adams persuaded the town meeting to create a "committee of correspondence" to spread news and coordinate defenses with other communities. The scheme created a political network that extended through New England and eventually to other colonies, bringing political issues into the lives of ordinary citizens and laying the basis for intercolonial cooperation.

The Colonies Move toward Independence

As politicians in the separate colonies responded to the imperial crisis, common interests gradually coalesced into a shared identity as aggrieved colonials. To be sure, at the beginning of 1773 a cautious calm prevailed throughout North America; no immediate issue demanded resolution. But by then colonials had developed a political perspective that made them wary of British politicians. Their faith in Parliament's wisdom had evaporated years before. As loyal colonials, however, they perceived the monarchy, now embodied by King George III, as the legitimate head of the English political family. In their religious sermons, political speeches, and private letters, they continued to view England as their mother country, the king as their political father, and themselves as dutiful colonial children. But many agreed that political harmony, like good families, depended on mutual benefits. Against that standard, colo-

nial leaders took the measure of a new series of English laws.

Tea and Protest

In this atmosphere of mutual mistrust, the English government announced passage of the Tea Act in 1773 to save the East India Company from financial ruin. The law reduced the tax on tea, but it also granted the company a monopoly of tea sales, threatening to undersell both smugglers and independent shopowners who could not compete with the company's prices. Once again, Parliament seemed more concerned with protecting English interests than the colonials'. More serious, the tea tax showed no retreat from Parliament's claims to tax the colonies.

The arrival of East India tea in 1773 precipitated a crisis. Determined to prevent importations, mobs in the port cities refused to allow ships to unload. In Boston harbor, an orderly group of fifty men, disguised as Mohawks, slipped aboard the tea ship and, as thousands watched from shore, dumped forty-five tons of tea into the sea. The Boston Tea Party alarmed conservative Americans no less than English officials, for the perpetrators had not only broken the law but also destroyed private property.

An enraged Parliament promptly passed the Coercive acts (called in America the "Intolerable" acts) in 1774. The first law closed Boston harbor until the citizens paid for the tea. A second law changed the structure of Massachusetts's government, restricting town meetings and strengthening the royal governor. To protect British officials from local juries, a third law allowed the transfer outside the colony of certain legal cases, such as a British soldier's killing a civilian. A fourth measure reenacted the Quartering Act to station redcoats in Boston at the colonists' expense. News of a fifth law, the Quebec Act, unrelated to New England, also alarmed colonial opinion because it increased Canadian land claims in the Ohio valley, reaffirmed the unrepresentative French government, and mandated toleration for Roman Catholics. To shocked colonial leaders, Parliament's attempt to alter a colony's government violated the basic principles of the English constitution—the belief that royal power needed to be balanced by elected representatives to protect the rights of Englishmen.

A Continental Congress

The Coercive acts aroused colonial anger, ignited popular fear of tyranny, and prompted organized opposition. In September 1774, the first Continental Congress, composed of fifty-six delegates from twelve colonies, met in Philadelphia to adopt a common response to the imperial crisis. In this emergency atmosphere the delegates quickly voted to endorse Massachusetts's "Suffolk Resolves," which denied the legality of the Coercive acts and authorized defensive military measures in the event of an English attack. The congress also adopted a "Declaration of Rights and Grievances," which avowed loyalty to the king but rejected Parliament's right to make laws for America. Yet many delegates still opposed separation from England. Seeking a moderate alternative, one group, led by Pennsylvania's Joseph Galloway, proposed a plan of union that would give the colonial legislatures veto powers over parliamentary laws, but the Galloway plan failed by a single vote.

The delegates proceeded to add economic bite to their protests. Instituting an economic boycott, Congress adopted the Continental Association to end trade with England. Imports would cease at the end of 1774; but to protect southern tobacco, rice, and indigo planters, exports would continue until September 1775. Colonials also agreed not to consume English products that avoided the ban. Unlike earlier embargoes, moreover, the Association would not be voluntary. Congress recommended the formation of local committees of safety

to enforce cooperation by confiscating contraband goods and boycotting defiant businesses. These committees, supervised by provincial councils, would form the basis of an extralegal government. Finally, Congress agreed to meet again in May 1775 if the controversy had not yet been settled.

While awaiting England's response to the protests, the colonials entered a period of public debate in the press and the pulpit. Adopting family metaphors, many conservatives opposed any "breach with the parent state," stressing the economic and military hazards of defying the mother country. "Even brutes do not devour their young," replied the uncompromising Thomas Paine, "nor savages make war upon their families." Meanwhile, the committees of safety enforced the economic boycott, sometimes using violence against reluctant merchants and consumers. When the king ordered more troops to New England, Massachusetts radicals formed militia companies, collected gunpowder, and prepared to fight.

The Second Continental Congress

"The shot heard 'round the world" exploded on April 19, 1775, when Massachusetts's military governor, General Thomas Gage, sent 700 redcoats to seize military supplies stockpiled at Concord. Warned by courier Paul Revere, the colony's militia (known as "minutemen" because of their readiness to fight at a minute's notice) exchanged shots with the British at Lexington. More skirmishes occurred at Concord, and the British retreated in a running battle back to Boston, taking heavy losses. As shocked Americans absorbed the news that military action had begun, the Boston militia readied for another battle. In Virginia the royal government guarded the public gunpowder, but in Vermont the Green Mountain Boys, led by Ethan Allen, captured the British forts at Ticonderoga and Crown Point on Lake Champlain.

On the threshold of war, the second Continental Congress opened sessions in Philadelphia on May 10, 1775. Of the sixty-five delegates, fifty had served in the first congress, evidence of the public's confidence in their elected representatives. Still hesitant to proclaim independence, the delegates agreed to send a conciliatory message directly to the king. This "Olive Branch Petition" pleaded to avert war but still demanded repeal of the Coercive acts and protection of colonial rights. But even as the appeal sailed to England, the congress assumed control of the provincial militias and dispatched the experienced military officer George Washington to Boston to act as commander-in-chief.

Before Washington arrived in Boston, New England troops had battled the redcoats at Bunker Hill in June 1775. Word of the engagement reached England by the end of the summer, destroying any interest in a political compromise. In October 1775, King George III told Parliament that the Americans "now openly avow their revolt, hostility, and rebellion." By the end of the year, king and Parliament declared America in a state of rebellion and forbade all commerce with the colonies. In January 1776, the colonists learned that England had hired German-speaking Hessian mercenaries to help subdue the rebels. Finally Americans began to see, in the words of Massachusetts's Abigail Adams, that England was "no longer [a] parent state, but a tyrant state."

Declaring Independence

"No longer piddle at the threshold," exclaimed Mercy Otis Warren to her friend, congressional delegate John Adams. "It is time to . . . open every gate that impedes the rise and growth of the American republic." But even as the king declared war on his American subjects, colonials hesitated to take the final step toward independence, still hoping that their benevolent political father, George III, would hear their pleas. The publication of Thomas Paine's pamphlet, *Common Sense,* in January 1776 helped overcome such illusions. The tract, which sold 150,000 copies in six months, proportionally rivaling today's bestsellers, drew no distinction between a bad parliament and a good king. According to Paine, monarchy itself was evil; George III was "the Royal Brute"! Urging immediate independence, Paine advocated the creation of a nonmonarchical form of government, a republic, in which citizens chose their own political fathers. As Paine's essay swayed public opinion and Americans prepared for a British invasion, the Continental Congress moved to decisive action. In March, Congress voted to send armed ships against "enemy" vessels. In April, the delegates opened American ports to all ships except England's. In May, Congress advised the separate colonial governments to draft new state constitutions that omitted any provision for royal power.

The next step was taken by Virginia, which authorized delegate Richard Henry Lee to present another resolution to the Continental Congress. On June 7, 1776, Lee introduced a motion declaring that "These United Colonies are, and of right ought to be, free and independent States." But Congress still hesitated to make the final move. Seeking to build a consensus of support, the delegates asked a committee of five, including Thomas Jefferson and John Adams, to draft a formal justification for this unprecedented step. Three weeks passed. Then, as encouragement poured into Philadelphia from local communities throughout the colonies, Congress voted to adopt Lee's resolution on July 2, 1776, formally creating the United States of America. The next day, Jefferson presented the document to Congress, and one day later the delegates approved the Declaration of Independence.

Jefferson's Declaration developed two lines of reasoning. The first drew on the political theories of John Locke and other English writer-philosophers, which held that governments existed by the consent of the governed and were intended to protect the natural rights of humankind, specifically the rights of "life, liberty, and the pursuit of happiness." When a government failed to protect such rights, "the people" had the right "to alter or to abolish" that government.

The second section of the Declaration contained a long list of examples of abuse, tyranny, and despotism by King George III to justify the decision to change the government. No word in the text referred to Parliament; it was sufficient to expose the failure of the evil political father, George III. In attacking the king, the Declaration personified the enemy and broke the last link of empire. Americans were now free to choose new political fathers.

The white male property holders who signed their names at the bottom of the Declaration did not intend to extend their "unalienable" rights to other social groups. As they all knew, the right to choose one's leaders did not exist widely in the 18th-century colonies. "I cannot say, that I think you are very generous to the ladies," remarked Abigail Adams to a signer of the Declaration, "for, whilst you are proclaiming peace and goodwill toward men, emancipating all nations, you insist on retaining an absolute power over your wives." Her husband, John Adams, merely laughed at the idea. And although some signers of the Declaration opposed slavery, they uncritically accepted the complaint that the king had "excited domestic insurrections," a reference to Virginia's royal governor, Lord Dunmore, who offered to liberate slaves who fled from their rebel owners. In defining the right to declare independence, the Declaration envisioned no social revolution, but merely a separation from the royal state.

The Legacy of Independence

As the founding document of a new nation, the Declaration of Independence achieved much more than the signers originally intended. The assertion that "the people" had the right to choose their leaders expressed a fundamental commitment to a representative, or republican, form of government. On July 4, 1776, no republic existed anywhere in the world, and it would take years of warfare with England before colonials won the right to build one. Nationhood and republicanism thus became inextricably intertwined, creating a unique identity for all citizens. By justifying independence in the universal language of "self-evident truths" and "unalienable rights," moreover, the Declaration presented a vocabulary that could be adopted by other groups of "the people" in different times and circumstances.

Although the so-called Founding Fathers had a narrow view of who was entitled to citizenship, other Americans and people around the world would later seize upon the Declaration to justify their own quests for self-government. In that vast ideological potential lay the great genius of Jefferson's words. But in 1776, the right of revolution was still a risky dream. To gain the government they wanted, colonials first had to win the war with England. That is why Jefferson added one final, solemn sentence to his document: "And for the support of this Declaration, with a firm reliance on the protection of divine providence, we mutually pledge to each other our lives, our fortunes, and our sacred honor."

INFOTRAC® COLLEGE EDITION EXERCISES

For additional reading go to InfoTrac College Edition, your online research library at *http://web1.infotrac-college.com.*

Keyword search: Patrick Henry

Keyword search: Seven Years' War

Keyword search: French and Indian wars

Subject search: Algonquians, reference book

Keyword search: Stamp Act

Keyword search: Boston Tea Party
Keyword search: Coercive acts
Subject search: Continental Congress
Keyword search: Thomas Jefferson
Keyword search: John Locke

ADDITIONAL READING

Gender and Politics

Philip Greven, *The Protestant Temperament: Patterns of Child-Rearing, Religious Experience, and the Self in Early America* (1977). A detailed interpretation of child-rearing practices that examines gender roles and their effects on religious beliefs.

Local Politics and Political Participation

Bernard Bailyn, *The Origins of American Politics* (1968). A thorough overview of provincial politics, emphasizing the built-in conflicts between colonists and royal authority.

Michael C. Batinski, *Jonathan Belcher: Colonial Governor* (1996). Following the research of the previous title, this biography studies provincial politics from the point of view of one royal governor.

Breen, T.H. *Tobacco Culture: The Mentality of the Great Tidewater Planters on the Eve of Revolution* (1985). A short study of the Virginia elite that explores the political and private problems of dependence on the English economy.

Richard L. Bushman, *King and People in Provincial Massachusetts* (1985). Focusing on one colony, this study explores public attitudes toward the English constitution and the growing conflict with royal power.

William D. Pierson, *Black Yankees: The Development of an Afro-American Subculture in Eighteenth Century New England* (1988). This study of African American life in the northern colonies includes a discussion of political activities.

Charles S. Sydnor, *Gentlemen Freeholders* (1952). A lively study of political practices in 18th-century

Virginia. For more recent analyses, see John Gilman Kolp, *Gentlemen and Freeholders: Electoral Politics in Colonial Virginia* (1998).

The War for Empire

Fred Anderson, *Crucible of War: The Seven Years' War and the Fate of Empire in British North America, 1754–1766* (2000). A thorough history of the French and Indian War, emphasizing the global impact of the conflict.

Eric Hinderaker, *Elusive Empires: Constructing Colonialism in the Ohio Valley, 1673–1800* (1997). Examines French, British, and U.S. efforts to control trade and land in the Ohio valley.

The Colonies Move toward Independence

Bernard Bailyn, *The Ideological Origins of the American Revolution* (1967). Building on Bailyn's survey of provincial politics (listed above), this book examines the development of American attitudes toward the English government, arguing that the political system bred a fondness for conspiracy theories.

Edward Countryman, *The American Revolution* (1985). A brief survey of the coming of the war for independence and its impact on American society, this lucid book includes an overview of the secondary writings about the subject.

Woody Holton, *Forced Founders: Indians, Debtors, Slaves, and the Making of the American Revolution in Virginia* (1999). Examines how nonleadership groups affected the decision of Virginia politicians to seek independence.

Pauline Maier, *The Old Revolutionaries: Political Lives in the Age of Samuel Adams* (1980). Examining the careers of such revolutionary leaders as Samuel Adams and Richard Henry Lee, Maier links political values and personal development.

Declaring Independence

Pauline Maier, *American Scripture: Making the Declaration of Independence* (1997). A thorough analysis of the drafting of the nation's founding document that traces the Declaration's symbolic legacy for later generations.

6

The Pennsylvania Packet, and Daily Advertiser.

[Price Four-Pence.]   MONDAY, JUNE 22, 1789.   [No. 3242.]

Sales at Auction.

THIS DAY,

Precisely at 9 o'Clock in the Morning—At the

Southwark Vendue Store,

Will begin the Sale of a General

Assortment of Merchandize,

Houshold Furniture, &c.

The stated Days of Sale are Mondays and Thursdays. The Public may rest assured that the greatest Attention and strictest Punctuality will invariably be pursued by

June 22   **A. Hubley & Co.** Auctioneers.

TO-MORROW,

The 23d Inst. at 9 o'Clock in the Morning,

At the City-Auction store,

Will be SOLD at PUBLIC SALE,

A LARGE and GENERAL

Assortment of Merchandize,

Consisting of

7-8 and yard wide cotton and linen checks	Brown do.
Cambric muslins	Sheetings
Striped persians	Striped lawns
Silk handkerchiefs	German dowlass
Linen and cotton handkerchiefs	Brown hollands
Shawls	Furniture checks
Manchester gown patterns	Sattinets
Cottons	Jeanets
Chintzes	Kentings
Callicoes	Thread and cotton hose
Jacket shapes	Cambricks & lawns
2-8 and yard wide Irish linens	Sewing silks
	Duroys
	Scotch carpets
	Hard ware, &c.

John Patton, Auctioneer.

June 22

To be Sold at Public Sale,

On WEDNESDAY the 24th Instant, at Elkton, Cæcil County—The

HOUSE and LOT,

With the Improvements, late the property of Thomas Huggins.

Robert Oliver,
William Matthews,
William Barroll,
⎫ Trustees.

June 4.   dtf

Vendue Sales

At Daniel Cooper's Ferry.

THE Subscriber having met with success in establishing his Vendue-Store in New-Jersey, is happy in the reflection, that he has hitherto afforded satisfaction to those who have honored him with their confidence, to whom, as also to those who have attended his Sales, he begs leave to return his most grateful acknowledgments; assuring them that the same candor and attention will be exerted to afford satisfaction to Buyer and Seller, that has hitherto been the ga-

On Thursday Next,

The 25th Instant, at 9 o'Clock in the Morning, At the House of Mr. JOHN BECK, deceased, in Front-street, nearly opposite the City Vendue Store,

Will be Sold by Public Sale,

A QUANTITY OF

New, ready-made Cloathing,

Houshold and Kitchen Furniture,

&c. &c.   June 22.   19.21 3sp

John Patton, Auctioneer.

On Saturday

The 27th inst. at 9 o'clock in the morning, At the House of WIDOW SUTTER, in Strawberry-Alley,

Will be sold by Public Vendue,

A QUANTITY OF

Houshold and Kitchen Furniture;

Consisting of—Beds, Bedding, Chairs, Tables, &c.

John Patton, Auctioneer.

June 22.

To be Sold by Public Vendue,

On Wednesday the 1st of July next, at 7 o'Clock in the Evening, at the COFFEE-HOUSE, in Second-street,

TWO undivided Third-Parts of 16,000 acres of Land, situate on Lechewaxin and Middle creeks, in the county of Northampton.

The Land is surveyed, and held under warrants from the Land-office; surveying fees and purchase money paid, but it is not patented.

A draft and description of the land may be now seen at the above Coffee House.

Conditions of sale are—One half of the purchase money to be paid at the time of sale, and the remaining half in 12 months, giving security if required.

June 15.   eop

John Patton, Auctioneer.

On Wednesday the 1st of July,

At 12 o'clock, will be sold at the Coffee House in Second-street, at Public Vendue—The

Ship Canton,

Lately commanded by Capt. Thomas Truxtun. The Canton was built by one of the first Carpenters in this Port, with uncommon care, and fitted in a very capital way for a London Trader, since which she has been supplied with many extra articles for her two voyages to China. Approved Notes at 60 days for one half, and at 90 days for the remainder, will be taken in payment.

June 16.   wfm

City Auction-Store,

THE Public are respectfully informed, that in future the stated Days of sale for Dry Goods at the above Store, will be on Tuesdays and Fridays, and those for Furniture on Wednesdays only—The sales to begin precisely at 9 o'Clock in the Morning.

All Sales of Groceries, Horses, Carriages, &c. formerly held at the Coffee House, will be continued at said Store on every Market Day, at Noon.

John Patton, Auctioneer.

Philadelphia, March 23

NOTICE.

THE First Company of Light Infantry will meet at the State-house on Monday next, the 22d inst. at 3 o'Clock, P. M. The Members are desired to be punctual in their Attendance as some Regulations for the Meeting to be on the 4th July next, will then be fixed upon.

By Order of Captain JAMES REES,

June 20   2sp   LEWIS KREIDER, Clerk.

THE Trustees of the University having fitted up the Rooms in the *Philosophical Hall,* in Fifth street, on the State-house square, for the accommodation of the several Schools, the Business of that Institution will be hereafter carried on at that Place, and the Students are desired to attend upon their respective Professors and Tutors, on Monday next, at 8 o'Clock in the Morning.

The State-house Bell will be rang at the usual Hours every Day, for the Meeting of the Students.

The Public Examination of the Senior Class in the University, will be held in the Hall on Thursday next at 10 o'clock, A. M. and the commencement for conferring degrees is appointed to be held on Thursday the 23d day of July next.

By order of the Board of Trustees.

June 18.   EDWARD FOX, Sec'ry.

A General Meeting of the subscribers to the Paper Money Fund will be held at the State-House on Monday, the 29th June, instant, at 11 o'clock in the forenoon, to take into consideration the state and circumstances of the said Fund, and what farther measures may be properly taken concerning the same. By order of the Trustees,

June 16.   3eo   RICHARD FULLERTON, Treasurer.

A Cook is Wanted.

Enquire of the Printers.   3t

WANTED IMMEDIATELY,

BY THE

Baltimore Manufacturing Company,

A PERSON well qualified to act as SUPERINTENDANT in the Manufacturing of Cotton, Flax and Wool, according to the present most approved methods in Europe. Proposals will be received by letter until 1st August, addressed to the Directors of the BALTIMORE MANUFACTORY. No Proposals will attended to but such as are accompanied with satisfactory testimonials of the abilities and characters of those who may apply.

LIKEWISE, WANTED,

A Number of skilful Manufacturers of Cotton, Flax and Wool, to whom, according to their abilities and characters, good Encouragement will be given, by applying as above.

Baltimore, June 11, 1789.   22w2w

Imported in the ship Canton,

AND FOR SALE BY

Coxe and Frazier,

FINE hyson teas, souchong, congo and bohea teas, in packages of various sizes; nankeens; enamelled tea cups and saucers; japan waiters—Also for sale, sheet copper, copper and iron nails; sheathing paper; Dutch dimities and linens; threads; French gauzes and flowers; superfine blue cloths; several parcels of excellent claret, and a quantity of new musquets and bayonets.   m&th3w

Carthagena Cotton.

John W. Swift, Junior,

HAS FOR SALE,

By WHOLESALE and RETAIL,

A FRESH ASSORTMENT OF

TEAS,

Of the first Quality, just imported in the last ships from CANTON,

At his STORE, between Market and Chesnut-streets.   dtf

NOW LANDING,

From the snow Oriana, captain Rogers, from England, Rochelle and Madeira,

BEST London market Madeira Wine (of vintages 1787 and 1788) in pipes, hogsheads and quarter casks

French brandy in pipes

Lead in bars, ingots and sheets

Red and white ditto in casks

Copperas and allum in ditto

Window glass in crates of 12 tables each

Ditto in boxes of 100 square feet

And a few tons of coals—FOR SALE by

Philip Nicklin.

May 9   4

Strong Beer in Casks

and Bottles,

Fresh Table Beer,

and Spruce Beer:

House-Keepers, Merchants and Captains of Vessels may be supplied by

WILLIAM INNES.

Vernon-street by South, between Front and Second streets, 12th June, 1789.   eu&t.22w4w.

By the ship Grange, from Liverpool,

Andrew Clow & Co.

HAVE IMPORTED,

PRINTED calicos, jeans, jeanets Fustians, beavers, velverets, and thicksets Broad and narrow, fine and superfine cloths Durants, callimancoes, shaloons and rattinets Black Barcelona, Bandano and Romal handkerchiefs With a Variety of other

Seasonable Goods.

May 1   dtf

Landing out of the Canton, from

China, and for SALE by

Sam. Wilcox & Arch. M'Call, junr.

The following Articles,

FINE Gunpowder, Hyson and Souchong Teas

Nankeens

Sattins

Taffeties

Lutestrings

Sensha

Pullicat Handkerchiefs

Hair Ribbon

Sewing Silks

Buge La Pour

June 9   dtf

Now LANDING, on Walnut-Street Wharf, from

Independence, Confederation, and the Republican Experiment, 1776–1787

CHRONOLOGY

1776	Washington avoids defeat in Battle of Long Island
	Pennsylvania adopts a democratic constitution
1777	Vermont constitution outlaws slavery
	Congress approves Articles of Confederation
	Burgoyne surrenders at Saratoga
1778	France joins military alliance with United States
	British army invades Georgia
1779	Spain supports United States
	George Rogers Clark defeats Native nations in Ohio valley
1780	British invade South Carolina
1781	States ratify Articles of Confederation
	Rhode Island blocks national tariff on imports
	Cornwallis surrenders at Yorktown
1783	Treaty of Paris ends war
1784	Economic downturn slows business
	Congress passes first Northwest Ordinance
1785	Land Ordinance creates grid land pattern in Northwest
1786	Virginia enacts statute of religious freedom
	Shays' Rebellion closes courts in Massachusetts
	Delegates attend Annapolis convention
1787	Northwest Ordinance creates territorial government
	Congress endorses constitutional convention

"Father!"

Captain Pipe, leader of the Delaware people, looked carefully at the warriors attending a peace council near Detroit. Then he returned his piercing gaze to the commander of the British troops. His lips curled in sarcasm, he spoke directly to the man with an eloquence that was punctuated with a far-from-respectful form of address.

"Father! Some time ago you put a war-hatchet into my hands, saying, 'take this weapon and try it on the heads of my enemies, the Long-Knives [colonial Americans]. . . .

"Father!—At the time when you gave me this weapon, I had neither cause nor wish to go to war against a foe who had done me no injury. But you say you are my father—and call me your child—and in obedience to you I received the hatchet. I knew that if I did not obey you, you would withhold from me the necessaries of life, which I could procure nowhere but here.

"Father! You may perhaps think me a fool, for risking my life at your bidding—and that in a cause in which I have no prospect of gaining any thing. For it is your cause and not mine—you have raised a quarrel among yourselves—and you ought to fight it out.

* * *

"... I may, perchance, happen to look back to the place from whence you started me, and what shall I see? Perhaps I may see my father shaking hands with the Long-Knives; yes, with those very people he now calls his enemies."

L ike the Delaware Captain Pipe, who seemed uncannily to foresee the events that would come to his people, Native groups residing near colonial borders had to choose between Britain and the United States, sometimes, as among the Iroquois, engaging in bitter disputes that sparked their own civil wars. And often, however they chose, these Native peoples would find themselves losers, abandoned equally by white allies and by the white enemies who coveted their lands.

The defense of colonial liberty also appeared hypocritical, if not absurd, to African slaves. As early as 1774, a young New England slave, Phyllis Wheatley, already a published poet, commented in a Boston newspaper that the colonists' "Cry for Liberty" masked "the reverse Disposition" to wield "oppressive Power over others." The next year, her owner set her free. Tens of thousands of other Africans took advantage of wartime disruptions to seek their freedom.

In declaring political independence from Great Britain in 1776, the American colonists went to war with the world's most powerful nation. But despite England's military superiority, the British government faced great obstacles in attempting to suppress the colonial rebellion, not least of which was the difficulty of transporting armies and supplies 3,000 miles across the Atlantic. The scattered, rural nature of American society gave the colonists important advantages. Colonial soldiers could be mustered from a friendly countryside and as easily dispersed after battle. Even decisive British victories, such as the military occupations of Philadelphia, New York, and Charleston, scarcely affected colonial troops elsewhere. Taking advantage of civilian supporters, General George Washington adopted brilliant guerrilla tactics to preserve the tattered Continental Army and avoid a major defeat.

But the dispersed American people were still far from united in 1776. Indeed, the war for independence resembled a civil war—a conflict not only between colonials and the mother country but also among social and political groups with different needs and expectations. Numerous Americans, known as Loyalists or Tories, opposed independence and remained loyal to the mother country. Even the desire to remain neutral was not always possible because the fortunes of war forced individuals and groups onto one side or the other. Certainly American political leaders worried about the lack of unanimity among colonials and acted harshly against suspected critics and enemies.

This demand for political conformity reflected important ideological beliefs. In separating from the British empire, the colonists had dismantled the existing type of political authority that linked citizens to the principles of monarchy. During the long struggle against royal power that led to the Declaration of Independence, Americans had discussed theories about non-monarchical republican governments—political systems based on the consent of the governed, in which free citizens chose their rulers. Republics seemed to offer maximum liberty to the citizenry, but political leaders debated whether large numbers of free people could be trusted to choose their rulers wisely. Only a highly moral citizenry, uncorrupted by material ambitions, they concluded, would overcome selfish interests and seek the benefit of the entire society. They doubted that all were so virtuous. From the birth of the American republic, the nation's leaders believed that morality and politics should be closely connected.

Political leaders also agreed that republican systems needed to keep government close to the people. In 1776, the same Congress that approved the Declaration authorized the separate states to create republican forms of state government. On the national level, Congress adopted the Articles of Confederation in 1777, deliberately establishing a weak federal system to prevent the abuse of power associated with the old monarchy. Under the Articles, Congress remained weak and the state governments became strong. But as unexpected political, economic, and diplomatic problems emerged in the 1780s, political leaders began to rethink these assumptions. The weakness of Congress and the independence of the states increasingly appeared as obstacles to effective government. By 1787, the political leadership was prepared to propose a new form of national government.

Choosing Sides: Social Divisions and Political Allegiances

"Rebellion is so odious," exclaimed one Massachusetts official. "It saps the foundation of moral virtue." Although colonial leaders, who called themselves patriots, overwhelmingly supported Congress and independence, a substantial portion of the population remained loyal to the king. Indeed, so vocal were the Loyalists in the months before Congress declared independence that the British government greatly exaggerated their strength. Believing that Congress consisted of rebellious conspirators rather than representatives of their communities, British strategists assumed that with armed support the Loyalist population would overthrow the rebels and return the colonies to the empire. But the strength of the Loyalists varied greatly: perhaps 6 percent in Connecticut, as many as half in New York. Elsewhere, regional pockets of strength reflected local issues and political disagreements. Overall, probably 20 percent of the colonists remained loyal to England.

Loyalism and Gender

Who were these Loyalists? Most royal government officials, such as Massachusetts's Thomas Hutchinson (whose home had twice been destroyed by colonial mobs) stayed with the king. So did merchants and large landholders who benefited from the government's patronage and grants. Recent British immigrants, including veterans of the Seven Years' War who had remained in America, retained allegiance to England.

Loyalism also appealed to social or cultural groups who felt oppressed by the colonial majority. In New England, worshippers in the Church of England resented tax discrimination by the Puritan Congregational churches, believed that English bishops could help them win tax relief, and tended to become Loyalists. Yet, ironically, New England Baptists, who also faced religious prejudice and tax discrimination, shared the Congregationalists' hostility to English bishops and so supported independence. Baptists thus gained greater respectability (though religious tax reforms would not come until the 1800s). Among non-English ethnic groups, assimilated colonists (such as English-speaking Germans and Dutch) supported independence, while isolated communities (such as Dutch-speaking members of the Dutch Reformed Church) backed the royal government. In New York, tenant farmers supported the king to oppose their landlords, who favored Congress; in the western Carolinas, small farmers were Loyalists in defiance of the wealthier planters who controlled their government.

Recognizing the strength of Loyalist opinion, Congress and the states tried to enforce political conformity. Some states banished Loyalists from their homes and exiled them to areas under British control. Other states passed laws confiscating Loyalist property. Even pacifists were suspect. The refusal of some Pennsylvania Quakers to support the war against England led to their banishment from the state. Members of the Shaker sect, a communal group led by the visionary Mother Ann Lee, faced arrest for refusing to support the fighting. By the end of the war, between 80,000 and 100,000 Loyalists followed the British armies into exile in

Some women served in the war as soldiers, by disguising themselves as men.

Canada, England, the West Indies, or the Spanish territories of Florida and Louisiana.

The persecution of Loyalists also affected women, who were presumed to share the political views of their fathers and husbands. Or course, women did chose sides during the war. Some, like Betsy Adams, the wife of Samuel Adams, shared the enthusiasm of their patriot spouses for independence; others, like Philadelphia milliner Margaret Hutchinson, aided British prisoners and carried messages for the redcoat army. Thousands of women made similar choices, serving in the war as cooks, nurses, washerwomen, and occasionally even as soldiers, by disguising themselves as men. Such involvement violated the widely held belief that women should not engage in political affairs. Yet some women used the presumed innocence of their gender to disguise their activities as spies and couriers. Women who rendered military service were often the wives of soldiers and followed the armies with their children. Others stood guard on the home front. "Imitate your husband's fortitude," wrote South Carolina's Eliza Lucas Pinckney to her daughter-in-law. "It is as much a female as a masculine virtue, and we stand in as much need of it to act our part properly."

Women's political views sometimes diverged from their husbands', and partisanship sometimes doomed their marriages. Such cases were rare, but significant. Whatever a woman's political views, the laws of most states assumed that married women shared the political positions of their husbands. Thus, with few exceptions, the confiscation of a Loyalist man's property included the possessions of his spouse, regardless of her politics. Patriot committees of safety, which tried to enforce a consensus among civilians, often ordered the wives and children of Loyalists into exile behind enemy lines. Without legal defense, such women lost their homes and property to the cause of liberty, and most never received recompense.

African Americans Choose Liberty

Among the Loyalists was a sizable proportion of Africans—approximately 25 percent of the total, or 20,000 people. Most were slaves who were compelled to accompany their pro-British owners into exile, but many had deliberately joined the British to gain their freedom. As early as 1775, Virginia's royal governor, Lord Dunmore, had offered emancipation to any slave who would fight for the king. In November 1775, the governor fielded a small army of ex-slaves who wore sashes declaring "Liberty to Negroes," but they were beaten by a patriot force. By the end of the war, Dunmore's proclamation attracted some 30,000 African Virginians who abandoned their masters. These included fighting men, but the entire slave population of a particular plantation often fled as a group. Similar offers of emancipation in other southern states encouraged thousands of slaves to take refuge behind British lines. Although some managed to keep their freedom and a few even returned as free people to west Africa, most were treated badly by the British and many were resold into slavery in the West Indies.

African Americans also fought for freedom in the patriot army and navy. Although free Africans had participated in the pre-war protests in northern cities, the slaveowning General Washington refused to allow Africans to serve in the Continental Army. Yet manpower shortages led the state militias to accept free Africans, although in some cases these recruits fought in segregated units. By the war's end, some 5,000 free blacks had served in the rebel ranks. Other African American soldiers were still slaves, sent as substitutes for their owners, and

some thereby obtained their freedom. For them, independence acquired a quite literal meaning.

Native Americans Choose Sides

The outbreak of war soon forced the various Native American nations to choose sides. Survivors of the coastal groups, surrounded by colonial settlers and dependent on local trade, usually supported the American cause. Mahican men from the praying village at Stockbridge, Massachusetts, for example, fought in the Continental Army and served as ambassadors to the nations of the Ohio valley; but the war did not improve their economic position and they migrated westward in the 1780s. By contrast, the Carolina Catawbas kept a precarious hold on their dwindling lands by joining the colonials against the hostile Cherokees.

Most Native groups, however, had no affection for the colonists. As 50,000 white settlers moved west of the Appalachians by 1774, the Ohio nations, such as the Shawnees and Delawares, and the Cherokees, Creeks, and Chickasaws of the south, fought to protect their lands from the colonial invaders. "The Rebels," a Seneca chief advised the Huron, "notwithstanding their fair speeches, wish for nothing more, than to. . . possess our lands, . . . which we are convinced is the cause of the present war between the king and his disobedient children." As a result, the British won many Native American allies and used their bases in Canada and Florida to provide ceremonial gifts, food, and ammunition. Even when a particular nation, such as the Iroquois Mohawks, preferred neutrality, colonial invasion of their lands propelled them to side with the British. The Great Spirit, one Cherokee told the Americans in 1777, "has given you many advantages, but he has not created us to be your slaves. We are a separate people!"

Colonial military tactics intensified problems within Native American communities. When Cherokee militants resisted colonial expansion by attacking border settlements, the militia retaliated violently, indiscriminately killing warriors and non-combatants, destroying Cherokee villages, and burning the growing crops. Americans waged similar wars of attrition against Iroquois and Shawnee villages, reporting the destruction of immense quantities of food. One campaign in Iroquois country in 1779 burned forty towns and 160,000 bushels of corn. The plundering of cornfields, timed late in the season to prevent replanting, brought widespread famine, suffering, and dispossession. It also upset the spiritual balance of groups like the Cherokees, Creeks, and Shawnees, who traced their origins to the corn goddess. Such attacks on Native life, while tactically successful, kept most Native American groups allied with the British and a continuing threat to the border settlers.

The alliance between the British and the Ohio peoples nevertheless failed to achieve a military victory in the west. In 1779, a colonial force under George Rogers Clark seized British supplies at Vincennes and prevented an attack by pro-British Shawnees. Americans then destroyed Shawnee villages and claimed title to the lands north of the Ohio River. Three years later, an American militia group gathered 96 Native American inhabitants from Moravian Christian villages at Gnadenhutten and slaughtered them all. Horrified survivors vowed that "no word of God should again be heard in the Indian land." Despite such bitterness, military victories strengthened American claims to Native lands, and the influx of American settlers continued.

The War for America

As the rebellious colonists prepared for a British military invasion, England faced problems of its own. King George may have had the best-trained soldiers in the world, but his military strategists used them poorly to suppress the rebellion in America. Since the British believed that most Americans were loyal to the empire, they ordered the redcoats into inhabited areas, expecting to be welcomed with open arms and civilian support. Instead, their very presence angered colonials and provoked rebel resistance.

Washington's Continental Army faced different problems. The colonial tradition of training adult men for militia duty provided adequate numbers of soldiers, but only for local defense. Throughout the war, the militias remained under state control, evidence that a national identity had not yet developed. To encourage recruitment of a national army, Congress offered bounties and promises of land after the war, but Washington never had enough reliable troops, and never more than 30,000 at one time. Still, the soldiers in the Continental Army repeatedly demonstrated courage and conviction, and as long as they fought somewhere the British could never claim victory.

The Early Battles

The ink on the Declaration of Independence was barely dry when Washington led the poorly trained 10,000-man Continental Army into battle against a superior force of redcoats on New York's Long Island in August 1776. Only the ineptness of British General William Howe permitted the defeated but resourceful American army to escape at night by evacuating to Manhattan. Stunned by this early failure, Washington explained to Congress that he was fighting a "defensive" war, retreating to buy time and trading territory to preserve the army. Howe pursued Washington north of New York City, forcing skirmishes at Harlem Heights and White Plains, but permitting an American retreat through New Jersey in the late autumn.

As the British went into winter quarters, Washington led a surprise attack against the king's Hes-

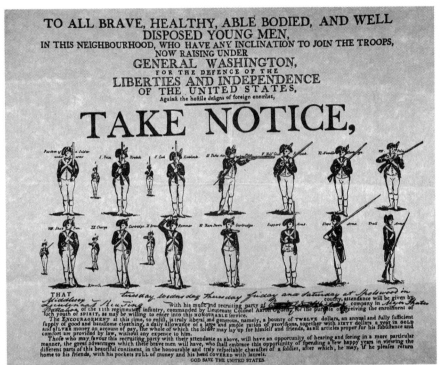

This recruiting poster summoned colonial troops to defend their liberty and independence "against the hostile designs of foreign enemies," which is how American leaders now viewed the mother country.

sian mercenaries at Trenton, New Jersey, by crossing the icy Delaware River on Christmas Day. He followed that triumph with a victory at Princeton three days after the new year. During the British occupation of New Jersey, the redcoats plundered civilians and raped young girls, politicizing the local population and gaining support for the rebel side. Washington's success boosted American morale and stimulated vigilance against the Loyalists. Thousands were sent into exile and others converted to the cause of independence.

In the spring of 1777, the British launched their next offensive in New York with an elaborate plan to split the colonies. Under the command of General John Burgoyne, a British force would march south from Quebec toward Albany, expecting to converge there with a smaller army of redcoats

and Mohawks led by General Barry St. Leger coming from Montreal and Lake Ontario. Meanwhile, General Howe would bring his army north from New York City. The combined British forces would end the rebels' military resistance, restore the Loyalists to power, and effectively separate New England from the other states. British maps, however, showed little knowledge of the local terrain. Even skillful military leaders would have had difficulty penetrating the area's dense forests that were inhabited by a hostile population—and the British generals were neither skillful nor resolute.

Rather than following the plan to bring his redcoats up the Hudson River toward Albany, General Howe decided to seize Philadelphia, home of the Continental Congress. Although the political leadership fled to safety, the city's boardinghouse keepers, many of them women, had to exchange patriot tenants for unwanted British officers. Such inconveniences appeared wherever the rival armies passed. Depending on the course of war, Loyalist or patriot families fled as refugees, carrying children and furnishings to safety. As Burgoyne's army marched through New York in 1777, one woman, whose companions "scattered like a flock of frightened birds," wandered alone through the forest for days and lost her baby daughter. "Alas! the wilderness is within," she grieved. For Philadelphia's African slaves, the British occupation provided an opportunity for immediate freedom, and many left their masters. "The defection of the Negroes," observed a Pennsylvanian, using the language of the Declaration, "showed what little dependence ought to be placed on persons deprived of their natural liberty."

While Howe's army settled into Philadelphia, Burgoyne captured New York's Fort Ticonderoga and proceeded toward his rendezvous with St. Leger near Albany. But patriot fighters felled trees to impede his progress and shot from ambush at his troops. Meanwhile, as St. Leger's army passed through Iroquois country, Native leaders argued bitterly about whether to join the British. As the League of Six Nations veered toward its own civil war, the sacred council fire that had symbolized Iroquois unity for centuries was ritually extinguished. Although older chiefs pleaded for neutrality, younger warriors accepted the British invitation "to come and see them whip the rebels." In the end, when American troops met St. Leger's army at Oriskany, New York, during the summer of 1777, the Iroquois were drawn into battle, where they shared a bloody defeat. Consequently, Burgoyne was left stranded near Saratoga. The Iroquois were left with a bloody civil war as the pro-British Senecas took revenge on the neutral Oneidas and the Oneidas retaliated against the Mohawks. Ignoring such tribal distinctions, New Yorkers raised arms against all Iroquois, attacking villages and crops for the remainder of the war. With the peace, even the Oneidas, who fought as patriot allies, found they had lost their lands in New York.

The War Becomes International

When Burgoyne finally surrendered at Saratoga in October 1777, the direction of the war changed dramatically. By defeating the British army, Americans had proven their ability to wage war and their determination to remain independent. The king of France, still bitter about the loss of French colonies in North America in 1763, now resolved to support the United States against his old British enemies. Indeed, the French had secretly been sending aid to America and had allowed the former colonists to launch warships to attack British commerce. After Saratoga, the American ambassador to France, Benjamin Franklin, persuaded Louis XVI to grant formal recognition to the new nation. The gesture prompted the British government to rethink the war. Fearing the expansion of French power, England's prime minister, Lord North, offered to meet all American demands, except that for independence. But Parliament moved slowly, and British ambassadors for peace did not reach Philadelphia until the summer of 1778. By then, France had signed a commercial treaty granting trade advantages to American merchants and had accepted a formal alliance, in which both nations agreed to fight together until Britain conceded the independence of the United States.

The French alliance of 1778 altered the political stakes of war. Besides sending men, money, munitions, and supplies to America, France represented a threat to Britain in Europe, forcing the mother country to maintain a large home army. When France and Spain formed an alliance in 1779, Britain faced another enemy not only in Europe but also on the colonial borderlands. From bases in Louisiana, Spanish troops fought against the British and their Choctaw and Chickasaw allies

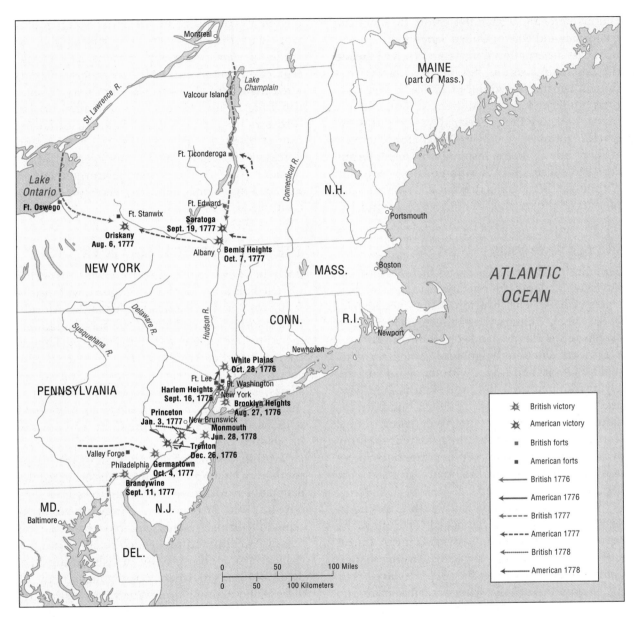

The War in the North, 1776–1778

in West Florida, destroying that colony as a refuge for Loyalist exiles and their slaves. The Spanish also moved against the Chickasaw capital at Natchez, ending pro-British interference with navigation of the Mississippi River. Britain's violation of neutral rights led other European nations to form a League of Armed Neutrality to protect their trade, a step that provoked war between Holland and England.

Dutch merchants extended credit to American companies and bought United States bonds.

These international maneuvers strengthened the American position, but the colonial war continued. During the winter of 1777-78, Washington's undernourished soldiers suffered in the frosts of Valley Forge, Pennsylvania. But when British troops moved from Philadelphia to New York in June 1778, the inspired Continental Army attacked successfully at Monmouth, New Jersey. Although the redcoats occupied New York City, the war in the north came to a virtual standstill.

The War Moves South

Seeking to encourage a rising of Loyalists, the British shifted military operations to the southern states in 1778. The invasion of the riverside city of Savannah, Georgia, brought the war home to slaveowning planters and their human property. Fleeing for safety to neighboring colonies, many planters took their slaves with them; others simply abandoned their holdings. Left behind, several thousand Georgia slaves, about one-third the state's total, fled to freedom, some taking refuge in remote areas, others trailing the redcoat army as noncombatant laborers. When American forces attacked the British armies, many Africans were captured and re-enslaved.

The British then invaded South Carolina in 1780. As the king's army attacked Charleston, the major port city, British General Henry Clinton stiffened Carolina's resistance by warning that all captured blacks would be sold as slaves, but promising that those who deserted from the rebels would be granted freedom. The policy outraged a plantation aristocracy already nervous about potential slave revolts. Thousands of Africans now escaped for freedom, some to serve with the redcoat army, others to seek refuge on abandoned plantations. After the British captured Charleston, the redcoats cynically returned those fugitives owned by Loyalists. Other fugitive slaves found work with the British army as artisans, nurses, guides, porters, or personal servants. Kept in segregated encampments, African Americans suffered high rates of disease and mortality. Despite these hardships, Africans accompanied British forces as the redcoats destroyed patriot farms, fought pitched battles against the militia, and defeated the Americans at Camden, South Carolina, in 1780. By the end of the year, the British marched into North Carolina, where the fighting continued.

THE WORLD TURNED UPSIDE DOWN

Early in 1781, British General Lord Cornwallis marched his army north into Virginia, with nearly 5,000 former slaves following his ranks. Already British forces had raided Chesapeake plantations, including one violent operation led by the famous traitor, Benedict Arnold. As the redcoats confiscated supplies, destroyed property, and seized slaves, Governor Thomas Jefferson, fearing that the British would instigate a slave revolt, pleaded with Washington to bring the Continental Army into battle.

Washington moved quickly, rushing the troops south from New York. As Cornwallis occupied the peninsula at Yorktown, expecting to receive support from the British navy, a French fleet intercepted the British rescuers and blocked an escape by sea. Washington proceeded to surround the redcoat army. The starving British soldiers ordered all blacks to depart, causing many to die of disease and malnutrition. When Cornwallis surrendered on October 19, 1781, patriotic Americans danced to the tune "The World Turned Upside Down."

The exhausted British empire, beaten by rebel forces, overwhelmed by war debts, confronted by France and Spain, now accepted the inevitability of United States independence. Negotiations among

The War in the South, 1778–1781

the British, the French, and three American agents (Benjamin Franklin, John Jay, and John Adams) opened in Paris in 1782, with various international claims complicating the question of territorial boundaries in America. The Treaty of Paris, formally signed in September 1783, reflected the facts of the American military victory. King George recognized the independence of the United States and agreed to remove British troops from his former colonies and territories.

The peace treaty established national boundaries: north to the Great Lakes, west to the Mississippi

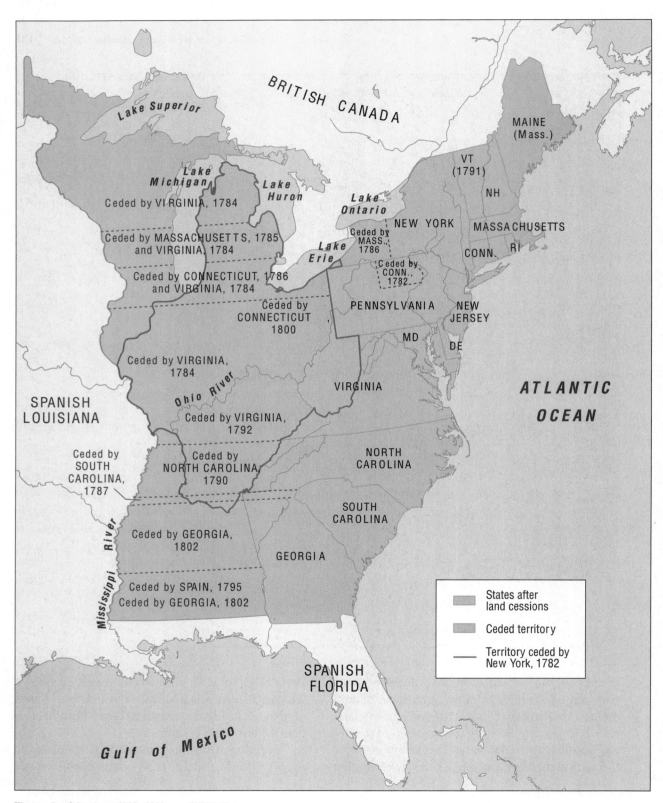

BRITISH CANADA

Lake Superior

Lake Michigan

Lake Huron

MAINE (Mass.)

VT (1791)

NH

Lake Ontario

Ceded by MASS. 1786

NEW YORK

MASSACHUSETTS

CONN. RI

Ceded by CONN., 1782

Ceded by VIRGINIA, 1784

Ceded by MASSACHUSETTS, 1785 and VIRGINIA, 1784

Lake Erie

Ceded by CONNECTICUT, 1786 and VIRGINIA, 1784

Ceded by CONNECTICUT 1800

PENNSYLVANIA

NEW JERSEY

MD

DE

Ceded by VIRGINIA, 1784

Ohio River

VIRGINIA

SPANISH LOUISIANA

Ceded by VIRGINIA, 1792

ATLANTIC OCEAN

Ceded by SOUTH CAROLINA, 1787

Ceded by NORTH CAROLINA 1790

NORTH CAROLINA

Mississippi River

Ceded by GEORGIA, 1802

SOUTH CAROLINA

GEORGIA

Ceded by SPAIN, 1795

Ceded by GEORGIA, 1802

States after land cessions

Ceded territory

Territory ceded by New York, 1782

SPANISH FLORIDA

Gulf of Mexico

Western Land Cessions, 1782–1802   OVERLAY 1

River, and south to the 31st parallel in Florida (this latter line, a figment of cartography rather than geography, would remain a bone of contention between Spain and the new nation until 1795). The peace also protected New England's historic fishing interests in Canadian waters; assured both countries rights of navigation on the Mississippi River; and guaranteed payment of pre-war debts and compensation for property confiscated during the war. Significantly, the treaty omitted any reference to Native American sovereignty or their claims to western lands. Shocked by Britain's betrayal of these allies, a northern chief condemned "this act of cruelty and injustice that Christians *only* were capable of doing." Although Britain proved slow to remove military posts from the Ohio valley, the Native peoples were left alone to confront an invading population of farmers and merchants.

Governing a Free People

Although winning independence had taken seven long years of warfare, American leaders had not waited to begin the great experiment in republican government. The creation of a new political system involved two overlapping realms of power. The first, and most important in the early phases of the war, led to the formation of republican governments in the states. Based on newly written constitutions in each state, these governments embodied the idea that political power ultimately rested on the consent of the governed. The second aspect of government making involved the creation of a national union to coordinate and, in some cases, oversee government activities in the separate states. In 1777, Congress had approved a written constitution of national union, the Articles of Confederation; but this charter was not ratified by the states until 1781, less than a year before the British finally surrendered. Through most of the war period, therefore, the second Continental Congress, first chosen to represent the people in 1775, had regulated the national government. The absence of a formal central government reflected the limited development of a national identity; most Americans still identified more closely with their states and regions than with a national political system.

Republicanism in the States

The delegates who represented the separate states in Congress were the first Americans obliged to deal with national problems. They learned the art of government as the fortunes of war demanded, using standing committees and ad hoc groups to handle administration and propose policy. To supply Washington's armies, Congress asked the states for requisitions of supplies and money, borrowed $15 million by selling bonds at home and overseas, issued paper money, and sent ambassadors to treat with European and Native American nations. Such functions required national coordination, but the heritage of colonial politics had made political leaders suspicious of a strong central government. Most Americans believed that power belonged close to home, in the state governments. Two months before adopting the Declaration, Congress had instructed the states to create new governments based on republican principles. With two exceptions, each newly independent state proceeded to draft a constitution providing for a popularly elected government that attempted to balance the necessities of political power with the rights of a free people.

Republican politics thus began, not in Congress but in the states. Having resisted the power of monarchy and royal governors, political leaders took care to weaken the executive branches of the new state governments. Pennsylvania's constitution even eliminated the office of governor, creating an elective executive council. Most states only limited the governors' judicial and legislative functions and weakened the executives' powers of appointment. Demonstrating optimism about popular politics, the states gave greatest power to the elected legislative branch, including the right to oversee foreign relations, to make executive and judicial appointments, and to regulate financial affairs.

The preeminence of the state legislatures encouraged other cautions. While many Americans believed that republican government would guarantee liberty, others worried that such popular governments might endanger the rights of property. Thus although Pennsylvania approved a single legislative house, all other states created a bicameral (two-chamber) system in which the assemblies represented "the people," while an upper house or senate served as an aristocracy of talent to check the power of the masses. Some state constitutions established different property requirements for members of each house in an attempt to formalize a division of social classes; in fact, the social composition of the two houses usually reflected similar affluence. Still, the membership of the legislatures did reflect a loosening of the old colonial system. Compared to the colonial assemblies, the state legislatures attracted men of lesser wealth, including those who had first participated in politics during the colonial protests.

To ensure a representative government, most states increased the frequency of elections and enlarged the size of the lower house to make government more responsive to constituents. Recognizing the importance of an informed public, the governments encouraged newspapers to publish their proceedings. As a further check on legislative power, each state constitution included a bill of rights that defined the civil liberties of citizens. Among the political innovations of the era were provisions to protect religious minorities. Many states still gave benefits to particular churches, and Massachusetts and Connecticut used public funds to support the Congregational churches

into the 19th century. But new measures, such as Virginia's 1786 statute of religious freedom, in the words of James Madison, "extinguished forever the ambitious hope of making laws for the human mind."

Property, Patriarchy, and Republican Women

Although the state republican governments derived their power from "the people," the new constitutions upheld the traditional concept of citizenship by limiting political participation to those who owned property. Moreover, the states often established even higher property ownership qualifications for those who sought public office. Such principles reflected the belief that voters had to remain completely independent in exercising political choices. By contrast, those who were dependent on others (the poor, children, servants, slaves, women) would not be able to make free choices. Even property-holding women were excluded from the suffrage on gender grounds—except in New Jersey, where the state constitution neglected to specify the gender of "free inhabitants." Because of this apparent oversight, some New Jersey women voted in local elections until an 1807 law explicitly disenfranchised both women and African Americans. Few Americans doubted that power belonged in the hands of propertied white male adults.

The commitment to property qualifications ironically stimulated other political reforms. Except in New England, colonial law had perpetuated two feudal types of land ownership: one, *primogeniture,* required that all inherited property pass to the first-born son; the second, *entail,* limited the division of estates among heirs. Such practices had effectively excluded widows and daughters from inheriting property, even though some colonial fathers made special provisions for younger sons. (New England's inheritance laws, by contrast, had customarily allowed widows one-third of a spouse's property.) Nearly all of the new state constitutions eliminated these feudal relics, making it easier for younger sons, daughters, and widows to acquire inherited property. Although women remained legally dependent on their husbands and fathers, changes in state property laws expanded their rights to control separate holdings, to enter contracts in the absence of husbands, and (in New England and Pennsylvania) to seek divorces. Most states still required private legislation for a couple to end a marriage or to live apart, and gave custody of children to the father.

By separating husbands from wives, the war encouraged women to exercise greater control over their households. "I hope you will not consider yourself as commander in chief of your own house," one wife wrote to her military spouse, "but be convinced. . . that there is such a thing as equal command." Although fathers still claimed a right to choose their daughters' husbands, women increasingly demanded more choice. Some evaded patriarchal authority by becoming pregnant and then marrying the man of their choice: during the late 18th century, a rising proportion of northern women delivered "seven-month" babies. A declining birthrate beginning near the end of the century suggests that married couples were deliberately practicing birth control, sometimes with syringes advertised in newspapers. With fewer children per household, parents could devote more attention to each child, a duty of growing importance for women in republican America.

As republican writers continued to emphasize women's domestic responsibilities, the burdens of family assumed a new political role. "Virtue alone," declared Pennsylvania's Benjamin Rush in 1778, ". . . is the basis of a republic." But if only a virtuous citizenry could be entrusted with liberty, republican leaders needed assurances that future generations would be worthy of their legacy. Republican mothers, viewed as the primary bearers

> "I hope you will not consider yourself as commander in chief of your own house," one wife wrote to her military spouse.

of moral lessons, appeared as the conveyors of republican morality.

Popular literature aimed at female readers advised mothers to assume responsibility for raising virtuous citizens. "The women, in every free country, have an absolute control of manners," declared a Fourth of July orator in 1790, "and . . . in a republic, manners are of equal importance with laws." Such ideas promoted an interest in women's education that, while preserving traditional female domestic roles, would contribute to a sound political system. Women's advancement as a group thus represented no threat to the patriarchal order. After the war, the expansion of female academies, mainly in the northern states, enabled women's literacy to reach equality with men's. Yet few women directly challenged the assumption that women's proper place was in the home. One exception was Judith Sargent Murray, who published essays, fiction, and poetry asserting women's intellectual equality. "Females," she noted tartly in 1786, "possess talents capable of extending their utility beyond the kitchen or the parlour." But even Murray made little effort to defy conventions within her own affluent Massachusetts family.

Slaves and the Ideal of Liberty

While educated women could find a vital, if subordinate, niche in republican America, the obvious inequality of African American slaves proved more difficult for republicans to excuse. Long before Jefferson spoke of the natural rights of human equality, Pennsylvania Quakers, believing in the inner light of each person's soul, had condemned ownership of human beings. Such humanitarian concerns coincided with a preference among urban merchants and artisans to employ free workers, who could be released during times of economic slowdown. African American participation in colonial protests against England proved their interest in the cause of liberty. As the African-born poet Phyllis Wheatley wrote in 1774: "In every human breast, God hath implanted a principle, which we call love of freedom." But when Congress discussed the status of slaves in 1776, the debate proved too explosive for compromise and the issue was dropped. Yet African Americans were keenly alert to the language of natural rights. "I have not yet enjoyed the benefits of creation," stated a Massachusetts slave women named Belinda in 1782. "I beg freedom."

The spirit of liberty moved some slaveholders, such as the Declaration signer Henry Laurens, to free their slaves; others provided in their wills for emancipation after their death. Such private emancipation increased in the 1780s, and in 1785 Virginia's College of William and Mary gave an honorary degree to antislavery activist Granville Sharp. In the Chesapeake states—Delaware, Maryland, and northern Virginia—declining tobacco production encouraged some planters to lease their slaves as urban workers, where they competed with free white labor. Sometimes the slaves would keep a portion of their wages and used these earnings to purchase their freedom. As rented labor, African American artisans mixed with free blacks and whites and enjoyed considerable freedom in their social activities.

Northern states, with smaller slave populations, also began to terminate slavery. Vermont became the first state to outlaw slavery in the constitution of 1777. In a series of legal cases brought by slaves, Massachusetts's courts ruled that slavery violated the state constitution of 1780. Other northern states, encouraged by local aboli-

tion societies, enacted laws mandating gradual emancipation. Choosing a particular date (often July 4), these laws declared that children born to slaves thereafter would be free, but only after serving their mother's owner for many years (21 for females, 28 for males). The parents of these children remained slaves for life. In 1810, there were 27,000 slaves in the northern "free" states. Gradual emancipation thus protected the property rights of slaveowners and meant that thousands of northern blacks remained slaves into the 1840s. All states prohibited the international slave trade, though some later repealed those laws.

As more African Americans obtained freedom, black communities sprouted around the country. Seeking jobs as mariners, day laborers, cooks, and domestics, African American men and women migrated from rural areas to the growing port cities such as Philadelphia, New York, and Baltimore. These ex-slaves moved quickly to stabilize family life, causing a surge in marriages. Emancipated slaves often marked their transition to freedom by choosing new names, most commonly English names—a sign of both independence and acculturation. "Robert," for example, adopted the surname "Freeman," and "Robin" became "Robin Justice." Others commonly took surnames that indicated their occupations, such as Carter, Mason, and Cook. Few kept slave names like Caesar or Pompey.

In 1787, ex-slaves in Philadelphia, the nation's largest free black community, founded the Free African Society; members of this organization established burial societies to continue traditional funeral rites, formed "African" churches, and supported mutual-aid groups. By 1790, nearly 60,000 African Americans, 8 percent of all blacks in the United States, were living free, and their number increased rapidly during the next two decades. As freed slaves continued to move to the cities for economic and cultural opportunities, however, most remained poor, experienced mortality rates twice as high as for whites, and faced discrimination in employment.

A Limited Revolution

Such changes appeared to contemporaries as "revolutionary." But to call the war for independence the "American Revolution" implies greater social change than actually occurred. Although the introduction of republican state governments encouraged citizens to reassess the relationship between property rights and liberty, most changes in American society appeared slight. While some African Americans achieved freedom, most—even those who followed the British into foreign countries—continued to labor as slaves. Women could claim some legal benefits and enjoy improved status as republican mothers, but full citizenship remained elusive. When republican governments confiscated Loyalist property, the lands were sold, not given freely to tenants or other claimants, and the beneficiaries usually were commercial land speculators who resold the real estate at a profit. Despite some laws that eased voting requirements, the electorate clung to old habits, choosing with few exceptions men of the "better sort" to represent them. Yet republican theories of government had great potential for social change, and that promise would emerge later as the powerful legacy of independence.

Launching the Confederation of States

Because of the preeminence of state governments in the lives of most citizens, few political leaders discussed a national union prior to the Declaration of Independence. But, as Congress led the nation into war with Britain, a committee headed by Pennsylvania's John Dickinson drafted Articles of Confederation to define an interstate or national union. The plan of government that emerged, and

that unified the country from 1781 to 1789, is best known for the powers that it lacked, for its "weakness" in comparison to the government that followed under the Constitution. But for Americans of that time, so recently a part of the British empire, the Confederation expressed their political preferences well. Mindful of the problems of Britain's rule, the Articles made state sovereignty the first defense of political liberty. Yet practical problems of finance, diplomacy, and administration ultimately revealed the Confederacy's inadequacy. Less than four years after the war ended, most political leaders were advocating a new and stronger national government.

The Confederation

For almost all citizens, local and state governments provided all the services they would ever need. Although war and diplomacy required interstate cooperation, these issues were considered exceptional matters. Consequently, the Articles of Confederation stated that Congress could exercise *only* those powers expressly delegated by the states to the national government. These included declarations of war and peace; conduct of foreign relations, including the negotiation of treaties with Native American nations; borrowing money; and the establishment of uniform coinage, weights and measures, and a postal service. Congress could not pass national taxes nor regulate interstate commerce; those powers remained in the states. Within Congress, moreover, each state carried a single vote, and nine states of the thirteen had to approve all laws. The national government had no executive or judicial branch. Instead, congressional committees handled administrative affairs such as diplomacy and finance. This weak central government, with sovereignty derived from the states, reflected the public's fear of power at a distance.

These limitations on national power nearly destroyed the young republic. Congress's paper

money, used to pay bills on the promise of future
redemption, gradually declined in value as citizens lost faith in the republic's ability to fulfill its
obligations. Toward the end of the war, frustrated
army recruits mutinied for back pay, forcing Congress to negotiate discharges, bonuses, and reen-
listments. In 1783, Washington's top officers,
encamped at Newburgh, New York, even suggested a coup d'etat to force the awarding of congressional pensions, but the prestigious general
simply stared them down. On the home front,
shortages of goods and inflation of prices created
conflicts between merchants and consumers that
occasionally flared into mob violence. Contemporaries fretted about lawlessness and the difficulty of reconciling conflicts of interest. "The few
. . . who act upon principles of disinterestedness,"
observed Washington, "are, comparatively speaking, no more than a drop in the ocean." Such
voices wondered whether the frail republic could
survive.

Approval of the Articles of Confederation,
which took four years of wrangling among the
states, revealed the difficulty of reaching political
compromise. The major stumbling block involved
control of the territory west of the Appalachians.
Despite the claims of Native American nations,
colonial charters had granted some states territory that stretched as far west as the Pacific ocean.
Consequently, Maryland, a small state with dubious claims to western lands, worried that the
larger states would obtain greater power in the
republic and refused to approve the Articles unless *all* western land claims were transferred to
the national government. But Virginia refused to
make that concession. The deadlock lasted until
1781, when Cornwallis's invasion of the Chesapeake persuaded Virginia's planters to relinquish
their claims to the west to ensure military assistance from the other states. Only then did Maryland ratify the Articles, launching the new nation
in 1781.

"The peacemakers and our enemies have talked away our lands at a rum drinking."

Diplomatic Disarray

The weakness of the new national government
also undermined efforts to enforce the Treaty of
Paris with England and Spain. Although both
countries formally acknowledged the sovereignty
of the United States, they ignored provisions of
the treaty, and then dared to use their question-
able policies as a basis for altering the treaty's
terms. United States diplomats struggled to protect the nation's interests, but the new country
lacked political respect abroad and the military
power to back up its demands.

During the 1780s, Britain stubbornly refused
to abandon its military and trading posts around
the Great Lakes, a territory now part of the United
States. Such violations benefited from Native
American objections to surrendering their lands
to either of the English-speaking rivals. "The
peacemakers and our enemies," complained a
Cherokee chief, "have talked away our lands at a
rum drinking." Despite protests to England, the
United States could not persuade the British to
leave the region. Britain also refused to provide
the promised compensation to American slaveowners for the slaves confiscated by the redcoats
during the war. To justify its refusal, Britain emphasized that the Americans had failed to com-
pensate the Loyalists for their losses and had
ignored promises to pay pre-war debts to British
merchants. That issue, too, pointed to the weakness of the Confederation, because Congress
lacked the power to force the states to honor
those obligations to Britain. England also forbade
the profitable U.S. trade with the West Indies, a
grievance that led Congress to send ambassador

John Adams to Britain to negotiate a new agreement. The British rudely rebuffed the offer.

On the southern borders, Spain threatened the nation's interests by refusing to permit American commerce on the Mississippi River, blocking Ohio valley farmers from bringing their produce to the port of New Orleans. In 1786, negotiations with U.S. ambassador John Jay complicated the crisis by proposing that Spain could close the Mississippi for 25 years if it opened Caribbean ports to U.S. shipping. The proposal, while beneficial to northern merchants and fishing interests, outraged southern and western farmers, whose prosperity depended on access to New Orleans. Although an angry Congress rejected the treaty, some frustrated Kentucky settlers proposed secession from the Confederation. The protest remained mostly talk, ending when Spain reopened the Mississippi in 1788.

Creating a Western Domain

The problems of western development remained the most pressing issue facing the Confederation Congress. Challenged not only by Spanish and British interests in the region, the new country also confronted the claims of Native American nations and a restless domestic population that wished to migrate west of the Appalachians. Without waiting for congressional approval, squatters and speculators flocked to the area. In western North Carolina and what is now Tennessee, illegal settlers organized a state called "Franklin"; by 1785, 30,000 migrants inhabited Kentucky. Conflicts over land, trespassing, and trade provoked innumerable acts of violence between U.S. citizens and Native Americans. When Native leaders protested the invasion of the Ohio valley, congressional agents replied that their nations had sided with Britain, "had desolated our villages and destroyed our citizens," and had, as a result, become "a subdued people." By right of conquest, the United States claimed the territory that England had ceded in the Treaty of Paris, even though the same territory was still claimed by the Native peoples.

The seizure of 160 million acres of tribal lands north of the Ohio river temporarily satisfied the demand for fertile acreage while providing an easy solution to problems of public finance. Rather than allowing individual settlers to occupy this valuable territory, Congress passed three laws, or ordinances, to promote what one investor called "the systematical mode of settlement." The first measure, proposed by Thomas Jefferson, was the Northwest Ordinance of 1784, which established the republican principle that any states formed from the territory north of the Ohio River would enter the United States as equals of the original thirteen.

Congress then approved the Land Ordinance of 1785, which provided for the sale, not the giveaway, of western lands to obtain revenue to run the government. This measure established a pattern for western development that mixed economic practicality with geographical symmetry. Whatever the particular contours of the land, surveyors would divide the public domain into square six-mile townships. These right-angle grids would then be subdivided into 640-acre (one square mile) sections. One section in each township would be reserved to support a school; four sections would be set aside for the United States; and the remainder would be sold at public auctions at no less than $1 per acre (equivalent to about $10 in today's money). So emerged the grid pattern of U.S. agriculture in the Midwest. But, since few farmers could afford to buy an entire section, wealthy investors reaped profits by purchasing sections and reselling the acreage in smaller parcels.

With western lands for sale, the Confederation extended political rights into the new territories. The revised Northwest Ordinance of 1787 divided the lands of the Shawnee, Mingo, and other Native American nations into no less than three and no more than five "territories." Jefferson's fanciful names for these units (Cherronesus, Assenisipia,

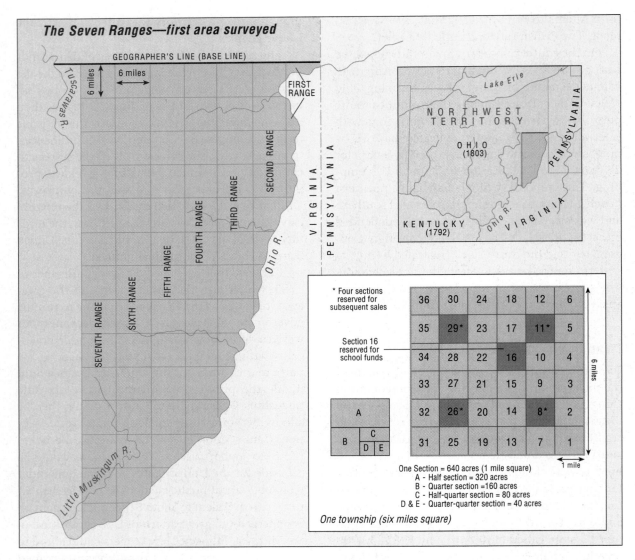

The Land Ordinance of 1785

Polypotamia, among others) eventually translated into Ohio, Indiana, Illinois, Michigan, and Wisconsin. Each territory would pass through three stages of political development. First, Congress would appoint territorial governors and judges; second, after the adult male population reached 5,000, citizens would elect a legislature and send a nonvoting delegate to Congress; and third, when the total population reached 60,000, the territory would achieve statehood by submitting a constitution for congressional approval. In another unprecedented step, the 1787 ordinance prohibited slavery in the

Northwest territories. While unwilling to eliminate slavery in the existing states, political leaders determined to restrict its expansion, hoping the institution would become unprofitable and disappear.

The Crisis of Money and Taxes

The Confederation Congress also confronted a deeper crisis of foreign trade. After the war for independence, new commercial relations with France, the French sugar islands, Holland, and even China expanded the U.S. marketplace. Optimists like Connecticut theologian Ezra Stiles saw the expansion of trade as part of the "great American revolution," in which "navigation will carry the American flag around the globe . . . and illuminate the world with truth and liberty." But the simultaneous loss of trade with Britain caused serious economic problems. To punish the ex-colonies, Britain barred U.S. fish and meat from the West Indies and permitted other imports only in British ships. Although northern shippers frequently violated these rules, the decline of business contributed to unemployment in the port cities. Without the protection of the royal navy, moreover, Mediterranean pirates preyed freely on American shipping.

During the war, the absence of British products had stimulated local manufacturing. On southern plantations from Virginia to Georgia, slave women learned the arts of spinning and weaving, establishing a local self-sufficiency that lasted until mass-produced textiles began to arrive in the early 19th century. Numerous northern farm families also began to manufacture local products (fermenting cider, nailing barrels, dressing animal skins) to supplement agricultural income. Even this resourcefulness could not satisfy consumer demands. As soon as the war ended, British merchants exported large surpluses, accumulated since the boycotts of 1775, into the warehouses of American importers. The merchandise moved quickly, going to retailers in the cities and in rural towns and villages, who found customers among farmers and small artisans. To pay the bills, hard cash flowed rapidly to Britain.

The postwar boom ended abruptly. Without markets in the West Indies, American importers lacked sufficient hard money to pay for additional imports. They called in debts from their rural retailers. But most country merchants had been paid with agricultural goods because few farmers had enough cash to pay all their bills. As debts mounted, business slowed. Pressed by creditors in England, large merchants squeezed the retailers; they, in turn, pushed the indebted farmers. "It's a common saying," one Massachusetts trader told his brother, "business before friends."

The states seemed equally stubborn in rejecting proposed remedies. Efforts by Congress to establish a national tariff (a duty on imported goods) failed when prospering Rhode Island alone blocked the measure in 1781; a second proposal stalled in New York. Instead, the separate states individually enacted tariffs to protect local business; but because these lacked uniformity, trade moved to low tariff areas. Some states responded to the commercial crisis by issuing paper money, which eased the currency shortage. Some states also passed *stay laws*, which prevented the foreclosure of farm mortgages to pay debts, and *tender laws*, which permitted payment in produce rather than hard currency. But paper money caused inflation, angered creditors, and failed to help large merchants involved in international trade. Farmers who were accustomed to bartering their goods with neighbors now felt threatened by more impersonal creditors who were prepared to prosecute debtors in court, seize their farms, or send them to jail.

The problem crystallized in western Massachusetts in 1786, when the state government enacted high land taxes to repay wartime debts and required payment in cash. Facing property seizures

SCENE IN SHAYS'S REBELLION.

A Massachusetts blacksmith served with a writ of attachment for debt during Shays' Rebellion in 1786.

for nonpayment, farmers in Massachusetts rallied behind war veteran Daniel Shays, formed an armed citizens' militia reminiscent of the pre-war crowds, and forced the local courts to halt debt collection. Although Congress tried to muster federal troops against the insurrection, other states refused to legislate taxes to pay for the army. Horrified merchants and political conservatives in Massachusetts privately subsidized the state militia to crush the rebels. After several pitched battles around the New England countryside, many of the Shaysites fled the state; a few were condemned and executed for treason. The return of prosperity in 1787 eventually eased the problem.

Reconsidering the Confederation

The Shays rebellion reflected and helped to stimulate an important shift in attitudes toward state government, all of which culminated in a proposal to restructure the national government. Since independence, political leaders had emphasized the value of decentralized power with supremacy placed in a legislative branch that was responsive to public pressure. The framers of the Confederation had deliberately created a weak central government—so much so that delegates frequently resigned their seats in order to return to their home states, where politics seemed more important. To be sure, a few leaders—Robert Morris, the superintendent of finance; Alexander Hamilton, an aide to General Washington; and Virginia delegate James Madison—had long advocated a strong national government. But when peace came in 1783, even these three departed from Congress and returned to private life. Through the 1780s, therefore, Americans measured their satisfaction with government based on what happened on the state and local level. Shays' rebellion, along with outbreaks of rural violence in other states, raised an old but alarming question: Were republican governments stable enough to survive?

Fears about the future of the republican experiment impelled a group of nationalist-minded leaders to consider a revision of the Articles of Confederation. Although still overwhelmingly a nation of farmers, the United States had already entered the commercial age. More citizens—merchants, artisans, export farmers—had developed interstate interests that could not be regulated by a single state legislature. Even Daniel Shays and his neighbors in rural Massachusetts were affected by international credit. In the border states of Georgia, western Carolina, and Pennsylvania, settlers looked to a central government to protect their holdings from attacks by Native American warriors. And political conservatives everywhere worried that the state governments had become overly responsive to popular opinion.

Such people responded to the call to revise the Articles. The movement began when representatives from Virginia and Maryland met in 1785 to discuss navigational improvements on the Potomac River and proposed a conference of all states to consider problems of interstate commerce. Only five states sent delegates to the gathering at Annapolis in 1786, an embarrassment that precluded any political action. Hamilton suggested that another conference be held the next year "to render the constitution of the federal government adequate to the exigencies of the union." In May 1787, after Congress endorsed the meeting, 55 delegates from every state except Rhode Island began their journeys to Philadelphia. The ensuing constitutional convention would stabilize a generation of revolutionary politics.

INFOTRAC® COLLEGE EDITION EXERCISES

 For additional reading go to InfoTrac College Edition, your online research library at *http://web1.infotrac-college.com*.

Keyword search: William Howe
Subject search: Battle of Trenton
Keyword search: American Revolution
Subject search: American Revolution, Loyalists
Keyword search: Yorktown
Subject search: Articles of Confederation, Reference
Keyword search: Shays' Rebellion [R]

ADDITIONAL READING

The War for America

Charles Royster, *A Revolutionary People at War* (1979). This innovative study of the military aspects of war stresses the political significance of the Continental army.

African Americans Choose Liberty

Sylvia R. Frey, *Water from the Rock: Black Resistance in a Revolutionary Age* (1991). Beginning with the effects of the British invasion on slavery, this study describes the evolution of black communities into the next century.

Native Americans Choose Sides

Colin G. Calloway, *The American Revolution in Indian Country: Crisis and Diversity in Native American Communities* (1995). A survey of the Native American response to the war for independence, emphasizing the variety of situations and the calamitous effects on Native peoples.

Property, Patriarchy, and Republican Women

Mary Beth Norton, *Liberty's Daughters: The Revolutionary Experience of American Women, 1750–1800* (1980). The first half of this pioneering book examines the private world of 18th-century women; the second half looks at their involvement in political issues.

Slaves and the Ideal of Liberty

Gary B. Nash, *Forging Freedom: The Formation of Philadelphia's Black Community, 1720–1840* (1988). Tracing the emergence of the nation's largest free community of African Americans, this book explores the impact of independence on black life.

Launching the Confederation of States

Jack N. Rakove, *The Beginnings of National Politics: An Interpretive History of the Continental Congress* (1979). Examines the political ideas of congressional delegates and how they shaped policy during the confederation.

Gordon S. Wood, *The Creation of the American Republic, 1776–1787* (1969). A thorough analysis of the drafting and ratification of state constitutions, focusing on changing attitudes toward republican governments.

The Crisis of Money and Taxes

David Szatmary, *Shays' Rebellion: The Making of an Agrarian Insurrection* (1980). Examining the clash between rural values and commercial interests, this study places the uprising in the context of changing political values.

THE
AMERICAN MUSEUM,
OR UNIVERSAL MAGAZINE,

For MAY, 1791.

CONTENTS.

ORIGINAL ARTICLES.

PROSE.

Building a Republican Government, 1787–1800

CHRONOLOGY

1787	Philadelphia convention drafts U.S. Constitution
1787–1788	Eleven states ratify Constitution
1789	George Washington inaugurated first president
	French Revolution overthrows monarchy
1790	Alexander Hamilton presents *Report on the Public Credit*
1790–1791	Native Americans defeat U.S. armies in Ohio
1791	States ratify first ten constitutional amendments (Bill of Rights)
1793	England and France go to war
	Washington issues Neutrality Proclamation
1794	Federal troops suppress Whiskey Rebellion
	U.S. troops win Battle of Fallen Timbers
	John Jay negotiates treaty with England
	Yellow fever epidemic rages in Philadelphia
1795	Treaty of Greenville ends warfare in Northwest territory
	Thomas Pinckney signs treaty with Spain
1796	John Adams elected president
1798	XYZ affair arouses public opinion
	Congress passes Alien and Sedition laws
1798–1799	Republicans offer Virginia and Kentucky resolutions
1800	Gabriel plans slave insurrection in Richmond, Virginia
	Thomas Jefferson elected president

His frilled neckpiece, wavy powdered wig, and serious expression placed him in the generation of the Founding Fathers, but Noah Webster's nationalism was more cultural than political. He grew from average colonial roots in a West Hartford, Connecticut, family engaged in farming and weaving. Despite financial shortages, Webster managed to attend Yale College (class of 1778), where he imbibed the patriotism of the war for independence and developed an intellectual passion for the new American nation.

As a young Connecticut school teacher, Webster became frustrated with the English books he had to use for his pupils, and in 1783 published his own textbook: *A Grammatical Institute of the English Language*, popularly known as "The Blue-Backed Speller." For 100 years it would teach children, including Ben Franklin's granddaughter, to read, spell, and pronounce words with a distinctive American syntax. Between its blue covers, Webster took up his lifelong mission of creating a unique "national language" with an American vocabulary and spellings. In the speller, as well as in his famous *American Dictionary of the English Language*

http://history.wadsworth.com

(1828), he used spellings like *color* instead of the English "colour," and *music* rather than "musick." He also added such uniquely American words as *skunk, squash, chowder,* and *hickory.*

"We ought not to consider ourselves as inhabitants of a particular state only, but as *Americans,* as the common subjects of a great empire," Webster urged. His ideas anticipated a time when the "United States" would be a singular noun—a country rather than a union of separate states. As Webster was developing his ideas about cultural nationalism, the Constitutional Convention of 1787 became a forum for discussing issues of political nationalism. The delegates who converged in Philadelphia to "form a more perfect union" struggled mightily to surmount traditions of local government and to replace state power with a stronger national government.

In the 1780s, a sense of American nationalism remained an aspiration for the future. Most citizens still identified with state politics, and many political leaders doubted that a republican government, elected by "the people," could survive in such a widely dispersed country. The lines of national communication remained rudimentary. In 1790, there were just seventy-five post offices in the country, and fewer than 2,000 miles of roads. It took four days for news to travel from the nation's first capital in New York City to James Madison and Thomas Jefferson in Virginia.

The political leaders who traveled to Philadelphia in 1787 thus had to bridge wide local and regional differences about social, political, and cultural values. Not least of these, perhaps, was the matter of punctuality. Benjamin Franklin, the oldest delegate to attend the constitutional convention, had made a virtue of keeping regular hours (see Chapter 4). Yet the convention opened eleven days late, for want of a quorum. Most delegates obviously were not in a rush to change the Articles of Confederation. "These delays greatly impede public measures," complained George Washington, "and serve to sour the temper of the punctual members, who do not like to idle away their time." The delay had its productive side, however, as James Madison drafted detailed proposals for the tardy delegates.

The many differences among the delegates provoked important philosophical debates about the essence of a republican government. The Articles of Confederation had created a "federal" union in which the national government depended on the approval of the separate state legislatures. Amendments required unanimous consent of the states. Politicians who opposed any changes in the Articles,

The convention opened eleven days late, for want of a quorum.

such as Virginia's fiery orator Patrick Henry, simply refused to attend the convention. By contrast, the political leaders who did attend the convention had a more national view of politics. Understanding *interstate* issues, they accepted the importance of giving greater power to the central government.

These delegates, who later achieved immortality as the Founding Fathers, were relatively young, averaging 42 years of age. Most had matured during the war against England rather than in the colonial period, and they understood the value of interstate cooperation. But, as products of their time, they accepted the existing basis for choosing political leaders. They expressed no interest in changing the political system within the separate states.

Among the most sensitive of the differences among the delegates would be the status of slavery. Many northern states had begun to abolish involuntary servitude, but southern states saw their prosperity linked to slave-based agriculture. Nor did northern delegates, who represented the merchant class involved in the Atlantic trade, share the concerns of southern delegates about protecting free navigation of the Mississippi River. Local interests also influenced the delegates' positions about strengthening the national government. The Georgia delegates represented white farmers interested in seizing Creek and Cherokee land and wanted a strong government to provide military support on their western borders. Delegates from states without western lands, such as New Jersey and Delaware, worried that a strong national government might submerge the interests of less populous states.

Although the first national leaders adopted the motto *e pluribus unum* ("from many, one"), most realized the danger of political disintegration. Washington, the most prestigious national figure, worried that western migration would weaken the country to the advantage of European nations with claims in the western territories. "No well informed mind need be told, that the flanks and rear of the United territory are possessed by other powers," he wrote in 1784, "and how entirely unconnected should we be . . . if the Spaniards on their right, or Great Britain on their left . . . should invite their trade and seek alliances with them." Washington's point of view ("Spaniards on their right" [Florida]; "Great Britain on their left [Canada]") shows that the man chosen to preside at the constitutional convention was facing east, looking across the Atlantic, and for good reason. During the next decade, Europe would profoundly affect the domestic politics and stability of the American republic. The danger of foreign influence would stimulate the formation of political parties in the 1790s and would ultimately strengthen a sense of national identity.

Designing a National Union

"Every man thinks himself at least as good as his neighbors," observed a New Englander in 1791, "and believes that all mankind have, or ought to possess equal rights." Two decades of political discussion had created a consensus about republican government: "the people" were the true source of political authority, and government depended on the consent of the citizens. To preserve those principles, two additional beliefs had emerged: first, citizens had to be protected from the arbitrary power of their elected leaders, and second, the people's representatives had to be protected from the whims of changing majorities. Political power, which might threaten minorities or even the government itself, had to be divided and balanced to

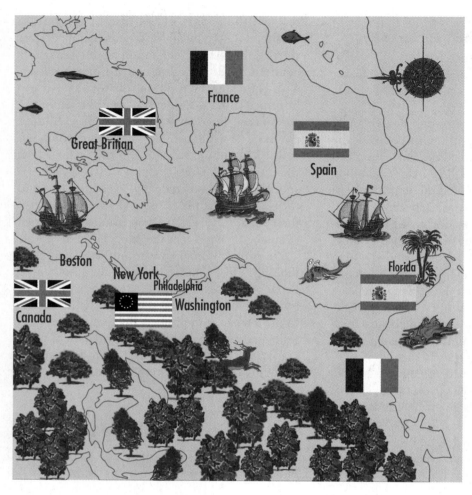

George Washington's View of the United States, 1784

prevent one interest group from achieving dominance over the political structure. Although the constitutional convention decided not to reform the Articles of Confederation, but to create a new political system, the delegates agreed to preserve state governments, dividing the power to govern between the states and the central government. (Even at the convention, delegates voted as state blocs, one vote per state, and not as individuals.) Within the national government, moreover, power would be divided and balanced among separate branches, each with distinct but overlapping re-

sponsibilities so that no one office could claim complete power.

Representation and Compromise

The drafters of the Constitution shared many ideas about republican government, but because they represented states with different interests, they soon split into two competing groups, disagreeing about the form such a government should take. The debate began when Virginia's James Madison, probably the most ardent supporter of a strong central government, introduced a plan of government known as the "Virginia Plan." Madison's proposal gave primary power to a two-house national legislature, in which members of the lower house would be chosen on the basis of each state's population, and the lower house would elect the members of the upper house or senate. Voting within the legislature would be by individuals rather than state delegations. Madison's plan gave the legislature unlimited powers to make laws, pass taxes, and veto state legislation. The legislature would also elect officials of separate judicial and executive branches.

The Virginia Plan aroused objections from the smaller states, which opposed representation based on population. These delegates preferred a plan of government proposed by William Paterson of New Jersey. The "New Jersey Plan" was closer to the Articles of Confederation, proposing a single-house legislature in which each state had an equal vote and provided for separately chosen judicial and executive branches.

Since both plans proposed to strengthen the legislative powers of the national Congress, disagreement focused on the question of representation within the legislature. The protracted debates ended with the "Great Compromise," proposed by the Connecticut delegation. This version provided for the election of a lower house of representatives based on population and the creation of an upper house or senate in which each state government (not the voters) chose two delegates who would vote as individuals. The lower house would thus represent "the people"; the senate would represent the states. The election of senators by the state legislatures would also protect the states from national power. Although both houses would have to approve all laws, a third provision required finance measures, including taxation, to originate in the lower house to protect citizens from taxation without representation.

The problem of representation introduced another dilemma: Who would count as citizens?

Southern states with substantial slave populations wanted to count slaves as persons for purposes of apportioning representation; they were not eager to count slaves as persons to apportion taxes. But delegates from states with few or no slaves protested the idea of giving representation to slaves who lacked any civil rights. If slaves were "not represented in the States to which they belong," asked New Jersey's Paterson, "why should they be represented in the General Government?" Another delegate from Philadelphia warned that his constituents "would revolt at the idea of being put on [an equal] footing with slaves."

Northern criticism of giving representation to slaves (who would have no political voice in choosing those representatives) provoked some southern delegates to threaten rejection of the whole Constitution. To remove that threat, the convention struck another bargain, called the "Three-Fifths Compromise": for purposes of determining representation and taxation, five slaves would count as three persons. To further protect investments in slave property, the delegates barred any state from blocking the return of a runaway slave to another state. The convention also refused to permit the national government to interfere with the importation of slaves prior to 1808, at which time Congress might enact prohibitions. In embodying this compromise in what became the nation's highest law, the Constitution allowed slavery to persist in the states as a "domestic" institution not subject to national law. The debate about slavery also showed that the delegates disagreed about which residents of the United States were entitled to be treated as citizens of the republic.

Devising Checks and Balances

By September 1787, after a hot, muggy summer of debate, the Philadelphia convention had drafted the Constitution of the United States. This document shifted power from the state governments to a national government consisting of a bicameral (two-chamber) Congress, an executive branch, and an independent judicial system. Under the Constitution, Congress had power to enact taxes (for example, on imported goods), borrow money, regulate interstate commerce and trade with foreign and Native American nations, coin money, establish uniform weights and measures, maintain military forces, declare war, and pass "all laws which shall be necessary and proper" to fulfill the responsibilities of the national government.

These extensive powers called for additional checks and balances to prevent one branch of government from becoming too powerful. To keep political oversight close to the people, the states would establish the qualifications for voting for delegates to the House of Representatives who would serve two-year terms. To ensure stability of government, senators would be chosen by the state legislatures and serve six-year terms. The Senate would approve appointments made by the president and would have the power to ratify treaties by a two-thirds vote. Such treaties, together with the Constitution, would stand as the supreme law of the land.

Accompanying the balance of power between the two houses of Congress, the Constitution established an independent executive branch led by a president. To keep this chief executive officer independent of those who chose him, the Constitution created an "electoral college," consisting of electors chosen by popular ballot and equal in number to each state's congressional representation. Every four years, each state's electors would meet, cast ballots for president and vice president, and then disband forever. In this way, the drafters of the Constitution expected to prevent a permanent alliance of politicians who could influence presidential decisions. Like most 18th-century thinkers, the founders feared the formation of political parties, or factions, which were considered inherently divisive and contrary to the ideal of public harmony. They believed

that a good ruler should reject all factions and seek the welfare of the whole. Thus, the president would be independent of both the Congress and the mass of citizens. The notion of lasting interstate political parties, which emerged later, had no place in the Constitution.

The Constitution gave the president the power to execute all laws, to negotiate and sign treaties with foreign nations, to act as commander-in-chief of the armed forces, to appoint judges and executive officers (subject to ratification by the Senate), and to approve or reject laws passed by Congress (presidential vetoes could be overridden by two-thirds vote of both houses of Congress). This strong executive diverged from the fear of monarchy that had influenced both the state constitutions and the Articles of Confederation. Now, after Shays' rebellion of 1786, the constitutional convention had more reason to fear the disruptive effects of popular unrest. The delegates also expected the first president to be George Washington, whose commitment to a republican government was beyond doubt.

The Constitution also established an independent judicial branch (distinct from the existing court systems in the states), which today is called the "federal judiciary." Giving Congress power to create a supreme court and lower courts, the document granted federal judges lifetime appointments (assuming only their good behavior in office; otherwise they might be impeached by Congress). These judges were thereby freed from executive or legislative interference. Reinforcing the ideas of federalism—that is, the division of power between state and national government—the Constitution preserved the judicial systems of the separate states but granted jurisdiction to the federal courts to resolve constitutional issues, interpret congressional laws and foreign treaties, and decide cases involving the separate states or citizens of more than one state. The Constitution made no provision for judicial review of the law (the power of judges to declare laws null and void for being "unconstitutional"), but federal judges subsequently assumed that power in interpreting the supreme law.

The Amendment Process

Anticipating the need to revise the basic system of laws, the Constitution provided for a process of amendment. Unlike the Articles of Confederation, constitutional changes did not require a unanimous vote, but they still had to gain substantial approval. Amendments could first be proposed, either in Congress by a two-thirds vote of both houses, or in conventions whose delegates were elected by the citizens of two-thirds of the states. Proposed amendments then had to be ratified by three-quarters of the states, either by the legislatures or by elected conventions. The complexity of the amendment process discouraged frequent changes, adding to the Constitution's stature as the law of the land. In later years, constitutional amendments often came in clusters as political leaders addressed fundamental changes in U.S. society.

What the Constitution did *not* do is equally significant. Not only did the founders preserve state governments and state judicial systems, but they also specifically reserved all powers *not* granted to the national government to the states. The debates at the constitutional convention assumed that citizens, regardless of their occupations as merchants or farmers, had primary loyalty to a state rather than to an economic interest group. Accordingly, the powers of the states included basic responsibilities that affected the ordinary citizen: voting procedures, property rights (including slavery), domestic laws (marriage, divorce, inheritance), administration of local affairs, and a concurrent right to tax the public. Legal inhabitants of the United States thus held dual citizenship within state and national governments.

Although national law assumed preeminence, and although the national government could compel enforcement of its laws in the states, such powers remained more *potential* than actual in 1787. In this rural country, the lives of most Americans remained focused on local matters.

The Struggle for Ratification

Assuming that the new government derived its powers from the sovereignty of its citizens—from "We, the people," as the Constitution's opening statement declared—the Constitution provided for the popular ratification of this basic document of law. Rather than relying on the separate state legislatures to approve the Constitution, the framers proposed that popularly chosen conventions in each state make that decision. Ignoring the Articles of Confederation's requirement that all thirteen states had to ratify changes, the constitutional convention decided that only nine states would need to approve the Constitution for the new government to take effect.

What followed was an impassioned debate in all states about the nature of the American republic. Because most citizens remained loyal primarily to their home states, they preferred to retain state sovereignty; in a literal sense, they believed in a federal form of government as a league of independent states rather than an all-powerful centralized unit. Realizing the popularity of the term *federal*, those who supported the Constitution called themselves "Federalists," even though that document greatly increased the authority of the national government. Their opponents, who desired stronger state governments, found themselves called "Anti-Federalists." The language was paradoxical, but voters in the states well understood the issues. To simplify matters further, the drafters of the Constitution proposed that citizens either approve or reject the entire document; amendments, such as a bill of rights, would only be considered after ratification.

Anti-Federalists versus Federalists

Faced with the all-or-nothing choice, critics of the Constitution mounted their attacks in the state ratifying conventions. Anti-Federalists, such as Virginia's Richard Henry Lee and New York's George Clinton, saw themselves as New Yorkers, Pennsylvanians, or Virginians, rather than as Americans; they expressed, in short, a limited national identity. As state-oriented politicians, they viewed the Constitution as a threat to the states and feared that a strong central government would neglect local interests in favor of national issues. Having adopted state bills of rights in the years after 1776, they also objected to the absence in the Constitution of a national bill of rights to protect civil liberties. "My primary objections," stated Massachusetts's influential Elbridge Gerry, "are that there is no adequate provision for representation of the people—that they have no security for the right of election."

At a time when most citizens pursued small-scale farming, Anti-Federalists spoke for those with little or no economic interest beyond their local communities and states. Regionally isolated, such farmers feared government at a distance, especially with leaders chosen indirectly for long terms of office. Anti-Federalists believed that republican governments should represent all community interests; government must be a perfect miniature of society. According to Anti-Federalist thinking, therefore, republics could function well only in small, fairly homogeneous units that allowed citizens to keep a close eye on their rulers. "The largest states," concluded one Anti-Federalist, "are the worst governed."

The Federalists, by contrast, were committed nationalists, men with interstate interests who advocated strengthening the central government. New York's Alexander Hamilton, for example, had served with Washington in the Continental Army and had suffered from Congress's inability to raise taxes for the war. Others, like Madison, believed that a national government could best protect property rights from majority rule. Believing that the state governments were overly democratic, Federalist leaders saw the Constitution's checks and balances as a protection against any politician's mere popularity.

Federalist supporters emerged among urban merchants and commercial farmers who transacted business in more than one state and therefore understood how national economic policies and a strong government could protect international trade. In the port cities, workers and artisans backed the Constitution because their prosperity, too, depended on interstate commerce. Investors who had purchased bonds issued by the Confederation government favored a stronger national government that might repay public debts at face value. Newspaper editors, with interests and influence in more than one state, lined up behind the Constitution. (Anti-Federalist writers complained, for good reason, of the difficulty of getting their ideas into print.) Other Federalist supporters came from areas with special interests, such as Georgia's farmers, who wanted military assistance for their border skirmishes against the Creeks, the Cherokees, and their Spanish allies in Florida.

To support their position, the Federalists offered a new theory of republican government. Whereas Anti-Federalists insisted that republics could survive only in small societies, Federalists argued that the best safeguard of republicanism lay in broad, diverse communities. During the ratification controversy, three leading Federalists—James Madison, Alexander Hamilton, and John Jay—published a series of newspaper essays, *The Federalist Papers,* in which they theorized that the larger and more pluralistic a country, the less likely it was that any one group could achieve a majority and force its will on the whole society. "The only remedy" to majority oppression, said Madison, "is to enlarge the sphere." Instead of being problems, the geographic dispersal of the American people and their multiple differences of interest, said the Federalists, precluded the tyranny of a majority and protected citizens from the abuse of power.

Ratification and Its Aftermath

These arguments prevailed in the state ratifying conventions. With Federalists seizing the initiative, the necessary nine states approved the Constitution by June 1788. But in two centrally located states, Virginia and New York, the Anti-Federalists attracted substantial support, leaving the survival of the new union uncertain. In Virginia, where the popular Patrick Henry looked at the Constitution and "smelled a rat," Federalist support came from western settlers, who wanted the national government's assistance in their conflicts with Native peoples. The Federalist victory in Virginia in turn strengthened the cause in New York, where the Anti-Federalists held an apparent majority. When Hamilton suggested that pro-Federalist New York City might secede from the state, the tide shifted. New York entered the union in July 1788, ensuring implementation of the republican experiment; but North Carolina did not join until 1789, and Rhode Island (the last of the thirteen original states to do so) waited until 1790 to ratify the Constitution.

Despite the great potential of the new centralized government, the Constitution did not significantly alter politics-as-usual in the states. By permitting the states to establish voting qualifications, the structure of political power remained unchanged. The same white male property owners who qualified as citizens in the 1780s participated politically in the 1790s. Those white men who were full citizens, moreover, continued to pay most taxes

to local and state governments, not to the national government, and voter participation in national elections remained lower than in state contests.

Meanwhile, women, slaves, Native Americans, and free African Americans won no additional liberties. Still described primarily by their domestic roles, white women measured their power by their ability to influence the next generation. African American slaves, such as Thomas Prosser's blacksmith, Gabriel, of Richmond, Virginia, exercised political power only by rebellious action. And Native Americans inhabiting the nation's borderlands fought bravely, but with mixed results, to keep their lands. Even free white men who lived far from the centers of power, such as the farmers of western Pennsylvania, possessed small power to oppose excise taxes that the new government imposed on whiskey production in 1794. Although denied equal rights by the Constitution, such people could hardly be viewed as invisible; indeed, their frustrations often drew violent attention from the leadership groups. Yet voters accepted the undemocratic elements of the new political system because the Constitution did not create, but merely expressed, the inequities of American society.

Equally striking was the absence of lasting recrimination. Once adopted, the Constitution became preeminent in the public mind, and the Anti-Federalists, as a group, disappeared from the political scene. Led by Madison, the first Congress soon approved ten constitutional amendments, known as the Bill of Rights, to guarantee basic civil liberties. Among property-holding white male citizens, the 1790s saw political participation increase as greater numbers voted, attended public meetings, wrote letters to newspapers, and held office. Although hardly democratic by today's standards, this rise of political activity quickly obliterated older traditions of monarchy and aristocracy. The Constitution's "We, the people" excluded many, yet strengthened the nation's commitment to an elected government. In time, too, this political inclusion would broaden the number of people who adopted a national identity.

Population Expansion and Migration

The creation of the new government coincided with a rapid expansion of the American population. Indeed, in 1790, "We, the people" were already diverse, though many areas remained homogenous. In New England, 80 percent of the people traced their ancestry to England (60 percent of the country's total population had an English lineage). New York remained heavily Dutch, while Pennsylvania was 40 percent German. And about 30 percent of the people of Georgia, the Carolinas, and Kentucky had roots in Ireland and Scotland. Despite such diversity, the nation's political and legal system remained overwhelmingly English, and British Americans dominated the national leadership. Indeed, the idea of a *written* Constitution, in contrast to the unwritten legal traditions that prevailed among Europeans and Native Americans, placed priority on literacy. Although the ability to read and write English was not a requirement for citizenship, those possessing such skills had obvious advantages. High literacy rates encouraged the expansion of newspapers, which spread information throughout the states. Yet unwritten oral traditions, such as Native American interpretations of treaties, lacked legal standing and could be dismissed as "hearsay evidence."

Immigrants from Europe and slaves from Africa continued to land on American shores, but the surge in population from 4 million in 1789 to 9 million in 1815 primarily reflected a high birthrate. Rural white women in the north were delivering seven to eight children, most healthy enough to reach maturity. Life expectancy for white adults averaged about 45. But the mortality rate of African American children was twice as high as for whites and life expectancy for blacks was only 35. The rising population also disguised (perhaps even caused) a decline in life expectancy among all Americans as infectious diseases spread more rapidly and took a higher toll.

Geographic Mobility and Society

The population boom within farm families created land shortages in settled areas, stimulating two economic trends: children of eastern farmers looked for land in western regions; others turned to nonagricultural employment, sometimes temporarily until they inherited or could afford to buy land, sometimes learning trades that brought them into towns and cities. Total urban growth remained small, yet the population of New York and Pennsylvania increased by 60 percent, while the rest of the nation grew 25 to 35 percent. Meanwhile, the price of public land rose to $2 per acre ($27 in today's money) for a minimum of 640 acres (or over $17,280 in today's money). Such prices primarily benefited land speculators who had money to invest. Migrants who settled the land bought smaller parcels at higher prices per acre.

In the coastal areas of the southern states, soil exhaustion encouraged tobacco planters to shift to grain production, while younger sons moved their families into the western foothills to transplant a tobacco economy there. Smaller farmers in western regions, many with Scots-Irish backgrounds, turned to livestock, fattening cows and pigs to feed the coastal towns. Such family farms seldom could afford to employ slaves. By contrast, tobacco planters who moved west either brought along their slaves or purchased them from dealers who operated an active domestic slave trade between the Upper South and Lower South. As white farmers built tobacco plantations in western Virginia, Carolina, Georgia, Kentucky, and Tennessee, some 40,000 African Americans were uprooted from their homes during the 1790s. Efforts by Quakers in Maryland to block this trade brought assurances from slaveowners that African Americans would thrive in the Gulf states' "warmer and more congenial climate." The demand for slave labor also resulted in the reopening of the foreign slave trade. Between 1783 and 1808, over 100,000 African slaves, mostly men and boys, entered the country through Savannah, Charleston, and New Orleans.

The enthusiasm for growing cotton increased substantially following the introduction of Eli Whitney's mechanical gin, which facilitated the separation of oily seeds from the cotton fibers. Stimulated by demand from English factories, western Georgia and South Carolina were producing 30 million pounds of cotton annually by 1800. The cotton boom encouraged expansion into the Alabama and Mississippi territories, where rivers linked planters to Gulf of Mexico ports. By 1800, cotton was the staple crop of Mississippi, and half the population in the Natchez district was African American.

Resistance to Westward Expansion

In the 1780s, the nation's 4 million inhabitants (including 700,000 African American slaves) were already looking beyond the frontiers of the thirteen states into areas claimed by other nations. Over 100,000 had crossed the Appalachians into Kentucky, Tennessee, and Spain's Louisiana territory. Territorial expansion brought the new nation into conflict with those already inhabiting the western regions.

New Spain, now a tottering empire, reluctantly permitted immigration into Mississippi, promising, in the words of Thomas Jefferson, "the means of delivering to us peaceably what may otherwise cost us a war." Treaties with Spain in the 1790s transferred some territorial claims to the United States. The collapse of the Spanish empire also became apparent in the Pacific northwest, where Great Britain successfully challenged Spain's claims to Vancouver in western Canada.

AMERICAN COOKERY,

OR THE ART OF DRESSING

VIANDS, FISH, POULTRY and VEGETABLES,

AND THE BEST MODES OF MAKING

PASTES, PUFFS, PIES, TARTS, PUDDINGS, CUSTARDS AND PRESERVES,

AND ALL KINDS OF

C A K E S,

FROM THE IMPERIAL PLUMB TO PLAIN CAKE.

ADAPTED TO THIS COUNTRY,

AND ALL GRADES OF LIFE.

By Amelia Simmons,

AN AMERICAN ORPHAN.

PUBLISHED ACCORDING TO ACT OF CONGRESS.

HARTFORD

PRINTED BY HUDSON & GOODWIN,

FOR THE AUTHOR.

1796

Title page from Amelia Simmons's *American Cookery* (1796). Styling herself as "an American orphan," Amelia Simmons performed a service for those American women who now needed cookbooks, because they were less likely to be geographically close to the source of their mothers' advice.

Some Americans were already eyeing nearby California, seeing the area as hopelessly undeveloped under Spanish rule. "The characteristics of the Californians," announced Jedediah Morse in his

> "The characteristics of the Californians are stupidity and insensibility . . . ; an excessive sloth and abhorrence of all labour."

ethnocentric book, *The American Geography* (1789), "are stupidity and insensibility . . . ; an excessive sloth and abhorrence of all labour."

More strenuous opposition to territorial expansion came from the Cherokees, Creeks, and Chickamaugas. American expansionists relied on trickery, whiskey, and force of arms to win their claims. ("I considered it in the interest of the United States to be . . . liberal," explained Tennessee's governor about dispensing corn liquor to a local chief and his thirsty party in 1793.) Military victories against Chickamauga towns on the Tennessee River, followed by the destruction of growing crops, effectively ended Native resistance. Forced treaties then gave Americans title to the lands in western Georgia, which rapidly became cotton fields.

Similar ambitions encouraged settlement of the Northwest Territory. "The original right of the aborigines to the soil," remarked a settler of western Pennsylvania, "is like the claim of children; it is mine for I saw it first." Making counter-claims, U.S. promoters stressed the superiority of developing the land for commercial purposes. As small farmers and organized land companies from New England claimed Native lands, Shawnee opposition provoked warfare. Between 1790 and 1796, the new nation spent five-sixths of the national budget for military action against the Ohio peoples. Expeditions in 1790 and 1791 brought U.S. defeats, and the victorious Shawnee warriors stuffed fertile soil into the mouths of slain U.S. soldiers to express their hatred of land hunger. President George Washington sent another army under General "Mad" Anthony Wayne, which won the

Row houses in Baltimore, built at the beginning of the nineteenth century. Each dwelling was constructed identically. With standard heights for roof lines, windows, and front steps, row houses revealed a cultural preference for geometric regularity.

Battle of Fallen Timbers in 1794 and then dictated the Treaty of Greenville to the Shawnees in 1795. The agreement gave the United States title to most of Ohio, and southern Indiana and Illinois. To preserve peace, Washington became the Shawnees' honorary "father" and agreed to provide annual payments to selected Native leaders.

Urban Geometry and Social Inequality

As some Americans migrated west, others headed for towns and cities. Here, problems of territoriality took different forms. "Curved lines symbolize the country, straight lines the city," observed Daniel Drake, a Cincinnati physician in 1794. Urban ar-

Andrew Ellicott's engraved map of 1792, based on Pierre L'Enfant's manuscript plan, which was adopted by the Congress as the final plan for the federal city of Washington. The plan deliberately placed the executive, legislative, and judicial branches of the government in separate parts of the city, mirroring the separation of powers in the Constitution.

chitecture of the period, the so-called Federal style, emphasized simplicity and uniformity. Municipalities initiated grid plans to facilitate real estate transactions and rationalize the use of urban space. New York introduced street numbering, with odds on one side, evens on the other. After political leaders agreed to move the nation's capital to the District of Columbia near the Potomac River in 1791, the new city's blueprint featured rectangular street plans and right-angle intersections.

The new urban growth underscored inequalities of wealth. As the nation's city population doubled during the 1790s and trade exports jumped fivefold, land values rapidly increased—by as much as 750 percent in Manhattan between 1785 and 1815. Few artisans and unskilled workers could afford to own a house; instead, they rented from more affluent landlords. The rising cost of housing provoked sporadic protests, but despite increasing rents, free African Americans migrated to the cities to take a growing number of unskilled jobs as dock workers and domestic servants. Some free blacks entered the skilled trades as shipbuilders and carpenters, but whites did not welcome their competition for jobs. Indeed, white workers excluded free blacks from annual July Fourth street celebrations, lest the principles of liberty attract enslaved blacks as well. The demand for labor was encouraging an increase in the number of urban slaves. As Richmond, Virginia, grew from 3,700 residents in 1790 to 5,000 in 1800 and nearly 10,000 by 1810, for example, the demand for construction workers stimulated the hiring of slaves owned by tobacco planters whose lands were losing fertility and value.

The increasing number of urban blacks, free and slave, encouraged the emergence of distinct African American institutions. Since the Great Awakening of the mid-18th century, a small proportion of blacks, probably less than 10 percent of the total black population, had converted to Christianity, joined racially mixed Baptist congregations, and developed an identity as black Christians. Despite Baptist tenets of Christian equality, many whites disliked racially integrated congregations; one white preacher in Richmond was pejoratively called "Negro George." Such prejudices, together with a growing sense of racial community, prompted the formation of separate black churches during the 1790s. Within these segregated institutions, slaves and free blacks enjoyed greater social independence. In New York City, however, African Americans encountered a distinctive type of vertical segregation and were obliged to live in unhealthy quarters. According to a medical report about an epidemic, numerous blacks "living in 10 cellars" died in great numbers, "while . . . whites living immediately above their heads in the apartments of the same houses" did not succumb to the fever.

Economic inequality in the cities accentuated the vulnerability of poor women of all races. In a celebrated New York City rape trial in 1793, a wealthy man, accused of seducing a poor 17-year old girl in a "bawdy" house, deflected blame by charging his victim with prostitution. "Could she imagine that a man of his situation would pay her any attention," asked the rich man's lawyer, "unless with a view of promoting illicit commerce?" The all-male jury could not, and voted for his acquittal, whereupon an angry mob of workers attacked both the bawdy house and the lawyers. The verdict was not changed.

Social and economic patterns of the period—urban growth, western migration, disruption of Native American life—existed in a distinct, parallel realm from problems of national government and political forms, though politics and society remained closely interrelated. For most citizens and noncitizens, social and economic issues remained more important than the affairs of state. Yet the nation's diversity reinforced the commitment to republicanism. A political system based

> **In frontier Kentucky, "the women . . . would follow their cows to see what they ate [so] that they might know what greens to get."**

on "the people" promised not only to represent the country's inhabitants, but also to encourage their social and economic liberty.

Launching the New Government

Although social institutions changed slowly, geographic mobility and political innovation constantly forced citizens to confront new challenges. In frontier Kentucky during the 1780s, recalled a pioneer settler, "the women . . . would follow their cows to see what they ate [so] that they might know what greens to get." Such prudence enabled migrating Americans to survive in unfamiliar territory. National politicians faced an equally strange landscape. "We are in a wilderness," remarked James Madison in 1789, "without a single footstep to guide us." The Constitution provided the blueprint; the nation's founders took tentative steps and built precedents.

Forging Political Precedents

George Washington was unanimously elected president by the first electoral college and took the oath of office in New York City, the nation's first capital, in 1789. Political leaders quibbled about what to call him; John Adams, the first vice president, proposed "His Elective Highness." Washington rejected this relic of monarchism; the democratic "Mr. President" would suffice. Although the Constitution did not provide for a presidential cabinet, Congress established executive departments of state, treasury, justice, and post office in 1789 and granted the president the right to appoint and dismiss the heads of these agencies. In selecting his cabinet, Washington chose men from geographically diverse backgrounds, thereby fulfilling the Federalists' notion of dispersing political power.

To establish a national legal system, Congress passed the Judiciary Act of 1789, creating district and appellate courts as well as the Supreme Court. The law also ensured that state courts would retain the bulk of original jurisdiction. Other legal precedents emerged less systematically. When Washington arrived in the Senate in 1789 to seek the constitutionally mandated "advice and consent" about a pending treaty with the Creek nation, the ensuing discussion proved unsatisfactory. The president retreated with "sullen dignity," creating the precedent of consulting with the Senate only *after* treaties had been negotiated and signed.

Congress established other legal precedents that revealed political values not explicitly included in the Constitution. The Naturalization Act of 1790 required two-year residency before immigrants could become citizens and reserved citizenship for applicants who were of good character and "white." The Militia Act of 1792, aimed at recruiting soldiers for wars against the Northwest nations, limited enrollment to able-bodied free white males. The Fugitive Slave Act of 1793 permitted an owner to seize a runaway slave in another state merely by presenting a sworn statement (oral or written), whereas a criminal fugitive from justice enjoyed rights of due process. Such racially discriminatory legislation reflected the views of the nation's first political leaders.

Although the Constitution had omitted a bill of rights, many states' ratification conventions assumed that basic protections of civil liberties would be added as amendments, and Washington's inaugural address recommended measures to protect the "characteristic rights of freemen." Accordingly, in the first session of the House of Representatives, Madison presented a dozen constitutional amendments to protect citizens from government. Ten were ratified by the states in 1791 and became part of the Constitution. These amendments, collectively known as the "Bill of Rights," guaranteed freedom of speech, the press, and religion; allowed the states to form citizen militias (to eliminate the need for standing armies); assured the right of trial by jury; protected citizens from unreasonable police search and seizure; and permitted individuals to refuse to give self-incriminating testimony. Together, they amounted to a defense of personal liberty against government power. During the 1790s, the Supreme Court extended citizens' rights to sue the states in federal courts. This expansion of federal judicial power alarmed Congress, leading to approval of the Eleventh Amendment, limiting such suits, in 1798.

Amendment XI (1798)

The judicial power of the United States shall not be construed to extend to any suit in law or equity, commenced or prosecuted against one of the United States by citizens of another state, or by citizens or subjects of any foreign state.

With the exception of the Twelfth Amendment of 1804, these were the last constitutional amendments until the 1860s, when the Civil War forced a redefinition of the rights of citizenship.

Hamilton's Financial Plan Provokes Debate

As political leaders formalized government operations, the nation's commercial interests looked to the new government to create a financial system that would ensure safe economic development based on foreign trade, primarily with England. The energetic and visionary secretary of the treasury, Alexander Hamilton, responded by designing an elaborate program to stabilize government credit at home and abroad. In 1790, Hamilton unveiled his ideas in a *Report on the Public Credit.* The plan proposed that the government pay or "fund" the entire existing national debt (the bonds and vouchers remaining from the Confederation government) at full face value. At a time when such paper money was worth a fraction of its printed value because few believed the Confederation would ever pay its debts, Hamilton's scheme would prove a windfall for speculators who had purchased these depreciated bonds at much less than their face value. By rewarding these wealthy citizens, Hamilton hoped his plan would marry the nation's business interests to the new government. In Congress, southern representatives, such as Madison, challenged the plan for its failure to reimburse the original holders of government bonds, among them war veterans who had been paid with promissory notes. In response, Hamilton emphasized the long-run advantages of stabilizing the nation's credit.

Hamilton's financial plan also proposed that the national government assume the outstanding debts of the state governments, even though those too were largely held by wealthy investors of the northeast. Yet Hamilton did not see his proposal merely as a benefit for Federalist business groups. He believed that the government's promise to pay the national debt would increase its credit—and so attract additional capital investment in the government. Since most southern states had already paid their debts, the debt-assumption plan aroused regional opposition. Hamilton eased those objections by making an agreement with the leading southern politicians, Madison and Jefferson. While New York and Philadelphia were competing to become the permanent capital of the United States, which would bring additional benefits to local businesses, Hamilton consented to move the capi-

tal to the banks of the Potomac in exchange for southern support of the debt-assumption program. The creation of the District of Columbia on federal lands further established the separation of the national government from state influence. The first Congress passed both the funding and debt-assumption measures in 1790. The resulting national debt would soon require Hamilton to propose new tax measures to balance the budget.

A third element of Hamilton's financial program emerged in 1791 with his request that Congress establish a national bank, the Bank of the United States, with power to raise $10 million by selling stock to the public. The government would hold one-fifth of the stock; investors would purchase the remainder. The bank would serve as a depository of government funds and would collect and dispense government monies. The bank's notes, backed by government deposits, would act as a legal currency. Thus the bank would both benefit stockholders and provide loans for business investment.

When Congress approved the Bank of the United States in 1791, however, President Washington raised questions about its constitutionality and sought the opinions of his cabinet. Secretary of State Jefferson, who believed that the nation's future lay in agriculture rather than in business, opposed the idea of using government funds to benefit private investors. He adopted a "strict" interpretation of the Constitution, arguing that anything the Constitution did not explicitly *permit* should remain outside the scope of government. Since the Constitution did not provide for a national bank, Jefferson denied its constitutionality. Hamilton, by contrast, adopted a "loose" interpretation of the Constitution and assured Washington that Congress could enact anything that was "necessary and proper" (in the words of the Constitution) as long as the Constitution did not explicitly *forbid* it.

The argument about the bank revealed rival ideas about the function of a republican government. To Hamilton, the issue hinged on stabilizing the nation; he did not care that certain business interests would benefit more than most citizens. To Jefferson, the matter involved the protection of the liberty of the citizens; he thought government should not play favorites. Washington listened to their pleas, then signed the bill into law. In the end, history vindicated both Jefferson and Hamilton. As Jefferson warned, individuals profited from doing the government's business; but, as Hamilton predicted, the expansion of credit boosted commerce around the country.

To complete the financial program, Hamilton issued a *Report on Manufactures* in 1791, stressing the advantages of tariffs (taxes on imports) to raise government revenue and to enable U.S. manufactures to compete against cheaper imported goods. Although Congress rejected high duties to stimulate manufacturing, the modest tariff of 1792 provided 90 percent of the national government's revenue. Most of that income came from duties on textiles and iron products imported from Great Britain. In this way, Hamilton's financial program linked the nation's budget with British trade. The merchants who dominated commerce with Britain, moreover, had benefited from Hamilton's funding plan. These connections would soon influence the nation's foreign policy. As Hamilton remarked to the British ambassador, "We think in English."

The Whiskey Rebellion

To keep tariffs low, Hamilton proposed a domestic excise tax on the manufacture of whiskey. Americans were famous for heavy drinking, but interest in whiskey reflected primarily the economics of transportation in rural areas such as western Pennsylvania. Farmers there relied on Ohio River flatboats to bring their produce to market and fermented their grain into whiskey to reduce freight charges. The 1791 excise tax, however, drew no distinction between home manufacturing and commercial distilleries. Struggling small farmers protested the new taxes, sometimes forming outlaw militias to harass government tax collectors.

Civilian violence alarmed government leaders, including the president, who thought the refusal to pay taxes was equivalent to sedition. To show the authority of the national government and prove its ability to enforce the law, Washington summoned the army in 1794 to suppress the so-called Whiskey Rebellion. Resistance quickly evaporated, but authorities imposed harsh penalties until Washington finally pardoned those convicted of treason. Soon afterward, the opening of the Northwest Territory to settlement eased the region's economic problems. Congress repealed the excise tax in 1800 and avoided such measures until the Civil War. But the turmoil over whiskey taxes demonstrated the limits of acceptable protest in a republican government.

Partisan Politics and Foreign Entanglements

Government fears about the Whiskey rebellion reflected a larger unease caused by the French Revolution of 1789, which dramatized class conflicts between the poor masses and their wealthy rulers. As president, Washington held the esteem of most citizens, and his birthday became a day of patriotic celebration. But when Hamilton proposed that Washington's face be stamped on U.S. coins, republicans objected to such "monarchical" poses, and Congress rejected the idea. Instead, a female representation of "Liberty" symbolized the new nation's ideology on U.S. money. The argument indicated a growing rift about other political issues. By the end of Washington's second term, his birthday had become a matter of partisan strife.

Conflicts over Foreign Policy

Foreign policy emerged as a prime topic of political disagreement. Although many Americans had welcomed the French Revolution as an extension of their own attack on King George III, the execution of the deposed French king in 1793 and the declaration of war between France and England forced a reappraisal of their initial enthusiasm. Washington issued a Proclamation of Neutrality in 1793 that rejected any obligations of the French alliance of 1778 and announced a desire to keep the country out of war. The arrival of the French ambassador Edmond Genêt soon afterward complicated the issue. Greeted as a hero by crowds as he traveled from Charleston to Philadelphia, Genêt overestimated the government's sympathy for revolutionary France. When the ambassador openly defied Washington's neutrality proclamation by outfitting ships to attack British commerce, the president demanded Genêt's recall.

The Genêt affair aroused public opinion. While the pro-British Hamilton organized mass meetings to denounce the French ambassador, pro-French sympathizers formed grassroots organizations, called Democratic Societies, to encourage support for France. Neutralists like Washington considered both sides potentially seditious. Since private political factions or parties were extralegal (that is, outside the constitutional system), these early steps in the formation of political parties appeared subversive to the nation's leaders. Ironically, both rival factions warned that their political enemies were threats to republican government. Both sides believed that any political discord endangered a republican system.

Yet the two political factions stood for different principles. The pro-French partisans claimed to defend republican principles of liberty (the "Spirit of '76") against a conspiracy of monarchist sympathizers. The anti-French partisans, such as Hamilton, claimed to defend the rights of property against radical revolutionaries. These differences involved not only political ideas but also strong emotions. Such passions intensified political debate and laid the basis of the first political party system: the pro-French "Democratic-Republicans" (later known simply as Republicans) versus the pro-English "Federalists."

The danger of radical politics crept closer to home when the slaves of Saint Domingue, a French Caribbean colony, erupted with violence in 1793. As French slaveowners (many with their slaves) sought refuge in North America, U.S. slaveholders worried that the spirit of insurrection would spread among their slaves. Saint Domingue, said Jefferson, was only "the first chapter." In New York City, a rising number of runaway slaves and outbreaks of arson fires terrorized the populace. In Philadelphia, a yellow-fever epidemic created an odd medical debate as anti-French doctors blamed the disease on the French refugees while pro-French physicians sought local explanations. Believing that Africans were immune to yellow fever, the nation's foremost physician, Dr. Benjamin Rush, persuaded blacks to assist the dying and remove the dead until they too began to succumb. Whatever the medical diagnosis, African Americans well understood the political crisis. Perhaps stimulated by the Caribbean revolt, cases of murder and poisoning of slaveowners rose dramatically and rumors of slave conspiracies abounded. Fear of slave revolts underscored the fragility of the nation's political structure. Throughout the decade, government leaders did not feel confident about the loyalty of their foes, whether slaves or free men.

The Jay Treaty and the Rise of Political Parties

Washington's policy of neutrality in the war between England and France increased U.S. shipping. Merchants took advantage of food shortages in Europe and expanded trade in the West Indies. But the risk of war increased when both Britain and France seized American ships on the high seas for trading with the enemy. Since the British navy dominated the seas, England's violations were more threatening to American interests. The two countries headed toward war.

To seek a peaceful settlement, Washington sent Ambassador John Jay to England. But British leaders showed little interest in negotiations, and Jay felt obliged to make concessions to avoid war. Instead of defending the principle that neutral nations could trade freely with warring countries, Jay accepted the British position that goods could not be carried to enemy ports and that trade with enemy colonies—the West Indies in particular—could not be legalized in time of war. England then promised reimbursement for lost cargoes and abandoned its claims to the Northwest Territory.

Jay's Treaty brought foreign controversy directly into domestic politics. As the ambassador's concessions to England inflamed public opinion, congressional opponents of the treaty clustered around the anti-British or "Republican" faction, led by Madison and Jefferson. Meanwhile, a pro-British "Federalist" faction, inspired by Hamilton, defended the treaty because it protected the lucrative trade with England. Both sides organized public rallies to petition the government; both used popular newspapers to sway citizen opinion. Both articulated distinctive political persuasions. The Federalists claimed that the commercial treaty would ensure stability and protect property; the Republicans pleaded for the commercial rights of a free nation and warned that the Federalists were monarchists who conspired with England to overthrow the republican experiment. What the two groups shared was a conspiratorial outlook, a belief that their opponents threatened the survival of republican government. Believing that factions were inherently subversive, neither side could accept the idea of a loyal opposition.

Beneath the rhetoric lay substantial differences of political interest. Federalist support for England obviously appealed to merchants who prospered with British trade. In New England, traditions of anti-French sentiment, dating to the colonial wars against Canada, made the region a Federalist stronghold. Small farmers in isolated areas tended to follow Federalist conservatism. Republicans, by contrast, appealed to farmers and merchants who sought economic opportunity by extending trade beyond the British marketplace; in urban areas, smaller merchants, manufacturers, and artisans opposed the Federalist leadership and expressed pro-French sentiment. Despite such public disagreements, neither side believed that their opponents were sincere or that their differences were based on interests and principles rather than some conspiratorial intentions. In this atmosphere of intense distrust, the Jay Treaty slipped through the Senate by a single vote in 1794.

Political leaders expressed greater unity in accepting Pinckney's Treaty of 1795, which settled the Florida boundary dispute with Spain and assured U.S. shipping rights on the Mississippi River. But national politics remained edgy, taut, and suspicious. When Washington retired after two terms as president, his farewell address of 1796 criticized the spirit of political parties and advised Americans to avoid entanglements with foreign nations because they imperiled domestic harmony.

Even as Washington spoke, the elections of 1796 intensified conflict between Federalists and Republicans. In the cities, Republicans attracted Irish (anti-British) immigrants and French refugees from Saint Domingue. But most voting followed regional lines, with Federalists strong in the northeast and Republicans successful in the south, rather than sharp party alignments. Indeed, half the candidates never clearly expressed a party identity. Nevertheless, Federalist sympathizers captured both houses of Congress. The outcome of the presidential contest revealed less clarity. While the Federalists nominated John Adams and Thomas Pinckney for the highest offices, the Republicans endorsed Jefferson and Aaron Burr. But the Constitution had made no mention of party affiliations in the electoral college vote. Consequently, the candidate with the majority of electoral votes, the Federalist Adams, became president; the second highest tally, just three votes short, went to the Republican Jefferson, who assumed the vice presidency.

Challenges to the Adams Administration

Despite the warning in Washington's farewell address, foreign entanglements soon swamped the Adams administration. As French privateers attacked U.S. ships in the West Indies, Adams dispatched negotiators to France in 1797 to reach agreement about neutral rights. In Paris, U.S. diplomats confronted the sly minister Talleyrand, who suggested that, instead of demanding monetary damages, the Americans would do well to offer a bribe to three French agents (later known as X, Y, and Z). "We are not a degraded people," exclaimed Adams, upon bringing the news of the XYZ affair to Congress. Infuriated by the insult to national honor, public opinion supported preparations for war. Congress voted to terminate the French Alliance of 1778, created a Department of the Navy to build warships and license privateers, and approved an army. Yet when influential Federalist leaders, including the retired Washington, forced Adams to appoint his rival, Hamilton, to head the troops, the second president hesitated to demand war. Fearful of open hostilities and mistrustful of Hamilton's intentions, Adams weighed his options.

The Alien and Sedition Acts

As an undeclared naval war commenced against France, bringing moments of glory to the new navy, Republicans and Federalists clashed about extending hostilities. One Federalist newspaper called the pro-French Republicans "democrats, mobocrats

and all other kinds of rats" and claimed that they intended to install French anarchy on the American republic. Without waiting for the president's decision to go to war, the Federalist Congress proceeded to enact four laws, the Alien and Sedition acts of 1798, to ensure political conformity and reduce foreign influence in domestic politics. First, the Naturalization Act aimed at what Federalists called "hordes of wild Irishmen" and other "turbulent and disorderly" immigrant groups (that is, those who opposed England's interests) by extending the period of probationary residence for citizenship to 14 years. Second, the Alien Act permitted the president to expel unnaturalized foreigners deemed "dangerous to the peace," but the measure expired in 1800 without ever being implemented. Third, the Alien Enemies Act allowed the president to apprehend, restrain, or remove dangerous foreign nationals, but only in wartime. Unlike the other statutes, this measure remained a permanent law, used by twentieth century presidents to restrict foreign groups during the world wars.

The fourth law, the Sedition Act, struck closer to home. Assuming that political dissent constituted a threat to legal order, this Federalist measure declared that any citizen who was guilty of writing, publishing, or speaking anything of "a false, scandalous or malicious" nature against the government or a government official faced stiff fines and imprisonment. The administration promptly issued indictments against Republican newspaper editors, sending several to jail.

As Hamilton proceeded to build the army, and Federalists pushed for a declaration of war against France, Republican leaders gathered support in the state legislatures. Fearing government suppression backed by the army, Madison and Jefferson wrote two resolutions that were passed by the Virginia and Kentucky legislatures in 1798. These resolutions argued that a state government had the power to nullify and refuse to obey congressional laws that threatened the people's liberties and were thus unconstitutional. The Adams administration made no effort to challenge this assertion of states' rights, but Virginians made preparations to meet a Federalist-led military attack. The peril of civil war seemed real to Republicans and Federalists alike.

Peace with France

While the constitutional squabble threatened domestic order, news from France suggested that negotiations might settle the foreign conflict. "The end of war is peace," Adams remarked, agreeing to send another ambassador to France in 1799. His decision outraged less conciliatory Federalists who broke with the president and looked to Hamilton for leadership. But the resolute Adams allowed diplomacy to proceed. By the time the ambassadors reached France, Napoleon Bonaparte had seized power and was eager for a truce. The Convention of 1800 did no more than guarantee neutral rights during wartime (indeed, the agreement angered Federalists by neglecting the matter of damage payments) but a grateful administration offered the treaty as a better alternative to war. Unknown to Adams, Bonaparte's designs were more ominous, for the day after signing the Convention he secretly persuaded Spain to cede the Louisiana territory to France, preparing to challenge American control of the Mississippi valley (see Chapter 8).

The Election of 1800

As the war clouds disappeared, the country focused on the 1800 presidential election. With Federalists divided between pro- and anti-Adams factions, Republicans built a coalition among commercial farmers, aspiring merchants and artisans, and non-English immigrants, all of whom had opposed recent Federalist war preparations, high taxes, and political persecution. Once again, Jefferson faced Adams in the presidential contest, this time gaining a majority of eight electoral votes.

The Constitution, conceived before the rise of political parties, made no distinction between presidential and vice-presidential ballots, and Jefferson and his running mate Aaron Burr of New York received the same number of electoral votes. Following the Constitution, the choice between Jefferson and Burr then moved to the sitting House of Representatives. Here, Federalist influence remained strong, and thirty-five ballots brought an unyielding deadlock. Since the new Congress would not take office for nearly a year, some Federalists saw an opportunity for remaining in power. But Hamilton's hatred of Burr, a New York rival, finally moved him to support Jefferson, who was named president on the thirty-sixth ballot. (Burr would later have his revenge, killing Hamilton in a duel.) To prevent any similar constitutional crisis, the Twelfth Amendment, adopted in 1804, separated electoral college balloting for president and vice president.

Amendment XII (1804)

The electors shall meet in their respective states and vote by ballot for President and Vice-President, one of whom, at least, shall not be an inhabitant of the same state with themselves; they shall name in their ballots the person voted for as President, and in distinct ballots the person voted for as Vice-President, and they shall make distinct lists of all persons voted for as President, and of all persons voted for as Vice-President, and of the number of votes for each, which lists they shall sign and certify, and transmit sealed to the seat of the government of the United States, directed to the President of the Senate;—The President of the Senate shall, in the presence of the Senate and House of

Representatives, open all the certificates and the votes shall then be counted;—the person having the greatest number of votes for President, shall be the President, if such number be a majority of the whole number of electors appointed; and if no person have such majority, then from the persons having the highest numbers not exceeding three on the list of those voted for as President, the House of Representatives shall choose immediately, by ballot, the President. But in choosing the President, the votes shall be taken by states, the representation from each state having one vote; a quorum for this purpose shall consist of a member or members from two-thirds of the states, and a majority of all the states shall be necessary to a choice. And if the House of Representatives shall not choose a President whenever the right of choice shall devolve upon them, before the fourth day of March next following, then the Vice-President shall act as President, as in the case of the death or other constitutional disability of the President. The person having the greatest number of votes as Vice-President, shall be the Vice-President, if such number be a majority of the whole number of electors appointed, and if no person have a majority, then from the two highest numbers on the list, the Senate shall choose the Vice-President; a quorum for the purpose shall consist of two-thirds of the whole number of Senators, and a majority of the whole number shall be necessary to a choice. But no person constitutionally ineligible to the office of President shall be eligible to that of Vice-President of the United States.

A Fragile Republic

The election of 1800, heralded as a peaceful transition of power from Federalists to Republicans, nonetheless revealed the shaky state of republicanism in the new nation. Not only did party leaders disagree about policies and programs but they also continued to doubt the essential loyalty of their political rivals. Indeed, fear of subversion dominated political discussion in both parties. Believing that republican governments were fragile entities, political leaders were not yet prepared to trust their opponents or accept the legitimacy of two-party politics.

Tension within the political leadership appeared slight compared to the potential conflict between citizens and racial outsiders. During the 1800 election campaign, slaveowners in Richmond, Virginia, discovered a slave conspiracy led by a blacksmith named Gabriel. The carefully planned uprising, thwarted at the last minute by a black informer, involved hundreds, perhaps thousands, of blacks and exposed the explosive contradictions of a republican government built on foundations of slavery. Adopting the slogan "Death or Liberty," African American rebels planned to spare the lives of Quakers, Methodists, and French persons because they were "friendly to liberty." But one African American insurrectionist confessed, "I could kill a white man as free as eat."

The state of Virginia soon hanged 27 blacks and sold hundreds into exile. Subsequent laws limited the freeing of slaves and restricted the movements of free blacks. Virginia Federalists blamed the crisis on the Jeffersonians for imparting "the French principles of Liberty and Equality . . . into the minds of the Negroes." Republicans replied by accusing the Federalist press of fomenting an "electioneering engine." Such partisan rhetoric belied the essential uncertainty of political life. As Federalists feared an epidemic of liberty, Republicans equally suspected a monarchist plot. Two hundred years ago, the stability of the new nation appeared doubtful, at best.

INFOTRAC® COLLEGE EDITION EXERCISES

For additional reading go to InfoTrac College Edition, your online research library at *http://web1.infotrac-college.com.*

Subject search: United States Constitution
Keyword search: Federalist Papers
Subject search: Hamilton and Jefferson
Subject search: Hamilton
Keyword search: George Washington

ADDITIONAL READING

Designing a National Union

Jack N. Rakove, *Original Meanings: Politics and Ideas in the Making of the Constitution* (1996). A careful analysis of the political ideas that produced the Constitution.

The Struggle for Ratification

Saul Cornell, *The Other Founders: Anti-Federalism and the Dissenting Tradition in America, 1788–1828* (1999). This study analyzes the opposition to ratification; see also the older but still-useful book by Jackson Turner Main, *The Antifederalists: Critics of the Constitution* (1961).

Geographic Mobility and Society

Joyce Appleby, *Inheriting the Revolution: The First Generation of Americans* (2000). Examines the liberating effects of republicanism on religion, business, and private life.

Malcolm J. Rohrbough, *The Trans-Appalachian Frontier: People, Societies, and Institutions, 1775–1850* (1978). Describes the American farmers who migrated into the Midwest.

Shane White, *Somewhat More Independent: The End of Slavery in New York City, 1770–1810* (1991). A study of the social and cultural conditions among African Americans in New York, contrasting with Gary Nash's *Forging Freedom* (1988), listed in the previous chapter.

Resistance to Westward Expansion

Gregory Evans Dowd, *A Spirited Resistance: The North American Indian Struggle for Unity, 1745–1815* (1992). This fine book links Native American resistance during the colonial period to conflicts during the early republic.

The Whiskey Rebellion

Thomas P. Slaughter, *The Whiskey Rebellion: Frontier Epilogue to the American Revolution* (1986). This analysis of rural America places the tax rebellion in the context of popular protest.

Partisan Politics and Foreign Entanglements

Stanley Elkins and Eric McKitrick, *The Age of Federalism* (1993). A thorough study of politics and diplomacy during the 1790s.

John R. Nelson, Jr., *Liberty and Property: Political Economy and Policymaking in the New Nation, 1789–1812* (1987). Describes the political and economic differences between Federalists and Republicans.

Simon P. Newman, *Parades and Politics of the Street: Festive Culture in the Early American Republic* (1997). This analysis of public symbols emphasizes the growing partisanship of public life in the 1790s.

James Roger Sharp, *American Politics in the Early Republic: The New Nation in Crisis* (1993). A study of partisan conflict that describes the tenuous stability of the republic.

A Fragile Republic

James Sidbury, *Ploughshares into Swords: Race, Rebellion, and Identity in Gabriel's Virginia, 1730–1810* (1997). An analysis of racial consciousness among African Americans, which explains the social dynamics of Gabriel's conspiracy. See also Douglas R. Egerton, *Gabriel's Rebellion* (1993).

The Connecticut Courant.

PRINTED AT HARTFORD, BY HUDSON & GOODWIN, OPPOSITE THE NORTH MEETING-HOUSE.

VOL. XXXV.]   MONDAY, MARCH 10, 1800.   [NUMBER 1883

PUBLISHED BY AUTHORITY.

SIXTH CONGRESS, OF THE UNITED STATES,

At the first session, begun and held at the city of Philadelphia, in the state of Pennsylvania, on Monday the second of December, 1799.

CHAPTER I.

An ACT for reviving and continuing suits and proceedings in the Circuit Court for the district of Pennsylvania.

Sec. 1. BE it enacted by the Senate and House of Representatives of the United States of America, in Congress assembled, That all suits, process and proceedings, of what nature or kind soever, which were pending in the Circuit Court of the United States, for the district of Pennsylvania, at the time appointed by law, for holding a session thereof in October, one thousand seven hundred and ninety-nine, and which were discontinued by failure to hold the said court, shall be, and they are hereby revived and continued, and the same proceedings may and shall be had in the same court, in all suits and process aforesaid, and in all things relating to the same, as by law might have been had in the same court, had it been regularly holden, at the time aforesaid.

Sec. 2. And be it further enacted, That all writs, and other process, which may have been, and which shall be issued, by the clerk of the said court, bearing teste of April session or October session, one thousand seven hundred and ninety-nine, shall be held and deemed of the same validity and effect, as if the same court had been regularly held on the eleventh day of October, one thousand seven hundred and ninety-nine.

Sec. 3. And be it further enacted, That it shall be lawful for the Judge of the District Court of the district of Pennsylvania, to direct the clerk of the said Circuit Court to issue such process, for the purpose of summoning jurors to be summoned to attend at the session of the said Circuit Court, on the eleventh day of April next, as hath heretofore been issued for the like purposes, returnable to any preceding session thereof; and the persons so summoned shall, in case of non-attendance, be liable to the same penalties as if such process had been issued in the ordinary course of proceeding.

THEODORE SEDGWICK,
Speaker of the House of Representatives.
SAMUEL LIVERMORE,
President of the Senate, pro tempore.
APPROVED—December 24th, 1799.
JOHN ADAMS,
President of the United States.

CHAPTER II.

An ACT extending the privilege of franking to William Henry Harrison, the delegate

dwelling houses in the same sub-division, shall not be changed or affected.

Sec. 2. And be it further enacted, That the said commissioners may direct the additions or deductions as aforesaid, to be made out and completed by the several principal assessors, or if they shall deem it more advisable, by their clerk and such assistants as they shall find necessary, and appoint for that purpose: Provided, That the compensation to be made to the said assistants shall not exceed the pay allowed to the assistant assessors, by the act to which this is a supplement.

THEODORE SEDGWICK,
Speaker of the House of Representatives.
TH: JEFFERSON,
Vice-President of the United States, and President of the Senate.
APPROVED—January 2d, 1800.
JOHN ADAMS,
President of the United States.

LANCASTER, (Penn.) Feb. 21.
FRACAS in the Chamber of the House of Representatives.

On Thursday evening last a very disagreeable fracas took place in the chamber of the House of Representatives of Pennsylvania. We have endeavored to collect the circumstances with accuracy, and believe them to be briefly as follows:

During the evening session of the House, Mr. Samuel H. Fisher was delivering his sentiments on a resolution which went to disfranchise all officers and soldiers under the United States. In the course of his arguments, Mr. Fisher was twice interrupted by a call for adjournment from one part of the House. Both calls were negatived. A third call was made, which Mr. Fisher and his friends acceded to, and the House adjourned.

As soon as the adjournment had taken place, Mr. Fisher observed to a number of the members who had repeatedly called for an adjournment, that they had acted cowardly, were unwilling and afraid to hear his arguments.

Dr. Logan remarked that such foolish, nonsensical arguments as those made use of by Mr. Fisher, were not worth attending to. The latter then replied that any man who would call his arguments foolish and nonsensical was a puppy. Dr. Logan rejoined and called Mr. Fisher a rascal! On this Mr. Fisher struck him. The Doctor returned the blow. The members on all sides immediately interfered, and the combatants were separated. A considerable deal of altercation took place among some of the members—and indeed we feel happy in being able to say that the battle was not more general.

While Mr. Fisher was aiming a blow at the Doctor, Mr. Wilson or Dauphin suddenly thrust himself in its road, and received a small contusion in or near the eye.

Another gentleman received a blow on his cheek but could not find his man. It was candle light, which rendered confusion the more confused. The members after some difficulty, found their hats, and dispersed.

Doctor Logan did not appear in the house on Friday, but addressed the following letter to Mr. Weaver, the Speaker.

Lancaster, February 21st, 1800.

SIR,

As a member of the House of Representatives, I complain to you as speaker of the House of Representatives, that yesterday, in the

the petition was referred to the Committee of Claims.

A message was received from the Senate, by Mr. Otis, their secretary, informing the house, that the Senate had passed the bill, intituled "An act further to suspend the commercial intercourse between the United States and France," with two amendments, to which they requested the concurrence of this house.

The first amendment, to strike out that part of the 4th section, which enabled citizens of the United States resident in France, to repair to this country, with vessels and other property bona fide belonging to them, was concurred in by the house—ayes 50, noes 36.

Previous to taking the question on concurring in this amendment, Mr. Macon made a motion, which superceded it, viz. "that the amendments of the Senate be postponed until the first Monday in December next"—which was negatived, only 30 members voting in favor of it.

The second amendment was to strike out the 10th section of the bill, by which it was enacted, that the Consul or Agent of the U. States shall receive an annual salary of 3000 dollars, and be restricted from trade, &c.

Mr. Otis moved that the House concur.

Mr. Champlin hoped not—and proceeded to give his reasons; by stating that great complaints had been made of the conduct of our agent at Hispaniola——that it had been insinuated he had entered into trade with the planters of that island, previous to public notice having been given that the trade was opened, and had monopolized a large portion of the produce, previous to the American merchant's having an opportunity of becoming purchasers—Mr. C. also mentioned the circumstance of a vessel having been overhauled by an American cruizer, who shewed a passport from Toussaint and one from Dr. Stevens, by which the war permitted to proceed—and thereby inferred that the vessel might have been employed in an illicit trade.

Mr. Smith also spoke in favor of continuing the section—It had been introduced upon the most mature consideration, to prevent what was considered a great evil, and was much cause of complaint. By the proclamation opening intercourse with St. Domingo, our vessels were restricted, Mr. S. said, from going to but two ports in that island, upon clearing out at our custom houses—viz. Port Republican and Cape Francois. Upon their arrival at either of those ports, if the supercargo wishes to seek farther for a market, application must be made to our agent for permission; who may delay granting it, and in the mean time, send to the place for which it is requested; buy up all the produce, and compel the merchant to purchase of him at an exorbitant price—this he had been informed had been done—but in mentioning it, Mr. S. said, he did not wish to be understood as criminating the person who did it. The agent was allowed to trade—he had no compensation from the government—and it was what every merchant in a similar situation might and would do. He tho't it a perfectly fair mercantile transaction. Hence arose the necessity of the section now under consideration.

But there was another transaction, Mr. S. said, the papers relating to which he had deposited with the proper executive officer.—A passport had been granted by our agent at Hispaniola; permitting the vessel of his partner to trade direct from the United States to

An Expanding Society, 1801–1815

"The Revolution of 1776 is now and for the first time arrived at its completion," trumpeted a Republican newspaper in 1801, "the sun of aristocracy [has] set, to rise no more." In Washington, D.C., the nation's new capital, Thomas Jefferson surveyed the muddy, undeveloped streets yet spoke glowingly of the country's future. Envisioning "a rising nation, spread over a wide and fruitful land," he predicted the expansion of agriculture, industry, and commerce "beyond the reach of mortal eye" and he frankly humbled himself "before the magnitude of the undertaking." To Jefferson, as he once put it, "those who labor in the earth are the chosen people of God," by which he meant the people of the United States.

And yet, Jefferson's optimism showed little sympathy for those who did not share the rights of citizenship. He saw Native Americans as a people doomed to disappear. "The backward [Native peoples] will yield," he vowed, "and we shall be obliged to drive them, with the beasts of the forest into the Stony [Rocky] mountains." Like most of his contemporaries, Jefferson also dismissed the political role of women, except as a moral presence

http://history.wadsworth.com

in the home. "Our good ladies ... have been too wise to wrinkle their foreheads with politics," he remarked. "They are contented to soothe and calm the minds of their husbands returning ruffled from political debate." When a shortage of civil service workers led a cabinet official to propose hiring women, Jefferson replied, "the appointment of women to office is an innovation for which the public is unprepared, nor am I."

Although the widowed Jefferson maintained an enduring relationship with his slave Sally Hemings, with whom he fathered children, he doubted too that African Americans could share the national identity—at least not for many generations. "From the experiments, which have been made," he wrote, "to give liberty, or rather, to abandon persons whose habits have been formed in slavery is like abandoning children."

Jefferson, author of the Declaraion of Independence, embodied the contradictions of a republican society, stressing the rights of self-government—but only for white men. As he prepared to take the oath of office as the nation's third president, he remained an enemy of recent Federalist policies, but he had no interest in attacking the party he had defeated. Rather, he expected his political foes to end their opposition and support his policies. "Every difference of opinion is not a difference of principle," Jefferson announced calmly. "We are all Republicans, we are all Federalists."

The transfer of power from Federalists to Republicans in 1800 was made easier by the relatively limited power of the national government, which dealt primarily with foreign affairs. During the previous decade, the war between England and France had drawn the United States into international conflicts, problems that would continue until 1815. Territorial expansion would also affect national policy and oblige the national government to confront the Native American nations fighting for their lands. The U.S. Supreme Court would issue precedent-setting decisions that affected interstate commerce and the law of contracts. National politicians, Federalists and Republicans, would disagree about such matters. But most domestic issues of this period—population migration, commercial growth, innovations in manufacturing—were local issues and did not involve national policy. In short, economic issues did not follow clear party lines.

Although Republicans increasingly replaced Federalists in public office (so much so that the Federalist party was nearly extinct outside New England by 1815), political power remained in the grip of property-holding white men in all regions. Slaveholding tobacco and cotton planters ruled the

> ## "We are all Republicans, we are all Federalists."

Thomas Jefferson (like George Washington, James Madison, and James Monroe) embodied the self-confident values of Virginia's slaveholding planter aristocracy.

southern states, while wealthier merchants dominated politics in the North. Republican ideology encouraged enterprise and economic advancement, though in many states propertyless people did not even have the right to vote or hold office. But during the eight years of Jefferson's presidency, and eight more under his colleague James Madison, the United States would come to fulfill its vast agricultural promise, extend its territorial limits, and accelerate its commercial development.

A Jeffersonian Agenda

Devoted to ideals of political simplicity, Jefferson promised "a wise and frugal Government" which would allow citizens "to regulate their own pursuits of industry and improvements." His administration proceeded to dismantle the most objectionable Federalist measures, repealing excise taxes, reducing military expenditures, and making it easier for immigrants to become citizens. But Jefferson proposed no changes in Hamilton's financial system or the national bank. Instead, a surge of overseas commerce brought surplus revenues, which shrank the national debt. Jefferson also preserved the young navy, sending warships against the Muslim states of North Africa (Tripoli, Morocco, Algeria), who were extorting payments for safe passage and sometimes seizing sailors to sell as slaves. Skirmishes around "the shores of Tripoli" ended the worst outrages.

Judicial Conflict

Jefferson showed less patience with the highly partisan, Federalist-dominated judiciary. Both Wash-

ington and Adams had appointed Federalist judges, some of whom had vigorously enforced the sedition laws against Republican critics. Reacting to Jefferson's election, the lame-duck, Federalist-controlled Congress had passed the Judiciary Act of 1801, which expanded the federal courts in time for Adams to fill the vacant positions with Federalist judges just before his term expired. These "midnight" appointments led the next Congress to repeal the law, and Jefferson refused to issue the appointment documents that Adams had lacked the time to distribute. One of Adams's appointees, a judge named William Marbury, appealed Jefferson's refusal to the Supreme Court (asking, in legal language, for a writ of mandamus that would require Secretary of State Madison to deliver Marbury's commission to hold office).

Chief Justice John Marshall, himself a recent Adams appointee, did not issue a verdict in *Marbury v. Madison* until 1803. But the decision in this seemingly inconsequential case altered the course of the country's legal history. Ruling that Marbury deserved his commission under the law, Marshall held nevertheless that the Supreme Court did not have proper jurisdiction in the case and therefore could not order Madison to comply. In effect, the decision declared that an earlier law of 1789 (which gave the Court jurisdiction of such cases) had exceeded the power of Congress under the Constitution and was consequently "unconstitutional." Marshall thus created the legal precedent of judicial review of congressional laws. Not until 1857 did the Court rule against another act of Congress. In other cases, the Marshall Court would later affirm its right to judge the constitutionality of state laws.

Jefferson did not object to Marshall's assertion of judicial power and thus endorsed the principle of judicial review. But some Republicans did challenge Federalist judges for expressing partisan prejudices in legal cases. In the most important impeachment case, involving Supreme Court Justice Samuel Chase, a rigid Federalist, Republican accusers appeared no less partisan than the judge. But when a Republican Senate failed to convict Chase in 1805, the proceedings confirmed that the judicial branch should be protected from partisan interference; for another half century, Congress would impeach no other federal judges.

The Louisiana Purchase

Jefferson's belief in a strict interpretation of constitutional powers soon clashed with his commitment to building a nation of farmers. Believing that the virtue of free citizens depended upon preserving their economic independence, Jefferson hoped that the country's "vacant lands" would provide for population growth and ensure the self-sufficiency of its inhabitants. As a tobacco planter, moreover, Jefferson understood the value of agricultural exports for domestic prosperity and he sympathized with western farmers who demanded that the Mississippi River remain open for U.S. shipping. But, after 1800, France owned the Louisiana territory and controlled river traffic on the Mississippi. Indeed, the French emperor Napoleon Bonaparte had plans for restoring a French empire in North America. When French officials in New Orleans closed the port to U.S. trade in 1802, Jefferson sent ambassador James Monroe to France to negotiate the purchase of that southern trading center.

By the time Monroe arrived in France, Bonaparte's plans had changed. The failure of a French military expedition to recapture Saint Domingue from rebel slaves and the threat of another war with England persuaded the French emperor to abandon his colonies. To Monroe's surprise, Napoleon offered to sell not just New Orleans, but the entire Louisiana territory, an area equal in size to the existing United States. While Jefferson appreciated the windfall, he faced a constitutional dilemma. The Constitution made no provision for the acquisition of new territory, and Jefferson hesitated to exceed the law; he even considered a constitutional amendment to permit the purchase. But, fear that Napoleon might withdraw the offer stretched his thinking. The Louisiana purchase would guarantee abundant land for the nation's farmers. Jefferson set aside his legal scruples to complete the transaction. Ironically, Federalists who preferred a loose interpretation of the Constitution objected to the Louisiana purchase because it promised to disperse population and erode the political influence of New England, the base of Federalist power. Such fears seemed justified. Already Ohio had entered

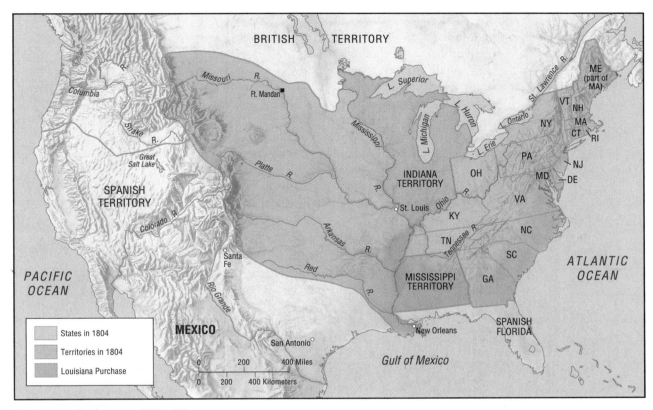

The Louisiana Purchase OVERLAY 2

the union in 1803, and westward migration underscored the Federalists' loss of national power. Yet Jefferson believed that the new territory would serve not to transplant independent farmers, but to resettle Native Americans west of the Mississippi, thus "filling up the eastern side, instead of drawing off its population."

Lewis and Clark Reach the Pacific

Jefferson's vision of western expansion, based on his philosophical speculation rather than geographical knowledge, stimulated a bold government project to explore the Louisiana territory. Led by two military officers, Meriwether Lewis and William Clark, an expedition consisting of 50 men departed from St. Louis in 1804, sailed up the Missouri River, then crossed the western mountains and descended the Columbia River to the Pacific Ocean. During the two-year journey, the explorers traded with Native American groups for food and shelter, cartographic information, and guides (such as the Shoshone woman Sacajawea, whose presence with her baby assured strangers of the group's peaceful purposes). Besides staking U.S. claims to the western shores, the expedition acquired geographical information, collected natural specimens, and served as early ethnographers, depicting the varieties of indigenous cultures they encountered.

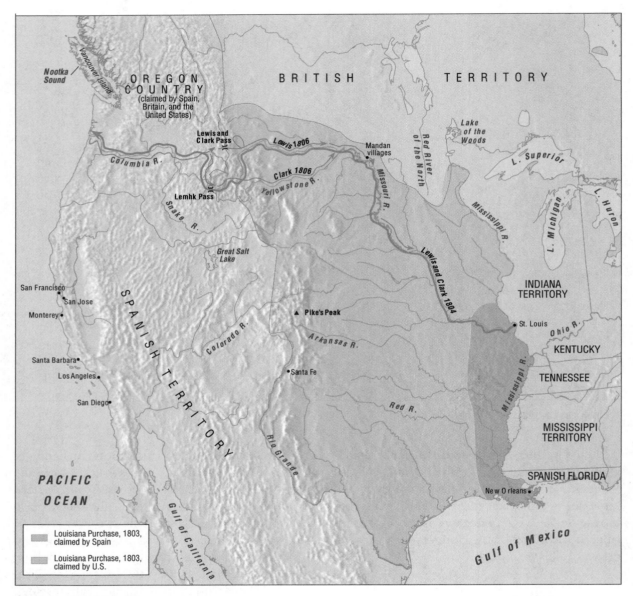

The Lewis and Clark Expedition

These discoveries in the heart of the continent mirrored the experiences of European explorers who had met the Atlantic coast peoples centuries earlier. Near the Missouri River, for example, the expedition observed the ruins of abandoned villages, remnants of a thriving Arikara population that had been devastated by smallpox just a decade before. These Plains people had thrived with mixed agriculture (corn, squash, beans) tended by women and buffalo hunting conducted by men. Living in dome-shaped earthen lodges, they had created compact villages that were surrounded by ditches and palisades as protection against the rival Sioux. By 1804, the Arikaras had dwindled to three large villages, composed of refugee remnants from numerous clans and kinship groups. Lewis and Clark assured "the red children" that "the great chief" of the United States, "impelled by his paternal regard," offered peace and profitable trade. Such messages were repeated on the long journey to the Oregon coast, as Jefferson's emissaries took the measure of Mandans, Shoshones, Nez Percés, and Chinooks along the way.

Reports of the Lewis and Clark expedition encouraged interest in western territories that were occupied not only by Native Americans but also by European settlers. By the beginning of the 19th century, Spain had planted twenty-one Franciscan missions in California, each a day's journey apart, plus a handful of military forts (presidios). But the non-Native population had climbed slowly from a mere 600 in 1781 to barely 3,000 thirty years later. "It would be as easy to keep California in spite of the Spaniards," remarked a visiting U.S. sailor, "as it would be to win it from them in the first place." Meanwhile, Great Britain used the 18th-century voyages of Captains James Cook and George Vancouver to claim the northwest regions, and Russian fur traders, seeking a food supply, planted a tiny colony in 1812 at Fort Ross, north of San Francisco Bay.

U.S. activity on the Pacific coast remained slight, though ships heading for China sometimes stopped for provisions. In 1816, two sailors, one an African American named Bob, took the opportunity to jump ship, be baptized as Catholics, take Spanish citizenship, and marry California women—apparently becoming the first U.S. settlers to stay in California. Farther north, the German immigrant John Jacob Astor planted a fur trading post, Astoria,

at the mouth of the Columbia River in 1811, but competition with British traders forced abandonment of the project.

Cultural Conflict on a Moving Frontier

Interest in the Louisiana territory and the Pacific reflected an acceleration of population migration from the settled states of the Atlantic seaboard. Jefferson himself believed that the newly acquired lands might become home to eastern Native Americans, who would surrender their traditional lands to migrating whites. Declining crop production, overcrowding, and a desire for land stimulated expansion across western New York and Pennsylvania and into the Ohio and Mississippi valleys. As Yankee farmers spread into Ohio and Indiana, pressing the Shawnees from their lands, southern migrants pushed across Creek and Cherokee country, bringing government roads that split Native lands. More ambitious southern planters headed to the Gulf plains, plowing cotton fields that tripled production in the first fifteen years of the century. By 1812, U.S. citizens who inhabited the area between the Appalachians and the Mississippi outnumbered Native Americans 7 to 1.

Western migration also brought conflicts between whites and blacks. Between 1800 and 1808, just before Congress voted to outlaw the international slave trade, 63,000 Africans entered the country, many of whom were transshipped into the western regions. In addition, slave traders moved over 100,000 Chesapeake blacks overland into the new territories. After Louisiana became American property, U.S. slaveowners joined French planters in boosting the region's sugar production. In this hot, humid climate, such manufacturing required strong male workers, who outnumbered women by a ratio of 3 or 4 to 1. In 1811, harsh labor conditions inspired the largest slave rebellion in U.S. history, when Charles Deslondes led as many as

A camp meeting in Indiana. As one observer described revivals, "A vast crowd, supposed by some to have amounted to twenty-five thousand, was collected together. The noise was like the roar of Niagara."

500 rebel slaves and fugitives in a bloody uprising against their masters. Armed militia finally ended the rebellion with violence and severe punishments. Whites in all the cotton states remained fearful of slave revolts.

Religious Revivalism

Geographic mobility also produced more subtle anxieties about social dislocation. By the 1820s, popular songs were expressing nostalgic lyrics, such as "How dear to this heart are the scenes of my childhood" ("Old Oaken Bucket") and "Be it ever so humble, there's no place like home" ("Home Sweet Home"). In newly settled areas, this concern about loss and a desire for stability contributed to a renewed interest in evangelical religions that stressed an individual's ability to find comfort in salvation. Seeking a personal religious conversion from sinner to saint, rural Americans increasingly moved away from the established Episcopalian, Congregational, and Presbyterian churches into less rigidly organized denominations, particularly the Baptists and Methodists, which emphasized a personal religious experience.

As itinerant preachers carried the gospel through scattered frontier villages, settlers sought spiritual expression in the electrifying Great Revivals at Cane Ridge, Kentucky, in 1801. These outpourings attracted some 20,000 enthusiasts, a dozen preachers, and converts by the hundreds. Within this evangelical Christianity, mobile people found not only a sense of personal salvation but also kinship and community, a voluntary joining of souls that merged an individualistic spirit with social responsibility. Congregations could scrutinize moral behavior, praise the faithful, and expel the sinful. Revivalism also stimulated the emergence of some women preachers, such as Harriet Livermore, known as "the Pilgrim Stranger," who in 1826 became the first woman to speak before Congress.

African American Christianity

The revival movement extended beyond white Christians and influenced the emergence of a distinctive African American Christianity. Responding to the Baptist and Methodist practices of communal prayer, exhortations, chanting, and clapping, which echoed the religious traditions of west Africa, blacks had joined those denominations during the late colonial period, often experiencing equality with fellow white parishioners. Even in southern states, some white evangelicals advocated the end of slavery. To blacks, evangelical Christianity had a familiar spiritual appeal. The practice of water baptism mirrored religious traditions in west African cultures, and the Christian belief of converting to a "new life" paralleled African beliefs in stages of spiritual development. The Christian idea of evil, though absent in African traditions, gave African Americans a context for understanding their enslavement. Nonetheless, only a small minority of slaves ever became Christians.

By 1800, southern evangelicals had retreated from supporting emancipation. Stressing the separation of church and state, these evangelicals described slavery as a strictly civil issue, not in the province of organized religion. While still emphasizing the universality of religious values, the churches created segregated congregations, seating black worshippers separately or holding different religious services for blacks and whites. From such pressure emerged the first African American Christian denominations, including the African Methodist Episcopal church founded by free blacks in 1816. Within their separate congregations, African Americans listened to female and male black preachers, preserved west African styles of prayer, such as call-and-response and the distinctive counterclockwise circle or ring dance, and perpetuated African funeral and mourning practices.

Christianity and Native American Conflict

Although migration across the Appalachians encouraged the mixing of diverse settlers, the westward movement brought newcomers into conflict with resident Native American communities. To aid white migrants, the U.S. government adopted a policy of divide-and-conquer, exploiting internal divisions within Native groups to seize their lands. In the Northwest territory, the national government began to make annual payments to selected "annuity" chiefs in exchange for tribal lands—a form of bribery that bitterly divided Native groups. With the white population spilling across the treaty boundaries of the 1790s, military officials and Christian missionaries pressed Native leaders to abandon their hunting economy and adopt agriculture. But since Native women traditionally attended to farming, Native men had no desire to assume female occupations; nor did Native women, who counted on men to supply skins for clothing and moccasins, wish to learn knitting and weaving. In other words, the proposed "civilizing" process, by which Native men adopted sedentary farming and women became "employed in our houses," involved a drastic reversal of gender roles. While some Native leaders who were beneficiaries of the government's annuity payments supported those changes, many leaders protested the abandonment of traditional beliefs.

One of the defenders of Native traditions was the Shawnee leader Tenskwatawa, known as the Prophet. Having experienced a religious vision around 1805, Tenskwatawa won a large following among the Northwest people by bringing a message from the Master of Life: "I will overturn the land," the prophecy declared, "so that all the white people will be covered and you alone shall inhabit the land." Under his guidance, imperiled Shawnees looked to traditional spiritual values to resist white expansion. Repudiating assimilation, the Prophet's supporters rejected the whites' food, alcohol, clothing, and utensils; curtailed sexual promiscuity with white traders; and resumed their traditional spiritual practices. Extinguishing what he considered

---

"They have driven us from the sea to the lakes. We can go no further."

---

to be the corrupt tribal fires, Tenskwatawa ritually relit the flames at Greenville, Ohio, site of the ignominious treaty of 1795 (see Chapter 7). Young warriors, disgusted by land sales made by the annuity chiefs, flocked like pilgrims to the Prophet's camp. So numerous were the visitors, from places as distant as Wisconsin and across the Mississippi River, that the Shawnee spiritualist had to move his camp to a larger site at Tippecanoe on the Wabash River in Indiana.

While government agents watched with alarm as the movement grew, the Prophet's brother, Tecumseh, traveled among the Northwest peoples trying to build a coalition that would refuse to sell any more land to whites. Rivalry among competing groups undermined Native American unity. In 1809, General William Henry Harrison persuaded friendly chiefs to transfer another 3 million acres in Indiana. "They have driven us from the sea to the lakes," protested Tecumseh, "We can go no further."

As tensions between government agents and Native American revivalists mounted, Tecumseh visited the English in Canada to seek military assistance, then embarked in 1811 on a bold journey to gain support among the southern nations. By then, both the southern Choctaws and Chickasaws had adopted an agricultural way of life and rebuffed Tecumseh's offer to join a confederation. Some militant Creeks expressed sympathy, but their distance from the Northwest made cooperation virtually impossible. During Tecumseh's absence, moreover, Harrison moved his troops against the Prophet's settlements, routing his followers in the battle of Tippecanoe in 1811. Frustrated by U.S.

policy, Tecumseh's Shawnee allies would fight with the British during the War of 1812.

A New Spirit of Enterprise

While western migrants sought land and economic opportunity, more subtle economic changes began to affect the country's attitudes toward business relations around the turn of the 19th century. Some observers began to complain about a rise of materialism and lamented what author Washington Irving called "the almighty dollar." Others criticized the growing impersonality of the marketplace and warned about the risks of doing business with strangers.

On family farms, especially in the northeast, rural women began to devote larger portions of their time to making cloth, buttons, and straw hats, not just for home consumption but for sale or trade. As in the colonial period, local governments continued to regulate the economy, seeking to protect the public interest from selfish entrepreneurs. Yet, the spirit of enterprise often seemed an end in itself, a release of individual energy from social control. Innovative economic activity reflected a subtle loosening of traditional business constraints.

The Market Economy Alters Domestic Life

Throughout the colonial period, successful commercial farmers had sold their surplus crops in an international marketplace, exporting tobacco, grains, and meat to the West Indies and Europe. Even small farmers had engaged in an exchange economy, trading small surpluses, agricultural tools, or day labor to obtain goods and services they could not provide for themselves. But, while commercial farmers often lamented the problems of debt and credit, most business between neighbors and kin involved noncommercial values of friendship and mutual assistance. To be sure, colonials were not shy about taking their neighbors to court to settle disputes about land and other property. But, with cash in short supply, most trade involved borrowing or barter, and creditors would carry small debts for months, even years, without charging interest. Such informal arrangements differed from long-distance business transactions, such as transatlantic trade, which involved more detailed accounting and prompter payments.

By the early 19th century, as population increased, bringing a rise in nonagricultural work and geographical dispersal, economic relations gradually became more formal—and more profitable. One congressman boasted that his constituents were "bred to commerce." "Barter and sale are their delight. The spirit of business warms them." In both western New England and western Virginia, for example, the growth of livestock production created greater dependency on the drovers who took cattle and pigs to market. Meat producers increasingly dealt, not with consumers but with merchants and butchers who bought the animals to feed the towns and cities. In other words, more producers were becoming wholesalers, while retail merchants dealt directly with consumers. Livestock also stimulated the dairy industry, enabling farm women to produce surplus butter and cheese for sale. Seeking to maximize agricultural production, New England families harvested broomcorn, the natural ingredient of the broom industry, and sold their wares to rural and urban merchants. Although commercial transactions often remained informal and prices were usually negotiable, some large merchants introduced a new, impersonal business ethic. As one of them advertised in 1802: "No trust, no goods sent out, no samples given, no abatement in price first asked, no goods delivered until paid for."

These emerging economic trends affected the quality of domestic life. Economic protests during the war for independence and the loss of trade with England afterward had stimulated home manufacturing. In rural families, men increasingly filled slack times by making shoes, tools, or furniture for trade or sale, while women integrated spinning and weaving into their daily routines. In 1810, 90 percent of the nation's total textile output was made at home. Even the early industrial mills, introduced between 1790 and 1815, produced yarns, which were then distributed to weavers who worked at home. Such activity often made the difference between a family's profit and loss, but put great pressure on women's time. "A woman's work is never done," sighed one diarist in 1795, "and happy [is] she whose strength holds out to the end of the [sun's] rays."

Despite this rise in home manufacturing, most housewives continued to stress their contributions to childcare and the rearing of good citizens. "You may benefit a nation, my dear Papa," one young mother wrote to her politician father, but "I may improve the condition of a fellow-being." Among poorer families, the limitations of economic resources, particularly in eastern areas, began to force young couples to delay marriage. Such decisions caused, in turn, a reduction in years of marital fertility and brought a shrinking of the size of rural white families outside the South.

The declining birthrate enabled parents to focus more attention on each child. Together with the rise of evangelical religion, which emphasized the possibility of individual salvation, parents came to see their children, not as naturally sinful but as potentially perfectible. Attitudes toward childrearing also began to change. Instead of beating children to break their evil wills, parents now endeavored to shape their children with more moderate discipline. "It is the fashion of the times to be lenient, loose, licentious," observed a disapproving writer in 1814, "and parents, out of mere *parental affection*. . . give their children some portion of that indulgence, which they allow themselves." Ironically, as the drop in birthrates diminished the number of children, parents also lost the free labor of older siblings. In subsequent decades, overworked housewives gladly surrendered time-consuming domestic textile work to buy their cloth in village stores.

The Dawn of a National Economy

Even as household production prospered, manufacturing underwent subtle but significant change, particularly in northern towns and cities. Skilled male artisans—carpenters, shoemakers, tailors—continued to dominate the urban crafts. These master craftsmen produced mahogany furniture, fine dinner plates, gilt-edged mirrors, and accurate eight-day clocks for well-to-do consumers. But the growing market for inexpensive products altered the nature of skilled work. Even before the introduction of machinery for mass production, the demand for ready-to-wear clothing and cheap shoes for slaves, for example, led innovative tailors and shoemakers to change the manufacturing process to improve the quantity, rather than the quality, of their products. Instead of one skilled worker's making an entire shoe, the division of labor allowed two or three workers to specialize in specific parts of the process. Such specialization led to the introduction of distinct left and right shoes, an advantage to consumers. Meanwhile, the opening of the first shoestores further separated the shoemaker from the retail consumer.

New manufacturing techniques altered the nature of labor. Instead of signing a contract with an apprentice worker and agreeing to teach him a skilled craft, master artisans preferred to hire free workers, even child and women laborers, who

Eli Terry clock. During the first years of the century, Connecticut clockmaker Eli Terry built specialized, mass-production machine tools that operated with a small tolerance of error, thereby producing intricate, inexpensive, and fully interchangeable clock parts. Nearly every household owned a timepiece by mid-century. Yankee peddlers distributing these clocks around the country also spread new attitudes about the importance of accurate time keeping. Here was the technological base that would make punctuality a national virtue.

could be paid less than men and be taught only the rudimentary skills necessary to make so-called slop goods. Although workers complained bitterly about the decline of traditional crafts, day laborers formed a growing class of employees who lived in rented rooms and faced layoffs during lean times. The worst jobs were reserved for Irish and African American workers. Not accidentally, the early decades of the century witnessed the outbreak of the first labor strikes (which the courts usually held to be illegal conspiracies) as workers developed an identity distinct from that of their employers.

The expansion of domestic trade and commercial agriculture also stimulated a revolution in transportation. "Things which twenty years ago a man would have been laughed at for believing," stated a government report in 1812, "we now see." Traditionally, water routes were the cheapest mode of commerce, especially between port cities, but the inland river systems remained slow and unreliable. Private investors increasingly formed joint-stock companies, backed by state and local government investments, to finance the construction of public roads and bridges. State charters established minimal standards for each project and permitted investors to charge tolls to users.

By the second decade of the century, this marriage of government and business had produced a network of turnpikes that connected the major towns of the northeast. The national government also financed interstate roads, including the Federal Road, which cut through Creek country in Georgia, and the National or Cumberland Road, begun in 1811, which linked Cumberland, Maryland, with Wheeling on the Ohio River.

More dramatic were experiments with steamboat technology, culminating in 1807 with Robert Fulton's *Clermont,* the first commercially successful steamboat, which ran on the Hudson River. Steamboat traffic drastically reduced the cost of shipping. By 1814, the price of sending a barrel of flour between Albany and New York City had fallen from $2 to 25 cents. Meanwhile, other innovators were already planning artificial canals, which would transform domestic commerce in later decades.

The national and state governments also supported business by issuing charters for corporations and banks, numbering some 1,800 companies be-

"The market house, like the grave, is a place of perfect equality."

tween 1800 and 1817. Although a Republican Congress allowed Hamilton's Bank of the United States to expire in 1811, other banks mushroomed within the states, increasing from 29 in 1800 to over 200 fifteen years later. These banks not only invested capital at interest but also issued bank notes (a form of paper money), which served as a circulating currency so long as people were confident that their notes could be redeemed. Government aid to manufacturing remained minimal. Tariffs on imported goods served primarily to raise revenue rather than to protect domestic industry. But states granted water rights, land, tax incentives, and exemptions from nuisance laws to help specific enterprises.

This new "spirit of enterprise" brought mixed responses from contemporary observers. While many saw business expansion as a sign of progress, others lamented the loss of an older morality. "The market house, like the grave," quipped one observer, "is a place of perfect equality." But if economic development appealed to individualistic values, the new economy brought failure as well as success. Businesses failed with unnerving frequency, casting entrepreneurs into debt. Although western migration and business investment permitted economic advancement, a smaller proportion of the population controlled a larger share of the national wealth. In New York, the number of paupers in the city's almshouses tripled between 1790 and 1817. At a time when people still went to jail for debt, investors had reason to worry about excessive economic optimism.

"Multitudes are undone," warned a southern newspaper, "by taking, as well as giving too much credit." As cash transactions eroded an older ethic of unwritten agreements, critics of the new economy stressed the importance of individual responsibility and self-discipline to avoid financial temptation and deceit. Thus when "Parson" Mason Locke Weems, an ambitious, bestselling book peddler, published his immensely popular *Life of Washington* in 1800, he depicted the first president as the embodiment of virtue—hardworking, self-controlled, impeccably honest (hence the story of the cherry tree)—a perfect model for children to imitate.

Tightening the Law of Contracts

The fear of credit, debt, and inadvertent ruin reinforced the law of contracts. On the national level, John Marshall's Supreme Court rigidly defended the sanctity of contracts, even in the face of obvious fraud. Thus, in *Fletcher v. Peck* (1810), the Court rejected the Georgia legislature's repeal of a corrupt land transaction, explaining that the Constitution protected the original contract. Similarly, in *Dartmouth College v. Woodward* (1819), the Court ruled that the state of New Hampshire had violated a colonial charter (which the Court said was a type of contract) by attempting to turn the private school into a state college. Such rulings laid the foundation of a national legal system at a time of expanding domestic commerce and provided important precedents for government relations with private business.

Strict rules of contract extended even to the most private of matters. State courts increasingly treated marriage as a consensual arrangement rather than a property settlement and held that a breach of promise to marry violated the sanctity of contract. The injured party (usually the woman) thus was entitled to sue, in the words of one Massachusetts judge, for such "losses" as "the wounded spirit, the unmerited disgrace, and the probable solitude" that would result from a broken engagement. Rejecting a world of informal promises where a person's word was his bond, Americans moved toward a code of ethics based on written contracts. No wonder, then, that the number of lawyers in the country grew four times faster than the population between 1783 and 1820.

A Second War for Independence

The outbreak of a new war between England and France in 1803 underscored the nation's involvement in European trade. Jefferson's goal of minimizing government activity while encouraging economic development thus collided with the risks of international commerce. The European war initially brought a boom to U.S. trade. Happy to receive agricultural exports, England, still mistress of the seas, permitted the United States to trade with France and its colonies. But as Napoleon's French armies established dominance on the European continent, England shifted to economic warfare and tried to block foreign commerce from reaching France. Napoleon retaliated by establishing boycotts against countries that traded with England. And then both European belligerents began to seize and confiscate U.S. ships; by 1807, some 700 U.S. vessels had surrendered their cargoes.

Defending Neutral Rights

Britain's naval supremacy also aroused opposition to a practice that began in colonial days: the seizure of alleged British deserters aboard U.S. ships for impressment into the service of the royal navy. Complicating the issue was Britain's refusal to recognize naturalized U.S. citizens and the difficulty of proving an individual's status. American citizens were sometimes forced at gunpoint to serve in the British navy. The issue drew public attention in 1807 when, within sight of Virginia shores, the British warship *Leopard* ordered the U.S. *Chesapeake* to allow a boarding party to search for deserters. The American ship's refusal to comply brought a rain of fire and an embarrassing surrender. While an outraged public called for war with England, the cautious Jefferson opted instead for negotiations.

Reluctant to enter a war that would require military mobilization, higher taxes, and a disruption of trade, Jefferson adopted a policy of peaceful pressure. In 1807, he persuaded Congress to pass an Embargo Act, which prohibited U.S. commerce with foreign ports. Since Britain had already interrupted U.S. trade with France, the measure was clearly aimed at England, with the expectation that British needs for agricultural produce would force England to recognize U.S. commercial rights. More practically, the embargo kept U.S. ships off the high seas, safe from further trouble. Underlying the embargo rested another idea, old as the colonial protests before independence, that American frugality would prove stronger than Britain's addiction to the fruits of commerce.

By congressional statute, U.S. foreign trade came to a halt. To be sure, some enterprising merchants developed a substantial smuggling business through British Canada. Together with the rapid increase of exports from Canada to England, this illegal trade greatly reduced the impact of the embargo. But as U.S. ships rotted at the docks, urban unemployment rose, exports sank, and the only business seemed to be bankruptcy proceedings and imprisonment for debt. Hardest hit were the shipping centers in New England. The 1808 elections tolled the result. Although Secretary of State Madison won the presidential election, Federalists returned to Congress in force, determined to repeal the hated embargo.

Although both England and France violated U.S. neutral rights, Republican leaders remained committed to peaceful maneuvers. After terminating the embargo, Congress passed the Nonin-tercourse Act of 1809, which resumed commerce with all nations, except England and France, and then promised to open trade with either of those countries after they ended commercial restrictions. When the British ambassador accepted the U.S. offer, President Madison thought the negotiations had succeeded. Six hundred American ships raced for England to cash in on the peace. But the British government abruptly rejected the settlement. A frustrated Congress then passed another compromise law in 1810, known as Macon's Bill Number 2, which lifted all restraints on U.S. shipping, but promised that if either England or France ended its commercial restrictions the United States would restore an embargo against the other country. Since England controlled the sea lanes to Europe, Napoleon offered to stop French violations *if* England did the same.

Declaring War on England

Madison knew that Napoleon's diplomatic overture did not involve a change in French policy; indeed, the French continued to seize U.S. ships. But pushing his toe in the door, the president used Napoleon's promise to stop seizing U.S. ships as an excuse to restore the nonintercourse measure against England in 1811. Public opinion, already anti-British, supported this step. Madison also resolved to fight for U.S. honor, and the nation moved closer to war. In the spring of 1812, Congress approved a 60-day embargo—time enough to allow U.S. ships at sea to return safely home—in preparation for declaring war against England. And, at last, the pressure against English merchants had the desired effect. With business in a slump, English manufacturers, desperate for southern cotton, persuaded the British government to end commercial restrictions in June 1812.

Americans found little satisfaction in the diplomatic victory. By then, the president had already persuaded Congress to declare war on England. While Federalists bitterly depicted the impending evils of conflict, "war hawks" in and out of Congress emphasized the revitalizing effects of going to war. "Forbearance has ceased to be a virtue," announced a congressional war report drafted by the young South Carolina representative John C. Calhoun. "There is an alternative only between the base surrender of their rights and a manly vindication." Madison's war message also mentioned British assistance to the Native Americans of the Northwest. Such factors (anti-Native sentiment, the defense of national honor, the ideology of republican virtue) surely contributed to the decision to fight. But, at bottom, the United States went to war in 1812 to defend its maritime rights on the high seas—rights that not only protected the interests of shipowners, merchants, and sailors but also access to markets for farmers with goods to sell abroad.

The War of 1812 Begins

Madison now led an ill-prepared nation into war against the mighty British empire. Despite seven years of commercial and diplomatic conflict, neither Congress nor the citizenry had prepared for war. When Congress approved the creation of a 35,000-man army (white male citizens between the ages of 18 and 45), barely 7,000 enlisted. The nation turned to the state militias, but encountered divided leadership, inexperience, and an attachment to local interests that led some volunteers to refuse orders to fight. The navy, well tested in wars with France and North African pirates, would protect merchant vessels hurrying home, but could hardly match the royal navy at sea.

Frugal Republicans had also weakened the economic apparatus necessary to wage war. Customs duties remained the main source of government income, but the war reduced trade, which in turn reduced revenues. Excise taxes, never very popular, brought small funds. The government turned to borrowing money. But a Republican Congress had permitted the Bank of the United States to expire in 1811, and state banks lacked sufficient capital. In the second year of the war, the administration reluctantly issued treasury bonds and certificates, which circulated below face value. Meanwhile, Federalist merchants, who opposed the war because it disrupted their trade with Britain, refused to contribute to the cause. In Connecticut, Federalist towns filed nuisance charges against the army for playing martial music during recruitment rallies. By 1814, as the government veered toward bankruptcy, Republicans proposed higher taxes. Only the end of the war spared the country worse financial embarrassment.

Native Americans Side with Britain

The outbreak of war intensified conflicts with the Native American nations. As the United States made plans to invade British Canada, Shawnee leaders in the Northwest argued about which side to support. Although many annuity chiefs defended their ties to the United States, Tecumseh pleaded for "us Indians of North America to form ourselves into one great combination" to fight against the United States. Tecumseh then formed an alliance with British military leaders and again visited the southern Creeks to make plans for a coordinated attack against American forces. He returned to the Northwest territory just as the United States prepared to invade Canada.

The weakness of U.S. military efforts exaggerated Native American strength. When U.S. General William Hull led an expedition from Detroit toward Canada in 1812, Tecumseh's warriors cut his supply lines, forcing U.S. troops to retreat and

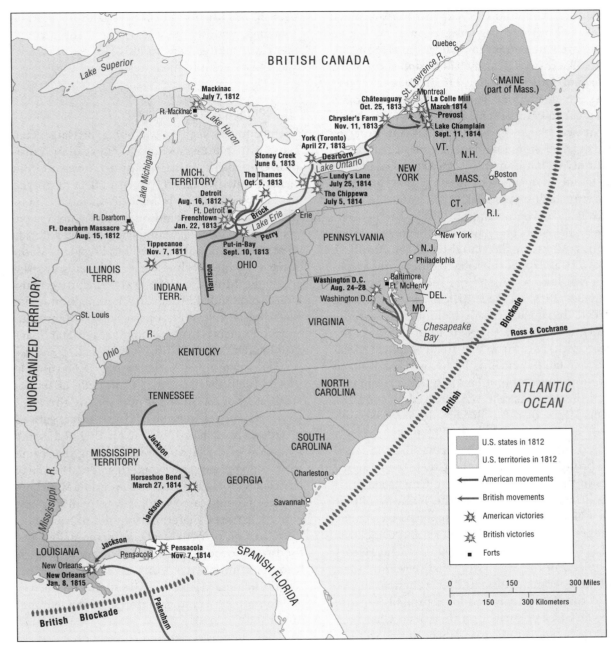

The War of 1812   OVERLAY 1

surrender. A second U.S. expedition to Canada succeeded in capturing Queenstown, but had to disengage when attacked by Britain's Mohawk allies. Still a third U.S. army had to stop short of the Canadian border when local militiamen refused to cross the state border. The land war thus appeared as a great embarrassment to the United States.

At sea, the navy fought well, but superior British forces won dominance in the Atlantic, subject only to harassment by an extensive fleet of American privateers. On inland waters, however, U.S. seamanship prevailed. In the critical Battle of Lake Erie in 1813, Captain Oliver Perry eliminated a British fleet. General William Henry Harrison, famous for the slaughter of the Prophet's followers at Tippecanoe, ferried his army across the great lake to pursue the redcoats and their Shawnee allies. As the British prepared a further retreat, Tecumseh pleaded eloquently for the chance to fight. "Our lives are in the hands of the Great Spirit," he cried. "We are determined to defend our lands, and if it be his will we wish to leave our bones upon them." In the ensuing battle of the Thames, the U.S. army destroyed the enemy. There died the Shawnee leader Tecumseh in 1813.

Futile in the Northwest, Tecumseh's resistance also brought calamity to the Creeks and Cherokees in the southeast. After the Creeks successfully attacked U.S. forces in the Tennessee River valley, General Andrew Jackson organized a counterattack, supported by Cherokees and Choctaws. In 1814, Jackson trapped 1,000 Creeks at Horseshoe Bend in the Mississippi territory and killed 800 men, women, and children. Then, after the Creek survivors scattered for refuge in Florida, Jackson's troops turned on their own Cherokee allies. When government agents protested this betrayal, Jackson replied, "No confidence can be placed in the honesty of an Indian!" The punitive Treaty of Fort Jackson, imposed in 1814, claimed over 20 million acres of Native land in Georgia, Alabama, and Tennessee. By then, the government was taking steps to move peaceful Creeks and Cherokees into the Louisiana territory.

Mr. Madison's War

Such triumphs kept the war going, but largely because British armies were still engaged on European battlefields. In 1814, a British invasion from Canada failed when an American fleet destroyed British supply ships in a battle on Lake Champlain. But another landing on the Chesapeake overwhelmed U.S. defenses, enabling the redcoats to march on the nation's capital. President Madison escaped just before the British set fire to the public buildings, including the executive mansion. An intended British attack on Baltimore did meet resistance from troops at Fort McHenry (inspiring Francis Scott Key to write "The Star Spangled Banner") and the British retreated.

The burning of Washington, D.C., underscored the humiliations of what Federalists derided as "Mr. Madison's War." During the 1812 elections, Federalist critics of the war had carried numerous state elections in New England, some by means of the creative redistricting that came to be known as *gerrymandering*. But the party lacked a national base, failed to prevent Madison's reelection, and scarcely influenced public policy. Some frustrated Federalists spoke of secession from the union. With legal commerce stalled and the British occupying nearby Maine, Federalist leaders summoned a convention at Hartford, Connecticut, in December 1814 to protest the war and to propose "a radical reform" of the national union.

The Federalists' Hartford convention proposed a series of constitutional amendments, which would, in effect, preserve the political power of this conservative regional minority. Among the propos-

The term *gerrymandering* was first coined in 1812, when Massachusetts Governor Elbridge Gerry had his state legislature favor a fellow Republican by engineering the oddly shaped district shown here—half salamander, half "Gerry"-mander.

als was the apportionment of representation and taxation based on the size of the white population, thus voiding the Three-Fifths Compromise which had given slave states greater influence (see Chapter 7). Reflecting their fear of regional isolation, the delegates suggested that the admission of new states require a two-thirds vote of Congress, which would slow territorial expansion. Two other measures would protect New England's economic interests by requiring a two-thirds majority for Congress to enact embargoes or declare war. To weaken the influence of Virginia, which had already produced three of the first four presidents, another proposal would limit presidents to a single term of office. Yet another recommended that naturalized citizens be barred from holding public office, to preserve the ethnic homogeneity of the leadership. In sum, the Federalists attempted to re-

Overnight, Jackson and his frontier riflemen became national heroes.

verse history, stop national development, and restore the old colonial hierarchy. That was no longer possible.

Federalist frustrations soon vanished, however, when U.S. troops scored a stunning triumph against the British at New Orleans in January 1815. Defeating a force of 10,000 redcoats, Andrew Jackson's militia from Georgia, Tennessee, and Kentucky gave the country a victory that transformed public opinion about the war. Overnight, Jackson and his frontier riflemen became national heroes, citizen-soldiers who had saved the embattled republic. Politicians and newspaper publishers gushed their thanks in verse and song. Patriotic enthusiasts claimed that "God had tested Americans and their government" to prove the superiority of republican virtue.

The Fruits of Peace

Despite such boasts, both the battle of New Orleans and the Hartford convention occurred after diplomatic negotiations had formally ended the war in the Treaty of Ghent in December 1814. When news of the peace finally reached America the following month, joyous citizens paid little attention to its ambiguous terms. Neither side had gained additional territory, though precise boundaries between the United States and Canada would be settled later by joint commissions. Nor did the British concede questions of neutral rights or impressment. Rather, the end of the European wars effectively eliminated the grievances that had provoked hostilities in the first place.

The war, in short, brought no tangible benefits except the indefinable pride of having avoided defeat against the most powerful European country. "Let any man look at the degraded condition of the country before the war," suggested Speaker of the House Henry Clay in 1816. "The scorn of the universe, the contempt of ourselves; and tell me we have gained nothing by the war?. . . . Our character and constitution are placed on a solid basis never to be shaken." In peace, the nation achieved what it had lacked during the recent war: a sense of purpose, self-confidence, and stability.

After the War of 1812, political leadership passed to a new breed of politicians. John Quincy Adams, son of the second president, and his chief political rival, Andrew Jackson, were both born in 1767; Kentucky's Henry Clay came ten years later; South Carolina's John C. Calhoun and Massachusetts' Daniel Webster were five years younger. Unlike the Founding Fathers—Washington, Adams, Jefferson, and Madison—this younger generation of national politicians had grown up with republican institutions and ideals and had learned almost with their first breath the principles of self-government and majority rule, without qualms or fear. Proud of a newfound "national character," the new generation boasted of the country's growth, mobility, even diversity, and promised to extend their institutions across the continent.

INFOTRAC® COLLEGE EDITION EXERCISES

 For additional reading go to InfoTrac College Edition, your online research library at *http://web1.infotrac-college.com.*

Keyword search: Anti-Federalist

Keyword search: Federalist

Keyword search: John Marshall

Keyword search: Marbury v. Madison

Keyword search: Lewis and Clark

Keyword search: James Madison

Subject search: United States History, War of 1812

Keyword search: Chesapeake

Keyword search: impressment

Keyword search: Tecumseh

ADDITIONAL READING

A Jeffersonian Agenda

Drew R. McCoy, *The Elusive Republic: Political Economy in Jeffersonian America* (1980). A study of economic values and ideas that links the republican tradition to political policy. See also Appleby's book listed in Chapter 7.

Lewis and Clark Reach the Pacific

James P. Ronda, *Lewis and Clark among the Indians* (1984). A study emphasizing the interaction with Native peoples; for a general overview, see Stephen E. Ambrose, *Undaunted Courage: Meriwether Lewis, Thomas Jefferson, and the Opening of the American West* (1996).

Religious Revivalism

Sylvia R. Frey and Betty Wood, *Come Shouting to Zion: African American Protestantism in the American South and British Caribbean to 1830* (1998). Traces the Christianization of African Americans from the colonial period through the great revivals of the early 1800s; see also the pioneering first chapter of Sterling Stuckey, *Slave Culture: Nationalist Theory and the Foundations of Black America* (1987).

Christianity and Native American Conflict

Allan W. Eckert, *A Sorrow in Our Heart: The Life of Tecumseh* (1992). A solid biography of the Shawnee leader; for a briefer study, see R. David Edmunds, *Tecumseh and the Quest for Indian Leadership* (1984).

R. David Edmunds, *The Shawnee Prophet* (1983). Examines the career of Tenskwatawa and explains the

Shawnee revival; see also Dowd's *Spirited Resistance,* listed in the previous chapter.

A New Spirit of Enterprise

Steven Watts, *The Republic Reborn: War and the Making of Liberal America, 1790–1820* (1987). This cultural history examines the expanding economy and its impact on American identity.

Nancy F. Cott, *The Bonds of Womanhood: "Woman's Sphere" in New England, 1780–1835* (1977). Based on women's writings, this book describes attitudes toward domesticity, education, religion, and sisterhood.

Cynthia A. Kierner, *Beyond the Household: Women's Place in the Early South, 1700–1835* (1998).

Depicts women's changing roles in the southern states. For the role of women in the northern maritime industry, see Lisa Norling, *Captain Ahab Had a Wife: New England Women and the Whalefishery, 1720–1870* (2000).

Jean V. Matthews, *Toward a New Society: American Thought and Culture, 1800–1830* (1991). A history of ideas, this book discusses such subjects as religion, science, art, and education.

A Second War for Independence

J. C. A. Stagg, *Mr. Madison's War: Politics, Diplomacy, and Warfare in the Early American Republic, 1783–1830* (1983). Examines the political background of the War of 1812.

The National Gazette

AND
LITERARY REGISTER.

PRINCIPLES *AND* MEN.

PHILADELPHIA, FRIDAY AFTERNOON, JUNE 7, 1822.

The National Gazette.

FOR THE NATIONAL GAZETTE.

THE FINE ARTS.

The Roman School is the most celebrated for beauty and correctness of design, elegance in composition, truth of
expression and intelligence in attitudes.
Its masters were fostered in the Greek
taste. They applied themselves less to
colouring, than to rendering with a kind
of solemnity, the grand ideas with which
they were penetrated; and in this they
have succeeded to a wonderful extent.
Rome has been, and must ever continue
to be, the best school for the fine arts,
so long as she retains the vestiges of
her greatness, and the monuments of
her former splendour and supremacy.
Where will the artist learn so well the
abridged history of Roman victory, of
the march of her legions, their banners,
and arms, and the costume of the nations
which she conquered, as on the trium-
phal arches of Severus and Constantine,
and the columns of Trajan and Antoni-
nus? In thus contemplating grandeur,
though amid ruins, his genius takes a
loftier flight, his mind is stored with
models for imitation, of a higher order,
and he labours in that spirit of enthusiasm which no other scenes could excite.
Let him walk through the halls of the
Vatican and Capitol, and his eye is met
by the personifications of divinity, high
and unbending in the Apollo, dignified
in the Juno, and graceful and lovely in
the Venus: the Emperor, the Philosopher and the Poet, are here present in
their busts and statues, which impart to
the spectator a portion of the respective
spirits which actuated them when living. Astonishment and admiration are
soon succeeded by a spirit of careful
discrimination, and a studious selection
of expressions, attitudes and disposition
of drapery: the memory filled with such
imagery and the internal sense rendered
acute, the hand soon executes what the
imagination devises, not the grotesque
vagaries of barbarism, but the sublime,
the beautiful and the true in nature. It
was in looking at the Pantheon, that
Michel Angelo formed the daring idea
of raising the dome of St. Peter's to tow-
er in the heavens, showing that not only

pupils. On the second story of these
lodges, in the first wing, are some of
his most celebrated productions, consisting of fifty two paintings, representing
some of the principal events recorded
in the old testament, and executed after
the cartoons of Raphael by Julio Roma-
na, Pietro del Vaga, Polidoro and Matu-
rin di Caravagio, and others. Of the
four first paintings that which is over
the door of the entry, and which represents the Almighty dispersing Chaos, is
entirely by Raphael. Few dare undertake such a subject, still fewer, none but
Raphael could have preserved in the
execution the sublimity of the concep-
tion. The Father is displayed darting
forward, in extending the arms and legs,
and by this single movement he separates the elements and arranges each in
its situation.

Between the first and second wing of
these lodges is a door opening into the
Rooms (*Camere*) of Raphael, containing
those paintings so celebrated in the an-
nals of the fine Arts, but which time,
humidity, and neglect, have much injured: the colouring is faded and of course
much of the effect must be lost, at least
the first impressions are not so favoura-
ble as would have been anticipated.

The greater part of these rooms was
already painted under Julius II. by Pietro de Borgo Bramante, of Milan, Pietro
Perugino and others, when at the instance of the celebrated Bramante Laz-
zari of Urbino, the Pope induced Raphael to come from Florence to Rome,
to paint also with the others a façade in
which he was to represent the Disputa-
tion on the Holy Sacrament. When
this work was finished, the Pope was so
much surprised and gratified that he
made all the other painters cease from
their labours, and even directed that the
whole of what they had done should be
effaced, and that Raphael should repaint
the entire series. This incomparable artist, however, out of respect to his pre-
ceptor Perugino would not suffer a ceiling
painted by him to be effaced. The
rooms are four in number, and named
after the subject represented in them.

The first is called the Hall of Constantine. On the wall opposite the windows is represented the victory of Constantine the Great, over the tyrant

Third room. One
works of Raphael
school of Athens or
ancient philosophers.
for the scene, is a fine
in a magnificent style
This painting includ
which, while it displa
of the ancient phi
also a true school
such is highly prize
look upon it as an
mance. In the figur
sages, he has given
some of the persona
Archimedes who is
ture, and marking o
a compass, we see An
friend and relation
young man who has
heart is Francis Du
Nephew to Julius II.
knee on the ground,
serve the last ment
attention is Frederic
tua.—The two figure
rooster who holds a g
are intended for Pic
Raphael himself, wh
countenance, and is s
cap.

The painting oppo
of Athens represents
the Holy Sacrament.
tioned, it is the first
Raphael, and one of
fine composition, co
and colouring.—The
in an altar in the mi
sun with the Holy S
above are seen the
Virgin and St. John
the sides of the altar
tors of the Latin Chu
fathers and saints wh
profound mystery.—
to the right, over the
Raphael, who has s
Mount Parnassus, wh
we see the nine Mu
the midst of them, pl
different parts of the
base are many of the
modern, among who
race, Virgil, Ovid,
Dante, Boccacio, an
poetess Sappho.

A Nation of Regions, 1816–1828

CHRONOLOGY

1816	Congress charters Second Bank of the United States
	Congress establishes protective tariff
	James Monroe elected fifth president
1817	American Colonization Society projects African colony
1819	*McCulloch v. Maryland* affirms constitutionality of bank
	Financial panic causes prolonged national depression
	Adams-Onís treaty transfers Florida, extends U.S. claims to Pacific
1819–1821	Congress debates Missouri compromise
1822	Denmark Vesey plots slave rebellion
1823	Monroe Doctrine rejects further colonization of Americas
1824	Congress raises tariff duties
	House of Representatives elects John Quincy Adams president
1825	Erie Canal links Albany and Buffalo
1826	John Adams and Thomas Jefferson die, July 4
	Treaty of Washington absorbs Creek lands
1827	Cherokees adopt formal constitution
1828	Congress passes high protective tariff
	Andrew Jackson elected president

"The war was finished in a blaze of glory," exclaimed a Republican newspaper editor in 1815, "as though God had tested Americans and their government. . . . America now stands in the first rank of nations." A spirit of nationalism echoed in pulpits, schoolrooms, and political gatherings, and inspired enormous economic and social growth in the shape of territorial expansion, domestic commerce, and business development. The new national self-confidence also prompted the expansion of suffrage for white men. "Enterprise walks forth unrestrained," boasted the happy editor, "*and the people are free.*"

After 1816, the decline of the Federalist party reinforced feelings of national unity. The Virginian James Monroe, elected in 1816 with hardly any opposition outside New England and reelected four years later with only one dissenting vote in the electoral college, presided over what was called in 1817 the "era of good feelings."

The new nationalism encouraged a spirited celebration of the country's brief history. When Congress commissioned the Connecticut painter John Trumbull to decorate the Capitol rotunda with historical paintings, the artist depicted life-sized scenes of the signing of the Declaration of Independence and the British surrender at Yorktown. In 1817, William Wirt's popular biography of Patrick Henry gave schoolchildren a model of republican virtue—and, along the way, rewrote the words of Henry's speech of 1765 (see Chapter 5) to become the stirring "Give me liberty or give me death!" Most celebrated was George Washington, immortalized in portraits by Gilbert Stuart, mythological biographies, and innumerable statues that showed the wooden-jawed Virginian in Roman togas (the 555-foot monument would come later). The Battle of New Orleans added Andrew Jackson to the list of national heroes. Like Washington, Jackson was a citizen-soldier, symbolizing the virtue of ordinary people. Such self-conscious nationalism appeared authentic and yet was deliberately manufactured in an effort to overcome people's attachments to their separate states.

Amid all this self-glorification, most citizens still clung to older habits of culture and politics, feelings of loyalty to their home states and regions. The new generation of political leaders— among them, Henry Clay of Kentucky, John Calhoun of South Carolina, and Daniel Webster of Massachusetts—spoke boldly of the nation's promise, but keenly guarded the interests of their local constituencies. Embracing the equality of all citizens, these younger politicians had put aside

George Washington before Yorktown, 1781, as depicted by Rembrandt Peale.

knee breeches, buckled shoes, and powdered wigs in favor of trousers, shoe laces, and short-clipped hair. Such democratic attitudes encouraged the expansion of the electorate, first in the Northeast in the decade after 1815, and later in the southern states.

Meanwhile, economic and social developments revealed increasing differences between regions of the country. In the South, the expansion of cotton reinforced slave agriculture; in the Northeast, textile manufacturing became more important and politically influential; in the Northwest, prosperous free-labor farming created surplus produce for export and trade. These trends forced national politicians to confront conflicts of regional interest. Legislation in Congress about economic policy or territorial expansion demanded extensive compromise; some differences, such as the status of slavery in the territories, truly imperiled national cohesion. And because regional differences had political consequences—and since the electorate grew substantially during this period—one-party politics soon disappeared. By the end of the 1820s, voters in the states and politicians in Washington had restored a vigorous two-party system.

The Politics of a National Economy

The spirit of nationalism that followed the War of 1812 encouraged Congress to address problems of a national economy. With the Federalist party in retreat, Republican leaders like President James Madison no longer worried about a monarchist conspiracy and accepted greater government power. Moreover, the recent war had exposed the problems of an uncoordinated financial policy. Thus, in 1815, Madison proposed the creation of a second national bank (to replace Hamilton's Bank of the United States, whose charter had expired in 1811); a tariff that would raise the price of imported goods and so protect the manufacturing businesses that had grown during the embargo and the war; and a program of federally financed internal improvements. In Congress, Henry Clay presented a similar legislative package, which he named the "American System."

The agenda appealed to the younger generation of politicians, not only because they embraced a stronger national government but also because the measures would benefit their home states. With manufacturers seeking protection for new industries, especially in New England, Congress passed the Tariff of 1816, which kept customs duties at the wartime levels. Clay, anticipating the growth of Kentucky's hemp industry, and Calhoun, imagining textile factories in South Carolina, supported the law. Congress also voted in 1816 to charter the second Bank of the United States to centralize currency and credit as a check against unregulated state banks. No one now questioned the bank's constitutionality. Since dividends from the bank promised to provide new revenues for government expenditures, Congress proposed in 1816 to use the bank "bonus" to develop roads, bridges, and canals to improve transportation and ease commerce. "Let us bind the Republic together," said Calhoun. "Let us conquer space." Although Congress passed the measure, Madison vetoed the Bonus bill in 1817, three days before leaving office, claiming the Constitution did not permit such federal expenditures.

Building the Erie Canal

The most dramatic transportation project of the age, the Erie Canal, was funded not by the federal government but by the state of New York. Yet even this effort promised greater national cohesion; in the words of the canal's chief promoter, Governor DeWitt Clinton, the resulting commerce would eliminate "the distinctions of eastern and western, of southern and northern interests." Laid out on the route of the old Iroquois fur trade, the $7 million, eight-year project, completed in 1825, extended 363 miles, linking Albany and the Hudson river with Buffalo and the Great Lakes. Besides its impressive technological achievement, which required such innovations as light wheelbarrows, tree-cutting pulleys, new mortar, and 83 locks, the canal symbolized the conquest of the wilderness. At the groundbreaking ceremony on the symbolic day of national unity, July 4, 1817, politicians raised toasts to the mixing of western and eastern waters. Workers in New York City paraded to salute the spirit of enterprise and progress, while newspapers in inland towns celebrated the arrival, for the first time in history, of fresh Long Island oysters. In this age before public zoos, one canal boat (appropriately named *Noah's Ark*) transported a living menagerie

The Erie Canal, 1829. The watercolor drawing by John William Hall contrasts the peaceful rural landscape with the bustle of canal commerce.

Newspapers in inland towns celebrated the arrival, for the first time in history, of fresh Long Island oysters.

of western species, including animals, birds, and even Seneca people to awe urban New Yorkers.

The Erie Canal strengthened economic ties between the Northeast and the Northwest. The result saw a dramatic rise in canal freight as westerners shipped their agricultural surplus to metropolitan centers and beyond. By 1827, New York City's flour exports exceeded the total shipped through all other U.S. ports. Such success stimulated a burst of similar canal projects in other northern states.

The National Economy and the Marshall Court

The failure of Congress to fund such internal improvements reflected both constitutional scruples about the legality of such expenditures and local resistance to national regulation of economic affairs. At issue was the larger question of whether national laws took precedence over state and local laws. Disagreements about such matters eventually reached the United States Supreme Court and came under the scrutiny of John Marshall, the chief justice for thirty-five years (1801–1835) and the last Federalist to hold high office. In a series of cases, the Marshall Court reaffirmed the supremacy of national government over the states. When, for example, the Pennsylvania state legislature passed a law intended to invalidate a federal court ruling, Marshall ruled in the *Peters* case (1809) that states could not legislate against federal law. Other decisions determined that the Supreme Court could overrule the judgment of a state court. These rulings were not popular, but by 1825, Marshall's court had overturned laws in ten states.

In other cases involving economic development, the Supreme Court upheld the power of Congress to regulate a national economy. When the state of Maryland imposed local taxes on the second Bank of the United States, Marshall warned in *McCulloch v. Maryland* (1819) that "The power to tax involves the power to destroy" and denied the right of state governments to tax institutions created by Congress. The ruling reaffirmed the constitutionality of the bank and asserted the superiority of federal power. In a later decision that had important implications for commercial development, *Gibbons v. Ogden* (1824), the Court rejected a New York state-chartered steamboat monopoly, which limited competition, by defining commerce on the Hudson river as *interstate* commerce, thus giving the national government jurisdiction over commerce on rivers that touched more than one state.

The Panic of 1819

Despite Marshall's assertions of national power, political commitments to state and regional interests continued to affect national politics, particularly when the economy took a nosedive in what was called the "Panic of 1819." Although the second Bank of the United States had been designed to regulate economic expansion, optimism after 1816 encouraged a flurry of investment and speculation by state banks and private investors. As American farmers found larger markets in Europe after the devastation of the Napoleonic wars, food and cotton prices surged upward, encouraging greater development of western lands. But when European farmers resumed production, the demand for U.S. produce abruptly dropped, reducing both prices and exports.

The resulting economic collapse demonstrated that an interlinked national economy already existed. Cotton sank from 33 cents a pound to 14 cents; tobacco fell from 40 cents to 4. As trade dwindled, the central Bank tightened credit, setting off a domino wave of credit contraction among the state banks. When banks called in their loans, business slowed, forcing bankruptcies and

defaults. Besides ruining merchants, wholesalers, and retailers, the downturn brought high unemployment among propertyless workers, who were forced to seek public relief. By 1820, commercial debtors (nearly 1,500 in Boston and 1,800 in Philadelphia) filled local jails.

This crisis, the first major depression in the nation's history, soon penetrated the rural economy. Farmers and land speculators, who had borrowed to expand agricultural holdings during years of prosperity, now faced eviction. Congress responded by revising western land laws to lower prices and permit farmers to liquidate some of their holdings to finance the remainder. State legislatures passed stay laws to prevent seizure of mortgaged property by creditors. These measures brought some relief, but the political consequences of the Panic endured. Cotton exporters and western farmers, for the first time facing the uncertainties of world markets, blamed their troubles on the national bank. Many became permanently anti-bank, and their feelings would affect later political alignments about rechartering the national bank.

Meanwhile, northern manufacturers, reeling from the loss of domestic markets and facing renewed foreign competition, appealed for higher protective tariffs (taxes that would increase the price of imported goods and so offer advantages to domestic products). However, southern interests realized that by raising the cost of finished goods, higher tariffs would only benefit the manufacturing states of the Northeast. Cotton, the South's main product, needed no protection. In 1820, southern senators defeated the proposed tariff. Four years later, a revised tariff bill added protection for western raw materials, such as wool and hemp, as well as northeastern textiles and iron products, thus creating a marriage of interests between western livestock producers and northern manufacturers. Although southern congressmen voted almost unanimously against the measure, Congress passed the 1824 tariff, which raised duties without offering benefits to southern agriculture.

Territorial Expansion and Regional Differences

Opinions in Congress about economic issues reflected the regional differences of specific constituencies, especially the contrast between the northern and southern parts of the western territories. With the return of peace in 1815, both areas attracted large numbers of settlers. Indiana entered the union in 1816, Mississippi in 1817, Illinois in 1818, Alabama in 1819. In the former Northwest territory, U.S. military actions had hastened the departure of Shawnees, Kickapoos, and other nations westward across the Mississippi River. In their place came farmers from New York and New England, seeking land and a free labor farm economy. Meanwhile, Andrew Jackson's defeat of the southern nations during the War of 1812 (see Chapter 8) opened Native American lands to cotton planters, who swarmed into the area and made Mississippi and Alabama slave states.

During the 1820s, 15,000 African American slaves were sold each year from the upper South to cotton plantations in the Gulf states. As a result, the cotton crop of Mississippi tripled to 30 million pounds annually between 1821 and 1826, and exports from New Orleans increased nearly tenfold during the decade. Although slaveowners dominated politics in the southwestern states, a majority of farmers in the region owned no slaves. Other white migrants from Kentucky crossed the Ohio River into southern Indiana and Illinois, where they converged with transplanted northerners to form "free" states. Yet African Americans in the Northwest remained second-class citizens, forced to post bonds for good behavior in Ohio and often laboring as contract workers for former

slaveowners in Illinois. Only a narrow vote prevented Illinois from legalizing slavery in 1824.

Free Society and the Paradox of Race

In contrast to the cotton planters of the Southwest, settlers in the Northwest tended to be more transient. Typical was Thomas Lincoln, father of the sixteenth president, who was born in Virginia, married in Kentucky, widowed and remarried in Indiana, and died on his second farm in Illinois. Government land surveys, which divided property into regular grids, facilitated real estate transfers. But although government land prices dropped to $1.25 an acre in 1820, prevailing wages made land purchases difficult. In Philadelphia, for example, day laborers earned only 75 cents per day and even along the booming Erie Canal workers could expect no more than a monthly income of $14 plus food, laundry, and a pint of whiskey. Families spent 80 percent of their income on food, clothing, and shelter. Although western settlers could buy a reasonable-sized farm for about $100, most frontier families could not save that much. Instead, they squatted on public lands for a limited time, then sold the "improvements" to a newcomer and moved on.

Despite this mobility, many western settlers migrated with or near other family members and friends, forming core communities that intermarried, built churches and schools, participated in political life, and shared "frolics," such as group corn-husking and house-raising. Early marriages in the new states encouraged high birthrates—6 to 8 children among first-generation settlers. Having small agricultural surpluses to sell, rural families engaged in a barter economy and worked hard. Those who owned their own land enjoyed both a sense of community and self-sufficiency.

The idea of a free society was nevertheless limited. Regional differences about the institution of slavery did not necessarily indicate differences about race prejudice. When a small group of African Americans in New England proposed a plan in 1815 to transplant free blacks to Sierra Leone on the west coast of Africa, white leaders gladly contributed to a project that would reduce the free nonwhite population. "We could be cleared of them," declared a white advocate of colonization; "we would send to Africa a population partially civilized and christianized . . . [and] blacks would be put in a better condition."

In 1816, leading national politicians, including Clay, Webster, Monroe, Jackson, and Marshall, joined in organizing the American Colonization Society to expedite the removal of free blacks to Africa. Significantly, the movement made no mention of emancipating slaves. The intent of white supporters was merely to remove part of the free black population. Moreover, most northern African American communities bitterly criticized the scheme. "Whereas our ancestors (not of choice) were the first successful cultivators of the wilds of America," declared a resolution approved by 3,000 black Philadelphians who crowded into the African Methodist Episcopal Church in 1817, "we their descendants feel ourselves entitled to participate in the blessings of her luxuriant soil." Although the federal government assisted colonizers in founding Liberia in west Africa, only 1,400 African Americans made the decision to migrate overseas during the 1820s; by 1856 the total number had reached only 9,500.

The Missouri Debates

The contrast between society north of the Ohio River, which was dominated by family farmers who cultivated grains and livestock, and southern society, which was dominated by cotton agriculture, provided the backdrop for a major debate about the status of slavery in the western territories.

Spurred by postwar expansion, over 60,000 whites, mostly small farmers from southern states, and 10,000 slaves had moved into the Missouri territory. In 1819, the territorial government petitioned Congress for admission into the union. This routine request suddenly exploded in the House of Representatives when New York's James Tallmadge ignored the views of territorial residents and presented two amendments to prohibit the importation of slaves into Missouri and to free the children of slaves already there when they reached the age of 25. These unprecedented motions aroused furious debate. In the House, where the more densely populated North had greater weight, the measures passed; but in the Senate, where North and South were equally represented, Tallmadge's amendments were defeated.

The Congress of 1820 soon faced Missouri again. As various state legislatures, county committees, benevolent organizations, slaveholders, and abolitionists transmitted opinions to Congress and the press, politicians in Washington debated the moral and constitutional issues. In the Senate, New York's Rufus King declared slavery "contrary to the law of nature, which is the law of God," while, according to John Quincy Adams, "the great slaveholders of the House gnawed their lips and clenched their fists as they heard him." Other senators described slavery as a benevolent institution: "Go home with me," said one to his northern colleagues, "and see the glad faces." The slave "is free from care," commented another. Southern politicians insisted that the Constitution protected slavery, and even northern critics were forced to agree: "our boasted Constitution connives" in slavery, admitted a New Englander. But now the issue exceeded constitutionality: "To tolerate slavery beyond the Constitution," stated the Congressman, referring to its extension into Missouri, "is a perversion."

Despite the moral arguments, the issue of Missouri appeared less a question of political principles

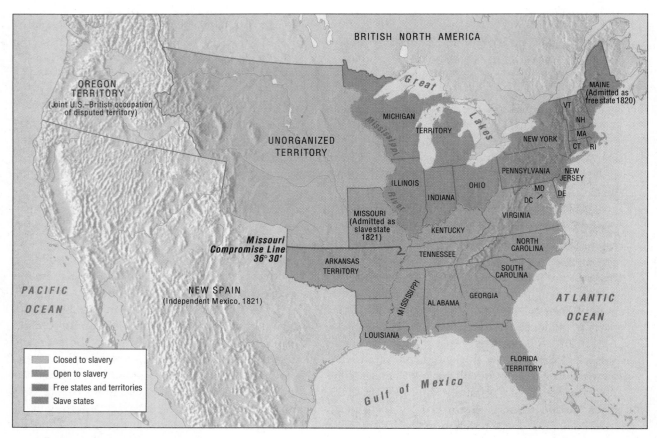

The Missouri Compromise, 1820   OVERLAY 2

than a matter of political power. The larger northern states already controlled the House of Representatives. But, in the Senate, the political match was clearly numerical: in 1820, eleven free states balanced eleven slave states. In the foreseeable future, only Florida and Arkansas promised to enter the slave column, whereas three free states waited in the wings. Missouri obviously held the future of southern power.

Reducing the Missouri question to such political numbers made the problem soluble. Since the district of Maine had also applied for admission to the union, politicians like Henry Clay saw a way of admitting the two states together—one slave, one free—to preserve the balance in the Senate, at least for a time. But, to appease the antislavery forces, Congress compromised by prohibiting slavery in the remainder of the Louisiana territory north of the latitude 36°-30" (the southern border of Missouri). This imaginary line, which had nothing to do with the feasibility of growing cotton west of the Mississippi River, established a mental division that dominated U.S. politics for the next generation. By 1821, slaveholding Missouri was a full member of the union.

Political leaders and newspaper editors congratulated the architects of the Missouri Compromise; Henry Clay acquired a proud reputation as the "great compromiser." But other observers realized that slavery still imperiled the union. Thomas

Jefferson, living in retirement at Monticello, heard "a fire bell in the night," which, he said ominously, "awakened and filled me with terror."

The Vesey Conspiracy

Jefferson's fears about slavery reflected not only political divisions between free and slave states but also the social tensions caused by the subjugation of African Americans, both slave and free, and the possibility of racial insurrection. In 1822, such fears surfaced in Charleston, South Carolina. Denmark Vesey, a free African American carpenter, had closely followed the Missouri debates in Congress. As a person who had purchased his own freedom after winning a lottery, and as a member of the African Methodist church, Vesey held strong antislavery sentiments and had urged other blacks to seek their freedom.

The expansion of slavery to Missouri impelled him to action. With other blacks, both slave and free, Vesey organized a conspiracy to seize the local arsenal, burn Charleston, and flee from slavery to black-controlled Haiti in the Caribbean. The plot would begin on July 14, 1822, the anniversary of Bastille Day, when French revolutionaries had stormed that Paris jail in 1789. Before Vesey's rebels could muster their forces, however, a black servant betrayed the plot. The state government quickly summoned the militia to arrest the rebels, resulting in the execution of 35 African Americans and the banishment of 37 more. "Let it never be forgotten," exclaimed a worried Carolinian soon afterward, "that OUR NEGROES are . . .the common *enemy of civilized society,* and the barbarians who would, IF THEY COULD, become the DESTROYERS of *our race.*"

As fear of slave insurrection permeated southern society, mysterious fires in Charleston kept the community on edge, and rumors of slave conspiracies abounded. Nor did the Missouri Compromise end the national debate about slavery. In Congress, various minor proposals (using profits from public land sales to finance emancipation or federal funding of colonization or restitution for damages to slave property) served as constant irritants that kept the argument alive. And free African Americans refused to be silenced. In 1827, black abolitionists in New York founded the newspaper *Freedom's Journal,* which stated "Too long have others spoken for us. . . . We abominate slavery, and all its advocates."

The Vesey plot and its anxious aftermath compelled many southern slaveowners to reconsider their involvement with human property. Since Vesey and his co-conspirators had belonged to an independent African American congregation, nervous southerners moved to discourage religious instruction, even Bible reading. Yet, as evangelical Christians, most southern leaders believed that eternal salvation, for black souls as well as white, depended on personal conversion. What did it mean, then, to deny religion to potential converts? Some relied on conservative preachers (rather than independent blacks) to emphasize biblical justifications of slavery. Others resolved the moral problem of slaveownership during the 1820s by defining slavery as a "necessary evil," a humane way of bringing Christianity and civilization to a supposedly inferior and degraded people. Others argued that emancipation was impractical: hundreds of thousands of ex-slaves could not be shipped to Africa nor left free in a white society. Significantly, few voices defended slavery as a positive good in itself.

Reshaping the Nation's Boundaries

The willingness of political leaders to colonize free black Americans in Africa coincided with efforts to expand the geographical borders of the republic. Like colonization, territorial expansion aimed at extending the power of free whites. Although southern expansionists wished to perpetuate slavery in the West, northern expansionists usually opposed the migration of free blacks. Such racial attitudes affected government policy about territorial expansion. On one hand, the United States recognized the power of the white nations of Europe by conducting legal negotiations and signing formal treaties that altered the nation's borders. On the other, white settlers and government officials disregarded the claims of the relatively powerless nonwhite nations of North America by engaging in illegal activities and violating formal treaties.

Negotiating with Britain and Spain

Negotiations with European nations, Britain and Spain, endeavored to remove competing claims to portions of the North American continent. Under President Monroe, Secretary of State John Quincy Adams developed a foreign policy to extend the country's territorial sovereignty and strengthen foreign commerce. In a series of treaties negotiated with Britain, Adams protected U.S. trading rights with British possessions and constructed a permanent peace along the Canadian border. The two countries agreed to demilitarize the Great Lakes, set the northern boundary of the Louisiana territory at the forty-ninth parallel, and subsequently provided for the joint occupation of the Oregon territory on the Pacific. Without consulting Native American groups, these agreements established precedents for westward expansion to the Pacific coast.

Adams also resolved differences with the Spanish empire about the status of Florida. That province had long served as a refuge for runaway slaves, who often entered Seminole society (sometimes as their slaves). Creeks fleeing U.S. armies also moved across the border. Hoping to limit U.S. expansion, these groups took assistance from Spanish authorities and British adventurers to raid U.S. settlements in Georgia. In 1818, Monroe ordered General Andrew Jackson to lead an expedition against Florida's Seminole-Creek-African communities. During the attack, Jackson seized Spanish garrisons and executed two British subjects who appeared to have instigated assaults against U.S. citizens. While some members of Congress denounced Jackson's aggression, fearing the incident would provoke hostilities with Spain and Britain, Adams defused the crisis by returning the Spanish towns and calming British outrage.

Jackson's expedition underscored the shaky state of Spain's remaining empire in North America. Already the Mexican province had rebelled against Spanish rule. Now Spain worried that the United States might seize not only Florida but also the northern portions of Mexico in Texas. Taking advantage of Mexican fears, Adams agreed to purchase eastern Florida for $5 million, which would be used to reimburse U.S. citizens for property damages. In exchange, the United States accepted a boundary division of Louisiana that assured Spanish control of Texas. But Adams bargained hard to persuade Spain to surrender claims in the far Northwest, beyond the Rocky Mountains, which gave the United States legal rights to the Pacific coast. This Adams-Onís treaty, also known as the Transcontinental Treaty, which was signed in 1819 and ratified two years later, formed the basis of the national empire. "A great epoch in our history," Adams wrote in his diary.

The Monroe Doctrine

Spain's concessions in North America reflected deeper fears of the upheavals occurring in the colonies of Latin America. After a decade of warfare, Mexico won its independence in 1821. As Spain faced other colonial rebellions, several European monarchs offered to support an army to reestablish Spanish control. Adams, already eyeing U.S. trade south of the border, saw no advantage in strengthening Spain's rule, and in 1822 encouraged Monroe to recognize the independence of the Latin American countries. The British

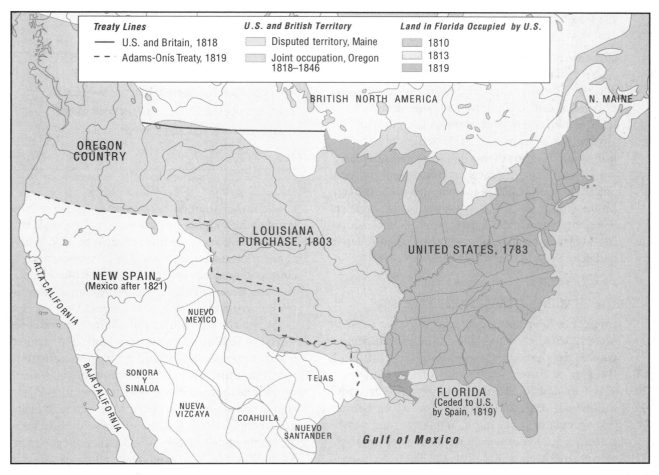

Spanish North America, 1819   OVERLAY 2

also wished to expand trade with Spain's former colonies and proposed that the Anglo-American nations cooperate in opposing European interference in South America, while repudiating any interest in annexing those countries. Adams quashed the idea. Recognizing that it was not in the United States' interests to support British trade with Latin America, nor advantageous to disavow any plans to annex areas of Mexico or Cuba, he also worried about recent Russian expansion on the Pacific coast. As the former minister to Russia, Adams knew about that country's fur-trading enterprises and colonial schemes in Alaska. The secretary of state also realized that whatever position the United States adopted, the

British navy would surely prevent unwanted military operations in South America.

Persuaded by Adams, the president announced what became known as the "Monroe Doctrine" in 1823. In his annual message to Congress, Monroe declared opposition to further colonization of the Western Hemisphere by any European power (a reference to Russian plans in the far Northwest), and renounced U.S. interference in European affairs (a reference to Greek and Spanish revolutions then occurring). More broadly, Monroe denied the right of European countries to interfere in political affairs in the Western Hemisphere.

The Monroe Doctrine had little immediate impact: the European monarchs made no serious effort to interfere in South America, and the colonial revolts ran their course. Meanwhile, Russia agreed to a treaty that set the southern boundary of Alaska. But in the long run, the Monroe Doctrine established precedents that enabled the United States to pursue an independent foreign policy throughout the Western Hemisphere, while promoting its own economic and political expansion into Spain's former colonies. Indeed, by the end of the 1820s, hundreds of U.S. settlers were entering Mexico's province in Texas, adopting Mexican citizenship and the Catholic faith, and scheming to overthrow Mexican rule.

Expelling the Creeks from the Southeast

Interest in developing new territory after the War of 1812 led the United States to repudiate several treaties that had been signed since the 1790s with the Native American nations of the Southeast. The war had forced these nations to surrender millions of acres to the United States, but farmers and speculators of Georgia, Tennessee, and nearby states wanted additional land for agricultural development. Although political leaders understood the contractual obligations of earlier treaties, government policy aimed at acquiring all Native lands, and as soon as possible. "The neighboring tribes are becoming daily less warlike, and more helpless and dependent on us," explained Monroe's secretary of war, John Calhoun, in 1818. "Our views of their interest, and not their own, ought to govern them."

Against the Creek nation, the government joined local officials, traders, and settlers (often the same individuals played all three roles) in depriving the tribal inhabitants of their land and formal treaty rights. By manipulating the agreed annual payments—for example, charging extravagant prices for manufactured cloth, treating personal debts as public credit, or distributing marked-up

> **Those who survived the Creek migration looked like "miserable and wretched . . . skeletons and their bones almost worn through the skin."**

goods rather than cash—government agents defrauded the supposed recipients of substantial public sums and lined their own pockets. To be sure, Creek protests to the national government brought clear policy directives prohibiting certain fraudulent practices. But the agents on Native lands simply ignored government instructions.

When the Creek national council formally resolved in 1820 to sell no further land to the United States, local politicians and developers conspired with renegade "chiefs" to sign fraudulent treaties, providing for enormous land transactions in exchange for personal cash payments. Although legitimate tribal leaders repudiated these transactions, government negotiators submitted an illegal document calling for the surrender of all Creek lands in Georgia and Alabama to the U.S. Senate, which promptly ratified the deal in 1825.

Meanwhile, the government of Georgia, in an assertion of state sovereignty, initiated land surveys to expedite the removal of Creek inhabitants to areas west of the Mississippi River. Hastening to Washington, Creek leaders persuaded President John Quincy Adams to reconsider the fraud. But the revised Treaty of Washington of 1826 merely protected Creek claims in Alabama. Forced to abandon all their lands in Georgia, the Creeks agreed to move to tribal territory farther west. But the promised government assistance for the forced march failed to arrive, and those who survived the migration looked, as one white observer put it, like "miserable and wretched. . . skeletons and their bones almost worn through the skin." These uprooted Creeks remained in Alabama for nine years, until another round of white fraud, theft, and military force drove them farther west.

Cherokee Nationalism

The Cherokee people faced similar pressure to abandon their homes. Yet the Cherokees were divided between traditionalists, who rejected Anglo American culture, and assimilationists, many of them children of interracial marriages, who endeavored to overcome cultural differences and become citizens of the United States. Cherokee policy thus followed two distinct paths—one traditionalist, one assimilationist.

To avoid further conflict with whites, Cherokee traditionalists, a minority of the nation, surrendered claims to their lands in the Southeast and migrated to Arkansas, where they promptly fell into conflict with the resident Osage and Quapaw peoples, as well as with white squatters who asserted prior rights to the lands. Meanwhile, assimilationist Cherokees fought to save their homes in Georgia. When Secretary of War John Calhoun declared in 1819 that "the Great Spririt has made our form of society stronger than yours and you must submit to adopt ours if you wish to be happy by pleasing him," Cherokee leaders in Georgia took his advice. Introducing political and cultural reforms, they hoped to make the nation appear less alien and threatening to U.S. interests. An independent national identity, based on self-government and economic self-sufficiency, would not only minimize cultural differences but also fulfill Cherokee claims to political sovereignty.

During the 1820s, these accommodating Cherokees adopted a formal book of laws, a legal court system, and a representative bicameral legislature, which conformed with Anglo American traditions by excluding Cherokee women from suffrage. In addition, the traditional clan relations and matrilineal obligations were replaced by a patriarchal system. Inheritance, for example, which traditionally had followed female lines, now became male-oriented, and children became dependents of fathers rather than mothers. To protect patriarchal lines of descent, Cherokee women lost traditional control of their pregnancies, and abortion became illegal for the first time. New laws also prohibited multiple marriages by men and barred rape, a crime previously unknown in Cherokee history and perhaps introduced by non-Cherokee intruders. To further conform to Anglo American standards, the Cherokees held a constitutional convention in 1827, adopting a formal constitution modeled on the United States' founding document. By then, Cherokee women had largely lost their political voice, and Cherokee citizenship was limited to adult men.

Besides these political innovations, assimilationists strove to imitate Anglo American cultural practices. In 1821, Sequoia, a previously illiterate Cherokee, developed a written Cherokee language based on 86 spoken syllables, each with a distinct symbol. (Ironically, some Cherokee leaders hesitated to endorse the system because the pictographic language would suggest something less than total assimilation by Anglo American standards of literacy.) By the end of the decade, the *Cherokee Phoenix,* a bilingual Cherokee-English newspaper edited by Elias Boudinot, served community needs. Christian missionaries, particularly Methodists, won numerous converts among Cherokee youth. In addition, Cherokees increasingly adopted Anglo American economic forms—men becoming farmers and artisans, women learning to spin and to weave. Such changes encouraged economic individualism, including the acceptance of African American slavery. Although 18th-century Cherokees had treated blacks as equals, efforts to embrace white values prompted new laws that prohibited intermarriage with blacks, forbade free blacks from joining the nation, and limited the rights of blacks to own property. Indeed, the *Phoenix* printed advertisements about runaway slaves and opportunities to purchase slaves from Cherokee traders.

Despite such assimilation, Cherokees were no more successful than Creeks at persuading the U.S. government, the southern states, or land hungry settlers to respect this cultural transformation, much less their treaty rights. In 1828, a majority of the Georgia state legislature demanded all Cherokee land and enacted provisions for immediate surveys and sales. Promises by the federal government of a 7 million-acre reservation "forever" failed to raise interest in migration. Cherokee appeals to Washington evoked no sympathy. "We have been far more successful in the acquisition of their land," admitted President Adams in 1828, "than in imparting to them the principles, or inspiring them with the spirit, of civilization."

Transforming National Politics

The unresponsiveness of the U.S. government to the problems of Creeks and Cherokees and the limited interest in Congress about the status of slaves and free blacks reflected the prevailing assumptions of white male superiority in the political world. Yet the same principle encouraged the extension of equal rights of citizenship to virtually all adult white men, regardless of their standing in the white community. Even the poorest white man, merely by possessing rights of citizenship, embodied racial, ethnic, and gender superiority over those residents who were denied full citizenship. Few worried about those left outside the political household. "If the time should ever arrive when the African shall be raised to the level of the white man," a New York politician proposed, "when the colours shall intermarry—when ne-

groes shall be invited to your tables—to sit in your pew, or ride in your coach, it may then be proper to. . . remodel the constitution to conform to that state of society." But the supposed inferiority of such people justified, at least for the immediate future, their exclusion from the political process.

After the War of 1812, the expansion of equal rights for white males transformed national politics. The first state government constitutions, established during the war for independence, had usually limited voting rights to propertied male citizens. But as population increased and moved westward, as multiple religious denominations (Congregationalist, Presbyterian, Baptist, Methodist, Episcopalian, even Catholic) competed for American souls, and as economic changes increased the number of propertyless workers, a younger generation of political leaders challenged the continuation of political representation based on property requirements, religious affiliation, and indirect elections. The new states that entered the union during the early 19th century opened the vote to all adult white males, regardless of whether they owned property, and many states adopted secret balloting instead of public polling to assure fair voting. By 1815, older states felt pressure from propertyless workers, religious minorities, and younger politicians to adopt political reform. Many state governments now summoned constitutional conventions to change the political order.

Broadening the Vote

"The principle of universal suffrage, which is now running a triumphant career from Maine to Louisiana, is an awful power," complained an old Federalist at the New York convention, "which, like gunpowder, or the steam engine, or the press itself, may be rendered mighty in mischief as well as in blessings." Warning that "governments are becoming downright democracies," such conservatives fought to limit the changes affecting elections, taxation, and office holding. By contrast, the reformers demanded that the right to vote be expanded not only because "life was as dear to a poor man as to a rich man" and "so was liberty," as one Boston politician declared, but also because these new leaders better represented a diverse citizenry and, incidentally, expected to win popular elections.

These democratizing pressures brought significant reforms, broadening the suffrage to include most white male citizens, making more offices elective rather than appointive, and reducing property requirements for holding office. But political leaders also preserved important limitations on political democracy. As one delegate remarked of the principle of "universal suffrage": "Women are excluded—minors are excluded." So, too, were other minorities. In Massachusetts, for example, Congregational churches retained tax advantages, to the dismay of smaller denominations. The New York convention established taxpaying and residency requirements uniquely for men "of colour." Those two words effectively took the vote away from 30,000 free African Americans, leaving only 298 African Americans who could meet the qualifications. "The minds of blacks," one politician observed, were "not competent to vote." Besides, another delegate declared, extending suffrage to blacks "would serve to invite that kind of population to this state, an occurrence which I should most sincerely deplore." Such attitudes disqualified Native American "aborigines"—though many whites considered them "more acute and discerning . . . [than] the African race."

Changes in voting requirements were important in state and local elections, but did not immediately affect national politics. In 1824, competition among four presidential candidates (William Crawford of Georgia, John Quincy Adams of Massachusetts, Henry Clay of Kentucky, and Andrew Jackson of Tennessee) still focused on issues of "character" rather than political ideas or programs. All were well-known figures, but voters were unimpressed by the choice. Fewer than 25 percent of eligible citizens bothered to vote. Only Jackson, the popular hero of New Orleans, drew support outside his home region. None of the four, therefore, captured a majority of electoral votes. For the second time in U.S. history, the presidential election went to the House of Representatives, where each state held a single vote. Although Jackson had outpolled Adams, political maneuvering in Congress put the Tennessee soldier at a disadvantage. Speaker of the House Clay wanted no western rivals and remained sympathetic to Adams's nationalism. Clay's support gave Adams the election. When Adams followed his victory by naming Clay his secretary of state, Jackson's supporters claimed that their candidate had been denied election by a "corrupt bargain" in Congress. The Jackson camp began preparing for the next election.

A statesman rather than a popular politician, John Quincy Adams did not favor a broadened electorate and viewed party politics as "a baneful weed." Failing to understand that "party strife" reflected the conflicting views of various interest groups, the president tried to rise above the factions, refusing to use political appointments to build alliances within Congress. Yet his nationalist political agenda—federal internal improvements, government support of agriculture and manufacturing, the creation of a national university—accentuated regional divisions and aroused congressional opposition. New Yorkers, for example, usually supported improvements in transportation, but now wanted no competition for the newly opened Erie Canal; southerners, who saw no benefits for their region, raised constitutional questions about government projects. Adams further aroused southern criticism by proposing that the United States participate in a conference of the newly liberated Latin American countries in Panama, whose aim was to pressure Spain to recognize their independence.

In the wake of the Missouri debates and the Vesey plot, southerners wanted no official contact with delegates from black-controlled Haiti, lest it imply formal recognition of a slave revolution. Although Congress eventually provided the funds in 1826, the meeting ended before the U.S. delegate arrived.

Contesting the Tariff

Regional divisions surfaced more bitterly in 1828 during debates about revising the tariff. Initially, the tariff proposal offered to protect both the finished manufactured goods of the Northeast and the raw products of the West, such as hemp, wool, and flax. But New England interests, which imported raw materials to manufacture textiles, opposed protection of raw commodities that would raise domestic prices and introduced amendments to lower those duties. Southern politicians opposed all tariffs and hoped to defeat the measure by splitting western and northeastern interests. Instead of supporting amendments to lower tariffs on raw goods, therefore, southerners expected to kill the entire tariff by supporting the higher rates favored by westerners, believing that the Northeast section would then vote against the bill.

By 1828, however, the interests of northeastern manufacturers were committed overwhelmingly to a policy of tariff protection, even though it would mean high duties on raw materials. Reluctantly, northeastern congressmen joined westerners in passing the high Tariff of 1828, which raised tariffs on most products. To frustrated southern leaders, this "tariff of abominations" demanded protest. South Carolina's John Calhoun, recognizing the increasing isolation of his region, drafted an elaborate defense of political minorities in an anonymously published essay called "Exposition and Protest." Attacking the new tariff, the southern spokesman elaborated a theory of states' rights in the tradition of Madison and Jefferson's Virginia and Kentucky resolutions, justi-fying the nullification of congressional laws by acts of the separate state legislatures (see Chapter 7). Yet Calhoun's argument remained only an intellectual statement. Believing that the next presidential administration would revise the offensive tariff, he proposed no further political action.

Strengthening the Political Parties

Political alignments in Congress revealed not only regional conflict, but also basic changes in the nation's political structure. Although voter participation had remained only around 25 percent in 1824, largely because of a lack of competition within the separate states, the increasing number of eligible voters encouraged state leaders, notably New York's Martin Van Buren, to form political organizations or parties to maintain discipline among the electorate. Yet parties remained slightly suspect. Voters rallied around individual leaders (Adams and Jackson) rather than taking a distinctive name or identity. All parties considered themselves "Republican."

Two instruments stimulated the emergence of political parties during the 1820s: partisan newspapers, which announced political positions and defined the issues for the public; and patronage appointments, such as jobs in the post office or in customs collection, to reward political loyalty. Unlike the political party leaders of the 1790s, politicians no longer felt embarrassed about organizing support to achieve their political objectives. Rejecting the older politics of *consensus,* which assumed a natural harmony of political interests among all citizens (perverted only by corrupt politicians, demagogues, or monarchists), party leaders of the 1820s saw politics as an arena of competition, in which the opinion of a *majority* appeared sufficient. Rather than undermining the nation's political virtue, parties would express the interests of the voters. Candidates stood for political office not as personalities (though individual images remained critical for gaining votes), but as supporters of particular programs.

Adams's rejection of the new party politics doomed his bid for reelection in 1828. While the president, identifying himself as a "National Republican," kept his political base in the Northeast, Van Buren skillfully built a political alliance between New York and like-minded "Democratic Republicans" in the southern states. By "substituting *party principles* for *personal preferences,*" he explained, "the planters of the South and the plain Republicans of the north" could rally behind Jackson not merely as a popular hero who could capture votes but also as the embodiment of a political position (what later would be called a party platform) dedicated to specific government programs.

The 1828 campaign left plenty of room for personal insult: Jackson's wife was accused of adultery, while Adams was charged with procuring a prostitute for the Russian tsar. But beyond personalities, the Democratic ticket of Jackson and Calhoun appealed to a coalition of western farmers interested in cheap land, southern slaveowners opposed to tariffs, and merchants in the middle states concerned with finance. With over 1 million voting—three times the number voting four years earlier—Jackson won 56 percent of the popular vote and two-thirds of the electoral college. The large turnout revealed not only the growth of the electorate but also greater public interest in national political issues. For the first time, questions of tariffs, internal improvements, banks, and western lands—subjects that had once seemed remote to ordinary citizens—had become topics of public debate.

Farewell to an Era

As Andrew Jackson ascended to power, the citizenry understood that they were coming to the end an era. The Founding Fathers' generation,

On the golden anniversary of the Fourth of July, the deaths of John Adams and Thomas Jefferson within hours of each other symbolized the end of an age.

which linked Americans of the 1820s to the birth of their nation, was rapidly passing from the stage. In 1825, the French patriot Lafayette returned to the land of his wartime triumphs, drawing crowds from Boston to New Orleans who gaped at this survivor of the French-American alliance. That year, on the fiftieth anniversary of the battle of Bunker Hill, the young Daniel Webster thrilled a crowd of tens of thousands by suddenly addressing the elderly war veterans standing on the slope before him. "Venerable men," he orated, "the great trust" of the republic "now descends to new hands." In 1826, on the golden anniversary of the Fourth of July, the deaths of John Adams and Thomas Jefferson within hours of each other symbolized the end of an age. Many wondered aloud whether the new generation could preserve the republican spirit of liberty. To keep the heritage alive, in 1827 Massachusetts became the first of many states to mandate instruction in American history in public schools.

The content of that schoolbook history extolled the progress of civilization from the landing of the Pilgrims at Plymouth Rock in 1620 to the construction of the Erie Canal by a "spirit of enterprise" that had "subdued the wilderness of the west." But some observers worried more about what was being lost by this passion for "progress" and individual achievement. New York novelist James Fenimore Cooper, born and raised in Erie Canal country, achieved literary fame by illuminating the darker side of progress. In *The Pioneers* of 1823, Cooper's first "Leather-Stocking" tale, his

James Fenimore Cooper's immensely popular Leatherstocking stories evoked the passage from "natural" society to "civilization."

frontier hero Natty Bumpo witnesses the wanton killing of enormous flocks of wild pigeons (passenger pigeons, which today are extinct) and remarks sadly: "This comes of settling a country!" The title of another popular Cooper novel, *The Last of the Mohicans* (1826) expressed the tragic plight of Native American cultures: "The pale faces are the masters of the earth," says the defeated chief. So, too, the New York poet William Cullen Bryant presented a saccharin farewell to a vanishing people: "A noble race!" he wrote, "but they are gone."

Such sentimentality greatly annoyed the writer William Apess, a New England Pequot, who had fought for the United States in the War of 1812. Comparing the "immortal Washington" to his own cultural hero, the Wampanoag King Philip, who led a bloody rebellion against the New England colonies in 1675 (see Chapter 3), Apess denounced the hero worship of his people's persecutors. His autobiography, *A Son of the Forest,* published in 1829, deplored the widely used and demeaning word *Indian.* "I could not find it in the Bible," he noted, "and therefore concluded that it was a word imported for the special purpose of degrading us." Apess was an exceptional person but not widely read. Rather, most readers shared the outlook of the nostalgic writers Bryant and Cooper, who like, Andrew Jackson, assumed that progress from wilderness to civilization was inevitable. Celebrating national values of territorial expansion, they saved their praise not for Native Americans, nor even for Leather-Stocking, who must depart toward the setting sun, but, as Cooper wrote, for "the march of the nation across the continent."

INFOTRAC® COLLEGE EDITION EXERCISES

 For additional reading go to InfoTrac College Edition, your online research library at *http://web1.infotrac-college.com.*

Keyword search: James Madison
Subject search: Bank of the United States
Subject search: Missouri Compromise
Keyword search: Denmark Vesey
Keyword search: Monroe Doctrine
Keyword search: John Quincy Adams

Subject search: Cherokees, periodicals
Subject search: Creeks, periodicals
Keyword search: Martin Van Buren

ADDITIONAL READING

The Politics of a National Economy

George Dangerfield, *The Awakening of American Nationalism, 1815–1828* (1965). This volume introduces the major political events of the period.

Building the Erie Canal

Carol Sheriff, *The Artificial River: The Erie Canal and the Paradox of Progress, 1817–1862* (1996). This survey places the canal in the context of changing cultural values about the economy; see also Ronald E. Shaw, *Erie Water West: A History of the Erie Canal, 1792–1854* (1966).

The National Economy and the Marshall Court

Francis N. Stites, *John Marshall: Defender of the Constitution* (1981). This succinct biography places the major Supreme Court cases in historical context.

Territorial Expansion and Regional Differences

John Mack Faragher, *Sugar Creek: Life on the Illinois Prairie* (1986). A social history of one community, the book describes problems of settling new lands.

Free Society and the Paradox of Race

William W. Freehling, *Prelude to Civil War: The Nullification Controversy in South Carolina, 1816–1836* (1966). Analyzes the role of slavery in the political culture of the 1820s.

Edward A. Pearson, ed., *Design against Charleston: The Trial Record of the Denmark Vesey Slave Conspiracy of 1822* (1999). Besides a fine essay about slave culture, this volume includes a transcript of the legal proceedings.

Expelling the Creeks from the Southeast

Michael D. Green, *The Politics of Indian Removal: Creek Government and Society in Crisis* (1982). A detailed examination of U.S. policy toward the Creeks, emphasizing the role of racism and fraud.

Cherokee Nationalism

William G. McLoughlin, *Cherokee Renascence in the New Republic* (1986). Examining Cherokee society, this study describes the effort to avoid forced removal; see also Theda Perdue, *Cherokee Women* (1998), listed in Chapter 1.

Strengthening Political Parties

Donald B. Cole, *Martin Van Buren and the American Political System* (1984). Focusing on New York's premier politician, this book examines the emergence of party politics during the 1820s. For the role of informal politics in Washington, D.C., see Catherine Allgor, *Parlor Politics* (2000).

Farewell to an Era

Barry O'Connell, ed., *On Our Own Ground: The Complete Writings of William Apess, A Pequot* (1992). This anthology introduces the remarkable work of a long-forgotten Native American author.

Alan Taylor, *William Cooper's Town: Power and Persuasion on the Frontier of the Early American Republic* (1995).Describes community development in rural New York and its impact on the writings of James Fenimore Cooper.

Hudson River near West Point, N. Y.

The Politics of Northern Development, 1815–1840

CHRONOLOGY

1828	Baltimore & Ohio becomes first railroad
	Congress passes "Tariff of Abominations"
	Andrew Jackson elected president, John Calhoun vice president
1830	Jackson vetoes Maysville Road project
1831	Cyrus McCormick patents mechanical reaper
1832	Jackson vetoes recharter of Bank of the United States
	Jackson defeats Henry Clay for presidency, Martin Van Buren is vice president
1834	First strike at Lowell textile mills
	Mob attacks Catholic convent in Charlestown, Massachusetts
1836–1837	Land boom absorbs capital investment
1836	Jackson issues Specie Circular
	Van Buren elected president
1837	Credit contraction causes economic depression
	Horace Mann heads Massachusetts Board of Education
	Supreme Court rules in *Charles River Bridge* case
1839	Mormons migrate to Nauvoo, Illinois

A ragged man in antique dress, carrying a rusty fowling-piece on his shoulder, stumbled down from a green knoll in the Catskill woods overlooking the Hudson River. He was decked with leaves, his grizzled hair and beard hung down to his knees, and his eyes teared in the bright sunshine of this morning after his twenty-year sleep. He made his way slowly to his native village in New York, where he was immediately struck by the newly "busy, bustling, disputatious tone" of the place.

"Strange names were over the doors—strange faces at the windows—everything was strange," moaned Rip Van Winkle. "Instead of the great tree that used to shelter the quiet little Dutch inn" in the center of town, "there now was reared a tall naked pole, with something on the top that looked like a red night-cap, and from it was fluttering a flag, on which was a singular assemblage of stars and stripes." He recognized on the sign, however, the ruby face of King George, under which he had smoked so many a peaceful pipe; but even this was singularly metamorphosed. The red coat was changed for one of blue and buff, a sword was held in the hand instead of a sceptre, the head was decorated with a cocked hat, and underneath was painted in large characters, GENERAL WASHINGTON. The poor creature cried in despair, "Every thing's changed, and I'm changed, and I can't tell . . . who I am!"

When Washington Irving's famous character entered the literary scene in 1832, Rip's confusion became part of the nation's folklore, echoing as he did the concern of early 19th-century readers about the political and economic changes that were altering rural communities, towns, and cities alike.

These changes would eventually reshape the economy in every corner of the nation, but in the beginning they were most noticeable in the northeastern states. As that area became more urbanized and industrialized, its inhabitants developed an identity as entrepreneurs and workers. They saw themselves as diligent, disciplined Yankees and contrasted their way of life with less economically developed Americans elsewhere. Because the Northeast was the most densely populated region, moreover, people in other areas could not ignore this transformation. Southern and western farmers saw the same kinds of changes spreading toward their own homes, though they did not necessarily want or welcome the invasion.

The Expanding Market Economy

Some of the changes could be measured statistically: the national population in 1815 numbered 8.4 million; 25 years later the total had more than doubled to 17.4 million. New York City, the nation's largest metropolis, grew from 156,000 in 1820 (equivalent today to a modest community like Fort Lauderdale, Florida, or Oxnard, California) to 391,000 in 1840 (the size of a modern city like Omaha, Nebraska, or Honolulu, Hawaii). Only 7 percent of the country's residents lived in large towns, but in 1820, for the first time in U.S. history, the urban population began to increase at a faster rate than the population in rural areas, a trend that would persist until the census of 1980 found urban dwellers returning to the countryside in greater numbers.

More subtle changes lay beneath the statistical surface. When the Erie Canal opened in 1825, one politician boasted that the waterway would "bring a market to every man's door." Yet expanding com-

"Have I the right to make as good a bargain as I can?"

merce also brought more impersonal economic relations. Traditional social ethics had emphasized fairness, justice, and "character" in doing business, but transactions between strangers encouraged mere monetary concerns. One horsetrader, living near the Erie Canal and misled by the promises of a well-dressed customer he had never seen before, complained bitterly about the unexpected "sharp tricks of the day." Thus the widening marketplace forced increasing numbers of producers and consumers to confront issues of economic development. As questions of credit, bank notes, and transportation affected more citizens, economic issues entered the political arena and became subjects of political debate.

Americans also faced moral dilemmas about economic change. "Have I the right to make as good a bargain as I can?" asked New England's *Christian Almanac* in 1830. The answer was resoundingly negative. "No man has the right to do anything which causes needless suffering." Yet the question itself testified to important changes in values, suggesting that many entrepreneurs were indeed pursuing "as good a bargain" as they could, at the cost of older social ethics. While some reached solely for profits, others, like the editor of *Christian Almanac,* recoiled from purely commercial transactions, stuck to old values, and protested the changes. Fearing that the country was losing its virtue, many evangelical Christians appealed for a revival of economic and social morality. Based largely among middle-class groups, these reformers pressed for moral change in society.

Attitudes about economic growth had direct political consequences. With the expanded electorate of the 1820s and the rise of two-party com-

petition in 1828, political leaders increasingly defined their differences about economic policies. Under President Andrew Jackson, the Democratic party questioned government support of economic development and opposed a strong national bank, high tariffs, and commercial "improvements." By contrast, Whig party leaders such as Henry Clay and Daniel Webster favored the central bank, modest tariffs, and congressional assistance for internal improvements. These political lines became clearer as the national economy touched the lives of more citizens. Yet regional economic differences—the South as slavery-based cotton producer, the Northeast as manufacturing center, and the Northwest as free-labor agriculture—continued to complicate national party alliances. On a broader level, these issues touched on competing definitions of the national identity: Were the American people merely materialistic? Could economic development be reconciled with traditional morality? Could two versions of the national identity coexist?

Economic Opportunity Stimulates Migration

The nation's growing population resulted primarily from a high birthrate, which despite a declining trend still averaged around five children per family. After the War of 1812, European immigration added to the growth, jumping tenfold from 8,000 in 1820 to 84,000 in 1840. Most newcomers in this period were skilled artisans from Britain and Germany, who could no longer compete with industrial factories, or farmers whose incomes suffered from declining food prices in their homelands. Such immigrants often traveled as families, though most were males. After a 4- to 6-week voyage at sea, most stayed in the ports where they landed, swelling the labor force of Boston, New York, Baltimore, and New Orleans. By 1840, over 40 percent of the residents of New York City and New Orleans were foreign-born (another 23 percent in New Orleans were African American slaves). Immigrants with cash often followed the river systems inland to the growing cities of Buffalo, Cincinnati, and St. Louis, and farmers bought acreage in the nearby hinterlands.

Economic opportunity also attracted the less fortunate. As high birthrates and land divisions caused overpopulation in Ireland, tens of thousands of single men and women sailed for American shores. Workers without money avoided the southern states, where slavery kept wages low. Most unskilled immigrants found jobs as manual laborers (such as digging the Erie Canal) or as domestic servants. By the 1830s, these propertyless Irish immigrants congregated in the cities, heralding the arrival of millions more when potato famines caused mass migration during the next decade.

Transportation and Mobility

The surge of population encouraged both geographical dispersal and innovative modes of transportation. The number of steamboats operating from New Orleans increased from 200 in 1820 to 2,000 in 1840. Meanwhile, the rage for canal building speeded western migration, as well as the shipping of agricultural products to inland ports and downriver cities. "Pork and Flour coming down—Tea and Sugar coming up," remarked a New York canal booster. "Things are as they should be; some up, some down." Canals also carried unhealthy cargo, such as the disease cholera, which raced in 1832 from the Atlantic seaboard to the Great Lakes in less than a month.

On July 4, 1828, the last surviving signer of the Declaration of Independence, Maryland's 91-year old Charles Carroll, flipped over a spadeful of sod to launch the Baltimore & Ohio, the nation's first railroad, boasting that the new technology would "perpetuate the union of the American

By 1840, railroad mileage had matched the total length of the nation's canals and would double that distance during the next decade.

states." As Baltimore merchants reached for the Ohio River, Boston's tracks headed to the Erie Canal and Charleston's extended toward the cotton belt. By 1840, railroad mileage had matched the total length of the nation's canals and would double that distance during the next decade. Other advances in agricultural technology—Cyrus McCormick's reaper (1831), the wheat thresher (1836), and John Deere's plow (1837)—enabled farmers to increase production by intensifying cultivation and by opening the thick-grassed prairie lands of Illinois. On the shores of Lake Michigan, the new city of Chicago spearheaded a vast commercial revolution.

Such growth doomed the Native American presence east of the Mississippi. Although Creeks, Cherokees, and Choctaws continued to wage legal battle to save their lands (see Chapter 11), the last resistance in the old Northwest territory flared in 1832 when a large group of Sauk crossed the Mississippi into Illinois "to make corn" on their traditional lands. "Land cannot be sold," said their leader, Black Hawk, in a comment about market values. "Nothing can be sold but such things as can be carried away." Black Hawk's violation of old treaties brought out the state militia, including the young Captain Abraham Lincoln. The future president saw little fighting and played no personal role in what was to follow: the 15-week Black Hawk war ended with the slaying of 500 Sauk, the capture of the chief, and the forced surrender of Sauk claims in Iowa. "Farewell, my nation!" cried the defeated warrior. Black Hawk's "sun is setting, and he will rise no more."

Transforming Northern Working Conditions

The expansion of western farming, together with the transportation boom, had immense consequences for the northern economy. First, more fertile western farms in the old Northwest territory resulted in greater competition for the older, less profitable farms of the Northeast; second, the total agricultural surplus provided food for the growing numbers in the nation's towns and cities. In the rural Northeast, population pressure had already encouraged a trend toward nonagricultural work, such as the home production of textiles. After the introduction of machine spinning, factories produced cotton yarn, which was then "put out" to farm women, who wove the yarn into cloth. Middlemen delivered the raw materials to farm families and collected the finished work. By 1830, however, the introduction of power looms had ended this type of textile outwork.

The Rise of Factories

Northeastern farm families had become increasingly dependent on some nonagricultural income to preserve their economic independence. Many rural women (and, to a lesser extent, men) shifted to small-scale forms of home production, such as the hand-braiding of split palm leaves into straw hats and the binding of shoes, for trade or sale. Such tasks were integrated into the domestic economy of small farms. Since agriculture remained a major source of income, rural women performed home manufacturing in the time available after finishing their other chores. This work primarily occupied unmarried daughters, who contributed their earnings to the family economy. Home manufacturing also proved a means of subsistence for widows. Instead of receiving cash wages, domestic workers usually exchanged the finished products for goods at local stores, which served as distributors of the raw materials. By 1837, home production of straw hats in Massachusetts employed over 50,000 women and children, reaching an annual value of nearly $2 million.

Although domestic outwork persisted through the century, the centralization of textile manufacturing drastically altered the nature of industrial work. During the 18th century, English manufacturers had successfully introduced mechanized factories and had maintained a monopoly of textile machinery by forbidding its export. In 1789, however, Samuel Slater, an English mechanic, memorized the complicated plans and migrated to Rhode Island. Backed by the wealthy merchant Moses Brown, Slater reconstructed the English plans and launched the first American spinning mill in 1790. New England soon became a textile center. Its many rivers provided water power, commercial profits created investment capital, and declining agricultural incomes tempted workers to leave the farms. To keep down labor costs, early factories employed entire families, including their children. Rather than receiving regular wages, factory families obtained housing, credit in company stores, and payment of any remaining balance at the end of a contracted period. These early mills produced only yarn. Through the putting out system, whereby weavers who worked at home turned the yarn into finished cloth, the factories remained integrated with the rural economy.

Trade restrictions imposed during the War of 1812 inspired a radically new approach to factory production. Francis Cabot Lowell, heir to one of the country's commercial fortunes, organized a group of investors called the Boston Associates and in 1814 established a textile factory at Waltham, Massachusetts, which combined the entire manufacturing process into a single operation. Instead of simply spinning yarn for home production, the Waltham system produced finished cloth for cheap

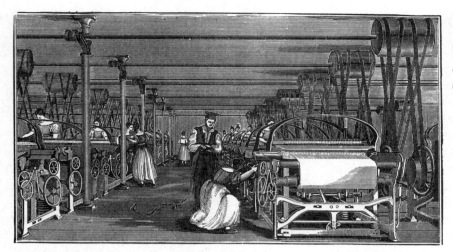

Mill workers, Lowell, Massachusetts, ca. 1820. "Consider the girls in a factory," suggested Henry David Thoreau in *Walden*, his classic critique of material values, "never alone, hardly in their dreams."

mass consumption. The sheer size of the factory's capital and output enabled the manufacturers to purchase raw cotton at reduced prices, while extending credit to wholesale consumers. The economic result was amazing. In the first eight years, annual sales climbed from $3,000 to over $300,000. During the 1820s, the Boston Associates opened larger plants at Lowell, Massachusetts, turning that rural village into the nation's textile center, employing over 6,000 workers by 1836.

The Mill Workers of Lowell

The most innovative feature at Lowell was the recruitment of a female labor force. Reversing the pattern of outwork production, textile factories advertised for workers among New England's "active and healthy" farm girls and invited them to move to town. Unmarried young women, aged between their late teens and early 20s, eagerly took the well-paying jobs and relieved their families of their expenses. This out-of-house employment of young women threatened traditional family oversight, but the mill owners tried to protect the workers' moral environment by placing them in well-supervised boarding houses. Yet

Factories advertised for workers among New England's "active and healthy" farm girls and invited them to move to town.

working conditions were quite different from rural life. Regulated by factory time clocks, the mill girls labored 75 hours per week at fast-paced tasks. Their pay, based on the output of the machines they tended, averaged between 40 and 80 cents a day (equivalent to $9 today), about half the income of male workers. Unlike later industrial workers, the Lowell women saw themselves as temporary laborers, and indeed the average span of mill work was less than three years. Most married at a rate comparable to non–mill workers, though at a slightly older age.

Mill work offered new opportunities for female independence. The women's wages were their own, sometimes sent home to augment family incomes, but more often spent on books, clothing, and entertainment, or saved for their subsequent marriages. Amidst a community of single women,

Lowell workers shared social activities, attended popular lectures, went to church, talked, read, and wrote poetry and stories for the magazine *Lowell Offering*. The contrast with the rural lifestyle they left behind appeared in a letter from a young girl in Vermont to her sibling at Lowell: "I dreamed the other night that you. . . brought twenty-five hundred dollars home with you. I thought if that was the case I should go to Lowell."

The fantasy of easy money contrasted with the realities of the factory regimen. The novelty of the work, the repetitive pace, the noisy machinery— "like frogs and jewsharps all mixed together," said one Lowell worker—contributed to a physical and mental exhaustion that the women called "mill fever." Twice during the 1830s mill workers took collective action when their managers increased the workload, ordered wage cuts, and raised boarding fees in the company dormitories. Identifying themselves as "daughters of freemen still" (that is, not permanently part of an industrial working class), 800 mill women defiantly organized a strike in 1834 to protest "the oppressing hand of avarice."

The first mill strike lasted but a few days, weakened by lack of cohesion. A second walkout two years later seriously cut textile production. That strike ended when management evicted the women from their rooms. During the 1830s, other factory disputes, some involving child workers, erupted around the country, winning small concessions. But a severe economic depression in 1837 caused widespread mill closings and broke the union movement. During the next decade, male immigrant workers, desperate for jobs and willing to work for lower wages, would displace Yankee farm women from the mills and form a permanent industrial labor force.

Urban Day Laborers

The emergence of factory work in New England coincided with dramatic and enduring changes in the skilled crafts, such as tailoring, carpentry, and shoemaking. Independent artisans, who did not compete directly with factories, could still make good livings by producing custom-made clothes or furniture for affluent consumers. Such master craftsmen retained a public identity based on their occupational skills. In the frequent public parades that marked urban life, for example, skilled craftsmen (never women) clustered together and carried banners that proclaimed their unique contributions to society. Nevertheless, the increase of mass produced goods intensified competition within most trades and reduced opportunities for younger skilled workers.

As artisans tried to reduce their production costs, the system of apprenticed labor, which had centered in the households of master craftsmen, became fragmented. Instead of teaching young boys (or, less frequently, girls) the skills of a trade, artisans divided the work into separate parts and then hired piece workers to perform portions of the job. This division of labor speeded production and reduced the cost of training a skilled craftsman. Piece workers no longer lived within the masters' households, but resided in rented rooms where they performed their tasks.

The physical separation of master craftsmen from day workers paralleled a similar splitting of their economic interests. Instead of the traditional protections that apprenticeships assured young workers, the free marketplace offered no guarantee of food, clothing, shelter, or even tutelage in a skilled trade. Although day laborers benefited indirectly from mass production by being able to purchase cheaper consumer goods, their own incomes remained precarious and tended to decline. Competing against other workshops, master artisans strove to keep wages low, and real earnings dropped substantially during the 1830s. Women workers, who were paid at one-third to one-half the rate of men, sank toward desperation; for seven days labor from before sunrise to after sunset,

Half the children brought to New York's charitable House of Refuge were committed by parents who could not support them.

women shoe binders might earn only 50 cents (about $8 in today's money). Working families could survive only by putting their children to work, scavenging in the streets (a common juvenile crime, often prosecuted), crowding into cheap tenement apartments (the first multifamily dwelling was erected in New York in 1833), and cutting expenditures for necessities. Half the children brought to New York's charitable House of Refuge were committed by parents who could not support them.

Lowest on the urban economic ladder were the free African Americans, who were disproportionately female. Although black women had opportunities for domestic work, black men were often excluded from good jobs. Undisguised racial discrimination permitted northern municipal officials to refuse business licenses to aspiring blacks, while the skilled trades routinely rejected African American apprentices. Social segregation was common—in churches, streetcars, and cemeteries. Because black women outnumbered black men in the cities, there were fewer opportunities for blacks to marry and to have children. Despite their small numbers, northern blacks were politically active, staging public celebrations of northern emancipation, supporting the movement to abolish slavery, and expressing opposition for African colonization. Yet when New York blacks organized a referendum in 1837 to eliminate property qualifications for African American voters, the predominantly white electorate defeated the measure by a margin of 2.6 to 1.

Race prejudice also prompted the appearance of minstrel shows, the most popular form of pub-

lic entertainment in 19th-century cities. Although theater owners usually required black spectators to sit in the segregated upper galleries, white audiences howled at the antics of white performers who blackened their faces with charcoal and presented musical comedies based on racial and sexual stereotypes. In 1832, a white actor named Thomas D. Rice captivated New York City audiences with the ridiculous dance steps of "Jim Crow," setting off a fad that dominated popular entertainment for decades. Using exaggerated physical gestures and contorted jumps, singing crudely in African American dialects, and brazenly depicting taboo topics of sexual promiscuity and cross dressing, white performers parodied the misunderstandings of a supposedly inferior people with names like Sambo, Zeke, and Zip Coon.

> I tell you what will happin den, now bery soon
> De Nited States Bank will be blone to de moon
> Dare General Jackson, will him lampoon,
> An de bery nex President will be Zip Coon.

Such song-and-dance routines allowed even the poorest whites to enjoy a sense of social superiority.

Early Trade Unions

Economic inequities encouraged white urban workers to form trade unions to protect their jobs. As early as the 1820s, labor unions, including a few women's trade organizations, went on strike in the larger cities to protest wage cuts and to demand a 10-hour workday. Such agitation was risky, not only because of the possible loss of jobs but also because the courts often held strikes to be criminal conspiracies.

Some middle-class reformers, who saw the emerging wage system as a threat to a republican society of equals, supported union demands. Workingmen's political parties appeared in Philadelphia and New York, appealing not only for economic benefits but also for free public education, abolition of imprisonment for debt, and lien laws to protect workers from employer bankruptcy. Headlining the crusade was the free-thinking socialist, Frances Wright, who electrified audiences by rejecting traditional female roles (she dared to lecture in public!) and condemned the inequalities of wealth and opportunity.

Such protests captured public attention, but brought few tangible reforms (though debt and lien laws were changed). During the 1830s, urban strikers successfully defended the 10-hour day, formed city labor councils, and established the National Trades Union. But, as in Lowell, the crushing depression of 1837 silenced the movement. Not until 1842 did a judicial decision in Massachusetts give labor unions legal standing and the right to strike.

Redefining the Middle Classes

The extremes of wealth and poverty that existed in the 1830s reflected a tightening of economic stratification, the increasing difficulty of achieving upward social mobility. Even the members of the middle classes—skilled workers, small merchants, and the emerging professions—felt the strains of economic change. As enterprising northern merchants and artisans became more involved in market activity, businesses tried to maximize profits and reduce economic uncertainty. In northern towns and cities, even in country stores, fixed retail prices replaced bargaining between buyer and seller. Hard cash, not country produce, became the preferred medium of exchange. As long-term credit arrangements between merchants and customers appeared undesirable, the first credit clearinghouse opened in New York City in 1841. Initially offering information about a borrower's personal "character," credit ratings soon shifted to an assessment of a client's assets and wealth. Yet, most businessmen agreed that self-discipline was the surest way to protect one's access to credit: establish sober rational practices; adhere to firm rules; avoid needless risk.

The Changing Household

The decline of the apprentice system of labor also changed the structure of the middle-class household. With new business operations expanding the range of occupations to include clerks, managers, and professionals, middle-class men now departed their place of residence to work in shops. Even lawyers who kept offices at home established business hours to distinguish their private lives from their professions. Thus, the middle-class household lost its economic cohesion. Meanwhile, the lack of supervision of young workers underscored the separation of "home" and "work." Living in boardinghouses and residential hotels, young workers formed distinct communities and participated in a lively public youth culture, which involved "walking out" with members of the opposite sex, attending the risqué theater (where prostitution thrived on the third balcony), and consuming alcohol at the omnipresent taverns.

The mass production of clothing, shoes, and household goods also encouraged middle-class women to give up home manufacturing. Instead, they concentrated on unpaid domestic tasks and purchased more household goods. A large number of advice books now told them that it was their duty to make their homes shelters from the cold and heartless world of business. As the business household, which had once been filled with nonkin members, became a private home, family relations also changed. In the past, abundant farmlands had encouraged large families, but the growth of urban society, with crowded housing and greater economic uncertainty, brought a steadily declining birthrate, which fell below five children per family by mid-century.

The Cult of Domestic Purity

The separation of middle-class women from the world of business encouraged a new emphasis on domestic purity. "In America," observed the New England essayist Ralph Waldo Emerson, "out-of-doors all seems a market, in-doors an air-tight stove of conventionalism. Everybody who comes into the house savors of these precious habits: the men, of the market; the women of the custom." Middle-class writers described virtuous women as sexless creatures: "Ever timid," in the words of one male writer, "doubtful and clingingly dependent, a perpetual childhood." Such mothers emerged as the primary parents, dedicated to imparting lessons of morality to their children and preserving their homes as spiritual centers for their "worldly" husbands. "The success of democratic institutions," asserted Catharine Beecher, author of *A Treatise on Domestic Economy* (1841), "depends upon. . . the moral and intellectual character of the young, [which] is committed mainly to the female hand." Borrowing from the male work ethic, such reformers urged housewives to inculcate principles of efficiency, punctuality, and cleanliness into the household routine.

Colonial parents had opposed birthday celebrations as signs of "worldliness" (too much concern with human affairs instead of God's) but 19th-century mothers marked their children's birthdays as spiritual occasions, days of prayer, even fasting, to encourage the youngsters' religious development. The editors of *Mother's Monthly Journal* reported the result: "Well, Ma, if you will go down and take something to eat," exclaimed a 3-year old in 1838, "I will henceforth be a good girl!" Such

precocious piety reinforced the evangelical Christian values that obliged adults to create a moral atmosphere in which virtue could flourish.

Middle-class families also expressed new attitudes toward sexuality. Although newspapers advertised various birth control products, including abortion remedies, couples increasingly practiced abstinence. One sign of this change was the decline of illegitimacy rates—the premarital pregnancies that in the late 18th century had led to marriage—which fell from about 33 percent to 23 percent for first births. Advice manuals, written by doctors and clergymen, warned young men of the dangers of masturbation, while medical literature viewed women's sexuality as diseased. In the cities, religious moralists targeted prostitution as a major evil. Meanwhile, male physicians, armed with obstetrical forceps and speculums, displaced midwives at middle-class births.

This emphasis on middle-class female purity encouraged more women, such as Catherine Beecher herself, to remain unmarried. Despite the negative connotations of "spinsterhood," over 7 percent of all American women (double that number in urbanized Massachusetts) opted not to wed. "A single lady, though advanced in life," rhymed one writer in 1817, "Is much more happy than an ill-match'd wife." Single women in the cities were usually among the poorest, but rising numbers of middle-class women found fulfillment (and low pay) as teachers, missionaries, social reformers, even pioneers in the professions. Among these was the educator Mary Lyon, who in 1837 founded Mt. Holyoke, the nation's first women's college. Another was Dorothea Dix, whose work as a Sunday school teacher exposed her to the poor treatment of insane people. Taking up their cause, Dix became an advocate for institutional reform, prompting the establishment of public asylums in several states.

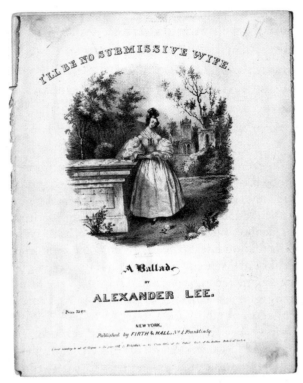

Cover of the popular song "I'll Be No Submissive Wife," which proclaimed, "Think you on a wedding day / That I said as others say / Love and honor and obey / . . . no no no not I. . . ."

Belief in a Perfectible Society

As the economy altered business relations and middle-class households, the prevailing religious values supported a secular creed of individualism, opportunity, and equality. By the beginning of the 19th century, the major Protestant denominations had moved in two directions. The first was a "rational" type of Protestantism, associated with the growing influence of Unitarianism and the Episcopal church among educated and affluent families. This religion emphasized the reasonableness of a benevolent God, freely offering love and salvation to those who pursued a good life. Such views made salvation appear possible for all godly citizens.

The second type was more "emotional" and emerged within evangelical denominations, especially the Methodists and Baptists. This type stressed God's power as well as his mercy, promised the possibility of religious conversion for all people, and inspired religious revivals throughout the country. "God has made man a moral free agent," declared the foremost evangelical preacher of the 1820s and 1830s, the Presbyterian Charles Grandison Finney. Since God had opened his heart to all sinners, Finney told his swelling congregations, the burden shifted to the sinners: They all could be redeemed if they would listen to the call, recognize their sinfulness, and avow a spiritual rebirth. Appealing to the possibility of individual self-improvement, Finney led a crusade through Erie Canal country and then into the poorest neighborhoods of New York City. Placing what he called an "anxious bench" in front of his congregation, the revivalist exhorted the unconverted to sit, focus on their peril, and come to God. Such pleas ignited spiritual fires, bringing a surge in church membership.

Finney's religion struck specific chords. First among Finney's converts were middle-class wives and mothers. Many kept the religious fires burning for years by encouraging their children to experience a feeling of salvation. Many women became religious missionaries, carrying a spiritual message to neighbors and strangers alike, as well as to their husbands. With religious self-confidence, rising businessmen could better face the uncertainties of a market economy and find justifications for their economic activities. "Only make it your invariable principle to do right and do business upon principle," Finney assured them, "and you can control the market." The gospel of self-discipline, sobriety, and avoidance of luxury and debt dovetailed with values of economic efficiency, orderliness, and good character.

Religion and Moral Reform

Belief in individual responsibility and the possibility of human perfectibility stimulated a movement to eliminate the ills and evils of society. Inspired by a sense of religious mission, middle-class women and, increasingly, men formed voluntary societies to bring Christianity to heathens and sinners. Some ventured to the Native American peoples, offering Christian schools to uplift Cherokees, Creeks, and other groups interested in assimilation; some boldly carried the gospel overseas. More frequently, evangelicals focused on the unconverted in the cities and countryside.

In the decade after 1825, the American Tract Society, backed by donations from the nation's richest merchants, such as Arthur and Lewis Tappan, printed and distributed over 30 million religious pamphlets, almanacs, and books. (The feat testified to the new technologies of steam-powered printing presses.) In addition, religious missionaries paid visits to the urban poor—giving away Bibles, kneeling in prayer, and offering relief to orphans, widows, and prostitutes. True to the evangelical creed, material assistance to the poor depended upon the recipient's moral character. Although rich evangelicals established charitable institutions, such as New York's Asylum for Lying-In Women, only expectant mothers with documentary proof of marriage could expect entry. Such moral criteria, however redeeming for the missionaries, barely affected the misery of the urban poor.

Evangelical efforts to curtail business on the Sabbath, including attempts to ban mail delivery on Sunday, failed to gain wide support. The single Erie Canal service that stood idle on the Sabbath

Workers commonly drank on the job; merchants conducted business over brimming glasses; working-class housewives interrupted their labors for a taste.

soon went out of business, and the proposed postal ban conflicted with the separation of church and state. But the marriage of business and moral reform did succeed in limiting the nation's thirst for alcohol. With whiskey prices as low as 25 cents (less than today's $5) per gallon, consumption of alcohol had soared. Workers commonly drank on the job; merchants conducted business over brimming glasses; working-class housewives interrupted their labors for a taste. In 1832, one New York worker beat his wife to death "because," he explained, "she was drunk & no signs of dinner." By 1835, ten years after the Erie Canal opened, 1,500 grog shops lined the right of way. Middle-class businessmen realized that drunkenness conflicted with rational business practices as well as evangelical morality. By 1830, a temperance crusade was trying to reform the nation's alcohol habits. As merchants and artisans banned alcohol from the workplace, religious groups launched local campaigns against Sunday tippling.

Most workers, accustomed to less disciplined labor habits, resisted efforts to impose sobriety, and voters usually rejected laws to prohibit alcoholic consumption. After the depression of 1837, however, workers responded to a campaign for voluntary abstinence and joined Washington Temperance societies, which mushroomed around the country. Women advocates formed Martha Washington societies. By the middle of the next decade, many members suffered relapses and the move-

The DRUNKARD'S PROGRESS,

(OR THE DIRECT ROAD TO POVERTY, WRETCHEDNESS & RUIN.)

The MORNING DRAM.   The CONFIRMED DRUNKARD.   CONCLUDING SCENE.

A temperance broadside expresses the viewpoint of a growing number of Americans in the 1820s.

ment disappeared. With this failure of voluntarism, reformers began to push for mandatory prohibition. Maine passed a prohibition law in 1846, and it was adopted by twelve states during the next decade. More impressive than legislation was the real decline in drinking. Where average annual alcohol consumption exceeded 7 gallons per adult in 1830, the quantity dropped to half in 1840 and half again by 1845.

The wide participation of middle-class evangelical women in moral campaigns expressed the limited range of female public life. Although it contradicted the domestic ideal that virtuous women should be sheltered from social vices, the missionary impulse enabled women reformers to assume public roles. Thus New York's Female Moral Reform Society, founded by evangelicals in 1833, sought not only to "rescue" prostitutes but also to shame their customers. Similarly, a few exceptional women (the African American Maria Stewart, for example, and the sisters Sarah and Angelina Grimké) rejected traditional roles to protest against slavery. These departures from so-

cial convention brought widespread criticism, which in turn contributed to a movement to improve women's rights in the next decade.

Reforming the Schools

Concern about public morality and business efficiency also inspired movements to create public schools for poor children. In 1825, New York City's business leaders persuaded the state to provide funds for eleven schools so "the indigent may be excited to emulate the cleanliness, decorum and mental improvement of those in better circumstances." Workers may have rejected such class snobbery, but they shared the belief that education offered an opportunity for social mobility. Most northern and western states now created public primary schools (only New England developed extensive public secondary schools) and extended the length of the school term. Yet no state made school attendance mandatory, and the quality of education varied widely. In the cities, racial segregation excluded most African American pupils

 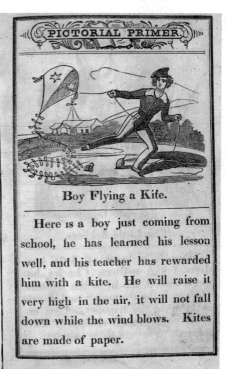

Pages from *American Pictorial Primer,* ca. 1845.

from public schools, though private classes provided elementary lessons for middle-class families. Well-to-do white families sent their children to private academies.

The nation's most prominent educator, Horace Mann, appointed head of the Massachusetts Board of Education in 1837, well understood that the lessons of public education served primarily to instill middle-class values among working families. "If the vicious and ignorant get possession of the [political] apparatus," said Mann of the risks of democracy, "the intelligent and the virtuous must take such shocks as the stupid . . . may choose to administer." Seeking to mold the character of the younger generation, William McGuffey's popular textbooks, which sold 120 million copies, offered a curriculum in patriotism, pru-

dence, and punctuality. "The good boy whose parents are poor, rises very early in the morning; and, all day long, does as much as he can to help his father and mother," read a typical story. "When he sees little boys and girls riding . . . in coaches, or walking with ladies and gentlemen, and having on very fine clothes, he does not envy them, nor wish to be like them."

Undemocratic Movements

The widely held values of individualism, opportunity, and equality did not always translate into practice, however. Although evangelical citizens celebrated the principle of voluntary association and formed a variety of societies, organizations, and political parties, they opposed groups that seemed to threaten egalitarian principles. During the 1820s, the Order of Masons appeared as one target. This secret male fraternal organization had hundreds of lodges with tens of thousands of members, including Washington, Jackson, and Clay. In 1826, a scandal erupted when an ex-member who was about to reveal the order's secrets was kidnapped and murdered with the collusion of government officials in western New York. The incident, showing signs of a widespread conspiracy, aroused public suspicions and inspired a popular anti-Mason movement, which spilled into local and national party politics. But why was Masonry seen as a threat? "IT IS POWERFUL," boasted one Mason. "It comprises men of RANK, wealth, office and talent, in power and out of power." To nonmembers, such a secret network of collaborators, working for self-advancement rather than an egalitarian community, seemed unduly conspiratorial.

Numerous Protestant groups viewed the Roman Catholic church with the same suspicion. In 1830, 300,000 Americans, only 3 percent of the population, were Catholics. Dating from colonial days, anti-Catholic feelings bubbled at the surface, evoking Protestant tirades against Catholic hierarchy, superstition, and alleged moral offenses committed in the secrecy of convents. To Protestants, the Catholic church appeared not only as a false religion but also as a threat to republican government—a foreign power cloaked in priests' robes and nuns' habits. As Catholic immigration increased in the 1830s, workers also saw a threat to their jobs. Ethnic antagonism provoked violence, dramatized one night in 1834 when a Protestant mob in Charlestown, Massachusetts, burned down the Ursiline convent and school. Respectable Protestants denounced the crime, but the climate of anti-Catholicism endured, feeding political movements in the following decades as Catholic immigration continued to climb.

Equally vulnerable was the Church of Jesus Christ of Latter Day Saints, known as the Mormons. This group had been founded in upstate New York in 1830 by Joseph Smith, who claimed to have been led by an angel to the hiding place of the Book of Mormon, where he discovered a divine revelation. The Mormons predicted that the creation of God's kingdom on earth would begin in North America. Unlike other evangelical churches, which appealed first to women, the Mormons initially attracted male followers, many of whom, like the prophet Smith, had been displaced by the new market economy. The Mormons' patriarchal communalism, permitting plural marriages, brought prosperity to members but attracted the hostility of suspicious neighbors. Facing attacks, the Mormons moved to Ohio, then to Missouri, and then to Nauvoo, Illinois, where they built a flourishing town in 1839. Violence followed them, culminating in the murder of Smith by a mob and the uprooting of the church once more as the new leader, Brigham Young, led 12,000 Mormons to Utah in 1847.

The social isolation of the Mormon church mirrored the experiences of other perfectionist groups that deliberately organized ideal or utopian communities outside existing social institutions. Often inspired by religious leaders, these groups withdrew from society to implement their ideals immediately and demonstrate that social perfection was possible. One social experiment began at New Harmony, Indiana, in 1825 when the English industrialist Robert Owen founded a socialist community that rejected private property, organized religion, and traditional marriage. New Harmony attracted wide attention, but internal divisions doomed the effort. One of Owen's disciples, the feminist Frances Wright, formed another community at Noashoba, Tennessee, which permitted African Americans to work for their freedom. Wright's radicalism offended potential supporters and this effort also failed.

Another example of perfectionism appeared when one of Finney's converts, John Humphrey Noyes, established a community at Oneida, New York, in the 1840s. Replacing private property with communal ownership and exclusive marriage with a system of "complex" marriage that permitted more than one partner, the Oneida reformers built a flourishing, self-sustaining community in rural New York that survived for decades. Other utopias were spiritually motivated, including the Amana Society, or "Community of True Inspiration," established near Buffalo, New York, in 1843. These diverse projects seldom succeeded, but they testified to a passionate desire among evangelical Americans to live in harmony with "natural" or divine principles. Their perfectionist impulse reinforced the idealism of the national identity, the widely held belief that Americans were a morally superior people.

Party Politics and the Market Economy

"It is said to be the age of the first person singular," noted the philosopher Ralph Waldo Emerson in 1827. As the expanding economy encouraged individual initiative and evangelical Protestantism emphasized personal responsibility for salvation, so the new national political parties, Democrats and Whigs, appealed to newly enfranchised voters to take stands on issues of economic development. The resulting political choices often reflected a citizen's position in the market economy. Facing new commercial activities, some citizens saw their fortunes decline, or feared that they would, and recoiled from the changes. Others rode the crest of financial speculation into realms of unimagined wealth or more modest middle-class occupations. Many more found themselves between those extremes.

In a nutshell, those who anticipated bettering themselves by means of commercial development (internal improvements, for example) supported policies to encourage change and found themselves aligned with what would be called, first, the National Republican and, later, the Whig party of Henry Clay and Daniel Webster. By contrast, people who felt threatened by government involvement in the economy (the regulation of credit by a national bank, for example) opposed public support of economic programs and aligned with Andrew Jackson and the Democratic party. Where Democrats supported a free-market economy and believed that people "looked to the government for too much," Whigs favored economic stimulation by tariffs and canal-building and proclaimed that the people were "entitled to the protecting care of a paternal government." Although local issues might affect voter opinion, party alignments cut across all regions. By the 1830s, both Whigs and Democrats competed for votes as *national* parties.

The Jackson Presidency

The inauguration of Andrew Jackson in 1829 demonstrated the power of political majorities. Having campaigned against the "corrupt bargain" that had deprived him of election in 1824, the new president claimed to embody the common citizenry. Jackson promptly redefined the meaning of a political "party" by opening the White House to inauguration day celebrants, according to one conservative "the most vulgar and gross in the nation," who got drunk, wrecked furniture, smashed china, and so introduced "the reign of King Mob." This welcoming of common people expressed the president's belief that "the duties of all public offices are . . . so plain and simple" that anyone of normal intelligence could perform them. Jackson proceeded to reward his political supporters with the "spoils" of politics—government jobs. Martin Van Buren, architect of the national party, became secretary of state, a rival to the succession of Vice President John Calhoun. Jackson also installed an informal "kitchen cabinet" of friends and supporters to give him counsel.

Jackson's political allies, chosen because of their position on party issues, nonetheless revealed the continuing role of personality and "character" in arousing political controversy. Indeed, party politics had nothing to do with Jackson's most debated appointment, Secretary of War John Eaton. What disturbed many contemporaries, including Calhoun and members of the cabinet, was the rumor that Eaton and his wife Peggy had had an affair while Mrs. Eaton's first husband was still alive. During the presidential campaign, Jackson's own wife had been accused of adultery and, when she died shortly after the election, Jackson blamed the rumormongers. As some administration wives started a moral crusade against Peggy Eaton, ostracizing the secretary of war from social affairs, a furious Jackson launched a personal campaign to restore her reputation. The issue, in this evangelical age, hinged on "virtue." Compromise proved impossible. The Eaton affair served mainly to split members of the administration, leaving Van Buren on the presidential side and Calhoun as an outsider.

Jackson and the Bank War

Jackson's suspicion of special privileges led him to oppose government support of economic development. Although the president praised the nation's commercial progress—while visiting the factories at Lowell, he marveled at the intricate machinery—Democrats questioned whether business interests deserved special government sup-

port. When Congress agreed to fund a turnpike linking Maysville and Lexington, Kentucky, in 1830, Jackson objected that the project was too costly and served only local needs. Van Buren, who desired no competition for New York's Erie Canal, drafted a veto message that challenged the constitutionality of such federal expenditures. Where politicians like Adams and Clay advocated ambitious programs to boost the market economy, Democrats opposed government favors to special interests.

This opposition came to a head in a "war" against the second Bank of the United States. Chartered for twenty years in 1816, the bank served as a depository of government funds and used its power to lend money to regulate the credit policies of smaller banks. But the bank had contributed to the sudden contraction of credit that had caused the Panic of 1819, creating abiding hostility among small businessmen and commercial farmers in the South and West. Jackson shared their antipathy to this "privileged" private institution and the benefits it brought to a "few monied capitalists." Yet by using its control of government revenues to extend credit, the bank had won supporters by stimulating economic development.

Among the defenders of the bank was Henry Clay, proponent of economic growth, who had his eye on the presidency. In 1832, four years before the bank's charter was scheduled to expire, Clay decided to make the institution an election issue. Passage of a recharter bill would assure continuation of Clay's program of economic development; a presidential veto, Clay believed, would offend the public and catapult him into the White House. With such assumptions, Congress passed the recharter bill four months before election day in 1832.

"Many of our rich men have not been content with equal protection and equal benefits, but have besought us to make them richer by act of Congress," Jackson replied in a ringing veto message that defined the fundamental conflicts of the age. Recognizing the growing importance of commercial activity, the president acknowledged the inevitable inequities caused by "superior industry, economy, and virtue." But government support of a particular bank, he said, introduced artificial advantages, favoring some citizens at the expense of others. "When the laws undertake . . . to make the rich richer and the potent more powerful," Jackson declared, "the humble members of society—the farmers, mechanics, and laborers—who have neither the time nor the means of securing like favors for themselves, have a right to complain of the injustice." Government, he said, should act as naturally, and neutrally, as the heavenly rains: "Shower its favor alike on the high and the low, the rich and the poor." Then, having thrown this challenge before Clay and the Bank of the United States, Jackson proceeded to throttle his opponents in the 1832 presidential election.

Voter endorsement of the bank veto expressed the public's ambivalence about economic development, desire for individual betterment coexisting with a fear of banks, credit, fluctuating prices, and the impersonal national economy. "You must recollect that the debt is due to the Bank, not to an individual," a nervous Virginia merchant informed his wife, "and we cannot get indulgence by promising to pay it tomorrow or next week, but it must be paid on the day it is due, or our credit must be ruined." To Jacksonians, the government-supported bank was evil, an artificial "Monster," that threatened "natural" economic operations. The bank reinforced those suspicions after the election by calling in loans and contracting credit. Fearing that the bank would destroy prosperity to save itself, Jackson resolved to withdraw government deposits and place them in state banks. He had to fire two secretaries of the treasury before finding a cabinet

To Jacksonians, the government-supported bank was evil, an artificial "Monster."

officer, Attorney General Roger B. Taney, willing to implement the scheme. This unprecedented presidential action brought condemnations of "King Andrew I"; Jackson's opponents proudly adopted the name of those who had criticized King George III and called themselves "Whigs."

The Panic of 1837

Ironically, by distributing government deposits to state banks, which the Whigs called "pet banks," Jackson did kill the national bank, but he also accelerated the economic trends that he opposed. Backed by government money, these state banks increased their loans, setting off an expansion of credit that encouraged investment and speculation. At the same time, unrelated changes in international markets (high British purchases of cotton, foreign investments in canals, importation of silver mined in Mexico) added to bank reserves, which in turn encouraged even more expansion of credit. The ensuing inflation had large repercussions. Rising cotton prices triggered a boom in land sales—38 million public acres were sold in 1836–37—while the inflation of food prices hit workers in the eastern cities, provoking numerous labor strikes for wage adjustments. Worried about inflationary land speculation, Jackson issued a Specie Circular in 1836, requiring that investors, but not actual settlers, pay for land with gold and silver coin, known as specie, rather than with paper money or with credit.

Jackson's financial policies—the removal of government deposits from the national bank, the promotion of pet banks, federal land sales—provided ammunition for a political war between Democrats and Whigs. But economic development reflected more complicated changes in international finance. As British bankers responded to falling cotton prices by reducing investments in the United States, American bankers called in their loans, reduced credit, and provoked a severe economic downturn, the Panic of 1837. Problems in the cotton trade perpetuated the crisis, which affected businesses, large and small, throughout the country. "Men could run away from the cholera," remarked a helpless businessman about the epidemic of failures, "but they can't run away from this distress."

Building a Competitive Society

Jackson's inability to control the economy testified to the intricacy of market relationships. Even the desire to end government support of special interests might serve cross purposes. Consider the legal implications of the Supreme Court's *Charles River Bridge* case of 1837. Although Massachusetts had granted a private company the right to build a toll bridge between Boston and Cambridge in 1785, the growth of trade and population led the state legislature to approve building another free bridge nearby, thus imperiling the profits of the first company. Two decades earlier, the Marshall Court had upheld the sanctity of contracts in the *Dartmouth College* case (see Chapter 8). But the Jacksonian Court, led by newly appointed Chief Justice Roger B. Taney, ruled that the original company constituted a privileged monopoly, just like the Bank of the United States, whose private interests remained secondary to the larger public benefit.

Reinforcing the ruling was a realization that government no longer had to grant special privileges to encourage capital investment. The deci-sion also encouraged basic changes in legislative regulation of new businesses. Instead of requiring a special law to create each private corporation, the states increasingly enacted general incorporation laws, which established uniform business codes that permitted virtually unlimited incorporation. In this way, the Jacksonian attack on privilege encouraged the types of commercial institutions (that is, private corporations) that Democrats usually opposed.

As the Panic of 1837 crippled the economy, Whigs and Democrats clashed about other economic issues. Believing that the federal government should support economic development, Whigs like Clay and Webster advocated government-funded internal improvements, tariffs, and the chartering of a third Bank of the United States. By contrast, Democrats saw monster banks and artificial privileges destroying the virtuous republic and demanded that government allow economic development to proceed without granting special favors. Yet neither party doubted that market values, for better or worse, pervaded society. "The question," explained an Indiana Democrat in 1838, "is not. . . whether the numerous family of banks should exist, but only whether government, out of that family, shall select one as a bride." One way or the other, business had become a crucial ingredient in the national identity.

The spread of commercial values highlighted differences of regional perspective. Although Democrats and Whigs won support in all sections of the country (both Tennessee's Jackson and Kentucky's Clay claimed to speak for the nation) business investment accentuated conflicts between the free-labor northern economy and the slave labor southern economy. If, for example, nonperishable southern cotton needed no haste to get to market, should southern politicians support federally funded roads and canals? If, for another example, western settlement depopulated the

Northeast and raised labor costs, should north-eastern politicians approve cheap western lands? If, for a third example, northern manufacturers needed tariffs to compete with British imports, should westerners pay more for the clothes they wore? During the 1830s, leading politicians debated these issues of regional self-interest and economic development.

Equally divisive was the issue of slavery. As citizens in all regions confronted impersonal market values, the treatment of human beings as labor commodities—as units of production to be bought and sold—raised moral issues about the country's claim to be a government of "the people." Yet, southerners vigorously denied that slaves existed only as economic entities, insisting that patriarchal owners looked after "their people." Such arguments, discussed often on the floors of Congress, set the stage for a growing debate about the South's "peculiar institution."

INFOTRAC® COLLEGE EDITION EXERCISES

For additional reading go to InfoTrac College Edition, your online research library at *http://web1.infotrac-college.com.*

Subject search: United States economic history, reference
Keyword search: Erie Canal
Keyword search: Lowell mills
Keyword search: Horace Mann
Keyword search: Andrew Jackson
Keyword search: bank war

ADDITIONAL READING

The Expanding Market Economy

Christopher Clark, *The Roots of Rural Capitalism: Western Massachusetts, 1780–1860* (1990). Describes a subtle transformation of economic behavior among farmers increasingly drawn into marketplace relations.

Charles Sellers, *The Market Revolution: Jacksonian America, 1815–1846* (1991). This survey examines economic issues, cultural values, and political conflict.

Susan Sessions Rugh, *Our Common Country: Family Farming, Culture, and Community in the Nineteenth-Century Midwest* (2001). Focusing on a single Illinois county, this study describes the impact of market values on the community.

Transforming Northern Working Conditions

Paul E. Johnson, *A Shopkeeper's Millenium: Society and Revivals in Rochester, New York, 1815–1837* (1978). Examining a single community, the book examines economic growth, religious values, and community life.

Sean Wilentz, *Chants Democratic: New York City and the Rise of the American Working Class, 1788–1850* (1984). Focusing on skilled workers, the author describes the changing nature of work and its economic consequences.

James Oliver Horton and Lois E. Horton, *In Hope of Liberty: Culture, Community, and Protest among Northern Free Blacks, 1700–1860* (1997). A thorough discussion of African American life in the North.

The Mill Workers of Lowell

Thomas Dublin, *Transforming Women's Work: New England Lives in the Industrial Revolution* (1994). Moving beyond his pioneering book, *Women at Work: The Transformation of Work and Community in Lowell, Massachusetts, 1826–1860* (1979), the author offers case studies of women's work in the 19th century.

Christine Stansell, *City of Women: Sex and Class in New York, 1789–1860* (1986). A study of the lives of working women, this book depicts the difficulties of urban life amidst rapid economic change.

Redefining the Middle Classes

Mary P. Ryan, *Cradle of the Middle Class: The Family in Oneida County, New York, 1790–1865* (1981). This book analyzes the connections of gender roles, religious awakening, and economic change. See also

Catherine E. Kelly, *In the New England Fashion: Reshaping Women's Lives in the Nineteenth Century* (1999).

The Cult of Domestic Purity

Lee Virginia Chambers-Schiller, *Liberty, A Better Husband: Single Women in America, the Generations of 1780–1840* (1984). Whereas Ryan's study (above) explores the changing situation of married women, this book depicts the lives of women, mostly middle-class, who did not marry.

Amy Gilman Srebnick, *The Mysterious Death of Mary Rogers: Sex and Culture in Nineteenth-Century New York* (1995). Focusing on a celebrated murder of 1840, the author explores the changing nature of urban life.

Party Politics and the Market Economy

Harry L. Watson, *Liberty and Power: The Politics of Jacksonian America* (1990). A lucid explanation of the assumptions and interests that motivated political alliances of the period.

THE NEW WORLD.

PARK BENJAMIN,
EDITOR.

J. WINCHESTER,
PUBLISHER.

"No pent-up Utica contracts our powers; For the whole boundless Continent is ours."

QUARTO EDITION.   OFFICE 30 ANN-STREET. $3 PER ANNUM.

VOLUME IV......No. 8.   NEW-YORK, SATURDAY, FEBRUARY 19, 1842.   WHOLE NUMBER 90.

ISLAND AND RUIN ON LOCH LOMOND.

With Ben Lomond in the Distance.

For the New World.

Oh! loveliest spot beneath the sun
    You never looked so bright before!
We left the lake's romantic side,
    And treading high yon mountain way,
Looked o'er the hills and waters wide,
    And vallies fair that round us lay;
And now we spread our wingèd sail
Free to the glad and bounding gale,
And wake from out their sunny sleep
The ripples of that tranquil deep.
And now an isle of verdant hue
Stands forth amid the waters blue,
A favored spot—where every tree
That Scotland boasts the eye may see,
And every tender flower doth blow
That Lomond's dells and forests know,
And here a gentle refuge find
From withering sun and blighting wind.
Lovely thou art, yet not alone,
Sweet isle, for beauty of thine own,
My earnest eye would fondly stray
To thy wild shore and rocky bay,
Where, through the mist of rolling years
To fancy's dreaming gaze appears,
Seated beneath the aspen bough,
A friendly band long severed now,
And hearts from friendship long estranged
Are smiling there in eyes unchanged:
'Tis gone——but I awake to greet
An hour than all the rest more sweet,
Whose perfect joy forbids a sigh
For future time or days gone by.

And dies in cadence sweet and low,
And the wild birds, in joyous crowd,
Soar upward to the summer cloud,
And warble forth their thrilling lays
To join the universal praise.
            VIII.
We leave the hallowed spot behind,
And on before the dancing wind
Joyously sweep, till high appear
Their lofty peaks uplifting near
Yon mountains dark, whose craggy height
Makes barrier for those waters bright.
But ere we turn our sail once more,
And sadly leave this lonely shore,
Rest in our course, and pause awhile
Beside the lady Ellen's isle.
With turret rent and roofless hall
A castle rears its crumbling wall,
Where the wild rose its blossoms pale
Hangs forth to meet the summer gale,
And in the rough and moss-grown floor,
Where human step resounds no more,
Fit tenant of such dreary ground,
The darksome yew hath refuge found.
In vain ye list to hear the swell
Of martial pipe or matin bell—
In vain, at twilight's haunted hour,
Soft notes to list from lady's bower—
The wind that sweeps these chambers gray
But tells of death and dark decay,
And glory passed in dust away.
            IX.

With him for whom she scarce could grieve,

Slavery and the Southern Economy, 1828–1844

"Suppose," asked the white southern Reverend Charles C. Jones in his published catechism, "the Master is hard to please, and threatens and punishes more than he ought, what is the Slave to do? Answer: Do his best to please him."

"Is it right for the Slave to run away . . . ?" he further inquired. "Answer: No." Indeed, another white southern minister warned that resistance to slavery was a sin: "It is the devil who tells you to try and be free."

Such Christian ministers articulated the core values of a southern regional identity, taking pains to explain to African American slaves why servants should obey their masters. As they interpreted the Bible, God had commanded servants to be obedient, to accept lowly stations in this world, and to conduct themselves with patience and humility so that they would receive a just reward in heaven. In the eyes of most white southerners, blacks could never participate as equals in this world or share a place in the national identity.

Biblical justifications for slavery may have eased the consciences of Christian slaveowners, but slaves responded with less enthusiasm to the doctrine of submission. Although the circumstances of slavery diminished opportunities for resistance, enslaved African Americans were slow to embrace religious tenets that demanded complete obedience to their masters. To avoid punishment, however, slaves usually told their masters what they thought their masters wanted to hear.

This desire to say what was expected adds irony to a conversation between a Methodist minister and a slave in Alabama:

Question: What did God make you for?
Answer: To make a crop.

This simple dialogue between slaveowner and slave underscored the essence of the South's "peculiar institution." Slavery existed "to make a crop"—that is, it existed to make money. And that material objective showed just how much the slave South resembled the rest of the country.

By the 19th century, the growth of commercial enterprise had crossed all geographic boundaries, even penetrating southern regions that claimed to despise northern material values. Southern leaders often said that agriculture was more natural than commerce and industry, and they saw themselves as rural patriarchs rather than as businessmen. But, while northern investors built steam-powered textile mills and interstate banking systems, dug canals and laid railroads, the South invested primarily in cotton, the essential raw material that fueled the nation's economic development. Although scarcely 10 percent of the country's manufacturing occurred in southern states, and southern production depended on northern credit, insurance, and shipping, the export of cotton kept European capital flowing into the United States. By mid-century, cotton production approached 3 million bales (1.5 billion pounds) per year and constituted nearly two-thirds of the nation's exports. "We could bring the whole world to our feet," asserted a southern senator. "Cotton is King."

With such economic power, cotton planters could deplore factories and big cities and yet remain committed to economic growth and business efficiency. "Time's money, time's money," cried an Alabama cotton planter, worrying about his farm's productivity. During the 1830s, agricultural reformers advised southern planters to increase productivity by "scientific" management of their farms.

Using improved agricultural technology and fertilizers, southern planters also aimed to enhance the productivity of their slave laborers. Imitating northern textile manufacturers who used clock-time instead of sun-to-sun to regulate the work hours of factory employees, southern cotton planters timed bells and bugles to their household clocks or carried watches into the fields to regulate the labor of their slaves. Lists of southern household items showed a correlation between a planter's wealth and the ownership of accurate timepieces.

What distinguished the southern economy was not so much the supremacy of cotton (southern farmers actually planted more acres of corn than cotton) as the investment of profits to acquire more land and more slaves. As one observer reported, the logic of southern agriculture was perfectly circular: "To sell cotton in order to buy negroes—to make more cotton to buy more negroes." Yet, the high price of slaves meant that the majority of white southerners could not afford to purchase even a single human being. Wealth and property were thus intertwined with cotton production and slave ownership. As the wealthiest citizens, moreover, slaveowners emerged as political leaders. Whigs and Democrats alike supported slavery; both the Democratic Andrew Jackson and the Whig Henry Clay owned slaves.

Slave ownership not only distinguished rich and prominent whites from the poorer groups but also created a unique regional society. Although southerners, no less than northerners, aggressively pursued economic gain (while citizens of both regions expressed prejudiced views of African Americans), the difference between free labor and slave labor established rigid social divisions that limited economic mobility to whites. Every white citizen, no matter how poor, stupid, or immoral, could claim to belong to a superior social group. Such attitudes helped tie the interests of nonslaveholders to the slaveowning elite.

Expanding Cotton Society

Successful cotton cultivation required three factors: fertile land, green seeds that produced the favored short-fiber variety, and a frost-free environment for at least 200 days after planting. Material success also demanded a willingness to pull up stakes and head west. Such requirements stimulated the expansion of cotton agriculture onto the Gulf plains and into territories west of the Mississippi River. But westward migration confronted an unmoving legal obstacle. For centuries, the Creeks, Cherokees, Choctaws, and Chickasaws had claimed lands now coveted by cotton planters. Indeed, leaders of these groups had even imitated southern whites by acquiring black slaves.

During the 1820s, southern farmers, speculators, and politicians had pressured the Native people to surrender their land in exchange for western acreage (see Chapter 10). By 1830, President Andrew Jackson decided to expedite the removal of these so-called civilized tribes from the southern states. Disregarding previous treaties and ample evidence of Creek and Cherokee assimilation, the president viewed "savage" peoples as doomed to extinction unless they migrated beyond the reach of Anglo American civilization. Despite the protests of northern evangelical missionaries, who had converted many Native Americans to the Protestant religion, Congress passed the Removal Act of 1830, which provided permanent reservation lands west of the Mississippi. "If they now refuse to accept the liberal terms offered they can only be liable for whatever evils and difficulties may arise," said the paternalistic Jackson. "I feel conscious of having done my duty to my red children."

Forced Removal of Native Americans

The federal government proceeded to coerce Native American leaders (some of whom were only

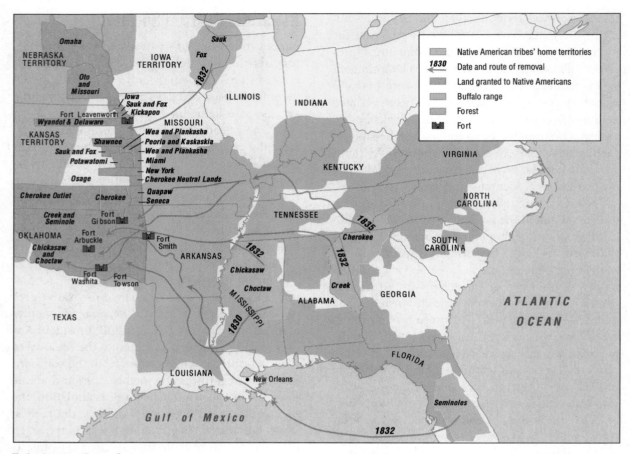

Native American Removals

self-appointed chiefs) to sign nearly seventy removal treaties. In 1831, Mississippi's Choctaws led the exodus to what is now Oklahoma. Inadequate food, clothing, and medicine brought immense suffering and high mortality en route, and when the Choctaws reached their destination, Jackson's promise of self-rule evaporated when federal officials refused to surrender supervision of tribal affairs. Meanwhile, the 7,000 Choctaws who had opted to remain on their lands in Mississippi fell victim to hostile squatters, fraudulent traders, and indifferent officials, who took advantage of local laws that forbade Native Americans

to testify against whites in court. A few half-bloods managed to hold onto their lands and even acquired slaves, but most Choctaws became landless agricultural workers who were treated no better than nearby African Americans.

In Georgia, efforts of the state government to establish sovereignty over Cherokee lands led to a legal battle that reached the U.S. Supreme Court. When a group of evangelical missionaries was arrested for violating a Georgia law that required whites living on Cherokee land to take an oath of allegiance to the state government, the pro-Cherokee defendants argued that federal

Suffering on the "Trail of Tears." Removed in a forced march to Oklahoma, one-quarter of the Cherokees lost their lives.

treaties superseded the state law. In 1832, John Marshall's Supreme Court agreed in *Worcester v. Georgia* that the Cherokees constituted a "domestic dependent" nation entitled to federal protection from Georgia jurisdiction. This statement of federal superiority should have won applause from Jackson, an avowed nationalist. But the president believed that no defeated Native American nation could claim sovereignty, and he ignored the Court's ruling. A treaty signed with a minority of Cherokees called for the departure of the entire tribe in 1838. "Doubtless it will be painful to leave the graves of their fathers," Jackson admitted. "But what do they [do] more than our ancestors did or than our children are now doing?. . . . Is it supposed that the wandering savage has a stronger attachment to his home than the settled, civilized Christian?" Despite Cherokee protests, Jackson's successor President Martin Van Buren, enforced the disputed removal treaty, ordering the military to compel the remaining Cherokees to leave their homes. The ensuing "Trail of Tears," a forced march to Oklahoma, brought starvation,

> **"Is it supposed that the wandering savage has a stronger attachment to his home than the settled, civilized Christian?"**

disease, and 25 percent mortality. Georgia farmers promptly settled on Cherokee lands.

The South's Agricultural Economy

The urge to remove Native Americans reflected the vitality of southwestern agriculture. With the demand for cotton increasing about 5 percent annually and offering an 8 percent annual return on investment, the acquisition of land promised both quick profits and long-term financial security. Indeed, the profitability of cotton agriculture discouraged southern investments in the types of commercial and manufacturing enterprise that altered the northern economy. Fresh land seemed

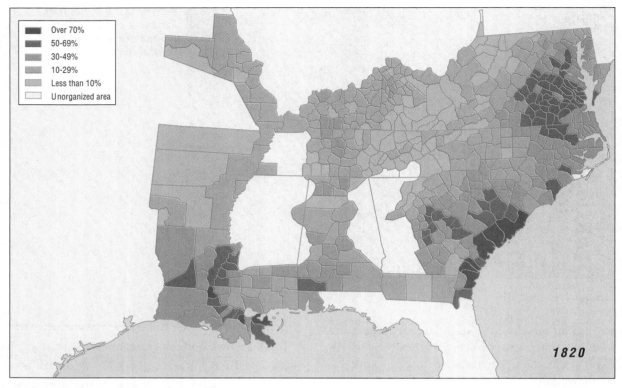

Over 70%
50-69%
30-49%
10-29%
Less than 10%
Unorganized area

1820

Percentage of Slave Population, 1820   OVERLAY 1

to offer its own reward. "The Alabama Fever rages here with great violence," remarked a North Carolinian who watched his neighbors migrating westward. "I am apprehensive . . . it will almost depopulate the country."

In this rural society, farming remained the primary occupation, and middle-class status depended on ownership of land. But ownership of slaves placed a farmer into a higher social category, and ownership of more than twenty slaves gave a farmer the prestigious status of "planter." In cotton-growing areas, 60 percent of all agricultural wealth took the form of slaves, while land and farm buildings contributed less than one-third of a plantation's value. Only about one-quarter of white families owned slaves, though slave owner-

ship in the cotton areas exceeded 40 percent. Half of all slaveowners held fewer than five slaves; three-quarters owned less than ten. Only 12 percent owned more than twenty. Yet this minority of white planters controlled the lives of a majority of the slaves and produced 75 percent of the region's cotton. Such economic power gave the planter elite disproportionate influence in southern society. Moreover, whether slaveowners were Whigs or Democrats, they had a larger percentage of seats in southern state legislatures than did nonslaveholding whites.

Outside the cotton regions, in the hill country of southern Appalachia (western Virginia, the Carolinas, and northern Georgia) farmers owned no slaves and concentrated on raising corn, live-

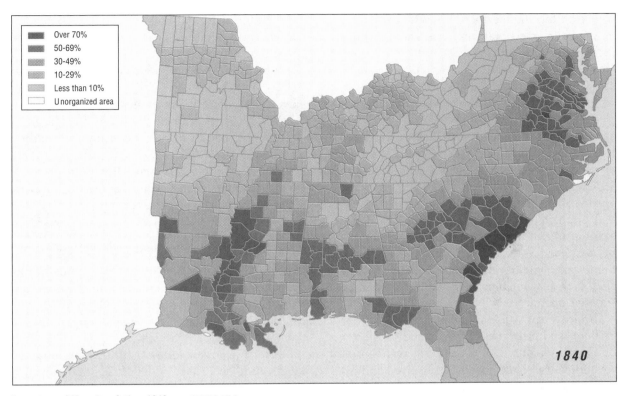

Percentage of Slave Population, 1840 OVERLAY 1

stock, and other subsistence crops. Less involved in commercial agriculture, these farmers grew crops to feed their households and exchanged small surpluses in local markets. Many were descendants of Scots-Irish immigrants who had come to America in the 18th century, and they created a distinctive self-sufficient society.

In plantation areas, by contrast, nonslaveholding farmers interacted closely with the larger cotton producers. They freely fished, hunted, and fed their livestock on any unfenced lands, treating such ground as common property. Smaller farmers also relied on nearby plantations to gin cotton, mill grains, and purchase their surplus produce. Some worked as overseers for wealthier planters; others rented slaves; most grew small quantities of

cotton and aspired to enter the planter class. During the 19th century, this desire for upward mobility collided with rising prices for land and slaves. But shared values of white supremacy reduced class conflict. Small farmers acknowledged the leadership of slaveholding planters, voted them into political office, and accepted the legal responsibility to support the slave system, for example by riding in night patrols that enforced slave curfews.

Southern Households

Although cotton sales brought the planters into the market economy, rural life discouraged changes in domestic arrangements. While economic changes were transforming northern households from economic units where craftsmen had worked at home into domestic institutions supervised by women (see Chapter 10), southern households maintained a traditional rural character, in which men and women mixed agricultural tasks with domestic crafts. On small farms with few or no slaves, wives and daughters often worked in the fields, especially at planting and harvest times. Even on large plantations with numerous slaves, the household served as an economic center. Planters' wives managed a diverse domestic economy, tending cows and poultry, making dairy products, gardening, sewing, and cooking for masters and slaves alike. Because the workplace was not separate from the home, the plantation household remained patriarchal, even as women participated fully in domestic supervision.

Southern white women continued to marry earlier than northern women, extending the years of marital fertility. The continuing availability of western cotton lands may have inspired optimism about their ability to support large families and the absence of birth-control information in rural areas, in contrast to cities, precluded much choice. Thus the southern birthrate did not show the decline occurring in the northern states. White families with eight children or more were not uncommon. In busy households many expressed obvious ambivalence: "My [menstrual] courses came on," wrote the wife of a Virginia slaveholder. "I felt so thankful. God is good and kind to me a sinner."

Since slave families had no legal status, individual members could be bought, sold, and separated from each other. Indeed, the disruption of slave families contributed to their smaller size, even though African American women tended to have babies at a younger age than whites. This disparity probably resulted from the unhealthy environment in which slave mothers lived. Experiencing nutritional deficiencies as well as hard work during their pregnancies, slave women had frequent miscarriages or delivered babies with low birthweights and high vulnerability to diseases. Half of all slave children died before age five, about twice the mortality rate for white children. "Celia's child died about four months old," noted one planter diarist, assessing the death of an infant slave. "This is two Negroes and three horses I have lost this year." But even southern white families suffered higher infant mortality rates than did those in the Northeast.

The Domestic Lives of Southern White Women

Although most southern white women, like northern women, embraced evangelical values, southern Protestants emphasized personal piety rather than social improvement. As a result, the evangelical reform movements that appeared in the North won few followers in the South. In any case, rural society provided little opportunity to form voluntary organizations for social activity. Outside the wealthy planter class, a lack of public schools limited female education, producing higher rates of illiteracy among southerners. Moreover, the frequency of westward migration and the demands of supervising slave households isolated southern white women from relatives and friends. Multiple pregnancies endangered their health and often caused severe calcium deficiency. "You would be shocked to see how old I look with one of my front teeth gone," lamented one woman about a common rite of passage. Yet most southern women idealized marriage and motherhood, viewing that status as their highest virtue. While poor women and slaves relied on female midwives to assist at births, more affluent southern women, like their sisters in the Northeast, summoned male doctors. Their medical expertise did not appreciably improve survival rates.

At a time when married women could not legally own property independently of their husbands, and when divorces usually required special acts of the state legislatures and were only granted in cases of idiocy, impotence, or bigamy, women were dependent on fathers and husbands to protect their economic interests. Such powerlessness, together with the pressure of household management, frequent pregnancy, and rural isolation produced chronic depression—what contemporaries called "melancholia." "I am continually oppressed by a feeling of *inability* to do what I ought," cried a frustrated housewife. "All is confusion, *all is wrong.*" Husbands were not necessarily sympathetic. "It is mere folly to be unhappy," wrote one annoyed spouse.

The Business of Slavery

While southern slaveholding women upheld values of domesticity, the slave economy continually threatened the bonds of African American families. Southern apologists claimed that most slave sales were made out of necessity to settle probate cases, but evidence of the slave trade between the Atlantic states and the cotton belt suggests that motives of commerce and profit were more common. Indeed, most sales occurred in times of prosperity. During the 1820s, 150,000 slaves were sold west, usually through a network of professional slave traders; in the next decade, the figure reached 250,000.

Contrary to slaveholders' claims, blacks did not typically move west with their owners or with kin. Twenty five percent of the interregional slave trade involved youngsters between the ages of 8 and 14, most of whom were purchased alone and separated from their mothers. About 10 percent of African American teenagers were sold from the Upper South, and 30 percent could expect to be transferred at least once during their lifetime. Children were seldom sold with their fathers, nor husbands with wives. When one state prohibited the importation of children under 10 without their mothers, the slave traders simply neglected to purchase the children in the first place, breaking up families at the initial place of sale.

For slaves, the possibility of being separated from their family instilled a pervasive fear and pain; the threat of being sold south or "down the river" served to discourage slave resistance. "Dear Husband," wrote a Virginia slave in 1840, "the trader has been here three times to look at me. . . . I expect I shall never see you all—never no more." "Dear Husband," wrote another Virginia slave, "A man . . . bought Albert and is gone. I don't know where." "Dear Husband," wrote yet another Virginia slave of her master's intentions, "I know not what time he may sell me, and then all my bright hopes of the future are blasted . . . for if I thought I should never see you, this earth would have no charms for me."

These sorrows, repeated innumerable times, contrasted with slaveowners' views of African American psychology. "The dance will allay his most poignant grief," observed a defender of slavery, "and a few days blot out the memory of his most bitter bereavement. His natural affection is not strong, and consequently he is cruel to his own offspring, and suffers little by separation from them."

The Conditions of Slavery

Such justifications could not disguise the essence of slavery: the control of human labor by compulsion and the lack of choice on the part of the enslaved. "We were worked in all weather," recalled the ex-slave Frederick Douglass. "It was never too hot or too cold; it could never rain, blow hail, or snow, too hard for us to work in the field. Work,

work, work. . . ." Such discipline commenced at an early age. "Us chillen start to work soon's us could toddle," recalled an ex-slave. "Iffen its freezin' or not us have to go to toughen us up."

Beyond this basic compulsion, the conditions of slavery varied immensely, depending on the nature of the work, the number of slaves, the temperament of the master, and the resourcefulness of the slave. One quarter of all slaves lived on small holdings of 1 to 9 slaves; half lived on larger holdings of 10 to 49 slaves; another quarter lived on big estates of over 50 slaves. The median number of slaves per holding was 32 in the cotton South and 23 in the region as a whole.

Most slaveholders viewed themselves as patriarchs, who used black labor not solely for their personal gain but also to regulate the lives of their supposedly inferior slaves. No rational person would deliberately imperil such valuable property—for economic, if not humanitarian, reasons. On small farms, slaves and masters often worked together, shared meals, and probably exchanged a degree of emotion. Slavery in those circumstances was personal, but whether relations were kind or brutal depended on intangible and capricious factors of personality. On small farms, slaves had less chance to develop families or unique institutions because of the day-to-day presence of their masters. Such owners were also less stable economically and more prone to sell their workers.

Slaves who did domestic work also interacted closely with whites. Freed from the drudgery of field labor, house servants enjoyed better food and clothing, but remained under the close oversight of master and mistress. In such proximity, it was easy to attract attention, and instant punishment. "I despise myself," admitted one planter's wife, "for suffering my temper to rise at the provocations offered by the servants." Believing that slaves were naturally lazy, slaveholders could

---

On small farms, slaves and masters often worked together, shared meals, and probably exchanged a degree of emotion.

---

justify their anger. Proximity to white men also exposed slave women to sexual assault. "I cannot tell how much I suffered, nor how much I am still pained by the retrospect," wrote ex-slave Harriet Jacobs of her experiences.

"If Cuffey won't work," went the slaveowners' motto, "you must make him work." While slaves on small farms or in plantation kitchens faced the spontaneous rage of masters and mistresses, field slaves were subject to the discipline of hired overseers. Whippings were frequent. "They'd never do any work at all if they were not afraid of being whipped," explained an overseer after thrashing a young woman with rawhide across her naked thighs. Even without violence, agricultural labor was harsh, from sun-up to sun-down, six days a week, a regimen that took women as well as men into the cotton fields. More arduous sugar production was largely male work.

Field workers wore slave-sewn clothing made from inferior "Negro" textiles or cheap ready-to-wear outfits and straw hats. Only in winter did slaves wear shoes, which were mass-produced and imported from the North. Slave cabins were drafty, windowless, crowded, and unsanitary. Slave diets, while usually sufficient in calories, lacked adequate protein and vitamins, causing chronic diseases that masters often attributed to laziness.

The desire for plantation self-sufficiency encouraged masters to allow some men to learn skilled trades (carpentry, masonry, blacksmithing), and their labor might be lent or leased to neighboring farmers. Women slaves sometimes acquired skill in spinning, weaving, and sewing. Artisans could occasionally negotiate to rent themselves out, earning money that they could use for self-purchase.

Slavery took a different form in towns and cities. One-fifth of southern slaveowners—artisans, merchants, lawyers, teachers, or doctors—lived in towns, but only 5 percent of the slave population were town dwellers. Urban slaves were usually domestic workers or tradesmen, sometimes factory workers. In the towns and cities, the proximity of slaveowners to each other served to reduce their brutality. "There is a vestige of decency, a sense of shame," explained the ex-slave Frederick Douglass, "that does much to curb and check those outbreaks of atrocious cruelty so commonly enacted on the plantation." Besides better food and clothing, urban slaves enjoyed the freedom to mingle with free blacks, attend churches, and experience public entertainment.

Defining African American Communities

In 1830, there were 2 million African American slaves in the United States. Although they traced their roots to diverse west African traditions, the conditions of servitude and work, for slaves and free blacks alike, had blurred their cultural differences. Just one generation after the legal closing of the African slave trade, African Americans had established a distinctive ethnic culture with unique patterns of language, religion, music, and family values.

Free Blacks in the South

Communities of free African Americans occupied most southern towns, even rural areas, and most lived in segregated sections that whites referred to by names like "Little Africa." In the Upper South, 20 percent of all blacks were free, but only 2 percent in the Lower South were free. The total number remained small—about 250,000 as late as 1860. Some free African Americans owned other blacks, though these were usually relatives or friends purchased from white owners. Half the free blacks in the southern states were mulattos, many of them liberated by their white fathers.

This free population encountered routine economic discrimination (they were the last hired and first fired) and constituted the poorest segment of southern society. Lighter-skinned women found work as domestics, darker-skinned as laundresses; free black men worked in fields or as casual laborers in town. Since more women than men were freed, most free black children inhabited female-headed households. During the 19th century, as slaveholders feared rebellions, the free population faced increasing restrictions on their movements. Free African Americans had to carry "freedom papers" to prove their status, and several states passed laws requiring emancipated slaves to migrate elsewhere. Free blacks had limited civil rights. They could not testify against whites in court, nor serve on juries.

Customary Rights and Slave Families

In most southern states, slaves could not legally marry, travel without permission, or learn to read and write, lest such activities disrupt the discipline of slave labor. Yet plantation slaves acquired many rights by custom. The selection of black slave drivers, respected leaders chosen informally by community approval, protected slaves from unusual burdens. Sunday work or nighttime work during the harvest time customarily brought extra rewards. Slaves also expected a traditional Christmas holiday, a labor-free week marked by gifts of food, clothing, and alcohol from their masters. Despite curfews and the vigilance of nightly patrols, slaves frequently traveled at night to neighboring plantations for social visits or religious meetings.

Viewing themselves as patriarchs, slaveowners routinely intervened in the private lives of their people. Most encouraged their slaves to form marriages, if only for convenience. On one plantation, a master arranged his newly acquired slaves in rows by sex, instructed each to find a mate, read aloud a marriage service, "and thus [saved] time by settling their matrimonial affairs." Such coercion was not typical. Plantation slaves usually chose their own partners, sometimes formally "jumping over a broom," a pagan European custom signifying that the relationship was more than casual. Nevertheless, plantation rules often undermined the creation of nuclear families.

Many slave families consisted of people owned by different masters. Such "abroad" marriages required permission from both partners' owners and often included strict rules preventing spontaneous meetings. Since children of slaves became the property of their mothers' owner, slave children usually lived with their mothers and their mothers' kin, and slave husbands traveled to visit their wives and children. To preserve a sense of family, many children were named after their fathers and grandfathers, and many slaves adopted surnames, often without their owners' approval, to signify family ties.

Long separations between husbands and wives encouraged serial relationships, which were sometimes monogamous, sometimes not. Since women slaves had work assignments, childcare passed to other female slaves, usually grandmothers or older children. When the young became old enough for field work, boys often moved into male dwelling units with or without their natural fathers, while girls undertook tasks that might separate them from

their mothers. To protect individuals from isolation, African Americans created elaborate networks of relationships with extended families or friends who served as kin and reinforced a sense of community.

African American Religion

Religion played an important part in African American culture. For most blacks, a belief in some aspects of African religion persisted, shaping a world-view that emphasized sacred elements of the natural world and the spiritual elements of human relations. Estimates suggest that between 10 and 20 percent of slaves brought from Africa were Muslims, some of whom surely continued to practice their religion in America. Masters sometimes assumed an obligation to instruct slaves in Christian doctrine, but so great was the fear that converted slaves might consider themselves spiritual equals and therefore deserving of freedom, slaveowners emphasized Christian virtues of humility, patience, and obedience. White missionaries occasionally visited slave plantations, preached a gospel of subjugation, and warned against stealing the masters' chickens. Slaves expressed little interest in such teachings and often preferred nonreligious owners who would be less scrupulous about punishing minor infractions. African Americans responded selectively to Christian teachings, embracing those principles that affirmed their humanity and offered the prospect not only of salvation but also of freedom. Within the slave communities, black preachers enjoyed both prestige and emotional power in interpreting religious subjects for fellow slaves.

Beyond formal church settings, slaves frequently held secret religious meetings in the woods at night, burying their dead with African customs that did not conflict with the daily work schedule of the plantations. In larger cities like New Orleans, free blacks and slaves continued the African tradition of elaborate funeral processions, marked by drumming, dancing, and singing through the streets. Other African religious practices, including call-and-response chants, ecstatic movement, and rhythmic cadence, clapping, and shouts, guided the slaves' religious experience. In addition, slaves chose aspects of Christianity that expressed the desire for freedom, preferring Old Testament stories about little David defeating Goliath, Moses leading the Hebrew slaves out of Egypt to the promised land, or Noah building an ark of deliverance from the sinful world. African American spiritual songs reiterated the chorus of freedom.

Slave Resistance

"Few people," wrote white South Carolina novelist William Gilmore Simms, were "so very well satisfied with their condition as the negroes,—so happy of mood, so jocund, and so generally healthy and cheerful." Singing, laughter, and storytelling among blacks might ease some owners' guilty consciences, but the content of African American culture reflected dual intentions, first, to assert the dissatisfaction with life under slavery and a hope for its abatement, and second, to distract the owners' attention from slave anger and resentment. The Br'er Rabbit stories, for example, which circulated during slavery days, typically described the success of weaker creatures outwitting stronger animals.

By pretending to be childlike, ignorant, or incompetent, slaves could thwart the masters' wishes without directly challenging their authority. Subtle forms of subversion abounded: damage to crops, broken tools, injury to farm animals, fires, pretended illness, self-inflicted injuries, and calculated laziness. "Negroes cannot, or will not—they do not—eat in as short a time as whites," complained a time-conscious planter, noting that what took him 10 or 15 minutes to eat required 30 to 45 minutes for his slaves to digest.

Slaves considered theft from their masters acceptable, even if they were punished when caught. The ultimate theft was to liberate one's labor, and oneself, by running away. Because they were more likely to have responsibility for their children, female slaves were less likely to run away than men. Hiding in nearby woods or swamps enabled runaways to avoid an impending punishment or burden, though masters responded severely to such infractions. Other runaways had specific destinations: to reach recently separated relatives, or the free states of the North. With the help of free blacks and southern Quakers, an "underground railroad" carried fugitive slaves into northern states or to Canada, where many became active in antislavery protests. Advertisements for runaway slaves also showed the brutality of slavery. In seeking their missing property, slaveowners identified personal characteristics—injuries, brands, or scars from whippings, as well as signs of intangible wounds such as stuttering or twitching.

Most runaways proved to be temporary fugitives, truants who returned after a few days of freedom or who were caught by slave trackers. Yet, despite the great difficulty of escaping through hostile territory, probably as many as 1,000 reached freedom each year. Other forms of resistance involved forceful confrontation with owners or overseers who, in the slaves' estimation, exceeded customary demands or punishments. Such spontaneous clashes were rare and could lead to severe punishment, even death. Sometimes the slaves prevailed, achieving an uneasy truce with their tormentors.

Nat Turner's Rebellion

"He who knoweth his master's will and doeth it not," slaveowners liked to quote from the scriptures, "shall be beaten with many stripes." One Bible-reading Virginia slave named Nat Turner put a different gloss on those words by taking God as his master. For years, the spiritual Turner had seen visions of retribution against slaveowners. In 1831, an eclipse of the sun, followed by atmospheric conditions that discolored the sky, came to Turner as an omen: "As the black spot passed over the sun, so shall the blacks pass over the earth." Turner struck in the late summer, leading fellow slaves in killing their masters and other whites, claiming sixty victims. Turner's ultimate goals remain unclear, but within two days slaveowners retaliated, capturing and executing about 120 rebels and selling others out of state. Turner hid in the woods for two months before he was caught. After a three-day interrogation, he was hanged for murder.

The Turner insurrection sent a chill through the South, alarming the nonslaveholding farmers, who questioned the wisdom of sustaining a hostile slave population. In 1832, anxious Virginia legislators debated a plan of gradual emancipation, much as northern states had once picked a future July 4 to liberate children of slaves. For a brief moment, the nonslaveholders challenged the value of slavery in southern society. But the slaveholders closed ranks and defeated the measure. Instead, Virginians encouraged free African Americans to depart for Liberia (see Chapter 10), though few accepted the offer of free transportation.

Meanwhile, in the wake of Turner's revolt, stricter enforcement of the slave codes limited slaves' travel, curtailed access to education, restricted church attendance, and made emancipation more difficult. "We must allay the fears of our own people," announced a southern newspaper. "We must satisfy them that slavery is of itself right—that it is not a sin against God—that it is not an evil, moral or political." Now slaveholders began to describe slavery not merely as a necessary evil but as a positive good. This change in attitudes about slavery foreshadowed a deepening conflict between southern and northern whites about the property rights of citizens.

The Antislavery Argument and National Politics

As the Turner rebellion undermined the confidence of slaveowners and showed that African Americans were not naturally content as slaves, antislavery reformers in the North expressed more militant criticism of southern society. Earlier critics of slavery, like Thomas Jefferson, had forecast the gradual eradication of slavery as African Americans acquired white civilization. But the spread of evangelical religion changed northern attitudes toward slavery. Sharing the slaveholders' belief that African Americans were inferior creatures and often incapable of moral choice, northern evangelicals nonetheless saw slavery as a sinful institution that corrupted the childlike slave. To be sure, many antislavery reformers had little experience with slaves or white southerners, and many northerners did not believe that slavery was unjust or morally wrong. In fact, northern businessmen made substantial profits selling cheap manufactured goods for slave apparel and shipped slave-grown cotton overseas without qualms. But for a small and passionate group of evangelical reformers, the commitment to creating a moral society demanded the *immediate* termination of the South's peculiar institution.

Free African Americans in the North moved to the forefront of protest. None was more bold than David Walker, a free black who had migrated from North Carolina to Boston and joined the antislavery Colored Association. His 1829 pamphlet, *Appeal . . . to the Colored Citizens of the World . . . and Very Expressly to Those of the United States of America,* minced no words. "The whites have always been an unjust, jealous, unmerciful, avaricious, and blood-thirsty set of beings," he wrote. Walker's solution was clear and simple. He advised American slaves to begin a rebellion: "Make sure work—do not trifle, for they will not trifle with you," he said. "Kill or be killed." Walker's *Appeal,* though reprinted three times, probably never reached Nat

TABLE 11.1

The Rise of Antislavery Societies, 1832–1838

	1832	1834	1835	1836	1837	1838
Maine	0	6	22	34	33	48
New Hampshire	0	9	12	42	62	79
Vermont	0	12	39	44	89	104
Massachusetts	2	23	48	87	145	246
Rhode Island	0	2	9	20	25	26
Connecticut	0	2	10	15	39	46
New York	0	7	42	103	274	369
New Jersey	0	2	3	6	10	14
Pennsylvania	1	2	6	32	93	126
Ohio	1	10	34	133	213	251
Michigan Terr.	0	0	2	4	17	19
Total	4	75	227	520	1000	1329

Source: Paul Goodman, *Of One Blood: Abolitionism and the Origins of Racial Equality,* University of California Press, 1998.

Turner. But his demand for immediate emancipation appealed to militant evangelicals, who believed that society was perfectible if only individuals would shun sin.

Evangelical Abolitionism

"I will be as harsh as truth, and as uncompromising as justice," declared the white abolitionist William Lloyd Garrison in launching his antislavery magazine, *The Liberator,* in 1831. "*I will be heard.*" Garrison had initially supported both colonization of free blacks and gradual emancipation, but the election of the slaveholding Andrew Jackson in 1828 showed the strength of proslavery interests. "I am ashamed of my country," Garrison said. "I am sick of our unmeaning . . . praise of liberty and equality." Converted to evangelical Christianity, he saw slavery as a sin, which made any compromise morally unacceptable. Indeed, because the Constitution permitted slavery, Garrison considered it sinful and burned the document in public on July 4, 1834.

Such religious views informed the many antislavery societies that sprang up in the 1830s (Table 11.1), including the new American Antislavery Society founded in 1833. That year, the country's most popular woman author, Lydia Maria Child, shocked her readers by publishing *An Appeal in Favor of That Class of Americans Called Africans.* The first book to advocate immediate emancipation, Child's work underscored the plight of women slaves and their sexual exploitation. "The negro woman is unprotected either by law or public

Lydia Maria Child (1802–1880) was at the height of her literary success when she published her attack on slavery and racial discrimination, prompting a reader boycott that undermined her earnings.

opinion," wrote Child. "She is the property of her master, and her daughters are his property. They are allowed to have no conscientious scruples, no sense of shame." The book also demanded the repeal of laws prohibiting interracial marriages. Such abolitionists appealed primarily to the consciences of other whites, the reformers in the North and slaveowners in the South. Their objective was to end slavery by moral persuasion.

Antiabolitionism

Northern whites did not usually welcome the antislavery movement. Conservatives—indeed, even some abolitionists—viewed blacks as "docile" and "childlike," considered interracial social activities "unwise," and questioned whether ex-slaves could handle the responsibilities of freedom. During the 1830s, violent mobs attacked antislavery leaders in northern cities. In Boston, a crowd dragged Garrison through the streets with a rope around his neck, while in 1837 a mob in Alton, Illinois, murdered Elijah Lovejoy, an abolitionist newspaper editor. Most anti-abolition mobs included respectable citizens, many of whom believed that emancipation would encourage racial mingling and thus supported African colonization. Northern cities established segregated schools, churches, even cemeteries. What northerners opposed was not so much the abolition of southern slavery as the equality of African Americans in northern society. Complained one white father, "If you educate these young blacks, they will soon know as much as our children!"

Violence against northern abolitionists mirrored the treatment of southern whites who dared to criticize slavery and faced beatings, tarring and feathering, even murder (averaging thirty cases of homicide a year in the three decades after 1830). Such intimidation demonstrated the commitment of most southern whites, slaveowners and nonslaveowners alike, to the slave system. Although a numerical minority, slaveowners dominated southern politics at all levels. The slaveowners' power partly reflected their wealth; smaller farmers had both economic and ideological ties to their richer neighbors.

The Tariff and the Nullification Crisis

The prominence of slaveowners among southern politicians accentuated regional conflicts about economic development, political power, and the national identity. The 1828 "tariff of abominations," which raised duties on imported manufactured goods and so raised prices for southern consumers, remained a serious grievance. Although southern

Democrats voted for Jackson in hopes of lowering the tariff, the economy-minded president preferred to eliminate the public debt before reducing customs taxes. Meanwhile, Vice President John Calhoun, who privately had asserted the rights of states to nullify obnoxious federal laws (see Chapter 10), muted his criticism of the tariff, in hopes of succeeding Jackson to the White House. With cotton prices lower than average for two years, however, southern leaders protested the hardships of a high tariff. Jackson sympathized with their complaints. "Those who have vested their capital in manufacturing establishments," he told Congress in 1831, "can not expect that the people will continue permanently to pay high taxes for their benefit." With such presidential support, Congress passed a tariff measure in 1832 that lowered the rates by half, to the levels of 1816.

For some southern leaders, even that reduction was not enough. The conflict had moved beyond tariff reform to states' rights. As Calhoun put it, "the issue is no longer one of free trade, but liberty and despotism." With northern free states controlling a majority of the House of Representatives and abolitionists attacking slavery, southern spokesmen worried about other unwanted national policies involving banks, internal improvements, and interference with slavery. Seeking to forestall the expansion of federal power, South Carolinians defended the right of a state to nullify a national law. In 1832, during the same month that Jackson won reelection with a new vice president, Martin Van Buren, South Carolina summoned an elected state convention to consider the national tariff. Challenging the legality of congressional policy, the convention voted to declare the nation's tariff laws null and void and forbade the collection of federal customs duties in the state. Jackson responded with cries of treason, threatening to hang the nullifiers for turning the "perpetual union" into "a rope of sand."

As South Carolina radicals threatened to follow nullification with secession, Jackson tried to defuse the crisis by focusing on tariff policy rather than abstract principles of states' rights. In a proclamation to the citizens of South Carolina, Jackson denounced nullification and appealed for demonstrations of loyalty to the union, but he also asked Congress to lower the tariff. The resulting compromise tariff of 1833 did not result in a clear victory for the nullifiers. Customs duties would decline gradually over the next ten years. Congress also passed the Force Act, authorizing the president to use military force to collect customs revenues in South Carolina. However, the provisions of the new tariff effectively undermined the economic complaint, and anti-nullifiers within the state, mostly from nonslaveholding farm areas, quieted the protest. Outside South Carolina, every southern legislature repudiated nullification, leaving the movement without support. Facing Jackson's wrath, South Carolina repealed the nullification of the tariff; as an act of defiance, however, the state legislature proceeded to nullify the Force Act, a gesture that Jackson chose to ignore.

Congress and the Gag Rule

The frustration of powerlessness that had provoked the nullification crisis followed southern politicians into the halls of Congress, where they confronted a mounting campaign against slavery. While Jackson's Democratic party involved a political alliance between southern planters and northern merchants, northern evangelicals who were opposed to slavery tended to be Whigs. Believing that southern Christians could be made to see the evils of slavery, the American Antislavery Society commenced a new crusade in 1835 by publishing thousands of abolitionist tracts and mailing them to citizens of the South. Outraged by such uninvited communications, mobs that included respectable citizens stormed southern post offices, seized the offensive publications, and lit public bonfires to destroy the inflammatory documents.

Such protests did not disturb the Democratic administration. Jackson's postmaster general instructed local post offices to detain abolitionist mail, and the president subsequently told Congress that antislavery activity was "unconstitutional and wicked." Northerners did not necessarily sympathize with abolitionism, but they did worry about government censorship; limits on mail delivery impinged on the rights of free northerners. In 1836, Congress forbade postal workers from deliberately detaining the mails. But when southern state laws prohibited such deliveries, federal officials permitted local postmasters to obey local law.

The question of censoring antislavery statements erupted again in Congress in 1835, when abolitionists presented citizens' petitions demanding legislation to end slavery in the nation's capital. Women played a key role in these protests, because petitioning was one of the few political rights that they possessed. Although Congress did not have the power to legislate against slavery in the states, it did have the right to make laws for the District of Columbia. But southern representatives insisted that such petitions be rejected without any consideration or debate. "A war of religious and political fanaticism," said Calhoun, was being "waged not against our lives, but our character. The object is to humble and debase us in our own estimation." Such defensiveness revealed the moral power of antislavery. But in 1836 an alliance between southern politicians, both Whigs and Democrats, and northern Democrats managed to pass the so-called gag rule, which automatically used parliamentary procedures to ignore, or table, public petitions about the status of slavery. Many northern Whigs perceived the rule

Former president John Quincy Adams (1767–1848) was an outspoken abolitionist in the House of Representatives when he posed for this daguerreotype in 1845.

as an attack on the right of free debate, and former president John Quincy Adams, now a Whig representative from Massachusetts, agitated against the measure until gaining its repeal in 1844.

The Presidency of "Van Ruin"

The struggle over slavery in Congress, by linking the South with northern Democrats, fortified that party for the election of 1836. Martin Van Buren, Jackson's hand-picked successor, avoided the specific issues of tariffs, national banks, and antislavery. But the Whigs failed to agree on a candidate, and three nominees, each strong in a separate region, divided the opposition vote. Although Van Buren's anti-abolitionism remained popular in the North, southern Democrats distrusted his support of slavery, and Democratic votes declined drastically in the South. In the end, Van Buren captured just 50.9 percent of the popular vote.

Economic Crisis and the Panic of 1837

The new administration proved incapable of coping with the Panic of 1837 and the ensuing economic depression that struck just as Van Buren was entering office. By the summer of 1837, a wave of business failures brought rising bankruptcies and unprecedented unemployment in the cities. In New York City, thousands of idle workers protested in the streets and broke into warehouses to steal food. "Loud cracks in the social edifice," sighed the philosopher Ralph Waldo Emerson. The economy recovered briefly in 1838, then collapsed the next year when cotton prices plummeted, causing a wider depression that lasted into the 1840s. Both southern planters and northern merchants suffered from the downturn, as unsold cotton accumulated at wharves and warehouses and the value of slaves declined. In the crisis, Whigs blamed the Jacksonians for dismantling the Bank of the United States and undermining the nation's credit with hard money policies (see Chapter 10).

Believing, like Jackson, that private interests had corrupted the banking system, Van Buren proposed an "independent treasury" plan in which public funds would be separated from private banks by depositing government revenue in vaults or sub-treasuries around the country. The proposal also required that all payments to the government be made in hard money. But that provision would reduce the circulation of bank notes, contract the national currency, and retard economic growth. Whig politicians, more attuned than the Democrats to the market economy and scornful

In New York City, thousands of idle workers protested in the streets and broke into warehouses to steal food.

of President "Van Ruin," thwarted the program until 1840. The long struggle showed the president's political weakness and his inability to meet the economic crisis.

Regional Discord: Texas, Slavery, and Race

Other aspects of Van Buren's policies revealed the difficulty of resolving fundamental regional differences. During the 1820s and 1830s, the expanding cotton economy had encouraged U.S. citizens to settle in the Mexican province of Texas. Many had joined the Missouri colonizer Stephen Austin, who obtained land grants from the Mexican government; others came as squatters. Both groups wanted slave-based agriculture, but Mexico outlawed slavery. Texans hoped that annexation to the United States would settle the dispute. Jackson shared that view. "The god of the universe," he had assured Van Buren in 1829, "intended this great valley to belong to one nation." Mexico, however, rejected Jackson's offer to purchase the territory. Frustrated by Mexican policy, Anglo Texans under the leadership of Sam Houston, declared independence from Mexico in 1836 and appealed to the United States for annexation as a state in the union.

As Mexico attempted to reconquer the newly proclaimed Republic of Texas, the Texas rebels, including Tennessee's Davy Crockett, took refuge in the Alamo, a mission in San Antonio. Mexico's General Antonio Santa Anna proceeded to attack the Alamo in 1836, killing all the rebels. Houston kept the insurrection alive by defeating other Mexican armies. In 1837, on his last day in office, Jackson recognized the independent Republic of Texas, but, fearing a war with Mexico, he rejected annexation. He left the Texas problem to his successor.

Under Van Buren, the Texas situation aggravated other regional disputes. Although southern expansionists supported the annexation of Texas to enlarge the domain of cotton and slavery, many northerners criticized an increase of slave territory. Caught in a crossfire, Van Buren opted to reject annexation, hoping to preserve his Democratic support in both regions. The result satisfied neither side. Van Buren's inability to bridge these regional differences did not indicate a lack of political skill, but rather the difficulty of achieving compromise on the issue of slavery in the territories.

Hesitancy to offend the South also shaped Van Buren's response to other controversial issues involving slavery and racial justice. When, for example, slaves aboard the Spanish ship, *Amistad,* rebelled in 1839 and brought the vessel ashore on New York's Long Island, Van Buren and proslavery members of his cabinet agreed to return the slaves to their owners in Cuba. Abolitionists challenged the decision, summoning John Quincy Adams to argue the case before the Supreme Court. Although the Court eventually ruled to release the slaves, Van Buren won applause in the South but earned the hatred of abolitionists.

Van Buren also continued Jackson's policy of removing the Creeks and Cherokees from their ancestral lands, overlooking the brutal Trail of Tears to tell Congress that the program had been "directed by the best feelings of humanity." Efforts to remove the Seminole people from Florida proved more difficult. Resistance by Seminole leader Osceola provoked open war in 1835. Although Osceola was captured and died in a federal prison, the Seminoles continued to fight under other leaders. The failure to achieve a military victory embarrassed the administration, and the use of bloodhounds against the Seminoles

aroused protests in the North. The war would continue into the next decade before the government could remove the Seminoles to Oklahoma.

Tippecanoe and Tyler, Too!

All Van Buren's problems—economic crisis, regional conflict, racial discord—crystallized in the election of 1840. When the Whig party passed over Henry Clay to nominate William Henry Harrison, victor in the battle of Tippecanoe against the Shawnees in 1811 (see Chapter 8), one disgruntled politician summed up the candidate: "Give him a barrel of hard cider and a pension . . . , [and] he will sit the remainder of his days in a log cabin." Intended as an insult, the image became a campaign theme, emphasizing Harrison's unpretentious democratic spirit. Whig enthusiasm exploded around the country with rallies and parades as well as slogans, cartoons, catchwords, and songs. "Farewell, dear Van / You're not our man: / To guide the ship, / We'll try old Tip." Women paraded, too, for the first time in a presidential campaign, carrying brooms to "sweep" the Democrats from office, baking cakes in the shape of log cabins, and vowing to marry "Whig husbands or none."

Issues were few, except for hard times and Van Buren's supposed aristocratic sensibilities. To attract southern votes, the Whigs chose Virginia's John Tyler, previously an avowed Democrat, as their vice-presidential candidate. About the campaign slogan "Tippecanoe and Tyler, Too!" admitted one Whig, "There was rhyme, but no reason." The election spirit was sensational. With a popular majority of only 145,000 votes, Harrison polled an electoral landslide, carrying Whig victories in both houses of Congress for the first and only time. A third presidential candidate, abolitionist James Birney, drew only 7,000 votes to the Liberty party in New York and Massachusetts, but even the existence of such a campaign indicated the growing sentiment against slavery in the North. Most significant, however, was the surge in public turnout. Up nearly 1 million voters from the last election, 2.4 million cast ballots in 1840, 80 percent of the eligible electorate.

The Politics of Stalemate

If the Whig Harrison carried a new agenda, it expired after he caught pneumonia during his inauguration and died just one month later. His successor, Tyler, still holding Democratic views against government support of economic development, had no interest in the Whig program of banks, tariffs, and internal improvements. Twice Henry Clay pushed legislation through Congress to establish a third Bank of the United States; twice Tyler vetoed the measure on constitutional grounds. The entire cabinet, except for Secretary of State Daniel Webster, denounced the new president and resigned from office. Webster stayed just long enough to complete negotiations with Great Britain about Canadian boundary disputes, extradition arrangements, and enforcement of laws against the slave trade. Then he, too, resigned. Thereafter, presidential vetoes and congressional deadlocks stalled most legislation. Indeed, the complicated political maneuvering in Congress testified to the strength of party discipline, as 90 percent of Democrats and Whigs voted as blocs on two-thirds of the votes.

The subjects of these legislative quarrels— banks, tariffs, and internal improvements—reflected fundamental disagreements between Whigs and Democrats about the nation's economic development and what each envisioned as the best type of society. Thus Whigs in all regions endorsed tariffs, banks, and internal improvements, praised economic nationalism, and promised that poor as well as rich would benefit by economic expansion.

Harrison caught pneumonia during his inauguration and died just one month later.

Democrats, in contrast, opposed government assistance to so-called privileged groups—bankers, manufacturers, and developers—who threatened independent farmers and merchants. Such disagreements partly reflected the regional differences between southern commercial agriculture and Northeast manufacturing. But southern Whigs and northern Whigs shared prodevelopment positions, just as southern Democrats and northern Democrats advocated low tariffs and free trade. Congress thus served as a battleground for competing interests. The stalemate under Tyler merely demonstrated the nearly equal strength of the rival positions.

Under Presidents Jackson, Van Buren, and Tyler, the art of politics hinged on compromise. Unlike their predecessors in the early years of the republic, politicians no longer expected to establish a broad consensus; mere majorities sufficed. Patronage, party loyalty, voter discipline—these threads enabled politicians to weave together national alliances that overcame regional differences. Political opponents no longer appeared as potential subversives but only as rivals for power; Whigs and Democrats could agree to disagree. Congressional politics could therefore reconcile disputes about banks, tariffs, and internal improvements.

The issues of tariffs, banks, and internal improvements drew the political lines between commercial opportunists and cautious farmers, between Henry Clay's Whigs and Andrew Jackson's Democrats. Yet both political parties claimed to speak for the nation, and both won support in all regions, despite obvious differences between the southern and northern economies. But, during the 1840s, as economic depression gave way to prosperity, investments in new technology (railroads, steamships, agricultural implements, telegraph lines) stimulated a surge of westward expansion. Geographic expansion, in turn, would imperil the two-party system.

Moral issues like slavery and abolition did not lend themselves to easy political compromises. Northern abolitionists condemned slavery as a sinful institution, and southern slaveholders defended their labor system as a positive good. These moral positions undercut the ground for political maneuvering. Van Buren's efforts to skirt the slavery issue weakened his strength in the North; his hesitation to defend slavery softened his standing in the South. Moreover, while party politicians tried to sidestep the slavery debate in the 1830s, the moral issues continually intruded into the political arena. Antislavery petitions aroused alarm in the South, just as the gag rule in Congress disturbed many in the North. Such tensions would not disappear. In the next decade, territorial expansion introduced new questions about the status of slavery and challenged Whigs and Democrats to reconsider their party loyalties. No longer a matter of political compromise, slavery emerged as a moral issue. The stalemate about how government could best promote economic development did not disappear, but the clash of regional interests increasingly focused not on wealth or poverty, boom or bust, but on slavery and abolition, matters of principle that could be neither ignored nor resolved.

INFOTRAC® COLLEGE EDITION EXERCISES

 For additional reading go to InfoTrac College Edition, your online research library at *http://web1.infotrac-college.com.*

Subject search: Native Americans, periodicals
Subject search: plantation
Keyword search: plantation women
Keyword search: slave culture
Keyword search: slave life
Keyword search: slave religion
Keyword search: abolitionist
Keyword search: William Lloyd Garrison
Keyword search: gag rule slavery

ADDITIONAL READING

Expanding Cotton Society

Mark M. Smith, *Mastered by the Clock: Time, Slavery, and Freedom in the American South* (1997). An imaginative study of timekeeping in southern life, the book shows the importance of clock-time in regulating economic activities.

The Domestic Lives of Southern White Women

Elizabeth Fox-Genovese, *Within the Plantation Household: Black and White Women of the Old South* (1988). Based on diaries and letters, this book is a superb study of slaveholding women and their interaction with their slaves.

Suzanne Lebsock, *The Free Women of Petersburg: Status and Culture in a Southern Town, 1784–1860* (1984). Another study of a single community, this book describes the differing experiences of white and black women.

The Business of Slavery

William W. Freehling, *The Road to Disunion: Secessionists at Bay, 1776–1854* (1990). A thorough examination of southern attitudes and values about slavery, society, and the political controversies of the period.

Kenneth S. Greenberg, *Masters and Statesmen: The Political Culture of American Slavery* (1985). This essay about southern political values links social behavior, such as dueling, with demands for political equality.

Peter Kolchin, *American Slavery: 1619–1877* (1993). A lucid survey of slavery stressing the differing perspectives of masters and slaves.

Michael Tadman, *Speculators and Slaves: Masters, Traders, and Slaves in the Old South* (1989). A careful analysis of the interregional slave trade, describing the disruptive effects of this profitable business.

The Conditions of Slavery

Eugene D. Genovese, *Roll, Jordan, Roll: The World the Slaves Made* (1974). This ground-breaking study stresses the creative interaction between slaves and masters.

Customary Rights and Slave Families

Wilma King, *Stolen Childhood: Slave Youth in Nineteenth-Century America* (1995). Focusing on the experiences of children, the author examines the social and psychological effects of slavery.

Brenda E. Stevenson, *Life in Black and White: Family and Community in the Slave South* (1996). This study of a single Virginia county describes the variety of family relationships among slaves and masters.

Slave Resistance

Lawrence W. Levine, *Black Culture and Black Consciousness: Afro-American Folk Thought from Slavery to Freedom* (1977). This brilliant interpretation of African American music, stories, and folk culture depicts the creative opposition to slavery and racial injustice.

Evangelical Abolitionism

Paul Goodman, *Of One Blood: Abolitionism and the Origins of Racial Equality* (1998). This analysis of the northern antislavery community links the movement to evangelical reformism. See also Henry Mayer, *All on Fire: William Lloyd Garrison and the Abolition of Slavery* (1998).

Congress and the Gag Rule

William Lee Miller, *Arguing about Slavery: The Great Battle in the United States Congress* (1996). This book describes the congressional debates about antislavery and the gag rule.

Manifest Destiny and the National Identity, 1844–1850

CHRONOLOGY

1844	Samuel Morse introduces telegraph
	James K. Polk elected president
	Treaty of Wangshia increases China trade
1845	Nativists gain political office in eastern cities
	Congress annexes Texas by joint resolution
1846	War begins between United States and Mexico
	U.S. settlers found Bear Flag Republic in California
	Congress ratifies Oregon treaty
	Wilmot Proviso seeks to prohibit slavery in new territories
1848	Treaty of Guadalupe Hidalgo ends Mexican war
	Californians discover gold at Sutter's Mill
	Women's rights convention held at Seneca Falls
1849	General Zachary Taylor inaugurated president
1850	Millard Fillmore succeeds Taylor
	Compromise of 1850 postpones crisis over slavery

Looking out over the green expanse of her Iowa home, now dotted with the blossoms of spring-flowering trees, the farm woman bewailed her husband's succumbing to an outbreak of "Oregon fever" in 1847.

"It seems to be contagious and it is raging terribly," she wrote. "Nothing seems to stop it but to tear up and take a six-month trip across the plains with ox teams to the Pacific Ocean."

"I said *O let us not go,*" wrote another farmer's wife, "but it made no difference."

"I am going with him," yet another woman told her mother, "as there is no other alternative."

The successive waves of "Texas fever," "Oregon fever," and "California fever" that comprised westward migration brought a new perspective to the nation's identity during the 1840s. While surveying the western lands sixty years earlier, George Washington had put Canada on his left hand and Florida on his right as he looked across the Atlantic toward Europe (see Chapter 7). By the 1840s, the country had reversed direction. "Behold," exclaimed a public orator about the new citizen. "He plants his right foot at the source of the Missouri—his left on the shores of the Gulf of Mexico; and gathers into his bosom the ever-flowing abundance of the fairest and richest valley on which the circling sun looks down." From that position, easterners' eyes now looked west.

Optimism about westward migration translated into a belief that expansion was inevitable. As the Democratic newspaper editor John L. O'Sullivan stated in 1845, the United States had a "Manifest Destiny"—a self-evident fate—"to overspread and to possess the whole of the continent which Providence has given to us for the development of the great experiment of liberty." Believing that the country had received a divine mission to expand across the continent, politicians, preachers, and promoters stressed three unique national blessings that would accompany the migration, words that would become a virtual cliché, "civilization, religion, and liberty."

Each of these advantages was loaded with nationalist values. *Civilization* meant the imposition of rational order on the natural landscape: schools and churches would edify future generations, and the surveyor's grid would produce rectangular farms that facilitated real estate transactions. *Religion* signified the Protestant gospel which, as one minister stated, guaranteed "the moral destiny of our nation" in the struggle against Native American devils, the "childish mummery" of Mexico's Catholics, and the spiritual views of California's Chinese immigrants, who were disparagingly called

"celestials." *Liberty,* to the expansionist mind, would bring republican institutions that assured equality—to white men. Such values justified settlement of the territories west of the Mississippi.

Having tied the national identity to the development of western lands, citizens discovered that geographic expansion aggravated tensions, not only with cultural outsiders but also among the most patriotic expansionists. To be sure, few complained that the annexation of Texas brought a war with Mexico and that the search for California gold created conflicts with the indigenous peoples of the Pacific coast (both Native and Mexican Americans) as well as with Chinese and South American immigrants. But political leaders were more disturbed by the growing conflict between northern and southern citizens over the status of slavery in newly acquired territories. Citizens of both regions believed in Manifest Destiny. But northern expansionists, dedicated to free labor and economic opportunity, saw the extension of slavery as a threat to their liberty, and southern expansionists, equally concerned about their rights, demanded constitutional protection of private property, including slaves. Such arguments had been submerged by the Missouri Compromise of 1820. By the end of the 1840s, the quarrel had resurfaced and threatened the survival of the union. The old party lines between Whigs and Democrats strained to contain this political conflict. Regional passions were finally cooled in 1850 by a political compromise, but only for a while.

Nature, Technology, and Expansion

Dozens of Native American nations inhabited the western territories in the 1840s, and Britain and Mexico challenged U.S. claims in the Pacific and Southwest. Still, the millions of undeveloped acres west of the Mississippi River appeared as a great temptation to eastern residents. "Everything . . . in

During the first half of the 19th century, the nation's population more than quadrupled, from 5 million to over 23 million.

the natural scenery is on a scale so vast and grand," remarked an Ohio minister in 1846, "the majestic rivers, the boundless prairies, the deep forest . . . as to make man vast in his schemes, gigantic in his purposes, larger in his aspirations, boundless in his ambitions." To Whigs and Democrats alike, the West beckoned as a region for human improvement, a land to sustain both population growth and economic opportunity. During the first half of the 19th century, the nation's population had more than quadrupled, from 5 million to over 23 million. Politicians now promised to lead the country to the Pacific coast.

The Paradox of Progress

"Nature," remarked the New England philosopher Ralph Waldo Emerson in 1836, "is to stand as the apparition of God." Emerson's ideas, which belonged to a school of thought known as *transcendentalism,* emphasized the spirituality of the natural world and viewed social institutions as stifling of the human spirit. During the 19th century, the exploration of untouched natural formations west of the Mississippi—vast mountains, cascading waterfalls, untracked prairies and deserts—dazzled the imagination of explorers, travelers, and artists. These natural wonders, said the painter Thomas Cole, "are of God the creator—they are his undefiled works, and the mind is cast into the contemplation of eternal things."

Visions of natural glories awakened a sad foreboding, for it was obvious that "the axe of civilization" was destroying old forests and landscapes. The

Asher Durand's Kindred Spirits (1849) places his friends, painter Thomas Cole and author William Cullen Bryant, amidst the natural grandeur of New York's landscape.

transformation of the wilderness into what one contemporary called "abodes of commerce and seats of manufactures" testified to the famous Yankee ingenuity. One Californian joked that "the Yankees will metamorphize the country over so that it will be showery the year round instead of [having a] rainy and dry season." The Hudson River painters, such as Cole and Asher Durand, saw no humor in the metamorphosis and resolved "to rescue" on canvas "the little that is left, before it is too late." Their paintings documented the price of technology.

The Wonders of Technology

Most citizens welcomed technology and its palpable improvements. "I hear the whistle of the locomotive in the woods," remarked Emerson. "Wherever the music comes it has a sequel. It is the voice of the Nineteenth Century saying 'Here I am.'" But to Emerson's literary friends Henry David Thoreau and Nathaniel Hawthorne, the whistle carried "the noisy world into the midst of our slumbrous peace." Women writers like Lydia Sigourney contrasted the subdued pleasures of domestic horticulture, "the sweet friendships of the quiet plants," with the "restlessness and din of the rail-road principle," which symbolized the pursuit of materialism. But most people simply expressed their wonder about technology, as did one little boy who was asleep when taken aboard for his first railroad trip in 1847, "and when he awoke," his mother wrote, "he looked around all surprised and said, 'Where is the horses?'"

Technology brought undeniable signs of progress. On the southern shores of Lake Michigan, the village of Chicago (named for the wild garlic used by the indigenous people) surged into a major metropolis, growing from 4,500 inhabitants to 30,000 during the 1840s. In the previous decade, a real estate boom encouraged Chicago builders to introduce a novel architectural design, known as the "balloon-frame" house. Built with pre-cut boards and nails, such structures could be made quickly and cheaply with a minimum of skilled labor. "We are proud of the flimsy, unsubstantial structures," boasted one local architect. "They are the homes of the people who will by-and-by build and own better ones." Chicago emerged as a major lumber center, where wood from midwestern forests provided not only homes and workshops but also the cross-ties for an expanding system of railroads.

The opening of the Galena and Chicago railroad in 1848, which was linked by canals to the Illinois river and to the steamships that sailed the great lakes, created a transportation network that turned the windy city into a year-round hub of economic enterprise. Financed by small farmers, who wanted to get their crops to market, the iron horse cut the

---

One little boy on his first railroad trip "looked around all surprised and said, 'Where is the horses?'"

---

journey to New York from two weeks to two days and eliminated seasonal slumps associated with bad weather. ("It's against the policy of Americans to remain locked up by ice over half of the year," quipped a railroad promoter.) Steam-powered grain elevators revolutionized the shipment of wheat, enabling Chicago to store and distribute 3 million bushels of grain annually by 1854.

Equally powerful was the telegraph introduced by Samuel F. B. Morse in 1844 with the haunting question "What hath God wrought?" Crowds flocked to telegraph offices to hear news of the 1844 presidential nomination, and newspapers predicted the "annihilation of time." For Chicago grain dealers, the telegraph initially enabled them to get price quotes from New York in 18 hours, but as wires followed the railroad tracks and became continuous, the interval was reduced to mere seconds. By 1860, the nation's 56,000 miles of wire were carrying 5 million messages a year. Few shared the pessimism expressed by the individualistic Thoreau: "We are in great haste to construct a magnetic telegraph from Maine to Texas," he observed; "but Maine and Texas, it may be, have nothing important to communicate."

Westward Migation and the Uprooted

Philosophical doubts about westward expansion could not compete with a popular desire to acquire land across the Mississippi. With federal land selling at $1.25 (about $19 in today's money) per acre for a minimum of forty acres, Congress passed the Preemption Act in 1841, which protected the

Deaths on the Oregon Trail averaged one every eighty yards.

claims of squatters, who could not afford to purchase their land but who "improved" its value by their settlement. "Come along, come along—don't be alarmed," said a popular song, "Uncle Sam is rich enough to give us all a farm." Westward migration nonetheless involved the pain of uprooting, as emigrants took their departures from family and neighbors, usually forever. More traumatic was the displacement of the Native Americans, whose lands were invaded, seized, and stolen. Although the federal government acknowledged the validity of some Native American claims in formal treaties, Manifest Destiny—the notion that expansion was ordained by God—permitted little respect for native cultures and jurisdiction.

Heading West

Heading west was usually a man's decision. Since most state laws considered the husband sole owner of family property, the sale of a farm and furnishings did not require the wife's agreement; some women learned of their imminent uprooting *after* their spouse had sold their home. Of course, many wives and daughters shared the men's enthusiasm, and many proved more than competent in assuming leadership when men died on the overland trails. All the same, women constituted only about 20 percent of those who moved west.

Migrants struggled to overcome their feelings of loss. Some admitted that their minds frequently wandered, "living once again the scenes of other days." Letters between emigrants and stay-at-homes included hair clippings, swatches of clothing, or photographs to preserve their connections. "Time, space, both are annihilated," wrote the young poet Walt Whitman about the craze for photography in 1846. "We identify the semblances with reality." Within a decade, photographers were developing 3 million daguerreotypes annually, almost all of them portraits rather than interiors or landscapes, to satisfy a yearning for family memory.

Besides their recollections, travelers who crossed the mountains and desert areas that formed the Great Plains carried heavy provisions, tools, clothing, and utensils, as much as a ton per wagon, to sustain them during a 2,000-mile journey that could last from six to eight months. No preparations seemed adequate for the ordeal. Daily domestic duties exhausted the strongest women, while men staggered under the burden of steering the "prairie schooners" across rough terrain and dangerous rivers. The toll was high. Every traveler noted that the route west was dotted with graves—mostly the result of disease, accidents, exhaustion, and starvation. One estimate suggests that deaths on the Oregon Trail averaged one every eighty yards.

Marking the Trails

The perils of migration marked people and land alike. The custom of naming babies after features of western geography (Nevada, Gila, Columbia) indicated a pride of achievement, though all too many infants and their mothers died en route and were buried hastily to spare their corpses from wolves or thieves. Naming the land also offered a modicum of immortality. In 1838, the young Abraham Lincoln linked the efforts of the nation's founders to the national geography. "If they succeeded," he remarked, "they were to be immortalized; their names . . . transferred to counties and cities, and rivers and mountains." Western migrants added a democratic touch to the fetish. At the cliffs at Independence Rock in Wyoming, travelers paused to inscribe personal names, initials, and dates. "Nothing escapes that can be marked upon," noted one emigrant; "even the slabs

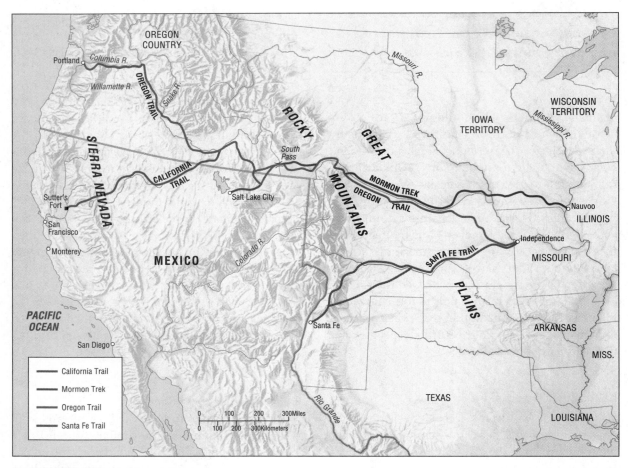

Overland Trails, 1846

of graves are all marked by this propensity for penciling." ("Each venturesome climber seems to wish to put his name above the last one," added the diarist. "One poor fellow fell and was killed.")

The graffiti proved less damaging to the landscape than the passage of thousands of wagon trains, together with flocks of sheep and herds of cattle, which in some years exceeded 150,000 head of livestock. Rotting carcasses of horses, mules, and oxen putrefied the air and water, while human excrement turned virgin canyons into

stinking pits that spread cholera and other diseases. The prairies became junk heaps of broken wagons, furniture, and assorted household litter discarded to lighten the load. Cattle and sheep ravaged the land, competing with native buffalo for scarce water and grasses.

Disrupting Native American Life

Even more devastating was the male sport of random killing. "Not less than fifty buffalo were slaughtered this morning, whereas not three in all were used," noted a California-bound traveler. "But the desire by the emigrant of engaging once at least in a buffalo chase can scarcely be repressed." Such play endangered the economies of Native Americans, intensifying competition among the nomadic Sioux and the settled Pawnees. (Sometimes, western migrants found fun in shooting the indigenous people, though one migrant reported that a white man who killed a Native woman like "a wild animal" was turned over to her kinsmen, who "skinned him alive.") When the Sioux complained to Washington about the disruption of hunting grounds, a government official replied, with the logic of Manifest Destiny, that "the injury complained of is but one of those inconveniences to which every people are subjected by the changing and constantly progressive spirit of the age."

Although overland emigrants prepared for armed conflicts, violence occurred infrequently, a fact that did not reduce the level of anxiety. Cross-cultural contacts often proved invisible and subtler. In 1837, a smallpox epidemic reduced the population of the Plains people by half, wiping out the Mandans and Hidatsas. By the late 1840s, annual cholera epidemics not only weakened the Plains' survivors but also made them wary of further contact with whites. "We are armed to the teeth," said one California emigrant, "but . . . we carry with us in their imagination a protection more formidable: the dread scourge which has spread among them." In eastern Washington, the tendency of white children to recover from measles, while Cayuse children died, prompted Native leaders to murder the local missionaries Marcus and Narcissa Whitman. In the Southwest, Apache raiders attacked stragglers and kidnapped children. For most emigrants, assaults involved only the nighttime theft of horses and livestock. In the light of day, emigrants mostly encountered omnipresent beggars seeking gifts, or Native American traders eager to swap sewn shirts for assistance crossing swollen rivers.

U.S. citizens also paid scant attention to the Spanish-speaking peoples of the Far West. "The greatest misfortunes of Spanish America," explained South Carolina's John Calhoun, "are to be traced to the fatal error of placing these colored races on an equality with the white race." Such racial attitudes justified their conquest, but drew a line at incorporating them into the national family. Northern expansionists shared Calhoun's views of Mexican inferiority. While attracted to California's outdoor festivals and "fandangos," eastern visitors like the author Richard Henry Dana concluded that "the women have but little virtue," an outlook that rationalized their sexual abuse. The absence of Yankee values—Protestantism, industry, and thrift—also persuaded expansionists that Californios were "an imbecile, pusillanimous race . . . and unfit to control the destinies of that beautiful country." By 1848, Yankee traders were exporting 6 million hides and 7,000 tons of tallow from California, a contrast with so-called California fever (laziness). As Dana exclaimed in his widely read *Two Years Before the Mast* (1840), "In the hands of an enterprising people, what a country this might be!"

Manifest Destiny, Ethnic Identity, and Social Reform

Since Manifest Destiny assumed the superiority of Anglo-Protestant culture, many political leaders worried that immigrant groups, especially Irish Catholics, would subvert the religious and political principles that defined the nation's identity. Protestants of all denominations viewed the Catholic church as an intolerant, undemocratic religion and questioned whether people who accepted the Pope's authority could be trusted to exercise republican rights of citizenship. Anglo-Protestants also doubted the ability of African Americans to become citizens. Although antislavery opinion increased in the northern states during the 1840s, criticism of the South's "peculiar institution" seldom acknowledged the equality of free blacks. When northern abolitionists did challenge such prejudices, they often provoked public hostility. In this way, women of the antislavery movement encountered discrimination against themselves, as women, and discovered the limitations of women's rights. Evangelical reformism thus linked the antislavery movement to a growing demand for women's equality.

The Rise of Irish Immigration

Public criticism of the Catholic church coincided with a surge of Irish immigration that rapidly increased the size of the Catholic population, especially in eastern cities. After 1815, economic depressions in Europe encouraged young Irish men and women to seek their fortunes in North America. Most were single people in their twenties who spoke English and wanted to acquire an "independence" instead of remaining landless tenants or underemployed trade workers. In the ten years after 1845, moreover, annual potato blights destroyed Irish agriculture, bringing famine that caused 1 million deaths and inspired nearly twice that number to seek refuge across the Atlantic. This wave of immigrants traveled as families, many suffering from malnutrition and shipboard diseases, and included non–English speaking people. Unlike most other immigrant groups, more than half the Irish newcomers were women. The simultaneous arrival of German immigrants, many fleeing the political rebellions that swept through Europe in 1848, aroused less concern because those newcomers were fewer in number, tended to be more prosperous, and settled in rural areas, not cities.

The famine-stricken Irish confronted an unfriendly economic and cultural environment. In the Atlantic port cities where they landed, Irish men

Slaveowners gave risky jobs in mining and construction to Irish workers to avoid endangering their slaves.

competed for low-paying manual jobs in construction and dock work; Irish women found domestic employment as maids, cooks, and laundry workers, displacing African American women from those occupations. Taking advantage of the transportation boom, many men found work building canals and railroads, which encouraged westward migration. When those jobs were finished, the Irish settled as farm workers or found occupations in the growing cities of the Midwest. Fewer Irish migrated to the southern states, where slaves and free blacks competed for manual work. Slaveowners sometimes gave more risky jobs in mining and construction to Irish workers to avoid endangering their slaves. For the Irish, traditional clannishness provided mutual support, but because they were the lowest-paid workers, their families often experienced the problems associated with poverty—alcoholism, violence, family desertion, and crime.

Skilled Irish immigrants also entered an economy of declining opportunity. As northern home manufacturing gave way to textile mills, Irish weavers had to abandon their trades for the routines and discipline of the factories. To support their families, the Irish accepted jobs at lower pay than native-born workers, often replacing New England farm girls in the mills. Meanwhile, the real wages of mill workers declined between 1830 and 1860. By the 1840s, entire families were forced to seek mill work, take in boarders to supplement their income, or find jobs for their children that included room and board. The low wages paid to Irish immigrants affected other groups as well: the distance between the richest and poorest Americans increased, reducing social mobility, and the competition for jobs among the poorest groups increased, sometimes provoking violent ethnic clashes.

Anti-Irish Nativism

Even before the floodtide of immigration, Irish Catholicism had aroused Protestant anger. Most citizens initially assumed that Irish "backwardness" reflected a deprived upbringing in Europe. "The sin of the Irish man is ignorance," declared a Harvard University commencement speaker in 1840, "the cure is Liberty." But as shiploads of Irish arrived in the 1840s, economic competition aggravated ethnic antagonism. In 1842, native-born citizens formed the American Protestant Association, an anti-immigrant group that opposed Irish Catholic culture, such as the reading of Catholic bibles in public schools. Street violence between anti-Catholic mobs and Irish gangs occurred frequently in the cities, climaxing in 1844 with organized riots in Philadelphia that left numerous dead and two Catholic churches burned to the ground. That year, a "nativist" candidate, campaigning to delay the naturalization of Catholic immigrants, won election as mayor of New York, prompting successful campaigns against immigration in other eastern cities.

Although many respectable citizens condemned the violence, anti-Irish views dovetailed with changing intellectual opinion. Instead of attributing Irish "deficiencies" to their environmental circumstances, during the 1840s nativist critics introduced racial and national characteristics to explain why the Irish appeared "ignorant . . . idle, thriftless, poor, intemperate, and barbarian." A stereotyped view of "Paddy" underscored physical differences in explaining ethnic behavior. Contemporary scientific theory reinforced such ideas. The popular fad of phrenology, involving pseudo-scientific measurement of skulls, suggested that

The influx of Irish immigrants prompted the stereotyped picture of an Irish "Paddy," with prominent nose and simian features.

psychological and cultural traits could be identified by the shape of the cranium and lent credence to the notion of permanent racial characteristics. More potent was the argument of Harvard's leading biologist, Louis Agassiz, who proposed a theory of *polygenesis,* the plural origins of mankind, which suggested racial differences among humans were God-given qualities of nature.

Native-born citizens usually viewed the Irish as an example of "otherness," of what they themselves were not. "All is noise and agitation, tumult and disorder," noted a Pennsylvania mechanic about the Irish immigrants he saw on a Mississippi steamboat; "nothing of composure or gravity, but the very reverse." Irish clannishness contrasted with Yankee individualism; their boisterous wakes and fraternal saloons clashed with the temperance crusade against alcohol; their shanty towns on the outskirts of town violated middle-class notions of domesticity; their tendency to support Democratic politics alarmed evangelical Whigs.

Irish family values, support of parochial schools, and ethnic societies offered protection and security for what one immigrant described as "a primitive people, wandering wildly in a strange land." After laboring for six days under harsh conditions, Irish workers wanted a Sunday of leisure, not an evangelical lecture about preserving the Sabbath. Yet, the desire to retain their ethnic identity did not preclude interest in assimilation. "Look to the Yankees as a model," advised one recent immigrant. "Imitate the energy, patience, and prudence of his character," said another. Assimilation and social mobility, however, depended not only on individual will but also on opportunity, and nativist attitudes kept the first generations of Irish outside society's mainstream. The federal census of 1860, for example, listed three national categories: "native," "foreign," and "Irish."

Challenging Racial Inequality

"I never hear an Irishman called Paddy [or] a colored person called nigger," wrote the abolitionist Lydia Maria Child in 1841, "without a pang in my heart, for I know that such epithets . . . are doing more to form the moral sentiments of the nation, than all the teachings of the schools." To evangelical reformers like Child, ethnic and racial discrimination contradicted the belief in human perfectibility. Yet if the Irish could anticipate a future time of cultural assimilation, African Americans faced deeper prejudices because of their race and skin color. During the 1830s, evangelical abolitionism had injected a moral imperative into antislavery agitation. But since most northerners continued to view African Americans as culturally, spiritually, and biologically inferior, public support of abolitionism remained marginal. Partly for this reason, radical abolitionists like William Lloyd Garrison opposed political activity, fearing that public hostility would drown the effort. Garrison also insisted that the evil of slavery was beyond political debate. Instead, he emphasized spiritual appeals: the emancipation of slaves depended first on the moral regeneration of free people, who would then voluntarily liberate all slaves.

During the 1840s, other abolitionists began to advocate political participation. Although the antislavery Liberty party's presidential candidate, James G. Birney, received only 7,000 votes in 1840, political abolitionists continued to agitate for specific objectives. Acknowledging that Congress lacked the constitutional power to interfere with slavery in the separate states, the Liberty party targeted government support of slavery in areas where congressional authority appeared unquestioned: slavery in the national capital; the interstate slave trade; the use of slave labor to build public works and military fortifications. The Liberty party also opposed the admission of new slave states and insisted that Congress should reject slavery in federal territories such as Florida. Yet, by 1845, every state that entered the union from the Louisiana territory—Louisiana, Missouri, Arkansas, and Texas—was a slave state.

Recognizing that antislavery measures depended on winning the support of northern voters, the Liberty party challenged the belief that blacks were innately inferior, arguing that the environment of slavery, not natural or racial deficiencies, had limited African American development. Free African Americans, including Henry Bibb, Henry Highland Garnet, and members of the National Convention of Colored Men, endorsed the

Liberty movement, though they preferred more militant action. In an 1843 "Address to the Slaves of the United States," Garnet echoed David Walker's appeal for slave rebellion (see Chapter 10) and declared, "It is sinful in the extreme for you to make voluntary submission." By the mid-1840s, however, most abolitionists were focusing on tamer electoral politics, seeking not so much to gain public office as to control the balance of power between the major parties and so obtain passage of antislavery laws.

Antislavery Issues and the Rights of Women

By emphasizing the equality of all human beings, the abolitionist movement awakened second thoughts about other social institutions—marriage, family, and sexual relationships. Garrison's newspaper *The Liberator* included a "Ladies Department," illustrated by a slave woman kneeling in chains and bearing the caption "Am I Not a Woman and a Sister?" Evangelical women, such as Lydia Marie Child and the Grimké sisters, fought actively in the abolitionist crusade, writing articles and pamphlets, and creating female auxiliaries to all-male antislavery societies. Such involvement enabled women to participate in public life despite the middle-class belief that a woman's proper sphere remained in the home.

The incipient conflict about women's roles crystallized in 1837 when Angelina and Sarah Grimké, the daughters of South Carolina slaveholders, embarked on an antislavery speaking tour of New England. Their willingness to address mixed audiences of men and women troubled orthodox clergymen, who considered such behavior "promiscuous." A Congregational ministers association protested that a woman who "assumes the place and tone of man as a public reformer . . . becomes unnatural." Such attacks exposed the limitations of women's public status, and the Grimké sisters began to speak not only about abolitionism

but also about the rights of women. The ensuing public debate divided the antislavery movement. "Is it not forgetting the great and dreadful wrongs of the slave in a selfish crusade against some paltry grievance of our own?" asked the abolitionist poet John Greenleaf Whittier. Angelina Grimké replied, "Are we aliens, because we are women?"

In working to free the slaves, the Quaker Abby Kelley remarked, "we [women] found that *we* were manacled *ourselves*." At the World Antislavery Convention held in England in 1840, male abolitionists voted against seating Lucretia Mott, Elizabeth Cady Stanton, and other women delegates, forcing them to attend the proceedings in a separate area. The insult reinforced their determination. "I was a woman before I was an abolitionist," said Lucy Stone. "I must speak for women."

During the 1840s, the Whig party took the lead in inviting women to form auxiliary clubs to campaign for presidential candidates. Evangelical women, who supported reform movements such as abolitionism and temperance, tended to be middle class and Whigs, and they used reform newspapers to argue for expanded political and legal rights. They wrote pamphlets, presented public lectures, and contributed to Amelia Bloomer's women's rights newspaper *Lily,* which by the mid-1850s reached a circulation of 6,000. Unsurprisingly, however, Bloomer acquired greater notoriety for proposing "short dress" costumes for women—loose fitting divided skirts called "bloomers" after their designer.

Women Democrats, in contrast, opposed government interference in private spheres such as the family, and generally opposed reform laws. So did most men in all parties. "Her speech like all others on Woman's Rights," remarked a Pennsylvania farmer who attended a feminist lecture, "was of very little practical use, being at least 5,000 years ahead of the time." Women often had a different reaction. "I really had thought we had all the rights that belonged to us," wrote a well-to-do

Bloomer acquired greater notoriety for proposing "short dress" costumes for women.

woman who attended a two-hour speech by Lucy Stone (who wore bloomers), "but . . . I find we are wronged and hope for a change in some respects."

The difficulty of altering male opinion inspired Stanton and Mott to organize a woman's rights convention at Seneca Falls, New York, in 1848. Seeking to appeal to women rather than men, the leaders nonetheless recoiled from drafting a manifesto ("as helpless and hopeless as if they had been suddenly asked to construct a steam engine," Stanton recalled) and persuaded Mott's husband to chair the meeting. The Seneca Falls convention soon found its voice. In a "Declaration of Sentiments," modeled on Jefferson's attack on King George III in the Declaration of Independence, the delegates offered an unwavering protest. "He," they declared, referring to men's treatment of women, "has endeavored, in every way that he could, to destroy her confidence in her own powers, to lessen her self-respect, and to make her willing to lead a dependent and abject life."

Having established that women were "aggrieved, oppressed, and fraudulently deprived of their most sacred rights," the Declaration of Sentiments demanded equal opportunities for professional careers and rights of citizenship. Among these was the right of married women to inherit and own property independent of their husbands. As women's rights meetings spread through the states, the movement clarified a critical element in the demand for political rights, including the vote: "We do not seek to protect women," an 1851 convention explained, "but rather to place her in a position to protect herself." By 1860, four-

teen states had enacted legislation establishing married women's property rights.

The Politics of National Expansion

Women's rights, abolitionism, anti-Catholicism, and Manifest Destiny—all these impulses were rooted in the popular belief that individuals should be made free, liberated from patriarchy, slavery, religious hierarchy, and political oppression. Social reformers stressed the superiority of U.S. culture and sought to "perfect" its essential goodness. During the 1840s, these views coalesced with the nationalist spirit of westward expansion. Believing that the nation's institutions—government, churches, commerce, and families—were superior to those of other nations, political leaders argued for spreading those virtues across the continent to ensure the future happiness of the citizenry. By the end of the decade, some expansionists even envisioned American trade and culture crossing the Pacific, from the harbors of San Diego, San Francisco, and Puget Sound, to Hawaii, China, and Japan.

Expansionist ideas soon aggravated quarrels about the contradictions between southern slavery and the free-labor economy of the North. Political leaders in both regions claimed to uphold *national* values, including the principle of westward expansion. In the early 1840s, southern leaders like Virginia's John Tyler and South Carolina's John Calhoun supported the annexation of Texas to obtain additional territory for the cotton and slave economy, arguing that such a society reflected the values of the nation's founders. By contrast, northern leaders like New York's Martin Van Buren and Pennsylvania's David Wilmot favored expansion only if slavery, which they deemed the antithesis of liberty, would be prohibited in the newly acquired territory. Indeed, northerners feared that the spread of slavery would interfere with a free labor economy and stifle the prospect of upward mobility for poorer whites. Pro-slavery leaders replied that any limitation of slavery violated the constitutional rights of free men to own private property, imperiling their own liberty. But the issue ran deeper than legal argument. "It is not a question of national politics," observed a northern Whig, "but of national identity." In short, the nation now faced its troubling paradox: Was the United States a country in which all men—or only some men—were free?

Texas and Oregon

The issue of territorial expansion exploded in 1844 when proslavery President Tyler authorized Secretary of State Calhoun to draft a treaty calling for the annexation of Texas. When Calhoun linked Texas to the survival of slavery, Whigs denounced annexation and the Senate refused to ratify the treaty. Texas then became the prime topic in the 1844 presidential election. Although the northern front runner, Van Buren, expected the Democratic nomination, southern party leaders abruptly dumped him because of his refusal to back annexation. Instead, the Democrats chose Tennessee's James K. Polk, a fervent expansionist who promised to bring both Texas and Oregon into the Union. Meanwhile, as the Whig candidate Henry Clay waffled on the Texas issue, many northern Whigs deserted the party to back the Liberty candidate James G. Birney. That shift proved decisive. Birney's 65,000 votes drained enough ballots from Clay in New York to give Polk the state's 36 electoral votes and the presidency. "Slavery," remarked the Whig William Henry Seward, "is now henceforth and forever among the elements of political action. . . . the ground the public mind has traveled cannot be retraced."

Despite the narrow election results, lame-duck President Tyler, who was determined to acquire Texas, took Polk's victory as proof of the popular view and urged Congress to annex the Lone Star republic by a joint resolution, which required a simple majority rather than two-thirds ratification of the Senate. Anger at this parliamentary strategy spread through the North, leading some anti-Texas politicians to accuse a so-called slave-power conspiracy of threatening constitutional checks and balances. But Congress approved annexation and Texas became a state in 1845.

President Polk then pressed ahead with claims to Oregon as far north as the latitude of the Alaska border ("54-40 or Fight" was his campaign slogan). In 1846, the White House accepted a compromise with rival British claimants, establishing the U.S. border with Canada at the 49th parallel and bringing Puget Sound into the union. The farming families who settled in Oregon proceeded to create a nonslave territorial government.

Polk's willingness to compromise about the Oregon boundary contrasted with his stubbornness in negotiating with Mexico. After the United States accepted Texas into the union, Mexico broke diplomatic relations and threatened war to recover its lost province. The United States also inherited Texas's bitter warfare with the Comanches, Kiowas, and other mounted peoples, who resisted encroachment on their lands. After annexation, Texas requested federal military forces to remove the native inhabitants. Amidst violent boundary disputes, the Comanches ignored national borders to raid Mexican territory for livestock and adding to Mexico's grievances about annexation.

Rejecting Mexico's objections, Polk claimed that the southern boundary of Texas was not the Nueces River, as Mexico claimed, but the Rio Grande, and he ordered General Zachary Taylor to occupy the disputed area. With that provocative step, the president also dispatched a special ambassador to Mexico City with instructions to purchase New Mexico and California and to settle the Texas boundary at the Rio Grande. Mexico's refusal to negotiate its dismemberment goaded Polk further. He instructed Taylor to move U.S. forces south, then used a minor military skirmish as an excuse to claim that Mexico had shed blood on U.S. soil and asked Congress to declare war.

The War with Mexico

"We are waging a most iniquitous war," cried the abolitionist Theodore Parker. Although the Democratic majority in Congress swiftly supported Polk's war message, opposition to the war was widespread. Abolitionists and antislavery "Conscience" Whigs denounced Polk's failure to seek a compromise with Mexico. To protest the war, Henry David Thoreau refused to pay his taxes, went to jail and there wrote his classic essay *Civil Disobedience,* defending conscientious objection to immoral actions of government. In Congress, the Illinois Whig Abraham Lincoln introduced a resolution asking the president to identify the spot of U.S. soil on which blood had been shed; the nickname "Spotty" Lincoln was the sole result.

Anti-war sentiment scarcely disrupted the war effort. Polk took command of military plans, sending Taylor's army south from Texas to seize Monterey, Mexico, where U.S. troops defeated a larger Mexican force under General Santa Anna at Buena Vista. Taylor's sudden fame ignited his presidential prospects, which Polk decided to cool by ordering him to await further orders. To secure New Mexico, Colonel Stephen Kearny marched 850 miles from Kansas into Santa Fe and raised the U.S. flag above the city's plaza. Kearny made peace agreements with the Pueblos, Apaches, and Utes, but needed a show of force to gain a settlement with the Navajos. Despite numerous treaties, neither the local peoples nor the federal government would surrender their claims to the lands, and the southwestern border remained dangerous for both peoples for years.

Kearny's troops then headed for California, where U.S. settlers led by the explorer John C. Frémont had declared independence from Mexico and founded the Bear Flag Republic in 1846. Meanwhile, U.S. naval forces captured Monterey, California. Mexican defenders battled Kearny's cavalry in southern California, but by early 1847 the U.S. army controlled the province. Polk then prepared to invade Mexico City, but to stifle General Taylor's political ambitions, he gave command of the army to General Winfield Scott. Landing at Vera Cruz, Scott's 14,000 soldiers fought their way over the mountains and laid siege to the Mexican capital. Santa Anna's superior numbers engaged U.S. soldiers in several bloody battles, but in the autumn of 1847 Mexico was forced to surrender. The war claimed 13,000 U.S. lives—2,000 killed on the battlefields, the remainder taken by disease.

While Polk's ambassador negotiated a treaty of peace in Mexico, a sharp political debate was brewing in Washington. Some expansionists called for the seizure of all Mexico. But a vocal antislavery group, fearful of extending slavery, joined racial purists like Calhoun in rejecting the absorption of Mexico's "colored" population. The demand for all Mexico passed. Instead, the Treaty of Guadelupe Hidalgo of 1848 required Mexico to cede California, New Mexico, and the Rio Grande region in exchange for $15 million and the U.S. assumption of claims against Mexico. These Mexican acquisitions, plus Texas and Oregon, brought 1.2 million square miles into the union, including 1,000 miles of Pacific shores.

Confronting Slavery and Race in the West

The acquisition of Mexican territory seemed to fulfill the promise of Manifest Destiny but quickly sparked a debate between northern and southern

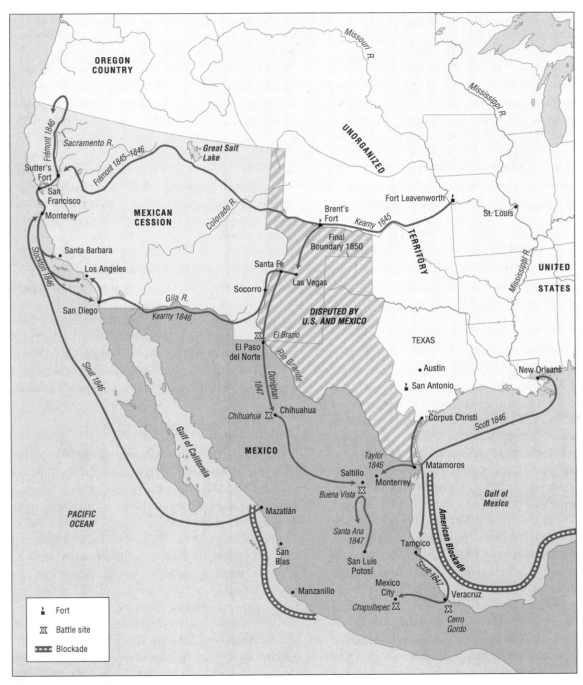

The Mexican War and Cession

versions of the national identity. The Missouri Compromise of 1820 had drawn a line through the Louisiana territory at the latitude 36°-30", prohibiting slavery north of that line. But, by the 1840s, northern opinion had turned against the spread of slavery anywhere. Rather than celebrating the acquisition of new lands, Congress became deadlocked in an effort to establish territorial governments. Complicating the crisis was the discovery of gold in California in 1848, which set off a mass exodus from around the world, brought new ethnic groups into the country, and underscored the importance of ending the congressional stalemate. Despite the presidential election that year, the national political parties failed to resolve the dispute. Not until 1850 did Congress find the basis for a compromise, trading political interests that offered a partial resolution of the territorial issue, but only for a decade.

Defining the Status of Slavery

"Slavery has within itself the seeds of its own dissolution," declared Pennsylvania Representative David Wilmot. "Keep it within limits, let it remain where it now is, and in time it will wear itself out." With such logic, the Democratic congressman introduced a resolution in 1846, known as the Wilmot Proviso, prohibiting slavery in all territory seized from Mexico. Disavowing any "morbid sympathy for the slave," Wilmot merely pleaded "the cause of white free men." As he assured his colleagues in the House of Representatives, "I would preserve to free white labor a fair country, a rich inheritance, where the sons . . . of my own race and color, can live without the disgrace which association with negro slavery brings upon free labor."

The ensuing debates revealed three competing views about the status of slavery in the territories. The first drew on the precedents of the Northwest Ordinance and the Missouri Compromise and insisted that Congress had the power and duty to

prohibit slavery in the territories. President Polk, who proposed extending the Missouri Compromise line to the Pacific, took that position. The second view, articulated by pro-slavery leaders like Calhoun, argued that the Constitution protected personal property in territories no less than in states and that Congress had an obligation to protect slavery in *all* U.S. territories. In Calhoun's view, the Missouri Compromise was unconstitutional. The third position, expressed by two midwestern Democrats, Lewis Cass of Michigan and Stephen Douglas of Illinois, was later known as "popular sovereignty"; it proposed that the voters in each territory, not Congress, should decide the issue of slavery for themselves.

These irreconcilable views did not encourage compromise. In the House, where northern constituencies held a majority, Wilmot's proposal passed in 1846. But in the Senate, where southern states had equal power with the North, the measure failed to carry. Yet the principles of Wilmot's proviso would be revisited on many occasions; it was a point of difference that would not fade away.

Defining the Status of Citizens

The Wilmot debates illuminated the high value that 19th-century politicians gave to the rights of citizenship. Significantly, no political leader on any side proposed extending full citizenship to African American men, or to women of any race. To the contrary, 19th-century politicians believed that the privileges of citizenship belonged only to adult white men. Neither the Constitution nor congressional law had ever drawn moral distinctions between citizens. To southern leaders, therefore, Wilmot's proviso broke all precedents, saying "in effect to the Southern man," as one Virginian put it, "You are not my equal, and hence to be excluded as carrying a moral taint with you." To Calhoun, the proviso pushed the South "from being equals into a subordinate and dependent

The Election of 1848

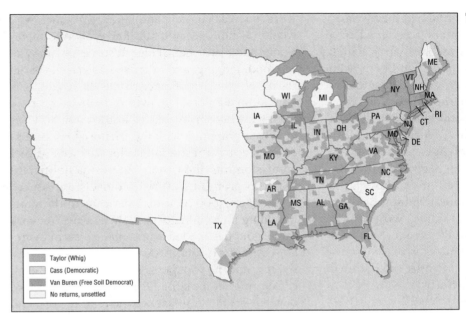

Taylor (Whig)
Cass (Democratic)
Van Buren (Free Soil Democrat)
No returns, unsettled

condition." This feeling of insult, of moral exclusion, of being denied the right to inhabit U.S. territory with one's private property in the form of slaves, threatened the foundations of republican politics, in which all white men possessed equal rights to life, liberty, and the pursuit of happiness. Even nonslaveholding southerners, interested in the opportunities of western expansion, shared this demand for equal status in the republic.

Northern politicians felt equally aggrieved by the proslavery leadership. Some, like Wilmot, objected to the immorality of slavery. Others opposed the increase of southern political power in Congress. The novel process of acquiring Texas by joint resolution, after the formal treaty had failed to win ratification, appeared to many northerners as an abuse of power. Then, the war with Mexico had brought vast territories into the union, most of which would prove inhospitable to cotton cultivation and slavery, but now proslave members of Congress were seeking to protect their power by admitting additional slave states. "They have trampled on the rights and just

claims of the North sufficiently long," a Massachusetts Whig wrote privately, "and have fairly shit upon all our Northern statesmen and are now trying to rub it in." Northerners might not share the abolitionist revulsion against slavery, but neither did they welcome competition with slave labor in the territories. "To contend that Congress should introduce, or engraft, Slavery upon territory now free," stated a northern Democrat, "is to ask the people of the union to consider and treat slavery as a positive benefit and blessing to be diffused and extended by the action of Congress."

As Washington remained deadlocked about territorial slavery, politicians prepared for the 1848 elections. Seeking southern votes, Democrats nominated the northerner Lewis Cass, whose support of popular sovereignty contradicted the Wilmot Proviso. The Whigs, by contrast, could achieve no unity on slavery and dodged the issue by nominating the military hero Zachary Taylor, who ran for president without a party platform. Thus the two major candidates had little appeal for Conscience

Whigs, antislavery Democrats, or Liberty party abolitionists. These dissenters converged in a third political party, the Free Soil party, which nominated the former Democrat Van Buren, who now endorsed the Wilmot Proviso. "The question is not whether black men are to be made free," averred a Free Soil Democrat, "but whether we white men are to remain free." African American leaders like Frederick Douglass welcomed the Free Soil movement as "the beginning [of] the end of . . . American slavery." And although the Free Soil party won no electoral votes, it held the balance of power in two states; with nearly 300,000 popular votes, half of them in New York and Massachusetts, Free Soilers spoke for one-tenth of the electorate. Meanwhile, the national majority elected General Taylor.

The California Gold Rush

Before Taylor or Congress could address the problem of new states, the California Gold Rush introduced a new element into the political equation. Ten days after Mexico surrendered California to Polk's diplomacy in 1848, a sawmill worker named James Marshall, employed by the entrepreneur John Sutter, had spotted gold nuggets in the sand near the American River. By 1849, the discovery had ignited an international race for fortune. "Forty-niners" flocked west by the tens of thousands, either along the overland trails or by ship to Panama and then across the isthmus and up the Pacific coast. In 1848, some 6,000 miners harvested gold worth $10 million; by 1850, the output had quadrupled to $42 million, and the number of miners had increased eightfold; in 1852, the peak year, gold values reached $81 million, but spread among 100,000 seekers.

The new Californians were overwhelmingly male—92 percent in 1850, and even higher in the mining camps. The shortage of women increased the value of what was usually considered women's work, such as cooking and laundry. Women who went to California could thus find economic opportunity, and many men achieved success by providing food, lodging, and other services in the boom towns, of which San Francisco was the largest.

California's rapid growth impelled settlers to form a civil government just at the moment Congress was grappling with the territorial issues. Encouraged by President Taylor to seek direct admission into the Union, California politicians voted to prohibit slavery. The decision assured freedom to 2,000 African Americans in the state, including those initially brought as slaves to work in the gold fields. Free status enabled them to create community institutions, such as churches, lodges, and newspapers. But, as the free black community complained, they continued to face racial discrimination, lacked the right to vote, and could not testify in state courts.

Even though California was a free state, political leaders made no effort to extend liberty to the indigenous population. State laws permitted the forced labor of any Native American found loitering, "strolling about," or "leading an immoral or profligate course of life." The state also approved a labor system that permitted white citizens to employ Native American children as involuntary "apprentices" at the minimal cost of giving them food, clothing, and "humane" treatment. Kidnapping proved a common way to acquire such youngsters to work as farmers, miners, ranchers, and domestic servants. With a shortage of white women, employers leased their female "apprentices" according to grade: "fair, middling, inferior, refuse."

Whites targeted "wild Indians" for violence, rape, and murder, and local governments offered bounties for their scalps. With such incentives, the Native American population of California dropped from 150,000 in 1845, to 100,000 in 1850, to 50,000 in 1855, to 35,000 five years later. Most died of imported illness (15 percent from sexually transmitted diseases) as well as alcoholism, murder, and

MINING LIFE IN CALIFORNIA.

CHINESE MINERS.

Chinese miners panned for gold on the American River in California in the 1850s.

abuse. Such distress aroused no interest from national politicians. When by the early 1850s federal officials appealed to Washington for aid in curbing these abuses, Secretary of War Jefferson Davis, a Mississippi slaveholder, declined to interfere.

East to Gold Mountain

One day a San Franciscan heard a man humming the homesick tune "Carry Me Back to Old Virginia," then looked twice to realize that the singer was Chinese. Forty-niners included several thousand men (very few women) who journeyed east to "Gold Mountain" from the province of Canton. Like Irish immigrants, Chinese peasants of the 1840s experienced overpopulation and food shortages caused both by drought and floods. China's opium wars with Britain in the 1840s and 1850s further disrupted the economy, while forced competition from foreign traders undermined local manufactures. Too weak to resist foreign pressure, China had signed the Treaty of Wangshia in 1844, opening several

ports to U.S. shipping. New York was already the home of a small Chinese community. Chinese merchants not only traded silks and other products but also sold the services of contract laborers who sailed to Australia, Latin America, and California.

"From far and near we came and were pleased," remarked an early Chinese merchant in San Francisco. But not for long. Protesting foreign competition in the gold fields, U.S.-born miners demanded restriction of the "Asiatic races . . . dissimilar from ourselves in customs, language, and education." In 1852, the state enacted a foreign miners' tax which targeted noncitizen miners, but particularly affected Chinese since a 1790 federal law had limited naturalization to white persons. By paying the discriminatory fees, Chinese miners provided nearly half the state government's annual revenue! After gold was discovered in Australia, many Chinese miners joined an outmigration. Those who remained in California worked in isolated, almost all-male communities. Spanish-speaking Forty-Niners from Mexico and Chile faced similar racial problems.

The Compromise of 1850

By 1850, the territories of California and New Mexico had drafted antislavery constitutions and applied for admission into the union. President Taylor's efforts to bypass the territorial stage (and so finesse congressional oversight of slavery) angered southerners of both political parties who saw the national balance of power tilting forever against them. Some extremists even spoke of leaving the union. Hoping to defuse another congressional deadlock, political moderates, led by Henry Clay, introduced a group of resolutions to permit the compromise of differences.

The resulting Compromise of 1850 provided for the admission of California as a nonslave state, but organized the remainder of the Southwest into a territory without restrictions about slavery; slaveowners could transport their human property into the region, but for reasons of climate and geography few expected to do so. The federal government would attach Texas's disputed western boundary lands to New Mexico, while assuming the state's public debt; this measure limited the size of Texas as a slave state, leaving the status of western Texas undecided, and satisfied Texas's northern creditors, who cared more about dividends than slavery. Two other key bills highlighted the impending conflict between northern and southern interests: one abolished the slave trade—but not slavery—in Washington, D.C.; the other mandated passage of a stricter fugitive slave law requiring free states to return runaways.

As the Senate, still balanced between slave and free states, considered the resolutions, the rhetoric of extremists in both regions exposed the fragility of the republic. "A single section, governed by the will of the numerical majority, has now, in fact, the control of the government," declared the aging John Calhoun; "the people of the southern states . . . cannot remain, as things now are . . . in the union." Jefferson Davis of Mississippi added a similar dissent. William Seward, a New York Whig, condemned the pending compromise, but for quite opposite reasons, decrying the refusal to confront the moral issue of slavery and declaring that there existed a "higher law" than the Constitution. Other senators spoke for the compromise, none more eloquently than Massachusetts' Daniel Webster, for which he earned the eternal malice of the abolitionists.

The sudden death of Zachary Taylor in 1850 abruptly removed presidential objections to the proposed compromise, and the new president, Millard Fillmore, backed Clay's proposals. Congressional managers swung into operation, dividing Clay's package into a series of distinct bills, each requiring a separate vote. The old party lines, dividing Whigs from Democrats, nearly disappeared. Southern Whigs and Democrats generally backed slavery; northern Whigs and Democrats largely opposed its extension. Consequently, neither region "compromised" its position. Instead, a small group of moderates held the balance on each measure, and the bills slipped through, one by one, each with a slim majority.

A Political Pause

Passage of the Compromise of 1850 generated a collective sigh of relief that echoed through the land. But no astute citizen could forget the tensions that had knotted Congress for more than a year. Regional politicians had not compromised their principles; they would monitor their opponents closely and demand that political promises to enforce the new laws be kept. Nor, ultimately, could lines drawn on the political map resolve the moral crisis that remained. "Slavery depends not on climate," observed the pedagogue Horace Mann, "but on conscience." The compromise thus brought not a resolution but only a temporary truce. What would happen when other western territories sought statehood? Exhausted political leaders could only wait.

INFOTRAC® COLLEGE EDITION EXERCISES

 For additional reading go to InfoTrac College Edition, your online research library at http://web1.infotrac-college.com.

Keyword search: Manifest Destiiny
Keyword search: westward expansion
Keyword search: James K. Polk
Keyword search: Mexican War
Keyword search: Zachary Taylor
Subject search: Treaty of Guadalupe Hidalgo
Keyword search: Irish immigration
Keyword search: potato famine
Keyword search: Thoreau
Keyword search: Emerson
Keyword search: Wilmot Proviso
Subject search: Compromise of 1850

ADDITIONAL READING

William R. Brock, *Parties and Political Conscience: American Dilemmas, 1840–1850* (1979). A good overview of national politics, emphasizing the relationship of ideas, interests, and national identity; see also the titles listed at the end of Chapter 13.

Nature, Technology, and Expansion

Barbara Novak, *Nature and Culture: American Landscape and Painting, 1825–1875* (1980). Based on art and literature, this analysis suggests the 19th-century ambivalence about territorial development and "progress."

The Wonders of Technology

William Cronon, *Nature's Metropolis: Chicago and the Great West* (1991). An economic and ecological history, the early chapters focus on railroads, grains, and lumber; the study extends to the end of the century.

Heading West

Lillian Schlissel, *Women's Diaries of the Westward Journey* (1982). Based on women's writings, the book provides an engaging account of the epic migration.

Anti-Irish Nativism

Dale T. Knobel, *Paddy and the Republic: Ethnicity and Nationality in Antebellum America* (1986). A study of changing images of Irish immigrants, this provocative work may be supplemented with Kerby A. Miller, *Emigrants and Exiles: Ireland and the Irish Exodus to North America* (1985).

Challenging Racial Inequality

Richard H. Sewell, *Ballots for Freedom: Antislavery Politics in the United States, 1837–1860* (1976). This book provides a clear account of the role of abolitionism in the political arena.

Antislavery Issues and the Rights of Women

Blanche Glassman Hersh, *The Slavery of Sex: Feminist Abolitionists in America* (1978). Tracing the origins of feminism within the evangelical abolitionist movement, this analysis should be supplemented with the first chapter of Ellen Carol DuBois, *Feminism and Suffrage: The Emergence of an Independent Women's Movement in America, 1848–1869* (1978). See also the relevant chapters of Paul Goodman, *Of One Blood* (1998), listed in Chapter 11.

Texas and Oregon

David J. Weber, *The Mexican Frontier, 1821–1846: The American Southwest under Mexico* (1982). A thorough history of Mexico's northern provinces, analyzing the impact of U.S. expansion into the region.

The California Gold Rush

Susan Lee Johnson, *Roaring Camp: The Social World of the California Gold Rush* (2000). A multicultural perspective of the mining camps; for the impact on Native Americans, see also James J. Rawls, *Indians of California: The Changing Image* (1984).

Malcolm J. Rohrbough, *Days of Gold: The California Gold Rush and the American Nation* (1997). Using letters and diaries of California gold miners, the book depicts the migration west and its consequences for those who stayed east.

13

The Collapse of the Union, 1850–1861

CHRONOLOGY

1850	Congress passes Compromise laws, including Fugitive Slave Act
	Illinois Central Railroad obtains federal lands
1852	Harriet Beecher Stowe publishes *Uncle Tom's Cabin*
	Franklin Pierce wins presidential election
1854	Senator Stephen Douglas introduces Kansas-Nebraska bill
	Massachusetts returns Anthony Burns to slavery
	Congress ratifies Gadsden Purchase
	Henry David Thoreau publishes *Walden*
	Know Nothings gain election victories
	Republican party emerges in Midwest
1855	Walt Whitman publishes *Leaves of Grass*
1856	James Buchanan defeats Frémont and Fillmore
1857	Supreme Court announces *Dred Scott* decision
	Economic downturn causes Panic and economic depression
	New York City begins to build Central Park
1858	Buchanan endorses Kansas's proslavery constitution
	Abraham Lincoln and Stephen Douglas debate for senate seat
1859	John Brown leads raid on Harper's Ferry
1860	Lincoln wins four-way presidential race
	South Carolina secedes from union
1861	Seceded states form Confederate States of America

Amid the strains of national politics in 1855, the country's foremost philosopher, Ralph Waldo Emerson, received from Walt Whitman a new book of poetry entitled *Leaves of Grass*. "I greet you at the beginning of a great career," he wrote the young author. While political leaders struggled to reconcile the contradictions of democratic sentiment—the divisions between southern and northern citizens, between cultures and classes—the 36-year-old New York poet's "Song of Myself" reveled in such paradoxes:

I am of old and young, of the foolish as much as the wise . . . ,
Maternal as well as paternal, a child as well as a man,
Stuffed with the stuff that is coarse, and stuffed with the stuff that is fine.

. . . .

A southerner soon as a northerner, a planter nonchalant and hospitable,
A Yankee . . . ready for trade.

. . . .

Of every hue and trade and rank, of every caste and religion,

Not merely of the New World but of Africa Europe
or Asia . . . a wandering savage.

. . . .

And am not stuck up, and am in my place.

Whitman's free verse celebrated the uncertainties of
the national identity—the coexistence of liberty and
slavery, of cultural toleration and intolerant nativism—
that made so many of his contemporaries uneasy. His
efforts to embrace all humanity seemed risky to a people fixated on "every hue and trade and rank." And
when the poet exulted, "I sing the body electric," he
touched on anxieties that were rooted both in the era's
sexual repression and in the "shock" of new technologies. Still, Whitman's work reaffirmed the uniqueness
of the country and its diverse inhabitants. "The genius
of the United States," he declared, "is not best or most
in its executives or legislatures, nor in its ambassadors
or authors or colleges or churches or parlors, nor even
in its newspapers or inventors . . . but always most in
the common people." This celebration of democracy
and cultural pluralism contrasted with the failure of
national politicians to resolve sectional disputes. Soon
after the decade ended, the poet's plea for union would
dissolve in a roar of cannons.

In his annual message to Congress in December
1850, President Millard Fillmore called the recent Compromise over extending slavery into
the new western territories "final and irrevocable."
His optimism was considerable, because most national politicians recognized that the political climate remained poisoned by regional conflicts.
Many northern leaders still refused to accept slavery in any unorganized territories, and southern
leaders equally condemned efforts to limit their
right to own slaves. Politicians in both regions
looked suspiciously at their opponents: some believed that a "slave power" conspiracy was seeking
to extend the South's peculiar institution; others
saw abolitionists laboring to deny the legitimate
rights of slaveholding citizens. The two regions
held different versions of the national identity;
each believed that the other's was immoral, if not
illegal. Yet, as government promoted westward expansion and citizens clamored for public lands, the
organization of new territories as either slave or
free could not be put off much longer.

Despite these tensions, most citizens of 1850
did not foresee a disruption of the union. Although slavery would dominate the nation's political life during the decade, a multitude of other
social issues competed for public attention. The
continuing immigration of foreign settlers, especially Catholic Irish and Germans, created social
tensions that affected voting alignments and political activity. Anti-immigration, or *nativism*, became a powerful political movement, attracting
voters from the old national parties. Whereas reformers of the previous decade had emphasized
moral persuasion alone to cure social and cultural
ills, during the 1850s citizens stressed legislative
solutions. Efforts to control foreign minorities
provoked both violence and political campaigns

Most citizens of 1850 did not foresee a disruption of the union.

to limit their influence. Yet, ironically, foreign immigration to free-labor states increased the North's population and its political representation in Congress, underscoring the South's minority status.

Political conflict about slavery, race, and ethnicity also obscured the decade's remarkable economic prosperity. California gold added a windfall to the nation's money supply, which, in turn, stimulated economic growth. In 1858, the discovery of gold in Colorado set off the cry "Pike's Peak or Bust!" The next year, silver finds in California and Nevada launched another mining boom. Economic optimism, in turn, encouraged investment in transportation, manufacturing, and commercial farming. Yet these economic developments, by stimulating western expansion, contributed to the sectional crisis. The question of slavery in the territories echoed behind every political issue.

The Ironies of Economic Prosperity

By 1850, half the nation's people lived west of the Appalachian Mountains. Most made their living in agriculture, but in two decidedly different economies. South of the Ohio River and extending toward Texas, the agricultural economy was based on cotton and slavery. Nonslaveholding southerners also migrated into this region, but many aspired to obtain land in order to improve their social position. Southwestern growers thus shared economic and cultural values with southeasterners. In the northwestern portion of the Mississippi valley, by contrast, free-labor agriculture prevailed, producing food crops for consumption in eastern cities and in Europe. Northern agricultural prosperity benefited from the growth of transportation systems, especially railroads, which increasingly bound the economic interests of northwestern farmers to northeastern markets. The economic boom thus accentuated sectional differences between North and South. What the two regional economies shared, however, was a disregard for Native American land claims, which stood in the way of western settlement. During the 1850s, the federal government coerced the Plains nations to accept treaties that limited access to their traditional lands.

The Agricultural Boom

A boom in cotton fueled a decade of national prosperity. Between 1850 and 1860, southern output increased from less than 3 million bales a year to nearly 5 million. By 1860, the value of cotton exports reached almost $200 million per year, accounting for nearly two-thirds of the country's total export trade. Three other southern products—sugar, tobacco, and rice—enjoyed a similar boom.

Indicative of southern prosperity was the doubling of the value of slaves during the decade. Some historians suggest that southern planters were not "landlords" but "labor lords." As the price of slaves rose, the proportion of whites who owned slaves declined from one-third to one-quarter. In other words, the economics of plantation agriculture enabled a smaller segment of southern society to control more of the region's total agricultural assets, indeed, as much as 90 to 95 percent of its wealth. A defender of southern agriculture described the planters as "unquestionably the most prosperous people on earth." But one consequence of investment in slaves was a proportionally smaller ownership of manufacturing, banking, and transportation, which attracted northern investors (Table 13.1). Southern leaders frequently complained of their dependence on northern capital to maintain their agricultural economy.

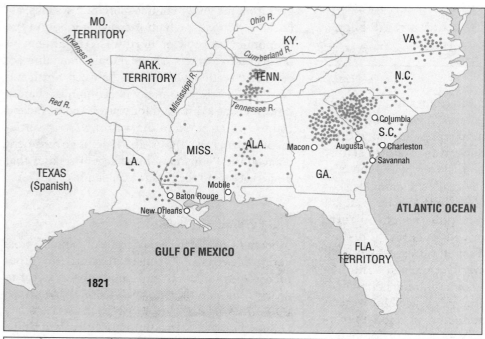

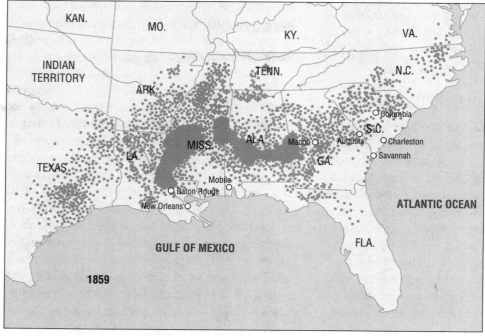

Cotton Production in the South, 1821 and 1859

TABLE 13.1

Regional Patterns of Manufacturing, 1850 and 1860

	Capital Invested by Manufacturing per Capita		Value of Manufacturing Output per Capita	
	1850	1860	1850	1860
New England	$57.96	$82.13	$100.71	$149.47
Middle States	35.50	52.21	71.24	96.28
Northwest	11.70	18.95	26.32	37.33
Pacific States	10.39	42.35	84.83	129.04
South	7.60	10.54	10.88	17.09
Cotton South	5.11	7.20	6.83	10.47
U.S.	22.73	32.12	43.69	59.98

Sources: U.S. Bureau of the Census, *Compendium of 1850 Census*, p. 179; Eighth U.S. Census, *Manufactures*, p. 725; Ninth U.S. Census, *Compendium*, p. 799.

Northern farmers were also affected by the operations of distant markets. The repeal of Britain's grain tariffs in 1846 and food shortages in Europe after the outbreak of the Crimean War in 1853 created new demands for northern corn, wheat, and pork. Since family farms, unlike southern plantations, faced perennial labor shortages, rising agricultural prices encouraged investment in farm machinery, which jumped over 60 percent to $250 million during the decade. Improved farming and crop specialization contributed to a doubling of production. Unable to compete with western grains, eastern farmers shifted to more specialized agriculture: vegetables, fruits, and dairy products. By 1860, local farmers were shipping nearly 200,000 quarts of milk to New York City every day. Areas of Massachusetts also enjoyed a small boom in tobacco production, though one college president expressed regret that tobacco farmers "sacrificed their luxuriant and lovely meadows to the growth of a narcotic."

The Economics of Railroad Expansion

Northern agricultural prosperity was closely tied to a boom in railroad construction, which reinforced the differences between the southern and northern economies. During the 1850s, railroad companies laid 20,000 miles of track worth $800 million of investments. The mileage of southern railroads increased 350 percent, but remained under one-third of the nation's total. By 1860, four major trunk lines linked the Atlantic ports of New York, Philadelphia, and Baltimore with the Ohio and Mississippi valleys. In 1856, the Chicago and Rock Island line opened the first railroad bridge across the Mississippi river, an engineering feat that required 1 million feet of lumber and over 300 tons of iron.

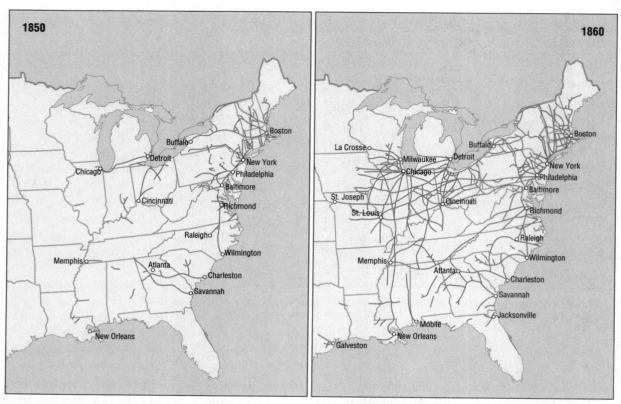

Railroads, 1850 and 1860

Meanwhile, the number of locomotives jumped from 3,000 to 8,500, and railroad employees increased from 4,800 to 90,000! Although freight traffic gradually surpassed passenger travel, the Erie line added a touch of professionalism by requiring conductors to wear uniforms. They were the first civilian employees so attired.

While the southern economy continued to rely on river transport to bring cotton to market, railroads began to weave inextricable ties between the Northeast and the Northwest. By 1860, eleven railroads and a hundred trains each day linked Chicago's massive grain elevators (with a total ca-

pacity of 4 million bushels) not only to transatlantic shipping companies but also to a commodities market that speculated in the future prices of grain. Similarly, the unprecedented amount of capital necessary to build the great trunk lines ($17 to $35 million each) required mass sales of railroad securities to domestic and foreign financiers. Boosted by railroad investment, by mid-decade the New York Stock Exchange was trading hundreds of thousands of shares each week. Meanwhile, new techniques of railroad finance—bond issues and subcontracted work—began to be used to fund northern municipal improve-

TABLE 13.2

Railroad Mileage in the United States, 1850–1860

Year	Miles of Line in Operation
1850	9,021
1852	12,908
1854	16,720
1856	22,016
1858	26,968
1860	30,626

Source: John F. Stover, *Iron Road to the West: American Railroads in the 1850s* (New York: Columbia University Press, 1978).

ments, enabling cities to pay for public works without raising taxes.

Track construction and railroad operations soon stimulated other industries. In rural Alabama, for example, woodburning locomotives and standard railroad ties demanded more logging and lumber mills. In the Great Lakes states, railroads virtually consumed the north woods. The shift to coal in the 1850s encouraged anthracite mining, particularly in Pennsylvania. Most important was the demand for iron rails. By 1854, investments in U.S. iron mills exceeded $10 million, achieving an industrial capacity of 100,000 tons a year. Yet railroads still had to import nearly twice that amount from British mills. Indeed, even with the low tariffs established in 1846, the duty on rail imports was large enough to produce a government surplus and a further lowering of tariff rates in 1857. Ironically, cotton exports supported this international trade, even though the immense profits from transporting the crop went to northern shippers and investors.

Railroads also had a cultural impact, stimulating a new preoccupation with timekeeping in all regions. "They come and go with such regularity and precision, and their whistles can be heard so far," remarked Henry David Thoreau in his 1854 book *Walden*, "that the farmers set their clocks by them, and thus one well-conducted institution regulates the whole country." By the 1850s, the nation's largest clockmaker was manufacturing 280,000 brass shelf clocks each year. Equally innovative was the mass production of pocket watches. Improving the technology of manufacturing 150 interchangeable parts, the Waltham Watch Company reduced the labor time for making each watch from 21 days in 1854 to 4 days in 1859 and advertised that broken parts could be replaced by mail with nothing more than the watch's serial number.

Despite the new national passion for punctuality, railroads still followed local sun time, which varied with geographical longitude, and efforts to standardize time zones were unsuccessful. Most citizens viewed timekeeping as a local, not a national, concern—an outlook that also applied to most political issues. Railroads would become an exception to local thinking, but not without consequences for sectional conflict.

Federal Support of Railroads

Railroads, claimed a Boston editor, "made the land a neighborhood," bringing local businesses into a national, even international, marketplace. Farmers and merchants living near projected rail lines became a major source of capital investment. By mortgaging their property to support railroad construction, farmers protected—indeed, increased—the value of their land and ensured their access to distant consumers. In this way, Chicago's aggressive railroad promoters overwhelmed the rival city of St. Louis, which relied on river transportation. While St. Louis doubled in size, the windy city quadrupled, as shipments of flour jumped sixfold and wheat increased five times. Chicago's merchants now sought to make their city the terminus of the nation's railroad network, especially for a transcontinental line that aimed west.

Because of greater distances and sparser populations, western railroad development required more funding than local sources could usually provide. State and local governments assisted new railroads with loans, tax exemptions, subsidies, and the purchase of stock. But, unlike the earlier government-backed turnpikes and canals, railroad companies rejected government regulation of fares and freight rates to protect private investors. Even state aid could not always satisfy the capital demands of extensive railroads. In 1850, Illinois's Democratic Senator Stephen Douglas persuaded Congress to give 2.5 million acres of land to the Illinois Central to construct a 700-mile railroad linking Lake Michigan with the Ohio and Mississippi rivers. With that precedent, the federal government proceeded to grant over 20 million additional acres of public lands (an area four times the size of Massachusetts) to eleven midwestern and southern states as well as a free right-of-way on the public domain during the decade. Such government gifts were quickly transformed into liquid assets. Besides using the land as security for railroad bonds, the companies sold the acreage to speculators and settlers. By 1859, the Illinois Central had disposed of 1.3 million government-bestowed acres at $12 each (a total of about $300 million in today's money).

Railroads and Territorial Expansion

Federal involvement appeared even more important as railroad investors envisioned a transportation system that would link commercial farmers with the Pacific coast and Asian markets. In 1853, eight years after Congress ratified a trade treaty with China, a squadron of U.S. warships, com-manded by Matthew Perry, entered Tokyo Bay in Japan and forced the *shogun* leadership to establish diplomatic relations. The ensuing treaty ensured that U.S. commerce obtained, as one American put it, "the entering wedge that will . . . open to us the interior wealth of these unknown lands." The same year, Congress authorized the War Department to undertake geographical surveys of four projected railroad routes across the Great Plains to the west coast. Secretary of War Jefferson Davis, a Mississippi slaveholder, favored a southern route that would connect Texas to San Diego. After he noticed that this route dipped below the border with Mexico, the federal government dispatched former South Carolina railroad president James Gadsden to Mexico to negotiate the purchase of territory south of the Gila river. It was an area so desolate, said the explorer Kit Carson, "a wolf could not make a living from it." But in 1854, the Senate ratified the Gadsden Purchase, exchanging $10 million for 30,000 square miles of railroad country.

As Washington politicians drew railroad lines on territorial maps, the original residents confronted threats to their survival. "Since the white man has made a road across our land," protested the Shoshone leader Washakie in 1855, "and has killed off our game, we are hungry, and there is nothing for us to eat." Four years earlier, in 1851, federal authorities had summoned the Plains nations to a conference near Fort Laramie in Wyoming to propose a new policy. The 10,000 Native Americans who attended learned that the government planned to confine them within distinct territorial boundaries—tribal reservations—to separate them from U.S. emigrants and from each other. Promising gifts and future annuities in exchange for the land, federal officials overcame the objections of unhappy Native leaders. Through the 1850s, U.S. expansion onto tribal territory brought further federal intervention, which compelled the Plains peoples to surrender another 1.5 million

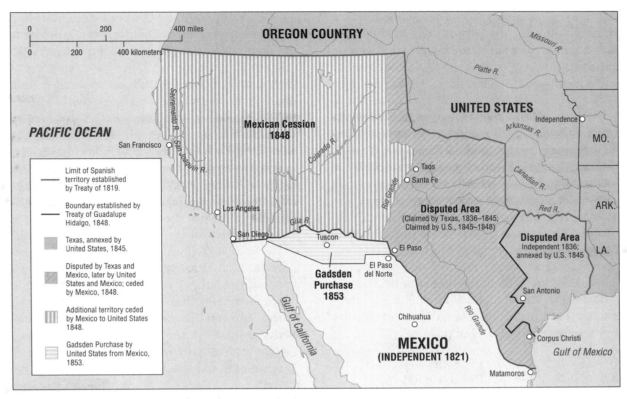

Southwestern Expansion and the Gadsden Purchase

"Since the white man has made a road across our land and has killed off our game, we are hungry, and there is nothing for us to eat."

acres. Those concessions opened the region west of Missouri, known as the Kansas and Nebraska territory, to settlement by whites. Kansas and Nebraska would soon become familiar names throughout the country as plans to build a railroad to the Pacific reawakened the conflicts between North and South about the status of slavery.

Redrawing Political Lines

Regional disagreements also arose about expansionist schemes south of the U.S. border. Interested in acquiring territory suitable for cotton and slavery, southern expansionists spoke about seizing Cuba and portions of Central America. "The path of our destiny on this continent," declared one Virginian, "lies in . . . tropical America, [where] we may see an empire . . . representing the noble peculiarities of southern civilization." When Spain rejected U.S. offers to purchase Cuba, southern expansionists organized illegal invasions of the island. But military failures and lack of congressional support ultimately thwarted the efforts.

Many northern expansionists shared the view that the supposedly superior Anglo-Saxon "race" was destined to conquer the peoples of the tropical areas. Indeed, some hoped that expansion southward would redirect slavery away from the West, where free blacks were also unwelcome. During the 1850s, Indiana, Illinois, Iowa, and Oregon prohibited further settlement by blacks. The decade also saw renewed interest in transplanting freed African Americans beyond U.S. territorial limits to Central America, but such colonization schemes aroused opposition. "We are Americans, having a birthright citizenship," responded the black nationalist author Martin Delany in 1852. "We must not leave this continent." Interest in expansion south ultimately failed, however, because the issues of the western territories absorbed national attention. With railroads stretching from east to west, expansion south seemed remote and impractical.

Resistance to the Fugitive Slave Act

As southern expansionists touted the advantages of extending slavery through the Western Hemisphere, northern critics resolved to draw strict boundaries against its spread. At the beginning of the 1850s, the first border of contention was the Mason-Dixon Line, which had been drawn nearly a century earlier to mark the southern boundary of Pennsylvania and which separated slave states from free soil. The Compromise of 1850 had included a Fugitive Slave Act that was stricter than the statute of 1793 (see Chapter 7). The new law required free states to cooperate in returning runaway slaves. Southern politicians repeatedly stressed the importance of that law, both legally and symbolically, as evidence of northern good faith. "Upon a faithful execution" of that law, warned a southern leader, "depends the preservation of our much beloved Union."

Although southern politicians demanded northern cooperation and northern politicians like Daniel Webster promised compliance, a significant constituency of free blacks, slaves, ex-slaves, and antislavery whites honored a long tradition of resistance to fugitive slave laws. For decades, an informal network called the "underground railroad," operated by ex-slaves like the celebrated Harriet Tubman, southern Quakers, and northern sympathizers, had assisted the escape of fugitives, harboring them quietly in northern communities or speeding them to freedom in Canada. To prevent the kidnapping of free blacks, many northern states had enacted personal liberty laws guaranteeing the civil rights of fugitive slaves and obstructing efforts to return them to previous owners. After 1850, threats to enforce the Fugitive Slave Act alarmed northern African American communities. Thousands of blacks immediately fled to Canada, while respectable antislavery leaders announced their refusal to obey "an immoral and irreligious statute." Some did not rule out violent resistance. "The only way to make the fugitive slave law a dead letter," advised ex-slave Frederick Douglass, "is to make half a dozen or more dead kidnappers."

African Americans and their supporters soon forced northern citizens to confront the issue. In 1851, the arrest of a runaway slave, Frederick "Shadrach" Minkins, in Boston brought a mob of angry blacks into the courtroom, where they beat a federal marshal, seized the prisoner, and transported him to Canada. President Fillmore denounced the violence, but a defiant jury acquitted the perpetrators. Federal enforcement succeeded in a second Boston case involving Thomas Sims, but it required a small army, which ferried the accused south at four in the morning. Other incidents involved shootouts with would-be slave catchers, jailhouse rescues, and vigilante attacks on the courts. When a runaway from Virginia named Anthony Burns was ordered back to slavery after a week-long trial in 1854 and marched in chains through the streets of Boston under guard of 1,000 federal troops, northern outrage exploded. "My thoughts are murder to the state," said Thoreau. But a Georgia student at Harvard who witnessed the protests now wrote to his parents, "Do not be surprised if when I return home you find me a *confirmed disunionist.*"

For northern whites, however, fugitives like Anthony Burns, Thomas Sims, and Shadrach Minkins—or more famous runaways like Frederick Douglass, Harriet Tubman, and Harriet Jacobs—gave the anonymous slave a human face. So, too, did the popular songs of the 1850s written by Stephen Foster, such as "My Old Kentucky Home" and "Beautiful Dreamer." Despite their stereotypes, the lyrics described African Americans experiencing human emotions and feelings. "They are heart songs," said Douglass in 1855. "They awaken sympathies for the slave, in which antislavery principles take root, grow and flourish." The publication of numerous autobiographies by ex-slaves not only showed the evils of slavery but also answered southern claims that unsupervised blacks could not achieve their human potential.

These themes culminated in the appearance of a stunning work of fiction, Harriet Beecher Stowe's *Uncle Tom's Cabin*, in 1852. The book sold 300,000 copies the first year, 2 million in a decade, and it became a stage play that captivated audiences for the remainder of the century. Inspired by the fugitive slave cases, Stowe condemned the human suffering, presenting the slave Uncle Tom as a Christ figure who transcends worldly evil through spiritual redemption. Passionately written and read, the scenes of Tom sold away from his children or the slave mother Eliza crossing the icy Ohio river for freedom etched the agony of slavery onto the northern conscience. Southerners attacked the novel for its distortions, even published counter-

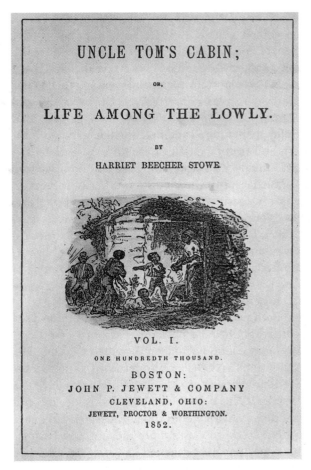

Title page of the 100,000th copy of the first edition of Harriet Beecher Stowe's *Uncle Tom's Cabin*, published at Boston in 1852.

novels to show the advantages of slavery. But Stowe's work remained a powerful indictment of the slave system, and she used her royalties to underwrite other antislavery protests.

The Weakening Party System

Despite the notoriety of the fugitive slave cases, most political leaders and voters hoped to preserve the Compromise of 1850. Off-year congressional elections in 1850 and 1851 showed support for the agreements, and in 1852 both national parties adopted platforms that accepted its principles. But the 1852 presidential election revealed strains in the political system, particularly among the Whigs. With the great compromisers Henry Clay and Daniel Webster dead in 1852, the Whig party had difficulty finding a candidate suitable to both southern and northern delegates. After 52 ballots, the party finally nominated the noncommittal General Winfield Scott over the pro-southern Fillmore to run for president. Scott would be the last Whig presidential candidate. Southern Whigs, frustrated at their failure to influence northern allies, began to abandon the party. The Democratic party also confronted a deadlock among competing factions before nominating New Hampshire's Franklin Pierce, a northerner with southern sympathies.

Both parties competed for the urban immigrant vote, though most newcomers from Ireland and Germany continued to identify with the Democrats. Van Buren's Free Soilers also returned to the Democratic fold. The splits in the Whig party gave the Democrat Pierce an electoral vote landslide, 254–42. But the popular vote was much closer, and in many areas eligible voters simply did not cast ballots. Voter participation reached its lowest levels since 1836 and would not be so low again until 1904. Some party regulars attributed the low turnout to the absence of issues. "General Apathy is the strongest candidate," remarked an Ohio politician. But it was the refusal of the national parties to address the real issues of the Compromise of 1850 that undoubtedly kept voters away.

"Party names of Whig and Democrat now mean nothing and point to nothing," observed a political commentator in 1853. The absence of national economic issues underscored the political intrigue of rival politicians competing for office. The parties had become "empty flesh, putrid mouths," said the poet Whitman, "the politicians standing back in the shadow telling lies." Cases of corruption emerged in local, state, and federal government, further weakening allegiance to the established parties. "Parties are broken up by local causes," lamented former President Fillmore at the end of 1853; only "some great national and centripetal force at Washington" could save them.

The Kansas-Nebraska Bill

National politics swiftly grabbed public attention in 1854 when Senator Stephen Douglas introduced legislation to organize the territories of Kansas and Nebraska. Seeking to secure Chicago's position as the terminus of the transcontinental railroad, Douglas saw no need to honor earlier pledges to protect the lands of the Plains nations, an omission that raised no congressional protests. But his willingness to tinker with the Missouri Compromise—under which both new territories would have become free states—soon aroused a political storm. The Missouri Compromise forbade slavery north of the line 36°30' but Southern Whigs, looking for an issue that would rejuvenate their party, now joined southern Democrats in demanding repeal of the Missouri line in exchange for their support of the Kansas-Nebraska bill. Douglas agreed to modify his proposal. Believing that neither territory was geographically suited to slave agriculture, he offered an alternative that he believed would satisfy southern demands for equal treatment in the West, while ensuring that the new states would adopt antislavery constitutions. His proposal reflected the idea of "popular sovereignty," which had already been part of the 1850 Compromise to regulate the New Mexico territory (see Chapter 12). Douglas proposed that the voters in each territory be allowed to decide the status of slavery. He never doubted the results: both Kansas and Nebraska would enter the union as free states.

Douglas underestimated the strength of antislavery opinion. Overnight, a group of antislavery Democrats, led by Ohio's Salmon Chase, published an "Appeal of the Independent Democrats," denouncing the proposed repeal of the Missouri Compromise "as a gross violation of a sacred pledge" and "part and parcel of an atrocious plot" to transform Kansas and Nebraska into slave states. To northern minds, the key word was *plot*; a conspiracy of slaveowners appeared ready to overthrow free republican institutions. "Past party lines will be obliterated with the Missouri line," predicted one politician—accurately, as it turned out.

The pro-southern Pierce administration worked with Douglas to muster a majority to pass the Kansas-Nebraska bill in both houses of Congress. Nevertheless, the Democratic party now began to divide along sectional lines. Meanwhile, Northern Whigs, realizing the unpopularity of the bill among antislavery constituents, voted against the measure. This trend prompted southern Whigs to announce "we will have no party association that will not . . . treat us as *equals*." Defending regional interests more than party ties, southern Whigs provided the critical votes needed to enact Douglas's plan into law. Frustrated northerners, Democrats and Whigs alike, began to form independent parties. Among these was the Republican party, born in the northern Midwest in 1854 and initially drawing support on a single issue: opposition to slavery in the territories. Thus passage of the Kansas-Nebraska act destroyed the Whigs as a national party and accelerated major political realignments.

Cultural Differences Become Political

As the slavery controversy disrupted both national parties, voters increasingly focused on political issues related to the changing ethnic composition of their communities. With 3 million immigrants arriving on Atlantic shores in the decade after 1845 (see Chapter 12), anti-foreign nativist politics assumed growing importance. When, for example, Irish and German immigrants showed indifference to evangelical temperance reformers, political leaders pushed for state legislation to outlaw alcohol consumption. During the 1850s, a dozen northern states passed prohibition laws. Ironically, the reluctance of traditional party leaders to take sides on prohibition contributed to the view that they were, as one reformer called them, "old fogies" who were oblivious to social problems. Protestant leaders frequently denounced a Catholic conspiracy against republican institutions, pointing, for instance, to Pierce's appointment of a Catholic postmaster general (a position with great patronage power) as a sign of impending subversion.

Growing anti-foreign sentiment encouraged a secret nativist club called the Order of the Star Spangled Banner to organize private lodges around the country, offering membership only to white Protestant men who had Protestant parents and who were "not united in marriage with a Roman Catholic." Members shared secret handshakes, passwords, and signals, strove for anonymity, and responded to outside inquiries by claiming to "know nothing." The Know Nothings, as they were called, sought to curb immigration and extend the probation period for naturalized citizenship. By early 1854, the Know Nothings tallied 50,000 members; half a year later, the secret group totaled over 1 million.

The election returns of 1854 awakened politicians to the strength of this political force, which many had not even realized existed. Selecting candidates from among their anonymous membership, the Know Nothings voted as a bloc in favor of temperance, against established politicians who depended on immigrant voters, and, in northern states, against repeal of the Missouri Compromise.

In Massachusetts, the Know Nothings captured the governorship, most of the state legislature, and the entire congressional delegation; in the South, many Whigs migrated to the movement as a way of competing with rival Democrats. The relationship between Know Nothings and slavery remained ambiguous. Southern Know Nothings supported slavery, but some northerners saw no difference between attacking slaveholders and Catholics. Others, like ex-Whig Republican Abraham Lincoln, wondered "How can any one who abhors the oppression of negroes be in favor of degrading classes of white people?"

Problems of Political Geography

By the mid-1850s, voters faced a widening array of political choices as new groups attempted to replace the Whigs as a national party and local issues complicated political alignments. In 1855, the nativist Know Nothings (now formally identified as the American party) tried to build a national organization by appealing to anti-immigration, anti-Catholic voters in all regions. Similarly, the small Republican party attempted to find allies among ex-Whigs, Free Soilers, antislavery Know Nothings, and anti-expansionist Democrats. "We are all very much in the dark as to the political future," confessed one politician.

While party leaders looked for a thread that would stitch national politics back together, one issue remained a powerful counterforce, ever dividing citizens along geographical lines: slavery in the territories. As more northern voters came to view slavery as a threat to wage labor, economic opportunity in the West, and civil liberties, and while southern politicians condemned the antislavery movement as a threat to property rights, slavery ignited deep passions that refused to be distracted by other issues. The one common concern of national politics, slavery split the country into two irreconcilable camps.

Bleeding Kansas and the Election of 1856

Stephen Douglas expected congressional approval of popular sovereignty to end the debate about slavery in Kansas. But the formation of a territorial government in 1855 triggered an explosion of violence that stunned the country and came to be known as "Bleeding Kansas." A majority of Kansas's settlers had migrated from free states and opposed slavery, but on election day slaveholders from Missouri rode across the state border to cast a majority of votes for a proslavery legislature to draft the state constitution. The legislature proceeded to enact proslavery laws, including one that prohibited antislavery men from holding office. This perversion of popular sovereignty outraged northern opinion. "We are for free Kansas," said an Illinois newspaper, "because we are for free white men." In Kansas, violence between proslavery and antislavery factions steadily escalated. Challenging the election fraud, the numerically larger antislavery settlers elected their own constitutional delegates and proceeded to form a territorial government in Topeka that prohibited slavery. Expressing widely held racist views, the same delegates also banned the immigration of free blacks.

President Pierce, now facing two rival constitutions, chose to support the proslavery legislature and warned the free-state claimants in Topeka that further opposition would be "treasonable insurrection." But violence between northern and southern settlers persisted. After a proslavery court in Kansas indicted antislavery leaders for treason, an armed proslavery posse attempted to arrest opposition leaders in the town of Lawrence, burned the Free Soil Hotel, and wrecked antislavery printing presses. Abolitionist

The Election of 1856

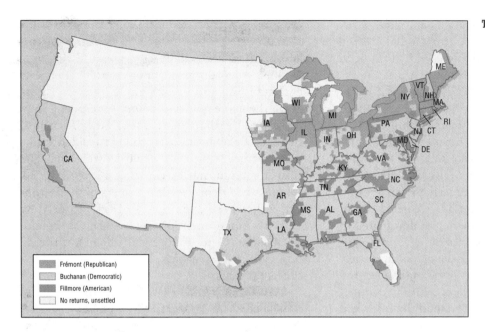

Frémont (Republican)
Buchanan (Democratic)
Fillmore (American)
No returns, unsettled

John Brown then took revenge by murdering five proslavery men at Pottawatomie Creek. Reacting to Bleeding Kansas, northerners and southerners cast blame on their opponents. In May 1856, Massachusetts's antislavery Senator Charles Sumner embarked on a two-day speech entitled "The Crime against Kansas." When Representative Preston Brooks learned that the senator's diatribe had insulted his cousin, South Carolina Senator Andrew Butler, he approached Sumner on the Senate floor and beat him into unconsciousness with a cane. It would take Sumner four years to recover from his injuries; northerners saw him as a martyr to the antislavery cause. Brooks emerged instantly as a southern hero.

The attack on Sumner infuriated the North, appearing as plain evidence of the barbarous effects of slavery and the threat to republican government: "Not merely an *incident,* but a *demonstration,*" said one politician, of a southern plan "to annihilate freedom." This sense of a southern conspiracy defined the 1856 presidential election. The Democrat Pierce's acceptance of slavery in Kansas ended his hopes for reelection in the North. The election fraud in Kansas also belied Douglas's optimism that popular sovereignty would make that state free and weakened his support in the North. The Democrats then nominated Pennsylvania's James Buchanan, a northerner with strong southern leanings. As ambassador to Britain, Buchanan had avoided the sectional debate. Meanwhile, the American party nominated its first presidential candidate, former President Millard Fillmore, but his refusal to condemn the spread of slavery destroyed his northern support. The new Republican party, committed unequivocally "to prohibit in the territories those twin relics of barbarism—polygamy and slavery," nominated John C. Frémont, famous as a military explorer of the West.

"You never saw so much enthusiasm in the people," noted a Republican politician. Although Frémont had no chance to carry the South, northern voters saw his candidacy as an alternative to traditional politics. In writing a campaign poem supporting Frémont, the abolitionist Lydia Child found that the only word she could think of to rhyme with Pierce (pronounced "purse") was "curse." Seeing Frémont as a moral politician, northern women flocked to his campaign rallies. Despite rumors of the nominee's Catholic ancestry, Republicans also won support from former Know Nothings in the North, showing that antislavery remained a more potent issue than nativism. With the slogan "Free Soil, Free Speech, Free Men, Frémont," the candidate carried eleven of the sixteen free states. Buchanan dominated in the South, where Frémont was not a serious candidate. Fillmore took only Maryland. With 45 percent of the popular vote, Buchanan won the election. But Republican leaders carefully counted their gains in the North, understood that they had absorbed their former rivals, the nativists, and pronounced the result "a victorious defeat." After the election, the Know Nothings disappeared as a political party.

The Dred Scott Decision

"May we not, then, hope," said Buchanan in his inaugural address of 1857, "that geographical parties . . . will speedily become extinct?" Such wishful thinking reflected the president's expectation that an imminent Supreme Court decision would resolve the issue of slavery in the territories once and for all. Members of the Court had leaked the outcome of a pending decision to the president-elect. However, when Chief Justice Roger Taney, the son of a Maryland slaveholding family, publicly announced the verdict two days after Buchanan's inauguration, the ruling—and the public outcry—thwarted any hopes for a sectional truce.

The case involved the family of Dred Scott, a Missouri slave who had once lived with his master in free territory north of 36°30' and on that basis now sued for his freedom. The Court answered by denying that slaves or even the descendants of emancipated slaves could become citizens. According to Taney, Scott lacked any legal standing and black people had "no rights which the white man was bound to respect." Having settled the immediate issue, Taney turned to the theoretical question of whether residence in a free territory entitled a slave to freedom. The Court declared that by drawing a line at 36°30' Congress had deprived slaveowners of their property without the due process of law required by the Fifth Amendment; therefore, the Court said, the Missouri Compromise was unconstitutional. Congress, in other words, lacked the authority to legislate the status of slavery in the territories.

By affirming that Congress had no right to limit slavery, the Court validated the extreme southern view and persuaded southern Democrats that they had heard "the funeral sermon of Black Republicanism." Yet Douglas Democrats insisted that the Court had upheld popular sovereignty because enforcement of slaveownership would depend on local laws. Slaveowners obviously understood that logic, for they made no move to bring their slaves into free territory. By contrast, many northern politicians saw in the ruling the hand of a "slave power" conspiracy. Antislavery leaders denounced the verdict as having "as much moral weight as . . . the judgment of a majority of those congregated in any Washington bar-room."

Nor did the *Dred Scott* ruling end the struggle in Kansas. When the proslavery territorial legislature called elections for delegates to ratify the territorial constitution in 1857, antislavery settlers boycotted the polls. Proslavery delegates then met in the town of Lecompton, drew up a constitution that legalized slavery, and—with free soilers still boycotting the proceedings—ratified the document. When the constitution went to voters for ratification, free soilers ended their boycott and carried a majority that rejected the proposal. Nevertheless, the proslavery faction applied for admission into the union.

Congress now had to decide which vote was valid. Buchanan's pledge to support popular sovereignty quickly evaporated. Instead of challenging the dubious voting in Kansas, the president endorsed the proslavery Lecompton constitution. Northern politicians, enraged at Buchanan's dismissal of the majority vote, charged the president with being part of the southern conspiracy. Douglas, facing pressure from his northern constituents, broke with the administration. Despite intense presidential lobbying, the House voted to reject the admission of Kansas as a slave state. By then, Douglas had lost his southern support. Not until 1861, after several southern states had seceded from the union, did Congress admit Kansas—as a free state.

The Politics of Economic Crisis

With political tempers afire, a sudden economic downturn (one New Yorker called it "a clap of thunder in a clear sky") accentuated sectional grievances. The financial Panic of 1857, followed by a severe depression, reflected distant economic factors, particularly the end of the Crimean War, which reduced the market for U.S. agricultural exports, and shifts in European investments. As U.S. businesses fell into bankruptcy and banks suspended payments, the price of western wheat and southern cotton plummeted. The slump in demand for farm production, in turn, affected railroad traffic and abruptly terminated the boom in new construction. This unexpected stagnation reawakened southern condemnation of the nation's financial institutions, what one planter criticized as "the wild speculations of Northern and

---

To provide jobs for the unemployed, New York City launched the construction of Central Park.

Western corporations." Yet, thanks to European demand, the southern cotton economy proved more resilient than western agriculture. While wheat prices remained depressed for two years, southern exports recovered by 1858, reaffirming the adage that "cotton is King."

Poverty in the Cities

The depression of the late 1850s proved much harder for city dwellers than for farmers. With over 5,000 business failures, urban unemployment skyrocketed. Jobless workers massed in the streets of most major cities, crying "Bread or Blood!" Challenging pay cuts, shoemakers, miners, female mill operators, and Irish construction workers organized trade unions and went on strike to demand better wages. But companies lacked the cash even to offer back pay, and charitable assistance was hopelessly inadequate. In New York, 40,000 homeless and poor people sought shelter in police stations, and newspapers routinely reported cases of unemployed workers and children starving to death.

To provide jobs for the unemployed, New York City launched a major public works project, the construction of Central Park. The idea of an urban park also addressed worsening problems of population density, commercial traffic, and noxious living conditions. Drawing 20,000 immigrants a year, the city had doubled in size to 1 million during the decade. Even in prosperous times, many workers barely eked out a living, and disparities of wealth and property ownership increased. Prostitution,

A fashionable crowd gathers to socialize on a Saturday afternoon near the music stand on the mall in New York City's Central Park, 1869.

alcoholism, and crime abounded, while sanitation, sewage, and garbage removal were left to roaming pigs. To New York's merchant princes and middle class planners, a landscaped urban park promised an island of tranquility to ease what one gentleman called the "heart-hardening and taste-smothering habits" of urban life.

Under the guidance of landscape architects Frederick Law Olmsted and Calvert Vaux, construction began in 1857. The city spent $5 million and hired some 20,000 workers to build the 800-acre park in the middle of Manhattan. The project was truly staggering, requiring 166 tons of gunpowder (more than would be expended in the Battle of Gettysburg) to blast out the bedrock, 6 million bricks, 40,000 cubic yards of manure, and 270,000 trees and shrubs. What distinguished this extraordinary engineering feat was the aesthetic approach to the land. Avoiding the rectangular lines associated with the city's street grid, Central Park's arrangement of sloping hills

and meadows, artificial ponds, and winding pathways offered refuge from the urban hubbub. But the park also placed a firm human hand on the irregularities of the natural landscape. Just as the entrepreneur P.T. Barnum presented "wild" animals in cages, so the urban park offered manicured "nature" to a people starved for sunlight and fresh air.

Reinforcing Regional Prejudices

The economic crisis in the North gave southern apologists cause for satisfaction. The problems of northern wage earners, a Virginia newspaper editorialized, contrasted with the "content and quiet" of southern slaves, who faced no "want and suffering." In a work entitled *Cannibals All!* Virginia's George Fitzhugh argued that northern wage labor lacked the inherent protections of a beneficent slave society. Southerners also used the Panic of 1857 as an opportunity to denounce northern business preferences, such as tariffs and western land speculation. The rapid recovery of cotton sales not only reinforced confidence in the southern economy but also convinced southern leaders that cotton was indispensable in the world market and that cotton importers, especially England, recognized their dependence on the crop.

Northerners also drew lessons from the economic crisis. Southern leaders had long supported low tariffs, including reduced rates in 1857. Northern business leaders blamed those lower rates for failing to protect industry and jobs and leaving the Treasury too depleted to ease eastern unemployment by financing internal improvements or encouraging settlement of the West. The belief that western lands could serve as a safety valve to absorb surplus free labor also reinforced northern opposition to extension of slavery in the territories. Responding to such pressure, the Republican party would endorse an economic program (higher tariffs, a homestead act to encourage westward migration, and internal improvements) that was opposed by most southern planters. In this way, economic regionalism reinforced the geography of political alignments.

Irreconcilable Differences

Sectional disagreements about the causes of the Panic of 1857, like the debate over slavery in the territories, reflected a polarization of opinion about recent laws. Although politicians in both regions shared political values about representative government, each side believed that its opponents had violated the principles of constitutional government. Accepting the *Dred Scott* decision, southerners perceived a conspiracy of northern extremists, fired by abolitionism, who refused to acknowledge, in the words of one politician, that

"southern opinion . . . is now the supreme law of the land." Antislavery northerners, frustrated by political defeats, saw a different conspiracy defeating the will of the majority. Challenging Stephen Douglas for the Senate in 1858, the Republican candidate articulated those fears. "When we see a lot of framed timbers . . . which we know have been gotten out at different times and places by different workmen—Stephen, Franklin, Roger, and James," remarked Abraham Lincoln (referring to Douglas, Pierce, Taney, and Buchanan), "and when we see these timbers . . . exactly make the frame of a house . . . we find it impossible to not believe that Stephen and Franklin and Roger and James . . . worked upon a common plan." In Lincoln's eyes, the secret plan aimed to bring slavery into the territories.

Lincoln versus Douglas

Lincoln's metaphor led into his famous statement that "A House divided against itself cannot stand" and that "this government cannot endure, permanently half slave and half free." Such moral rhetoric denied the ambiguous compromise language that, despite fundamental differences, had existed since the birth of the republic. Douglas's notion of popular sovereignty—the view that slavery and antislavery were equally valid political choices—attempted to perpetuate the advantages of imprecision and paradox.

In an 1858 public campaign debate at Freeport, Illinois, however, Lincoln forced Douglas to resolve the ambiguity. Could a territory voluntarily exclude slavery? asked Lincoln. To answer yes would cost Douglas his southern support; to say no would mean that he repudiated popular sovereignty and would cost him the north. "Slavery," replied Douglas, clinging to his ambiguous doctrine, "cannot exist a day in the midst of an unfriendly people with

An artist's reconstruction of the Lincoln-Douglas debates of 1858 during the campaign for senatorship of Illinois.

unfriendly laws." The Illinois state legislature, controlled by Democrats, soon sent Douglas back to his Senate seat in Washington. Northern Democrats still hoped that the ambiguity of popular sovereignty could bridge regional differences in the next presidential election, in 1860.

Lincoln's skillful oratory in his debates with Douglas catapulted him into presidential contention. The Illinois lawyer had entered politics as a Whig but, with the party's demise, he had followed his antislavery principles into the Republican party in 1856. Douglas's idea of popular sovereignty offended Lincoln's moral opposition to a slave society. To be sure, Lincoln had no quar-

rel with white supremacy. He doubted that African Americans could achieve social and political equality, though he believed that black people had certain natural and economic rights. He favored colonization as a way of removing free blacks from the country. Yet, he saw the geographical spread of slavery as a threat to a free labor society, equal opportunity, and majority rule in Congress. Believing that southerners were conspiring to nationalize slave holding, Lincoln saw a political plot to make slavery legal everywhere, even in Illinois.

John Brown's Raid

Proslavery southerners, meanwhile, saw "Black Republicans" like Lincoln conspiring to end slavery—not only in the territories but also in the South. Such fears gained terrifying credibility one October night in 1859, when the zealous abolitionist John Brown led eighteen armed men in a raid on the federal arsenal at Harper's Ferry, Virginia, in hopes of igniting a slave rebellion. Local blacks showed no interest in the suicidal mission. Brown was soon captured, tried for treason, and hanged. The daring raid sent shock waves through the South, arousing nightmares of slave insurrection. The price of slaves began to fall. In the wake of Harper's Ferry, rumors of slave conspiracies raced through the southern states, instigating vigilante attacks on alleged abolitionist villains, African Americans, even Native American communities; most of those rumors, admitted a southern editor, "turned out to be totally false, and all of them grossly exaggerated." Although many northern politicians, including Lincoln, condemned Brown's raid, southern leaders were appalled to learn that many northern churches tolled John Brown's death as a martyrdom. "Nobody cares a damn if the union is dissolved," snapped a slave trader bitterly. "Virginia can whip the whole North herself."

Women, Slaves, and White Male Dominance

The debate about slavery stimulated controversy about other so-called domestic institutions, such as marriage, the family, and household relations. "The black man and the woman are born to shame," Elizabeth Cady Stanton told the American Antislavery Society six months after Brown's execution. "The badge of degradation is the skin and sex—the 'scarlet letter' so sadly worn upon the breast." During the 1850s, women's rights advocates like Stanton and Susan B. Anthony assiduously petitioned state legislatures to pass laws for women's equality, seeking the right to divorce immoral men, to own property, and to vote. Such pleas brought widespread condemnation—but especially in the southern states, where slaveowning patriarchs defended their households. At the same time that some northern states passed divorce laws that protected women's claims to property, South Carolina prohibited legal divorce. Massachusetts became the first state to legalize interracial marriage in 1843, followed in the next decade by Iowa and Kansas. Southerners were horrified.

"The people of our Northern States, who hold that domestic slavery is unjust and iniquitous," said Virginia writer George Fitzhugh in 1854, "are consistent in their attempts to modify or abolish the marriage relation." Free women, no less than slaves, Fitzhugh insisted, required male authority: "Woman . . . has but one right and that is the right to protection." When one southern woman expressed concern that marriage would destroy her freedom, her fiancé quieted those fears by vowing to be her "protector and defender when all friends and relations fail." Like other troubled women, in the North as well as the South, this

"Woman [is] more fully identified with the slave than man can possibly be."

prospective bride accepted marriage without rights as better than its alternative, because, she said, "We poor women have no name or existence of our own, we pass silently down the stream of time without leaving a single trace behind—we die unknown."

In exchange for assuming responsibility for the "weaker" sex, however, men demanded women's subordination, what Fitzhugh called "the obligation to obey." Such ideas pervaded the country. "Woman [is] more fully identified with the slave than man can possibly be," Stanton told her northern audience. "She early learns the misfortune of being born an heir to the crown of thorns . . . , to womanhood." Ironically, the wives of slaveowners often agreed with this pessimistic view. Although Mary Chesnut, a well-to-do South Carolinian, wielded no small power over her slaves, she claimed that women like herself were oppressed by "a swarm of blacks about them as children under their care . . . hard, unpleasant, unromantic, undeveloped savage Africans." Another southern bride, twenty-two-year-old newlywed Tryphena Fox, explained her role: "Having two servants to do the work, I do but little myself and that particular things which I do not like to trust to them, but I have to watch them and tell them every little item to be done, for a negro never sees any dirt or grease, so if a *Southern lady* does not do much manual labor, she has head-work enough to keep her busy." Such racism made slaveholding women loathe the presence of slaves; yet these same women almost never challenged the institution of slavery. Rather, they shared with abolitionist women a sense of powerlessness over their own lives. Husbands, south and north, continued to rule the domestic realm.

The Election of 1860

In 1860, a presidential election year, southern leaders prepared to fight an expected attack on slavery. When the Democrats gathered at their nominating convention in Charleston, South Carolina, extremist delegates demanded a platform protecting slavery in the western territories. But Douglas supporters carried a majority in favor of popular sovereignty, and their victory provoked half the southern delegates to leave the Democratic convention. Unable to choose a candidate after fifty-nine ballots, the Democrats adjourned to a later meeting in Baltimore. When Douglas won the nomination there, the remaining southern Democrats quit the national party and chose their own candidate, Buchanan's vice president, John C. Breckinridge. The issue of slavery had torn apart the last national party. Although many southern rank-and-file Democrats remained loyal to the national party, Douglas could no longer expect to carry the southern states. Meanwhile, a splinter group of die-hard southern Whigs and nativists formed the Constitutional Union party and nominated Tennessee's John Bell.

To match Douglas's strength in his home region, Republicans nominated Lincoln. Although firmly opposed to the expansion of slavery, the candidate shared the racial views of his Illinois neighbors. "There must be a position of superior and inferior," he had declared in the recent senatorial election, "and I . . . am in favor of having the superior position assigned to the white race." Yet Lincoln had repudiated the racial exclusionism of the nativist movement, and he scoffed at the notion that "all men are created equal, except negroes, and foreigners, and catholics." Such ideas endeared Lincoln to the German farmers of the midwest. The Republican candidate also affirmed a commitment to free labor, describing himself as an example of someone who had risen from humble beginnings to national stature. To reinforce the message of economic opportunity, the Republicans adopted a party platform calling for a homestead law to promote free lands for settlers, a tariff to protect manufacturing and workers, and a transcontinental railroad.

The election of 1860 reflected the deepening sectional divisions. Douglas, understanding his chances were slim, nonetheless traveled south as well as north, defining himself as the only national candidate. Lincoln did not campaign in the South; his name did not even appear on most southern ballots. Breckinridge made no appeals in the North; his supporters warned that Lincoln's election would force the South to choose secession. That year, voters well understood the choices, and over 80 percent cast ballots.

In the South, Breckinridge defeated Bell everywhere except three border states; outside the South, Lincoln lost only the border state Missouri to Douglas. To be sure, Lincoln carried less than 40 percent of the popular vote to Douglas's 29.5 percent and Breckinridge's 18 percent. But the electoral score was decisive. Thanks to the dominance of the densely populated industrial states of the North, Lincoln received 180 electoral votes; everyone else's electoral votes totaled 123. "A party founded on a single sentiment . . . of hatred of African slavery," exclaimed a southern newspaper, "is now the controlling power."

Desperation shot through the South. "Nothing short of separation from the Union can save us!" cried one editor. Some were convinced that the Republican victory sounded the end of slavery. "Then every negro . . . will be his own master," warned a Baptist minister; "nay, more than that, will be the equal of every one of you." The

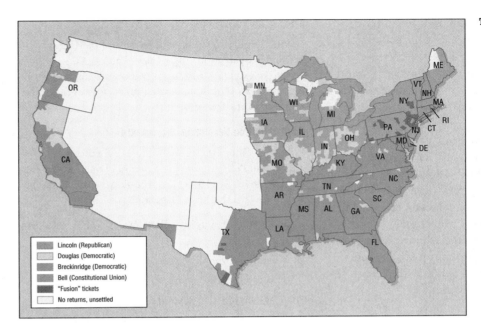

governors of three southern states quickly summoned special conventions to consider secession from the union. One month after the election, South Carolina's convention voted unanimously to secede from the federal government, setting off a hooplah of fireworks, rallies, and parades. Within weeks, the six Deep South states of Mississippi, Florida, Alabama, Georgia, Louisiana, and Texas followed South Carolina out of the union. In February 1861, delegates met in Montgomery, Alabama, to found the Confederate States of America and choose Jefferson Davis to head the new republic.

A Failure to Compromise

Eight Border States remained loyal to the union. Hoping to heal the breach, Kentucky's John Crittenden offered resolutions in Congress to reestablish the Missouri Compromise line all the way to the Pacific and enact a constitutional amendment to preserve slavery wherever it existed. But neither secessionists nor those opposed to extending slavery into the territories would compromise their principles. Lincoln, moreover, refused to allow the rebels to hold the government hostage. Already the seceding state governments had seized federal forts, customs houses, and other federal buildings. "If we surrender," said Lincoln, "it is the end of . . . government."

In his inaugural address of March 4, 1861, the new president reiterated his willingness to protect slavery in the southern states, and he promised to enforce the Fugitive Slave Act. "We must not be enemies," he pleaded. "Though passion may have strained, it must not break our bonds of affection." Through such peaceful gestures, the sixteenth president hoped to heal the nation's wounds. But, as Walt Whitman remarked about Lincoln, "the only thing like passion or infatuation in the man was the passion for the union of these states." Lincoln's commitment to constitutional government was unswerving, and he would go only so far to accommodate the secessionists. "The Union of these states is perpetual," he insisted.

Southern leaders showed no sign of retreat, no desire to reenter the union. As the crisis intensified during the winter of 1860–1861, the country perched on the edge of civil war. Herman Melville's *Moby Dick,* published nearly a decade earlier, had forecast the collision course. "Swerve me?" exclaims Captain Ahab ominously as the whaling ship pursues its own destruction. "Ye cannot swerve me. . . the path of my fixed purpose is laid with iron rails, whereon my soul is grooved to run."

INFOTRAC® COLLEGE EDITION EXERCISES

 For additional reading go to InfoTrac College Edition, your online research library at *http://web1.infotrac-college.com.*

Keyword search: Harriet Tubman

Keyword search: Frederick Douglass

Keyword search: underground railroad

Keyword search: Harriet Beecher Stowe

Keyword search: Franklin Pierce

Subject search: slavery history

Keyword search: Bleeding Kansas

Keyword search: Kansas/Nebraska Act

Subject search: Dred Scott

Subject search: Lincoln-Douglas Debates, reference books

Subject search: United States history, Civil War

ADDITIONAL READING

David S. Reynolds, *Walt Whitman's America: A Cultural Biography* (1995). This exquisite study places the poet and his writings in the context of his times.

The Agricultural Boom

Gavin Wright, *The Political Economy of the Cotton South: Households, Markets, and Wealth in the Nineteenth Century* (1978). A statistical study comparing southern economic development with agricultural patterns in the free states.

Railroads and Territorial Expansion

Robert A. Trennert, Jr., *Alternative to Extinction: Federal Indian Policy and the Beginnings of the Reservation System, 1846–51* (1975). This book describes national policy toward the Plains nations.

Resistance to the Fugitive Slave Act

Albert J. Von Frank, *The Trials of Anthony Burns: Freedom and Slavery in Emerson's Boston* (1998). Depicts the capture and trial of a fugitive slave in 1854.

The Weakening Party System

Michael F. Holt, *The Political Crisis of the 1850s* (1978). A study of two-party politics describing the disintegration of the Democrat-Whig system and the emergence of new political alliances.

Cultural Differences Become Political

Tyler Anbinder, *Nativism and Slavery: The Know Nothings and the Politics of the 1850s* (1992). This careful analysis of party politics explores the emergence of the nativists and their relationship to antislavery issues.

Problems of Political Geography

Eric Foner, *Free Soil, Free Labor, Free Men: The Ideology of the Republican Party before the Civil War* (1970). A lucid study of the ideas that defined the nation's first sectional party.

William E. Gienapp, *The Origins of the Republican Party: 1852–1856* (1987). A detailed state-by-state study analyzing the emergence of Republican parties amid a welter of local and ethnocultural issues.

The Dred Scott Decision

Don E. Fehrenbacher, *The Dred Scott Case: Its Significance in American Law and Politics* (1978). Analyzes the constitutional implications of the landmark Supreme Court decision.

The Politics of Economic Crisis

James L. Huston, *The Panic of 1857 and the Coming of the Civil War* (1987). Describes the economic crisis and its political impact.

Poverty in the Cities

Roy Rosenzweig and Elizabeth Blackmar, *The Park and the People: A History of Central Park* (1992). A fine example of social and cultural history, examining the values that inspired the nation's first urban park.

Lincoln versus Douglas

Douglas L. Wilson, *Honor's Voice: The Transformation of Abraham Lincoln* (1998). Focusing on Lincoln's early career, this insightful study explores the background of a rising politician.

14

War for the Union, 1861–1865

CHRONOLOGY

1861	Abraham Lincoln takes office as sixteenth president
	Confederacy fires on Fort Sumter, South Carolina
	Confederates defeat Union army at First Battle of Bull Run
	U.S. Congress passes first Confiscation Act
1862	Union wins victory at Shiloh, Tennessee
	Gen. George McClellan leads Union army into Virginia
	U.S. Congress passes Legal Tender and Homestead acts
	Santee Sioux attack Minnesota farmers
	Union stops Confederate advance at Antietam, Maryland
1863	Emancipation Proclamation frees slaves behind Confederate lines
	Union wins at Gettysburg; Grant captures Vicksburg
	New York City workers riot against draft
1864	William T. Sherman takes Atlanta and marches to sea
	Lincoln wins reelection over ex-General George McClellan
	Colorado militia massacres Cheyennes at Sand Creek
1865	Lee surrenders at Appomattox Court House
	Actor John Wilkes Booth assassinates Lincoln
	States ratify Thirteenth Amendment

War clouds hovered over the nation's capital as the newly inaugurated President Abraham Lincoln adopted a firm stand against southern secession. One afternoon in March 1861, Ohio's Senator John Sherman introduced Lincoln to his brother, William Tecumseh Sherman, who might be of assistance should a war begin. Indeed, in expectation that war would soon commence, Sherman had resigned as head of the Louisiana Military Academy. "How are they getting along down there?" asked Lincoln. "They are preparing for war," replied the soldier. But apparently Lincoln was not yet interested in acquiring the services of the man who would prove to be an invincible military leader for the Union. "Oh, well," the president responded, "I guess we'll manage to keep house." After they had parted and William Sherman found a civilian job in St. Louis, he summed up his impression of the national predicament: "You have got things in a hell of a fix," he told his politician brother, John, "and you may get them out as best you can."

By then, the United States was already split in two, but whether the secession of seven southern states would lead to a permanent division of the Union remained uncertain. In February 1861, delegates from the seceded states had met in Montgomery, Alabama, formed an independent republic called the Confederate States of America, and elected former Mississippi Senator Jefferson Davis as president. Eight other slave states of the Upper South remained in the Union, but watched carefully as northern and southern leaders attempted to resolve the political crisis.

Hoping to keep the border states in the Union, Lincoln promised to preserve slavery where it existed. But he rejected the legality of secession and he vowed to "hold, occupy, and possess" all federal property within the seceded states. President Davis, for his part, defended the principle of states' rights and insisted that it was legal for a state to vote openly to secede from the Union and to form a new government. On these grounds, he refused to surrender federal property as a violation of his nation's sovereignty.

By April, the eyes of all citizens, North and South, turned toward an island in the middle of Charleston harbor in South Carolina, where the red-brick, federal Fort Sumter lay within range of Confederate artillery. As southern leaders demanded that Lincoln surrender the fort to the Confederacy, the fort's Union defenders informed the president that they lacked provisions to hold out much longer.

"The military excitement here is intense," Senator Sherman wrote from Washington, as Lincoln ordered a relief ship to bring food to Fort Sumter and prudently notified the state governor of his peaceful intentions. Davis countered by instructing Confederate commanders to take immediate control of the fort. When federal officers refused southern demands to surrender, Confederate artillery commenced firing on the morning of April 12. "Civil war is actually upon us," exclaimed Sherman, "and,

"Civil war is actually upon us and, strange to say, it brings a feeling of relief."

strange to say, it brings a feeling of relief: the suspense is over."

Thus the Civil War began as a contest of political rights between the North and the South. The two regions had already been separated by differences of society and economics; their residents held different views of what ought to be the national identity. As the North adopted principles of free wage labor and the South defended unfree agricultural slavery, their political differences became more difficult to compromise. Yet, to most contemporaries, slavery was only indirectly the cause of the war. Northerners and southerners alike saw themselves defending common political principles of citizenship and the rights of free white men. Indeed, even as the end of slavery eventually became one of the North's war goals, many northern unionists opposed the emancipation of blacks and expressed sentiments of white supremacy.

In firing the first shots of the Civil War, southern leaders defined their action as a defense of republican citizenship, including the right to create a government that protected private property in the form of slaves. In their speeches and letters, Confederates saw themselves defending "liberty" against northern "tyranny," and they appealed frequently to the spirit of 1776. "Sooner than submit to Northern slavery," declared a slaveowning South Carolina officer, "I prefer death." In the words of President Davis, the Confederacy fought for "the holy cause of constitutional liberty." Such patriotic rhetoric fired the consciences of Confederate volunteers and homefront supporters through four years of fighting, sacrifice, and the loss of 260,000 Confederate lives.

Northerners, too, fought for the principles of republican citizenship, charging that the South's secession imperiled free elections and majority rule. In his first Civil War message to Congress on July 4, 1861, Lincoln declared that "when ballots have fairly and constitutionally decided, there can be no successful appeal back to bullets." Believing that secession violated the sacred constitutional compact that had created the United States in 1787, the northern president appealed to the traditions of the nation's founders and summoned loyal citizens to save the Union. Northern patriotism prompted volunteer soldiers and civilians to battle through four years of fighting, sacrifice, and the loss of nearly 370,000 Union lives.

The bravery of those who fought and died would become legendary, embodying the power of self-governing peoples to wage wars of ideology. The Civil War became a "total" war—not just a clash of governments and armies, but of entire populations, affecting civilians and noncombatants as much as those who wore uniforms and fired weapons. Intangible factors, such as morale and loyalty, assumed new importance on battlefield and homefront, and the strength of will of government and military leaders on both sides often proved decisive. Total war also brought unexpected social consequences as vast armies crossed civilian terrain. Death seemed to be everywhere.

Although Confederate secessionists had seldom mentioned slavery as a reason for leaving the Union and few northerners had defined the war as an attack on that institution, the crisis forced the issue to center stage. As Union leaders waged total war, slavery seemed to give the South military advantages, and Lincoln decided to attack the institution to weaken the enemy. The result was a redefinition of the purposes of the war. By the time the war ended in 1865, the Union fought not only to restore the national government but also to emancipate the slaves. Thereafter, U.S. citizens would confront a different type of republi-can government—no longer merely for white men, but for black men too. The Civil War would forever change the national identity.

Mobilizing for Victory

As the war began, each side had cause for optimism. With vastly larger numbers and potential military power, Union leaders expected a quick victory. Even if the Union could not win a decisive battle, northern strategists hoped to use the North's economic advantages to crush southern opposition. Adopting the so-called Anaconda plan, named for the deadly snake that strangled its victims, Union leaders aimed to choke southern trade by establishing coastal blockades, controlling the Mississippi river, and capturing the Confederate capital at Richmond. By causing economic hardships, the Union hoped to persuade southern leaders to abandon the fight. But the Anaconda plan required time to succeed, and time played into southern plans. To achieve its objectives, the Confederacy merely had to survive. Rather than invading enemy territory, the Confederates would adopt what President Davis called an "offensive defensive" strategy: beat back Union attacks and undermine the North's will to fight. Confederate optimism also expressed faith in the power of cotton. Believing that the European economy would stagnate without cotton exports, southerners expected England and France to assist the Confederacy. Within a year, it was clear that both sides had exaggerated their strengths; yet even in 1862 both believed that victory might be just around the corner.

Arousing the Citizenry

"War!" cried the poet Walt Whitman in 1861. "An armed race is advancing! the welcome for battle, no turning away." With the shots of Fort Sumter echoing in the land, Lincoln summoned 75,000

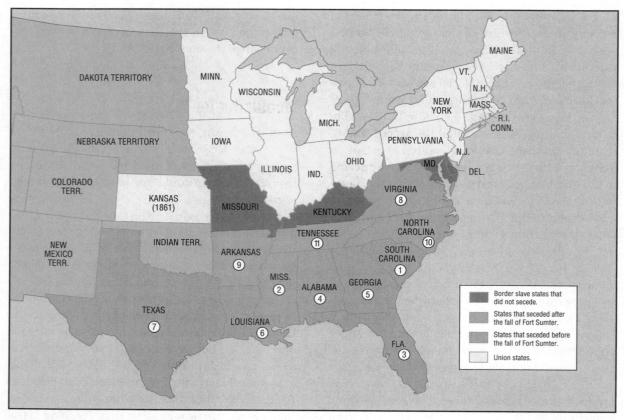

The Progress of Secession. Circled numbers indicate order of secession.

volunteers for 90-day duty, igniting patriotic fervor throughout the North. Enthusiastic communities soon organized local and state military units and proudly sent their sons to defend the Stars and Stripes. But northern mobilization ironically strengthened the Confederacy. Lincoln's call to arms prompted four more states—Virginia, Arkansas, Tennessee, and North Carolina—to secede from the Union. "Lincoln may bring his 75,000 troops against us," declared Confederate Vice President Alexander Stephens. "We fight for our homes. . . . We can call out a million . . . if need be, and when they are cut down we can call another, and still another, until the last man of the

South finds a bloody grave." Southern women vowed that "none but the brave deserve the fair," and sent women's undergarments as a rebuke to men who were slow to enlist.

The strength of southern defiance surprised Lincoln, and the president soon called for more volunteers for three years of military service. The northern states rushed to fill their quotas. In 1861, volunteering became a male rite of passage on both sides; 18-year-olds were the largest age group during the first year of war. African Americans were still unwanted by either army.

With Virginia out of the Union, the Confederacy moved its capital from Montgomery to Richmond, barely 100 miles from Washington and close to Maryland, a "border" slave state, whose loyalty remained uncertain. When Massachusetts volunteers passed through Baltimore in April 1861, an anti-Union mob attacked the soldiers with rocks and rifle fire, provoking an armed response that left a dozen dead. Lincoln declared martial law, suspending the right of habeas corpus (which protected citizens from arbitrary arrest), and ordered the seizure of pro-secession leaders. Chief Justice Roger Taney ruled that the president was violating basic civil rights, but Lincoln insisted that the crisis demanded special executive powers and ignored a Court order to lift martial law. Military power kept Maryland in the Union. Lincoln also used troops to ensure loyalty of other border states, such as Kentucky and Missouri, though guerrilla warfare in those states indicated a deep division of opinion. Meanwhile, the Washington government encouraged the pro-Union mountainous portion of Virginia to become the separate state of West Virginia in 1863.

Economic and Diplomatic Issues

As the armies prepared for conflict, the Union held obvious material advantages. The North's population greatly exceeded the Confederacy's (22 million northerners to the South's 9 million whites, 4 million slaves, and 250,000 free blacks), and the North had more than four times as many white men of military age (18 to 45). Two-thirds of the nation's railroad lines lay in the North. The Union's industrial capacity showed even greater strength: 97 percent of the total firearms production, 96 percent of locomotives, 94 percent of iron, 94 percent of clothing, 90 percent of shoes. Even agricultural production was much greater in the North, except for cotton. This economic superiority inspired the Anaconda plan, the Union's primary military strategy to surround the southern states and strangle the Confederacy into

submission. Yet southerners fought for their home territory. They believed that by prolonging the conflict, they could compel the North to abandon the fight.

Southern hopes also depended on economic power. Believing that cotton was "King," the Confederacy deliberately withheld exports of cotton to Britain and France to accentuate European dependence on southern agriculture and to persuade those nations to break the northern blockade of southern ports. Yet large surpluses from previous years enabled European textile manufacturers to remain in business—indeed, to earn greater profits than expected from the southern embargo and the consequent rise in cotton prices. Britain also had other sources for cotton in Egypt and India. Moreover, Britain remained dependent on U.S. grain production; 40 percent of Britain's wheat and flour came from northern farms.

Instead of choosing sides, Britain and France jointly declared neutrality, treating the Confederacy as an equal belligerent without granting diplomatic recognition or providing material aid. The ambiguous policy nearly led to hostilities in the fall of 1861, when a U.S. naval vessel intercepted two Confederate agents bound for Europe aboard the British ship *Trent*. Prudent apologies from the Lincoln administration avoided conflict, but the British continued to outfit southern warships, which preyed on northern shipping.

"The Red Business" Begins, 1861–1862

"Forward to Richmond," cried Horace Greeley's New York *Tribune* in the summer of 1861, as the Confederate congress prepared to meet in the southern capital. The first Union army moved into action in July amid so much optimism that civilians went out with picnic lunches to watch the battle. At Manassas Junction (also known as

Bull Run) in northern Virginia, 35,000 hastily trained Union soldiers charged 22,000 Confederates. So began what Whitman called "the red business." After nearly gaining a victory, Union forces collapsed under a flank attack, causing a terrified stampede all the way back to Washington. Union casualties (the killed, wounded, and missing) numbered nearly 2,900, and Confederate losses exceeded 1,900. "Times were too wild with excitement to stay in bed," exulted Mary Chesnut in Charleston, South Carolina. Meanwhile, in the North, "All is quiet and sad, and the mourners go about the streets," wrote nurse Clara Barton from Washington. A stunned Congress immediately summoned another half-million three-year recruits. "We now see the magnitude of the contest," admitted the chastened Senator John Sherman.

As volunteers joined Union regiments, Lincoln named General George McClellan to command the Army of the Potomac in an invasion of Virginia. A disciplined West Point graduate, McClellan transformed the raw recruits into soldiers by endless marching and drilling. But long preparations allowed the rebellion to continue, and Lincoln pleaded for action. Not until April 1862, nearly a year after the war began, did the 120,000 man Union army land on the Virginia peninsula, a logistical feat that required 400 ships and three weeks. Slowly McClellan inched toward Richmond. But the Union general exaggerated the size of the enemy and decided to wait for reinforcements.

Union soldiers loved McClellan for his professionalism and his caution. In the face of new rifled weapons, which fired expanding minié bullets with greater accuracy and speed than older weapons, frontal assaults would prove exceptionally deadly. But as McClellan hesitated, a Confederate army under Thomas "Stonewall" Jackson moved north through Virginia's Shenandoah valley, as if to cross the Potomac to attack Washington. Lincoln ordered

---

Civilians went out with picnic lunches to watch the battle.

---

reserve troops to meet Jackson, but the Confederates won tactical victories and eluded capture. Soon after, southern troops under Virginia's Robert E. Lee took the initiative, driving McClellan's Union forces into retreat in the Seven Days' Battles. Lincoln ordered McClellan to halt the campaign. A year's planning had brought 16,000 Union casualties, 20,000 Confederate.

While McClellan's army had prepared to invade Virginia, another Union army under General Ulysses S. Grant was fighting for control of the Mississippi valley. Victories in Tennessee early in 1862 forced the Confederates to retreat, but Union soldiers pursued them, finally meeting the Confederates at Shiloh, Tennessee, where two days of fighting in April left a combined total of 23,000 casualties. After the rebels withdrew, Grant marched west toward Memphis, gaining control of the great river from that city northward. Meanwhile, U.S. naval forces had entered the Mississippi from the south, seizing New Orleans in April 1862. But the middle stretch of the river remained in southern hands. Hoping to divide the Confederacy along the river, Union armies struggled to take the southern fortress at Vicksburg, Mississippi. Farther west, a Colorado militia defeated rebel troops in New Mexico.

Late in the summer of 1862, military action resumed in northern Virginia. In August, Confederate armies under Lee and Stonewall Jackson moved north to the second battle of Bull Run (Second Manassas), where they defeated Union forces. Another 25,000 men fell. Emboldened by victory, Lee carried the war into Union territory, advancing into Maryland in September 1862. A southern

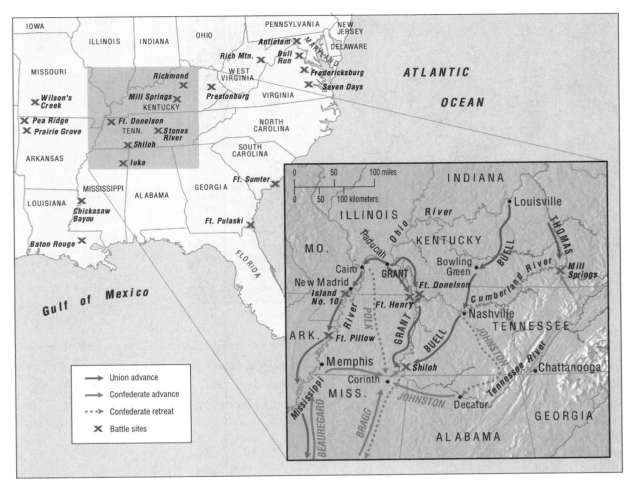

Civil War in the East and West

victory there might bring that border state into the Confederacy, weaken the northern will, or win British recognition of the southern nation. The ensuing battle at Antietam Creek became a bloodbath, claiming 23,000 casualties on the single deadliest day of the war, leaving bodies "thick as autumn leaves." McClellan's Union army came close to victory, but Lee managed to withdraw his troops to Virginia. Lee's failure to advance persuaded Britain and France to remain neutral.

Union armies still lacked a decisive victory. Two months later, at Fredricksburg, Virginia, they sustained another defeat. Union soldiers, including New York City's Irish regiment, were bled white by a series of uphill charges against entrenched infantry. "It will be a sad, sad Christmas by many an Irish hearthstone," wrote a Union officer. "It is well that war is so terrible," observed the victorious Lee, otherwise "we should grow too fond of it."

Scenes of battlefield carnage, such as this at the Battle of Bull Run, brought the war shockingly close to home.

A People's War

These early battles shocked combatants and civilians on both sides. "I shall never forget how awfully I felt on seeing for the first time a man killed in battle," reported one soldier. "I stared at his body, perfectly horrified! Only a few seconds ago that man was alive and well, and now he was lying on the ground, done for, forever!" That primal horror never stopped, recurred on every battlefield, and expressed an omnipresent sense of fear about the precariousness of survival. For some, facing battle became impossible. About 200,000 Union soldiers deserted the army (80,000 were caught) and 104,000 left Confederate ranks (21,000 were returned). Those who stayed often felt the same impulse to run, though they remained to fight. Union soldiers spoke often of the obligations of "duty"; Confederates mentioned the importance of "honor." "I never could rid myself of a sneaking desire to turn and run for all I was worth," admitted a sergeant from Connecticut, "but I wouldn't have run for a good deal more than

> **"Only a few seconds ago that man was alive and well, and now he was lying on the ground, done for, forever!"**

I was worth." "Tell my father," said a mortally wounded North Carolina officer, "I died with my face to the enemy."

Field hospitals could do little to relieve the suffering. The standard medical treatment for wounded limbs was amputation, usually performed without anaesthetics. "The screams and groans of the poor fellows undergoing amputation are sometimes dreadful," said one soldier, "and then the sight of arms and legs surrounding these places, as they are thrown into great piles, is something one . . . can never forget." Because ambulance service was primitive, most casualties bled to death where they fell. Behind the lines, hospitals became death houses. Upon arriving at a Union hospital in Washington in 1862, the novelist Louisa May Alcott was struck first by the odor of rotten flesh. Lacking understanding of antiseptic treatment, medical aides inadvertently carried infection from patient to patient; often, second amputations had to be performed. Contagious diseases proliferated: dysentery, typhoid, malaria, even epidemics of mumps and measles ravaged the hospitals. Twice as many soldiers died of disease as from battle injuries. By 1865, the total number of dead was 620,000; the number of wounded reached a million, or 3.4 percent of the entire U.S. population.

Another casualty of war was the northern belief that victory depended merely on beating the rebel army. At the beginning, Lincoln called the war "a people's contest" that would determine "whether a constitutional republic . . . can, or cannot maintain its territorial integrity, against its own domestic foes." By emphasizing limited political objectives and affirming his willingness to protect slavery where it already existed, Lincoln hoped to coax the seceded states back into the Union. Ultimately, he believed, the decision depended on the southern citizenry, which accepted Confederate leadership, but might be persuaded to reject it.

The tragedy of warfare made a political compromise less likely. Increasingly, northern leaders saw the Confederacy not as a misguided political entity but as the enemy. "I gave up all idea of saving the Union except by complete conquest," Grant reported after the battle of Shiloh. As early as August 1861 Congress passed the first Confiscation act, which permitted the seizure of all property, including slaves, that could aid the military rebellion. This expedient measure allowed Union armies to use freed slaves in limited ways (as cooks, laborers, and laundry workers) but prudently avoided a direct attack on slavery per se.

During the first years of the war, Union armies did not forage widely in southern territory for food. Grant in the west and McClellan in the east worried about protecting their lines of supply. By the end of 1862, however, Grant had resolved "to consume everything that could be used to support or supply armies." Thereafter, wherever possible, Union soldiers would live off the land. In calculating the supplies needed by his troops, Grant began to study local maps together with 1860 census data to determine the economic resources of particular southern counties. This linking of civilian property and military policy, the assumption that southern citizens were responsible for their government's actions, reflected the shift to total war.

The War for Freedom

Although Lincoln hesitated to attack slavery, hoping that moderate policies would end the rebellion, Confederate stubbornness and military success encouraged the North to take stronger measures against a valuable southern resource. In small steps, the North extended its antislavery policies, restricting slavery in federal territories and allowing freed slaves and free blacks to serve in Union armies. Black military service, in turn, reinforced attacks on slavery as an institution. Even before the war was over, the northern Congress approved a Thirteenth Amendment to the Constitution and sent its antislavery provisions to the states for ratification. Thus the war for the Union became a war for freedom, redefining the conflict's political and moral issues and ultimately changing the definition of republican citizenship.

These developments did not necessarily alter public attitudes about racial differences. African Americans and Native Americans, to name the most prominent wartime examples, still confronted prejudice, discrimination, and violence in the North, which belied the promises of freedom. Yet the war irrevocably altered the position of black Americans, the first non-white racial group to become eligible for U.S. citizenship. This new northern version of republicanism would ultimately determine the national identity.

The Politics of Emancipation

Despite Lincoln's personal rejection of slavery, the president faced political obstacles to authorizing emancipation, especially the importance of keeping the border slave states—Delaware, Kentucky, Maryland, and Missouri—loyal to the Union. When General John C. Frémont, the Republican candidate for president in 1856, ordered the liberation of slaves owned by rebels in Missouri in 1861, Lincoln quickly overruled the order. Yet more radical Republicans in Congress felt fewer restraints. The first Confiscation Act, in 1861, not only permitted seizure of slaves working for the Confederacy but also prohibited slavery in the western territories and abolished slavery in Washington, D.C. The next year, Congress voted to prohibit the return of fugitive slaves to their former masters.

Meanwhile, abolitionists continued to press the president to take a bolder stand—on grounds of military advantage, if not political principle. "My paramount object . . . is to save the Union," Lincoln responded in 1862. "If I could save the Union without freeing *any* slave I would do it; and if I could save it by freeing *all* the slaves I would do it; and if I could save it by freeing some and leaving others alone I would also do that." Nevertheless, the president did persuade Congress to authorize government compensation to states that voluntarily abolished slavery, and he pleaded with members of congress from the border states to support a program of gradual emancipation. To ease the objections of whites to living among free blacks, Lincoln even proposed the colonization of African Americans to Haiti or Panama, though black leaders angrily rejected the idea.

"If I could save the Union without freeing *any* slave I would do it; and if I could save it by freeing *all* the slaves I would do it; and if I could save it by freeing some and leaving others alone I would also do that."

It was African Americans themselves—slaves, ex-slaves, and free blacks—who influenced Lincoln and the North to change their policies. Whenever Union armies approached slave regions, some slaves felt emboldened to seek refuge and freedom behind Union lines. Northern leaders called these fugitives "contraband of war" and initially limited their use in the war effort. But as both armies demanded the full resources of civilian society, African Americans assumed greater importance in tipping the scales of war. Rather than permitting southern slaves to contribute to the rebellion, northern leaders began to use blacks to help the Union.

By 1862, Lincoln decided to announce a formal change of policy. Waiting until after the victory at Antietam in September 1862 (lest he appear too desperate), Lincoln issued a presidential proclamation, proposing to make all slaves in the rebellious states "forever free," unless those states returned to the Union by January 1, 1863. The president said nothing about the status of slaves in the loyal border states. Even that tentative step, according to a white eyewitness, brought "joy and thanksgiving" among northern African Americans. But many northern whites opposed emancipation, and Lincoln's critics advised "every white laboring man" to vote for Democrats. This anti-abolition sentiment in the North contributed to Democratic victories in the 1862 congressional elections.

Racist attitudes obviously pervaded the southern cause as well. In the words of Vice President Alexander Stephens, the Confederacy was dedicated to the proposition "that the negro is not equal to the white man; that slavery . . . is his natural and normal condition." Southern leaders made no effort to respond to Lincoln's preliminary emancipation offer. On New Year's Day 1863, therefore, the president's Emancipation Proclamation went into effect. "All night they tooted and tramped, fired crackers, sung 'Glory Hallelujah,'" reported Louisa May Alcott about Washington's black population. (In contrast, an indignant Jefferson Davis called the order the "most execrable measure recorded in the history of guilty man.") Yet Lincoln freed only those slaves in areas of rebellion—not in the border states, nor even in southern territory already held by Union troops. In other words, the Emancipation Proclamation did *not* free slaves in any area where the government could implement the policy. Keenly aware of the discrepancy, Republican radicals would continue to press for passage of a constitutional amendment to outlaw slavery throughout the nation.

Blacks Enter the Ranks

When the war began, many northern African Americans volunteered to fight, only to be turned away because it was a "white man's war." As one Union soldier explained, "The Southern people are rebels . . . but they are white, and God never intended a nigger to put white people down." Questioning the courage of black men, the War Department initially employed them as civilian workers, but not as fighters. Some African Americans did serve in the navy, but usually as noncombatants. The slaughter of war soon altered northern sentiments, if only for reasons of self-interest. "When this war is over and we have summed up the entire loss of life," wrote the governor of Iowa in 1862, "I shall not have any regrets if it is found that a part of the dead are niggers." Or as one northern Irish song put it, "I'll let Sambo be murdered instead of myself/on any day of the year."

By 1862, even before emancipation, Congress repealed a 1792 law that limited military service to white men and authorized the enlistment of black troops. During the fall of 1862, Lincoln permitted the formation of a regiment of freed slaves to serve under white officers on the Sea Islands off the South Carolina coast. After Lincoln issued the Emancipation Proclamation, the War Department began to raise regiments of black volunteers in the northern states. In 1864, Congress offered freedom to African American soldiers from the border states (which were not covered by the Emancipation Proclamation), and the next year extended that right to their families. By the war's end, about 15 percent of the entire northern black population served in Union armies. White officers who volunteered to lead these troops, many of whom came from principled abolitionist families, faced considerable ridicule. Most famous of the black regiments was the 54th Massachusetts. Northern states also hired agents to recruit freed slaves in the South, who served instead of local white volunteers.

Black soldiers faced special problems in the military. Of the 180,000 African Americans who joined the northern armies, 37,000 died, mostly from disease rather than bullets, a deathrate much higher than that of white soldiers. Military leaders often assigned blacks to manual labor and other unpleasant duties. Black recruits also received lower pay than white troops. Seven times the 54th Massachusetts protested that unequal distinction by refusing to accept any pay, eventually persuading Congress to change the policy, but only for blacks who had been free at the war's outset. African American complaints about discrimination in the ranks often brought harsh punishments, including charges of mutiny, for which blacks received physical discipline, imprisonment, even execution. Black volunteers believed nonetheless that they were fighting for the freedom of their people. "Once let the black man get upon his person the brass letters, U.S., let him get

On April 12, 1864, black soldiers who had already surrendered were wiped out by Confederates at Fort Pillow, Tennessee. General Nathan Bedford Forrest, who ordered the massacre, later became the head of the Ku Klux Klan. After the incident, "Remember Fort Pillow!" became a rallying cry for black troops.

an eagle on his button, and a musket on his shoulder," declared ex-slave Frederick Douglass, "and there is no power on earth which can deny that he has earned the right to citizenship." Indeed, African American military service transformed the nature of the war.

Given the chance to fight, black soldiers quickly proved their valor. In 1863, for example, the 54th Massachusetts advanced on Fort Wagner, South Carolina, in the face of withering fire—a military disaster that belied the myth of black cowardice. "I have no tears to shed over their graves," wrote the abolitionist Angelina Grimké Weld, "because I see that their heroism is working a great change in public opinion, forcing all men to see the sin and shame of enslaving such men." By the end of the war, African Americans constituted about 12 percent of the Union armies and a quarter of the Navy, and they earned innumerable citations for bravery.

The use of black troops brought condemnation from the Confederacy, and in 1863 the south-

ern Congress authorized the execution of white Union officers who were captured while leading black troops. African American prisoners of war faced the death penalty for insurrection or a return to slavery. Lincoln responded by threatening to execute a Confederate prisoner for every Union prisoner killed, white or black, and to sentence a southern prisoner to hard labor for every black prisoner returned to slavery. Forced to moderate its official policy, the Confederacy still winked at atrocities committed against African Americans. In 1864, at Fort Pillow, Tennessee, to name the most notorious example, Confederate General Nathan Bedford Forrest permitted the killing of nearly 300 black Union soldiers who had already surrendered.

Nor did the courage shown by northern blacks persuade the Confederacy to enlist African Americans in their fight, at least until the war—and slavery—was virtually lost. Fearing a slave insurrection, southern leaders resisted changes in domestic life, relying on slaves to maintain the civilian economy. In 1864 the Confederate Congress agreed to accept blacks for noncombat assignments as teamsters, cooks, nurses, and laborers. But, despite severe manpower shortages, proposals to arm slaves with incentives of fighting for freedom drew hostile responses. "If slaves will make good soldiers," admitted one Georgia politician, "our whole theory of slavery is wrong." Not until the last month of the war did a desperate government offer emancipation in exchange for military service. Watching some "Confederate darkeys" on drill parade, a Virginia officer concluded, "this is but the beginning of the end."

War on Native Grounds

Both the U.S. government and the Confederacy competed for the support of Native Americans who had been expelled from their eastern lands during the 1820s and 1830s (see Chapters 8 and 9). Ironically, many Cherokee, Creek, Chickasaw, and Choctaw people owned African American slaves. They also felt an abiding hostility to the Washington government for forcing their removal from their homes. "Our geographical position, our social and domestic institutions, our feelings and sympathies, all attach us to our southern friends," declared the Chickasaw nation. But although Native leaders signed formal treaties with the Confederacy in 1861, significant numbers opposed those alliances and migrated elsewhere to preserve their neutrality.

Pro-Confederate Cherokees consulted oracle stones, engaged in war dances, and went into battle against Union forces in Missouri and Arkansas in 1861. Later, these Cherokees attacked the neutrals' encampments and drove them from the reservation. Fleeing to Kansas, Cherokee and Creek refugees endured extreme hardship without food, clothing, or shelter, and many joined the

Trader Myrick, who stated of the Sioux, "let them eat grass or their own dung," was found dead two weeks later with prairie grass stuffed in his mouth.

Union armies against their Cherokee cousins. Despite such demonstrations of loyalty to the Union, the federal government treated all the southern groups as rebels. Forcing them to enter new treaties with the United States in 1865, the government ended slavery within the Native groups, granted tribal citizenship to former slaves, and compelled Native Americans to surrender about half their reservation land. During the four years of war, the western Cherokees lost more than a quarter of their population, dwindling to 15,000.

Northern tribes fared no better. During the 1850s, the federal government had forced the Santee Sioux of Minnesota to cede 24 million acres in exchange for annuities, reservation lands, and promises to establish mills, schools, and farms that would, in the words of the local Sioux agent, "make white men of them." But the annuity system was riddled with fraud, and crop failures aggravated the shortages caused by the war. By 1862, the Sioux faced mass starvation. Some broke into government warehouses and stole food; others pleaded for assistance. "If they are hungry," replied a trader named Myrick, "let them eat grass or their own dung." Two weeks later, the Sioux attacked local farmers; Myrick's body was found with prairie grass stuffed in his mouth.

The Sioux uprising terrified white Minnesotans, and uninformed Washington officials feared the influence of Confederate instigators. "Attend to the Indians," Lincoln telegraphed to Union generals, "necessity knows no law." Military leaders responded with promises to treat the Sioux "as maniacs or wild beasts." After skirmishing in the Minnesota woods, some Sioux fled to the Dakotas; most surrendered to face Union justice. In ten days' work, a military tribunal heard 392 cases and sentenced 303 to death. Lincoln commuted most sentences, except for cases of murder and rape. On the day after Christmas 1862, the government hanged thirty-eight Santee Sioux in the largest public execution in U.S. history. Soon afterward, Minnesotans grabbed Sioux lands and subsequently persuaded Congress to order removal of the peaceful Winnebagos to unfertile parts of the Dakotas. "Although we are now engaged in a great war between one another," said Lincoln with no trace of irony, "we are not as a race so much disposed to fight and kill one another as our red brethren."

Despite the government's preoccupation with the war, Washington continued to press the Plains Cheyenne and Arapahoe to abandon buffalo hunting for farming. As with the Sioux, shortages of food during the 1860s provoked a crisis of survival at the Sand Creek camp in the Colorado territory, and Cheyenne hunters began to raid local farms in 1864. When a rancher accused some Cheyennes of stealing livestock, the governor ordered a military attack on the unprotected village. When negotiations failed, a Colorado cavalry unit entered the Sand Creek camp. Firing cannons and rifles among sleeping people, the militia then attacked survivors with knives: castrating men, ripping open pregnant women, slaughtering children in the snow. Although a congressional committee later condemned the massacre, the federal government merely offered the survivors new treaties, exchanging claims in Colorado for promised reservations in Texas and Oklahoma. The Senate later changed the documents unilaterally to eliminate those promises. "I live in hopes," commented a Cheyenne leader; "but . . . it is hard for me to believe white men any more."

The War on the Home Front

As military casualties climbed to the hundreds of thousands, the sense of personal suffering and sacrifice moved from the battlefields to the homefronts on both sides. The war now involved whole societies, affecting civilian employment, local politics, and individual psychology. This private participation underscored the war's ideological passion; virtually no one could avoid taking sides. Yet the demand for civilian sacrifice affected groups unevenly, often accentuating social and economic divisions that had existed before the war. For the most part, civilian morale on both sides remained high, and the soldiers, Union and Confederate, believed that they were fighting for their families at home.

Facing the Death Toll

"News of the War!" exclaimed *Harper's Weekly* in 1862. "We all live on it. Few of us but would prefer our newspaper in these times to our breakfast." Total war involved not only mobilization of troops and industry but also of people's minds and beliefs. With homes everywhere containing the "vacant chair" of a son, father, or husband, civilians devoured newspapers for casualty lists, scoured correspondence from the campgrounds as soldiers reported gossip about their neighbors, and read avidly the descriptions of battle. "The only news I know," wrote the young Massachusetts poet Emily Dickinson,

> Is Bulletins all Day
> From Immortality

Newspaper circulation skyrocketed into the tens, even hundreds, of thousands for single issues, enabling enterprising publishers to boast about the advantages of this remarkable "advertising medium."

Winslow Homer drew this picture of a sharpshooter on picket duty.

Besides published information, civilians craved visual evidence of the war. Newspapers and magazines dispatched painters, such as the young Winslow Homer, to depict battle scenes and to sketch soldiers at rest. Mathew Brady's photographs of dead soldiers, exhibited in New York galleries, drew large crowds. "Minute as are the features of the dead," advised one newspaper, "you can, by bringing a magnifying glass to bear on them, identify not merely their general outline but actual expression." There was no romanticism about such details. A similar realism emerged in Civil War cemetery architecture. Although prewar "rural" cemeteries, such as Cambridge, Massachusetts's Mount Auburn, Chicago's Rose Hill, and Cincinnati's Spring Grove, used landscaping and statuary to evoke the naturalness of death, battlefield cemeteries, such as Gettysburg, appeared stark and impersonal, expressing an unvarnished egalitarianism. And Lincoln's famous eulogy for the dead at Gettysburg in November 1863 sought no higher meaning than the secular ends of the war. "We cannot hallow this ground," he said; the dead had already done that. Lincoln asked only that the living give the same devotion "to that cause" for which so many brave soldiers had died.

Citizens on both sides, however, believed fervently in the religious purposes of the war. Julia Ward Howe's "The Battle Hymn of the Republic," written in 1862, linked the northern cause to divine retribution, serving to rationalize total war. (Soldiers preferred less militant, sentimental songs, such as "Tenting Tonight" and "Just Before the Battle, Mother.") In 1864 alone, evangelicals distributed 6 million Christian books (such as *Come to Jesus*) as well as 1 million hymnals, 1 million Bibles, and 11 million tracts. Southern women also defined the war as a sacred cause, seeing the Confederacy as God's chosen nation and assuring soldiers that "piety will not make you effeminate or cowardly." Religious revivals spread through the Confederate ranks during seasons of military defeat, but Union armies experienced no major "awakenings." In his second inaugural address, Lincoln acknowledged the irony that both enemies "read the same Bible and pray to the same God, and each invokes His aid against the other." The president made the November harvest thanksgiving a national holiday in 1864, and that year the Treasury Department ordered all U.S. currency to bear the words "In God We Trust." Such evangelical imperatives inspired volunteers, civilian no less than soldiers.

Woman and the War

White women on both sides lamented their exclusion from the male adventure. "I never before wished I was a man," confessed a Tennessee woman. "Now I feel so keenly my weakness and dependence." Some 400 women managed to disguise themselves as men to enlist in the military; most were soon discovered and dismissed, though a few not before they were killed in action. More typically, women used their traditional skills to support the war, forming sewing and knitting societies to replenish supplies. Although northern textile manufacturers met the Union army's requirements, shortages of cloth in the Confederacy obliged southern women to make a virtue of wearing homespun outfits. "Our needles are now our weapons," explained one group.

Southern women often assumed the responsibilities of their absent husbands—taking over field work, running shops, and supervising slaves. Such role shifts brought identity problems for some; one wife and mother who assumed responsibility for 11 slaves admitted "I am so sick of trying to do a man's business when I am nothing but a poor contemptible piece of multiplying flesh." Others gladly took work in previously male occu-

Four hundred women disguised themselves as men to enlist in the military; most were soon discovered, a few not before they were killed in action.

pations, as teachers or as government clerks, inscribing tens of thousands of signatures on Confederate treasury bills. "No one said I was unladylike," remarked a volunteer nurse, "to climb into cattle cars . . . to feed those who cannot feed themselves." Yet most military nurses in the South were African American women and men, not white women.

Some northern women also found opportunities working for the philanthropic United States Sanitary Commission, which collected and distributed food, clothing, and medical supplies to the Union armies. By 1863, "Sanitary Fairs" appeared in northern cities, offering civilians evening entertainment while raising funds for the war. When the War Department appointed the humanitarian reformer Dorothea Dix to organize military hospitals and recruit female nurses in 1861, volunteers flocked to Washington. Dix supervised the selection and assignment of women nurses, taking pains to remind them to uphold their morality.

For many young women, the war provided escape from traditional female roles: "So sorry for the necessity," as the Massachusetts-born Clara Barton put it, "so glad for the opportunity." In 1863, for example, Cornelia Hancock, a 23-year old New Jersey Quaker volunteered to tend the wounded and soon confronted the terrible suffering and death. But she also reported discovering an inner resiliency and a feeling that "my past life was a myth." To her worried parents, she wrote,

"I feel like a new person. . . . I feel so erect." Although both Union and Confederate volunteers remained subordinate to male doctors and bureaucrats, the war released them from domestic roles and provided public tasks to fulfill. "We are changed by all this contact with terror," explained a northern nurse. Many Union nurses, such as Barton and Hancock, remained active reformers in the postwar years.

CONFLICTS IN THE CONFEDERACY

The Confederacy's martial spirit on the home front could not conceal cracks in the South's political consensus. Although the Confederate constitution described the southern government as a group of "sovereign and independent states," wartime pressure often forced the Richmond government to adopt policies that strengthened the central government, regardless of states' rights. Manpower shortages prompted the Confederacy to introduce military conscription in 1862, one year before the Union, but the laws permitted exemptions for slave overseers (requiring one white man for every twenty slaves) and allowed men who were drafted to hire substitutes. The cost of such replacements soon exceeded the reach of most people and brought complaints from poorer whites. Such inequities and favoritism toward slaveowners encouraged draft evasion and military desertions. Southern governors also resisted the use of state militia outside their state boundaries.

Although pre-war southern politicians had opposed the national government's support of economic development, such as tariffs and internal improvements, mobilization led the Confederacy to intervene directly in economic affairs. To improve transportation, the southern government gave subsidies for railroad construction and regulated the use of railroad equipment. Protective tariffs, long hated in the South and prohibited in the Confederate constitution, nonetheless served during wartime as a source of revenue. The Confederate government also supervised military production, even financing government-owned factories to manufacture gunpowder and munitions. To feed the Confederate army, the government "taxed" food production by seizing crops and claimed other goods-in-kind. Meanwhile, several states mandated limits in cotton acreage to encourage food production. Even so, wartime scarcity encouraged a huge inflation of food prices, and the resulting complaints from the home-front often triggered military desertions as soldiers worried about their families. In 1863, bread riots erupted in several southern cities as women stole loaves for their families. Jefferson Davis personally intervened in the Richmond riot, then persuaded newspapers and telegraph operators to censor the story lest it weaken southern morale.

The Northern Economy

The strength of the northern economy, by contrast, enabled the Union to mobilize industry and agriculture through capitalist incentives rather than government coercion. Such policies fit the Republican party agenda, which favored tariffs, national banking, internal improvements, and western settlement. With southern Democrats out of Congress, the Republican majority enacted laws that both supported the war and stimulated economic growth. The Tariff of 1861 raised duties on imports, not just for revenue purposes but also to protect northern industry. In 1862, Congress passed the Morrill Land Grant Act, giving the states public lands to support agricultural education and the "mechanical arts." The Homestead Act of 1862 offered free land to farmers who developed 160 acres and reduced the five-year residency requirements for war veterans. Envisioning a transcontinental railroad, Congress offered immense acreage to railroad companies to stimulate construction, though most development awaited the postwar years.

Other wartime financial legislation had tremendous social implications. To help finance the war, the Legal Tender Act of 1862 authorized the Treasury to issue paper currency (known as "Greenbacks"), which circulated to pay all taxes and debts except interest on government bonds. While facilitating public and private transactions, the currency steadily depreciated in value, nearly doubling the cost of living by 1865. Yet wealthy bondholders, whose interest payments came in hard specie, enjoyed great prosperity. To raise additional revenue, Congress also enacted the first federal income tax (3 percent for those earning over $800) as well as excise taxes, which affected all consumers, on almost every manufactured commodity.

Wartime demands proved a stimulus for most northern manufacturing. Although the absence of southern cotton weakened the textile industry, government purchases of uniforms, shoes, and munitions boosted production. In response to military needs, manufacturers created standard sizes for ready-to-wear clothing, which continued to be used after the war. Civilian workers also adopted what became "uniform" dress in business offices: jacket, pants, white linen shirt, and necktie. Shoes, manufactured on newly invented sewing machines, were made to fit either foot. Union officers also appreciated the advantages and prestige of personal timepieces, boosting the pocket watch industry. After battles, the watches became booty for thieves; as one looter explained, "where he is gone . . . time is nothing."

The war affected every aspect of economic development. Unable to ship their corn down the blockaded Mississippi River, farmers fed the corn to pigs and then brought the pigs to market. As the Union army consumed over half a billion pounds of packed meat during the war, Chicago stockyards emerged as the largest food processors in the nation. Meanwhile, the shortage of farm workers encouraged the mechanization of northern agriculture, and sales of farm implements soared. Coal, iron, and steel production also responded to enormous military demands.

Aggravating Social Tensions

Northern business prosperity contrasted with the condition of industrial workers, especially in the cities. As inflation sharply raised the price of goods (over 50 percent between 1862 and 1864), workers' wages lagged behind and their standard of living fell. Children, drawn into the labor force by the departure of soldiers, joined women at the bottom of the economic ladder. Women umbrella workers, for example, worked 16-hour shifts for wages of about $10 per day in today's currency. Seamstresses worked 14-hour days for the equivalent of $12.75 per week in today's money. Meanwhile, prison records showed a rise in the proportion of women and children charged with crimes relating to poverty; many were struggling relatives of absent soldiers.

Although labor unions greeted the war with patriotic enthusiasm, economic hardships ignited numerous labor disputes and strikes. Complicating these concerns was the northern Conscription Act of 1863, enacted over Democratic objections, which drafted "citizens" (not blacks) and permitted men to hire replacements for $300, about half a year's wages for unskilled workers. Passed just after Lincoln issued the Emancipation Proclamation, the law aroused indignation among workers who could not afford to pay for substitutes, hated the black exemption, and opposed the new war objective of freeing the slaves. Employers' use of African American strikebreakers intensified ethnic grievances. During an 1863 New York dock strike, predominantly Irish longshoremen used violence to clear black workers from the wharves.

These racial and class resentments exploded into riots in Manhattan in July 1863 when federal officials started the draft lottery. Enraged at the inequities, organized mobs disrupted the draft, burned factories, invaded the homes of abolitionists, and attacked men in business suits, presumably because they had paid their way out of military service. Angry mobs assaulted blacks indiscriminately—men, women, and children. Over 100 died during four days of street violence, requiring the use of Union troops to pacify the city.

The War of Conquest, 1863–1864

Despite growing frustration about the length of the war, both sides still fielded strong armies capable of winning tactical advantages that could lead to peace, if not victory. At the beginning of 1863, the Union's Army of the Potomac under "Fighting Joe" Hooker once again prepared to invade northern Virginia in hopes of capturing the Confederate capital. Against these forces, Confederates under Lee and Stonewall Jackson continued the offensive-defensive strategy to protect southern territory while striking opportunistically at northern units. Meanwhile, in the western theater, General Ulysses Grant advanced toward the Confederate fortress at Vicksburg, hoping to achieve Union control of the Mississippi River. This steady clash of military force had lasted for nearly two years, but in 1863 the Union began to break the Confederate defensive ring. The next year, despite heavy casualties, Union armies drove deeper into southern territory, steadily advancing against Confederate defenders. By the end of 1864, Union armies held Atlanta and were marching northward toward Charleston.

As the tide of battle turned, Union spirits rose. Although Lincoln had faced harsh criticism from anti-abolitionists, urban workers, and "peace" Democrats, the success of Union armies brought the Republican president and his party victories in the elections of 1864. By the time Lincoln pre-

sented his second inaugural address in March 1865, the war was nearly over. Already Congress had begun to debate postwar reconstruction of the Union. Questions about the status of ex-rebels and ex-slaves would shape the nation's politics for another decade. But the course of the war—the defeat of Confederate armies, the liberation of slaves—would determine the acceptable options. In fighting for the union, African Americans had established their claim to national citizenship.

Turning the Tide: Vicksburg and Gettysburg

In the spring of 1863, Union armies invaded northern Virginia, only to be stopped once again by Lee's tactical skills at Chancellorsville. But while the battle soured Union optimism, the South lost Stonewall Jackson, and Lee had still not tasted a clear victory. Nevertheless, the strategic stalemate in the eastern theater suggested the effectiveness of the offensive-defensive plan. Simultaneously, the Union failure to defeat Lee fueled criticism of Lincoln's leadership, and war-weary civilians denounced both the emancipation of slaves and the conscription of whites.

In the Mississippi valley, Union forces fared no better. Although the Confederate fortress at Vicksburg prevented Union control of the river, Grant used the Union navy to transport troops south of the fortress and then attacked from the east. Failing to conquer southern defenses, Grant established a siege that starved the post into surrender on July 4, 1863. The victory, followed by the capture of Port Hudson, gave the Union control of the river and split the western Confederacy (Louisiana, Arkansas, and Texas) from the eastern states. This part of the Anaconda strategy had finally prevailed.

Just days before Vicksburg fell, the Union's Army of the Potomac and the Confederacy's Army of Northern Virginia engaged in a ferocious battle at Gettysburg, Pennsylvania. During the siege at Vicksburg, Lee had proposed an invasion of the North, partly to demoralize the Union, partly to

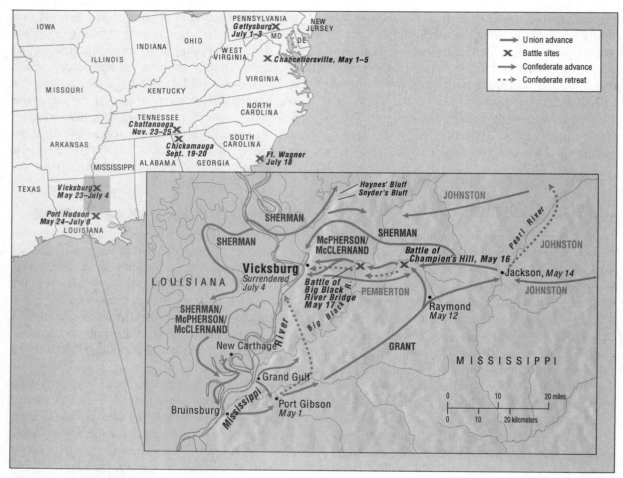

Vicksburg, Summer 1863

influence European opinion about assisting the South. In June 1863, as Grant was establishing his siege in Mississippi, Lee marched his army north through Maryland into Pennsylvania, finally encountering the Union army, now led by General George Meade, at Gettysburg. The ensuing battle epitomized the war's bitter fighting and foreshadowed its final outcome. For three days, outnumbered Confederate soldiers charged bravely into the blazing Union guns, until Lee had lost one-third of his army. Union troops suffered, too, but

the North had more resources and men to sacrifice. Forced at last to retreat, Lee might have lost all his troops had the Union armies pursued more aggressively. Lee managed his escape, however, and the war went on.

War of Invasion

The Confederate hope that war weariness would persuade the North to seek a peaceful compromise was running out of time. By the end of 1863,

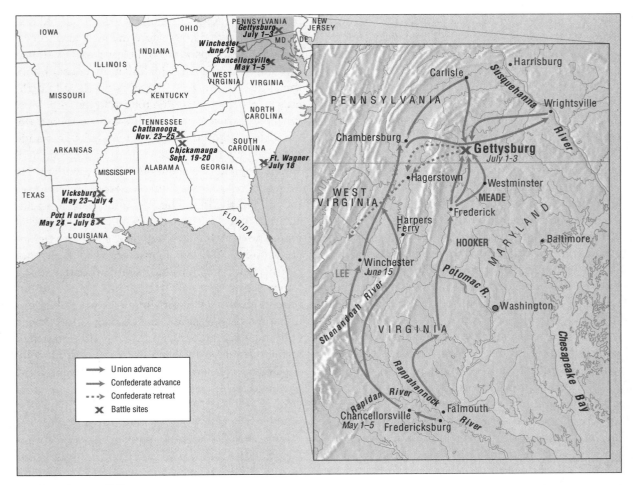

Gettysburg, Summer 1863

Union victories at Chattanooga, Tennessee, had opened the Confederacy for invasion. Preparing for a spring campaign, Lincoln promoted Grant to lead the Union armies and shifted him to the eastern sector, where the tough, resolute general would contend against the skillful Lee. The western command passed to William Tecumseh Sherman, whose sense of relentless discipline embodied the principles of total war. "The South has done her worst," he said to Grant, "now is the time for us to pile on our blows thick and fast."

Grant needed no encouragement. His goal was to defeat Lee's army in northern Virginia and capture the Confederate capital at Richmond. With 115,000 soldiers to Lee's 75,000, the Union general counted on numerical superiority to launch frontal attacks against Lee's weakened forces. In the Battle of the Wilderness in May 1864, Lee's armies benefited from the wooded terrain and inflicted 18,000 casualties, while losing 12,000. But this apparent Confederate victory failed to stop the Union advance. The fighting continued at Spotsylvania, where Grant lost another 18,000; Lee 12,000, but the result remained indecisive. Three weeks later, the armies clashed again at Cold Harbor, a vicious three-day battle in which Union forces sustained 7,000 losses in a single hour. Less than two weeks later, Grant attacked Lee at Petersburg, losing another 11,000 men. The six weeks' campaign cost the Union over 60,000 soldiers, while the Confederacy lost 37,000. By the fall of 1864, the two armies dug in for a long siege near Petersburg, Virginia.

Sherman, meanwhile, had begun to march from Tennessee to Atlanta, Georgia. "We have devoured the land," the general wrote to his wife. Killing farm animals for food, feeding their horses and mules from growing crops, looting and burning deserted buildings, Sherman's soldiers sent terror through the Confederacy. Southern women feared the pillage and spread rumors of rape. Northern soldiers generally proved respectful of white women, but freed slaves were sometimes targeted for sexual abuse. Indeed, Union courtesy toward whites permitted some southern women to step out of their traditional roles to act as spies or to insult the invading forces. Sometimes the tables were turned. When one Mississippi woman spat in the face of a Yankee prisoner, she did not expect him to return with Sherman's army; when he did, he reminded her of their previous meeting and burned her house to the ground. "Thus may it be with all who descend from their high pedestal of womanhood," said the arsonist. Whatever the limits of Union chivalry, by the summer of 1864 Sherman stood inside Atlanta, having caused 29,000 casualties and sustained 23,000. Meanwhile, General Philip Sheridan led Union forces through Virginia's Shenandoah valley, burning Confederate farms.

Seeking a Northern Consensus

"The cannon will not suffer any other sound to be heard for miles and for years around it," said the author Ralph Waldo Emerson during the battle of Spotsylvania. "Our chronology has lost all old distinctions in one date—before the War, and since." By 1864, the tremendous toll of war had frustrated civilians in the North. High inflation, conscription, the attack on slavery—these issues fueled northern grievances against Republican leadership. Most criticism focused on Lincoln's failure to end the bloodshed. "Stop the War," demanded Democratic newspapers as the 1864 election approached. When Confederate agents indicated a willingness to negotiate for peace, Lincoln sent representatives to talk. But the Republican commitment to emancipation, like the Confederacy's insistence on total independence, blocked any deal. Lincoln's Democratic opponents were themselves divided. A peace faction demanded an immediate armistice, but a larger group of "war" Democrats primarily opposed Lincoln's management of the war, violations of habeas corpus rights, and emancipation. In the end, the war Democrats prevailed and nominated former General McClellan to run against Lincoln.

During the campaign, Democrats invented the term *miscegenation* to refer to interracial sexual relations and accused Lincoln of advocating the practice. Republicans smeared Lincoln's critics as "Copperheads" (deadly snakes, easily camouflaged). Democrats also criticized the administration's inability to arrange prisoner exchanges. In prison hellholes like Georgia's Andersonville, Richmond's Libby, and Illinois's Camp Douglas, prisoners of war died like flies (30,000 Union; 26,000 Confederate). But Republicans rejected Confederate demands that African Americans be excluded from any prisoner returns. As with emancipation, Lincoln would not compromise the war's goals. Ultimately, it was the fortunes of war that determined the political outcome in November 1864. Bolstered by Sherman's victories in Georgia, the Republicans swept the presidential election. Lincoln won 55 percent of the popular vote, including 78 percent of the ballots cast by soldiers. The Republicans also carried both houses of Congress.

This Republican victory had vast political consequences. First, Lincoln treated the election as a mandate from the citizenry; he promptly urged the sitting lame-duck Congress, in which Democrats had substantial strength, to pass a constitutional amendment ending slavery throughout the nation. Only after intense administration pressure did enough Democrats agree to enact the Thirteenth Amendment in January 1865. Ratification by the states would be completed by the end of the year.

Amendment XIII (1865)

Section 1.
Neither slavery nor involuntary servitude, except as a punishment for crime whereof the party shall have been duly convicted, shall exist within the United States, or any place subject to their jurisdiction.

Section 2.
Congress shall have power to enforce this article by appropriate legislation.

Second, Lincoln had made a strategic decision during the campaign to choose a new vice-presidential running mate, Tennessee's Andrew Johnson, a lifelong Democrat and the only southern senator to remain in Washington after secession. Lincoln had brought Johnson aboard to strengthen his chances for reelection. But, as the postwar years would reveal, the new vice president did not share Lincoln's sympathy for the freed slaves nor accept Republican views of how best to reconstruct the shattered South.

The Confederacy Falls

"We cannot change the hearts of those people of the South," remarked Sherman as the war continued, "but we can make war so terrible and make them so sick of war that generations would pass away before they would again appeal to it." After burning large sections of Atlanta, Sherman's army commenced a devastating 280-mile march to the sea, destroying everything of military value on the way to Savannah. By January 1865, the seasoned troops were heading north toward South Carolina, birthplace of secession, and chanting, "Hail Columbia, happy land; if we don't burn you, I'll be damned." Columbia, South Carolina, fell in February, and Union soldiers, drunk on glory and confiscated whiskey, scribbled graffiti and "foul comments" on the public walls. The South had lost the power, though not the will, to fight.

"Fondly do we hope—fervently do we pray—that this mighty scourge of war may speedily pass away," said Lincoln in his second inaugural address in March 1865. As mass desertions weakened the remaining southern armies in Virginia, Grant finally turned Lee's flank at Petersburg. The Confederate government in Richmond abandoned the city, setting fires to prevent Union troops from capturing military supplies and records. Union cavalry prevented Lee's forces from escaping into North Carolina. At the village of Appomattox, the Confederate general reached the end of the fight. On April 9, 1865, Grant and Lee arranged a formal surrender. After a few weeks of mop-up skirmishing, the Civil War was over.

"No howling!" observed South Carolina's Mary Chesnut of the Confederate defeat. "Our poverty is made a matter of laughing. . . . Of the country, we try not to speak at all." Northerners could not contain their joy, nor forget, in Lincoln's words, "the loved and lost." To the victorious Union, Lincoln embodied the suffering and sacrifice of the war as he felt the strain of sending boys and men to their death, commuted sentences of deserters or Sioux warriors, and even lost a young son to malaria during his presidency. Yet Confederate loyalists remained bitter. Five days after Appomattox, while the president watched a play at

Ford's Theater in Washington, one unrepentant southern sympathizer, the actor John Wilkes Booth, crept behind Lincoln's seat and fired a bullet into the president's head.

The Unfinished War

The public mourning that followed Lincoln's assassination helped northern hearts recover from the horror of the war. As the president's black-draped funeral train moved on a 1600-mile journey from Washington through the nation's major cities to Springfield, Illinois, some 7 million citizens paused to pay homage (though municipal officials in New York, sharing the racist views that had prompted the draft riots, barred the city's African Americans from visiting the funeral cortege). Outside the ruined Confederacy, Lincoln's reputation rose to mythic heights; his name was placed on streets, counties, and towns; monuments were built in his honor; and his words were repeated so often that they became cliches. Southerners, by contrast, took solace in a cult of "the lost cause." Believing in the honor of secession and their defense of southern liberty, die-hard Confederates acknowledged only the superiority of Union power. "One thing I shall glory in to the latest hours of my life," wrote one Georgia woman. "We never yielded in the struggle until we were bound hand and foot and the heel of the despot was on our throats."

Conflicts between the North and the South thus endured, but the war had transformed the nation's political life. Until the Civil War, the noun "United States" was considered a plural phrase, but never so afterward. The defeat of secession had permanently altered the federal balance of power. Now a centralized government would determine constitutional rules of law, compelling the southern states to accept northern terms of recon-

struction. To be sure, those conditions remained subject to debate. In 1864, Lincoln had vetoed a congressional plan of reconstruction, beginning a decade-long political struggle over the nature of the federal Union. After the war, moreover, Lincoln's Republican party would maintain a firm grip on national power and would continue to legislate policies that promoted industrial development. Republicans would demand justice for the former slaves. The war for freedom not only destroyed slavery but also killed the ante-bellum assumption that the government existed only to serve white people. In the end, the Civil War proved what Lincoln had only proposed in his Gettysburg Address of 1863: ". . . that government of the people, by the people, and for the people, shall not perish from the earth." The phrase would become a benchmark for postwar generations.

INFOTRAC® COLLEGE EDITION EXERCISES

 For additional reading go to InfoTrac College Edition, your online research library at *http://web1.infotrac-college.com*.

Keyword search: Confederate states
Keyword search: Jefferson Davis
Keyword search: Fort Sumter
Keyword search: Civil War draft
Keyword search: Robert E. Lee
Keyword search: Emancipation Proclamation
Keyword search: Ulysses S. Grant
Keyword search: Appomattox
Keyword search: Lincoln assassination

ADDITIONAL READING

James M. McPherson, *Battle Cry of Freedom: The Civil War Era* (1988). A clear overview of the war's political, social, and military history.

Economic and Diplomatic Issues

Howard Jones, *Abraham Lincoln and a New Birth of Freedom: The Union and Slavery in the Diplomacy of the Civil War* (1999). This book places political and ideological issues in the international context.

A People's War

Gerald F. Linderman, *Embattled Courage: The Experience of Combat in the American Civil War* (1987). This study examines warfare from the perspective of the fighting soldiers; for ideological motives in the armies, see also James M. McPherson, *For Cause and Comrade: Why Men Fought in the Civil War* (1997).

Charles Royster, *The Destructive War: William Tecumseh Sherman, Stonewall Jackson, and the Americans* (1990). Analyzes the social and cultural implications of the Civil War's violence.

The Politics of Emancipation

William K. Klingaman, *Abraham Lincoln and the Road to Emancipation, 1861–1865* (2001). The author traces the president's growing commitment to ending slavery.

Leon F. Litwack, *Been in the Storm So Long: The Aftermath of Slavery* (1979). A superb account of southern African Americans carries the story into the era of reconstruction. See also an excellent anthology of contemporary documents in Ira Berlin and Leslie S. Rowlands, eds., *Families and Freedom: A Documentary History of African American Kinship in the Civil War Era* (1997).

Blacks Enter the Ranks

Joseph T. Glatthaar, *Forged in Battle: The Civil War Alliance of Black Soldiers and White Officers* (1990). This book discusses the experience of black Union soldiers and their white leaders; see also Christopher Looby, ed., *The Complete Civil War Journal of Thomas Wentworth Higginson* (1999).

War on Native Grounds

Philip Weeks, *Farewell, My Nation: The American Indian and the United States, 1820–1890* (1990). A succinct study of U.S.–Native American relations, the book's Civil War chapter offers an excellent summary.

The War on the Home Front

Phillip Shaw Paludan, *"A People's Contest": The Union and the Civil War, 1861–1865* (1988). A thorough survey of the war's impact on the North, summarizing recent scholarship.

Facing the Death Toll

Garry Wills, *Lincoln at Gettysburg: The Words That Remade America* (1992). This analysis of the Gettysburg Address places Lincoln in the context of 19th-century culture.

Women and the War

Drew Gilpin Faust, *Mothers of Invention: Women of the Slaveholding South in the American Civil War* (1996). This analysis takes a fresh look at how Confederate women responded to the military crisis.

Judith Ann Giesberg, *Civil War Sisterhood: The U.S. Sanitary Commission and Women's Politics in Transition* (2000). A study of middle-class northern women, this book links wartime activism with postwar reformism.

Conflicts in the Confederacy

Emory M. Thomas, *The Confederate Nation: 1861–1865* (1979). This volume provides a detailed survey of southern history; see also Gary W. Gallagher, *The Confederate War* (1997), which discusses the relationship between southern society and Confederate military strategy.

The Northern Economy

Iver Bernstein, *The New York City Draft Riots: Their Significance for American Society and Politics in the Age of the Civil War* (1990). This work provides an analysis of ethnic, economic and political tensions in the North.

15

Reconstructing the National Identity, 1865–1877

CHRONOLOGY

1865	Congress establishes Freedmen's Bureau
	Andrew Johnson succeeds slain President Lincoln
	Johnson issues amnesty proclamation
	States ratify Thirteenth Amendment
1865–1866	Southern states enact Black Codes
1866	Ku Klux Klan and vigilante groups appear in South
	Congress passes Civil Rights Act over Johnson's veto
	Women reformers organize American Equal Rights Association
1867	Congress passes Reconstruction Acts
	Farmers form Patrons of Husbandry
1868	House impeaches President Johnson; Senate votes acquittal
	States ratify Fourteenth Amendment
	Congress reseats southern representatives
	Fort Laramie treaty establishes Sioux reservation
	Ulysses S. Grant wins presidential election
1869	Transcontinental railroad completed in Utah
1870	States ratify Fifteenth Amendment
1871	Fire destroys Chicago; scandals topple New York Tweed Ring
1872	Grant defeats Liberal Republican Horace Greeley
1873	Wall Street panic precipitates economic downturn
	Slaughterhouse ruling limits enforcement of Fourteenth Amendment
1875	Congress passes Civil Rights Act
1876	Sioux warriors defeat U.S. cavalry at Little Big Horn
1877	Rutherford B. Hayes chosen president by electoral commission
	Hayes withdraws last federal troops from South

The boy was six or seven years old—he didn't know exactly the year of his birth—when he and his brother, sister, and mother, and all the other slaves on the Virginia plantation were summoned to the master's "big house" to hear the news of their freedom. "All was excitement and expectancy," recalled Booker T. Washington. The master's family stood or sat on the veranda, their faces clouded with sadness. A Union officer made a short speech, read aloud the Emancipation Proclamation, and advised the anxious slaves that they were free and could go where and when they pleased. Washington's mother, tears of joy streaming down her cheeks, leaned over her children, and kissed them tenderly. "For some minutes, there was great rejoicing, and thanksgiving, and wild scenes of ecstasy," Washington remembered. And then the former slaves retreated soberly to their cabins, feeling for the first time "the great responsibility of being free."

http://history.wadsworth.com

The metamorphosis of ex-slaves mirrored the transformation of the entire nation in 1865, as whites and blacks, southerners and northerners, faced a new sense of national identity. "The territorial, political, and historical oneness of the nation is now ratified by the blood of thousands of her sons," declared a new magazine, appropriately named *The Nation,* in 1865. In the same year, an Illinois editor boasted of "the mysterious but unmistakable homogeneity of [the] people." To be sure, such hyperbole ignored obvious disagreements about race, class, and gender. "Verily," observed the black abolitionist Frederick Douglass, "the work does not end with the abolition of slavery, but only begins."

A new sense of federal power now stimulated a vast quantity of national legislation. In the decade after 1865, the number of bills introduced to Congress tripled over the previous ten years, and the number of laws that were passed doubled. A growing federal bureaucracy—beginning with the Bureau of Statistics in 1866, the Department of Justice and the Weather Bureau in 1870, and the expanded 1870 national Census—greatly increased national record-keeping. Meanwhile, in 1866, the Western Union telegraph company, the nation's first major monopoly, knit together the strands of national communication.

If the Civil War produced an enlarged national government, the death of the Confederacy raised divisive questions about the definition of U.S. citizenship. Whom did the federal government now represent? How should the seceded states be "reconstructed" as members of the national Union? What was the legal status of ex-Confederates, and should all ex-rebels be treated alike? The end of slavery prompted additional questions about the status of ex-slaves and free blacks. Should African Americans be considered citizens? Should black women enjoy the status of black men? Should white women obtain the same privileges of citizenship as African American men?

These political questions touched the core of the national identity, forcing all Americans to consider their own status and rights. The Fourteenth Amendment, which gave citizenship to African Americans in 1868, introduced the word *male* into the U.S. Constitution for the first time, but ignored women like Elizabeth Cady Stanton, who demanded "government by . . . the whole people; for . . . the whole people." An Oregon newspaper carried the matter to a logical, and unpopular, conclusion: "If we make the African a citizen, we cannot deny the same right to the Indian and the Mongolian."

Public debate about citizenship did not necessarily affect the country's social and economic development. Indeed, the political nationalism expressed by leadership groups—party politicians, newspaper writers, businessmen, and their supporters at the polls—often contrasted with the concerns of political outsiders, such as immigrants, ex-slaves, women, and Native Americans, who experienced a contrary pattern of exclusion, separation, and persecution. Moreover, persistent local issues involving land use, economic development, or ethnic conflict often seemed more important to diverse communities than did the affairs debated in Washington, D.C.

The extraordinary economic growth after the Civil War, notably the completion of a transcontinental railroad, a burst in urbanization, and agricultural expansion at the expense of the Plains nations, distracted attention from political questions of citizenship, suffrage, and civil rights. And, because national politicians usually responded to the concerns of their separate constituencies, the lack of interest in the hinterlands about national politics made it difficult for leaders in Washington to fulfill the promises of equal rights for ex-slaves.

Yet by 1877, when the era of reconstruction ended, the contours of the national identity had assumed a new form, laying the basis for a multicultural government for future generations.

The Promise of Reconstruction

In 1865, the U.S. government had to determine the conditions for readmitting the seceded states into the Union and restoring political rights to ex-rebels. Even before the Civil War ended, President Abraham Lincoln had offered a general amnesty to Confederates, exempting only high political and military leaders, and proposed that as few as 10 percent of eligible voters, once they affirmed their loyalty to the Constitution, might create new state governments. Lincoln also indicated an interest in extending the vote to some southern blacks—at least those who were educated, had served in the Union army, and owned property. Yet Lincoln's plan was designed as much to encourage Confederate surrender as to restore the Union. More radical Republicans in Congress, concerned that Lincoln's easy terms for readmitting southern representatives would weaken their party's position, subsequently offered a stricter plan of reconstruction. As passed in the Wade-Davis bill of 1864, Congress demanded that a majority (not just 10 percent) of southern voters take "iron-clad" oaths of loyalty to the Union, repudiate Confederate debts, disenfranchise Confederate leaders, and accept the end of slavery. Lincoln considered these terms too rigid and refused to sign the bill into law.

After the Confederate surrender and Lincoln's assassination, the issue of reconstruction could no longer be avoided. The new president, Tennessee Democrat Andrew Johnson, distrusted the Republican-controlled Congress. Since the new Congress would not come into session until December 1865, the president initiated his own policies to restore the Union. Johnson's conciliatory approach to most ex-Confederates encouraged the southern states to pass discriminatory laws against the former slaves. Such disregard for black rights aroused criticism in the North, and congressional Republicans prepared to challenge the president's version of reconstruction.

At the end of the Civil War, moreover, the southern states were in a ruined condition. Damage to towns, fields, fences, and plantations had shattered the southern economy. Not only did investors lose the value of Confederate money, but the emancipation of 4 million slaves eliminated the basis of most southern wealth. The freed slaves, meanwhile, lost the minimal security and subsistence that slavery had provided. One month before the war ended, Congress had established the Bureau of Freedmen, Refugees, and Abandoned Land, known as the Freedmen's Bureau. The bureau's mission was to assist ex-slaves and poor whites with food, transportation, and legal advice; to help them obtain work or settle on abandoned lands; and to establish schools to prepare them to live independently. Such federal intervention in the realm of social welfare was unprecedented. Yet most ex-slaves did not await government instruction to explore their freedom. Indeed, African American initiatives in 1865 revealed so much passion for self-determination that white southerners became alarmed.

A Passion for Freedom

Freed slaves quickly asserted their independence. Many took new surnames that identified kinship and family connections; others took the last names of their former owners or of some famous personage. The desire for family ties prompted many

Former slaves who went to the Freedmen's Bureau could expect help with food, transportation, and legal advice; finding work or settling on abandoned lands; and schooling to prepare them to live independently.

ex-slaves to search for spouses, children, and parents who had been sold away during slavery. African Americans also endeavored to stabilize their family lives. In rural areas, where most blacks lived, married women tried to avoid field work, instead assuming domestic roles in their families. Black domestics who worked for whites chose to dwell at home, not with their employers. Such decisions reflected a deliberate effort to strengthen their own families, although poverty often forced them back into the labor force.

Whites encouraged ex-slaves to legalize their marriages, partly for reasons of morality, partly to relieve governments of responsibility for illegitimate children, and partly to enable public officials to enforce the legal responsibilities between husbands and wives for financial support. Formal marriage also gave black men the legal standing to protect their children against apprenticeship laws that permitted the seizure of minors who were without legal guardians to become wards of the state. Yet legal marriage raised new problems. Since state laws presumed that men were heads of the household, married black women, who had considerable family responsibility during slavery, now faced a state-imposed patriarchal family structure.

African Americans also departed from the white-controlled Christian churches of slavery days, effectively evading oversight of their spiritual lives. They now established independent congregations, usually within the Methodist or Baptist churches. In this way, freed African Americans continued to develop a distinct religious system that perpetuated African-derived styles of Christian worship services, such as singing, clapping, and call-and-response.

The abrupt independence of former slaves disrupted old assumptions about the social order. Former slaveholding women, once spared the drudgery of housework, discovered the "same old tune of washing, ironing and cooking . . . of being maids of all work." When young freed women appeared in public wearing stylish black veils, offended white women boycotted the fashion. Recognizing the importance of harnessing black labor to assure their own economic survival,

"I's free. Ain't wuf nuffin."

white landowners complained that "Negroes know nothing of the value of time," slept after sunrise, and demanded Saturdays without labor.

"Where shall Othello go?" remained, however, a serious question for one paternalistic planter, who doubted the ability of African Americans to survive on their own. "Poor elk—poor buffalo—poor Indian—poor Nigger—this is indeed a white man's country." Indeed, former slaves confronted a new and unfriendly world of economic relations. "I's free," observed one ex-slave. "Ain't wuf nuffin." Such vulnerability enabled unscrupulous whites to cheat the newly freed workers, refuse to pay wages, or commit violence against those who protested new forms of economic exploitation.

Johnson's Policy of Restoration

President Johnson's policy of "restoration" accentuated the problems of southern blacks. With Congress out of session in the spring of 1865, Johnson offered amnesty to southern rebels who agreed to a loyalty oath, restoring their property and political rights to all but the richest southern leaders. A second presidential proclamation called for the creation of new state governments, limiting the vote to pardoned white men; it also demanded ratification of the Thirteenth Amendment, which abolished slavery, as a condition for a state's readmission to the Union. When African American leaders like Frederick Douglass appealed to Johnson to extend voting rights to blacks, the former Tennessee slaveowner refused and defended white supremacy. Johnson also ordered the return of lands confiscated by the Union armies to pardoned ex-Confederates, even when freed slaves already inhabited those lands.

Johnson's views emboldened southern voters to elect ex-Confederates to draft new state constitutions. Rather than meet the president's conditions, moreover, the southern constitutional conventions hesitated to repudiate secession and the abolition of slavery. In addition, the first postwar southern governments sought to control the freed slaves by enacting restrictive laws known as "Black Codes." These laws gave African Americans minimal rights, such as the right to marry, own property, make contracts, bring lawsuits, and testify in court against other blacks. But the codes excluded African Americans from juries and the right to vote, rejected black testimony against whites, and provided more severe penalties for black criminals than for white ones.

The new codes limited the freedom of black workers. By defining black unemployment as vagrancy, southern laws permitted the courts to impose fines on idle blacks and to contract their labor to private citizens to repay the fines. Black children without adequate parental support could be apprenticed to businessmen and forced into involuntary labor. Some codes prohibited land ownership or leases, compelling ex-slaves to work for wages on other people's land. Black workers had to sign annual labor contracts or face high penalties, which could only be paid by additional labor. Although Freedmen's Bureau courts suspended some of these restrictions, military authorities endorsed the labor contracts both to protect blacks' rights and to assure economic stability. To African Americans and their northern sympathizers, the Black Codes seemed like a retreat toward reenslavement of black workers.

Congress Challenges Johnson

While the southern governments attempted to thwart political change, northern leaders prepared to enforce fundamental reforms. As the first postwar Congress convened in December 1865, the

Republican majority divided into two camps. The smaller group, called "Radicals," included Massachusetts's Charles Sumner and Ohio's Ben Wade in the Senate and Pennsylvania's Thaddeus Stevens in the House; this group believed fervently in protecting equal rights for all citizens, blacks as well as whites. The larger Republican wing, known as "Moderates," wanted assurances that secession and slavery were dead, but felt no commitment to black equality and hoped to cooperate with the president. But Johnson's generous amnesty, followed by the Black Codes, alarmed even Moderate Republicans, who assessed the newly elected southern representatives and refused to seat them.

Recognizing that southern whites were threatening the freedom of ex-slaves, Moderate Republicans supported Illinois Senator Lyman Trumbull's proposal to extend the term of the Freedmen's Bureau to offer federal protection for southern blacks. While promising to continue programs for education, supervision of labor contracts, and food and transportation for ex-slaves, the Freedmen's Bureau bill of 1866 also supported President Johnson's order restoring confiscated land to pardoned rebels and limited black settlement on other federal lands. Protection of black labor, not seizure of white-owned land, remained the Moderates' goal. In the end, the only pro-Confederates forced to surrender land to former slaves were the southern Native Americans in Indian territory. The subsequent Southern Homestead Act of 1866 merely offered undeveloped public lands for purchase by blacks and other Unionists, most of it too costly for former slaves. But even the Moderate version of the Freedmen's Bureau bill offended Johnson, who viewed any social aid to ex-slaves as a violation of constitutional limits on government authority. He vetoed the measure, and a stunned Congress initially failed to override the veto.

Moderate Republicans also sought to protect southern blacks by passing the Civil Rights bill of 1866, which disallowed discrimination in state laws. Congress limited this bill to those states that refused to guarantee civil rights to their own citizens. But Johnson vetoed the proposal as an unnecessary expansion of federal power. For the first time in U.S. history, Congress mustered two-thirds majorities to override a presidential veto of major legislation. By the summer of 1866, Congress also mustered the votes to pass the Freedmen's Bureau bill and override another presidential veto of the measure. This defiance of presidential leadership reflected growing resentment of Johnson's personal arrogance as well as his refusal to compromise with the congressional majority. The political rift would soon grow.

During the spring of 1866, Congress proceeded to draft a Fourteenth Amendment to the Constitution, establishing the citizenship of all people born or naturalized in the United States, which included blacks but not "Indians." This provision overturned the principles of the Dred Scott decision of 1857 (see Chapter 13). The Fourteenth Amendment also addressed the matter of black suffrage. With the end of slavery, southern states were no longer limited by the Three-Fifths Compromise to count black residents as a fraction of whites in apportioning representation in Congress; instead, southern blacks would count as whole persons, thus increasing southern representation. Republicans realized that white southerners would back Democratic candidates. To balance white voters, therefore, the proposed Amendment authorized congressional representation to be based on the number of "male" inhabitants allowed to vote, an effort to induce states to give the suffrage to black men. This provision was not necessarily popular in the northern states, of which only six gave black men the ballot. Eventually eight other northern states would vote on the issue of black suffrage, but it passed in only two, Iowa and Minnesota. Finally, the Fourteenth Amendment disqualified former

Confederate officials from holding office. Congress promptly sent the Fourteenth Amendment to the states for ratification. But of the former Confederate states, only Tennessee voted to ratify, stalling approval and angering Republican leaders.

The split between Congress and the president widened during the 1866 congressional elections. Seeking to build a coalition of Democrats and conservative Republicans, Johnson challenged the Republican majority, purging opponents from government jobs and embarking on an unprecedented—and unseemly—campaign tour that newspapers derided as the "Swing around the Circle." During the campaign, moreover, violent race riots by whites in Memphis and New Orleans revealed the terror that afflicted southern blacks. The violence undermined Johnson's political support and swept Republicans back into office.

Congressional Reconstruction

Frustrated by the South's refusal to ratify the Fourteenth Amendment, the new Republican-dominated Congress introduced its own program of reconstruction in 1867. Its aim was to end the Johnson-approved southern governments, whose representatives had still not been seated in Congress. The plan emerged in a series of Reconstruction acts, passed in 1867 over the Democratic president's vetoes. Denying the legality of the previous southern governments, Congress divided the South into five military districts to ensure enforcement of federal laws and established strict criteria for the election and admission of representatives to Congress. The measures required that black men be allowed to vote; took political rights from leading Confederates; required elected conventions to draft new state constitutions that would guarantee black male suffrage; mandated ratification of the Fourteenth Amendment; and, finally, allowed the election of state government officials and congressional representatives. In providing for reunion based on black suffrage, the act gave Republican leaders the possibility of countering white southern political power in Congress. Far more radical than the Fourteenth Amendment, congressional reconstruction brought black citizens directly into the nation's political structure.

Amendment XIV (1868)

Section 1.
All persons born or naturalized in the United States, and subject to the jurisdiction thereof, are citizens of the United States and of the state wherein they reside. No state shall make or enforce any law which shall abridge the privileges or immunities of citizens of the United States; nor shall any state deprive any person of life, liberty, or property, without due process of law; nor deny to any person within its jurisdiction the equal protection of the laws.

Section 2.
Representatives shall be apportioned among the several states according to their respective numbers, counting the whole number of persons in each state, excluding Indians not taxed. But when the right to vote at any election for the choice of electors for President and Vice President of the United States, Representatives in Congress, the executive and judicial officers of a state, or the members of the legislature thereof, is denied to any of the male inhabitants of such state, being twenty-one years of age, and citizens of the United States, or in any way abridged, except for participation in rebellion, or other crime, the basis of representation therein shall be reduced in the proportion which the number of such male citizens shall bear to the whole number of male citizens twenty-one years of age in such state.

Section 3.

No person shall be a Senator or Representative in Congress, or elector of President and Vice President, or hold any office, civil or military, under the United States, or under any state, who, having previously taken an oath, as a member of Congress, or as an officer of the United States, or as a member of any state legislature, or as an executive or judicial officer of any state, to support the Constitution of the United States, shall have engaged in insurrection or rebellion against the same, or given aid or comfort to the enemies thereof. But Congress may by a vote of two-thirds of each House, remove such disability.

Section 4.

The validity of the public debt of the United States, authorized by law, including debts incurred for payment of pensions and bounties for services in suppressing insurrection or rebellion, shall not be questioned. But neither the United States nor any state shall assume or pay any debt or obligation incurred in aid of insurrection or rebellion against the United States, or any claim for the loss or emancipation of any slave; but all such debts, obligations and claims shall be held illegal and void.

Section 5.

The Congress shall have power to enforce, by appropriate legislation, the provisions of this article.

The split between Johnson and Congress provoked a constitutional crisis. Hostile to congressional efforts to strengthen the power of southern blacks at the expense of whites, Johnson used his executive authority to grant thousands of pardons to ex-Confederates and to make appointments to undermine Congress's reconstruction program.

Republicans countered by enacting such laws as the Tenure of Office Act of 1867, which limited the president's right to dismiss executive officers. When Johnson defied that law by dismissing Secretary of War Edwin M. Stanton, a supporter of congressional reconstruction, Radical Republicans pushed for the president's impeachment.

After the House of Representatives voted to impeach Johnson for violating the Tenure of Office Act, the Senate held formal hearings in 1868. Although Johnson insisted that he had committed no crimes, he agreed privately to accept the Reconstruction acts. Moderate Republicans then became less hostile. The Senate finally voted 35–19 for conviction, but fell one vote short of the two-thirds majority necessary to remove the president from office. Johnson lost any hope of gaining reelection in 1868. Instead, Republicans backed war hero Ulysses S. Grant, who supported congressional reconstruction. Although politically inexperienced, Grant won the election.

Debating the Votes for Blacks and Women

As the presidential crisis ended in 1868, nearly all the southern states had adopted constitutions providing for black suffrage, ratified the Fourteenth Amendment, and returned delegates to Congress. But the 1868 elections underscored political trends that alarmed Republican leaders. First, in the southern states, violence against black voters showed that many whites did not accept the political settlements; second, in sixteen northern and border states where blacks were denied the suffrage, Democrats had made election gains. Republicans therefore proposed a Fifteenth Amendment, which prohibited both federal and state governments from interfering with suffrage on racial grounds. Although Democrats denounced this "most revolutionary measure," the Fifteenth Amendment actually threatened no existing power, for the proposed Amendment did not outlaw non-racial voting restrictions, such as literacy, education, or wealth, nor did it extend the franchise to women. Even so, western states, whose citizens were opposed to Chinese or Mexican voting, refused to ratify the Amendment.

Amendment XV (1870)

Section 1.
The right of citizens of the United States to vote shall not be denied or abridged by the United States or by any state on account of race, color, or previous condition of servitude.

Section 2.
The Congress shall have power to enforce this article by appropriate legislation.

Women reformers, such as Elizabeth Cady Stanton, Susan B. Anthony, Lucretia Mott, and Lucy Stone, had formed the American Equal Rights Association in 1866 to merge the campaigns for black and female voting. But a statewide referendum in Kansas in 1867 revealed that women's suffrage was even less popular than the black vote. Congress extended the franchise to African American men in Washington, D.C., but showed no interest in accommodating women's demands.

The language of the Fourteenth Amendment specifically referred to "male" voters. "On what principle of justice or courtesy," demanded Mrs. Stanton, "should woman yield her right of enfranchisement to the negro?" Furious that former Republican allies gave preeminence to African American men over Anglo Saxon women, some women appealed to racial prejudices in arguing against ratification of the proposed amendment. "American women of wealth, education, virtue and refinement," said Stanton, "do not wish the lower orders of Chinese, Africans, Germans and Irish . . . to make laws for . . . your daughters." Such opinions split the women's suffrage campaign into rival groups. Male reformers, such as Frederick Douglass, who publicly supported woman's suffrage, endorsed the Fifteenth Amendment, even though it omitted the women's vote. "Woman has a thousand ways by which she can attach herself to the ruling power of the land," Douglass explained to justify his position.

In 1868, reformers who opposed compromise formed the National Woman Suffrage Association, dedicated to passage of a Sixteenth Amendment for the women's vote. When Congress refused to consider the idea, some dissatisfied women decided to ignore male-only voting laws. In 1871 and 1872, hundreds of women attempted to cast ballots. One result was Susan B. Anthony's arrest and trial for illegal voting. In 1869, Mormon-dominated Utah granted women the franchise to strengthen conservative power, followed in 1870 by Wyoming, where the women's vote was seen as a moral force against social disorder. This growing awareness of women's potential power encouraged activists to seek reforms outside the ballot box. Although some groups continued to demand the vote, women reformers increasingly focused on social legislation, such as divorce reform, that would help women without changing the political system.

Reconstruction Comes to the South

The political environment in the southern states accentuated the economic problems faced by the freed slaves. Since southern blacks remained loyal to their Republican emancipators and southern whites clung to the Democratic party, state politics embodied fundamental racial conflicts. Hostile whites organized violent vigilante groups such as the Ku Klux Klan to keep blacks from voting, holding political office, or obtaining economic independence. Meanwhile, new state laws about marriage, apprenticeship, and land reinforced white economic supremacy. Such policies often worked against the interests of poor whites, who ironically identified with white leaders rather than with blacks who had similar problems. This oppression of southern blacks aroused northern criticism and justified the continuing presence of federal troops in the southern states. But northern interest in southern problems was easily distracted by other issues. Increasingly, southern blacks could challenge their status only at the peril of life and property.

Reconstruction Leadership

Congressional reconstruction initially disenfranchised ex-Confederates (about 15 percent of southern white men) and gave the vote to some 700,000 African Americans, thus assuring Republican majorities. Identifying with the party of Lincoln, blacks formed the majority of southern Republicans. Yet blacks constituted voting majorities in only five states. As the new state constitutions restored voting rights to most former Confederates (excluding only high ranking Confederate officers from holding public office), southern whites supported the Democratic party, with two significant exceptions.

One white group that supported the Republican party consisted of transplanted northerners, many of them ex-Union army officers or Freedmen's Bureau officials, who sought opportunity in the South. Democrats labeled this group *carpetbaggers*, implying that they were opportunists with no stake in southern society. A second group of southern Republicans had roots in the Whig party and favored regional economic development or came from nonslaveholding regions that had remained Unionist during the Civil War. Many were small farmers who opposed the restoration of

planter leadership. Their Democratic opponents called them *scalawags*—contemporary slang that meant "mean fellows" or "disgraces"—suggesting that these native-born southerners were betraying their region by supporting outsiders.

Despite the Democrats' negative views, southern Republicans formed complicated coalitions that transcended racial and class divisions. Although African Americans provided nearly 80 percent of the Republican vote, southern whites dominated officeholding, partly because of traditions of deference and partly to increase the party's appeal to white voters. Yet blacks participated actively in the political process, attending party conventions and holding local offices. By the end of Reconstruction in 1877, Republicans had sent 16 African Americans to Congress, including two Mississippi Senators, and elected nearly 700 blacks, most of them former slaves, to state government. Many more served in local government. Black officials, though always a minority among whites, enjoyed respect within black communities and ensured the basic fairness of government services.

Southern Politics and Economy

The Republican party's agenda in the South reflected the needs of its diverse constituency. Following the success of Freedmen's Bureau schools, and educational efforts by northern charitable organizations that sent teachers into the South, every southern state established a system of tax-supported public schools, which greatly increased literacy and provided primary education for a generation of African Americans. To be sure, the schools were usually poorly financed and racially segregated. Most southern states maintained segregated prisons, orphanages, and railroad cars, but Republican majorities legally ended discrimination in many public accommodations, such as streetcars and municipal employment, though such laws were not enforced.

Republican lawmakers also supported economic development. Democrats objected to growing state indebtedness and higher taxes, but shared the enthusiasm for certain public works, such as railroads. To attract private investment, the states eased restrictions on interest rates, donated public lands to factories, and enacted general incorporation laws. Yet northern capital remained scarce, largely because of better investment opportunities in the western states and in northern cities. Consequently, southern economic development rested on frail credit and bonds, and was further weakened by legislative bribery and graft. During the early 1870s, a national financial contraction pushed southern municipal and state governments toward bankruptcy, undermining public support of Republican policies.

Efforts to stimulate southern business hardly affected rural agriculture. Although the Union army had threatened rebels with land confiscation and sometimes allowed ex-slaves to work on confiscated lands, President Johnson restored most property to the original holders in 1865. Despite the help of northern philanthropists and the Freedmen's Bureau, very few ex-slaves ever managed to acquire their own holdings. Freed black workers thus had to find work on land owned by whites, often former slaveowners. Although landowners initially kept the paid workforce in large groups, or gangs, African Americans objected to the rigid supervision, which they associated with slavery. Instead, black field workers preferred smaller units, or squads, directed by a chosen leader.

 Tensions arose frequently between white landowners and the black labor force. Freed slaves not only resisted strict supervision but also chose to work fewer hours than slavery had demanded, closer to the sunup-to-sundown schedule of white hired hands. In addition, women opted to work at home, rather than in the fields, and ex-slave children often left the fields to attend school. The result was a significant decline in labor productivity.

To regulate the freed labor force, the Freedmen's Bureau joined white planters in encouraging ex-slaves to sign annual labor contracts, usually exchanging specified work for wages. Since many former slaveowners resented paying for black labor, however, the system was subject to abuse. Blacks complained of nonpayment, or eviction for trifling offenses, after they had planted their crops. Meanwhile, failure to work at all opened blacks to charges of vagrancy and forced labor.

Eventually, a system evolved that was based on sharing the profits of land and labor. Two patterns emerged. The most common type was called *sharecropping*. In exchange for a year's labor, landowners provided food, supplies, tools, and seed, and paid workers with a portion of the crop (a "share") after the annual harvest was sold. The sharecropping system encouraged individual families to contract with landowners to grow specific crops. As family workers, rather than paid labor, women and children joined the men in fields. Although sharecroppers sometimes enjoyed independence from direct supervision, they remained workers, not tenants, and the crops belonged to the landowners, who settled accounts only after deducting expenses, including carrying charges, interest, and high markups. It was not uncommon for workers to obtain a smaller return than their cost of living during a year. Thus sharecroppers could easily become debtors and be obliged to work the next year under the same, or worse, terms to repay previous debts. The second, less common arrangement was called *tenant farming*. Farmers rented land for a specified sum and then repaid the landowner after the harvest. Tenants usually owned their own tools, farm animals, and seed, and were therefore less dependent on landowners and could plant what they wished.

African Americans who left the plantations for urban centers faced similar problems of protecting their independence. Housing segregation in southern towns forced blacks to live in crowded, unsanitary neighborhoods where epidemic diseases took their toll. In Nashville, Tennessee, for example, where many blacks inhabited shacks originally built for animals, the black mortality rate was double that of whites. Legal segregation of public facilities further restricted black activities. In cities like Atlanta, Richmond, and Nashville, however, ex-slaves found strength in numbers, forming community institutions, such as churches, schools, and burial societies. Religious organizations also founded teachers' training colleges, including Fisk and Atlanta Universities. Within a decade of emancipation, ex-slaves joined an older community of free blacks to build their own class system and cultural institutions within the larger segregated society.

Despite changes in labor practices, southern staple crops dominated the economy. With cotton the most valuable commodity per acre, southern farmers intensified production to cover wartime losses and the effects of a postwar drought. With payoffs based on the harvest sale prices, sharecropping also encouraged cotton production. In 1876, 60 percent of the black labor force was planting cotton. This emphasis on cotton undermined food production; the agricultural South actually had to import food from other regions.

High cotton prices suited the Republican agenda of stimulating economic development, especially investment in railroads to carry southern crops to market. Indeed, northern railroads saved Georgia's peach industry by bringing that perishable commodity more quickly to urban consumers. Atlanta, burned by Sherman's army during the Civil War, emerged as a rail center for southern commerce and soon became a model for other towns that vied for railroad lines. Republicans and Democrats alike supported government aid to railroads, giving tax breaks, public lands, and convict labor for private companies, while ignoring cases of bribery and corruption. Such practices greatly increased the states' debt, and left local governments vulnerable when the economy faltered in the early 1870s.

The penetration of railroads into the mountainous counties of the South, where nonslaveholding farmers had practiced subsistence agriculture before the Civil War, altered the small farm economy. As upcountry farmers turned to cotton to recover from wartime debts, postwar crop failures worsened their economic position. Using newly developed commercial fertilizers (delivered by railroads), planting fewer acres of corn and grains (and importing food from the Midwest by rail), and cultivating previously unproductive fields, small farmers became increasingly dependent on merchants' credit to obtain supplies and tools. "Nearly everybody has abandoned the ways of their fathers, and caught the cotton planting mania," lamented a Georgia newspaper. When cotton prices hit a plateau in the mid-1870s, overly specialized farmers went deeper into debt, often losing their land and becoming tenants or sharecroppers.

Poor farm workers, white and black alike, also lost an economic step when landowners began to demand fence laws in the 1870s to restrict open grazing on private property. In addition, seasonal game laws, designed to protect dwindling numbers of deer, fish, and birds, removed a significant source of nutrition for poorer families. When whites complained that blacks hunted singing birds that had "claims upon human sympathy, and are besides unfit for food," they were overlooking the importance of such dietary supplements. Despite common economic problems of rural poverty, abiding racial tensions between whites and blacks prevented political cooperation.

Rebuilding the National Economy

Amid the political and constitutional crises of Reconstruction, the country embarked on an era of unprecedented economic growth. Indeed, one reason for the weakness of the southern economy

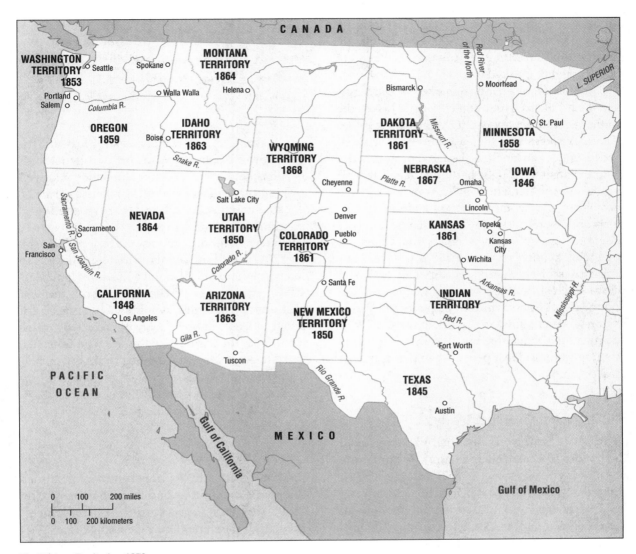

The Western Territories, 1870

after the Civil War was that northern investors saw greater profits in western development. The great railroad boom, interrupted by the war, now moved to completion, linking eastern cities with western agriculture. Railroads, in turn, stimulated agricultural expansion, not only by more easily bringing southern cotton to northern markets and western food to southern cotton growers but also by encouraging an international migration of farmers into the western territories. Instead of joining the underpaid farm labor of the southern states, European and Chinese immigrants found opportunities in the West. Commercial farming also demanded organized markets for wholesale distribution, boosting the growth of rail centers like Chicago and Atlanta.

The creation of a national marketplace accentuated the problems of cultural outsiders. Just as the southern cotton economy limited the opportunities of former slaves and increased friction between landed whites and landless blacks, so postwar westward expansion brought battle-hardened federal troops into conflict with the Plains nations. While most citizens welcomed immigrants from Scandinavia and western Europe, anti-Asian sentiments provoked opposition to newcomers from China. Yet the preoccupation of post–Civil War Americans with issues of economic development deflected public interest from questions of Reconstruction and the rights of nonwhites. The politics of Washington—even the historic issues of the Civil War constitutional amendments—ultimately seemed less important to most people than did mundane local concerns.

Building a National Rail Network

"The whole country is opening up," exclaimed the hustler Colonel Sellers in Mark Twain's satire of post–Civil War greed, *The Gilded Age* (1874). "Slap down the rails and bring the land to market." Such rhetoric captured the national mood. Between 1862 and 1873, Congress gave 100 million acres of public land, plus $100 million of federal loans and bonds, to feed the railroad fever that doubled the length of the nation's tracks. Nearly $20 million of that sum lined the pockets of dishonest investors—and several congressmen who greased the wheels of public spending. But federal subsidies represented only a fraction of public investment. Small town boosters and ambitious farmers joined land speculators and politicians in endorsing railroad construction.

"Nothing so rapidly pushes forward the car of progress and civilization as the railroad locomotive."

"Nothing . . . so rapidly pushes forward the car of progress and civilization," coaxed a Minneapolis newspaper, "as the railroad locomotive." Hoping that railroads would bring prosperity to isolated communities, boosters persuaded local governments to grant special tax advantages to encourage building. European investors also sank over $500 million (equivalent to $5 billion in today's money) into U.S. rail companies in the late 1860s. Such vast sums encouraged both speculation and corruption, as lobbyists appealed for public aid. The bubble finally burst in 1873 when Jay Cooke, the nation's leading railroad financier, failed to cover his overextended credit, precipitating a panic on Wall Street: "A monstrous yell," according to one observer. The Panic of 1873 brought the railroad boom to an abrupt halt.

Chinese Immigration

The construction of the transcontinental railroad epitomized the effort to create a national geography. "They are laying siege to Nature in her strongest citadel," declared a California newspaper in 1865 as workers of the Central Pacific began cutting roadbeds through the rugged high Sierra. With gold and silver mines attracting white laborers, western railroad builders set aside their prejudices and recruited Chinese immigrants. Using newly invented nitroglycerin, Chinese workers blasted through sheer rock, dug perilous snow tunnels, hung off mountain cliffs, and kept on laying track. "Their quiet efficiency," observed one employer, "was astounding." In 1868, U.S. ambassador

"Little Indian Boy, Step Out of the Way for the Big Engine," declared one promotional placard, demonstrating the railroads' lack of sympathy for the Plains peoples through whose lands they passed.

Anson Burlingame negotiated a treaty with China, expanding trade and permitting unrestricted immigration, which annually brought 18,000 Chinese workers into the country. Yet the 1790 Naturalization Act still prohibited Chinese from becoming U.S. citizens, and no politician endorsed extending the Fourteenth Amendment to cover Chinese settlers.

Chinese railroad workers also confronted racist violence, went on strike for equal pay, and demonstrated great technical skill, but their achievements earned little applause. Just before the symbolic golden spike linked the transcontinental railroad at Promontory Point, Utah, in May 1869, Chinese workers were moved out of camera range. After the completion of the major railroads, the Chinese found employment on California land reclamation projects; in San Francisco factories making shoes, cigars, or clothing; and as farmers specializing in Chinese vegetables and fruits. On the east coast, some businesses used Chinese as strikebreakers, fueling public hostility to "coolie"

labor. Whites resented Chinese competition, and the California Workingmen's party demanded their exclusion. By 1882, Congress voted to restrict most Chinese immigration.

Pacifying the Plains

The imperatives of railroad building also changed the government's relations with Native American inhabitants near the lines. Few railroad developers considered the Plains peoples anything but an obstacle. As new track extended onto the Plains, railroad crews became targets for warriors who resisted the invasion of their buffalo hunting grounds. General William Tecumseh Sherman, appointed in 1865 to command the U.S. Army between the Mississippi and the Rocky Mountains, quickly perceived a solution to the impending conflict. He proposed that the Sioux be moved to northern reservations and the Arapaho, Cheyenne, and Comanche peoples be pushed to the south, leaving a corridor for westward migrants. The policy required revisions of earlier treaties, but Sherman demanded cooperation. "The road must be built," he told the Lakota Sioux, "and you must not interfere with it."

U.S. peace commissioners opened negotiations to restrict the Sioux on the northern Plains, but the Army did not wait for their approval before building a line of forts along the Powder River, or Bozeman trail. Sioux leader Red Cloud then broke off talks and began to harass the outposts. In 1866, the Sioux lured an overeager cavalry contingent into an ambush and killed the entire force. General Sherman, well known for his advocacy of total warfare, vowed revenge, "even to their extermination." Moderate voices in Washington demanded a peaceful settlement, but skirmishing continued, and Red Cloud refused to negotiate until the Army abandoned the Powder River forts. In 1868, the U.S. government accepted that condition. The new treaty of Fort Laramie established the "Great Sioux Reservation" in western South Dakota, allowing unceded territory west of the reservation to be closed to whites, and permitted the Sioux to hunt in this region "so long as buffalo may range there in numbers sufficient to justify the chase."

Other Native American groups also signed reservation treaties, but the decentralized nature of tribal politics made compliance impossible. As Native warriors continued to attack white settlements, military leaders launched a winter campaign against the southern Cheyenne in 1868. Realizing that peaceful people would surely suffer, the Army found justification in the recent war against the Confederate South. "Did we cease to throw shells into Vicksburg or Atlanta because women and children were there?" asked General Philip Sheridan. The cavalry proceeded to attack the southern groups in north Texas, slaughtering indiscriminately and forcing survivors onto reservations. When the Comanche leader Tosawi asked Sheridan, "Why am I and my people being tormented by you? I am a good Indian," the Civil War hero purportedly replied, "The only good Indians I ever saw were dead."

Whatever his exact words, Sheridan's deeds outraged humanitarian opinion, particularly among Quakers, who pleaded in Washington for a more benevolent policy. Such reformers hoped to eliminate the corruption associated with federal payments to the tribes. At the same time, Christian organizations hoped to "civilize" Native peoples by replacing their community orientation with an individualistic identity. These reformers urged instruction of English to undermine the "mythology and sorcery" of Native languages, which articulated an alternative world-view. To hasten the erosion of group loyalty, Congress ended the treaty-making relationship in 1871, thus transforming Native American *nations* into individual "wards" of the federal government. Instead of negotiating through Native leaders, Washington could now legislate directly for all its dependents.

Despite government efforts to confine the Plains peoples on reservations, inadequate government assistance forced them to hunt buffalo on the plains. To end such practices and establish tribal dependency on the government, U.S. leaders decided to destroy the plains' primary resource: the buffalo. Railroad companies hired hunters to shoot the animals by the thousands, using some to feed their workers but leaving most carcasses to rot. Upon encountering herds, railroad passengers would open the windows and commence firing. Cashing in on the fad, the Kansas Pacific introduced excursion trains for weekend sportsmen. When improvements in tanning techniques increased the value of buffalo hides after 1871, commercial hunters used fast-loading rifles to kill dozens of animals in mere minutes. The annual number of slaughtered buffalo reached 2.5 million

Upon encountering herds, railroad passengers would open the windows and commence firing.

in 1871 and exceeded 7 million by 1874. The hunters "are destroying the Indians' commissary," gloated General Sheridan. By 1876, the last of the great herds had vanished.

As long as buffalo remained on the northern Plains, the 1868 treaty gave the Sioux the right to hunt off their reservations. Four years later, the Northern Pacific railroad announced plans to construct a line through nonreservation territory. When federal officials requested a concession for the right-of-way, Sioux leaders refused to negotiate. But after a military survey discovered gold in the Black Hills, an area considered sacred by the Sioux, the government could not stop whites' invasion of Sioux lands. The Sioux still refused to cooperate, leading the War Department to announce a state of war. During the spring of 1876, the U.S. 7th Cavalry, under the command of George Armstrong Custer, rode into the Black Hills to enforce compliance. Encountering a party of Sioux and Cheyenne warriors near the Little Big Horn River, Custer attacked, only to be forced to retreat. The Oglala Sioux Crazy Horse then led an attack on Custer's troops, annihilating the regiment. The disastrous defeat intensified military resolve, and continuing warfare finally forced the Sioux to accept new treaties in 1878.

Farmers Settled the Plains

The military campaigns against the Plains peoples cleared U.S. claims to vast territories and accelerated railroad development. With immense acreage to sell and prospects of carrying western farm produce, the railroads encouraged settlement by European immigrants. Promising prosperity, the companies distributed promotional tracts in multiple languages (English, Swedish, Danish, Norwegian, and Dutch). Although the Homestead Act of 1862 offered free land to settlers, most farmers bought property from the railroads in order to live near the tracks and reduce their shipping costs. In farmhouse kitchens, one visitor noted in 1870, "the railway timetable hangs with the almanac." Despite rising land prices, the white population of the northern Plains (Minnesota, the Dakotas, Nebraska, Kansas) jumped from 300,000 in 1860 to over 2 million twenty years later. In 1870, Kansas farmers grew 17 million bushels of corn; by 1872, Minnesotans harvested 22 million bushels of wheat.

Kansas growers also competed with another railroad commodity: cattle. During the Civil War, Texas cowboys lost their export markets in New Orleans and held enormous herds by the war's end. As the Union Pacific railroad inched westward toward the town of Abilene, Kansas, local investors encouraged cattle drovers to bring their herds to the railhead there for shipment to urban markets. In 1867, 35,000 cows were shipped out of Abilene; one year later, the demand for cattle cars exceeded the supply.

The cattle industry soon collided with agricultural interests. Fearing that Texas cattle would spread disease, Kansas farmers imposed quarantine lines, known as "deadlines," to regulate the cattle trade. Farmers also demanded fence laws to protect their crops, but the shortage of trees made the cost of fencing prohibitive. In 1873, Congress passed the Timber Culture Act, offering free land for planting trees. In 1874, Nebraska's Governor J. Sterling Morton proposed a special day for tree planting, Arbor Day, which later became a legal holiday in many states. Meanwhile, the problem of fencing attracted widespread interest; in the decade after the Civil War, the federal Patent Office issued 800 new patents for fencing. Finally, in 1874, the introduction of barbed wire—flexible, cattle resistant, nearly invisible—provided the long-awaited solution. As the buffalo declined, fenced cattle took over the ranges, and intensive grazing eliminated the natural tall grasses. Prairie fires, a much-feared hazard of the Plains, disappeared.

Most settlers knew enough to expect periods of extreme heat and drought, but few anticipated the severe Plains weather that killed crops and livestock, and nothing presaged the grasshopper invasions of 1873 and 1874. "They came upon us in great numbers, in untold millions, in clouds upon clouds, until their fluttering wings looked like a sweeping snowstorm in the heavens, until their dark bodies covered everything green upon the earth," wrote a Wichita newspaper reporter. "In a few hours many fields that hung thick with long ears of golden maize were stripped bare of their value and . . . in their nakedness mocked the tiller of the soil."

Such disasters accentuated the fragility of farm life. Without adequate public assistance, growers formed cooperative groups to share information and marketing. In 1867, a Department of Agriculture official, Oliver H. Kelley, founded the Patrons of Husbandry, also known as the Grange. This network of social organizations, modeled on the Masons, claimed over 1 million members by the early 1870s. With the goal of protecting self-sufficient family farms, the Grange organized cooperative stores and grain elevators to eliminate the commercial middlemen, who seemed to be taking agricultural profits. Targeting bankers, merchants, and especially railroads, the Granger movement persuaded several midwestern states to prohibit discounts for large shippers or lower charges for long hauls than short trips, and to set maximum freight rates. These "Granger laws" on railroad pricing initially won approval from the Supreme Court in

Munn v. Illinois (1877), though later rulings prohibited states from regulating interstate commerce.

Organizing Urban Life

Rising agricultural production in the western states provided the stimulus for rapid urban expansion. After the Civil War, cities assumed a major role in building a national economy by importing raw produce and selling finished products. To contemporaries, the complexity of the urban economies encouraged comparisons to technological machinery; the burgeoning cities appeared immense, complicated, inhuman—and fast.

When Mrs. O'Leary's cow purportedly kicked over a kerosene lamp and ignited the great Chicago fire of 1871, the city's official weatherman described the ensuing firestorm as a "column of flame and smoke, which was [spinning] contrary to the hands of a watch." In the city, keeping time now depended less on clocks than on watches: portable, personal, pocket-held timepieces, which symbolized a new, speedier pace of urban life. "Atlanta is certainly a fast place in every sense of the word," remarked a local newspaper. Its residents "live fast and they die fast. They make money fast and they spend it fast. . . . The whole city seems to be running on wheels, and all of the inhabitants continually blowing off steam." The illusion of prosperity belied great disparities of urban wealth; most fatalities in the Chicago fire occurred in poor neighborhoods where flimsy construction and crowded conditions gave residents little time to escape. Afterwards, efforts to impose fire-resistant architecture failed because most residents lacked the resources to rebuild with anything but wood.

Newly invented steam-powered elevators offered the possibility of building vertically, but urban planners preferred geographical dispersal. To open new residential areas, New York City launched an elevated train system in 1868 and introduced an experimental subway two years later. San Francisco's

The Chicago Fire destroyed 17,000 buildings and left 100,000 residents—one-third of the city's population—homeless on October 8 and 9, 1871.

cable cars began running in 1873, stimulating residential construction on the city's hills. To ease health problems associated with urban congestion, New York adopted the Tenement House law in 1867, requiring improved ventilation, lighting, and sanitation in these multistoried residential buildings. Taking advantage of new streetcars, middle-class city dwellers were already fleeing to suburbs, where landscape architects introduced contour designs instead of rectangular streets.

The most dramatic urban developments remained commercial. For cattle, horses, pigs, and sheep, Chicago stood at the end of the line. The Union stockyards, begun in 1865, covered 100 acres, used three miles of troughs and half a million gallons of water to process tens of thousands of animals each day. The vast disassembly lines, notorious for their stench, and the introduction of refrigerated railcars in the 1860s, made Chicago the meat-packing center of the nation, if not the world.

New York's municipal development projects—street grading, dock renovations, and new transit lines—offered opportunities for a different kind of profiteering. Financed by municipal bonds instead of taxes, construction projects gave Mayor William Marcy "Boss" Tweed and his cronies an opportunity to dispense 60,000 patronage jobs while inflating the city debt by $60 million. The political organization, one contemporary boasted, "works with the precision of a well-regulated machine." Revelations of Tweed Ring graft in 1871 brought public outrage, and the corrupt mayor ended his days in prison. Yet municipal "machine" politics, supported by expensive public works projects, dominated the nation's cities well into the next century.

The End of Reconstruction

The creation of a national economy did not overcome ingrained traditions of local politics. Municipal government, county seats, and state legislatures remained the locus of power to resolve most economic issues. To be sure, post–Civil War citizens understood that the federal government had a responsibility to settle constitutional issues in the seceded states and to protect the rights of freed slaves. But after ratification of the Fourteenth and Fifteenth Amendments, preoccupation with economic development, together with the frustrations of supervising southern government, discouraged federal involvement in southern politics.

The Grant Years

In 1868, the Republican party nominated Civil War hero Ulysses S. Grant to run for president. His campaign slogan "Let Us Have Peace" characterized the climate of national politics. Although

The Election of 1868

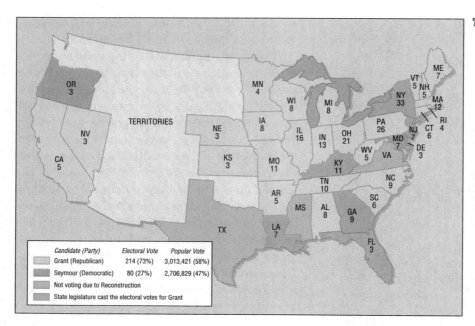

Candidate (Party)	Electoral Vote	Popular Vote
Grant (Republican)	214 (73%)	3,013,421 (58%)
Seymour (Democratic)	80 (27%)	2,706,829 (47%)
Not voting due to Reconstruction		
State legislature cast the electoral votes for Grant		

Democrats attacked Republican Reconstruction as a violation of constitutional principles, Civil War patriotism assured Republican majorities in the northern states and in the electoral college. Southern blacks also voted Republican. Yet, in 1868 Grant's popular majority was only 300,000. Despite his fine military leadership, moreover, the new president proved a poor administrator, appointing officials who would taint his tenure with scandal. Such political trouble further weakened public interest in a rigorous program of continued reconstruction.

Although Grant himself seemed above corruption, he remained loyal to cabinet officers, the vice president, and his personal secretary, even after their acceptance of bribes became public knowledge. The president's use of the spoils system to reward his supporters angered members of his own party, and Congress created a Civil Service Commission in 1871 to encourage appointments to public office on the basis of merit. Such reforms threatened the nation's party system, however, and political leaders allowed the commission to expire. Frustration with Grant's leadership finally inspired a party rebellion by self-styled "Liberal Republicans," who promised to provide government by "the best men." In 1872, the Liberal Republicans broke with Grant and nominated Horace Greeley, editor of the New York *Tribune,* for the presidency. Their criticism of "bayonet rule" in the South broadened their appeal among Democrats. But Grant, the Union hero, had the confidence of the North. In addition, the Republican platform favored women's rights, persuading women to campaign for the regular party. Grant easily won reelection.

Redeeming the South

Even before the Liberal Republican rebellion, Democrats had made major gains in the former Confederate states. As early as 1866, the violent Ku Klux Klan and other white vigilante groups had successfully intimidated Republican voters in areas where the political balance was uncertain. Congressional investigations led in 1871 to passage of the Ku Klux Klan Act and other enforcement laws, which made interference with civil and political rights a federal crime. Washington proceeded to prosecute hundreds of cases, and Grant sent federal troops to occupy violent areas. Such acts pacified the South, but accentuated the racial divide between the political parties. In 1872, Congress passed the Amnesty Act, which restored political rights to almost all ex-Confederates, excluding only 500 leading rebels from holding government office. Liberal Republicans worried that these new voters would back Democratic candidates and thus proposed "home rule," the removal of all federal troops from the South, to attract white voters to the Republican party.

"We must make the issue White and Black, race against race," countered a Virginia Democrat in 1873. "The position must be made so odious that no decent white man can support the radical [Republican] ticket and look a gentleman in the face." Calling themselves "Redeemers," Democrats appealed to white supremacy to disrupt the Republican coalition, and persuaded many white Republicans to vote Democratic. The Democrats also made major gains in the northern states. In the 1874 congressional elections, Democrats won control of House of Representatives for the first time since 1861. Thus Republicans lost their ability to coerce the South. Although the lame-duck Republican Congress passed the Civil Rights Act of 1875, outlawing racial discrimination in public places, enforcement required blacks to file legal complaints, a complicated procedure that seldom occurred. The law was virtually dead, even before the Supreme Court ruled it unconstitutional in 1883.

As conservative Democrats regained control of the southern states between 1869 and 1875, African Americans lost both white allies and na-

tional support. In states like Mississippi, whites used economic pressure and intimidation to bring carpetbaggers and scalawags into the Democratic party, while threatening blacks with violence to keep them from voting. Meanwhile, the second Grant administration gave patronage favors to southern Democrats; the Justice Department dropped civil rights cases; and the president refused to send troops to quell violence against black voters.

Such policies received sanction from the Supreme Court, which ruled in the *Slaughterhouse* cases of 1873 that the Fourteenth Amendment protected only national citizenship, not the rights that were traditionally monitored by the states. In 1876, the Court announced in *U.S. v. Cruickshank* that the new Amendments applied only to actions by the *states,* not private individuals, and thus restricted federal enforcement of civil rights laws. In addition, the Court held that the Fifteenth Amendment did not guarantee the right to vote. Although civil rights laws would remain on the books, white supremacy, racial segregation, and restrictions on black voting could now be imposed informally without risk of reprisal from the federal government.

The Compromise of 1877

The election of 1876, which pitted Ohio Republican Rutherford B. Hayes against New York Democrat Samuel J. Tilden, spelled the end of Reconstruction. Running on vague promises of political reform, neither candidate achieved a clear victory. Although Tilden led by 250,000 popular votes, his electoral college total of 184 fell one short of the necessary majority. Hayes could claim 165 electoral votes. Twenty disputed electoral votes remained in three southern states and Oregon. As inauguration day approached without a clear winner, Congress appointed an electoral committee to resolve the deadlock. Party loyalty continued to block a solution.

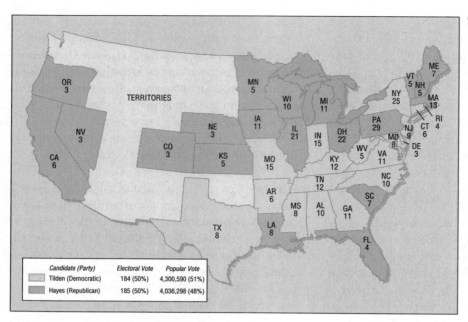

The Election of 1876

Candidate (Party)	Electoral Vote	Popular Vote
Tilden (Democratic)	184 (50%)	4,300,590 (51%)
Hayes (Republican)	185 (50%)	4,036,298 (48%)

Hayes finally agreed to a compromise in order to gain the contested southern electors. In exchange for the presidency, Republicans agreed to appoint a southerner to the cabinet, appropriate funds for public improvements in the South, and adopt a policy of noninterference in southern politics. Shortly after taking office, Hayes consummated the deal by removing the last federal troops from Louisiana and South Carolina, facilitating Democratic electoral victories in both states.

Although southern whites returned to political power and white property owners continued to control the southern economy, the constitutional changes made during Reconstruction had given African Americans a bedrock of civil rights, which, while often ignored, were never effaced. Racial prejudice against nonwhites certainly did not diminish, but racism no longer had legal sanction in the U.S. Constitution. Moreover, ex-slaves used the advantages of civil rights to build independent cultural institutions (families, churches, schools) that offered them some protection and autonomy. To be sure, many political outsiders were not content with the Reconstruction settlement and continued to demand equal rights. This dissatisfaction with second-class citizenship would flower in the civil rights movements of later generations.

The National Union

Pride in economic growth and progress, not the reconstruction of a national identity, set the tone of the hundredth anniversary celebrations of the Declaration of Independence. In 1876, Philadelphia opened a six-month Centennial Exposition that drew nearly 10 million spectators to celebrate the nation's historical development. Here the "progress of the age," in the words of the fair's promoters, could be seen in a panoply of in-

President Grant and the emperor of Brazil officially opened the Philadelphia Centennial Exhibition by starting the great Corliss engine in Machinery Hall.

technology epitomized a dynamic vision of the future.

Visitors to the Centennial Exposition looked backward as well. Anthropological displays depicted the work of more primitive peoples who had first inhabited the continent, showing tipis and canoes, pottery and tools, and life-size figures made of wax and papier-mache, to contrast with the symbols of modern industry. Most observers lauded the change. "The red man," remarked the writer William Dean Howells, "as he appears in effigy and in photograph . . . is a hideous demon, whose malign traits can hardly inspire any emotion softer than abhorrence." African Americans were also seen at the fair, though they were not permitted to work on the construction projects that built the exposition, and a guidebook promised "a band of old-time plantation 'darkies' who will sing their quaint melodies and strum the banjo before visitors of every clime." Frederick Douglass was invited to sit on the dignitaries' platform, but was not permitted to speak.

The presence of foreign nationals (Chinese, Japanese, Egyptians, Turks, Spaniards) amused Philadelphia's visitors; boys and men pursued these strangers, hooting and shouting, according to one observer, "as if they had been animals of a strange species." A woman's pavilion, which had been added as "an afterthought," showed needlepoint, weaving, and power looms supervised by a "lady engineer." On July 4, five women reformers, including Susan B. Anthony and Elizabeth Cady Stanton, interrupted ceremonies to distribute copies of a Declaration of Rights for Women. It included demands that women be allowed to serve on juries and vote for government representatives, and that the word *male* be deleted from legal codes. Meanwhile, the public was fascinated by an off-limits side-show strip that featured "wild men of Borneo, and wild children of Australia, the fat

ventions: the telephone, typewriter, electric light, Westinghouse's railroad air brake, Fleischmann's yeast, linoleum. All stood in wonder, even the poet Walt Whitman, before the 700-ton Corliss steam engine that silently powered the fair. Equally impressive was the 700-pound electric pendulum clock, which governed 26 other clocks precisely to the second. "Yes," said a visitor, "it is still in these things of iron and steel that the national genius most freely speaks." The promise of woman . . . heavy enough to entitle her a place in Machinery Hall." Popular with the poor, a meeting point for "tramps, peddlers, and boot-blacks" as well as tipplers, prostitutes, and others labeled "pests and nuisances," the district was demolished by public order.

The Centennial Exposition thus embraced the contradictions of the national society: rich and poor, male and female, white and a rainbow of other colors. But, significantly, some groups were better represented than others. So it appeared within the nation's political system. In 1876, African Americans remained on the threshold of national citizenship; women, as the Fifteenth Amendment made manifest, were clearly excluded. Nor were Asians welcome: "The Chinese will not assimilate with our population," stated a Philadelphia newspaper in 1876. "From a plaything and curiosity [he] has become a vexing problem." Most citizens viewed Native Americans only as hostile, never more so than when the telegraph brought the shocking news that Custer's cavalry had been annihilated by the Sioux at the Little Big Horn. As the government celebrated a century of independence, the country remained culturally fragmented, the meaning of the past as uncertain as the shape of its future.

INFOTRAC® COLLEGE EDITION EXERCISES

For additional reading go to InfoTrac College Edition, your online research library at *http://web1.infotrac-college.com.*

Subject search: Ku Klux Klan, history
Keyword search: black codes
Subject search: Reconstruction
Keyword search: Fourteenth Amendment
Keyword search: Johnson impeachment
Keyword search: William Marcy Tweed

Keyword search: transcontinental railroad
Subject search: Ulysses S. Grant
Keyword search: Little Big Horn
Keyword search: Rutherford B. Hayes

ADDITIONAL READING

Eric Foner, *Reconstruction: America's Unfinished Revolution, 1863–1877* (1988). A comprehensive study of the era, this book illuminates the political struggles produced by the Civil War and the end of slavery.

Michael Perman, *Emancipation and Reconstruction: 1862–1879* (1987). This brief book summarizes the political and historiographical issues of the period.

John Brinckerhoff Jackson, *American Space: The Centennial Years, 1865–1876* (1972). This study explores the relationship of geography and culture.

Debating the Vote for Blacks and Women

Ellen Carol DuBois, ed., *Elizabeth Cady Stanton, Susan B. Anthony: Correspondence, Writings, Speeches* (1981). This collection of primary sources provides a good complement to DuBois's earlier book, *Feminism and Suffrage* (1978), which begins with pre–Civil War reformism.

Reconstruction Comes to the South

Laura F. Edwards, *Gendered Strife and Confusion: The Political Culture of Reconstruction* (1997). This book examines the effect of legal changes on southern domestic life.

Howard N. Rabinowitz, *Race Relations in the Urban South: 1865–1890* (1978). This social history of five southern cities should be supplemented by Leon F. Litwack's *Been In the Storm So Long* (1979), listed in Chapter 14.

Southern Politics and Economy

William Cohen, *At Freedom's Edge: Black Mobility and the Southern White Quest for Racial Control, 1861–1915* (1991). Analyzes African American labor opportunities and the prospects of postwar migration.

Steven Hahn, *The Roots of Southern Populism: Yeoman Farmers and the Transformation of the Georgia Upcountry, 1850–1890* (1983). This book examines economic changes among small farmers and their effect on social relations.

Building a National Rail Network

David Haward Bain, *Empire Express: Building the First Transcontinental Railroad* (1999). This narrative describes the vast technological undertaking.

Chinese Immigration

Sucheng Chan, *This Bittersweet Soil: The Chinese in California Agriculture, 1860–1910* (1986). This study moves beyond issues of discrimination to consider the forging of Chinese American communities.

Pacifying the Plains

Ralph K. Andrist, *The Long Death: The Last Days of the Plains Indians* (1964). This narrative describes U.S. policy toward the Plains nations.

Organizing Urban Life

Karen Sawislak, *Smoldering City: Chicagoans and the Great Fire, 1871–1874* (1995). Focusing on Chicago's calamity, the author analyzes the related social, economic, and political issues. See also William Cronon's *Nature's Metropolis* (1991), listed in previous chapters.

The Declaration of Independence*

In Congress, July 4, 1776.

A Declaration by the Representatives of the United States of America, in General Congress assembled.

When in the Course of human Events, it becomes necessary for one People to dissolve the Political Bonds which have connected them with another, and to assume among the Powers of the Earth, the separate and equal Station to which the Laws of Nature and of Nature's God entitle them, a decent Respect to the Opinions of Mankind requires that they should declare the causes which impel them to the Separation.

We hold these Truths to be self-evident, that all Men are created equal, that they are endowed by their Creator with certain unalienable Rights, that among these are Life, Liberty, and the Pursuit of Happiness—That to secure these Rights, Governments are instituted among Men, deriving their just Powers from the Consent of the Governed, that whenever any Form of Government becomes destructive of these Ends, it is the Right of the People to alter or to abolish it, and to institute new Government, laying its Foundation on such Principles, and organizing its Powers in such Forms, as to them shall seem most likely to effect their Safety and Happiness. Prudence, indeed, will dictate that Governments long established should not be changed for light and transient Causes; and accordingly all Experience hath shewn, that Mankind are more disposed to suffer, while Evils are sufferable, than to right themselves by abolishing the Forms to which they are accustomed. But when a long Train of Abuses and Usurpations, pursuing invariably the same Object, evinces a Design to reduce them under absolute Despotism, it is their Right, it is their Duty, to throw off such Government, and to provide new Guards for their future Security. Such has been the patient Sufferance of these Colonies; and such is now the Necessity which constrains them to alter their former Systems of Government. The History of the present King of Great Britain is a History of repeated Injuries and Usurpations, all having in direct Object the Establishment of an absolute Tyranny over these States. To prove this, let facts be submitted to a candid World.

He has refused his Assent to Laws, the most wholesome and necessary for the public Good.

He has forbidden his Governors to pass Laws of immediate and pressing Importance, unless suspended in their Operation till his Assent should be obtained; and when so suspended, he has utterly neglected to attend to them.

He has refused to pass other Laws for the Accommodation of large Districts of People, unless those People would relinquish the Right of Representation in the Legislature, a Right inestimable to them, and formidable to Tyrants only.

*The spelling, capitalization, and punctuation of the original have been retained here.

He has called together Legislative Bodies at Places unusual, uncomfortable, and distant from the Depository of their Public Records, for the sole Purpose of fatiguing them into Compliance with his Measures.

He has dissolved Representative Houses repeatedly, for opposing with manly Firmness his Invasions on the Rights of the People.

He has refused for a long Time, after such Dissolutions, to cause others to be elected; whereby the Legislative Powers, incapable of Annihilation, have returned to the People at large for their exercise; the State remaining in the mean time exposed to all the Dangers of Invasion from without, and Convulsions within.

He has endeavoured to prevent the Population of these States; for that Purpose obstructing the Laws for Naturalization of Foreigners; refusing to pass others to encourage their Migration hither, and raising the Conditions of new Appropriations of Lands.

He has obstructed the Administration of Justice, by refusing his Assent to Laws for establishing Judiciary Powers.

He has made Judges dependent on his Will alone, for the Tenure of their offices, and the Amount and payments of their Salaries.

He has erected a Multitude of new Offices, and sent hither Swarms of Officers to harass our People, and eat out their Substance.

He has kept among us, in times of Peace, Standing Armies, without the consent of our Legislatures.

He has affected to render the Military independent of, and superior to the Civil Power.

He has combined with others to subject us to a Jurisdiction foreign to our Constitution, and unacknowledged by our Laws; giving his Assent to their Acts of pretended Legislation:

For quartering large Bodies of Armed Troops among us:

For protecting them, by a mock Trial, from Punishment for any Murders which they should commit on the Inhabitants of these States:

For cutting off our Trade with all Parts of the World:

For imposing Taxes on us without our Consent:

For depriving us, in many cases, of the Benefits of Trial by Jury:

For transporting us beyond Seas to be tried for pretended Offences:

For abolishing the free System of English Laws in a neighbouring Province, establishing therein an arbitrary Government, and enlarging its Boundaries, so as to render it at once an Example and fit Instrument for introducing the same absolute Rule into these Colonies:

For taking away our Charters, abolishing our most valuable Laws, and altering fundamentally the Forms of our Governments:

For suspending our own Legislatures, and declaring themselves invested with Power to legislate for us in all Cases whatsoever.

He has abdicated Government here, by declaring us out of his Protection and waging War against us.

He has plundered our Seas, ravaged our Coasts, burnt our towns, and destroyed the Lives of our People.

He is, at this Time, transporting large Armies of foreign Mercenaries to compleat the works of Death, Desolation, and Tyranny, already begun with circumstances of Cruelty and Perfidy, scarcely paralleled in the most barbarous Ages, and totally unworthy the Head of a civilized Nation.

He has constrained our fellow Citizens taken Captive on the high Seas to bear Arms against their Country, to become the Executioners of their Friends and Brethren, or to fall themselves by their Hands.

He has excited domestic Insurrections amongst us, and has endeavoured to bring on the Inhabitants of our Frontiers, the merciless Indian Savages, whose known Rule of Warfare is an undistinguished Destruction, of all Ages, Sexes and Conditions.

In every state of these Oppressions we have Petitioned for Redress in the most humble Terms: Our repeated Petitions have been answered only by repeated Injury. A Prince, whose Character is thus marked by every act which may define a Tyrant, is unfit to be the Ruler of a free People.

Nor have we been wanting in Attentions to our British Brethren. We have warned them from Time to Time of Attempts by their Legislature to extend an unwarrantable Jurisdiction over us. We have reminded them of the Circumstances of our Emigration and Settlement here. We have appealed to their native Justice and Magnanimity, and we have conjured them by the Ties of our common Kindred to disavow these Usurpations, which would inevitably interrupt our Connections and Correspondence. They too have been deaf to the Voice of Justice and of Consanguinity. We must, therefore, acquiesce in the Necessity, which denounces our Separation, and hold them, as we hold the rest of Mankind, Enemies in War, in Peace, Friends.

We, therefore, the Representatives of the UNITED STATES OF AMERICA, in General Congress Assembled, appealing to the Supreme Judge of the World for the Rectitude of our Intentions, do, in the Name, and by Authority of the good People of these Colonies, solemnly Publish and Declare, That these United Colonies are, and of Right ought to be, Free and Independent States; that they are absolved from all Allegiance to the British Crown, and that all political Connection between them and the State of Great Britain, is and ought to be totally dissolved; and that as Free and Independent States, they have full Power to levy War, conclude Peace, contract Alliances, establish Commerce, and to do all other Acts and Things which Independent States may of right do. And for the support of this declaration, with a firm Reliance on the Protection of divine Providence, we mutually pledge to each other our Lives, our Fortunes, and our sacred Honor.

Constitution of the United States of America*

We the people of the United States, in Order to form a more perfect Union, establish Justice, insure domestic Tranquility, provide for the common defence, promote the general Welfare, and secure the Blessings of Liberty to ourselves and our posterity, do ordain and establish this Constitution for the United States of America.

Article I

Section 1. All legislative Powers herein granted shall be vested in a Congress of the United States, which shall consist of a Senate and House of Representatives.

Section 2. The House of Representatives shall be composed of Members chosen every second Year by the People of the several States, and the Electors in each State shall have the Qualifications requisite for Electors of the most numerous Branch of the State Legislature.

No person shall be a Representative who shall not have attained to the Age of twenty-five Years, and been seven Years a Citizen of the United States, and who shall not, when elected, be an Inhabitant of that State in which he shall be chosen.

Representatives and direct [Taxes][1] shall be apportioned among the several States which may be included within this Union, according to their respective Numbers [which shall be determined by adding to the whole Number of free Persons, including those bound to Service for a Term of Years, and excluding Indians not taxed, three fifths of all other Persons].[2] The actual Enumeration shall be made within three Years after the first Meeting of the Congress of the United States, and within every subsequent Term of ten Years, in such Manner as they shall by Law direct. The Number of Representatives shall not exceed one for every thirty Thousand, but each State shall have at Least one Representative; and until such enumeration shall be made, the State of New Hampshire shall be entitled to chuse three, Massachusetts eight, Rhode Island and Providence Plantations one, Connecticut five, New-York six, New Jersy four, Pennsylvania eight, Delaware one, Maryland six, Virginia ten, North Carolina five, South Carolina five, and Georgia three.

When vacancies happen in the Representation from any State, the Executive Authority thereof shall issue Writs of Election to fill such Vacancies.

The House of Representatives shall chuse their Speaker and other Officers; and shall have the sole Power of Impeachment.

*The spelling, capitalization, and punctuation of the original have been retained here. Brackets indicate passages that have been altered by amendments to the Constitution.

1. Modified by the Sixteenth Amendment.
2. Modified by the Fourteenth Amendment.

Section 3. The Senate of the United States shall be composed of two Senators from each State [chosen by the Legislature thereof],[3] for six Years; and each Senator shall have one Vote.

Immediately after they shall be assembled in Consequence of the first Election, they shall be divided as equally as may be into three Classes. The Seats of the Senators of the first Class shall be vacated at the Expiration of the second year, of the second Class at the Expiration of the fourth Year, and of the third Class at the Expiration of the sixth Year, so that one third may be chosen every second Year [and if Vacancies happen by Resignation, or otherwise, during the Recess of the Legislature of any State, the Executive thereof may make temporary Appointments until the next Meeting of the Legislature, which shall then fill such Vacancies.][4]

No Person shall be a Senator who shall not have attained to the Age of thirty Years, and been nine Years a Citizen of the United States, and who shall not, when elected, be an Inhabitant of that State for which he shall be chosen.

The Vice President of the United States shall be President of the Senate, but shall have no Vote, unless they be equally divided.

The Senate shall chuse their other Officers, and also a President pro tempore, in the Absence of the Vice President, or when he shall exercise the Office of President of the United States.

The Senate shall have the sole Power to try all Impeachments. When sitting for that Purpose, they shall be on Oath or Affirmation. When the President of the United States is tried, the Chief Justice shall preside: And no Person shall be convicted without the Concurrence of two thirds of the Members present.

Judgment in Cases of Impeachment shall not extend further than to removal from Office, and disqualification to hold and enjoy any Office of honor, Trust or Profit under the United States; but the Party convicted shall nevertheless be liable and subject to Indictment, Trial, Judgment and Punishment, according to Law.

Section 4. The Times, Places and Manner of holding Elections for Senators and Representatives, shall be prescribed in each State by the Legislature thereof; but the Congress may at any time by Law make or alter such Regulations, except as to the Places of chusing Senators.

[The Congress shall assemble at least once in every Year, and such Meeting shall be on the first Monday in December, unless they shall by Law appoint a different Day.][5]

Section 5. Each House shall be the Judge of the Elections, Returns and Qualifications of its own Members, and a Majority of each shall constitute a Quorum to do Business; but a smaller Number may adjourn from day to day, and may be authorized to compel the Attendance of absent Members, in such Manner, and under such Penalties as each House may provide.

Each House may determine the Rules of its Proceedings, punish its Members for disorderly Behaviour, and, with the Concurrence of two thirds, expel a Member.

Each House shall keep a Journal of its Proceedings, and from time to time publish the same, excepting such Parts as may in their Judgment require Secrecy; and the Yeas and Nays of the Members of either House on any question shall, at the Desire of one fifth of those present, be entered on the Journal.

Neither House, during the Session of Congress, shall, without the Consent of the other, adjourn for more than three days, nor to any other Place than that in which the two Houses shall be sitting.

3. Repealed by the Seventeenth Amendment.
4. Modified by the Seventeenth Amendment.

5. Changed by the Twentieth Amendment.

Section 6. The Senators and Representatives shall receive a Compensation for their Services, to be ascertained by Law, and paid out of the Treasury of the United States. They shall in all Cases, except Treason, Felony and Breach of the Peace, be privileged from Arrest during their Attendance at the Session of their respective Houses, and in going to and returning from the same; and for any Speech or Debate in either House, they shall not be questioned in any other Place.

No Senator or Representative shall, during the Time for which he was elected, be appointed to any civil Office under the Authority of the United States, which shall have been created, or the Emoluments whereof shall have been encreased during such time; and no Person holding any Office under the United States, shall be a Member of either House during his Continuance in Office.

Section 7. All Bills for raising Revenue shall originate in the House of Representatives; but the Senate may propose or concur with Amendments as on other Bills.

Every Bill which shall have passed the House of Representatives and the Senate, shall, before it become a Law, be presented to the President of the United States; If he approves he shall sign it, but if not he shall return it, with his objections to that House in which it shall have originated, who shall enter the Objections at large on their Journal, and proceed to reconsider it. If after such Reconsideration two thirds of that House shall agree to pass the Bill, it shall be sent, together with the Objections, to the other House, by which it shall likewise be reconsidered, and if approved by two thirds of that House, it shall become a Law. But in all such Cases the Votes of both Houses shall be determined by yeas and Nays, and the Names of the Persons voting for and against the Bill shall be entered on the Journal of each House respectively. If any Bill shall not be returned by the President within ten Days (Sundays excepted) after it shall have been presented to him, the Same shall be a Law, in like Manner as if he had signed it, unless the Congress by their Adjournment prevent its Return, in which Case it shall not be a Law.

Every Order, Resolution, or Vote to which the Concurrence of the Senate and House of Representatives may be necessary (except on a question of Adjournment) shall be presented to the President of the United States; and before the Same shall take Effect, shall be approved by him, or being disapproved by him, shall be repassed by two thirds of the Senate and House of Representatives, according to the Rules and Limitations prescribed in the Case of a Bill.

Section 8. The Congress shall have Power To lay and collect Taxes, Duties, Imposts and Excises, to pay the Debts and provide for the common Defence and general Welfare of the United States; but all Duties, Imposts and Excises shall be uniform throughout the United States;

To borrow Money on the credit of the United States;

To regulate Commerce with foreign Nations, and among the several States, and with the Indian Tribes;

To establish a uniform Rule of Naturalization, and uniform Laws on the subject of Bankruptcies throughout the United States;

To coin Money, regulate the Value thereof, and of foreign Coin, and fix the Standard of Weights and Measures;

To provide for the Punishment of counterfeiting the Securities and current Coin of the United States.

To establish Post Offices and post Roads;

To promote the Progress of Science and useful Arts, by securing for limited Times to Authors and Inventors the exclusive Right to their respective Writings and Discoveries;

To constitute Tribunals inferior to the supreme Court;

To define and punish Piracies and Felonies committed on the high Seas, and Offences against the Law of Nations;

To declare War, grant Letters of Marque and Reprisal, and make Rules concerning Captures on Land and Water;

To raise and support Armies, but no Appropriation of Money to that Use shall be for a longer Term than two Years;

To provide and maintain a Navy;

To make Rules for the Government and Regulation of the land and naval Forces;

To provide for calling forth the Militia to execute the Laws of the Union, suppress Insurrections and repel Invasions;

To provide for organizing, arming, and disciplining the Militia, and for governing such Part of them as may be employed in the Service of the United States, reserving to the States respectively, the Appointment of the Officers, and the Authority of training the Militia according to the discipline prescribed by Congress;

To exercise exclusive Legislation in all Cases whatsoever, over such District (not exceeding ten Miles square) as may, by Cession of particular States, and the Acceptance of Congress, become the Seat of the Government of the United States, and to exercise like Authority over all Places purchased by the Consent of the Legislature of the State in which the Same shall be, for the Erection of forts, Magazines, Arsenals, dockYards, and other needful Buildings;—And

To make all Laws which shall be necessary and proper for carrying into Execution the foregoing Powers, and all other Powers vested by this Constitution in the Government of the United States, or in any Department or Officer thereof.

Section 9. The Migration or Importation of such Persons as any of the States now existing shall think proper to admit, shall not be prohibited by the Congress prior to the Year one thousand eight hundred and eight, but a Tax or duty may be imposed on such Importation, not exceeding ten dollars for each Person.

The Privilege of the Writ of Habeas Corpus shall not be suspended, unless when in Cases of Rebellion or Invasion the public Safety may require it.

No Bill of Attainder or ex post facto Law shall be passed.

[No Capitation, or other direct, Tax shall be laid, unless in Proportion to the Census or Enumeration herein before directed to be taken.][6]

No Tax or Duty shall be laid on Articles exported from any State.

No Preference shall be given by any Regulation of Commerce or Revenue to the Ports of one State over those of another; nor shall Vessels bound to, or from, one State, be obliged to enter, clear, or pay Duties in another.

No Money shall be drawn from the Treasury, but in Consequence of Appropriations made by Law; and a regular Statement and Account of the Receipts and Expenditures of all public Money shall be published from time to time.

No Title of Nobility shall be granted by the United States; and no Person holding any Office or Profit or Trust under them, shall, without the Consent of the Congress, accept of any present, Emolument, Office, or Title, of any kind whatever, from any King, Prince, or foreign State.

Section 10. No state shall enter into any Treaty, Alliance, or Confederation; grant Letters of Marque and Reprisal; coin Money; emit Bills of Credit; make any Thing but gold and silver Coin a Tender in Payment of Debts; pass any Bill of Attainder, ex post facto Law, or Law impairing the Obligation of Contracts, or grant any Title of Nobility.

---

6. Modified by the Sixteenth Amendment.

No State shall, without the Consent of the Congress, lay any Imposts or Duties on Imports or Exports, except what may be absolutely necessary for executing its inspection Laws; and the net Produce of all Duties and Imposts, laid by any State on Imports or Exports, shall be for the Use of the Treasury of the United States; and all such Laws shall be subject to the Revision and Controul of the Congress.

No State shall, without the Consent of Congress, lay any duty of Tonnage, keep Troops, or Ships of War in time of Peace, enter into any Agreement or Compact with another State, or with a foreign Power or engage in War, unless actually invaded, or in such imminent Danger as will not admit of delay.

Article II

Section 1. The executive Power shall be vested in a President of the United States of America. He shall hold his Office during the Term of four Years, and, together with the Vice President, chosen for the Same Term, be elected, as follows.

Each State shall appoint, in such Manner as the Legislature thereof may direct, a Number of Electors, equal to the whole Number of Senators and Representatives to which the State may be entitled in the Congress; but no Senator or Representative, or Person holding an Office of Trust or Profit under the United States, shall be appointed an Elector.

[The Electors shall meet in their respective States, and vote by Ballot for two Persons of whom one at least shall not be an Inhabitant of the same State with themselves. And they shall make a List of all the Persons voted for, and of the Number of Votes for each; which List they shall sign and certify, and transmit sealed to the Seat of the Government of the United States, directed to the President of the Senate. The President of the Senate shall, in the Presence of the Senate and House of Representatives, open all the Certificates, and the Votes shall then be counted. The Person having the greatest Number of Votes shall be the President, if such Number be a Majority of the whole Number of Electors appointed; and if there be more than one who have such Majority, and have an equal Number of Votes, then the House of Representatives shall immediately chuse by Ballot one of them for President; and if no Person have a Majority, then from the five highest on the List the said House shall in like Manner chuse the President. But in chusing the President, the Votes shall be taken by States, the Representation from each State having one Vote; A quorum for this Purpose shall consist of a Member or Members from two thirds of the States, and a Majority of all the states shall be necessary to a Choice. In every Case, after the Choice of the President, the Person having the greatest Number of Votes of the Electors shall be the Vice President. But if there should remain two or more who have equal Votes, the Senate shall chuse from them by Ballot the Vice President.][7]

The Congress may determine the Time of chusing the Electors, and the Day on which they shall give their Votes; which Day shall be the same throughout the United States.

No person except a natural born Citizen, or a Citizen of the United States, at the time of the Adoption of this Constitution, shall be eligible to the Office of President; neither shall any Person be eligible to that Office who shall not have attained to the Age of thirty five Years, and been fourteen Years a Resident within the United States.

---

7. Changed by the Twelfth Amendment.

[In Case of the Removal of the President from Office, or of his Death, Resignation, or Inability to discharge the Powers and Duties of the said Office, the same shall devolve on the Vice President, and the Congress may by Law provide for the Case of Removal, Death, Resignation or Inability, both of the President and Vice President, declaring what Officer shall then act as President, and such Officer shall act accordingly, until the Disability be removed, or a President shall be elected.][8]

The President shall, at stated Times, receive for his Services, a Compensation, which shall neither be encreased nor diminished during the Period for which he shall have been elected, and he shall not receive within that Period any other Emolument from the United States, or any of them.

Before he enter on the Execution of his Office, he shall take the following Oath or Affirmation:—"I do solemnly swear (or affirm) that I will faithfully execute the Office of President of the United States, and will to the best of my Ability, preserve, protect and defend the constitution of the United States."

Section 2. The President shall be Commander in Chief of the Army and Navy of the United States, and of the Militia of the several States, when called into the actual Service of the United States; he may require the Opinion, in writing, of the principal Officer in each of the executive Departments, upon any Subject relating to the Duties of their respective Offices, and he shall have Power to grant Reprieves and Pardons for Offences against the United States, except in Cases of Impeachment.

He shall have Power, by and with the Advice and Consent of the Senate, to make Treaties, provided two thirds of the Senators present concur;

8. Modified by the Twenty-fifth Amendment.

and he shall nominate, and by and with the Advice and Consent of the Senate, shall appoint Ambassadors, other public Ministers and Consuls, Judges of the supreme Court, and all other Officers of the United States, whose Appointments are not herein otherwise provided for, and which shall be established by Law; but the Congress may by Law vest the Appointment of such inferior Officers, as they think proper, in the President alone, in the Courts of Law, or in the Heads of Departments.

The President shall have Power to fill up all Vacancies that may happen during the Recess of the Senate, by granting Commissions which shall expire at the end of their next Session.

Section 3. He shall from time to time give to the Congress Information of the State of the Union, and recommend to their Consideration such Measures as he shall judge necessary and expedient; he may, on extraordinary Occasions, convene both Houses, or either of them, and in Case of Disagreement between them, with Respect to the Time of Adjournment, he may adjourn them to such Time as he shall think proper; he shall receive Ambassadors and other public Ministers; he shall take Care that the Laws be faithfully executed, and shall Commission all the Officers of the United States.

Section 4. The President, Vice President and all civil Officers of the United States, shall be removed from Office on Impeachment for, and Conviction of, Treason, Bribery, or other high Crimes and Misdemeanors.

Article III

Section 1. The judicial Power of the United States, shall be vested in one supreme Court, and in such inferior Courts as the Congress may from time to time ordain and establish. The Judges, both of the supreme and inferior Courts, shall hold their Offices during good Behaviour, and shall, at stated Times, receive for their Services, a Compensation, which shall not be diminished during their Continuance in Office.

Section 2. The judicial Power shall extend to all Cases, in Law and Equity, arising under this Constitution, the Laws of the United States, and Treaties made, or which shall be made, under their Authority;—to all Cases affecting Ambassadors, other public Ministers and Consuls;—to all Cases of admiralty and maritime Jurisdiction;—to Controversies to which the United States shall be a Party;—to Controversies between two or more States;—[between a State and Citizens of another State;][9]—between Citizens of different States,—between Citizens of the same State claiming Lands under Grants of different States, [and between a state, or the Citizens thereof, and foreign States, Citizens or Subjects.][10]

In all cases affecting Ambassadors, other public Ministers and Consuls, and those in which a State shall be Party, the supreme Court shall have original Jurisdiction. In all the other Cases before mentioned, the supreme Court shall have appellate Jurisdiction, both as to Law and Fact, with such Exceptions, and under such Regulations as the Congress shall make.

The Trial of all Crimes, except in Cases of Impeachment, shall be by Jury; and such Trial shall be held in the State where the said Crimes shall have been committed; but when not committed within any State, the Trial shall be at such Place or Places as the Congress may by Law have directed.

Section 3. Treason against the United States, shall consist only in levying War against them, or in adhering to their Enemies, giving them Aid and Comfort. No Person shall be convicted of Treason unless on the Testimony of two Witnesses to the same overt Act, or on Confession in open Court.

The Congress shall have Power to declare the Punishment of Treason, but no Attainder of Treason shall work Corruption of Blood, or Forfeiture except during the Life of the Person attainted.

Article IV

Section 1. Full Faith and Credit shall be given in each State to the public Acts, Records, and judicial Proceedings of every other State. And the Congress may by general Laws prescribe the Manner in which such Acts, Records and Proceedings shall be proved, and the Effect thereof.

Section 2. The Citizens of each State shall be entitled to all Privileges and Immunities of Citizens in the several States.

A Person charged in any State with Treason, Felony, or other Crime, who shall flee from Justice, and be found in another State, shall on Demand of the executive Authority of the State from which he fled, be delivered up, to be removed to the State having Jurisdiction of the Crime.

[No Person held to Service or Labour in one State under the Laws thereof, escaping into another, shall, in Consequence of any Law or Regulation therein, be discharged from such Service or Labour, but shall be delivered up on Claim of the Party to whom such Service or Labour may be due.][11]

---

9. Modified by the Eleventh Amendment.
10. Modified by the Eleventh Amendment.

11. Repealed by the Thirteenth Amendment.

Section 3. New States may be admitted by the Congress into this Union; but no new State shall be formed or erected within the Jurisdiction of any other State; nor any State be formed by the Junction of two or more States, or Parts of States, without the Consent of the Legislatures of the States concerned as well as of the Congress.

The Congress shall have Power to dispose of and make all needful Rules and Regulations respecting the Territory or other Property belonging to the United States; and nothing in this Constitution shall be so construed as to Prejudice any Claimes of the United States, or of any particular State.

Section 4. The United States shall guarantee to every State in this Union a Republican Form of Government, and shall protect each of them against Invasion, and on Application of the Legislature, or of the Executive (when the Legislature cannot be convened) against domestic Violence.

Article V

The Congress, whenever two thirds of both Houses shall deem it necessary, shall propose Amendments to this Constitution, or on the Application of the Legislatures of two thirds of the several States, shall call a Convention for proposing Amendments, which, in either Case, shall be valid to all Intents and Purposes, as Part of this Constitution, when ratified by the Legislatures of three fourths of the several States, or by Conventions in three fourths thereof, as the one or the other Mode of Ratification may be proposed by the Congress; Provided that no Amendment which may be made prior to the Year One thousand eight hundred and eight shall in any Manner affect the first and fourth Clauses in the Ninth Section of the first Article; and that no State, without its Consent, shall be deprived of its equal Suffrage in the Senate.

Article VI

All Debts contracted and Engagements entered into, before the Adoption of this Constitution, shall be as valid against the United States under this Constitution, as under the Confederation.

This Constitution, and the laws of the United States which shall be made in Pursuance thereof; and all Treaties made, or which shall be made, under the Authority of the United States, shall be the supreme Law of the Land; and the Judges in every State shall be bound thereby, any Thing in the Constitution or Laws of any State to the Contrary notwithstanding.

The Senators and Representatives before mentioned, and the Members of the several State Legislatures, and all executive and judicial Officers, both of the United States and of the several States, shall be bound by Oath or Affirmation, to support this Constitution; but no religious Text shall ever be required as a Qualification to any Office or public Trust under the United States.

Article VII

The Ratification of the Conventions of nine States, shall be sufficient for the Establishment of this constitution between the States so ratifying the Same.

Done in Convention by the Unanimous Consent of the States present the Seventeenth Day of September in the Year of our Lord one thousand seven hundred and Eighty seven and of the Independence of the United States of America the Twelfth. IN WITNESS whereof we have hereunto subscribed our Names.

Go. WASHINGTON
Presid't. and deputy from Virginia

Attest
William Jackson
Secretary

Delaware
Geo. Read
Gunning Bedford jun
John Dickinson
Richard Basset
Jaco. Broon

Massachusetts
Nathaniel Gorham
Rufus King

Connecticut
Wm. Saml. Johnson
Roger Sherman

New York
Alexander Hamilton

New Jersey
Wh. Livingston
David Brearley
Wm. Paterson
Jona. Dayton

Pennsylvania
B. Franklin
Thomas Mifflin
Robt. Morris
Geo. Clymer
Thos. FitzSimons
Jared Ingersoll

James Wilson
Gouv. Morris

Virginia
John Blair
James Madison Jr.

North Carolina
Wm. Blount
Richd. Dobbs Spaight
Hu. Williamson

South Carolina
J. Rutledge
Charles Cotesworth
Pinckney
Charles Pinckney
Pierce Butler

Georgia
William Few
Abr. Baldwin
New Hampshire
John Langdon
Nicholas Gilman

Maryland
James McHenry
Dan of St. Thos. Jenifer
Danl. Carroll

Amendment I[12]

Congress shall make no law respecting an establishment of religion, or prohibiting the free exercise thereof; or abridging the freedom of speech, or of the press; or the right of the people peace-

12. The first ten amendments were passed by Congress on September 25, 1789, and were ratified on December 15, 1791.

ably to assemble, and to petition the Government for a redress of grievances.

Amendment II

A well regulated militia, being necessary to the security of a free State, the right of the people to keep and bear arms, shall not be infringed.

Amendment III

No Soldier shall, in time of peace be quartered in any house, without the consent of the owner, nor in time of war, but in a manner to be prescribed by law.

Amendment IV

The right of the people to be secure in their persons, houses, papers, and effects, against unreasonable searches and seizures, shall not be violated, and no warrants shall issue, but upon probable cause, supported by oath or affirmation, and particularly describing the place to be searched, and the persons or things to be seized.

Amendment V

No person shall be held to answer for a capital, or otherwise infamous crime, unless on a presentment or indictment of a Grand Jury, except in cases arising in the land or naval forces, or in the militia, when in actual service in time of war or public danger; nor shall any person be subject for the same offence to be twice put in jeopardy of life or limb; nor shall be compelled in any criminal case to be a witness against himself, nor be deprived of life, liberty, or property, without due process of law; nor shall private property be taken for public use, without just compensation.

Amendment VI

In all criminal prosecutions, the accused shall enjoy the right to a speedy and public trial, by an impartial jury of the State and district wherein the crime shall have been committed, which district shall have been previously ascertained by law, and to be informed of the nature and cause of the accusation; to be confronted with the witnesses against him; to have compulsory process for obtaining witnesses in his favor, and to have the assistance of counsel for his defence.

Amendment VII

In Suits at common law, where the value in controversy shall exceed twenty dollars, the right of trial by jury shall be preserved, and no fact tried by a jury, shall be otherwise reexamined in any Court of the United States, than according to the rules of the common law.

Amendment VIII

Excessive bail shall not be required, nor excessive fines imposed, nor cruel and unusual punishments inflicted.

Amendment IX

The enumeration in the Constitution, of certain rights, shall not be construed to deny or disparage others retained by the people.

Amendment X

The powers not delegated to the United States by the Constitution, nor prohibited by it to the States, are reserved to the States respectively, or to the people.

Amendment XI
(Ratified February 7, 1795)

The Judicial power of the United States shall not be construed to extend to any suit in law or equity, commenced or prosecuted against one of the United States by Citizens of another State, or by Citizens or Subjects of any Foreign State.

Amendment XII
(Ratified June 15, 1804)

The Electors shall meet in their respective states, and vote by ballot for President and Vice-President, one of whom, at least, shall not be an inhabitant of the same state with themselves; they shall name in their ballots the person voted for as President, and in distinct ballots the person voted for as Vice President, and they shall make distinct lists of all persons voted for as President, and of all persons voted for as Vice-President, and of the number of votes for each, which lists they shall sign and certify, and transmit sealed to the seat of the government of the United States, directed to the President of the Senate;—The President of the Senate shall, in the presence of the Senate and House of Representatives, open all the certificates and the votes shall then be counted;—The person having the greatest number of votes for President, shall be the President, if such number be a majority of the whole number of Electors appointed; and if no person have such majority, then from the persons having the highest numbers not exceeding three on the list of those voted for as President, the House of Representatives shall choose immediately, by ballot, the President. But in choosing the President, the votes shall be taken by states, the representation from each state having one vote; a quorum for this purpose shall consist of a member or members from two-thirds of the states, and a majority of all the states shall be necessary to a choice. [And if the House of Representatives shall not choose a President whenever the right of choice shall devolve upon them, before the fourth day of March next following, then the Vice-President shall act as President, as in the case of the death or other constitutional disability of the President.]¹³—The person having the greatest number of votes as Vice-President, shall be the Vice-President, if such number be a majority of the whole number of Electors appointed, and if no person have a majority, then from the two highest numbers on the list, the Senate shall choose the Vice-President; a quorum for the purpose shall consist of two-thirds of the whole number of Senators, and a majority of the whole number shall be necessary to a choice. But no person constitutionally ineligible to the office of President shall be eligible to that of Vice-President of the United States.

Amendment XIII
(Ratified on December 6, 1865)

Section 1. Neither slavery nor involuntary servitude, except as a punishment for crime whereof the party shall have been duly convicted, shall exist within the United States, or any place subject to their jurisdiction.

Section 2. Congress shall have power to enforce this article by appropriate legislation.

Amendment XIV
(Ratified on July 9, 1868)

All persons born or naturalized in the United States, and subject to the jurisdiction thereof, are citizens of the United States and of the State wherein they reside. No State shall make or enforce any law which shall abridge the privileges or immunities of citizens of the United States; nor shall any State deprive any person of life, liberty, or property, without due process of law; nor deny to any person within its jurisdiction the equal protection of the laws.

Section 2. Representatives shall be apportioned among the several States according to their respective numbers, counting the whole number of persons in each State, excluding Indians not taxed. But when the right to vote at any election for the choice of electors for President and Vice President of the United States, Representatives in Congress, the Executive and Judicial officers of a State, or the members of the Legislature thereof, is denied to any of the male inhabitants of such State, being [twenty-one]¹⁴ years of age, and citizens of the United States, or in any way abridged, except for participation in rebellion, or other crime, the basis of representation therein shall be reduced in the proportion which the number of such male citizens shall bear to the whole number of male citizens twenty-one years of age in such State.

Section 3. No person shall be a Senator or Representative in Congress, or elector of President and Vice President, or hold any office, civil or military, under the United States, or under any State, who having previously taken an oath, as a member of Congress, or as an officer of the United States, or as a member of any State legislature, or as an executive or judicial officer of any State, to support the Constitution of the United States, shall have engaged in insurrection or rebellion against the same, or given aid or comfort to the enemies thereof. But Congress may by a vote of two-thirds of each House, remove such disability.

13. Changed by the Twentieth Amendment.

14. Changed by the Twenty-sixth Amendment.

Section 4. The validity of the public debt of the United States, authorized by law, including debts incurred for payment of pensions and bounties for services in suppressing insurrection or rebellion, shall not be questioned. But neither the United States nor any State shall assume or pay any debt or obligation incurred in aid of insurrection or rebellion against the United States, or any claim for the loss or emancipation of any slave, but all such debts, obligations and claims shall be held illegal and void.

Section 5. The Congress shall have power to enforce, by appropriate legislation, the provisions of this article.

Amendment XV
(Ratified on February 3, 1870)

Section 1. The right of citizens of the United States to vote shall not be denied or abridged by the United States or by any State on account of race, color, or previous condition of servitude.

Section 2. The Congress shall have power to enforce this article by appropriate legislation.

Amendment XVI
(Ratified on February 3, 1913)

The Congress shall have power to lay and collect taxes on incomes, from whatever source derived, without apportionment among the several States, and without regard to any census or enumeration.

Amendment XVII
(Ratified on April 8, 1913)

The Senate of the United States shall be composed of two Senators from each State, elected by the people thereof, for six years; and each Senator shall have one vote. The electors in each State shall have the qualifications requisite for electors of the most numerous branch of the State legislatures.

When vacancies happen in the representation of any State in the Senate, the executive authority of such State shall issue writs of election to fill such vacancies: *Provided,* That the legislature of any State may empower the executive thereof to make temporary appointments until the people fill the vacancies by election as the legislature may direct.

This amendment shall not be so construed as to affect the election or term of any Senator chosen before it becomes valid as part of the Constitution.

Amendment XVIII
(Ratified on January 16, 1919)

Section 1. After one year from the ratification of this article the manufacture, sale, or transportation of intoxicating liquors within, the importation thereof into, or the exportation thereof from the United States and all territory subject to the jurisdiction thereof for beverage purposes is hereby prohibited.

Section 2. The Congress and the several States shall have concurrent power to enforce this article by appropriate legislation.

Section 3. This article shall be inoperative unless it shall have been ratified as an amendment to the Constitution by the legislatures of the several States, as provided in the Constitution, within seven years from the date of the submission hereof to the States by the Congress.[15]

Amendment XIX
(Ratified on August 18, 1920)

The right of citizens of the United States to vote shall not be denied or abridged by the United States or by any State on account of sex.

15. The Eighteenth Amendment was repealed by the Twenty-first Amendment.

Congress shall have power to enforce this article by appropriate legislation.

Amendment XX
(Ratified on January 23, 1933)

Section 1. The terms of the President and Vice President shall end at noon on the 20th day of January, and the terms of Senators and Representatives at noon on the 3rd day of January, of the years in which such terms would have ended if this article had not been ratified, and the terms of their successors shall then begin.

Section 2. The Congress shall assemble at least once in every year, and such meeting shall begin at noon on the 3rd day of January, unless they shall by law appoint a different day.

Section 3. If, at the time fixed for the beginning of the term of the President, the President elect shall have died, the Vice President elect shall become President. If a President shall not have been chosen before the time fixed for the beginning of his term, or if the President elect shall have failed to qualify, then the Vice President elect shall act as President until a President shall have qualified; and the Congress may by law provide for the case wherein neither a President elect nor a Vice President elect shall have qualified, declaring who shall then act as President, or the manner in which one who is to act shall be selected, and such person shall act accordingly until a President or Vice President shall have qualified.

Section 4. The Congress may by law provide for the case of the death of any of the persons from whom the House of Representatives may choose a President whenever the rights of choice shall have devolved upon them, and for the case of the death of any of the persons from whom the Senate may choose a Vice President whenever the right of choice shall have devolved upon them.

Section 5. Sections 1 and 2 shall take effect on the 15th day of October following the ratification of this article.

Section 6. This article shall be inoperative unless it shall have been ratified as an amendment to the Constitution by the legislatures of three-fourths of the several States within seven years from the date of its submission.

Amendment XXI
(Ratified on December 5, 1933)

Section 1. The eighteenth article of amendment to the Constitution of the United States is hereby repealed.

Section 2. The transportation or importation into any State, Territory, or possession of the United States for delivery or use therein of intoxicating liquors, in violation of the laws thereof, is hereby prohibited.

Section 3. This article shall be inoperative unless it shall have been ratified as an amendment to the Constitution by conventions in the several States, as provided in the Constitution, within seven years from the date of the submission hereof to the States by the Congress.

Amendment XXII
(Ratified on February 27, 1951)

No person shall be elected to the office of the President more than twice, and no person who has held the office of President, or acted as President, for more than two years of a term to which some other person was elected President shall be elected to the office of the President more than once. But this Article shall not apply to any person holding the office of President when this Article was proposed by the Congress, and shall not prevent any person who may be holding the office of President, or acting as President, during the term within which this Article becomes operative from holding the office of President or acting as President during the remainder of such term.

Amendment XXIII
(Ratified on March 29, 1961)

Section 1. The District constituting the seat of Government of the United States shall appoint in such manner as the Congress may direct:

A number of electors of President and Vice President equal to the whole number of Senators and Representatives in Congress to which the District would be entitled if it were a State, but in no event more than the least populous State; they shall be in addition to those appointed by the States, but they shall be considered, for the purposes of the election of President and Vice President, to be electors appointed by a State; and they shall meet in the District and perform such duties as provided by the twelfth article of amendment.

Section 2. The Congress shall have power to enforce this article by appropriate legislation.

Amendment XXIV
(Ratified on January 23, 1964)

Section 1. The right of citizens of the United States to vote in any primary or other election for President or Vice President, for electors for President or Vice President, or for Senator or Representative in Congress, shall not be denied or abridged by the United States or any State by reason of failure to pay any poll tax or other tax.

Section 2. The Congress shall have power to enforce this article by appropriate legislation.

Amendment XXV
(Ratified on February 10, 1967)

Section 1. In case of the removal of the President from office or of his death or resignation, the Vice President shall become President.

Section 2. Whenever there is a vacancy in the office of the Vice President, the President shall nominate a Vice President who shall take office upon confirmation by a majority vote of both Houses of Congress.

Section 3. Whenever the President transmits to the President pro tempore of the Senate and the Speaker of the House of Representatives his written declaration that he is unable to discharge the powers and duties of his office, and until he transmits to them a written declaration to the contrary, such powers and duties shall be discharged by the Vice President as Acting President.

Section 4. Whenever the Vice President and a majority of either the principal officers of the executive departments or of such other body as Congress may by law provide, transmit to the President pro tempore of the Senate and the Speaker of the House of Representatives their written declaration that the President is unable to discharge the powers and duties of his office, the Vice President shall immediately assume the powers and duties of the offices as Acting President.

Thereafter, when the President transmits to the President pro tempore of the Senate and the Speaker of the House of Representatives his written declaration that no inability exists, he shall resume the powers and duties of his office unless the Vice President and a majority of either the principal officers of the executive department or of such other body as Congress may by law provide, transmit within four days to the President pro tempore of the Senate and the Speaker of the House of Representatives their written declaration that the President is unable to discharge the powers and duties of his office. Thereupon Congress shall decide the issue, assembling within forty-eight hours for that purpose if not in session. If the Congress, within twenty-one days after receipt of the latter written declaration, or, if Congress is not in session, within twenty-one days after Congress is required to assemble, determines by two-thirds vote of both Houses that the President is unable to discharge the powers and duties of his office, the Vice President shall continue to discharge the same as Acting President; otherwise; the President shall resume the powers and duties of his office.

Amendment XXVI
(Ratified on July 1, 1971)

Section 1. The right of citizens of the United States, who are eighteen years of age or older, to vote shall not be denied or abridged by the United States or by any State on account of age.

Section 2. The Congress shall have the power to enforce this article by appropriate legislation.

Amendment XXVII
(Ratified on May 7, 1992)

No law, varying the compensation for the services of the Senators and Representatives, shall take effect, until an election of Representatives shall have intervened.

Presidential Elections, 1789–2000

Year	President	Vice President	Party of President	Election Year	Winner's Electoral College Vote %	Winner's Popular Vote %
1789–1797	George Washington	John Adams	None	(1789)	*	No popular vote
				(1793)	*	No popular vote
1797–1801	John Adams	Thomas Jefferson	Fed	(1797)	*	No popular vote
1801–1809	Thomas Jefferson	Aaron Burr (to 1805)	Dem-R	(1801)	HR*	No popular vote
		George Clinton (to 1809)		(1805)	92.0	No popular vote
1809–1817	James Madison	George Clinton (to 1813)	Dem-R	(1809)	69.7	No popular vote
		Elbridge Gerry (to 1817)		(1813)	59.0	No popular vote
1817–1825	James Monroe	Daniel D. Tompkins	Dem-R	(1817)	84.3	No popular vote
				(1821)	99.5	No popular vote
1825–1829	John Quincy Adams	John C. Calhoun	Nat R	(1824)	HR	39.1**
1829–1837	Andrew Jackson	John C. Calhoun (to 1833)	Dem	(1828)	68.2	56.0
		Martin Van Buren (to 1837)		(1832)	76.6	54.5
1837–1841	Martin Van Buren	Richard M. Johnson	Dem	(1836)	57.8	50.9
1841	William H. Harrison	John Tyler	Whig	(1840)	79.6	52.9
1841–1845	John Tyler	(No VP)	Whig	(1840)	—	52.9
(1845–1849)	James K. Polk	George M. Dallas	Dem	(1844)	61.8	49.6

*Electoral College system before the Twelfth Amendment (1804). The original Constitutional provisions called for the person with the second highest total Electoral College vote to be the Vice President.

**Received fewer popular votes than an opponent. HR: Election decided in House of Representatives.

Year	President	Vice President	Party of President	Election Year	Winner's Electoral College Vote %	Winner's Popular Vote %
1849–1850	Zachary Taylor	Millard Fillmore	Whig	(1848)	56.2	47.3
1850–1853	Millard Fillmore	(No VP)	Whig	—	—	—
1853–1857	Franklin Pierce	William R. King	Dem	(1852)	85.8	50.9
1857–1861	James Buchanan	John C. Breckinridge	Dem	(1856)	58.8	45.6
1861–1865	Abraham Lincoln	Hannibal Hamlin (to 1865)	Rep	(1860)	59.4	39.8
		Andrew Johnson (1865)		(1864)	91.0	55.2
1865–1869	Andrew Johnson	(No VP)	Rep	—	—	—
1869–1877	Ulysses S. Grant	Schuyler Colfax (to 1873)	Rep	(1868)	72.8	52.7
		Henry Wilson (to 1877)		(1872)	81.9	55.6
1877–1881	Rutherford B. Hayes	William A. Wheeler	Rep	(1876)	50.1	47.9**
1881	James A. Garfield	Chester A. Arthur	Rep	(1880)	58.0	48.3
1881–1885	Chester A. Arthur	(No VP)	Rep	—	—	—
1885–1889	Grover Cleveland	Thomas A. Hendricks	Dem	(1884)	54.6	48.5
1889–1893	Benjamin Harrison	Levi P. Morton	Rep	(1888)	58.1	47.8**
1893–1897	Grover Cleveland	Adlai E. Stevenson	Dem	(1892)	62.3	46.0
1897–1901	William McKinley	Garret A. Hobart (to 1901)	Rep	(1896)	60.6	51.0
		Theodore Roosevelt (1901)		(1900)	64.7	51.7
1901–1909	Theodore Roosevelt	(No VP, 1901–1905)	Rep	—	—	—
		Charles W. Fairbanks (1905–1909)		(1904)	70.6	56.4
1909–1913	William Howard Taft	James S. Sherman	Rep	(1908)	66.4	51.6
1913–1921	Woodrow Wilson	Thomas R. Marshall	Dem	(1912)	81.9	41.9
				(1916)	52.2	49.3
1921–1923	Warren G. Harding	Calvin Coolidge	Rep	(1920)	76.1	60.3
1923–1929	Calvin Coolidge	(No VP, 1923–1925)	Rep	—	—	—
		Charles G. Dawes (1925–1929)		(1924)	71.9	54.0
1929–1933	Herbert Hoover	Charles Curtis	Rep	(1928)	83.6	58.2
1933–1945	Franklin D. Roosevelt	John N. Garner (1933–1941)	Dem	(1932)	88.9	57.4
		Henry A. Wallace (1941–1945)		(1936)	98.5	60.8
		Harry S Truman (1945)		(1940)	84.6	54.7
				(1944)	81.4	53.4

*Electoral College system before the Twelfth Amendment (1804). The original Constitutional provisions called for the person with the second highest total Electoral College vote to be the Vice President.

**Received fewer popular votes than an opponent. HR: Election decided in House of Representatives.

Year	President	Vice President	Party of President	Election Year	Winner's Electoral College Vote %	Winner's Popular Vote %
1945–1953	Harry S. Truman	(No VP, 1945–1949)	Dem		—	—
		Alban W. Barkley		(1948)	57.1	49.5
1953–1961	Dwight D. Eisenhower	Richard M. Nixon	Rep	(1952)	83.2	55.1
				(1956)	86.1	57.4
1961–1963	John F. Kennedy	Lyndon B. Johnson	Dem	(1960)	58.0	49.7
1963–1969	Lyndon B. Johnson	(No VP, 1963–1965)	Dem		—	—
		Hubert H. Humphrey (1965–1969)		(1964)	90.3	61.6
1969–1974	Richard M. Nixon	Spiro T. Agnew	Rep	(1968)	55.9	43.4
		Gerald R. Ford (appointed)		(1972)	96.7	60.7
1974–1977	Gerald R. Ford	Nelson A. Rockefeller (appointed)	Rep		—	—
1977–1981	Jimmy Carter	Walter Mondale	Dem	(1976)	55.2	50.1
1981–1989	Ronald Reagan	George Bush	Rep	(1980)	90.9	50.7
				(1984)	97.4	59.8
1989–1993	George Bush	J. Danforth Quayle	Rep	(1988)	79.0	53.4
1993–2001	William J. Clinton	Albert Gore	Dem	(1992)	68.8	43.2
				(1996)	70.4	49.9
2001–	George W. Bush	Richard Cheney	Rep	(2000)	50.3	48**

*Electoral College system before the Twelfth Amendment (1804). The original Constitutional provisions called for the person with the second highest total Electoral College vote to be the Vice President.

**Received fewer popular votes than an opponent. HR: Election decided in House of Representatives.

Source for election data: Svend Peterson, *A Statistical History of American Presidential Elections.* New York: Frederick Ungar Publishing, 1963. Updates: Richard Scammon, *America Votes* 19. Washington D.C.: Congressional Quarterly, 1991; *Congressional Quarterly Weekly Report,* Nov. 7, 1992, p. 3552.

Abbreviations:

Dem = Democratic
Dem-R = Democratic-Republican
Fed = Federalist
Dem-J = Jacksonian Democrats
Nat R = National Republican
Rep = Republican
Union = Unionist

Presidential Administrations

President	Vice President	Secretary of State	Secretary of Treasury
George Washington 1789–1797	John Adams 1789–1797	Thomas Jefferson 1789–1794	Alexander Hamilton 1789–1795
		Edmund Randolph 1794–1795 Timothy Pickering 1795–1797	Oliver Wolcott 1795–1797
John Adams 1797–1801	Thomas Jefferson 1797–1801	Timothy Pickering 1797–1800 John Marshall 1800–1801	Oliver Wolcott 1797–1801 Samuel Dexter 1801
Thomas Jefferson 1801–1809	Aaron Burr 1801–1805 George Clinton 1805–1809	James Madison 1801–1809	Samuel Dexter 1801 Albert Gallatin 1801–1809
James Madison 1809–1817	George Clinton 1809–1813 Elbridge Gerry 1813–1817	Robert Smith 1809–1811 James Monroe 1811–1817	Albert Gallatin 1809–1814 George Campbell 1814 Alexander Dallas 1814–1816 William Crawford 1816–1817
James Monroe 1817–1825	Daniel D. Tompkins 1817–1825	John Quincy Adams 1817–1825	William Crawford 1817–1825

Secretary of War	Secretary of Navy	Postmaster General	Attorney General
Henry Knox 1789–1795		Samuel Osgood 1789–1791	Edmund Randolph 1789–1794
Timothy Pickering 1795–1796 James McHenry 1796–1797		Timothy Pickering 1791–1795 Joseph Habersham 1795–1797	William Bradford 1794–1795 Charles Lee 1795–1797
James McHenry 1797–1800 Samuel Dexter 1800–1801	Benjamin Stoddert 1798–1801	Joseph Habersham 1797–1801	Charles Lee 1797–1801
Henry Dearborn 1801–1809	Benjamin Stoddert 1801 Robert Smith 1801–1809	Joseph Habersham 1801 Gideon Granger 1801–1809	Levi Lincoln 1801–1805 John Breckinridge 1805–1807 Caesar Rodney 1807–1809
William Eustis 1809–1813 John Armstrong 1813–1814 James Monroe 1814–1815 William Crawford 1815–1817	Paul Hamilton 1809–1813 William Jones 1813–1814 Benjamin Crowninshield 1814–1817	Gideon Granger 1809–1814 Return Meigs 1814–1817	Caesar Rodney 1809–1811 William Pinkney 1811–1814 Richard Rush 1814–1817
George Graham 1817 John C. Calhoun 1817–1825	Benjamin Crowninshield 1817–1818 Smith Thompson 1818–1823 Samuel Southard 1823–1825	Return Meigs 1817–1823 John McLean 1823–1825	Richard Rush 1817 William Wirt 1817–1825

President	Vice President	Secretary of State	Secretary of Treasury	Secretary of War
John Quincy Adams 1825–1829	John C. Calhoun 1825–1829	Henry Clay 1825–1829	Richard Rush 1825–1829	James Barbour 1825–1828 Peter B. Porter 1828–1829
Andrew Jackson 1829–1837	John C. Calhoun 1829–1833 Martin Van Buren 1833–1837	Martin Van Buren 1829–1831 Edward Livingston 1831–1833 Louis McLane 1833–1834 John Forsyth 1834–1837	Samuel Ingham 1829–1831 Louis McLane 1831–1833 William Duane 1833 Roger B. Taney 1833–1834 Levi Woodbury 1834–1837	John H. Eaton 1829–1831 Lewis Cass 1831–1837 Benjamin Butler 1837
Martin Van Buren 1837–1841	Richard M. Johnson 1837–1841	John Forsyth 1837–1841	Levi Woodbury 1837–1841	Joel R. Poinsett 1837–1841
William H. Harrison 1841	John Tyler 1841	Daniel Webster 1841	Thomas Ewing 1841	John Bell 1841
John Tyler 1841–1845		Daniel Webster 1841–1843 Hugh S. Legaré 1843 Abel P. Upshur 1843–1844 John C. Calhoun 1844–1845	Thomas Ewing 1841 Walter Forward 1841–1843 John C. Spencer 1843–1844 George M. Bibb 1844–1845	John Bell 1841 John C. Spencer 1841–1843 James M. Porter 1843–1844 William Wilkins 1844–1845
James K. Polk 1845–1849	George M. Dallas 1845–1849	James Buchanan 1845–1849	Robert J. Walker 1845–1849	William L. Marcy 1845–1849
Zachary Taylor 1849–1850	Millard Fillmore 1849–1850	John M. Clayton 1849–1850	William M. Meredith 1849–1850	George W. Crawford 1849–1850
Millard Fillmore 1850–1853		Daniel Webster 1850–1852 Edward Everett 1852–1853	Thomas Corwin 1850–1853	Charles M. Conrad 1850–1853
Franklin Pierce 1853–1857	William R. King 1853–1857	William L. Marcy 1853–1857	James Guthrie 1853–1857	Jefferson Davis 1853–1857

Secretary of Navy	Postmaster General	Attorney General	Secretary of Interior
Samuel Southard 1825–1829	John McLean 1825–1829	William Wirt 1825–1829	
John Branch 1829–1831 Levi Woodbury 1831–1834 Mahlon Dickerson 1834–1837	William Barry 1829–1835 Amos Kendall 1835–1837	John M. Berrien 1829–1831 Roger B. Taney 1831–1833 Benjamin Butler 1833–1837	
Mahlon Dickerson 1837–1838 James K. Paulding 1838–1841	Amos Kendall 1837–1840 John M. Niles 1840–1841	Benjamin Butler 1837–1838 Felix Grundy 1838–1840 Henry D. Gilpin 1840–1841	
George E. Badger 1841	Francis Granger 1841	John J. Crittenden 1841	
George E. Badger 1841 Abel P. Upshur 1841–1843 David Henshaw 1843–1844 Thomas Gilmer 1844 John Y. Mason 1844–1845	Francis Granger 1841 Charles A. Wickliffe 1841–1845	John J. Crittenden 1841 Hugh S. Legaré 1841–1843 John Nelson 1843–1845	
George Bancroft 1845–1846 John Y. Mason 1846–1849	Cave Johnson 1845–1849	John Y. Mason 1845–1846 Nathan Clifford 1846–1848 Isaac Toucey 1848–1849	
William B. Preston 1849–1850	Jacob Collamer 1849–1850	Reverdy Johnson 1849–1850	Thomas Ewing 1849–1850
William A. Graham 1850–1852 John P. Kennedy 1852–1853	Nathan K. Hall 1850–1852 Sam D. Hubbard 1852–1853	John J. Crittenden 1850–1853	Thomas McKennan 1850 A. H. H. Stuart 1850–1853
James C. Dobbin 1853–1857	James Campbell 1853–1857	Caleb Cushing 1853–1857	Robert McClelland 1853–1857

President	Vice President	Secretary of State	Secretary of Treasury	Secretary of War
James Buchanan 1857–1861	John C. Breckinridge 1857–1861	Lewis Cass 1857–1860 Jeremiah S. Black 1860–1861	Howell Cobb 1857–1860 Philip F. Thomas 1860–1861 John A. Dix 1861	John B. Floyd 1857–1861 Joseph Holt 1861
Abraham Lincoln 1861–1865	Hannibal Hamlin 1861–1865 Andrew Johnson 1865	William H. Seward 1861–1865	Salmon P. Chase 1861–1864 William P. Fessenden 1864–1865 Hugh McCulloch 1865	Simon Cameron 1861–1862 Edwin M. Stanton 1862–1865
Andrew Johnson 1865–1869		William H. Seward 1865–1869	Hugh McCulloch 1865–1869	Edwin M. Stanton 1865–1867 Ulysses S. Grant 1867–1868 John M. Schofield 1868–1869
Ulysses S. Grant 1869–1877	Schuyler Colfax 1869–1873 Henry Wilson 1873–1877	Elihu B. Washburne 1869 Hamilton Fish 1869–1877	George S. Boutwell 1869–1873 William A. Richardson 1873–1874 Benjamin H. Bristow 1874–1876 Lot M. Morrill 1876–1877	John A. Rawlins 1869 William T. Sherman 1869 William W. Belknap 1869–1876 Alphonso Taft 1876 James D. Cameron 1876–1877
Rutherford B. Hayes 1877–1881	William A. Wheeler 1877–1881	William M. Evarts 1877–1881	John Sherman 1877–1881	George W. McCrary 1877–1879 Alexander Ramsey 1879–1881
James A. Garfield 1881	Chester A. Arthur 1881	James G. Blaine 1881	William Windom 1881	Robert T. Lincoln 1881
Chester A. Arthur 1881–1885		F. T. Frelinghuysen 1881–1885	Charles J. Folger 1881–1884 Walter Q. Gresham 1884 Hugh McCulloch 1884–1885	Robert T. Lincoln 1881–1885
Grover Cleveland 1885–1889	T. A. Hendricks 1885	Thomas F. Bayard 1885–1889	Daniel Manning 1885–1887 Charles S. Fairchild 1887–1889	William C. Endicott 1885–1889

Secretary of Navy	Postmaster General	Attorney General	Secretary of Interior	Secretary of Agriculture
Isaac Toucey 1857–1861	Aaron V. Brown 1857–1859 Joseph Holt 1859–1861 Horatio King 1861	Jeremiah S. Black 1857–1860 Edwin M. Stanton 1860–1861	Jacob Thompson 1857–1861	
Gideon Welles 1861–1865	Horatio King 1861 Montgomery Blair 1861–1864 William Dennison 1864–1865	Edward Bates 1861–1864 James Speed 1864–1865	Caleb B. Smith 1861–1863 John P. Usher 1863–1865	
Gideon Welles 1865–1869	William Dennison 1865–1866 Alexander Randall 1866–1869 William M. Evarts 1868–1869	James Speed 1865–1866 Henry Stanbery 1866–1868 O. H. Browning 1866–1869	John P. Usher 1865 James Harlan 1865–1866	
Adolph E. Borie 1869 George M. Robeson 1869–1877	John A. J. Creswell 1869–1874 James W. Marshall 1874 Marshall Jewell 1874–1876 James N. Tyner 1876–1877	Ebenezer R. Hoar 1869–1870 Amos T. Akerman 1870–1871 G. H. Williams 1871–1875 Edwards Pierrepont 1875–1876 Alphonso Taft 1876–1877	Jacob D. Cox 1869–1870 Columbus Delano 1870–1875 Zachariah Chandler 1875–1877	
R. W. Thompson 1877–1881 Nathan Goff, Jr. 1881	David M. Key 1877–1880 Horace Maynard 1880–1881	Charles Devens 1877–1881	Carl Schurz 1877–1881	
William H. Hunt 1881	Thomas L. James 1881	Wayne MacVeagh 1881	S. J. Kirkwood 1881	
William E. Chandler 1881–1885	Thomas L. James 1881 Timothy O. Howe 1881–1883 Walter Q. Gresham 1883–1884 Frank Hatton 1884–1885	B. H. Brewster 1881–1885	Henry M. Teller 1881–1885	
William C. Whitney 1885–1889	William F. Vilas 1885–1888 Don M. Dickinson 1888–1889	A. H. Garland 1885–1889	L. Q. C. Lamar 1885–1888 William F. Vilas 1888–1889	Norman J. Colman 1889

President	Vice President	Secretary of State	Secretary of Treasury	Secretary of War	Secretary of Navy
Benjamin Harrison 1889–1893	Levi P. Morton 1889–1893	James G. Blaine 1889–1892 John W. Foster 1892–1893	William Windom 1889–1891 Charles Foster 1892–1893	Redfield Procter 1889–1891 Stephen B. Elkins 1891–1893	Benjamin F. Tracy 1889–1893
Grover Cleveland 1893–1897	Adlai E. Stevenson 1893–1897	Walter Q. Gresham 1893–1895 Richard Olney 1895–1897	John G. Carlisle 1893–1897	Daniel S. Lamont 1893–1897	Hilary A. Herbert 1893–1897
William McKinley 1897–1901	Garret A. Hobart 1897–1899 Theodore Roosevelt 1901	John Sherman 1897–1898 William R. Day 1898 John Hay 1898–1901	Lyman J. Gage 1897–1901	Russell A. Alger 1897–1899 Elihu Root 1899–1901	John D. Long 1897–1901
Theodore Roosevelt 1901–1909	Charles Fairbanks 1905–1909	John Hay 1901–1905 Elihu Root 1905–1909 Robert Bacon 1909	Lyman J. Gage 1901–1902 Leslie M. Shaw 1902–1907 George B. Cortelyou 1907–1909	Elihu Root 1901–1904 William H. Taft 1904–1908 Luke E. Wright 1908–1909	John D. Long 1901–1902 William H. Moody 1902–1904 Paul Morton 1904–1905 Charles J. Bonaparte 1905–1906 Victor H. Metcalf 1906–1908 T. H. Newberry 1908–1909
William H. Taft 1909–1913	James S. Sherman 1909–1913	Philander C. Knox 1909–1913	Franklin MacVeagh 1909–1913	Jacob M. Dickinson 1909–1911 Henry L. Stimson 1911–1913	George von L. Meyer 1909–1913
Woodrow Wilson 1913–1921	Thomas R. Marshall 1913–1921	William J. Bryan 1913–1915 Robert Lansing 1915–1920 Bainbridge Colby 1920–1921	William G. McAdoo 1913–1918 Carter Glass 1918–1920 David F. Houston 1920–1921	Lindley M. Garrison 1913–1916 Newton D. Baker 1916–1921	Josephus Daniels 1913–1921
Warren G. Harding 1921–1923	Calvin Coolidge 1921–1923	Charles E. Hughes 1921–1923	Andrew W. Mellon 1921–1923	John W. Weeks 1921–1923	Edwin Denby 1921–1923
Calvin Coolidge 1923–1929	Charles G. Dawes 1925–1929	Charles E. Hughes 1923–1925	Andrew W. Mellon 1923–1929	John W. Weeks 1923–1925	Edwin Denby 1923–1924

Postmaster General	Attorney General	Secretary of Interior	Secretary of Agriculture	Secretary of Commerce	Secretary of Labor
John Wanamaker 1889–1893	W. H. H. Miller 1889–1893	John W. Noble 1889–1893	Jeremiah M. Rusk 1889–1893		
Wilson S. Bissel 1893–1895 William L. Wilson 1895–1897	Richard Olney 1893–1895 Judson Harmon 1895–1897	Hoke Smith 1893–1896 David R. Francis 1896–1897	J. Sterling Morton 1893–1897		
James A. Gary 1897–1898 Charles E. Smith 1898–1901	Joseph McKenna 1897–1898 John W. Griggs 1898–1901 Philander C. Knox 1901	Cornelius N. Bliss 1897–1898 E. A. Hitchcock 1898–1901	James Wilson 1897–1901		
Charles E. Smith 1901–1902 Henry C. Payne 1902–1904 Robert J. Wynne 1904–1905 George B. Cortelyou 1905—1907 George von L. Meyer 1907–1909	Philander C. Knox 1901–1904 William H. Moody 1904–1906 Charles J. Bonaparte 1906–1909	E. A. Hitchcock 1901–1907 James R. Garfield 1907–1909	James Wilson 1901–1909	Secretary of Commerce and Labor George B. Cortelyou 1903–1904 Victor H. Metcalf 1904–1906 Oscar S. Straus 1906–1909	
Frank H. Hitchcock 1909–1913	G. W. Wickersham 1909–1913	R. A. Ballinger 1909–1911 Walter L. Fisher 1911–1913	James Wilson 1909–1913	Charles Nagel 1909–1913	
Albert S. Burleson 1913–1921	J. C. McReynolds 1913–1914 T. W. Gregory 1914–1919 A. Mitchell Palmer 1919–1921	Franklin K. Lane 1913–1920 John B. Payne 1920–1921	David F. Houston 1913–1920 E. T. Meredith 1920–1921	W. C. Redfield 1913–1919 J. W. Alexander 1919–1921	William B. Wilson 1913–1921
Will H. Hays 1921–1922 Hubert Work 1922–1923 Harry S. New 1923	H. M. Daugherty 1921–1923	Albert B. Fall 1921–1923 Hubert Work 1923	Henry C. Wallace 1921–1923	Herbert C. Hoover 1921–1923	James J. Davis 1921–1923
Harry S. New 1923–1929	H. M. Daugherty 1923–1924	Hubert Work 1923–1928	Henry C. Wallace 1923–1924	Herbert C. Hoover	James J. Davis 1923–1929

President	Vice President	Secretary of State	Secretary of Treasury	Secretary of War	Secretary of Navy	Postmaster General	Attorney General
Calvin Coolidge 1923–1929	Charles G. Dawes 1925–1929	Frank B. Kellogg 1925–1929		Dwight F. Davis 1925–1929	Curtis D. Wilbur 1924–1929		Harlan F. Stone 1924–1925 John G. Sargent 1925–1929
Herbert C. Hoover 1929–1933	Charles Curtis 1929–1933	Henry L. Stimson 1929–1933	Andrew W. Mellon 1929–1932 Ogden L. Mills 1932–1933	James W. Good 1929 Patrick J. Hurley 1929–1933	Charles F. Adams 1929–1933	Walter F. Brown 1929–1933	J. D. Mitchell 1929–1933
Franklin Delano Roosevelt 1933–1945	John Nance Garner 1933–1941 Henry A. Wallace 1941–1945 Harry S Truman 1945	Cordell Hull 1933–1944 E. R. Stettinius, Jr. 1944–1945	William H. Woodin 1933–1934 Henry Morgenthau, Jr. 1934–1945	George H. Dern 1933–1936 Harry H. Woodring 1936–1940 Henry L. Stimson 1940–1945	Claude A. Swanson 1933–1940 Charles Edison 1940 Frank Knox 1940–1944 James V. Forrestal 1944–1945	James A. Farley 1933–1940 Frank C. Walker 1940–1945	H. S. Cummings 1933–1939 Frank Murphy 1939–1940 Robert Jackson 1940–1941 Francis Biddel 1941–1945
Harry S Truman 1945–1953	Alben W. Barkley 1949–1953	James F. Byrnes 1945–1947 George C. Marshall 1947–1949 Dean G. Acheson 1949–1953	Fred M. Vinson 1945–1946 John W. Snyder 1946–1953	Robert P. Patterson 1945–1947 Kenneth C. Royall 1947 **Secretary of Defense** James V. Forrestal 1947–1949 Louis A. Johnson 1949–1950 George C. Marshall 1950–1951 Robert A. Lovett 1951–1953	James V. Forrestal 1945–1947	R. E. Hannegan 1945–1947 Jesse M. Donaldson 1947–1953	Tom C. Clark 1945–1949 J. H. McGrath 1949–1952 James P. McGranery 1952–1953
Dwight D. Eisenhower 1953–1961	Richard M. Nixon 1953–1961	John Foster Dulles 1953–1959 Christian A. Herter 1957–1961	George M. Humphrey 1953–1957 Robert B. Anderson 1957–1961	Charles E. Wilson 1953–1957 Neil H. McElroy 1957–1961 Thomas S. Gates 1959–1961		A. E. Summerfield 1953–1961	H. Brownell, Jr. 1953–1957 William P. Rogers 1957–1961
John F. Kennedy 1961–1963	Lyndon B. Johnson 1961–1963	Dean Rusk 1961–1963	C. Douglas Dillon 1961–1963	Robert S. McNamara 1961–1963		J. Edward Day 1961–1963 John A. Gronouski 1961–1963	Robert F. Kennedy 1961–1963
Lyndon B. Johnson 1963–1969	Hubert H. Humphrey 1965–1969	Dean Rusk 1963–1969	C. Douglas Dillon 1963–1965 Henry H. Fowler 1965–1968 Joseph W. Barr 1968–1969	Robert S. McNamara 1963–1968 Clark M. Clifford 1968–1969		John A. Gronouski 1963–1965 Lawrence F. O'Brien 1965–1968 W. Marvin Watson 1968–1969	Robert F. Kennedy 1963–1965 N. deB. Katzenbach 1965–1967 Ramsey Clark 1967–1969

Secretary of Interior	Secretary of Agriculture	Secretary of Commerce	Secretary of Labor	Secretary of Health, Education and Welfare	Secretary of Housing and Urban Development	Secretary of Transportation
Roy O. West 1928–1929	Howard M. Gore 1924–1925 W. J. Jardine 1925–1929	1923–1928 William F. Whiting 1928–1929				
Ray L. Wilbur 1929–1933	Arthur M. Hyde 1929–1933 Roy D. Chapin 1932–1933	Robert P. Lamont 1929–1932 William N. Doak 1930–1933	James J. Davis 1929–1930			
Harold L. Ickes 1933–1945	Henry A. Wallace 1933–1940 Claude R. Wickard 1940–1945	Daniel C. Roper 1933–1939 Harry L. Hopkins 1939–1940 Jesse Jones 1940–1945 Henry A. Wallace 1945	Frances Perkins 1933–1945			
Harold L. Ickes 1945–1946 Julius A. Krug 1946–1949 Oscar L. Chapman 1949–1953	C. P. Anderson 1945–1948 C. F. Brannan 1948–1953	W. A. Harriman 1946–1948 Charles Sawyer 1948–1953	L. B. Schwellenbach 1945–1948 Maurice J. Tobin 1948–1953			
Douglas McKay 1953–1956 Fred Seaton 1956–1961	Ezra T. Benson 1953–1961	Sinclair Weeks 1953–1958 Lewis L. Strauss 1958–1961	Martin P. Durkin 1953 James P. Mitchell 1953–1961	Oveta Culp Hobby 1953–1955 Marion B. Folsom 1955–1958 Arthur S. Flemming 1958–1961		
Stewart L. Udall 1961–1963	Orville L. Freeman 1961–1963	Luther H. Hodges 1961–1963	Arthur J. Goldberg 1961–1963 W. Willard Wirtz 1962–1963	A. H. Ribicoff 1961–1963 Anthony J. Celebrezze 1962–1963		
Stewart L. Udall 1963–1969	Orville L. Freeman 1963–1969	Luther H. Hodges 1963–1965 John T. Connor 1965–1967 Alexander B. Trowbridge 1967–1968 C. R. Smith 1968–1969	W. Willard Wirtz 1963–1969	Anthony J. Celebrezze 1963–1965 John W. Gardner 1965–1968 Wilbur J. Cohen 1968–1969	Robert C. Weaver 1966–1968 Robert C. Wood 1968–1969	Alan S. Boyd 1966–1969

President	Vice President	Secretary of State	Secretary of Treasury	Secretary of Defense	Postmaster General	Attorney General	Secretary of Interior	Secretary of Agriculture
Richard M. Nixon 1969–1974	Spiro T. Agnew 1969–1973 Gerald R. Ford 1973–1974	William P. Rogers 1969–1973 Henry A. Kissinger 1973–1974	David M. Kennedy 1969–1970 John B. Connally 1970–1972 George P. Schultz 1972–1974 William E. Simon 1974	Melvin R. Laird 1969–1973 Elliot L. Richardson 1973 James R. Schlesinger 1973–1974	Winton M. Blount 1969–1971	John M. Mitchell 1969–1972 Richard G. Kleindienst 1972–1973 Elliot L. Richardson 1973 William B. Saxbe 1974	Walter J. Hickel 1969–1971 Rogers C. B. Morton 1971–1974	Clifford M. Hardin 1969–1971 Earl L. Butz 1971–1974
Gerald R. Ford 1974–1977	Nelson A. Rockefeller 1974–1977	Henry A. Kissinger 1974–1977	William E. Simon 1974–1977	James R. Schlesinger 1974–1975 Donald H. Rumsfeld 1975–1977		William B. Saxbe 1974–1975 Edward H. Levi 1975–1977	Rogers C. B. Morton 1974–1975 Stanley K. Hathaway 1975 Thomas D. Kleppe 1975–1977	Earl L. Butz 1974–1976
Jimmy Carter 1977–1981	Walter F. Mondale 1977–1981	Cyrus R. Vance 1977–1980 Edmund S. Muskie 1980–1981	W. Michael Blumenthal 1977–1979 G. William Miller 1979–1981	Harold Brown 1977–1981		Griffin Bell 1977–1979 Benjamin R. Civiletti 1979–1981	Cecil D. Andrus 1977–1981	Robert Bergland 1977–1981
Ronald W. Reagan 1981–1989	George H. Bush 1981–1989	Alexander M. Haig, Jr. 1981–1982 George P. Shultz 1982–1989	Donald T. Regan 1981–1985 James A. Baker 1985–1988 Nicholas F. Brady 1988–1989	Caspar W. Weinberger 1981–1987 Frank C. Carlucci 1987–1989		William French Smith 1981–1985 Edwin Meese 1985–1988 Richard Thornburgh 1988–1989	James G. Watt 1981–1983 William P. Clark 1983–1985 Donald P. Hodel 1985–1989	John R. Block 1981–1986 Richard E. Lyng 1986–1989
George H. Bush 1989–1993	J. Danforth Quayle 1989–1993	James A. Baker 1989–1992 Lawrence S. Eagleburger 1992–1993	Nicholas F. Brady 1989–1993	Richard Cheney 1989–1993		Richard Thornburgh 1989–1990 William Barr 1990–1993	Manuel Lujan 1989–1993	Clayton Yeutter 1989–1990 Edward Madigan 1990–1993
William Clinton 1993–2001	Albert Gore 1993–2001	Warren M. Christopher 1993–1996 Madeleine K. Albright 1997–2001	Lloyd Bentsen 1993–1994 Robert E. Rubin 1994–1999 Lawrence H. Summers 1999–2001	Les Aspin 1993–1994 William J. Perry 1994–1996 William S. Cohen 1997–2001		Janet Reno 1993–2001	Bruce Babbitt 1993–2001	Mike Espy 1993–1994 Dan Glickman 1995–2001
George W. Bush 2001–	Richard B. Cheney 2001–	Gen. Colin L. Powell 2001–	Paul H. O'Neill 2001–	Donald H. Rumsfeld 2001–		John Ashcroft 2001–	Gale A. Norton 2001–	Ann M. Veneman 2001–

Secretary of Commerce	Secretary of Labor	Secretary of Health, Education and Welfare	Secretary of Housing and Urban Development	Secretary of Transportation	Secretary of Energy	Secretary of Veterans Affairs
Maurice H. Stans 1969–1972 Peter G. Peterson 1972 Frederick B. Dent 1972–1974	George P. Shultz 1969–1970 James D. Hodgson 1970–1973 Peter J. Brennan 1973–1974	Robert H. Finch 1969–1970 Elliot L. Richardson 1970–1973 Caspar W. Weinberger 1973–1974	George W. Romney 1969–1973 James T. Lynn 1973–1974	John A. Volpe 1969–1973 Claude S. Brinegar 1973–1974		
Frederick B. Dent 1974–1975 Rogers C. B. Morton 1975 Elliot L. Richardson 1975–1977	Peter J. Brennan 1974–1975 John T. Dunlop 1975–1976 W. J. Usery 1976–1977	Caspar W. Weinberger 1974–1975 Forrest D. Matthews 1975–1977	James T. Lynn 1974–1975 Carla A. Hills 1975–1977	Claude S. Brinegar 1974–1975 William T. Coleman 1975–1977		
Juanita Kreps 1977–1981	F. Ray Marshall 1977–1981	Joseph Califano 1977–1979 Patricia Roberts Harris 1979–1980	Patricia Roberts Harris 1977–1979 Moon Landrieu 1979–1981	Brock Adams 1977–1979 Neil E. Goldschmidt 1979–1981	James R. Schlesinger 1977–1979 Charles W. Duncan, Jr. 1979–1981	

		Secretary of Health and Human Services	Secretary of Education			
		Patricia Roberts Harris 1980–1981	Shirley M. Hufstedler 1980–1981			

Secretary of Commerce	Secretary of Labor	Secretary of Health and Human Services	Secretary of Education	Secretary of Housing and Urban Development	Secretary of Transportation	Secretary of Energy	Secretary of Veterans Affairs
Malcolm Baldridge 1981–1987 C. William Verity, Jr. 1987–1989	Raymond J. Donovan 1981–1985 William E. Brock 1985–1987 Ann Dore McLaughlin 1987–1989	Richard S. Schweiker 1981–1983 Margaret M. Heckler 1983–1985 Otis R. Bowen 1985–1989	Terrell H. Bell 1981–1985 William J. Bennett 1985–1988 Lauro Fred Cavazos 1988–1989	Samuel R. Pierce, Jr. 1981–1989	Drew Lewis 1981–1983 Elizabeth H. Dole 1983–1987 James H. Burnley 1987–1989	James B. Edwards 1981–1982 Donald P. Hodel 1982–1985 John S. Harrington 1985–1989	
Robert Mosbacher 1989–1991 Barbara Franklin 1991–1993	Elizabeth Dole 1989–1990 Lynn Martin 1992–1993	Louis Sullivan 1989–1993	Lamar Alexander 1990–1993	Jack Kemp 1989–1993	Samuel Skinner 1989–1990 Andrew Card 1990–1993	James Watkins 1989–1993	Edward J. Derwinski 1989–1993
Ronald H. Brown 1993–1996 William M. Daley 1997–2000 Norman Y. Mineta 2000–2001	Robert B. Reich 1993–1996 Alexis M. Herman 1997–2001	Donna E. Shalala 1993–2001	Richard W. Riley 1993–2001	Henry G. Cisneros 1993–1996 Andrew M. Cuomo 1997–2001	Federico F. Peña 1993–1996 Rodney E. Slater 1997–2001	Hazel O'Leary 1993–1996 Federico F. Peña 1997–1998 Bill Richardson 1998–2001	Jesse Brown 1993–1997 Togo D. West, Jr.[2] 1998–2001
Donald L. Evans 2001–	Elaine L. Chao 2001–	Tommy G. Thompson 2001–	Roderick R. Paige 2001–	Melquiades R. Martinez 2001–	Norman Y. Mineta 2001–	Spencer Abraham 2001–	Anthony Principi 2001–

PHOTO CREDITS

Title page, The Morgan Collection. Author photo, Jeannette Ferrary.

Chapter 1: Opener, Serpent Mound in Ohio (800 B.C.—A.D. 100), The Morgan Collection. Page 5, Warren Morgan/Corbis. Page 11, The Morgan Collection. Chapter 2: Opener, Map of the World, 1529, after Diego Ribero's "Mappa Mundia," Stock Montage. Page 41, The Mariners' Museum/Corbis. Page 43, Tecmap Corporation/Corbis. Chapter 3: Opener, The marriage of John Rolfe and Pocahontas, The Morgan Collection. Page 49, Bettmann/Corbis. Page 62, The Newberry Library. Chapter 4: Opener, Act Concerning Tithables, 1748, The Morgan Collection. Page 76, Stock Montage, Inc. Page 78, N. Carter/North Wind. Chapter 5: Opener, The Battle of Lexington, The Morgan Collection. Page 93, Christie's Images/Corbis. Page 99, The Granger Collection, New York. Page 103, The Granger Collection, New York.

Chapter 6: Opener, *The Pennsylvania Packet,* 1789, The Morgan Collection. Page 117, The Granger Collection, New York. Page 132, The Granger Collection. Chapter 7: Opener, The American Museum, 1791, The Morgan Collection. Page 138, fantasy map, Pat Rogondino. Page 145, *American Cookery,* 1796, Peter Carroll. Page 146, SuperStock. Page 147, The Granger Collection, New York. Chapter 8: Opener, *The Connecticut Courant,* 1800, The Morgan Collection. Page 161, The Granger Collection. Page 166, The Granger Collection.

Page 170, Underwood & Underwood/Corbis. Page 177, Stock Montage. Chapter 9: Opener, The National Gazette, 1822, The Morgan Collection. Page 182, The Granger Collection, New York. Page 184, The Granger Collection, New York. Page 198, The Granger Collection. Chapter 10: Opener, The Hudson River near West Point, New York, The Morgan Collection. Page 206, Stock Montage, Inc. Page 211, The Morgan Collection. Page 213, Stock Montage, Inc. Page 214, The Granger Collection, New York.

Chapter 11: Opener, *The New World,* 1842, The Morgan Collection. Page 227, The Granger Collection, New York. Page 238, Corbis. Page 240, The Granger Collection, New York. Chapter 12: Opener, Westward-bound Conestoga wagon, The Morgan Collection. Page 249, The Granger Collection, New York. Page 255, The Morgan Collection. Page 265, The Granger Collection, New York. Chapter 13: Opener, Homestead in the Kansas Territory, 1856, The Morgan Collection. Page 279, The Granger Collection, New York. Page 286, The Granger Collection, New York. Page 288, The Granger Collection, New York. Chapter 14: Opener, Civil War-era woman, The Morgan Collection. Page 302, The Granger Collection, New York. Page 306, The Granger Collection, New York. Page 309, The Morgan Collection. Chapter 15: Opener, Plains bison, The Morgan Collection. Page 324, The Granger Collection, New York. Page 335, Bettmann/Corbis. Page 339, Stock Montage, Inc. Page 343, The Morgan Collection.